Contents

Feasting in northern France colour section following p.176

Megaliths and monuments colour section following p.304

◄◄ Cornouaille, Finistère ◄ The Vieux Bassin at Honfleur

Weymouth
Plymouth
Rosslare
Cork & Rosslare
ENGLISH CHANNEL
Alderney
Cap de le Hague
Guernsey
Sark
Barneville-Carteret
Jersey
Îles Chausey
Baie de Mont-St-Michel
Côte de Granit Rose
Perros-Guirec
Île de Batz
Île de Bréhat
Roscoff
Lannion
Paimpol
Côte d'Emeraude
L'Aber-Wrac'h
Ouessant
Molène
Brest
Le Conquet
N12
Morlaix
N12
Guingamp
St-Brieuc
Erquy
St-Malo
Dinard
Cancale
Dol
N176
Dinan
Huelgoat
Monts d'Arrée
Carhaix-Plouguer
Crozon Peninsula
Crozon
Châteaulin
N165
Baie de Douarnenez
Douarnenez
Sein
Pointe du Raz
Audierne
D765
N164
R. Aulne
Gouarec
Lac du Guerledan
Loudéac
R. Rance
N137
N12
R. Odet
Montagnes Noires
N164
Quimper
Pontivy
Nantes-Brest Canal
Rennes
Bénodet
D785
Concarneau
Le Guilvinec
Pont-Aven
N165
Lorient
R. Blavet
Josselin
Forêt de Paimpont
BRITTANY
R. Vilaine
Auray
Vannes
Île de Groix
Carnac
Redon
Quiberon
Golfe de Morbihan
Île Houat
Belle Île
Île Hoëdic
Guérande
Grande Brière
N165
A84
La Baule
St-Nazaire
Pornic
Nantes
Île de Cape
N
Metres
200
100
0
0
50 km

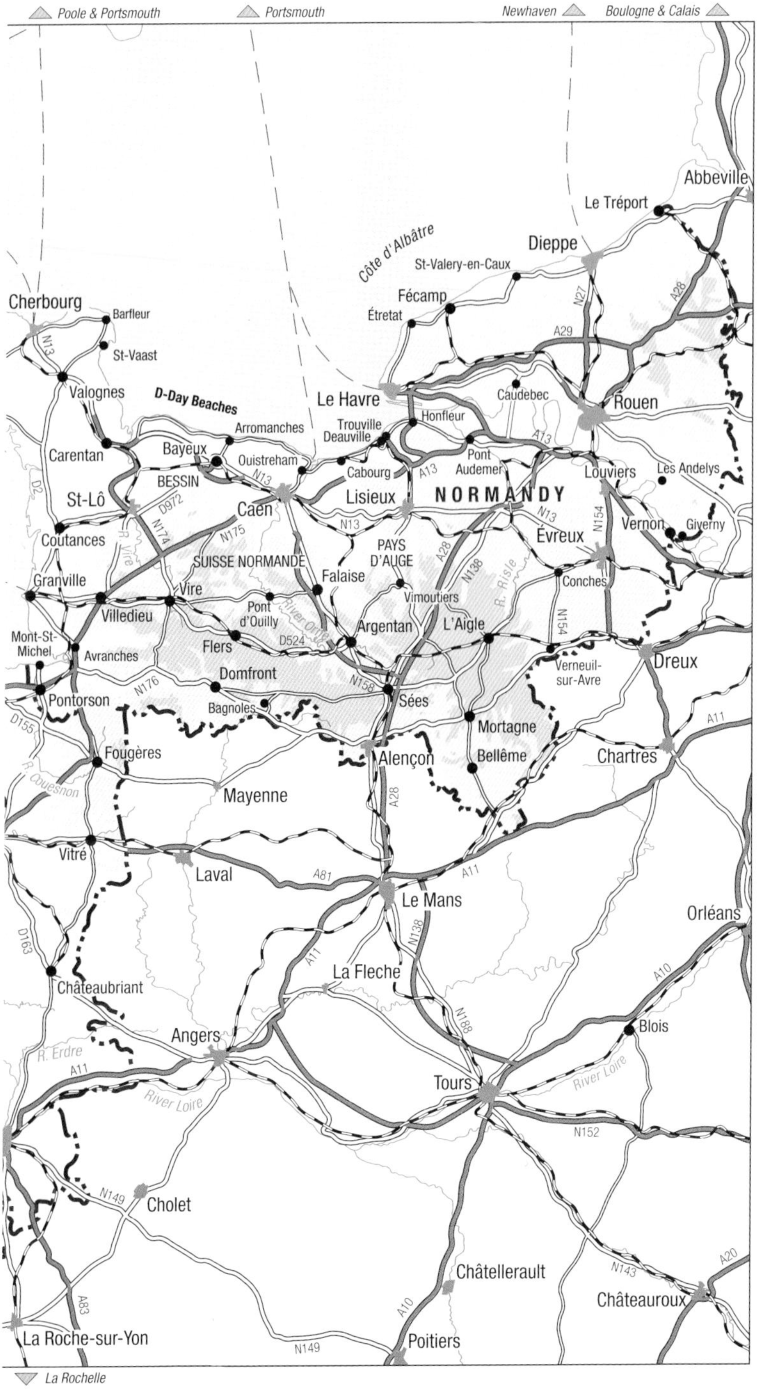
Poole & Portsmouth
Portsmouth
Newhaven
Boulogne & Calais
Abbeville
Le Tréport
Dieppe
Côte d'Albâtre
St-Valery-en-Caux
Fécamp
Étretat
Cherbourg
Barfleur
St-Vaast
N13
Valognes
D-Day Beaches
Arromanches
Le Havre
Caudebec
Rouen
A29
A28
N27
Honfleur
Trouville
Deauville
A13
Carentan
Bayeux
Ouistreham
Cabourg
Pont Audemer
Louviers
Les Andelys
BESSIN
N13
St-Lô
D972
Caen
Lisieux
NORMANDY
N13
Vernon
Giverny
Paris
D2
N174
N175
N13
Évreux
N154
Coutances
R. Vire
SUISSE NORMANDE
PAYS D'AUGE
A28
N138
R. Risle
Granville
Falaise
Conches
Vire
Vimoutiers
Villedieu
Pont d'Ouilly
River Orne
L'Aigle
N154
Mont-St-Michel
Avranches
Flers
D524
Argentan
Dreux
Verneuil-sur-Avre
N176
Domfront
N158
Sées
Pontorson
Bagnoles
Mortagne
D155
A11
Fougères
Alençon
Bellême
Chartres
R. Couesnon
Mayenne
A28
Vitré
Laval
A81
A11
Le Mans
Orléans
D163
N138
A11
La Fleche
A10
Châteaubriant
N188
Blois
Angers
R. Erdre
A11
River Loire
Tours
River Loire
N152
N149
Cholet
Châtellerault
N143
A20
A83
A10
Châteauroux
La Roche-sur-Yon
N149
Poitiers
La Rochelle

Introduction to

Brittany and Normandy

Of the many strongly individual regions of France, Brittany and Normandy rank among the most distinct. Each sustains its own proud identity, in terms of culture, peoples, landscape and history. A journey through both offers visitors a wonderful opportunity to experience much of the best that France has to offer: wild coast and sheltered white-sand beaches; sparse heathland and dense forests; medieval ports and relics of the prehistoric past; and, just as important, abundant seafood and a compelling and exuberant cuisine.

Both provinces are ideal for **cycle** touring, with superb scenery yet short distances between each town and the next, so you're never too far from the next hotel, restaurant or market. Otherwise, a **car** is the best alternative; public transport options tend to be very limited.

Where to go

Brittany is the more popular of the two regions, with both French and foreign tourists. Its most obvious attractions lie along the **coast**, speckled with offshore islands and islets, which makes up over a third of the seaboard of France. In parts of the north, and in Finistère to the west, the shoreline can be nothing but rocks and cliffs, its exposed

▲ Les Andelys

headlands buffeted by the full force of the Atlantic and swept by dangerous currents. But elsewhere, especially in the sheltered southern resorts around the Morbihan and La Baule, it is caressed by the gentlest of seas, with the sands rambling for kilometres or nestling into coves between steep cliffs.

Thanks to the sheer extent of the Breton coastline, it's always possible to walk alone with the elements. Although in high season solitude can be scarce there could never be enough visitors to cover every twist of the Finistère coast. As well as exploring the mainland resorts and seaside villages – each of which, from ports the size of **St-Malo** or **Vannes** down to little-known communities such as Erquy or L'Aber Wra'ch, can be relied upon to offer at least one welcoming hotel or restaurant – be sure to take a boat trip out to at least one **island**. The magical Île de Bréhat is just a ten-minute crossing from the north coast near Paimpol, while historic Belle-Île, to the south, is under an hour from Quiberon. Other islands are set aside as bird sanctuaries, while, off Finistère, the Îles d'Ouessant, Molène and Sein are as remote and strange as Orkney or the Shetland Isles.

A vast wealth of **megalithic remains** scattered across Brittany evoke the prehistoric past. The single most famous site is **Carnac**, whose spectacular alignments of menhirs may have been erected as part of an ancient observatory. Equally compelling remains include the pyramid-like burial tumuli on the island of **Gavrinis**, in the gulf of Morbihan, and at **Barnenez** outside Morlaix in the north. Not all such relics are found near the sea; the moors and woodlands of **inland Brittany** are the realm of legend, with the **forests** of Huelgoat and Paimpont in particular being identified with the tales of Merlin, the Fisher King and the Holy Grail. In the "Little Britain" of King Arthur's domain – Petite Bretagne, as opposed to Grande Bretagne

Fact file

- The historic terms **Normandy** and **Brittany** remain in constant use, although for centuries the original boundaries of the regions have not been recognized in French law.
- Normandy is split between **Haute Normandie** (Upper Normandy), which consists of the *départements* of Seine Maritime and Eure, and **Basse Normandie** (Lower Normandy), made up of the *départements* of Calvados, Orne and Manche. Taken together, these two regions cover just under 30,000 square kilometres, and are home to 3.4 million people.
- Brittany is officially a single region – **Bretagne** – that combines the *départements* of Ille-et-Vilaine, Côtes d'Armor, Finistère and Morbihan. Since 1973 it has excluded its historical capital, Nantes, and the *département* of Loire-Atlantique; that anomaly may shortly be corrected, but in any case Bretons themselves continue to regard Brittany as comprising all five *départements*. By that reckoning, Brittany occupies 34,000 square kilometres, with a population of 4.4 million.
- **French** is used everywhere; tourists are unlikely to encounter spoken Breton.

– an otherworldly element still seems entrenched in the land and people.

Normandy, on the other hand, has a less harsh appearance and a more mainstream, prosperous history. It too is a seaboard province, first colonized by Norsemen and then colonizing in turn; the ruthless Norman formula for success was exported in the eleventh and twelfth centuries to England, Sicily and parts of the Near East, and later on to Canada. Normandy has always boasted large-scale **ports**: Rouen, on the Seine, is as near as ships can get to Paris, while Dieppe, Cherbourg and Le Havre have important transatlantic trade. **Inland**, it is a wonderfully fertile belt of tranquil pastureland, where most visitors head straight for the restaurants of the Pays d'Auge and the Suisse Normande.

The pleasures of Normandy are perhaps less intense than those of Brittany. Much of its **seaside** is a little overdeveloped. However, the ancient ports – **Honfleur** and **Barfleur** especially – are delightful, and numerous coastal villages remain unspoiled by crowds or affectations. Lovely little towns lie tucked away within 20km of each of the major Channel ports – the **Cotentin peninsula** around **Cherbourg** is among the best, and least explored, areas – while the banks of the **Seine**, too, hold several idyllic resorts.

Normandy also boasts extraordinary **architectural** treasures, although only its much-restored traditional capital, **Rouen**, has preserved a complete medieval centre. Most famous of all is the spectacular *merveille* on the island of **Mont-St-Michel**, but there are also the monasteries at Jumièges and Caen, and Richard the Lionheart's castle above the Seine at Les Andelys,

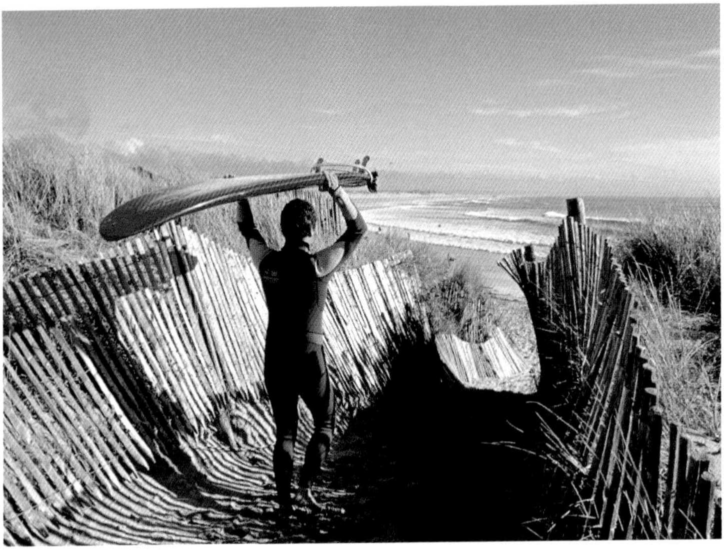

Audierne

while **Bayeux**, in addition to its vivid and astonishing **Tapestry**, holds a majestic cathedral. Many other great Norman buildings survived into the twentieth century, only to be destroyed during the Allied landings in 1944 and the subsequent **Battle of Normandy**, which has its own legacy in a series of war museums, memorials and cemeteries. While hardly conventional tourist attractions, as part of the fabric of the province these are moving and enlightening.

When to go

Every French town or district seems to promote its own *micro-climat*, maintaining that some meteorological freak makes it milder or balmier than its neighbours. On the whole, however, Normandy and Brittany follow a broadly set pattern. **Summer**, more reliable than in Britain, starts around mid-June and can last through to mid-October. **Spring** and **autumn** are mild but sporadically wet. If you come for a week in April or November, it could be spoiled by rain, though rainy spells seldom last more than a couple of days. **Winter** is not too severe, though in western Brittany especially the coast can be damp and very misty.

Sea temperatures are not Mediterranean; any greater warmth felt in the Channel waters off the Norman coast as opposed to the south of England is probably more psychological than real. The south coast of Brittany is a

▲ Fishing boat at Port-en-Bassin

different matter – consistently warm through the summer months, with no need for you to brace yourself before going into the sea.

On the coast, the **tourist season** gets going properly around July, reaches a peak during the first two weeks of August and then fades quite swiftly; try to avoid the great *rentrée* at the end of the month, when cars returning to Paris jam the roads. Inland, the season is less defined; major attractions can be crowded in midsummer but some smaller hotels close in August when their owners are on holiday. Conversely, seaside resorts take on a distinctly ghostlike appearance in winter, and can often be entirely devoid of facilities.

Average daily temperatures (°C) and monthly rainfall (mm)

	Jan	Feb	Mar	Apr	May	Jun	Jul	Aug	Sep	Oct	Nov	Dec
Brittany												
Brest												
Av Temp °C	6	6	7	9	12	14	15	16	15	12	9	7
Rainfall mm	132	106	101	73	72	58	49	68	85	110	127	148
Nantes												
Av Temp °C	5	6	8	10	13	17	19	19	16	12	8	6
Rainfall mm	78	60	60	53	60	53	50	53	68	88	91	86
Normandy												
Cherbourg												
Av Temp °C	5	5	6	7	11	13	15	16	14	12	8	6
Rainfall mm	90	79	78	56	65	48	44	47	80	99	110	103
Rouen												
Av Temp °C	3	3	6	8	12	14	17	17	15	11	6	4
Rainfall mm	59	47	46	47	52	54	58	61	57	65	66	64

19 things not to miss

It may not be possible to sample everything that Brittany and Normandy have to offer in a single trip – but you can have a great time trying. What follows, in no particular order, is a selective taste of the regions' highlights: outstanding scenery, picturesque villages, remarkable history and fabulous fresh produce. Each entry has a page reference to take you straight into the guide.

01 **The Grand Éléphant** Page **335** • Trumpeting, squirting water, and carrying 49 passengers on its mighty back, Nantes' sensationally preposterous pachyderm is worth travelling a very, very long way to see.

02 Cycling Page **27** • Slow your pace and cycle through quiet country lanes, undulating hills and enchanted forests.

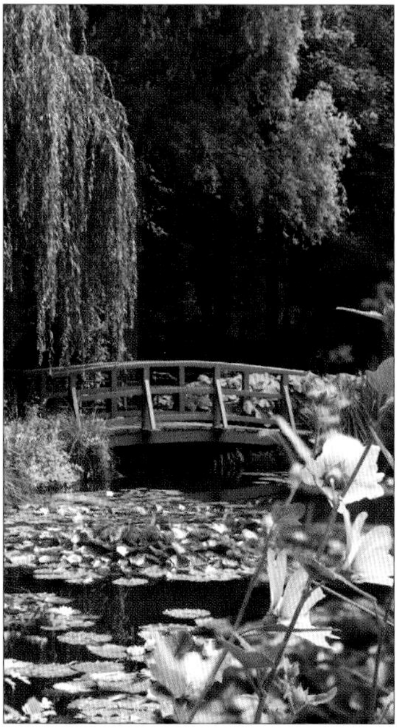

03 Waterlily pond at Giverny Page **95** • Despite the summer crowds, the waterlily pond at Claude Monet's Normandy home remains as spellbinding as ever.

04 The megaliths of Carnac Page **361** • Europe's oldest town remains surrounded by enigmatic reminders of its prehistoric inhabitants.

05 **The Seine** Page **73** • Broadening as it approaches the Channel, the premier river of northern France becomes languidly rural, lined by lovely little-known villages such as Villequier.

06 **Mont-St-Michel** Page **148** • The glorious medieval abbey that tops this tiny Norman island ranks among the most recognizable silhouettes in the world.

07 **The Inter-Celtic Festival** Page **346** • For anyone who loves Breton music, or all things Celtic, Lorient's August extravaganza is the unmissable highlight of the year.

08 **The Bayeux Tapestry** Page **120** • Now almost a thousand years old, this colourful embroidery celebrates the Norman Conquest of England in every fascinating detail.

09 Nantes-Brest Canal Page **309** • Meander along Brittany's inland waterways and soak up the stunning scenery.

10 Honfleur Page **102** • Normandy's most charming little port has long attracted artists and photographers.

11 The cliffs at Étretat Page **67** • Wind and tide have sculpted the chalky cliffs to either side of the delightful Norman resort of Étretat into extraordinary shapes.

12 Hiking the Côte de Granit Rose Page **247** • Lined by bizarre rock formations, this stretch of the northern Breton seashore offers dramatic coastal hikes.

13 Rouen Page **77** • Explore the vibrant medieval core of Rouen, which contains a superb cathedral as well as the spot where Joan of Arc met her death.

14 The Pays d'Auge Page **168** • With its crumbling half-timbered farmhouses, lush meadows and fertile orchards, the Pays d'Auge encapsulates Normandy's rural splendour.

15 St-Malo Page **197** • The finest town on the Breton coast, walled St-Malo proudly commands a lovely estuary.

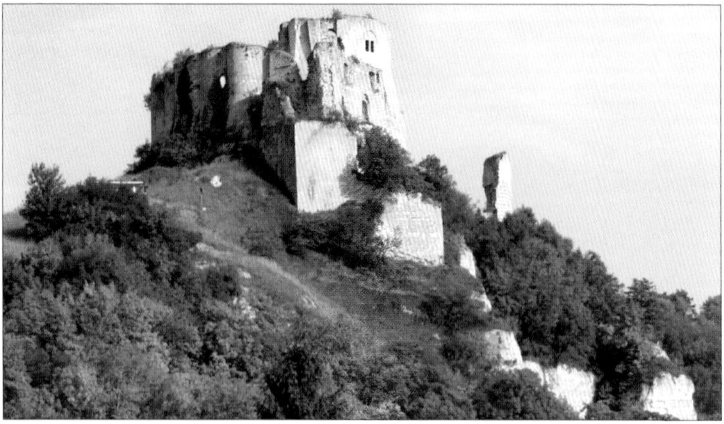

16 **Château Gaillard** Page 92 • The stark white ruins of Richard the Lionheart's fortress still dominate a dramatic curve of the Seine.

17 **The Dance of Death** Page 237 • A haunting and extraordinary medieval relic, discovered by chance in the tiny village church of Kermaria-an-Isquit.

18 **Memories of D-Day** Page 122 • Every June, veterans and their families return to the beaches of Normandy to remember the events of June 6, 1944.

19 **A boat trip to the Île de Sein** Page 291 • Of the many beautiful and remote islands that lie off the coast of Brittany, none is more hauntingly atmospheric than Finistère's tiny Île de Sein.

Basics

Basics

Getting there

Travelling to Brittany and Normandy from Britain is extremely easy. The main ferry operator, Brittany Ferries, crosses to Caen, Cherbourg, St-Malo and Roscoff, while other ferries connect Newhaven with Dieppe, and Portsmouth with Le Havre, and the Channel Tunnel provides rapid access to Normandy. In addition, budget airlines offer cheap flights to Brest, Dinard, Nantes and Rennes.

Irish visitors can choose between a handful of direct ferry services between Ireland and France, most active in summer; flying with Ryanair to Nantes; or travel via England and/or Paris.

If you're coming to Brittany and Normandy from anywhere outside Europe, then you'll almost certainly have to start by flying to Paris, and travel onwards from there.

From the UK

Six commercial ferry ports line up along the coastline of Brittany and Normandy, and four regional airports are served by budget airlines. While the cheapest ferry routes cross the Channel further east, between Dover and Calais, and the Channel Tunnel starts outside Folkestone, which route is most convenient for you will depend on where you're starting from.

Ferries

The most direct route to Normandy or Brittany, for motorists, cyclists and pedestrians, is still to take a ferry to any of four Norman and two Breton ports. However, it's generally cheaper to cross the Channel further east, and travel via Calais or Dunkerque. All these services are detailed in the box on p.21.

Ferry fares vary so enormously with the season – each sailing tends to be priced individually – that it's all but impossible to predict what you will actually pay. Most operators charge a flat fare for a vehicle with two adults, then additional per-person charges for further passengers, and for any "accommodation" required, from a seat for £5 to £40 for a cabin berth.

Booking ahead is strongly recommended for motorists, certainly in high season; foot passengers and cyclists can normally just turn up and board, at any time of year. You can compare prices and find cut-price fares online at Ⓦferrysavers.com.

The Channel Tunnel

The Channel Tunnel, which burrows beneath the English Channel at its narrowest point – the Pas-de-Calais, well to the east of Normandy – plays host to two distinct services. Eurostar trains carry foot passengers only, with its principal routes being from London to Paris or Brussels, while Eurotunnel simply conveys cars and other vehicles between Folkestone and Calais, in direct competition with the ferries.

Eurostar

Eurostar **trains** from London St Pancras International take two hours twenty minutes to reach **Paris** Gare du Nord. Travellers heading for Brittany and Normandy can change at Lille, 1 hour 20 minutes out from

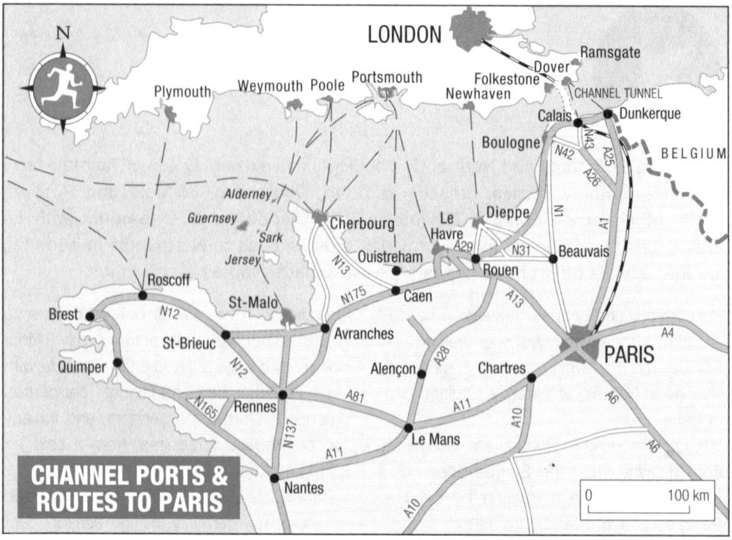

London, for destinations in the two regions. Tickets can be bought directly from Eurostar (Ⓣ0870/518 6186, Ⓦeurostar.com), or from all main train stations in Britain; for lesser-known destinations you may well have to call rather than use the website.

Eurostar offers concessionary fares to young people (under 26), over-60s, and holders of international rail passes. Bicycles can be carried free of charge in the carriage provided that they can fold; if not, they should be declared as "Registered Baggage" a day in advance (£20 per cycle per journey).

Eurotunnel

The Channel Tunnel also provides the fastest and most convenient way to take your car to France. For motorists, the tunnel entrance is less than two hours' drive from London, off the M20 at Junction 11A, just outside Folkestone. Once there, you drive your car onto a two-tier railway carriage; you're then free to get out and stretch your legs during the 35 minutes (45min for some night trains) before you emerge from the darkness at Coquelles, just outside Calais. The sole operator, **Eurotunnel** (Ⓣ0870/535 3535, Ⓦeurotunnel.com), offers a continuous service with up to four departures per hour (1 per hr midnight–6am). While it's not compulsory to buy a ticket in advance, it's highly advisable in midsummer or during school holidays. You must arrive at least thirty minutes before departure.

Fares are calculated per car, regardless of the number of passengers. Rates depend on time of year, time of day and length of stay (the cheapest ticket is for a day-trip, followed by a five-day return). In low season, travelling at antisocial hours, you can make the round trip for around £100; a return fare in July or August, with weekend departures, can reach £400. Bikes are carried on a specially adapted carriage that makes the crossing twice a day – it costs £32 for bike and person if you are staying more than five days, £16 if it's just a short break (all bike reservations on Ⓣ01303/282 201).

While the tunnel journey itself is fast and efficient, drivers heading for Brittany or Normandy should not underestimate the length of time it takes to drive across northern France from the tunnel exit. Just to reach Le Tréport, the eastern extremity of Normandy, takes a good two hours, while western Brittany would take more like eight hours.

Combined train/ferry routes

You can buy connecting tickets from any British station to any French station, via any

Sea crossings from the UK

Route	Operator	Crossing Time	Frequency
Brittany			
Portsmouth–St-Malo	Brittany Ferries	10hr 45min	1 daily
Poole–St-Malo (via Jersey or Guernsey)	Condor Ferries	4hr 35min	2–6 daily May–Sept
Plymouth–Roscoff	Brittany Ferries	6–8hr	0–2 daily March–Oct
Weymouth–St-Malo (via Jersey or Guernsey)	Condor Ferries	5hr 15min	2–7 weekly, May–Dec
Normandy			
Newhaven–Dieppe	Transmanche	4hr	1–2 daily
Portsmouth–Cherbourg	Brittany Ferries	3hr*–7hr	1–2 daily
Portsmouth–Cherbourg	Condor Ferries	5hr	Sun, late May to early Sept
Poole–Cherbourg	Brittany Ferries	2hr 15min*–5hr	1–3 daily
Portsmouth–Caen	Brittany Ferries	3hr 30min*–6hr	2–4 daily
Portsmouth–Le Havre	LD Lines	5hr 30min	1 daily
Pas-de-Calais			
Dover–Calais	P&O Ferries	1hr 30min	23 daily
Dover–Calais	Sea France	1hr 30min	15 daily
Dover–Dunkerque	NorfolkLine	2hr	9–12 daily

*These services use high-speed catamarans

Ferry operators

Brittany Ferries	ⓣ0871 244 0744	ⓦbrittanyferries.com
Condor Ferries	ⓣ0845 609 1024	ⓦcondorferries.co.uk
LD Lines	ⓣ0844 576 8836	ⓦldlines.co.uk
NorfolkLine	ⓣ0844 847 5042	ⓦnorfolkline.com
P&O Ferries	ⓣ0871 664 5645	ⓦpoferries.com
Sea France	ⓣ0871 423 7119	ⓦseafrance.com
Transmanche Ferries	ⓣ0800 917 1201	ⓦtransmancheferries.com

of the ferry routes. Details and prices (again with various special and seasonal offers) are obtainable from any British Rail travel centre. Students and anyone under 26 can buy heavily discounted tickets from Eurotrain outlets such as STA Travel and most student travel agents.

Rail travellers catching ferries from Portsmouth should be warned that "Portsmouth Harbour" station is nowhere near the cross-Channel ferry terminals. The only connecting bus service is very intermittent; contact Bailey's Transport (ⓣ07721/877722) for details.

By air

Air France (ⓦairfrance.com) offer daily flights from London City Airport to **Nantes**. In addition, two budget airlines operate flights from Britain to Brittany and Normandy. Ryanair (ⓦryanair.com) fly from London Stansted to Dinard; from London Luton to Brest; from East Midlands airport to Dinard and Nantes; and from both Leeds and Liverpool to Nantes. British European (ⓦflybe.com) fly to Brest from Birmingham and Southampton, and to Rennes from Southampton and Edinburgh. At times the quoted fares drop to zero, but by the time taxes are included you're very unlikely to pay under £50 return, and £100 is generally more realistic.

By coach

Eurolines coach services (ⓣ08717 81 8181, ⓦwww.eurolines.co.uk) connect London with only the main towns in Brittany and Normandy. Typical adult single fares in

Sea crossings and fares from Ireland

Route	Operator	Crossing Time	Frequency
Cork–Roscoff	Brittany Ferries	14hr	Mid-March to Oct, Sat 4.30pm
Rosslare–Cherbourg	Irish Ferries	18hr 30min	3–4 weekly
Rosslare–Cherbourg	LD Lines	17hr	0–6 weekly
Rosslare–Roscoff	Irish Ferries	16hr	2 weekly May–Sept

Ferry operators

Brittany Ferries	ⓣ021/427 7801	ⓦbrittanyferries.ie
Irish Ferries	ⓣ0818/300 400	ⓦirishferries.com
LD Lines	ⓣ0844/576 8836	ⓦldlines.co.uk

summer from London are £80 to Rennes and Nantes, £50 to Rouen and £25 to Calais, from where you can make train connections to Normandy and Brittany.

From Ireland

As detailed above, three operators run ferries direct to Brittany and Normandy from Ireland. Services between Rosslare and both **Cherbourg** and **Le Havre** operate year-round, while in summer it's also possible to sail from Cork or Rosslare to **Roscoff**.

By air

Aer Lingus (ⓦaerlingus.ie) fly direct from Dublin and Cork to Paris CDG, while Ryanair (ⓦryanair.com) fly from Dublin and Shannon to Nantes, and from several Irish airports to London Stansted, where you can pick up onward flights to Dinard as well.

From the US and Canada

Getting to France from the US or Canada is straightforward; direct flights connect over thirty major North American cities with Paris. From there, it's simple to continue to Brittany or Normandy by rail – Rouen is just over an hour away, while super-fast TGV trains get to either Rennes or Nantes in around two hours – or by air. A connecting flight to Brest, the remotest Breton city, costs approximately US$150 extra.

Although flying to London is usually the cheapest way to reach Europe, price differences are so minimal that there's no point travelling to France via London unless you've specifically chosen to visit the UK as well.

A return midweek flight to Paris typically costs around $850 from Los Angeles, $750 from Houston and $650 from New York. From Canada, prices to Paris are in the region of Can$850 from Montréal and Toronto and Can$1100 from Vancouver.

From Australia, New Zealand and South Africa

Most travellers from **Australia** or **New Zealand** choose to fly to France via London; the majority of airlines can add a Paris leg to an Australia/New Zealand–Europe ticket. Flights via Asia or the Middle East, with a transfer or overnight stop in the airlines' home ports, are generally the cheapest option; those routed through the US tend to be slightly pricier. The cheapest return fares start at around Aus$2000 from Sydney, Perth and Darwin and NZ$2000 from Auckland.

From **South Africa**, Johannesburg is the best place to start, with Air France flying direct to Paris from around R8000 return; from Cape Town, they fly via Amsterdam and cost from around R11,000. BA, flying via London, comes in slightly more expensive, at upwards from R11,000 from Johannesburg and R12,000 from Cape Town.

Airlines, agents and operators

Airlines

Air Canada ⓦaircanada.com
Air France ⓦairfrance.com
Air Transat ⓦairtransat.com
American Airlines ⓦaa.com
bmi ⓦflybmi.com

bmibaby ⓦbmibaby.com
British Airways ⓦba.com
British European ⓦflybe.com
Continental Airlines ⓦcontinental.com
Delta ⓦdelta.com
easyJet ⓦeasyjet.com
Jet2 ⓦjet2.com
Northwest/KLM ⓦnwa.com
United Airlines ⓦunited.com
US Airways ⓦusair.com

Travel agents

North South Travel ⓦnorthsouthtravel.co.uk
STA Travel ⓦstatravel.com
Trailfinders ⓦtrailfinders.com

Tour and package operators

UK

Blakes Holidays ⓣ0845/604 3985, ⓦblakes.co.uk. Self-catering canal trips in Brittany, starting from Redon. Typical high-season rental rates range from £1200 per week for a two-berth boat to £2200 for a twelve-berth vessel.
Brittany Travel ⓣ0845/230 1380, ⓦbrittany.co.uk. Self-catering holidays throughout Brittany, and especially the Morbihan; typical summer rentals for four-person cottages and apartments cost £500–700 weekly.
French Connections ⓦfrenchconnections.co.uk. Website offering holiday rentals throughout Brittany and Normandy, arranged direct with the owners at advantageous rates.
Gîtes de France ⓦgites-de-france.fr. Comprehensive list of houses, cottages and chalets throughout France that can be booked online, or through Brittany Ferries (ⓣ0871/244 0744) in the UK.
Holiday France ⓦholidayfrance.org.uk. Online search for French tour operators by holiday type and location; run by Association of British Tour Operators.
Holt's Battlefield Tours ⓣ01293/865000, ⓦholts.co.uk. Definitive guided battlefield tours; five-day tours to Normandy covering the D-Day landings or other aspects of the invasion, for around £750.
Matthews Holidays ⓣ01483/284044, ⓦmatthewsholidays.co.uk. Self-drive mobile-home holidays on good-quality campsites in southern Brittany; a week for a family with two children, staying in Benodet and including ferry travel with car, ranges from £300 to £700 depending on the season.
Saddle Skedaddle ⓣ0191/265 1110, ⓦskedaddle.co.uk. A week's self-guided cycle tour in northern Brittany – six days cycling, seven nights in hotels – costs £530 per person for two travelling together.

Six steps to a better kind of travel

At Rough Guides we are passionately committed to travel. We feel strongly that only through travelling do we truly come to understand the world we live in and the people we share it with. But the extraordinary growth in tourism has also damaged some places irreparably, and of course **climate change** is exacerbated by most forms of transport, especially flying. This means that now more than ever it's important to **travel thoughtfully** and **responsibly**, with respect for the cultures you're visiting – not only to derive the most benefit from your trip but also to preserve the best bits of the planet for everyone to enjoy. At Rough Guides we feel there are six main areas in which you can make a difference:

- Consider what you're contributing to the **local economy**, and how much the services you use do the same.
- Consider the **environment** on holiday as well as at home. The biodiversity of local flora and fauna can be adversely affected by tourism. Try to patronize businesses that take account of this.
- Travel with a purpose, not just to tick off experiences. Consider **spending longer** in a place, and getting to know it and its people.
- Give thought to how often you **fly**. Try to avoid short hops by air and more harmful night flights.
- Consider **alternatives to flying**, travelling instead by bus, train, boat and even by bike or on foot where possible.
- Make your trips "**climate neutral**" via a reputable carbon offset scheme. All Rough Guide flights are offset, and every year we donate money to a variety of charities devoted to combating the effects of climate change.

VFB Holidays ⓣ01452/716840, ⓦvfbholidays.co.uk. Cottages all over Brittany and Normandy, especially southern Finistère, and also self-drive hotel holidays. Prices, including ferry travel, for a two-week cottage stay for two range seasonally £250–750.

UK Camping operators

Canvas Holidays ⓣ0845/268 0827, ⓦcanvas.co.uk
Eurocamp ⓣ0844/406 0402, ⓦeurocamp.co.uk
Keycamp ⓣ0844/406 0200, ⓦkeycamp.co.uk
Vacansoleil ⓣ0333/7005050, ⓦvacansoleil.co.uk

US and Canada

Backroads ⓣ1-800/GO-ACTIVE, ⓦbackroads.com. Cycling and hiking tours for families and singles, with the emphasis on going at your own pace. Accommodation ranges from campsites to luxury hotels.
Classic Journeys ⓣ1-800/200-3887, ⓦclassicjourneys.com. Seven-day coastal walking holidays in Normandy and Brittany, incorporating 3–4 hours of walking a day and costing $3895.
EC Tours ⓣ1-800/388-0877, ⓦectours.com. Two and eight-day tours of Normandy, Brittany and the Loire from Paris, for $230 and $1650 respectively.
France Vacations ⓣ1-800/539-7098, ⓦfrancevacations.net. Air/hotel and fly-drive packages to Normandy.
The French Experience ⓣ1-800/283-7262, ⓦfrenchexperience.com. Flexible escorted and self-drive tours, châteaux, apartment and cottage rentals, airfare arrangements, plus day-trips from Paris to Norman destinations.
Infohub ⓦinfohub.com. Web portal with a huge range of escorted and self-guided cultural, gastronomy and activity French holidays.
Viking River Cruises ⓣ1-800/304-9616, ⓦvikingrivercruises.com. French river cruises, including a week-long trip from Paris to Honfleur along the Seine, starting at $1399 in low season.

Australia and New Zealand

Travel.com Australia ⓣ1300/130 483, ⓦtravel.com.au. Comprehensive online travel company.
Viatour Australia ⓣ02/8219 5400, ⓦviator.com. Bookings for hundreds of travel suppliers worldwide, covering all regions of France.

Getting around

The best way to travel around Brittany and Normandy is with a car or a bike. Public transport is far from impressive. SNCF trains are efficient, as ever in France, and the Atlantique TGV has reduced the Paris–Rennes journey to a mere two hours fifteen minutes, but the rail network circles the coast and, especially in Brittany, barely serves the inland areas.

Buses do complement the trains to some extent – SNCF buses often pick up routes that trains no longer follow – but on the whole their timetables are geared much more to market, school or working hours than to the needs of tourists, and it can take a very long time to get where you want to go. If you come without your own transport, the ideal solution is to make longer journeys by train or bus, then to rent a bike (never a problem) to explore a particular locality.

Approximate journey times and frequencies for trains, buses and boats can be found under "Travel details" at the end of each chapter in this book.

Driving

Car rental in France costs upwards of €250 per week (from around €70 a day); few British travellers see it as an economic alternative to bringing their own vehicle across the Channel. However, the major international rental chains are found throughout the region, including at the ferry ports. Booking online, through the websites of the major chains (see opposite), is usually cheaper than renting on the spot.

North Americans and Australians should be forewarned that it is very difficult to rent a car with **automatic transmission**; if you can't drive a stickshift, try to book an automatic well in advance, and expect to pay a much higher price for it. Most rental companies will only rent cars to customers aged under 25 on payment of a young driver surcharge of around €20–25 per day; you still must be over 21 and have driven for at least one year.

Petrol/gas (*essence*) or diesel fuel (*gazoil*) is least expensive at out-of-town superstores, and most expensive on the autoroutes. At night, many stations are unmanned, and often their automated 24 hour pumps will only accept French bank cards. Typical fuel prices as this book went to press were around €1.40 a litre for unleaded (*sans plomb*), €1.35 for four-star (*Super*) and €1.15 for diesel; for British motorists, that made it cheaper to fill up in the UK than in France.

Autoroute driving, while fast, tends to be boring when it's not hair-raising, and the tolls in Normandy are expensive.

If you run into **mechanical difficulties**, all the major car manufacturers have garages and service stations in France. You can find them in the phone book under "Garages d'automobiles". For breakdowns, look under "Dépannages". If you have an accident or break-in, make a report to the local police (and keep a copy) in order to make an insurance claim.

For motoring vocabulary, see p.413.

Car rental agencies

Alamo Ⓦalamo.com
Auto Europe Ⓦautoeurope.com
Avis Ⓦavis.com
Budget Ⓦbudget.com
Dollar Ⓦdollar.com
Enterprise Rent-a-Car Ⓦenterprise.com
Europcar Ⓦeuropcar.com
Europe by Car Ⓦeuropebycar.com
Hertz Ⓦhertz.com
Holiday Autos Ⓦholidayautos.co.uk
National Ⓦnationalcar.com
Thrifty Ⓦthrifty.com

Legal requirements

British, Irish, Australian, Canadian, New Zealand and US **driving licences** are valid in France, though an International Driver's Licence makes life easier. If the vehicle is rented, its registration document (*carte grise*) and the insurance papers must be carried. The **minimum driving age** is 18, and provisional licences are not valid.

The vehicle registration document and the **insurance papers** must be carried; only the originals are acceptable. It's no longer essential for motorists from other EU countries to buy a green card to extend their usual insurance. If you have insurance at home then you have the minimal legal coverage in France; whether you have any more than that, and (if not) whether you want to buy more, is something to discuss with your own insurance company.

If your car is right-hand drive, you must have your **headlight dip** adjusted to the right before you go and as a courtesy change or paint them to yellow or stick on black glare deflectors. Shops at the ferry terminals sell headlight deflectors that achieve both aims – you basically pay £8 for two small pieces of sticky yellow plastic, but they do the job.

Similarly, you must also affix **GB plates** if you're driving a British car, and carry a red warning triangle, a reflective jacket and a spare set of headlight bulbs in your vehicle.

Seat belts are compulsory for the driver and all passengers; children under 10 can only sit in the front seat if they're in approved rear-facing child seats.

Rules of the road

The French **drive on the right**. Most drivers used to driving on the left find it easy to adjust. The biggest problem if you're driving a British car tends to be visibility when you want to overtake; you can buy special forward-view mirrors that may help.

Although the law of *priorité à droite* – which said you have to give way to traffic coming from your right, even when it is coming from a minor road – has largely been phased out, it still applies on some roads in built-up areas, so be vigilant at junctions. A sign showing a yellow diamond on a white background indicates that you have **right of way**, while the same sign with an oblique black slash warns you that vehicles emerging from the right have priority. **Stop signs** mean stop completely; *Cédez le passage* means "Give way". Other signs warning of potential

Road information

Up-to-the-minute traffic information for all French roads can be obtained from the Bison Futé free-dial recorded information service (ⓣ08.00.10.02.00; French only) or website ⓦwww.bison-fute.equipement.gouv.fr. Information on autoroutes is also available on the bilingual website ⓦautoroutes.fr.

dangers include *déviation* (diversion), *gravillons* (loose chippings), *boue* (mud) and *chaussée déformée* (uneven surface).

The main French national **speed limits**, which apply unless otherwise posted, are 130kph (80mph) on the tolled autoroutes; 110kph (68mph) on dual carriageways; and 90kph (56mph) on other roads. In wet weather, and for drivers with less than two years' experience, these limits are 110kph (68mph), 100kph (62mph) and 80kph (50mph) respectively. There's also a ceiling of 50kph (31mph) in towns and on autoroutes when fog reduces visibility to less than 50m. Stiff **penalties** for driving violations can mean fines of up to €75,000 and a suspended licence. The standard **fine** for exceeding the speed limit by 20kph (12mph), for example, is €90; above 40kph (25mph) you will not only be fined but will also have to go to court. The legal **blood alcohol limit** is 0.05 percent (0.5 grams per litre, which is lower than in the UK and North America), and random breath tests are common.

By scooter and motorbike

Scooters are relatively easy to find, and are ideal for pottering around local areas. Places that rent out bicycles often also rent scooters; expect to pay around €45 a day for a 50cc machine, less for longer periods. You only need a **motorbike licence** for bikes larger than 50cc. Rental prices for a motorbike are around €65 a day for a 125cc bike; expect to leave a hefty deposit – over €1000 is the norm – by cash or credit card too. **Crash helmets** are compulsory on all bikes, whatever the size, and the headlight must be switched on at all times. You are recommended to carry a first-aid kit and a set of spare bulbs.

Trains

French **trains**, operated by the nationally owned SNCF (ⓣ08.05.90.36.35, ⓦsncf.com), are by and large clean, fast and frequent, and their staff both courteous and helpful. All but the smallest stations (*gares SNCF*) have an information desk, while many also rent out bicycles.

Regional **timetables** and leaflets covering particular lines are available free at stations. "Autocar" (often abbreviated to "car") at the top of a column means it's an SNCF bus service, on which rail tickets and passes are valid. **Fares** are reasonable; children under 12 travel half-price and under-4s free. The ultra-fast TGVs (*Trains à Grande Vitesse*) require a supplement at peak times. The slowest trains, marked *Autotrain* in the timetable, stop at all stations.

Try to use the counter service for buying tickets, rather than the complicated computerized system; the latter changes the price of TGV tickets depending on demand, and you may find you've bought an expensive ticket without realizing that a later train is cheaper.

All tickets – but not passes – must be date-stamped in the orange machines at station platform entrances. It is an offence not to follow the instruction to *Compostez votre billet* ("Validate your ticket"). Train journeys may be broken for up to 24 hours at a time for as long as the ticket is valid (usually two months); if you plan longer stopovers, it's best to indicate this when buying your ticket.

For details on taking your bicycle by train, see opposite.

Discounts and rail passes

French train **timetables** are divided into *période blanche* (normal or white period), and the cheaper *période bleue*, (off-peak or blue period). In conjunction with this, a large number of **discounts** are available. SNCF itself offers a range of travel cards, which can be purchased online or from main *gares SNCF*, and are valid for one year. Over-60s can get the Carte Senior (€56), which entitles the holder to up to fifty percent off tickets on TGVs, subject to availability, or other journeys starting during blue periods, and a 25 percent reduction on normal, white-period fares. The same percentage reductions are available for anyone under 26 (Carte 12–25; €49) and for up to four people travelling with a child under 12 (Carte Enfant Plus; €65). Those aged between 26 and 59 years can purchase a Carte Escapades (€85), but this only entitles the holder to a forty percent reduction on normal, white-period fares.

Buses

Buses cover far more Breton and Norman routes than the trains – and even when towns do have a rail link, buses are often quicker, cheaper and more direct. They are almost always short distance, however, requiring you to change if you're going further than from one town to the next. And timetables tend to be constructed to suit working, market and school hours – often dauntingly early when they do run, and prone to stop just when tourists need them most, becoming virtually nonexistent on Sundays.

Larger towns usually have a central **gare routière** (bus station), most often found next to the *gare SNCF*. However, the private bus companies (who provide most of the Breton services) don't always work together and may leave from an array of different points. The most convenient lines are those run by SNCF as an extension of rail links, which always run to/from the SNCF station (assuming there is one).

Cycling

Bicycles have high status in France. The car ferries and SNCF trains carry them for a minimal charge, and the French respect cyclists – both as traffic, and, when you stop off at a restaurant or hotel, as customers. French drivers normally go out of their way to make room for you; it's the great British caravan you might have to watch out for.

Most importantly, distances in Brittany and Normandy are not great, the hills are sporadic and not too steep, cities like Rennes and Nantes have useful networks of **cycle lanes**, and the scenery is nearly always a delight. Even if you're quite unused to it, cycling sixty kilometres per day soon becomes very easy – and it's a good way to keep yourself fit enough to enjoy the rich regional food.

Most cyclists use **mountain bikes**, which the French call VTTs (*Vélos Touts Terrains*), for touring holidays, although if you've ever made a direct comparison you'll know it's much less effort, and much quicker, to cycle long distances and carry luggage on a traditional touring or racing bike. Whichever you prefer, do use cycle panniers; a backpack in the sun is unbearable.

Restaurants and hotels along the way are nearly always obliging about looking after your bike, even to the point of allowing it into your room. Most large towns have well-stocked retail and repair shops, where parts are normally cheaper than in Britain or the US. However, if you're using a foreign-made bike, it's a good idea to carry spare tyres, as French sizes are different. Neither is it easy to find parts for mountain bikes, the French enthusiasm being directed towards racers instead. Inner tubes are not a problem, as they adapt to either size, though you should always be sure that you get the right valves. The best places to find foreign parts are in Raleigh stockists.

The **train network** runs various schemes for cyclists, outlined in the free leaflet *Train et Vélo*, available from most stations. Trains marked with a bicycle in the timetable, and some TGVs, carry bikes free, either in the dedicated bike racks or in the luggage van so long as there's space; in the latter case, reserve a slot several days in advance (for €10). Otherwise, you can take your dismantled bike, packed in a carrier, on TGVs and other trains with sufficiently large luggage racks. Another option is to send your bike parcelled up as registered luggage for a fee of €39; delivery should take two days, with no service at weekends. **Eurostar** allows you to take your bicycle provided it's dismantled and packed in a bag no more than 120cm by 90cm. However, they encourage people to send their bikes unaccompanied with Eurostar's registered baggage service, Esprit Europe (ⓣ0870/585 0850, ⓦespriteurope.co.uk) for £20 one way, with a guaranteed arrival time of 24 hours; you can register your bike, which does not need to be dismantled, up to 24 hours before departure.

Bikes are often available to **rent** from campsites and hostels, as well as from cycle shops, some tourist offices and train stations and from seasonal stalls on islands, from perhaps €12 per day.

The UK's national cyclists' association, the CTC (Ⓣ0844/736 8451, Ⓦctc.org.uk), can suggest routes and supply advice for members (£36 a year or £58.50 for a family of four, and £12 for under 26 years). They run a particularly good insurance scheme. Companies offering specialist bike touring holidays are listed on pp.23–24.

For cycling vocabulary, see p.414.

Boat trips and inland waterways

Boat trips on many of Brittany and Normandy's rivers, as well as out to the islands, are detailed throughout this book. More excitingly, you can **rent a canoe**, boat or even **houseboat** and make your own way along sections of the Nantes–Brest canal. French Government Tourist Offices have lists of French and foreign operators who arrange boat rental, as do websites like Ⓦwww.france-nautic.com, Ⓦbretagne-info-nautisme.fr and Ⓦbretagne-fluviale.com. You can also contact Blakes Holidays in the UK (Ⓣ0845/604 3985, Ⓦblakes.co.uk; see p.23).

There is no charge for use of the waterways in Brittany or Normandy, and you can travel by boat without a permit for up to six months in a year. For information on maximum dimensions, documentation, regulations and so forth, see Ⓦvnf.fr.

Walking

Neither Brittany nor Normandy is serious hiking country. There are no mountains or extensive wilderness areas, and casual rambling along the clifftops and beside the waterways is the limit of most people's aims. However, 21 of the French GR long-distance walking trails – the *sentiers de grande randonnée* – run through the area. The GRs are fully signposted and equipped with campsites and rest huts along the way. The most interesting are the GR2 (*Sentier de la Seine*), which runs from Le Havre to Les Andelys; the GR341 (*Sentier de Bretagne*) along the Granit-Rose coast between Lannion and St-Brieuc; and the GR347 (*Val d'Oust au pays Gallo*) between Josselin and Redon.

Each GR path is described in a *Topo-guide*, which gives a detailed account of the route (in French), including maps, campsites, sources of provisions and so on. These are produced by the principal French walkers' organization, the Fédération Française de la Randonnée Pédestre (Ⓣ01.44.89.93.93, Ⓦffrandonnee.fr).

In addition, many tourist offices provide guides to their local footpaths.

Accommodation

Most of the year, accommodation is plentiful in both Brittany and Normandy, and visitors can expect to be able just to turn up in a town and find a room in a hotel or a place on a campsite.

The Language section at the back should help you make any necessary phone calls if you're uncertain of your French, though many hoteliers and campsite managers, and almost all hostel managers, speak some English.

Problems arise mainly between July 15 and the end of August, when the French take their own vacations en masse – the first weekend of August is the busiest time of all. That said, the whole of July and August, extending in the more touristy areas to the period from mid-June to mid-September, is **high season** for the hotels. With campsites, which are generally open from around Easter to October or November, you can be more relaxed, unless you're touring with a caravan or camper van.

The tourist season in Brittany and Normandy runs roughly from Easter until the end of September; while hotels in the cities remain open all year, those in smaller towns and, especially, seaside resorts often close for several months during the winter (Nov–March, for instance). It's quite possible to turn up somewhere in January or February to find that every hotel is closed; in addition, many family-run places close each year for two or three weeks some time between May and September, and some hotels in smaller towns and villages close for one or two nights a week, usually Sunday or Monday.

Hotels

French **hotels** tend to be better value for money than they are in Britain and much of northern Europe, but not as good as in North America. In most towns, you'll be able to get a double room for around €50 (£42), or a single for around €40 (£33), though this will typically mean sharing a shower and/or toilet.

All French hotels are graded from zero to five stars. The price more or less corresponds to the number of stars, though the system is a little haphazard, having more to do with ratios of bathrooms per guest than genuine quality; ungraded and single-star hotels are often very good. North American visitors accustomed to staying in hotel rooms equipped with items like coffee-makers, safes and refrigerators should not automatically expect the same facilities in French hotels however, even the more expensive ones. Lifts

Accommodation price codes

All **hotel prices** in this book have been coded using the symbols below. The price shown is for the **least expensive double room in high season**, which, for categories ❶ and ❷ may well mean a room without private bath, shower or toilet, though there's usually a washbasin, and it's surprisingly common to have a shower but not a toilet. Reviews in this guide make it clear whether rooms have en-suite facilities. In any case, even cheaper hotels usually also have rooms with en-suite facilities, which typically cost around €15–25 extra. In the ❸ category and above, all rooms tend to be equipped with private facilities.

Although many hotels offer rooms at differing prices, ranges (such as ❷–❼) are only indicated when the spectrum is especially broad, or where there are relatively few rooms in the lowest category.

❶ €40 and Under	❹ €66–80	❼ €121–150
❷ €41–50	❺ €81–100	❽ €151–200
❸ €51–65	❻ €101–120	❾ €200 and Over

are also very much the exception rather than the rule in Normandy and Brittany. Genuine single rooms are rare; lone travellers normally end up in an ordinary double let at a slightly reduced rate. On the other hand most hotels willingly equip rooms with extra beds, for three or more people, at a good discount.

Breakfast, which is never included in the quoted price, can add €7–15 per person, though there is no obligation to take it. The cost of eating dinner in a hotel's restaurant can be a more important factor to bear in mind when picking a place to stay. Officially hotels are not supposed to insist that you take meals, but they often do, and in busy resorts you may not find a room unless you agree to *demi-pension* (half-board). If you are unsure, ask to see the menu before checking in; cheap rooms aren't so cheap if you have to eat a €30 meal.

One of the great pleasures of travelling in the region is the sheer quality of **village hotels**. The fixtures and fittings may not always date from the twentieth century, let alone the twenty-first – at the bottom of the range, you'll find corduroy carpets creeping up the walls, blotchy linoleum curling from buckled wooden floors and clanking great brass keys that won't quite turn in the ill-fitting doors. However, the standards of service are consistently high, and it's rare indeed to stay in a hotel that doesn't take pride in maintaining a well-appointed and good-value restaurant serving traditional local food. **Wi-fi** is very widely available in hotels.

In recent years, outlets of several French **motel** chains have begun to proliferate, usually located alongside major through-routes on the outskirts of larger towns. Other than close to the ferry ports, there are fewer of these in Brittany and Normandy than elsewhere in the country, but those that do exist make a good alternative option for motorists, especially late at night.

The largest and most useful of the French **hotel federations** is Logis de France (Ⓦlogis-de-france.fr), an association of over 3500 independent hotels, promoted together for their consistently good food and reasonably priced rooms; they're recognizable on the spot by a green-and-yellow logo of a hearth. They produce a free annual guide, available from French tourist offices (see p.45), Logis de France itself, or from member hotels. Two other, more upmarket federations worth mentioning are Châteaux & Hôtels de France (Ⓦchateauxhotels.com) and the Relais du Silence (Ⓦrelaisdusilence.com).

Bed and breakfast, rented accommodation and gîtes

In country areas, in addition to standard hotels, you will come across *chambres d'hôtes*, **bed-and-breakfast** accommodation in someone's house or farm. These vary in standard, but are rarely an especially cheap option; they usually cost the equivalent of a two-star hotel. However, if you strike lucky, they can be good sources of traditional home cooking. Average prices range between €60 and €100 for two people including breakfast; payment is almost always expected in cash. Some offer meals on request (*tables d'hôtes*), usually evenings only.

It's also worth considering renting **self-catering** accommodation. This will generally consist of self-contained country cottages known as *gîtes* or *gîtes ruraux*. Many *gîtes* are in converted barns or farm outbuildings, though some can be quite grand.

Lists of both *gîtes* and *chambres d'hôtes* are available from Gîtes de France (Ⓣ01.49.70.75.75, Ⓦgites-de-france.fr); you can search their website for accommodation by type or theme as well as area, for example choosing a *gîte* near fishing or riding opportunities. Tourist offices maintain lists of places in their area that are not affiliated to Gîtes de France, and you can also find self-catering accommodation, often foreign-owned, advertised online, including through the outlets listed on pp.23–24.

Hostels, foyers and gîtes d'étapes

Auberges de Jeunesse – **hostels** – are invaluable for single travellers on a budget, costing anything from €10 up to €20 per night for a dormitory bed. For couples, however, and certainly for groups of three or more people, they'll not necessarily work out less than the cheaper hotels – particularly if you've had to pay a bus fare out to the edge of town to reach them. However, many of the hostels in Normandy and Brittany are beautifully sited, and they do allow you to cut costs by preparing your own food in their kitchens, or eating in cheap canteens.

As well as the two rival **French hostelling associations** – the Fédération Unie des Auberges de Jeunesse (FUAJ; ⓦfuaj.org), and the much smaller Ligue Française pour les Auberges de Jeunesse (LFAJ; ⓦauberges-de-jeunesse.com) – there are now also plenty of independent hostels, where dorm beds cost €15–20 with breakfast thrown in, though these tend to be party places with an emphasis on good times rather than sleep.

Normally, to stay at FUAJ or LFAJ hostels you must show a current Hostelling International (HI) **membership card**. Visit ⓦhihostels.com for details of your national youth hostel association and membership prices, as well as for worldwide booking facilities.

A few large towns provide a more luxurious standard of hostel accommodation in Foyers des Jeunes Travailleurs/euses, residential hostels for young workers and students, where you can usually get a private room for €12 or more. Most have good cafeterias or canteens.

A further hostel-type alternative exists in the countryside, especially in hiking or cycling areas, in the form of the **gîtes d'étapes**. Less formal than hostels, these are often run by the local village or municipality, and provide basic hospital-style beds and simple kitchen facilities from around €10. They are marked on the large-scale IGN walkers' maps and listed in individual GR *Topoguides*. For more information, visit ⓦwww.gites-refuges.com.

Camping

Practically every village and town in the country has at least one **campsite**, to cater for the thousands of French people who spend their holiday under canvas. The tourist boards for both Brittany and Normandy produce full lists of sites in their regions.

The cheapest – at around €12 per site per night – is usually the **Camping municipal**, run by the local municipality. In season or when they are officially open, they are always clean, with plenty of hot water, and often situated in the prime local position. Out of season, many of them don't even bother to have someone around to collect the overnight charge.

At superior categories of campsite, found especially on the coast, you'll pay prices similar to those of a budget hotel for the facilities – bars, restaurants, sometimes swimming pools. Many visitors spend their whole holiday at one site. If you plan to do the same – particularly if you've a caravan, camper van or substantial tent – book ahead. Reckon on paying at least €15 per head with a tent, €20 with a vehicle. Inland, *camping à la ferme* – on somebody's farm – is another (generally facility-less) possibility. The *Camping Qualité* designation (ⓦwww.campingqualite.com) indicates campsites with particularly high standards of hygiene, service and privacy, while the *Clef Verte* (ⓦlaclefverte.org) label is awarded to sites run along environmentally friendly lines.

Lists of sites are available from the Camping France website (ⓦwww.campingfrance.com), Gîtes de France (ⓦgites-de-france.fr), or at local tourist boards.

If you plan to do a lot of camping, an **international camping carnet** is a good investment. The carnet gives discounts at member sites and serves as useful identification. Many campsites will take it instead of making you surrender your passport during your stay, and it covers you for third-party insurance when camping. In Britain, it costs £4.95 from the **Camping and Caravanning Club** (ⓣ0845/130 7701, ⓦcampingandcaravanningclub.co.uk).

Lastly, a word of caution: never camp rough (*camping sauvage*, as the French call it) on anyone's land without first asking permission.

Food and drink

The superb range of food available has to rank among the principal reasons to visit Brittany and, especially, Normandy. You'll find a fully illustrated account of the characteristic cuisines of the two regions in the colour section *Feasting in Northern France*. With restaurant quality remaining consistently high, there are, to be honest, towns and villages where just about the only source of excitement is their gastronomic output.

With no wine production in Normandy, and only the Muscadet-style whites coming from the southeast of Brittany, the most interesting local **alcohol** is derived from the region's orchards. Cider is made everywhere, along with its pear equivalent, *poiré*, while Normandy is renowned for its **Calvados** (apple brandy) and Fécamp's **Benedictine** liqueur.

Restaurants

Both Brittany and Normandy hold countless **restaurants**, and in many towns **brasseries** add to the choice. There's no distinction between the two in terms of quality or price range, though brasseries, which resemble cafés, serve quicker meals at most hours of the day; restaurants tend to stick to the traditional meal times of noon until 2pm and 7 to 9.30pm. After 9pm or so, restaurants often serve only à la carte meals – invariably more expensive than choosing a set menu. For the more upmarket places it's wise to make reservations – easily done on the same day. In small towns it may be impossible to get anything other than a bar sandwich after 10pm; in major cities, central brasseries will serve until 11pm or midnight and one or two may stay open all night. Restaurants will usually be closed on one day of the week (often Mon), in addition to the odd lunchtime or evening. During low season (in other words, outside of July & Aug) in seasonal resorts, closing times might extend to a couple of days per week. Don't forget that hotel restaurants are open to non-residents, and are likely not only to offer the best food in town but also to do so at good-value prices; the green-and-yellow **Logis de France** symbol is always worth looking out for.

For a comprehensive glossary of French food and drink terms, see p.415.

Prices have to be posted outside. Normally there's a choice between one or more *menus fixes* (set menus) – where the number of courses has already been determined, the choice is limited, and service is included – and the *carte*, the full menu.

At the bottom price range, say below €17, *menus fixes* revolve around standard dishes, such as steak and chips (*steak frites*), chicken and chips (*poulet frites*), or various offal concoctions, though it's always worth looking out for the *plat du jour*, which may be more appealing. For €18 to €30, virtually any of the restaurants recommended in this guide will serve you a good three-course meal, while four-course blowouts, including a starter as well as separate meat and fish courses, cost from €28 to €60. Most expensive of all are the special seafood menus, offering giant platters of assorted crustaceans; away from the big centres such as Cancale and St-Malo, it pays to be wary of these, as the stuff may have been waiting around for several days for someone foolhardy enough to order it.

Going à la carte offers greater flexibility and, in the better restaurants, access to the chef's specialities, but you can expect to pay heavily for the privilege. A simple and perfectly legitimate ploy is to have just one course instead of the expected three or four. You can share dishes or just have several starters – a useful strategy for vegetarians. There's no minimum charge.

Weekly markets

The list below features the biggest and best markets of Brittany and Normandy, with an emphasis on those specializing in **fresh food** and **local produce**.

Bear in mind that in addition to the specific days listed here, most large cities – **Rennes**, **Rouen** and **Caen**, for example – tend to have markets every day (with the occasional exception of Mon).

	Normandy	Brittany
Monday	Bricquebec, Carentan, Pont-Audemer, Pont d'Ouilly, Pont-L'Êveque, St-Pierre-sur-Dives, Torigni-sur-Vire, Vimoutiers	Auray, Combourg, Concarneau, Douarnenez, Moncontour, Ploërmel, Questembert, Redon, Vitré
Tuesday	Alençon, Argentan, Bagnoles, Brionne, Caen, Cherbourg, Deauville, Grandcamp-Maisy, Lessay, Portbail, Thury-Harcourt, Villedieu-les-Poêles	Dinard, Le Conquet, Locmariaquer, Paimpol, Pont-Aven, St-Malo, St-Pol, La Trinité
Wednesday	Cabourg, Granville, Isigny-sur-Mer, Lisieux, Orbec, Pirou, Pontorson, St-Lô, St-Hilaire	Carnac, Douarnenez, Guérande, Piriac-sur-Mer, Quimper, Roscoff, St-Brieuc, Tréguier, Vannes
Thursday	Alençon, Carolles, Carteret, Cherbourg,Coutances, La Ferté-Macé, Forges-les-Eaux, Houlgate, Livarot Ste-Mère-Église	Binic, Dinan, Dinard, Hennebont, Huelgoat, Lamballe, Lannion, Malestroit Pont l'Abbé
Friday	Alençon, Argentan, Deauville, Eu, Langrune, Pont-Audemer, St-Hilaire, St-Valery, Valognes, St-Lô, Vimoutiers, Vire	Concarneau, Douarnenez, Guingamp, Jugon-les-Lacs, Perros-Guirec, Quimper, Quimperlé, St-Malo, Le Val-André
Saturday	Avranches, Bagnoles, Caudebec, Cherbourg, Coutainville, Dieppe, Domfront, Falaise, Granville, Honfleur, Lisieux, Ry, Sées, St-Lô, St-Vaast	Audierne, Dinard, Dol, Douarnenez, Erquy, Fougères, Guérande, Guingamp, Josselin, Locmariaquer, Morlaix, St-Brieuc, Quimper, Rennes, Vannes, Vitré
Sunday	Alençon, Argentan, Brionne, Cabourg, Cherbourg, Caen, La Ferrière-sur-Risle, Port-en-Bessin, St-Valery (summer), Trouville	Auray, Cancale, Carnac, Quimper

North American visitors should bear in mind that in France an *entrée* is an appetizer or starter; the main course of the meal is the *plat principal*. In the French sequence of courses, any salad (sometimes vegetables, too) comes separate from the main dish, and cheese precedes a dessert. You will be offered coffee, which almost always costs extra, to finish off the meal.

Service compris (*s.c.*) means the **service charge** is included, which is usually the case on all set menus; *service non compris* (*s.n.c.*), or *service en sus*, means that it isn't, and you need to calculate an additional fifteen percent. **Wine** (*vin*) or a drink (*boisson*) is unlikely to be included, although a glass is occasionally thrown in with cheaper menus.

The French not only offer reduced-price children's menus but also create an atmosphere, even in otherwise fairly snooty establishments, that positively welcomes kids. It is regarded as self-evident that large family groups should be able to eat out

Vegetarians

On the whole, **vegetarians** can expect a somewhat lean time in Brittany and Normandy. One or two towns have specifically vegetarian restaurants (detailed in the text), but elsewhere you'll have to hope you find a sympathetic restaurant (crêperies can be good standbys). Sometimes they're willing to replace a meat dish on the *menu fixe* with an omelette; other times you'll have to pick your way through the *carte*. Remember the phrase "*je suis végétarien(ne); il y a quelques plats sans viande?*" (I'm a vegetarian; are there any non-meat dishes?).

If you are **vegan**, however, you should probably forget about eating in French restaurants altogether and try to cook your own food.

together. That said, you may well be obliged to order the children's menu rather than a single, cheaper item à la carte, so things can work out expensive. A rather murkier area is that of **dogs** in the dining room; it can be quite a surprise in a provincial hotel to realize that the majority of your fellow diners are attempting to keep dogs concealed beneath their tables. One final note is that you should always call the waiter or waitress *Monsieur* or *Madame* (*Mademoiselle* if a young woman), never *garçon*, no matter what you were taught in school.

Cafés and snacks

The days when hotels gave you piles of croissants or *brioches* for **breakfast** are long gone; now it's virtually always bread, jam and a jug of coffee or tea for at least €7. If you're on the road, it makes more sense to pick up a croissant, *pain au chocolat* or sandwich in a bakery, for a fraction of the price.

For **midday meals** and **light snacks**, most bars and cafés – there's no real difference – advertise *les snacks*, or *un casse-croûte* (a bite), with pictures of omelettes, fried eggs, hot dogs or various sandwiches. Even when they don't, they'll usually fill a half or third of a baguette with such ingredients as *jambon* (ham), *fromage* (cheese), *thon* (tuna), *saucisson* (sausage) or *poulet* (chicken). Toasted sandwiches – most commonly *croques-monsieur* (cheese and ham) or *croques-madame* (cheese and bacon or sausage) – are also invariably on offer. Especially in rural areas, small bars may serve a moderate-priced *plat du jour* (chef's daily special) or *formule* (a limited or no-choice menu).

Crêpes, pancakes both sweet or savoury that are a traditional Breton speciality, are another very popular lunch. Almost every town has at least one crêperie, often serving set menus featuring a filled buckwheat *galette* as a main course and a sweet crêpe for dessert. You can also buy ready-cooked pancakes by the dozen.

For **picnic** and **takeaway food**, nothing beats buying fresh ingredients in one of the numerous local **markets** listed on p.33. If there isn't a market around on the day you need it, you'll find **charcuteries** everywhere – even in small villages. These sell cooked meats, prepared snacks such as *bouchées de la reine* (seafood vol-au-vents), ready-made dishes and assorted salads. You can buy by weight or ask for *une tranche* (a slice), *une barquette* (a carton) or *une part* (a portion). The cheapest, in towns, are the supermarkets' charcuterie counters.

Salons de thé, which open from mid-morning to late evening, serve brunches, salads, quiches, etc, as well as cake and ice cream and a wide selection of teas. They tend to be a good deal pricier than cafés or brasseries – you're paying for the ritzy surroundings.

Patisseries, of course, have impressive arrays of cakes and pastries, often using local cream to excess. In addition to standard French pastries, the Bretons specialize in heavy, pudding-like affairs, dripping with butter, such as *kouïgn-amann* and *gaufres* – cream-drenched waffles.

Drinking

Where you can eat you can invariably **drink**, and normally vice versa. Drinking is done at a leisurely pace, whether as a prelude to food (*apéritif*), a sequel (*digestif*), or the accompaniment.

Every bar or café is obliged to display a full price list, which will usually show progressively increasing prices for drinks at the bar (*au comptoir*), sitting down (*la salle*), and on the terrace (*la terrasse*).

Wine (*vin*) is the regular drink. Red is *rouge*, white is *blanc*, or there's *rosé*. *Vin de table* – plonk – is generally drinkable and always cheap. Restaurant mark-ups for quality wines can be outrageous, in a country where wine is so cheap in the shops; if you're worried about the cost, ask for *vin ordinaire*. You should in any case be given the house wine (or *cuvée*) unless you specify otherwise. When ordering, ask for *un quart* or *un pichet* (quarter-litre), *un demi-litre* (half-litre) or *une carafe* (a litre). In bars, you normally buy by the glass.

Strictly speaking, no wine is produced in Brittany or Normandy. However, along the lower Loire Valley, the *département* of Loire-Atlantique, centred on Nantes, is still generally regarded as "belonging" to Brittany – and is treated as such in this book. Vineyards here are responsible for the dry white **Muscadet** – which is what normally goes into *moules marinières* – and the even drier **Gros-Plant**. You'll find a brief account of how to visit some of the vineyards where they are made on p.339.

Cider (*cidre*) is extremely popular. In Brittany it's a standard accompaniment to a meal of crêpes and may be offered on restaurant *menus fixes*. Normans more often consume it in bars. Most of the many varieties are very dry and very wonderful. *Poiré*, pear cider, is also produced, but on a small scale and is not commercially distributed.

The familiar Belgian and German brands account for most of the **beer** you'll find. Draught (*à la pression*, usually Kronenbourg) is the cheapest drink you can have next to coffee and wine – ask for *un demi* (defined as 25cl). Bottled beer is exceptionally cheap in supermarkets.

British-style ales and stouts are also popular. Every town seems to have some Celtic-affiliated bar that sells Guinness, and good pubs can be found in cities like Brest, Rennes and Quimper. There are even home-grown Breton beers, such as Coreff from Morlaix, and Britt, a white beer brewed in Concarneau.

Strong alcohols are drunk from 5am as pre-work fortifiers, right through the day; Bretons have a reputation for commitment to this. Brandies and dozens of *eaux de vie* (spirits) and liqueurs are always available. In Normandy, the most famous are **Calvados**, brandy distilled from apples and left to mature for anything upwards of ten years, and **Benedictine**, distilled at Fécamp from an obscure mix of ingredients (see p.64). Measures are generous, but they don't come cheap, especially in restaurants (where Calvados is traditionally drunk as the *trou Normand*, or "hole", between courses). The same applies to imported spirits like whisky (Scotch).

On the soft drink front, you can buy cartons of unsweetened fruit juice in supermarkets, but bottled nectars such as apricot (*jus d'abricot*) and blackcurrant (*cassis*) still hold sway in cafés. Some cafés serve tiny glasses of fresh orange and lemon juice (*orange/citron pressé*); otherwise it's the standard fizzy cans. Bottles of mineral water (*eau minérale*) and spring water (*eau de source*) – either sparkling (*pétillante*) or still (*eau plate*) – abound, from the best-seller Perrier to the obscurest spa product. But there's not much wrong with the tap **water** (*eau du robinet*).

Coffee in Normandy is invariably espresso and very strong; in Brittany, particularly in villages, it is sometimes made in jugs, very weak. *Un café* or *un express* is black, *un crème* is white, *un café au lait* (served at breakfast) is espresso in a large cup or bowl filled up with hot milk. Most bars will also serve *un déca*, decaffeinated coffee. You can get ordinary **tea** (*thé*), usually Lipton's, everywhere, while herb teas (*tisanes*) are also widely available. The more common ones are *verveine* (verbena), *tilleul* (lime blossom) and *tisane* (camomile). *Chocolat chaud* (hot chocolate) lives up to the high standards of French food and drink, and can be ordered in any café.

The media

For anyone who can read French, or understand it when spoken, the print and electronic media in France match any in the world. English-language newspapers are usually available, many hotels offer English-language TV and BBC radio can easily be picked up.

Newspapers and magazines

British and North American **newspapers** – at the very least, the *International Herald Tribune* – are generally widely available, especially in summer and especially also in the larger towns such as Nantes and Rouen.

As for the **French press**, the widest circulations are enjoyed by the regional dailies. Throughout Normandy and Brittany, the most important and influential paper is *Ouest-France* (ouest-france.fr). Based in Rennes, this publishes numerous local editions, worth picking up for their listings supplements, at the very least. Of the national dailies, *Le Monde* (lemonde.fr) is the most intellectual and respected, with few concessions to entertainment, but a correctly styled French that is probably the easiest to understand. *Libération* (liberation.com; *Libé* for short), which has its own Rennes edition, is moderately left-wing, pro-European, independent and more colloquial, with good, if specific, coverage.

Weeklies, on the *Newsweek/Time* model, include the wide-ranging left-leaning *Le Nouvel Observateur* (nouvelobs.com), its right-wing counterpoint *L'Express* (lexpress.fr) and the centrist with bite, *Marianne* (marianne2.fr). The best, and funniest, investigative journalism is in the satirical *Canard Enchaîné* (lecanardenchaine.fr), unfortunately almost incomprehensible to non-native speakers.

Monthlies include the young and trendy *Nova* (www.novaplanet.com), which has excellent listings of cultural events.

Radio

The main **radio** provider, Radio France (radio-france.fr), operates seven stations, including the regional France Bleu network, France Culture, France Info for news and France Musique. Other major private stations include Europe 1 (europe1.fr) for news, debate and sport and NRJ (nrj.fr) for relentless chart music.

English-language broadcasts are available from the BBC (bbc.co.uk/worldservice), Radio Canada (rcinet.ca) and Voice of America (voa.gov). See their websites for local frequencies.

TV

French **terrestrial TV** has six channels: three public (France 2, France 3 and Arte/France 5); one subscription (Canal Plus – with some unencrypted programmes); and two commercial open broadcasts (TF1 and M6). Of these, TF1 and France 2 are the most popular, showing a broad mix of programmes.

Arte/France 5 (also known as La Cinquième) is a joint Franco-German cultural venture that transmits simultaneously in French and German; offerings include documentaries, art criticism, French and German movies and complete operas. During the day (7am–7pm), France 5 uses the frequency to broadcast educational programmes. Canal Plus is the main movie channel, with repeats of foreign films usually shown at least once in the original language. France 3 is strong on regional news and more heavyweight movies, including undubbed foreign films. The main French news broadcasts are at 8pm on France 2 and TF1.

Cable and **satellite** channels you may find available in hotels include CNN, BBC World and BBC Prime, Eurosport, MTV, Planète, which specializes in documentaries, Ciné Première and Canal Jimmy. The main French-run music channel is MCM.

Festivals and events

The most interesting Breton events are without doubt the region's cultural festivals. At the largest, the Lorient Festival Inter-Celtique (Aug), music, performance, food and drink of all seven Celtic nations are featured in a completely authentic gathering that pulls in cultural nationalists (and ethnic music fans) from Ireland to Spain. There are two smaller – and more particularly Breton – alternatives in the Nantes Quinzaine Celtique (June/July) and Quimper's Festival de Cornouaille (July).

Look out also for local club events put on by individual **Celtic folklore** groups – Cercles, Bagadou or, best of the lot, **Festou-Noz**. These are most prolific in Nantes, but wherever you are in the province, the listings pages of *Ouest-France* are worth scrutiny. The "Breton music" section at the end of this book recommends clubs and venues to check out.

Religious **pardons**, sometimes promoted as tourist attractions in Brittany, are rather different affairs. These are essentially church processions, organized by a particular community on the local saint's day. Though generally small-scale, some, like that at Ste-Anne-d'Auray, have over the centuries taken on more region-wide status as pilgrimages. Rather than being carnivals or fêtes, they are primarily very serious, centred on lengthy and rather gloomy church services. If you're not interested in the religious aspects, only the food and drink stalls are likely to hold any great appeal.

By and large, **Normandy** lacks any specific cultural traditions to celebrate, but does its best to make up with celebrations of related historic events – births and deaths of William the Conqueror, Ste Thérèse, etc. The **D-Day** (June 6) landings along the Invasion Beaches are always marked in some way. The regional and *départemental* tourist boards listed on p.45 are the best source of information.

In both Normandy and Brittany, avoid the *Spectacles*, camp and overpriced outdoor shows on some mythical theme or other, held most regularly (and most tackily) at Bagnoles and Elven.

On the more mainstream cultural side, the larger cities – Rouen, Rennes and Nantes – have active theatre, opera and classical music seasons, though little happens during the summer. Cinema is most interesting in these cities, too, and the region is host to perhaps the most accessible French **film festival** – Deauville's American Film Festival (Sept). Almost all foreign films will be dubbed into French; "v.o." in the listings signifies original language.

Both Rennes and Rouen lay claim to be "the capital of French rock"; Rennes is increasingly the one to watch, with its December *Transmusicales* (Ⓦ lestrans.com) attracting international stars to share the stage with local groups. Meanwhile, Carhaix's *Vieilles Charrues* (Ⓦ www.vieillescharrues.asso.fr) has established itself very rapidly as the biggest French **rock festival** of all.

Calendar of events

January to April

Carnival Granville, Feb. See p.144.
Scallop Festival Erquy, early April. See p.230.

May to August

Jazz Sous Les Pommiers Coutances, May. See p.143.
St-Yves Pardon Tréguier, third Sun in May. See p.243.
Art Rock Festival St-Brieuc, end May/early June. See p.235.
Étonnants Voyageurs St-Malo, end May/early June. See p.200.
D-Day Ceremonies Invasion Beaches, June 6. See p.122.
Pardon Le Faouët, last Sun in June. See p.313.
Tombées de la Nuit theatre and music festival Rennes, first ten days of July. See p.223.

Troménie Pardon Locronan, second Sun in July. See p.287.
Fête de Ste-Claire La Haye du Routot, July 16. See p.75.
Festival de Cornouaille Quimper, third week in July. See p.299.
Fête des Remparts Dinan, third weekend in July. See p.212.
Les Vieilles Charrues Rock festival Carhaix, third weekend in July. See p.313.
Pardon Ste-Anne-d'Auray, July 26. See p.366.
Pont du Rock festival Malestroit, last weekend in July. See p.326.
Festival of the Sea Locquirec, last Sun in July. See p.250.
Jazz Festival Vannes, end July. See p.370.
World Music Festival Crozon, end July/early Aug. See p.281.
Blessing of the Sea Le Tréport, Aug 2. See p.58.
Cheese Fair Livarot, first weekend Aug. See p.172.
Medieval Fair Moncontour, Aug. See p.233.
Festival Inter-Celtique Lorient, first to second Sun, Aug. See p.346.
Fête de la Brière Île de Fedrun, first fortnight in Aug. See p.378.
Semaines Musicales Quimper, first three weeks in Aug. See p.299.
La Route du Rock St-Malo, middle weekend in Aug. See p.197.
Normandy Horse Show Saint-Lô, mid-Aug. See p.185.
Saint Loup Breton Dance Festival Guingamp, mid-Aug. See p.234.
Horse Festival Lamballe, mid-Aug. See p.232.
Festival of the Sea St-Valery, mid-Aug. See p.62.
Folk-music Festival Île de Tatihou, mid-Aug. See p.139.
Onion Festival Roscoff, late Aug. See p.259.

September to December

Horse Show Le Pin, first Sun in Sept. See p.177.
Pardon Le Folgoët, first Sun in Sept. See p.268.
Kite-flying festival Dieppe, early Sept. See p.55.
American Film Festival Deauville, first week in Sept. See p.107.
Pardon Josselin, Sept 8. See p.321.
Holy Cross cattle and animal fair Lessay, second weekend in Sept. See p.142.
Archangel Michael Festival Mont-St-Michel, Sun nearest Sept 29. See p.148.
Cider Festival Caudebec, last Sun in Sept. See p.73.
Mycology Festival Bellême, late Sept/early Oct. See p.208.
British Film Festival Dinard, first week in Oct. See p.168.
Cider Festival Beuvron-en-Auge, last Sun in Oct. See p.171.
Herring Festival St-Valery, mid-Nov. See p.62.
Les Transmusicales international rock festival Rennes, first week in Dec. See p.223.

Travel essentials

Beaches

Beaches are public property within 5m of the high-tide mark, so you can walk past private villas and set foot on islands. Another law, however, forbids you to camp.

Children

Children and babies are generally welcome everywhere, including most bars and restaurants. Hotels charge by the room, and many either hold a few large family rooms, or charge a small supplement for an additional bed or cot. Family-run places will often babysit or offer a listening service while you eat or go out. Especially in seaside towns, most restaurants have children's menus or cook simpler food on request. SNCF charge nothing on trains and buses for under-4s, and half-fare for 4–11s. If you're renting a car, however, baby seats will normally cost extra. Most tourist offices have details of specific activities for children – in particular, many resorts supervise "clubs" for children on the beach. Something to be aware of – not that you can do much about it – is the difficulty of negotiating a child's buggy over the large cobbles that cover many of the older streets in town centres.

Costs

Changes in the euro exchange rate have made Brittany and Normandy significantly more expensive for foreigners to visit in recent years. However, distances (and transport costs) remain relatively small, while the price of food and accommodation is still lower than in Britain and much of northern Europe.

On a shoestring level, camping and eating at least one picnic meal a day, taking buses or cycling, two people travelling together could get by easily enough on €60 (£55/$90) per person per day. Moving slightly more upmarket, staying in modest hotels, spending a bit on restaurants and driving, you should reckon on around €90 (£80/$135) per person per day.

Accommodation is likely to represent the bulk of your expenditure. Hotels average around €45 (£40/$67) for the simplest double room in the cheapest places (note that in this book all hotels are given price codes, as explained on p.29). If you're sharing, that works out at little more per person than the €12–25 per person charged by hostels. Camping, of course, can cut costs dramatically, so long as you avoid the plusher private sites; the local *Camping municipal* rarely asks for more than €10 a head.

As for eating out, you should always be able to find a good three-course meal for around €20, or a takeaway for a lot less. Fresh food from shops and markets is surprisingly expensive in relation to low restaurant prices, but it's always possible to save money with a basic picnic of bread, cheese and fruit. More sophisticated meals – takeaway salads and ready-to-heat dishes – can be put together for reasonable prices if you shop at charcuteries (delis) and supermarkets. On the other hand, drinks in cafés and bars can make a severe hole in your pocket. Nowhere in the region matches Paris prices, but €5 cups of coffee are not unheard of, and a cognac costs double that. Note, however, that drink prices in most cafés are lower when ordering and drinking at the bar as opposed to occupying a table and being served by a waiter.

Transport costs obviously depend entirely on how (and how much) you travel; for details see p.24.

Admission charges for sites and museums can be high enough to make you picky as to what you visit – even with a student card (many museums have reduced admission for all under-26s, and not just students). But this is no special hardship: the region's attractions lie as much in its towns and landscapes as in anything fenced off or put in a showcase.

Discounts

Various official and quasi-official **youth/student ID cards** soon pay for themselves in savings. Full-time students are eligible for the International Student ID Card (ISIC, Ⓦisiccard.com, or Ⓦisic.org in the US and Canada), which entitles the bearer to special air, rail and bus fares and discounts at museums, theatres and other attractions. For Americans there's also a health benefit, providing up to $3000 in emergency medical coverage and $100 a day for sixty days in the hospital, plus a 24-hour emergency hotline.

You only have to be 26 or younger to qualify for the **International Youth Travel Card** (**IYTC**), which carries the same benefits. Teachers qualify for the **International Teacher Card (ITIC)**, offering similar discounts; see Ⓦmyisic.com or Ⓦisic.org for details.

Crime and personal safety

Although compared to Paris or the south of France, crime is a low-key problem, you still need to take normal precautions against petty theft – keep your wallet in your front pocket or your handbag under your elbow. To report a theft, go to the local *gendarmerie* (police station), and ask for the requisite piece of paper (the *constat de vol*) for a claim. The two main types of French police, the Police Nationale and the Gendarmerie Nationale, are for all practical purposes indistinguishable; you can go to either.

Drivers are obviously vulnerable, with the ever-present risk of a break-in. Vehicles are rarely stolen, but luggage left in cars makes a tempting target, and foreign number plates are easy to spot. Good insurance is the only answer (see opposite) but, whether you have it or not, make sure you don't leave your valuables in sight.

If you have an accident while driving, you have to fill in and sign a *constat à l'aimable* (jointly agreed statement); car insurers are supposed to give you this with a policy, though in practice few seem to have heard of it.

For non-criminal driving violations such as speeding, the police can impose on-the-spot fines. Should you be arrested on any charge, you have the right to contact your nearest consulate. Although the police are not always as cooperative as they might be, it is their duty to assist you – likewise in the case of losing your passport or all your money.

As for offences of your own making, treatment by the police is little different from anywhere else in Europe. Camping outside unauthorized sites can bring you into contact with the authorities, though it's more likely to be the landowner who tells you to move off. Topless sunbathing is acceptable within reason, but nudity is limited to a few specifically naturist beaches.

Officially, you're supposed to carry identification documents at all times, and the police are entitled to stop you and demand it.

From a safety point of view, hitching is definitely not advisable.

Electricity

Almost always 220V, using plugs with two round pins. If you need a transformer, it's best to buy one before leaving home, though you can find them in big department stores in France.

Entry requirements

Citizens of **European Union** (EU) countries can travel freely in France, while those from Australia, Canada, New Zealand and the United States, among other countries, do not require visas for a stay of up to ninety days. South African citizens require a short-stay visa for up to ninety days, which costs €60.

All **non-EU citizens** who wish to remain longer than ninety days must apply to the local *mairie* or town hall for a residence permit (a *titre de séjour*, also known as a *carte de séjour*), for which you will have to show proof of – among other things – a regular income or sufficient funds to support yourself, evidence of medical insurance and the appropriate visa (if required).

Visa regulations are always liable to change; check for up-do-date information on ⓦdiplomatie.gouv.fr.

French embassies and consulates

Australia Canberra ⓣ02/6216 0100, ⓦambafrance-au.org.
Canada Montréal ⓣ514/878-4385, ⓦconsulfrance-montreal.org; Québec ⓣ418/694-2294, ⓦconsulfrance-quebec.org; Toronto ⓣ416/925-8041, ⓦconsulfrance-toronto.org; Vancouver ⓣ604/681-4345, ⓦconsulfrance-vancouver.org.
Ireland Dublin ⓣ01/277 5000, ⓦambafrance-ie.org.
New Zealand Wellington ⓣ04/384 2555, ⓦambafrance-nz.org.
South Africa Johannesburg ⓣ11/778 5600, ⓦconsulfrance-jhb.org.
UK London ⓣ020/7073 1200, ⓦambafrance-uk.org; Edinburgh ⓣ0131/220 6324, ⓦconsulfrance-edimbourg.org.
US Washington ⓣ202/944-6200, ⓦambafrance-us.org.

Fishing

You get fishing rights by becoming a member of an authorized fishing club – tourist offices have details. The main areas for river fishing are in Brittany, in the Aulne River around Châteaulin and in the Morbihan.

Gay and lesbian travellers

France tends to have liberal attitudes to homosexuality. The age of consent is 16, and same-sex couples have been able to form civil partnerships, called PACs, since 1999. Brittany and Normandy, however, have little conspicuous gay life; the best source for clubs and meeting places is the *Gai Pied Guide*, widely available in French newsagents and bookshops (or online at ⓦgaipied.fr). The English-language *Spartacus International Gay Guide* (ⓦspartacusworld.com) has an extensive section on France and contains some info for lesbians. *Têtu* (ⓦtetu.com) is a highly rated gay/lesbian magazine with events listings and contact addresses; you can buy it in bookshops or through their website, which is also an excellent source of information. Dyke-plaNET (Ⓦdykeplanet.com), produces the annual *dykeGuide*, a guidebook listing lesbian-friendly places across France.

Health

Visitors to France have little to worry about as far as health is concerned. No vaccinations are required, there are no nasty diseases and tapwater is safe to drink. The worst that's likely to happen to you is a case of sunburn or an upset stomach from eating too much rich food. And if you do need treatment, you should be in good hands.

Under France's excellent **health system**, all services, including doctor's consultations, prescribed medicines, hospital stays and ambulance call-outs, incur a charge which you have to pay upfront. EU citizens are entitled to a refund (usually between 70 and 100 percent) of medical and dental expenses, providing the doctor is government-registered (*un médecin conventionné*) and provided you have the correct documentation (the European Health Insurance Card – EHIC; application forms available from main post offices in the UK or on Ⓦwww.dh.gov.uk). Note that every member of the family, including children, must have their own card. Even with the EHIC card, it's a good idea to have additional insurance to cover the shortfall, which can be especially substantial after a stay in hospital. All non-EU visitors should ensure they have adequate medical insurance cover.

For **minor complaints**, go to a *pharmacie*, signalled by an illuminated green cross. There's at least one in every small town, and even some villages. They keep normal shop hours (roughly 9am–noon & 3–6pm), though some stay open late. In larger towns, at least one (known as the *pharmacie de garde*) is open 24 hours according to a rota; details are displayed in all pharmacy windows.

For anything more serious you can get the name of a **doctor** from a pharmacy, local police station, tourist office, the Yellow Pages or your hotel. Consultation fees are usually €21–25. You'll be given a *Feuille de Soins* (Statement of Treatment) for later insurance claims. Any prescriptions will be fulfilled by the pharmacy and must be paid for.

In serious **emergencies** you will always be admitted to the nearest general hospital (*centre hospitalier*). For an ambulance, call Ⓣ15.

Insurance

Even though **EU citizens** are entitled to healthcare privileges in France, it's worth having insurance against theft, loss, illness or injury. Before paying for a new policy, however, check whether you are already covered: some all-risks home insurance policies cover your possessions when overseas, and many private medical schemes include cover when abroad. In Canada, provincial health plans usually provide partial cover for medical mishaps overseas, while holders of official student/teacher/youth cards in Canada and the US are entitled to meagre accident coverage and hospital in-patient benefits. **Students** will often find that their student health coverage extends during the vacations and for one term beyond the date of last enrolment.

A typical travel insurance policy usually provides cover for the loss of baggage, tickets and – up to a certain limit – cash or cheques, as well as cancellation or curtailment of your journey. Most exclude so-called dangerous sports unless an extra premium is paid, and many policies can be chopped and changed to exclude coverage you don't need – for example, sickness and accident benefits can often be excluded or included at will.

If you do take medical coverage, ascertain whether benefits will be paid as treatment proceeds or only after you return home, and if there is a 24-hour medical emergency number. When securing baggage cover, make sure that the per-article limit will cover your most valuable possession. If you need to make a claim, you should keep receipts for medicines and medical treatment. In the event you have anything stolen, you must obtain an official statement from the police (called a *constat de vol*).

Internet

Internet access is relatively easy to come by; you'll find internet cafés in most towns and cities, as well as points (*point internet*) in hotels, hostels, tourist offices and many of the larger post offices. The great majority of hotels have **wi-fi**, as do many cafés and bars.

Living in Brittany and Normandy

Although EU citizens are in theory free to move to France and find jobs with exactly the same pay, conditions and union rights as French nationals, for anyone who isn't a specialist, casual work in Brittany or Normandy is hard to come by and poorly paid.

Visitors from North America or Australasia without a prearranged job offer would be foolish to imagine they have any chance of finding paid employment. For EU citizens who arrange things in advance, however, there are work possibilities in au-pairing, teaching English as a foreign language and in the holiday industry.

The **national employment agency** (Ⓦanpe.fr), with offices all over France, advertises temporary jobs in all fields and, in theory, offers a whole range of services to job-seekers open to all EU citizens, but is not renowned for its helpfulness to foreigners. Non-EU citizens will have to show a work permit (*autorisation de travail*) to apply for any of their jobs.

Finding a job **teaching English** is best done in advance, in late summer. Courses and jobs are listed on Ⓦelgazette.com and Ⓦtefl.com, while the **British Council** (Ⓦbritishcouncil.org) recruits and helps train TEFL teachers for work abroad. The best places to live and teach are probably St-Malo, Quimper, Rennes and Rouen.

Au pair work is usually arranged through an agency, who should sort out any necessary paperwork; you'll find agencies listed on Ⓦwww.iapa.org. **Terms and conditions** are never very generous, but should include board, lodging and pocket money. Prospective employers are required to provide a written job description, so there is protection on both sides.

It's relatively easy to be a **student** in France. Foreigners pay no more than French nationals to enrol for a course, and the only problem then is to support yourself, though you'll be eligible for subsidized accommodation, meals and all the student reductions. For details and prospectuses of French universities, contact the Cultural Service of any French embassy or consulate (see p.40). The **British Council** (Ⓦbritishcouncil.org) runs a programme for British university students who want to spend some time studying in France.

Language schools all along the coast provide intensive French courses for foreigners. The most popular are organized each summer at St-Malo by the University of Rennes (Ⓦwww.uhb.fr). The École des Roches, in Verneuil-sur-Avre in Normandy (Ⓣ02.32.23.40.00, Ⓦecole-des-roches.com), runs intensive three- to nine-week summer courses in French for pupils aged 11 to 19.

Mail

As a rule, post offices (*bureaux de poste* or PTTs) in Brittany and Normandy are open from around 8am until noon and 2 to 6pm on weekdays, and 8am until noon only on Saturday; look for bright yellow *La Poste* signs. However, main offices in larger towns remain open throughout the day (8am–7pm), while lunch hours and closing times in the villages can vary enormously. Most larger offices also offer internet access.

Sending letters, the quickest international service is by *aérogramme*, sold at all post offices. You can buy ordinary stamps (*timbres*) at any *tabac* (tobacconist). When this book went to press, the rates for standard letters (*lettres*, weighing 20g or less) and postcards (*cartes postales*) were €0.65 for the UK and Europe, and €0.85 for North America, Australia and New Zealand. For further information, log on to Ⓦlaposte.fr.

Maps

Though their town maps are often very good, tourist office handouts rarely contain usable regional maps. To supplement them – and the maps in this guide – you will probably want a reasonable road map. The *Michelin* 1:200,000 area maps of Brittany (512) and Normandy (513) are very good for driving and other purposes; virtually every road they show is passable by any car, and those that are tinged in green are usually reliable as "scenic routes". Rough Guides also offers its own map of Brittany, printed on waterproof and rip-proof paper.

If you're planning to walk or cycle, check the *IGN* maps – either the green (1:100,000 and 1:50,000) or the more detailed purple (1:25,000) series. The *IGN* 1:100,000 is the smallest scale available with contours marked, though the bizarre colour scheme makes it hard to read. *Michelin* maps have little arrows to indicate steep slopes, which is all the information most cyclists will need.

Money

France's currency, the **euro**, is divided into 100 cents (often still referred to as *centimes*). There are seven notes – in denominations of 5, 10, 20, 50, 100, 200 and 500 euros – and eight different coins – 1, 2, 5, 10, 20 and 50 cents, and 1 and 2 euros. At the time of writing, the **exchange rate** for the euro was around €1.10 to the pound sterling (or £0.91 to one euro) and €1.50 to the dollar (or $0.67 to one euro). See Ⓦxe.com for current rates.

By far the easiest way to access your money in France is to use your credit or debit card to withdraw cash from an **ATM** (known as a *distributeur* or *point argent*); machines are every bit as ubiquitous as in Britain or North America, and most give instructions in several languages. Check with your bank before you leave home if you're in any doubt, and note that there is often a transaction fee, so it's more efficient to take out a sizeable sum each time rather than making lots of small withdrawals.

Similarly, all major **credit cards** are almost universally accepted in hotels, restaurants and shops, although some smaller establishments don't accept cards, or only for sums above a certain threshold. Visa – called Carte Bleue in France – is almost universally recognized, followed by MasterCard (also known as EuroCard). American Express ranks a bit lower.

Usual banking hours are Monday to Friday 9am to noon and 2 to 4.30pm. Some branches, especially those in rural areas, close on Monday, while those in big cities may remain open at midday and may also open on Saturday morning. All are closed on Sunday and public holidays.

Opening hours and public holidays

Basic **hours of business** are Monday to Saturday 9am until noon, and 2 to 6pm. In big city centres, shops and other businesses stay open throughout the day, while in July and August most tourist offices and museums are open without interruption. Otherwise almost everything – shops, museums, tourist offices, most banks – closes for a couple of hours at midday.

If you're looking to buy a picnic lunch, you'll need to get into the habit of buying it before you're ready to eat. Small food shops often don't reopen until halfway through the afternoon, closing around 7.30 or 8pm just before the evening meal.

The standard closing days are Sunday and Monday. Food shops tend to close on Monday rather than Sunday, but in smaller towns you may well find everything except the odd *boulangerie* (bakery) shut on both days.

Museums are not very generous with their hours, tending to open at around 10am, close for lunch at noon until 2pm

Public holidays

January 1 New Year's Day
Easter Sunday
Easter Monday
Ascension Day (forty days after Easter)
Pentecost or Whitsun (seventh Sunday after Easter, plus the Monday)
May 1 May Day/Labour Day
May 8 Victory in Europe Day
July 14 Bastille Day
August 15 Assumption of the Virgin Mary
November 1 All Saints' Day
November 11 Armistice Day 1918
December 25 Christmas Day

(sometimes 3pm) and then run through until only 5 or 6pm. Summer opening times, usually applicable between mid-May or early June and mid-September, but sometimes only during July and August, often differ from winter times; variations are indicated throughout this book. The closing days are usually Monday or Tuesday, sometimes both.

Phones

To call **to France** from your home country, dial ⓣ00 33 from the UK or Ireland, ⓣ011 33 from the USA, Canada or Australia, or ⓣ00 44 33 from New Zealand, and then the last nine digits of the ten-digit French number (thus omitting the initial 0).

To make a phone call **within France** – local or long-distance – simply dial all ten digits of the number. Numbers beginning with ⓣ08.00 up to ⓣ08.05 are free; those beginning ⓣ08.10 and ⓣ08.11 are charged as a local call; anything else beginning ⓣ08 is premium-rated (typically €0.34 per minute). None of these ⓣ08 numbers can be accessed from abroad. Calls to mobile phones (numbers starting with ⓣ06) are also charged at premium rates.

To speak to the operator dial ⓣ13; directory enquiries, both national and international, are on ⓣ12; medical emergencies, ⓣ15; the police, ⓣ17; fire, ⓣ18.

Mobile or cell phones

If you want to use your **mobile/cell phone**, contact your phone provider to check whether it will work in France and what the call charges are – they tend to be pretty exorbitant, and remember you're likely to be charged extra for receiving calls. French mobile phones operate on the European GSM standard, so US cellphones won't work in France unless you have a tri-band phone.

If you are going to be in France for any length of time and will be making and receiving a lot of local calls, it may be worth buying a **French SIM card** (which will give you a local phone number) and pre-paid recharge cards (*mobicartes*). You can buy a SIM card from any of the big mobile providers (Orange, SFR and Boygues Telecom), all of which have high-street outlets. They cost from around €30, and you'll need to have an address in France to register – that of your hotel or a friend will usually suffice.

Calling home from France

You can make international calls using either a standard *télécarte*, as sold at *tabacs*, newsagents and post offices, which will work with almost all payphones (coin-operated payphones are becoming rare), or a pre-paid phone card, also sold in *tabacs*, which can be used from both payphones and private phones.

Smoking

Smoking is banned in all public places, including public transport, museums, cafés and restaurants.

Time

France is in the Central European Time Zone (GMT+1). This means it is one hour ahead of the UK, six hours ahead of Eastern Standard Time and nine hours ahead of Pacific Standard Time. Daylight Saving Time (GMT+2) in France lasts from the last Sunday of March to the last Sunday of October. Between March and October France is one hour behind South Africa, eight hours behind eastern Australia and ten hours behind New Zealand; from October to March it is the same time as South Africa,

Calling home from France

Note that the initial zero is omitted from the area code when dialling the UK, Ireland, Australia and New Zealand from abroad.

UK international access code + 44 + city code
Republic of Ireland international access code + 353 + city code
US and Canada international access code + 1 + area code
Australia international access code + 61 + city code
New Zealand international access code + 64 + city code
South Africa international access code + 27 + city code

ten hours behind southeastern Australia and twelve hours behind New Zealand.

Tourist information

The **French Government Tourist Office** (Maison de la France) has offices throughout the world, each with its own website holding general country-wide information. For practical details on a specific location, such as hotels, campsites, activities and festivals, contact the relevant regional or departmental tourist offices; contact details can be found online at ⓦfncrt.com and www.fncdt.net respectively.

In France itself, practically every town and many villages have a tourist office – usually an **Office du Tourisme** (OT) but sometimes a **Syndicat d'Initiative** (SI). These provide local information, including hotel and restaurant listings, leisure activities, car and bike rental, bus times, laundries and countless other things; many can also book accommodation for you. Most can provide a town plan, and sell maps and local walking guides.

French Government tourist offices abroad

Australia and New Zealand ⓦau.franceguide.com
Britain ⓦuk.franceguide.com
Canada ⓦcanada.franceguide.com
Ireland ⓦie.franceguide.com
South Africa ⓦza.franceguide.com
USA ⓦus.franceguide.com com

Regional tourist boards

Brittany Tourist Board ⓦwww.brittanytourism.com
Normandy Tourist Board ⓦnormandy-tourism.org
Calvados (Normandy) ⓦcalvados-tourisme.info
Côtes d'Armor (Brittany) ⓦwww.cotesdarmor.com
Eure (Normandy) ⓦtourisme28.com
Finistère (Brittany) ⓦwww.finisteretourisme.com
Ille-et-Vilaine (Brittany) ⓦbretagne35.com
Manche (Normandy) ⓦmanchetourisme.com
Morbihan (Brittany) ⓦwww.morbihan.com
Orne (Normandy) ⓦwww.ornetourisme.com
Seine Maritime (Normandy) ⓦwww.seine-maritime-tourisme.com

Travellers with disabilities

The French have made concerted efforts to improve facilities for travellers with disabilities. Though haphazard parking habits and stepped village streets remain serious obstacles for anyone with mobility problems, ramps or other forms of access are gradually being added to hotels, museums and other public buildings. All but the oldest hotels are required to adapt at least one room to be wheelchair accessible. APF, the French paraplegic organization, is the most reliable source of information on accommodation with disabled access and other facilities (see p.46).

Eurotunnel (see p.20) offers the simplest option for **travelling to France** from the UK, as you can remain in your car. Alternatively, Eurostar trains have a limited number of wheelchair spaces in first-class for the price of the regular second-class fare; reserve well in advance. While airlines are required to offer access to travellers with mobility problems, the level of service provided by discount airlines may be fairly basic. All cross-Channel ferries have lifts to and from the car deck, but moving between the different passenger decks may be more difficult.

Within France, most train stations make provision for travellers with mobility problems. Spaces for wheelchairs are available (but must be booked in advance) in first-class carriages of all high-speed TGVs for the price of the regular second-class fare. For other trains, a wheelchair symbol in the timetable indicates services offering special on-board facilities; double check when booking.

Drivers of **taxis** are legally obliged to help passengers in and out of the vehicle and to carry guide dogs. Specially adapted taxi services are available in some towns: contact the local tourist office for further information, or one of the organizations listed below. The big **car rental** agencies such as Hertz and Europcar provide automatic cars and cars with hand controls, but only in certain locations and you'll need to reserve well in advance.

As for finding suitable **accommodation**, guides produced by Logis de France and Gîtes de France (see p.30) indicate places with specially adapted rooms, though it's advisable to double check when booking that the facilities meet your needs.

Up-to-date **information** about accessibility, special programmes and discounts is best obtained before you leave home from the organizations listed below. French readers might want to get hold of the *Handitourisme* guide, published by Petit Futé (ⓦpetitfute.fr). Tour operators specializing in holidays for the disabled are listed below.

Useful contacts

Access Travel ⓦ**access-travel.co.uk.** UK tour operator that can arrange flights, transfer and accommodation in various locations around France.

Association des Paralysés de France (APF) ⓦ**apf.asso.fr.** National association that can answer general enquiries and put you in touch with their departmental offices.

Fédération Française Handisport ⓦ**handisport.org.** Among other things, this federation provides information on sports and leisure facilities for people with disabilities.

Mobile en Ville ⓦ**mobile-en-ville-normandie.over-blog.com.** Information on wheelchair access throughout Normandy (French only).

Society for the Advancement of Travellers with Handicaps (SATH) ⓦ**sath.org.** US non-profit educational organization with information and tips on travelling abroad.

Tourism For All ⓦ**tourismforall.org.uk.** Masses of information, including useful advice for prospective travellers to France.

Travelling with pets from the UK

If you wish to take your dog or cat to France, the **Pet Travel Scheme** (**PETS**) enables you, so long as certain conditions are met, to avoid putting your pet in quarantine when you re-enter the UK. Current regulations are available on the Department for Environment, Food and Rural Affairs (DEFRA) website ⓦwww.defra.gov.uk, or through the PETS Helpline (ⓣ0870/241 1710).

Guide

Guide

Normandy

Brittany

1

Seine Maritime

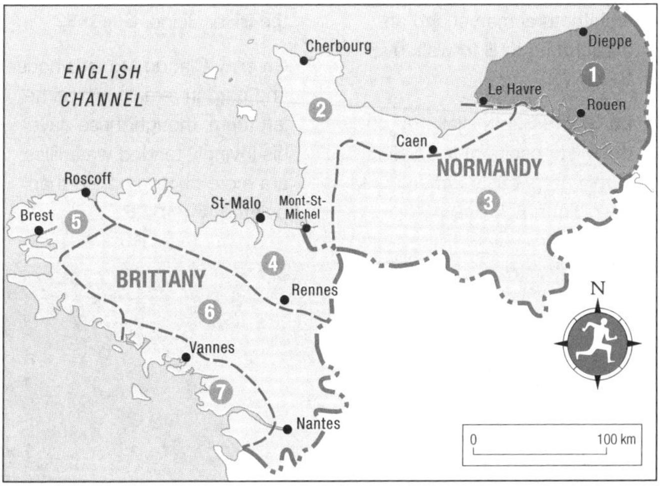

CHAPTER 1 Highlights

✱ **Hôtel de la Terrasse** Lovely clifftop hotel in Varengeville that makes a perfect first- or last-night stopover for ferry passengers. See p.61

✱ **Étretat** Normandy's most attractive little resort, offering great walks to admire its spectacular cliff formations. See p.66

✱ **Pont de Normandie** Vertiginous bridge across the Seine that's both an architectural marvel and an exhilarating thrill to walk over. See p.72

✱ **Le Grand Sapin** Wake up on the misty banks of the Seine in this gorgeously romantic old riverfront hotel. See p.73

✱ **Rouen** Despite war damage, this fine old medieval city would still seem familiar to Joan of Arc, who perished in its main square. See p.77

✱ **Aître St-Maclou** Ghoulish Dance of Death carvings adorn this centuries-old courtyard in central Rouen. See p.83

✱ **Château Gaillard** The atmospheric ruins of Richard the Lionheart's mighty fortress dominate a sweeping curve of the River Seine. See p.92

✱ **Giverny** Claude Monet's house and garden remain just as he left them, though these days his lovingly tended waterlilies are more photographed than painted. See p.93

▲ Le Grand Sapin, Villequier

1

Seine Maritime

Stretching north from the fertile Seine Valley to the undulating cliffs that line the Channel coast, the *département* of **Seine Maritime** is largely distinct from the rest of Normandy. Though scattered with the usual Norman half-timbered houses and small farms, the landscape is stark along the seashore, while relentlessly flat on the chalky Caux plateau behind. Only along the sheltered ribbon to either side of the **Seine** do you find the greenery, and profusion of flowers and fruit, that you might expect of the province.

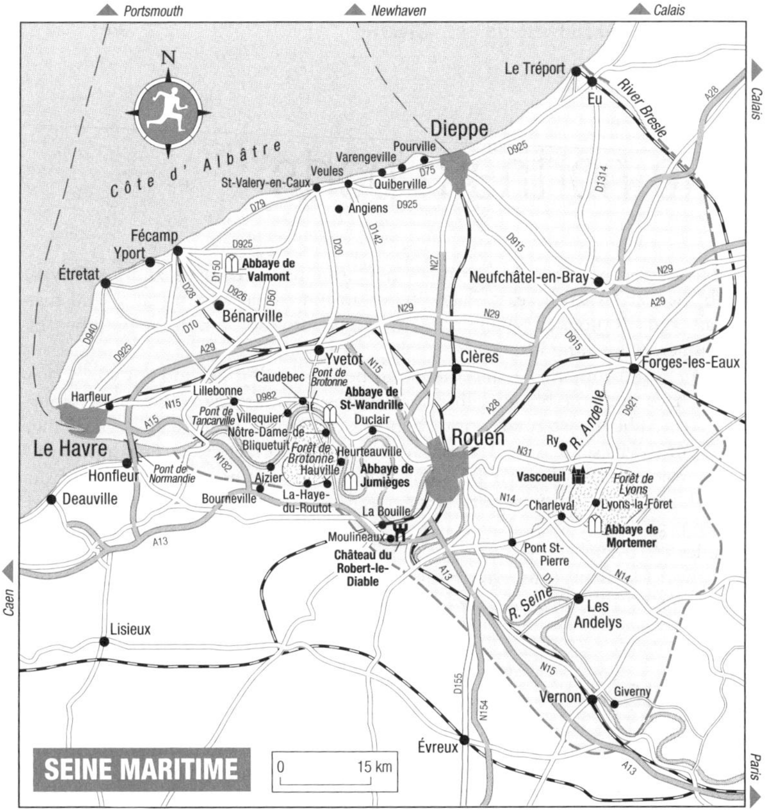

It's well worth taking time to explore, however. If you arrive at the pleasant port of **Dieppe**, several low-key but popular resorts along the **Côte d'Albâtre** make appealing overnight stops, with occasional surprises behind their windswept and tide-chased walks. **Étretat**, for example, boasts spectacular stacks and arches of rock, flanking one of the nicest little coastal towns in Normandy; **Fécamp** holds the absurd Gothic monstrosity of the Benedictine distillery; and **Varengeville** offers the wonderful house designed by architect Edwin Lutyens at **Bois des Moutiers**.

While motorists tend to hurry through the hinterland just south of the coastal cliffs, for **cyclists** the gentle valleys and expansive grain fields are ideal for a few days' undemanding pedalling through pastoral French countryside. Even **Le Havre**, on the Seine estuary, while hardly conventionally attractive, is home to some noteworthy modern architecture and art.

The extravagant meanders of the **River Seine**, however, shape most itineraries. **Rouen**, by far the largest of the river towns, was the scene of the trial and execution of Joan of Arc, and remains one of the major provincial capitals of France; a combination of contemporary verve with its restored medieval centre makes it by far the most interesting city in Normandy. Elsewhere along the valley and riverbanks there is plenty to delay your progress: tranquil villages such as **Villequier** and **La Bouille**; the evocative Romanesque abbey ruins of **St-Wandrille** and **Jumièges**; the English frontier-stronghold of **Château Gaillard** looming above **Les Andelys**; and, an unmissable last stop before Paris, **Monet's garden** and waterlilies at **Giverny**.

The northern ports

There is no confusing Normandy's northern ports, **Dieppe** and **Le Havre**, with their rivals to the east. Each retains an individual identity of a kind that Calais and Boulogne, which have to cope with ten times the number of passengers, have long lost.

Setting off from either – and there's no need to rush off as soon as you arrive – you have the same obvious choice of **routes**: inland towards Rouen, or along the coast. The **coast road** from Dieppe is the most immediately gratifying. Harbour towns such as **Le Tréport** to the east, and **Étretat** and **Fécamp** to the west, make diverting overnight stops, whereas the plains of the Caux plateau inland hold few diversions until you get as far south as Rouen. Both Étretat and Fécamp also lie within easy reach of Le Havre, at the mouth of the Seine. Besides the towns along the river itself, places such as Honfleur (see p.102) on the lower Norman coast, covered in Chapter Two, are just a few minutes from Le Havre, via the huge Seine bridges.

Dieppe

Squeezed between high cliff headlands, **DIEPPE** makes an enjoyably small-scale port at which to arrive in France, quintessentially French yet long associated with England. As the closest harbour and beach to Paris, 170km southeast, it has had an eventful history. The abbey of Mont Ste-Catherine-de-Rouen acquired the area in 1030, for an annual rent of five thousand smoked herrings. As king of England, William the Conqueror used the port regularly, and it returned to French control in 1195 when Philippe Auguste burned Richard the Lionheart's fleet in the harbour.

Adventurers from Dieppe were at the forefront of French **naval explorations**. Dieppois navigators supposedly reached the coast of Guinea in 1384, and Brazil in 1488; less questionably, the Italian Giovanni da Verrazzano sailed from here in 1524 to found the settlement that later became New York. Early emigrants to Canada used the port, too, establishing links with the French colony there that endured long after the French lost Canada to the British in 1759.

Soon after the railway from Paris reached Dieppe in 1848, the Newhaven Packet started a daily cross-Channel service from England. The town became a fashionable **seaside resort**, attracting French aristocracy and British royalty; the French would promenade along the seafront, while the English colony indulged in the peculiar pastime of bathing.

Modern Dieppe has a population of around 35,000. Though ferry services have diminished in recent years, it remains one of the nicer northern French ports, and you won't regret spending an afternoon or evening here. With kids in tow, the aquariums of the **Cité de la Mer** (see p.56) are the obvious attraction; otherwise, you could settle for admiring the cliffs and the castle as you stroll the seafront lawns.

Arrival and information

The only **ferry** services between Dieppe's **gare maritime**, east of the centre, and Newhaven in England, are the four-hour crossings operated by Transmanche Ferries, using conventional vessels (1–2 daily; Ⓣ08.00.65.01.00, Ⓦwww.transmancheferries.com). Motorists coming off the boats are directed away from the town, and have to double back west to reach it; foot passengers can walk the 500m to the centre.

Dieppe's **gare SNCF** is on boulevard Clemenceau, 1km inland. Trains are by far the quickest way to get to Rouen or Paris, while buses head along the coast from the **gare routière** alongside (CNA run services to Fécamp and St-Valéry; Ⓣ08.25.07.60.27). All **local buses** stop at the *gare SNCF*, as well as next to the tourist office on pont Ango.

Dieppe's **tourist office** (May, June & Sept Mon–Sat 9am–1pm & 2–7pm, Sun 10am–1pm & 2–5pm; July & Aug Mon–Sat 9am–7pm, Sun 10am–1pm & 3–6pm; Oct–April Mon–Sat 9am–noon & 2–6pm; Ⓣ02.32.14.40.60, Ⓦwww.dieppetourisme.com) is on the pont Ango, which separates the ferry harbour from the pleasure port. **Bicycles** can be rented very cheaply from Vélo Service, operating out of a bus just across the bridge (€1 per hr, €5.50 per day; Ⓣ06.24.56.06.27, Ⓦwww.veloservice.fr.tc). **Internet access** is available at the main **post office**, 2 bd Maréchal-Joffre (Mon–Fri 8am–6pm, Sat 8am–12.30pm; Ⓣ02.35.04.70.14).

Accommodation

Dieppe holds plenty of **hotels**. The more expensive options are concentrated along the seafront – which is surprisingly quiet at night – especially at its western end, closest to the château. Hotels with their own restaurants tend to insist on half board, or even full board, in season.

EATING
Le Bistrôt du Pollet	6
Diverne Traiteur	8
Le Festival	5
La Marmite Dieppoise	9
Le New Haven	3
L'Océan	4
Le Sully	1

DRINKING
Cactus Café	2
Café des Tribunaux	11
Epsom	7
Scottish Pub	10

DIEPPE

ACCOMMODATION
Les Arcades de la Bourse	C
Captain House	E
Grand Duquesne	D
La Plage	A
Windsor	B

Hostel & Camping ▼ ▼ Paris & Auchan Hypermarket

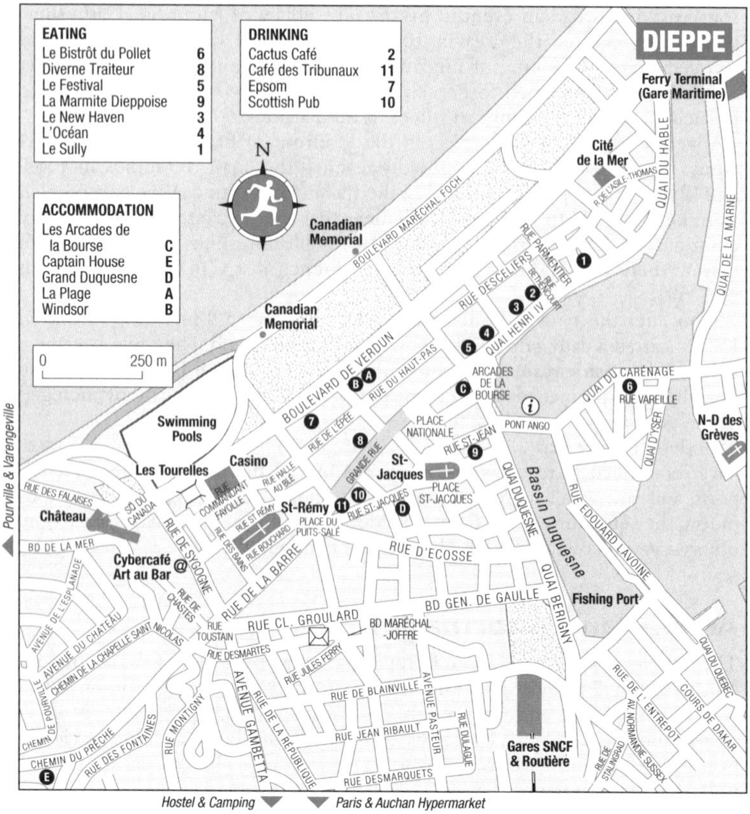

Hotels

Les Arcades de la Bourse 1–3 arcades de la Bourse ☎02.35.84.14.12, ⊛lesarcades.fr. Long-established hotel, under the eponymous arcades facing the port; you couldn't ask for a more central location. Cheaper rooms face the street. Restaurant with full, good-value menus from €18. ❸

Captain House 4 Chemin du Prêche ☎02.35.40.31.96. Two spacious *chambres d'hôtes* decorated in country-chic style in a pretty old house below the castle. ❹

Au Grand Duquesne 15 pl St-Jacques ☎02.32.14.61.10, ⊛augrandduquesne.free.fr. This small, central hotel is unusually plain for the Logis de France organization, but offers twelve slightly old-fashioned but acceptable en-suite rooms at bargain rates, and good food in the downstairs restaurant (full menus from €18.90). ❷

La Plage 20 bd de Verdun ☎02.35.84.18.28, ⊛plagehotel.fr.st. Seafront hotel with something

to suit all budgets, from the upmarket sea-view rooms, and family rooms, to smaller but perfectly pleasant courtyard-facing doubles. No restaurant. ❸–❺

Windsor 18 bd de Verdun ☎02.35.84.15.23, ⊛hotelwindsor.fr. You pay higher rates for the superior sea-facing rooms in this *logis*, where the glass-fronted first-floor dining room has lunch menus from €19.50, dinner from €25 weekdays, €34 weekends. The cheaper "classic" rooms, facing inwards, can be pretty grim, even if they do have baths and cable TV. ❺

Campsite

Camping Vitamin Chemin des Vertus ☎02.35.82.11.11, ⊛www.camping-vitamin.com. Three-star site, well south of town in an unremark-able setting in St-Aubin-sur-Scie that's really only convenient for motorists, even if it is served by the #2 bus route. Open April to mid-Oct.

The Town

Dieppe remains a busy port; its sheer bustle and verve is striking to any visitor. Vast quantities of fruit from all over the world – and forty percent of all shellfish eaten in France – are unloaded at its commercial docks, but the quayside fish stalls near the tourist office are what really grab the eye. Each morning the previous night's catch is displayed with mouthwatering French flair, an appetizing profusion of sole, turbot and the local speciality, scallops.

Early in the nineteenth century, Dieppe was radically re-shaped when its ancient circuit of walls were knocked down. The twin turrets of the only one of seven city gates to survive, **Les Tourelles**, still guard the western end of the seafront, below the fifteenth-century château and alongside the casino. Modern Dieppe was laid out along three still-evident axes. The **boulevard de Verdun** runs for over a kilometre along the seafront, from the château to the port entrance. A short way inland, the **rue de la Barre** and its pedestrianized continuation, the **Grande Rue**, run parallel to the seafront. That line is extended along the harbour's edge by **quai Henri IV**, with its colourful backdrop of cafés, brasseries and restaurants.

The place du Puits-Salé and around

At the heart of the old town, the spruce half-timbered *Café des Tribunaux* dominates the **place du Puits-Salé**, its outdoor tables spilling out into the pedestrianized streets, and its cavernous interior the late-night preserve of college students. Built as an inn in the seventeenth century, the *Café* briefly became Dieppe's town hall after the previous one was bombarded by the British in 1694. In the nineteenth century, it was favoured by painters such as Renoir, Monet, Sickert, Whistler and Pissarro, and the unhappy Oscar Wilde drank here regularly while living in exile (as M. Melmouth) at Berneval, 10km east, which was where he wrote *The Ballad of Reading Gaol*.

Rue St-Jacques leads from the *Café* to **St-Jacques church**. The original church, built in the twelfth century to greet English pilgrims heading for the shrine of St James at Santiago de Compostela, burned down a hundred years later, so its oldest part today is the fourteenth-century lantern tower. Inside, a chapel to the "Canadian Martyrs" neighbours the usual ones to Ste-Thérèse and the Sacred Heart. Dedicated in 1951, this has nothing to do with World War II; instead it's devoted to two Dieppe priests, shown in modern stained glass being hacked to death by "Mohawks" in 1648. Nearby, the **Mur de Trésor** bears intricate and potentially fascinating carvings of Brazilian Indians dating from the seventeenth century. Unfortunately they're too high and weathered to see clearly.

Northwest of the place du Puits-Salé, **rue Bouchard** heads to the sixteenth-century **church of St-Rémy**, which was partly destroyed when, used as an arms dump by the Germans, it was blown up the day before the town was liberated in August 1944. Now restored, organ and all, it's occasionally used for special events, such as August's Festival of Ancient Music.

The beach

Dieppe's wide, steeply shelving **shingle beach** was deposited by a freak tide long after the rest of the town took shape. Hence the extravagant clear space between the seafront and the first buildings, taken up partly by the windswept grassy lawns that make an ideal venue for the town's biennial **kite festival** (spread across two weekends in early Sept of even-numbered years), and partly by car parks where departing ferry passengers munch last-minute picnics. A large area at the western end has been re-landscaped to hold

Les Bains, a massive complex of indoor and outdoor swimming pools, kitted out with water slides and the like, and a salt-water therapy centre (daily, hours vary enormously; pool access €5.90; Ⓣ02.32.82.80.90, Ⓦvert-marine.com/les-bains-dieppe-76).

The château

Dieppe's most conspicuous sight is the medieval **château** that overlooks the seafront from the west. Though most visitors make the stiff climb up simply to enjoy the view, the château also serves as home to the **Musée de Dieppe** (June–Sept daily 10am–noon & 2–6pm; Oct–May Mon & Wed–Sat 10am–noon & 2–5pm, Sun 10am–noon & 2–6pm; €3.60). In addition to its exhibition on local history – which stretches, thanks to Dieppe's maritime past, to encompass pre-Columbian pottery from Peru – the museum houses two showpiece collections. The first is a group of **carved ivories**. Dieppois "explorers" shipped ivory home from Africa in such quantities that during the seventeenth century over three hundred craftsmen-carvers lived here. Earlier pieces tend to be exquisite miniature portraits and classical scenes; by the nineteenth century, the sculptors were concentrating instead on souvenirs.

The other permanent exhibition is made up of a hundred or so prints by the co-originator of Cubism, **Georges Braque**, who went to school in Le Havre, spent his summers in Dieppe, and is buried nearby at Varengeville-sur-mer (see p.61). Around a quarter tend to be displayed at any one time. Other galleries upstairs hold assorted paintings of local scenes, while a separate, much newer wing stages temporary exhibitions.

The Cité de la Mer

The grandly named **Cité de la Mer**, or "City of the Sea", 37 rue de l'Asile-Thomas (daily 10am–noon & 2–6pm; €5.80; Ⓦestrancitedelamer.free.fr), is in fact simply a museum. Housed in a white concrete block, tucked away in the tangle of streets just west of the harbour mouth, it's designed both to entertain children and serve as a centre for scientific research.

Kids are bound to enjoy learning the principles of navigation by operating radio-controlled boats (€2 for 3min). The museum then traces the history of

Operation Jubilee

At the foot of the château, the **square du Canada** originally commemorated the role played by sailors from Dieppe in the colonization of Canada. After the last war, however, it acquired an additional significance, thanks to **Operation Jubilee**, the Allied commando raid on Dieppe, on August 19, 1942. In the first large-scale assault on the continent since Dunkerque, almost five thousand Canadian troops launched a near-suicidal series of landings and attacks up sheer and well-fortified cliff faces. Many were cut down as soon as they left their landing craft, before they even touched dry land, while some German defenders are reputed not to have bothered with firing their weapons, and simply dropped projectiles over the edge. In total, 907 Canadians were killed and 1874 captured.

The Allied Command later justified the carnage as having taught valuable lessons; according to Lord Mountbatten, "for every soldier who died at Dieppe, ten were saved on D-Day". The Channel ports were shown to be too heavily defended to be vulnerable to frontal attack, and the invasion plan was changed to one that required the amphibious landing armies to bring their own harbour with them. It was the 2nd Canadian Infantry Division who ultimately liberated Dieppe, on September 1, 1944.

seagoing vessels, leading from the great Norman voyages of exploration and conquest up to a sketchy account of the insides of a nuclear-powered submarine. Next comes a very detailed geological exhibition covering the formation of the local cliffs, from which we learn how to convert shingle into sandpaper.

Visits culminate with the large **aquariums**, filled with the marine life of the Channel: flatfish with bulbous eyes and twisted faces, retiring octopuses, battling lobsters, and hermaphrodite scallops (a caption helpfully explains that the white part is male, and the orange, female).

Eating

The most promising area to look for **restaurants** in Dieppe is along the quai Henri IV, which, although it overlooks the port rather than the open sea, makes a lovely place to stroll and compare menus of a summer's evening. Competition for ferry passengers keeps prices relatively low. The beach itself, by contrast, offers no formal restaurants, just a couple of open-air bistro-type cafés and a handful of crêpe stands.

Dieppe's main shopping streets are rue de la Barre and the Grande Rue; Saturday sees an all-day open-air **market** in the place Nationale and along Grande Rue. L'Épicier Oliver at 18 rue St-Jacques sells specialist items such as wines and cheeses, while the largest of several local **hypermarkets** is Auchan (Mon–Sat 8.30am–9.30pm), out of town at the Centre Commercial du Belvédère on the route de Rouen (RN 27), or reached by bus #2 from the tourist office.

Le Bistrot du Pollet 23 rue du Tête du Boeuf ⓣ02.35.84.68.57. Little local restaurant just east of Pont Ango, especially cosy on a winter's evening, which sells fresh seafood at low prices. Closed Sun, Mon, second fortnight in April and second fortnight in Aug.

Diverne Traiteur 138 Grande Rue ⓣ02.35.84.13.87 Chic *patisserie* and tea room serving up delicious cakes.

Le Festival 11 quai Henri IV ⓣ02.35.40.24.29. Quick-fire brasserie at the busiest end of the quayside that delivers its fishy goods at top speed without skimping on quality. *Moules frites*, at €8, comes in blue china ships, while the €12.90 and €17.90 menus are also dominated by seafood.

La Marmite Dieppoise 8 rue St-Jean ⓣ02.35.84.24.26. Rustic, busy little restaurant between St-Jacques church and the arcades de la Bourse. Menus are on the pricey side, starting at €29, while the €36 one features the local speciality *marmite Dieppoise* (seafood pot, with shellfish and white fish), followed by apple tart. Closed Sun eve & Mon, plus Thurs eve out of season.

Le New Haven 53 quai Henri IV ⓣ02.35.84.89.72. Reliable seafood specialist, towards the quieter end of the quayside, with good menus from €18. The €22 *menu de la Jetée* is fine if you hanker after fish livers, the house speciality, while €19 buys you a *choucroute de la mer* (seafood sauerkraut). Closed Tues eve, plus Mon & Wed in winter.

L'Océan 23 quai Henri IV ⓣ02.32.90.97.80. Big, sprawling quayside bistro that's ideal for a large group; its long menu offers every imaginable permutation of meat, fish and shellfish, with set menus from €10.50 to €32.

Le Sully 97 quai Henri IV ⓣ02.35.84.23.13. This smart indoor restaurant offers some of the finest seafood along the quayside – none of it frozen – served either on bargain menus, ranging from just €12 up to €34, or in lavish platters; there's also a €15 vegetarian menu.

Drinking and nightlife

Things tend to shut early in Dieppe. Apart from the **Cinema Rex** on the place Nationale (ⓣ08.92.68.69.02), and the slot machines at the **casino** at the western end of boulevard de Verdun, there's little incentive to abandon your comfortable restaurant terrace of an evening. However, in addition to the *Café des Tribunaux* (see p.55), a handful of **bars** do manage to keep busy.

Cactus Café 71 quai Henri IV ⓣ02.35.82.59.38. Lively café, squeezed between the quayside restaurants with plenty of outdoor seating, offering a regular diet of reggae and Latin music.
Epsom 11 bd de Verdun ⓣ02.35.84.12.27. Dieppe's most enticing venue, this *café littéraire* puts on live jazz on some Thurs.
Scottish Pub 14 rue St-Jacques ⓣ02.35.84.13.16. Also known for good measure as the *Irish Pub*, this British-style pub caters to a mainly Anglo-Saxon clientele in search of beer and football.

The Côte d'Albâtre

Thanks to its consistently high white cliffs, the Norman coast between Picardy in the east and Le Havre in the west is known as the **Côte d'Albâtre** – the Alabaster coast. This whole shoreline is eroding at such a ferocious rate that the small resorts here, tucked in at the mouths of successive valleys, may not last another century. For the moment, however, they are quietly prospering, with casinos, sports centres and yacht marinas ensuring a modest but steady summer trade.

If you're setting out to tour Normandy, it might seem counter-intuitive to head **east** from Dieppe towards Calais and Boulogne, but doing so gives the opportunity to see a couple of surprising old towns: venerable **Le Tréport** and, just inland, the village of **Eu** with its thick forest surround. Head **west**, on the other hand, and the coast road dips into a series of pretty little ports, with **Étretat** the pick of the bunch.

Le Tréport

Thirty kilometres east of Dieppe, at the mouth of the River Bresle – the border with Picardy – **LE TRÉPORT** is an atmospheric old seaside resort that springs creakily to life each summer. Already something of a bathing spot when the railways arrived in 1873, it was duly promoted as "the prettiest beach in Europe, just three hours from Paris", and remained the capital's favoured resort until the 1950s.

Le Tréport divides into three distinct sections: the flat wedge-shaped seafront area, bounded on one side by the Channel, on another by the harbour at the canalized river mouth, and on the third by imposing hundred-metre chalk cliffs; the old town, higher up the slopes on safer ground; and the modern town further inland.

The actual **seafront** is entirely taken up by a pink and orange concrete 1960s apartment block, with one or two snack bars but no other sign of life, facing the casino and a drab grey shingle beach. It's the more sheltered harbourside **quai François 1er** around the corner that holds most of the action, lined with restaurants, souvenir shops and cafés. A venerable little brick fish market stands across the road by the water, alongside a hundred-year-old carousel. The assorted stone jetties and wooden piers around the harbour are enjoyable to stroll around, as you watch the comings and goings of the fishing boats that still keep Le Tréport bustling. It's even more fun to take a free ride up (indeed through) the cliffs on the restored **téléphérique**, a funicular railway that tunnels into the rock to re-emerge in the open air up top (July & Aug daily 7.45am–12.45am; Sept–June Sun–Thurs 7.45am–8.45pm, Fri & Sun 7.45am–12.45am). As well as views to either side of the decaying mansions of Le Tréport, you can see across to the longer beach of **Mers-les-Bains**, which, being in Picardy, falls outside the scope of this book.

If you walk to the top of the cliffs instead, climbing a total of 365 steps, not far up from the *quai* you'll pass the heavily nautical **Église St-Jacques**, built in the fifteenth century to replace an eleventh-century original that crumbled into the sea, along with the cliff on which it stood.

Practicalities

Trains and **buses** arrive in Le Tréport on the far side of the harbour, a short walk from the main *quai*. Turn left as you hit the main drag to reach the **tourist office** on quai Sadi-Carnot (April–June & Sept Mon–Thurs 10am–noon & 3–6pm, Fri & Sat 10am–12.30pm & 2.30–6.30pm, Sun 10am–1pm & 3–5pm; July & Aug daily 9.30am–7pm; Oct–March Mon–Sat 10am–noon & 3–6pm; Ⓣ02.35.86.05.69, Ⓦwww.ville-le-treport.fr). Le Tréport's major annual **festival** is the Blessing of the Sea on August 2.

The best **hotel** option is the refurbished *Hôtel de Calais*, overlooking the port at 1 rue de Paris, where the cheapest of several distinct grades of room lack en-suite facilities, while the fanciest have whirlpool baths and great sea views (Ⓣ02.27.28.09.09, Ⓦwww.hoteldecalais.com; ❶–❺). Numerous consistently tempting seafood **restaurants** line the *quai*, each boasting of its fresh *assiette de fruits de mer* and serving similar meals from around €18. At the top-notch *St-Louis*, 43 quai François 1er (Ⓣ02.35.86.20.70; closed mid-Nov to mid-Dec), the meat is every bit as good as the fish.

Eu

Queen Victoria twice visited Le Tréport with Albert; she didn't come to play on the beach, though, but to stay at the château at **EU**, a couple of kilometres inland. When she did so the first time, in the original "Entente Cordiale" in 1843, she became the first English monarch to make an official visit to France since Henry VIII arrived for the Field of the Cloth of Gold.

Today, Eu is something of a backwater, consisting of a few pedestrian streets at the top of a hill, and a straggle of newer districts reaching down the slopes. The sixteenth-century **château** at its heart holds a museum devoted to its glory years as the summer residence of French monarch Louis Philippe, between 1830 and 1848 (mid-March to early Nov Mon, Wed, Thurs, Sat & Sun 10am–noon & 2–6pm, Fri 2–6pm; €4). Of Eu's previous château, burned in 1475, only the tiny chapel remains, which was the site of William the Conqueror's marriage to Mathilda.

Unlikely as it may sound, Eu's Gothic church, **Notre-Dame et St-Laurent**, is dedicated to St Lawrence O'Toole, an archbishop of Dublin who died here in 1181 while en route to visit Henry II of England in Rouen. His effigy still lies in the brightly lit and eerie crypt.

For an enjoyable afternoon, venture into the **forest of Eu**, a mysterious and ancient tangled woodland dominated by tall beeches, where a lost Roman city supposedly lies hidden.

Practicalities

Eu is on the Le Tréport rail line, with its **gare SNCF** 500m down the hill from the centre. The **tourist office** is in the central place Guillaume le Conquérant (May, June & Sept to mid-Nov Mon–Sat 9.30am–12.30pm & 2–6.30pm, Sun 10am–1pm; July & Aug Mon–Sat 9.30am–6.30pm, Sun 10am–1pm; mid-Nov to April Mon–Sat 9.30am–noon & 2–5.30pm; Ⓣ02.35.86.04.68, Ⓦville-eu.fr). The best-value central **hotel** is the *Maine* at 20 av de la Gare (Ⓣ02.35.86.16.64, Ⓦwww.hotel-maine.com; ❸; restaurant closed Sun eve), a seductively faded Logis de France, with Art Deco trimmings, in a slightly dilapidated red-brick town house next to the *gare SNCF*, which offers top-quality menus from €16. There's also an FUAJ **hostel** in the former royal kitchens in rue des Fontaines, the *Centre des Fontaines* (ⓣ02.35.86.05.03, ⓦwww.centredesfontaines.fr; HI members €12.60), which serves meals, offers free internet access, and acts as a general resource for local youngsters. Eu is generally rather short of places to **eat**, but *La Bragance*, in what used to be an icehouse in the gardens of the château (ⓣ02.35.83.47.70; closed Sat lunch & Sun), serves good-value alfresco lunches on its terrace, and pricier dinners.

Pourville-sur-mer

West of Dieppe, the coastal D75 drops in a majestic sweep after 3km down a steep green hill, to reach the resort of **POURVILLE-SUR-MER**. An extremely tranquil last- or first-night stop for ferry passengers, it's no more than a long straight beach at the mouth of a broad valley that briefly interrupts the line of cliffs. It lacks any form of port, but the wave conditions are enough to attract hordes of **surfers**. The beach itself was painted by Monet, a reproduction of whose *La Plage à Pourville* is displayed at the centre of the promenade.

Most of the few buildings lining the road through Pourville are **hotels**, including a *logis* confusingly named *Produits de la Mer* (ⓣ02.35.84.38.34; ❷; closed Dec & Jan), where all eight rooms have showers or baths, and the plainest seafood menu costs €25. Next to it is a crazy-golf course. Other good **restaurants** along the front include the ugly white concrete *l'Huitrière* (ⓣ02.35.84.36.20), which as the name suggests serves delicious fresh oysters on its raised sea-view terrace. The two-star *Le Marqueval* **campsite** (ⓣ02.35.82.66.46, ⓦwww.campinglemarqueval.com; closed mid-Oct to mid-March), set in the fields further back from the sea, has cabin rentals as well as tent places.

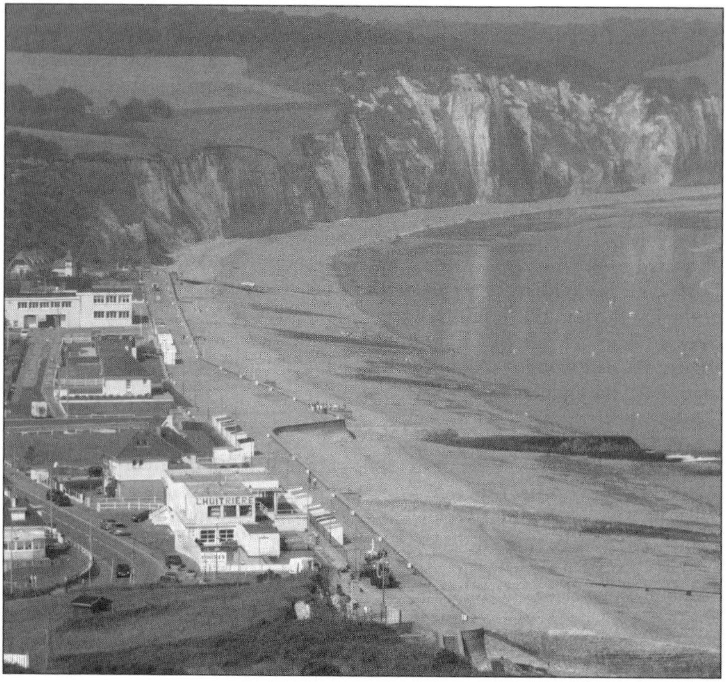

▲ Pourville-sur-mer

Varengeville-sur-mer

The straggling clifftop community of **VARENGEVILLE-SUR-MER**, 8km west of Dieppe, has long been popular with **artists**, including at different times Monet, Dufy, Miró and the painter parents of British Prime Minister Anthony Eden, who was born here. Its greatest devotee, however, was the pioneer Cubist **Georges Braque** (1882–1963), whose **grave** is situated outside a church perched spectacularly above the cliffs a couple of kilometres north of the main road, a smooth marble tomb topped by a sadly decaying mosaic of a white dove in flight. More impressive is his vivid-blue *Tree of Jesse* stained-glass window inside the church, through which you can see the sun rise in summer.

Back along the road towards town from the church, the house at the **Bois des Moutiers**, built for Guillaume Mallet from 1898 onwards and un-French in almost every respect, was one of architect **Edwin Lutyens**' first commissions. Then just 29, and heavily influenced by the "Arts and Crafts" ideas of William Morris, Lutyens was at the start of a career that culminated during the 1920s when he laid out most of New Delhi. The real reason to visit, however, is to enjoy the magnificent **gardens**, designed by Mallet in conjunction with Gertrude Jekyll, and at their most spectacular in the second half of May (tickets on sale mid-March to mid-Nov daily 10am–noon & 2–6pm; house open those hours, gardens open April–Oct 10am–8pm; €8 during May & June, otherwise €7). Enthusiastic guides lead you through the highly innovative engineering of the house and grounds, full of quirks and games. The colours of the Burne-Jones tapestry hanging in the stairwell were copied from Renaissance cloth in William Morris's studio; the rhododendrons were chosen from similar samples. Paths lead through vistas based on paintings by Poussin, Lorrain and other eighteenth-century artists; no modern roses, with their anachronistic colours, are allowed to spoil the effect.

Also in Varengeville, 300m south of the D75, is the **Manoir d'Ango**, the "summer palace" of sixteenth-century Dieppe's leading shipbuilder (mid-April to Sept daily 10am–12.30pm & 2–6pm; Oct Sat & Sun 10am–12.30pm & 2–6pm; €5; Ⓦwww.manoirdango.fr). Jean Ango outfitted such major expeditions as Verrazzano's, which "discovered" the site of New York in 1524, and made his riches from pillaging treasure ships out on the Spanish Main. His former home consists of a rectangular ensemble of fine brick buildings arranged around a central courtyard. The intricate patterning of red bricks, shaped flint slabs, stone blocks and supporting timbers is at its finest in the remarkable central **dovecote**, topped by a dome that rises to an elegant point, which is aflutter with pigeons. Parts of the various houses are given over to temporary art exhibitions each summer.

While the village of Varengeville offers little choice of **accommodation**, its one available option is absolutely irresistible – the lovely *Hôtel de la Terrasse*, a *logis* set amid the pines on the route de Vastérival, (Ⓣ02.35.85.12.54, Ⓦwww.hotel-restaurant-la-terrasse.com; ❸; closed mid-Oct to mid-March). Reached via a right turn off the main highway as you head west of town, it's perched high above the cliffs, with great sea views. Fish menus in its panoramic dining room start at €22, and you can follow footpaths down through narrow cracks in the cliffs to reach the rocky beach below.

Veules-les-Roses

As you follow the coastal road immediately beyond Varengeville, **Quiberville**, the main name on the map, is popular with windsurfers, but in itself is little more than an overgrown caravan park. **VEULES-LES-ROSES** is rather more promising, a delightful little seaside town that boasts of being located on the shortest river in France, the kilometre-long Veules itself. Apart from walks along the riverbank and the wide shingle beach, the chief pleasure here is dining at superb seafood **restaurants** like *Les Galets*, footsteps from the sea at 3 rue Victor-Hugo (Ⓣ02.35.97.61.33), and the nearby *Victor Hugo*, 1 place Mélingue (Ⓣ02.35.97.98.98). **Angiens**, not far beyond, is another attractive village with a flower-bedecked square.

St-Valery-en-Caux

The first sizeable community west of Dieppe, **ST-VALERY-EN-CAUX**, is a rebuilt but still attractive port where open-air stalls along the quayside of the narrow harbour sell fresh-caught fish daily. Busy with tourists in summer, St-Valery provides a clear reminder of the fighting – and massive destruction – during the Allied retreat of 1940. To either side of the shingle beach rise crumbling brown-stained cliffs. A monument on the western heights pays tribute to the French division who faced Rommel's tanks on horseback, brandishing their sabres with hopeless heroism, and beside the ruins of a German artillery emplacement on the opposite cliffs a second monument commemorates a Scottish division, the 51st Highlanders, rounded up while fighting their way back to the boats home.

A characterless casino stands in the centre of the seafront, east of the port entrance, with an even newer church a little way behind, on the northern edge of the main market square. Made almost entirely of stained glass, it holds a giant sailing boat motif above its entrance.

Practicalities

By far the most attractive house to survive in St-Valery is the Renaissance **Maison Henri IV** on the quai d'Aval, with its intricately carved wooden facade. It's now the **tourist office** (daily: July & Aug 10am–1pm & 2–7pm; Sept–June 10am–12.30pm & 2–6.30pm; Ⓣ02.35.97.00.63, Ⓦville-saint-valery-en-caux.fr), though some rooms serve as a separate museum with changing exhibits on local history (same hours; €2). No trains serve the town, but SNCF **buses** connect with trains to and from Rouen at Yvetot, 27km south.

The only **hotel** facing the sea, *La Maison des Galets* at 22 rue le Perrey, has recently been refurbished to a high standard, with a lovely breakfast room but no restaurant; the rooms that face inland are less appealing (Ⓣ02.35.97.11.22; ❸). A cheaper *logis*, the seven-room *La Marine*, 113 rue St-Léger (Ⓣ02.35.97.05.09; ❷; closed Fri in low season), is tucked away in a backstreet on the west side of the harbour, while several more small hotels surround the market square, including the *Eden*, above a brasserie at 21 place du Marché (Ⓣ02.35.97.11.44, Ⓦeden76.com; ❶), where the cheapest rooms are not en suite. Otherwise, head for the huge *Hôtel du Casino*, 500m back along the pleasure port at 14 av Clemenceau (Ⓣ02.35.57.88.00, Ⓦhotel-casino-saintvalery.com; ❺). Its 149 rooms are faultlessly comfortable, if a little characterless, and can be a godsend in high season, when the few resources along this stretch of coast are strained to the limit.

St-Valery also holds two municipal **campsites**, the one-star *Falaise d'Amont* (Ⓣ02.35.97.05.07; closed mid-Nov to mid-March), on the eastern cliffs, and the larger three-star *d'Étennemare* (Ⓣ02.35.97.15.79), set back from the sea southwest of the harbour.

A couple of good **restaurants** stand to either side of the harbour. The *Restaurant du Port*, 18 quai d'Amont (Ⓣ02.35.97.08.93; closed Sun eve, Thurs eve, and all Mon), offers a simple but delicious €23.50 menu, and a more extravagant five-course €42 one, centring on grilled turbot. In a pretty blue half-timbered house near the tourist office, *La Boussole*, 1 rue Max-Leclerc (Ⓣ02.35.57.16.28; closed Mon–Wed in winter), has tables in a narrow conservatory or outdoors on the terrace, and serves menus at €16 and €26, which include curry and tajine dishes as well as the expected seafood.

Markets take place on Fridays and summer Sundays, and the town plays host to both a **festival of the sea** in mid-August, and a **herring festival** in mid-November.

Fécamp

FÉCAMP, roughly halfway between Dieppe and Le Havre, is, like Dieppe, a serious fishing port, albeit one with a modern sideline as a holiday resort. First chartered in 875 AD as Fiscannum, from the Germanic for "fish", it has been a centre for shipbuilding ever since. These days, it's a striking rather than pretty town, surrounded by high cliffs so that, approaching from inland, you don't see the sea until you're right upon it. It was fortunate enough to sustain very little damage during World War II, though the Germans did destroy its Belle Époque casino, fearing it could serve as a landmark for Allied invaders.

Fécamp still has its **railway link**, the tracks running right up to the small harbour, where fishing boats and yachts jostle for position. The town's long promenade fronts a uniform steep beach of shingle, framed by crumbling and overhanging cliffs. As ever along this coast, windsurfing is more appealing than bathing. In the absence of any major attraction out to sea, the tourist boats or *vedettes* offer cruises to watch the sun set.

Arrival and information

Approaching from the south, whether by road or rail, you'll come into Fécamp alongside the Valmont River. As the coastline runs north to south at this point, however, the river is in fact flowing westward, and it disappears into successive canalized channels and artificial harbours when it reaches the port. Trains from the south and buses along the coast from Dieppe pull in at the **gares SNCF** and **routières** respectively, both located on its left bank between the port and the town centre on boulevard de la République. Buses from Le Havre arrive on avenue Gambetta, opposite St-Étienne church.

The main **tourist office** is on quai Sadi-Carnot (April–June Mon–Fri 9am–6pm, Sat & Sun 10am–6.30pm; July & Aug daily 9am–6.30pm; Sept–March Mon–Fri 9am–6pm, Sat 9.30am–12.30pm & 2–6pm; Ⓣ02.35.28.51.01, Ⓦwww.fecamptourisme.com).

Accommodation

Fécamp's **hotels** tend to be set back away from the sea, on random side streets. It's a popular place, so you'll need to reserve a room in summer.

Hotels

Angleterre 91–93 rue de la Plage Ⓣ02.35.28.01.60, Ⓦhotelangleterre.com. Long-established hotel, just back from the sea above a crêperie, which looks unattractive from the outside but holds nicely refurbished sea-view rooms, all en suite, as well as a lively "English pub" with a large outdoor terrace. The ambience is more suited to young budget travellers than those seeking seaside tranquillity. ❹

La Ferme de la Chapelle Côte de la Vierge Ⓣ02.35.10.12.12, Ⓦfermedelachapelle.fr. This ancient converted farmhouse, overlooking Fécamp from high on the Falaise d'Amont, offers 22 clean, modern rooms – though sadly not with sea views – a peaceful atmosphere, and a fine restaurant, with menus from €25. ❺

De la Mer 89 bd Albert 1er Ⓣ02.35.28.24.64, Ⓦhotel-dela-mer.com. Simple but good-value hotel on the seafront, adjoining *La Frégate* bar just short of the casino. It's nicer inside than it looks from the outside; some of the bright rooms have balconies overlooking the sea, not all have en-suite facilities. Closed first three weeks of Feb. ❷

De la Plage 87 rue de la Plage ⓣ02.35.29.76.51, ⓦhoteldelaplage-fecamp.com. The smartest option close to the beach; only the higher rooms have sea views, but almost all have been well refurbished and the location is quiet. The welcome is very friendly and helpful, and there's a nice little restaurant. ❷

Campsite

Camping de Reneville ⓣ02.35.28.20.97, ⓦcampingdereneville.com. A lovely campsite with beautiful views of the coast, a short walk out of town on the western cliffs; it also has some simple two- and three-bedroom chalets, rented for €425–620 per week in summer. Closed mid-Nov to mid-March.

The Town

Although Fécamp proper, focused on the venerable **Église de la Trinité**, sprawls up the slopes near the port, the sea lies a few hundred yards further west, along a harbourside promenade that holds most of Fécamp's best restaurants. A sturdy sea wall shields the main road from the Channel itself. Throughout the summer, visitors stroll along the top, above the steeply shelving shingle beach. Immediately inland, however, everyday life continues year-round; only a block or two back from the sea, you'll find rundown residential terraces.

Musée des Terres-Neuvas et de la Pêche

Sealed from view of the Channel by the high sea wall, the modern **Musée des Terres-Neuvas et de la Pêche**, 27 bd Albert 1er (July & Aug daily 10am–7pm; Sept–June daily except Tues 10am–noon & 2–5.30pm; €3, under-18s free), commemorates Fécamp's association with the sea from the Viking invasions onwards. It focuses in particular on the long tradition whereby the fishermen of Fécamp decamped en masse each year to catch cod in the cold, foggy waters off Newfoundland. Life on board was both brutal and lonely, and the work was hard, with the fish being cleaned and salted on deck, and then sold in Spain or Portugal rather than being carried back to France. Sailing vessels continued to make the trek from the sixteenth century right up until 1931; today, vast refrigerated container ships have taken their place.

A fascinating scale model shows the port and town in 1830, shortly before Fécamp was transformed by the arrival of the first railway. At that point, it entirely lacked docks and warehouses; in fact nothing stood on the far side of the river, and the whole town was still surrounded by agricultural land.

The Benedictine Distillery

Fécamp's most distinctive tourist attraction is the **Benedictine Distillery**, at 110 rue Alexandre-le-Grand, a backstreet parallel to the port (daily: early Feb to March & mid-Oct to Dec 10.30–11.45am & 2–5pm; April to mid-July & Sept to mid-Oct 10am–noon & 2–5.30pm; mid-July to Aug 10am–6pm; €6.50; ⓦbenedictine.fr). This bizarre mock-Gothic monstrosity was built at the end of the nineteenth century for the manufacture of the sweet liqueur known as Benedictine which had been invented three hundred years earlier in the local abbey. To see inside, you have to join a ninety-minute guided **tour**, which starts by trekking through a museum of local antiquities and oddments. The tour does have its moments, including headless statues (mostly of bishops), serpentine musical instruments, and a kitsch stained-glass window in which Alexandre le Grand, former owner of the Benedictine company (no relation to Alexander the Great), is treated to a bottle of his liqueur by a passing angel.

Eventually you pass on to the distillery section (although commercial operations have moved to a new factory outside town), where bucket-loads of exotic herbs are thrown into great copper vats and distillation vessels. Then comes a massive surge drinkwards, for the (modest) *dégustation* across the road; it must be said it's nice stuff, especially the "B&B", Benedictine and brandy, served either neat or on crêpes. Hang on to your admission ticket to get the free drink.

Église de la Trinité

The medieval abbey church of the **Église de la Trinité**, inland on place Général Leclerc, is light and almost frail with age, its bare nave echoing to the sound of birds flying free beneath the high roof. The wooden carvings are tremendous, in particular the dusty wooden bas-relief *Dormition of the Virgin*. The abbey also has a fine selection of saintly fingers and sacred hips, authenticated with wax seals, and even a drop of the Precious Blood itself, said to have floated all the way here in a fig tree dispatched by Joseph of Arimathea. Until Mont-St-Michel was built, this was the religious centre of Normandy; Edward the Confessor may have lived here at some point before his coronation as king of England.

Eating

In summer, Fécamp welcomes enough visitors to keep several **restaurants** in business; not surprisingly, the fish tends to be good. The most promising area is along the *quais* fronting the harbour; the seafront boulevard has a relatively meagre selection.

Chez Nounoute 3 pl Nicolas-Selle ⓣ02.35.29.38.08. The blue chairs of this friendly, good-value bistro, housed in a former fishmongers, spread across a nice little square by the port; fill yourself up with *moules frites* for €10. Closed Sun eve.

La Marée 77 quai Bérigny ⓣ02.35.29.39.15. Very good fish restaurant, enjoying harbour views from a grand upstairs dining room above a wonderful fish shop. The only set menu, at €30, features all kinds of pescatorial pleasures – the one meat option is foie gras – plus a *Bénédictine crême brûlée*. Closed Sun eve & Mon.

La Marine 23 quai de la Vicomté ⓣ02.35.28.15.94. Friendly little quayside restaurant, not far from the beach, but with indoor seating only. It's open daily for mainly seafood €15 lunches and dinners up to €25; the excellent *choucroute de la mer* is €18.

Les Terres-Neuvas 63 bd Albert 1er ⓣ02.35.29.22.92. The one high-class seafood option on Fécamp's seafront; menus at €23 and €35, and lovely sunset views. Closed Sun eve & Mon.

Yport

The tiny fishing port of **YPORT**, tucked into a narrow gap in the chalky cliffs 6km west of Fécamp, is something of a cross between Fécamp and Étretat. It's much smaller and more attractive than Fécamp, from which it's actually visible along the shoreline, without being nearly as photogenic (or crowded) as Étretat. Local legend has it that Yport was colonized over two thousand years ago by Greek fishermen from Asia Minor, who for some reason were not deterred by its complete lack of a harbour. Their descendants have remained ever since, meaning that Yport has a reputation for being an insular community. While it's not a place to spend your entire holiday, it makes an appealing and very peaceful overnight stop.

Practicalities

Yport's **tourist office** is on rue Afred-Nunes (June–Aug daily 9.30am–12.30pm & 2.30–6.30pm; Sept–May Mon–Sat 9.30am–12.30pm & 2–6pm; ⓣ02.35.29.77.31, ⓦtourisme-yport.info). Both the main **hotels** are painted to appear half-timbered. The *Hôtel Normand*, 2 place J-P Laurens (ⓣ02.35.27.30.76,

Ⓦwww.hotel-normand.fr; ❸; closed mid-Jan to mid-Feb), is a Logis de France with menus from €14; *La Sirène*, 7 bd Alexandre-Dumont (Ⓣ02.35.27.31.87, Ⓦwww.hotel-sirene.com; ❹; closed Mon and all Dec, plus Tues–Thurs in winter), enjoys sweeping beachfront views, and serves the usual seafood menus at €15 and upwards.

Étretat

Delightful little **ÉTRETAT** is very different to Fécamp. Here the alabaster cliffs are at their most spectacular – their arches, tunnels and the solitary "needle" out to sea adorn countless tourist brochures – and the town itself has grown up simply as a pleasure resort.

Étretat doesn't even have a port of any kind; the seafront consists of a sweeping unbroken curve of concrete above the shingle beach. Traditionally, wooden boats were hauled up onto the promenade each summer and thatched over to serve as seasonal bars. These days, the boats are permanently beached, cemented into place and roofed over, but they still add a charming touch. However, it's not just the waterfront that makes Étretat truly special, but its central core of attractive old timber buildings, grouped around the market square a few metres inland, along with the breathtaking clifftop walks to either side of town.

Arrival and information

The biggest drawback to visiting Étretat is that it gets so **crowded**; in theory there's plenty of central **parking**, especially at the northern end of the seafront, but in summer you may have to use overflow car parks that stretch back a *long* way from the sea. The **tourist office** is beside the main through road, on place M. Guillard (mid-June to mid-Sept daily 10am–7pm; mid-March to mid-June & mid-Sept to mid-Nov Mon–Sat 10am–noon & 2–6pm; mid-Nov to mid-March Fri & Sat 10am–noon & 2–6pm; Ⓣ02.35.27.05.21, Ⓦetretat.net). Coastal **buses** stop just outside.

Accommodation

Though Étretat is hardly short of **hotels** – four crowd onto the corners of place Foch alone – they struggle to cope with demand during high season. It makes a lovely place to stay, however, so it's well worth booking in advance. For **campers** there's the *Camping Municipal* spreading beside the D39, 1km out of town (Ⓣ02.35.27.07.67; closed mid-Oct to mid-April).

Le Corsaire rue Général Leclerc Ⓣ02.35.10.38.90, Ⓦwww.lecorsaire-etretat.com. Seafront hotel, in the thick of things alongside the casino. All the rooms are en suite, but those that enjoy sea views are more luxurious, and considerably more expensive, than plainer counterparts facing inland. The beach terrace restaurant serves good menus from €18. ❹–❼

Dormy House rte du Havre Ⓣ02.35.27.07.88, Ⓦdormy-house.com. Grand modern establishment perched above town on the coastal road to the west, situated as much for the golf course as the beach. Comfortable rooms, some with superb views, and a good restaurant with lovely outdoor seating. ❹–❾

L'Escale pl Foch Ⓣ02.35.27.03.69. Twelve simple but pleasant rooms on the main square, above a snack restaurant specializing in *moules frites* and crêpes. ❸

Hôtel la Résidence 4 bd René-Coty Ⓣ02.35.27.02.87, Ⓦwww.hotels-etretat.com. Dramatic half-timbered old mansion just off place Foch, moved in its entirety from Lisieux a century ago, with beautiful wooden carvings decorating its every nook and cranny. Though recently refurbished, the guest rooms vary enormously; the cheapest option lacks en-suite facilities, while others are positively luxurious. ❶–❼

Taverne des Deux Augustins pl Foch Ⓣ02.35.27.06.99. Hybrid structure on the main square, with the pink brick of the hotel proper rising above the sprawling wood-panelled frontage of the (rather ordinary) *choucroute* restaurant downstairs; reasonable rates for such a good central location. ❸

The Town

Étretat is a very pretty little place, thanks partly to its superb setting, and also to the lovely architectural ensemble that surrounds its central **place Foch**, just back from the sea. The old wooden market *halles* still dominate the main square, the ground floor now converted into souvenir shops, but the beams of the balcony and roof are bare and ancient. **Market** day locally is Thursday, with most of the stalls spreading across the larger car park to the west.

As soon as you step onto the beach you're confronted by Étretat's stunning **cliffs**. The coastline here runs roughly north to south; the largest arch, and the lone needle, thrusting out to the **south**, is known as the **Falaise d'Aval**. A straightforward if precarious walk leads up the crumbling side of the cliff. On the inland side lie the lush lawns and pastures of a golf course, while on the shore side down, at the foot of the cliff, German fortifications extend to the point where the turf abruptly stops. From the windswept top you can see further rock formations and possibly even glimpse Le Havre, but the views back to the town sheltered in the valley, and the **Falaise d'Amont** on its northern side, are what stick in the memory.

Maupassant compared the profile of the smaller arch at the base of the **northern** cliffs – as painted by Monet, among others – to an elephant dipping its trunk into the ocean. Except at high tide, it's possible to stroll along the shingles beyond the town proper to within a few metres of the arch. Alternatively, an extraordinarily picturesque footpath winds to the top of the cliff on this side as well, another demanding climb up the green hillside that leads to the little chapel of **Notre Dame**. Just beyond that, a futuristic white arch commemorates French aviators **Nungesser and Coli**, who set out from Paris in the *Oiseau Blanc* in May 1927, hoping to make the first east–west transatlantic flight, and were last seen over Étretat. What happened to them is not known – there are suggestions that they crashed somewhere in deepest Maine, New England – but a mere eighteen days later Charles Lindbergh arrived coming from the opposite direction (see p.142) and went into the history books. In the turf alongside the arch, a life-size aeroplane is set in concrete relief, and a tiny museum nearby tells the story (daily 10am–6pm; free).

▲ Falaise d'Amont, Étretat

Eating

Fierce competition keeps **restaurant** prices in Étretat appealingly low. Even the succession of seafront terraces offer good value for money, while away from the sea bargains can be had at both ends of the spectrum.

Crêperie Lann-Bihoué 45 rue Nôtre-Dame ⓣ02.35.27.04.65. Cheerful traditional crêperie, at the south end of town, that's Étretat's best bet for a good-value family meal. Closed Wed and all Dec, plus Tues in low season.

Le Galion 4 bd René-Coty ⓣ02.35.29.48.74. Étretat's finest restaurant adjoins the *Résidence* hotel and has a similar antique-filled ambience. The €22 menu makes a definitive introduction to all that's best in Norman cuisine, while the €32 and €39 options are increasingly more refined. Closed Tues & Wed in low season.

La Huitrière pl de Gaulle ⓣ02.35.27.02.82. Panoramic first-floor dining room, at the foot of the steps up the Falaise d'Aval, which makes the perfect setting for an absolute blowout on seafood. As well as menus from €23 to €44, it offers an enormous range of seafood platters, up to the €75-per-person *Abondance*, which comes with half a lobster each and a scattering of caviar.

La Salamandre 4 bd René-Coty ⓣ02.35.27.17.07. This organic restaurant, downstairs from the *Résidence* hotel but run by separate management, serves stylish modern cuisine amid ravishing medieval trappings, on menus from €16 to €34.

Le Havre

While **LE HAVRE** – Normandy's largest town, at the mouth of the Seine – may not be the most picturesque or tranquil place in the region, neither is it the soulless urban sprawl some travellers suggest. Yes, its port, the second largest in France after Marseille, takes up half the Seine estuary, but the town itself at the core, home to a population of 191,000, has become a place of pilgrimage for devotees of contemporary architecture.

The city was originally built by François I in 1517, to replace the ancient ports of Harfleur and Honfleur, then already silting up. Its name soon changed from Franciscopolis to Le Havre – "the Harbour" – and it became the principal trading post of northern France, importing cotton, sugar and tobacco. In the years before the outbreak of war in 1939, it was the European home of the great trans-Atlantic liners such as the *Normandie*, *Île de France* and *France*.

During World War II, Le Havre suffered heavier damage than any other port in Europe. Following its all but total destruction by Allied bombing, it was rebuilt by a single architect, **Auguste Perret**, between 1946 and 1964. That makes it a rather rare entity, and one that with its utter dependence on **reinforced concrete** is visibly circumscribed by constraints of time and money. Nonetheless, its sheer sense of space can be exhilarating, the showpiece monuments have a dramatic and winning self-confidence, and the few churches and other relics that survive of the old city have been sensitively integrated into the whole. While the skyline has been kept deliberately low, the endless mundane residential blocks, which simply had to be erected as economically and swiftly as possible, can get dispiriting. However, with the sea visible at the end of almost every street, and open public space and expanses of water at every turn, even those visitors who ultimately fail to agree with Perret's famous dictum that "concrete is beautiful" may enjoy a stroll around his city. UNESCO added the entire town centre to its World Heritage List in 2005.

Arrival and information

The only current **ferries** to Le Havre are one or two sailings daily from Portsmouth in England, operated by LD Lines (ⓣ08.25.30.43.04, ⓦldlines.co.uk).

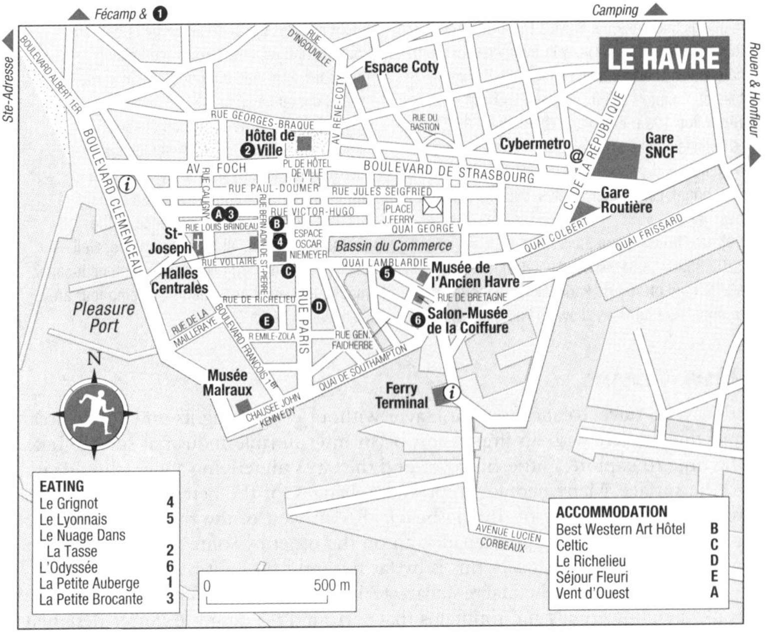

Shuttle buses connect the ferry terminal with the **gare SNCF**, 1.5km east of the Hôtel de Ville on cours de la République. Fast **trains** (though not TGV) go to Rouen (1hr) and Paris (a further 1hr 15min). If you're travelling west, you have to change at Rouen – a very circuitous route. Commuter services run regularly to Harfleur in around five minutes. Alongside the *gare SNCF*, the **gare routière** is the base for local **bus** services in the Bus Océane network (ⓣ02.35.22.35.00, ⓦwww.bus-oceane.com). Heading further afield, express buses from here, run by Bus Verts du Calvados (ⓣ08.10.21.42.14, ⓦwww.busverts.fr), take advantage of the Pont du Normandie to connect Le Havre with Honfleur seven times daily, with two services continuing as far as Caen.

Le Havre's modern, helpful **tourist office** is in an inconspicuous and not very central location on the main seafront drag, at 186 bd Clemenceau, near avenue Foch (July & Aug Mon–Sat 9am–7pm, Sun 10am–12.30pm & 2.30–6pm; May, June, Sept & Oct Mon–Sat 9am–6.45pm, Sun 10am–12.30pm & 2.30–5.45pm; Nov–April Mon–Fri 9am–6.30pm, Sat 9am–12.30pm & 2–6.30pm, Sun 10am–1pm; ⓣ02.32.74.04.04, ⓦwww.lehavretourisme.com).

Accommodation

One consequence of Le Havre's lack of idiosyncratic old buildings is that its **hotels** tend to be hidden away behind indistinguishable concrete facades. There are two main concentrations of hotels: one group faces the *gare SNCF*, while most of the rest lie within walking distance of the ferry terminal.

Best Western Art Hôtel 147 rue Louis-Brindeau ⓣ02.35.22.69.44, ⓦwww.bestwestern.com. Smart, comfortable, non-smoking hotel, on the north side of the Espace Oscar Niemeyer, facing the Volcano cultural centre. All rooms have flat-screen LCD TVs and wi-fi access. 5

Celtic 106 rue Voltaire ⓣ02.35.42.39.77, ⓦhotelceltic.com. Facing the *Art Hôtel*, in the long buildings that flank the Espace Oscar Niemeyer, this hotel tells it like it is, with three distinct room categories: "budget" (with showers but sharing toilets); "comfort"; and "pleasure". ❶–❸

Richelieu 135 rue de Paris ⓣ02.35.42.38.71, ⓔhotel.lerichelieu@orange.fr. If you're looking for a friendly mid-priced hotel in a very central location with bright, comfortable rooms, this one is hard to beat. ❸

Séjour Fleuri 71 rue Émile-Zola ⓣ02.35.41.33.81, ⓦwww.hotelsejourfleuri.fr. On a side road off rue de Paris, close to the ferry terminal; not quite as "flowery" as the name might suggest but cheered up by bright red shutters and window boxes, and holding minimally furnished but perfectly clean rooms inside, not all en suite. ❶

Vent d'Ouest 4 rue de Caligny ⓣ02.35.42.50.69, ⓦventdouest.fr. Le Havre's smartest hotel is a stylish boutique affair, housed in a cream-coloured cement building beside the main entrance to the St-Joseph church. All the comfortable, well-equipped rooms are decorated with a nautical or mountain theme. Apartments sleeping four are also available. ❻

The Town

It's easy to travel to and from Le Havre without ever seeing its downtown area, and thus be left with an impression of an interminable industrial sprawl. Take the time to explore a little, however, and the city's underlying appeal should rise to the surface. Many people's impression changes for the better as soon as they reach the 2km stretch of shingle **beach**, 1.5km west of the *gare SNCF*, fronted on one side by a lively promenade and on the other by some surprisingly clean water. In summer especially, this is by far the most pleasant part of town.

A good example of Le Havre's characteristic **urban greenery** is in the pergola walkways, flowerbeds and fountains that surround the Auguste Perret-designed **Hôtel de Ville**, halfway between the beach and the *gare SNCF*: a low, flat-roofed building stretching for over 100m and topped by a seventeen-storey concrete tower. Not that Perret himself would have approved; he considered trees and plants to be unnecessary obstacles that would impair the appreciation of his edifices, and they were added after his death in 1954.

The steeple of Perret's other major creation, the church of **St-Joseph**, rises not far southwest. Instead of the traditional elongated cross shape, the four arms of the cross on which this church is built are equally short. From the outside, it's a very plain mass of speckled concrete, almost Egyptian in its simplicity, the main doors thrown open to the street to hint at dark interior spaces. Once you get inside, it all makes sense. The altar is in the centre, with the hundred-metre bell tower rising directly above it. Simple patterns of stained glass, all around the church and right the way up the tower, produce a bright interplay of coloured light, all focusing on the altar to create the effect of a church in the round.

Le Havre's boldest example of modern architecture is considerably more recent – the cultural centre known as the **Volcano** (or less reverentially as the "yoghurt pot"), dominating the **Espace Oscar Niemeyer** at the end of the Bassin du Commerce. The Brazilian architect after whom the *espace* is named – who is best known for overseeing the construction of Brasilia, and was at the time this book went to press still hard at work, having recently celebrated his 101st birthday – designed this slightly asymmetrical smooth gleaming white cone during the 1970s. Cut off abruptly just above the level of the surrounding buildings, its curving planes are undisturbed by doors or windows; the entrance is concealed beneath a white walkway in the open plaza below. A large green copper hand emerges from the Volcano just above its base, slightly cupped and pouring out water as a fountain, inscribed with the sentiment that "One day, like this water, the land, beaches and mountains will belong to all".

The **Bassin du Commerce**, which stretches away from the Espace Oscar Niemeyer, is in fact of minimal commercial significance; a couple of larger boats

Harfleur

The once-great port of **Harfleur** is now no more than a suburb of Le Havre, 6km upstream from the centre. While visibly older than the modern city that engulfs it, it's no longer sufficiently distinctive to be worth visiting. It earned an undying place in history, however, as the landing place of Henry V's English army in 1415, en route to victory at Agincourt. During a month-long siege of the town, two thousand English soldiers died from eating contaminated seafood from the surrounding marshes. Harfleur surrendered in late September, following a final English onslaught spurred on – according to Shakespeare – by Henry's cry of "Once more unto the breach, dear friends...".

are moored permanently to serve as clubs or restaurants. It's all surprisingly quiet, existing mainly as an appropriate stretch of water for the graceful white footbridge of the Passarelle du Commerce to cross.

Musée Malraux

The modern **Musée Malraux** (Mon & Wed–Fri 11am–6pm, Sat & Sun 11am–7pm; €5, under-18s free), overlooking the harbour entrance at 2 bd Clemenceau, ranks among the best designed art galleries in France. It uses natural light to full advantage to display an enjoyable assortment of nineteenth- and twentieth-century French paintings. The principal highlight upstairs is a collection of over two hundred canvases by **Eugène Boudin**. Two years after the painter's death, his brother Louis gave the museum the entire contents of Eugène's studio. Although many of the works were neither signed nor dated, and some are no bigger than postcards, they range from throughout the artist's career. Most are arranged by theme, so one wall consists almost entirely of miniature cows, but there are also greyish landscapes from all along the Norman and Breton coastlines, including views of Trouville, Honfleur and Étretat.

Downstairs, the focus shifts to a lovely set of works by **Raoul Dufy** (1877–1953). In his case, the artist's widow left two hundred of his paintings to be divided between three museums – the national modern art museum in Paris, the one in Nice, and this gallery in Dufy's home town. Each curator was allowed to pick a single piece in turn, with the result that Le Havre ended up with a collection of images of itself that make it seem positively radiant. Dufy depicts his native city at play, with drawings and paintings of festivals and parades, and even a panorama of the whole city framed beneath an arching rainbow. Among other treasures are a Gauguin from Tahiti, several Monets – including scenes of Westminster and Varengeville, plus a few waterlilies and a snowscape sunrise – as well as works by Corot, Courbet, Pissarro (including one painted within a few metres of this spot), Sisley, Léger, Braque and Lurçat.

Eating

Few of Le Havre's **restaurants** are worth making a fuss about, except perhaps for some near the suburb of **Ste-Adresse**, northwest along the coast towards Étretat. There are, however, lots of bars, cafés and brasseries around the *gare SNCF*, and all sorts of crêperies and ethnic restaurants – North African, South American, Caribbean – in the backstreets of the St-François quarter opposite the ferry terminal.

The larger of the two local Auchan **hypermarkets** (both Mon–Sat 8.30am–10pm) is at the Mont Gaillard Centre Commercial; reached by following cours de la République beyond the *gare SNCF*, through the tunnel, it holds an outlet of the chain self-service cafeteria, *Flunch*. The other, at Montivilliers, is signposted off the Tancarville road, east of the centre. In the town centre, on rue Bernadin de St-Pierre just east of the Espace Oscar Niemeyer, the **Halles Centrales** is a good place to buy fresh fruit and vegetables, fish and meat.

Le Grignot 53 rue Racine ⓣ02.35.43.62.07. Traditional brasserie, with brisk, efficient service and good food at very reasonable prices.

Le Lyonnais 7–9 rue de Bretagne ⓣ02.35.22.07.31. Small, cosy restaurant with chequered tablecloths and an English-speaking owner (hence the menu translated into English). The house speciality is baked fish, though dishes from Lyon, such as *andouillettes*, are also available on menus which start at €12.50 for lunch, €16 for dinner. Closed Sun & Mon eve.

Le Nuage Dans La Tasse 93 av Foch ⓣ02.35.21.64.94. Huge salads and simple, good-value bistro meals near the town hall. Closed Sun & lunchtime Mon–Wed.

L'Odyssée 41 rue Général-Faidherbe ⓣ02.35.21.31.42. First-rate seafood restaurant close to the ferry terminal in the old town, serving a reliable €24 weekday lunch menu and a more adventurous €30 dinner option. Closed Sat lunch, Sun eve, Mon & first three weeks in Aug.

La Petite Auberge 32 rue de Ste-Adresse ⓣ02.35.46.27.32. High-class traditional French cooking, aimed more at local businesspeople than at tourists, and offering few surprises but no disappointments. Menus at €23 (lunch), €30 and €43. Closed Sun eve, Wed lunch & Mon.

La Petite Brocante 75 rue Louis Brindeau ⓣ02.35.21.42.20. Lively central bistro, where the set menus are a little pricey at €25 and up, but there's always a good-value *plat du jour*, as often as not fresh fish. Closed Sun & first three weeks in Aug.

The Seine Valley

As far back as the Bronze Age, the **River Seine** was a crucial part of the "Tin Road" linking Cornwall to Paris. Fortresses and monasteries lined its banks from the Roman era onwards. Now, with the threat of its tidal bore and treacherous sandbanks a thing of the past, heavy ships make their serene way up its sinuous course from the Channel to the provincial capital of **Rouen**.

Following the river by car, bus or bicycle, it's worth taking this journey equally slowly, savouring such highlights as the riverside towns of **Villequier** and **Caudebec** or the abbey of **Jumièges**. Rouen itself is the major attraction, nonetheless, as one of France's most vibrant medieval cities. Beyond it, en route to Paris, things if anything get even better, in the shape of the dramatic castle fortress above **Les Andelys** and Monet's celebrated gardens at **Giverny**.

Along the Seine to Rouen

Even though Le Havre and Rouen have become vast industrial conurbations, long stretches of the riverbank between the two remain remarkably unspoiled and tranquil. As you first leave Le Havre, however, the refineries and cement works seem to go on forever; to reach the river, drivers have first to negotiate a long approach road that twists its way over the Canal du Havre. Beyond that, the huge, humpback **Pont de Normandie** spans the mouth of the Seine to connect Le Havre with Honfleur, offering direct access between the coasts of Upper and Lower Normandy. An amazing spectacle, it stretches 853m across, with the roadway climbing 50m above sea level. When completed, it was the longest cable-stayed bridge in the world, but it has since lost that record to a rival in Hiroshima, Japan. Crossing either that bridge – which incurs a one-way toll of €5 – or the similarly immense **Tancarville** suspension bridge, 20km upriver, brings you to the **south** (**left**) **bank** of the Seine. This holds the vast majority of the **Parc Naturel Régional de Brotonne**, where peaceful rolling hillsides are evenly divided between bucolic agricultural fields and dense woodlands.

By far the quickest route up the Seine Valley, however, is to follow the dramatic chalky bluffs along the **north** (**right**) **bank**. This side offers richer scenic and historic rewards, with the road that sticks firmly to the riverbank leading past such sights as the venerable towns of **Villequier** and **Caudebec**, and the magnificent ruined abbey of **Jumièges**.

Only one more bridge crosses the river in the extravagant loops that lie between Tancarville and Rouen – the **Pont de Brotonne**, near Caudebec, which leads to the heart of the park (€5). Further upstream, however, there are also intermittent *bacs* (car **ferries**) across the river, which charge smaller tolls, and tend to leave on the hour (and to have long lunch breaks).

Villequier

The first of the riverbank towns you come to on the D982 along the north bank is quite undeservedly one of the least known – **VILLEQUIER**. There's nothing really to do in Villequier, but watching the extraordinary array of boats great and small that pass by, towering above the riverbank, is deliciously hypnotic. An enjoyable riverside pedestrian promenade runs the length of the village, which has a bohemian vibe with its higgledy-piggledy old houses. Several hundred metres upstream from the centre, near the southern end of the waterfront, a mournful statue of Victor Hugo, so weathered as to make the author appear naked, peers out into the Seine, to the spot where his daughter and her husband drowned in 1843, just six months after their marriage. The couple's former home, back in town, now serves as the **Musée Victor Hugo**, probably of interest only to fluent French speakers with a passion for Hugo's writings (April–Sept Mon & Wed–Sat 10am–12.30pm & 2–6pm, Sun 2–6pm; Oct–March Mon & Wed–Sat 10am–12.30pm & 2–5.30pm, Sun 2–5.30pm; €3, under-18s free).

Wherever you may be heading, it's worth making a considerable detour to stay at Villequier's one, delightfully quirky, **hotel**: *Le Grand Sapin*, 12 rue Louis le Gaffrie (Ⓣ02.35.56.78.73, Ⓦlegrandsapin.free.fr; ❷), is a gorgeous rambling old building, where three of the bedrooms have rickety gingerbread balconies overlooking the river. The fixtures and fittings are showing their age, but the whole place is absolutely magical on a misty morning – and exceptional in the evening, when the wood-panelled restaurant (closed Tues eve & Wed except July & Aug) is in full swing (menus range from €22 up to €37). Tables in the riverside garden are laid out under the shade of the eponymous *grand sapin* itself – not the original, but a rather frail pine that has had its thunder stolen by a giant magnolia nearby.

Villequier also holds a riverside **campsite**, halfway to Caudebec: the two-star *Barre Y Va* (Ⓣ02.35.96.26.38, Ⓦwww.camping-barre-y-va.com; closed Nov–March).

Caudebec-en-Caux

Just over 4km upstream from Villequier, **CAUDEBEC-EN-CAUX** is significantly bigger and busier. The thirteenth-century **Maison des Templiers** on rue Thomas Bassin, 100m back from the river, was one of the few buildings in this old town to survive the firestorm devastation of World War II. It now serves as a museum of local history, with plenty of old photos and "one of the most important collections of chimney plaques in France" (Wed–Sun 2–6pm; €5). A more specific and contemporary look at the role of the Seine in Norman history is taken by the **Musée de la Marine de Seine**, avenue Winston-Churchill (daily: April–Sept 2–6.30pm; Oct–March 2–5.30pm; €3.50). The magnificent flamboyant **Notre Dame church**, with its octagonal spire circled by three separate *fleurs-de-lis* crowns, still dominates the main square, which has been the site of a **market** every Saturday since 1390.

A little way south of town, a **stone aeroplane** propels itself out of the cliff face across the water. In 1928, a plane was being prepared here for an attempt at what would have been the first east–west transatlantic flight. But shortly before it was due to set off, the Norwegian polar explorer Amundsen issued a worldwide appeal for help to rescue some Italian sailors who had been shipwrecked off Spitzbergen in the Arctic. The French government offered the plane, and its four crewmen left with Amundsen. Two days later they were lost.

Practicalities

Caudebec's **tourist office** is slightly south of the centre, in place Charles de Gaulle by the river (April–Sept daily 9.30am–6.30pm; Oct–March Mon–Sat 9.30am–12.30pm & 2–6pm; ⓣ02.32.70.46.32, ⓦwww.caudebec-en-caux.com). Two indistinguishable Logis de France stand side by side facing the river on quai Guilbaud, identical buildings with identical balconies, and all but identical prices – the *Normotel La Marine* at no. 18 (ⓣ02.35.96.20.11, ⓦwww.normotel-lamarine.fr; ❹; restaurant closed Fri eve, Sat lunch & Sun eve), and the *Normandie* at no. 19 (ⓣ02.35.96.25.11, ⓦwww.le-normandie.fr; ❸; r estaurant closed Sun eve). Both hotels offer en-suite rooms with phone, TV and free parking, while the on-site restaurants have menus ranging from €20 to €45 and are slightly more formal than the several other brasseries and cafés that line the *quai*. Another *logis*, the *Cheval Blanc*, is a little way back from the river at 4 place René-Coty, 200m north of the Hôtel de Ville on the western edge of town (ⓣ02.35.96.21.66, ⓦwww.le-cheval-blanc.fr; ❸; closed late Dec).

On the last Sunday in September of each year, Caudebec comes alive with a large **Cider Festival**.

The Pont de Brotonne

Slightly upstream from Caudebec, the magnificent span of the **Pont de Brotonne**, completed in 1977 as the world's highest and steepest humpback bridge (€5 toll for motorists), climbs out above the Seine. It has an unexpectedly appealing colour scheme – the suspension cables are custard yellow, the rails pastel green, the walkway maroon, and the vast concrete columns left bare. If you don't lose both heart and hat to the sickening drop and the seaborne winds, walking across it is one of the big treats of Normandy. From a distance, its stays refract into strange optical effects, while far below small tugs flounder in the wash of mighty cargo carriers.

Parc Naturel Régional des Boucles de la Seine Normande

The **Parc Naturel Régional des Boucles de la Seine Normande** – most but not quite all of which lies south of the Seine – ranks among the most beautiful tracts of the Norman countryside. While not entirely rural, it shelters a wide range of conservation projects and traditional industry initiatives, run by local people, alongside its more obvious abbey and château sites. Full details on all its aspects can be obtained from the very helpful Maison du Parc in the small village of **NÔTRE-DAME-DE-BLIQUETUIT**, immediately east of the southern end of the Pont de Brotonne (April–June, Sept & Oct Mon–Fri 9am–6pm, Sat & Sun noon–6pm; July & Aug Mon–Fri 9am–6.30pm, Sat & Sun 10am–6.30pm; Nov–March Mon–Fri 9am–6pm; Ⓣ02.35.37.23.16, Ⓦwww.pnr-seine-normande.com).

The most compelling section of the park is concentrated into a mighty meander on the southern bank of the Seine, across from Caudebec. Here the slopes are covered by the deep thick woods of the **Forêt de Brotonne**, perfect for cyclists and hikers. The pretty little village of **AIZIER** nestles beside the river at the western limit of the forest, with the edges of the Vernier marshes, grazed by Camargue horses and Scottish Highland cattle, just beyond.

Hauville

The southern border of the Forêt de Brotonne marks the dividing line between the *départements* of Seine-Maritime and Eure. Still under the auspices of the park, outside the small community of **HAUVILLE** (and signposted towards the even tinier village of La Mare-Guérard), you can look round what's said to be the oldest still-functioning **windmill** (*moulin*) in France. One of six owned by the monks of Jumièges, who farmed and forested this area in the Middle Ages, its outline – based on contemporary castle towers – looks like a kid's drawing (mid-April to June & first three weeks in Sept Sun 2.30–6.30pm; July & Aug daily 2–6.30pm; €6 with museums in La Haye du Routot, see below).

La Haye du Routot

The churchyard in the village of **LA HAYE DU ROUTOT**, 4km west of Hauville, is a real oddity, featuring a pair of thousand-year-old yew trees that are still alive but have been sufficiently hollowed out to shelter a chapel and grotto. Every year, on July 16, the feast of St Clair, the village stages the dramatic **Fête de St-Clair**. Its centrepiece is a towering, conical bonfire, topped by a cross which must survive to ensure a good year. The smouldering logs are taken home to serve as protection against lightning. Should you miss the big day, they show footage in the local crafts **museum**, which numbers among its separate sections a traditional functioning bread oven, adjacent to the church, and a clog-specialist shoemaker opposite (both April–June & Sept Sun 2–6.30pm; July & Aug daily 2–6.30pm; March, Oct & Nov Sun 2–6pm; combined admission €2, or €6 with windmill in Hauville, see above).

Abbaye de St-Wandrille

Just beyond the Pont de Brotonne on the north bank of the Seine, a side road (marked "St-Wandrille-Rançon") climbs 2km up to the **Abbaye de St-Wandrille**. So legend has it, the abbey was founded by a seventh-century count who, with his wife, renounced all earthly pleasures on the day of their wedding. It remains an active monastery, home to fifty or so Benedictine monks who, in addition to their spiritual duties, turn their hands to money-making tasks that range from candle-making to running a reprographic studio. It's not such an obvious tourist destination as nearby Jumièges (see p.76), but the abbey complex nonetheless makes an attractive if curious architectural ensemble: part ruin, part restoration and, in the case of the main buildings, part transplant – a fifteenth-century barn brought in a few years ago from another Norman village.

Throughout the year, monks show visitors around the abbey on **guided tours** (Easter–Oct Mon & Wed–Sat 3.30pm, Sun 11.30am & 3.30pm; Nov–Easter Sun

11.30am; €3.50; Ⓦwww.st-wandrille.com); in addition it's possible to wander through the grounds on your own for no charge (daily 5.15am–1pm & 2–9.15pm). You can also hear **Gregorian chanting** at services in their new church (Mon–Sat 5.25am, 7.30am, 9.45am, 12.45pm, 2.15pm, 5.30pm & 8.35pm; Sun 5.25am, 7.30am, 10am, 12.45pm, 2.30pm, 5pm & 8.35pm).

For something to **eat**, there's a crêperie opposite the abbey, while the more upmarket *Auberge des Deux Coronnes* restaurant (Ⓣ02.35.96.11.44; closed Sun eve & Mon), a few doors along in the place de l'Église, is a half-timbered seventeenth-century inn, where delicious menus start at €15 for lunch and €25 for dinner.

Abbaye de Jumièges

In the next loop of the Seine, 12km upstream from St-Wandrille, squats the more famous **Abbaye de Jumièges** (mid-April to mid-Sept daily 9.30am–6.30pm; mid-Sept to mid-April daily 9.30am–1pm & 2.30–5.30pm; €5, ages 18–25 €3.50, under-18s free). Deliberately destroyed during the Revolution, it's now a haunting ruin. Founded by St Philibert in 654 AD, just five years after St-Wandrille, it was burned by Vikings in 841, then rebuilt a century later. Its main surviving shell, however, as far as it can still be discerned, dates from the eleventh century; William the Conqueror attended its reconsecration in 1067. The twin towers, over 52m high, are still standing. So too is one arch of the roofless nave, while a one-sided yew tree stands in the centre of what were once the cloisters.

Hailed as "the most beautiful ruins in France", these bleached stones can be explored on hourly guided tours, in French only, or you can take an unescorted ramble across the lawns; in either case, you're obliged for the most part to keep well clear of the precarious walls themselves. Though it survived the Revolution intact, the grand **abbot's residence** that commands a nearby eminence – built in the seventeenth century, by which time the abbot was appointed directly by the king rather than being elected by his fellow monks – is not open to visitors. The grounds, however, are sometimes used for temporary art exhibitions.

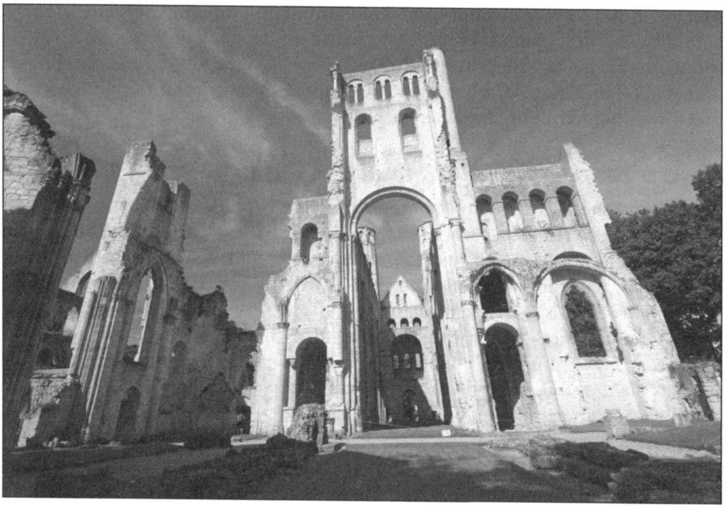

▲ Abbaye de Jumièges

The *Auberge des Ruines*, across from the abbey at 17 place de la Mairie (Ⓣ02.35.37.24.05, Ⓦwww.auberge-des-ruines.fr; closed Sun eve, Tues eve, Wed and second fortnight of Aug), is a truly superb **restaurant**, with outdoor seating on a shaded terrace. Its dinner menus range from €35 up to €70.

The river itself now flows roughly a kilometre west of the ruins. A tiny *bac* (ferry) crosses the Seine at this point to Heurteauville on the left bank, half-hourly in summer and hourly in winter; the riverbank *Auberge du Bac* (Ⓣ02.35.37.24.16; closed Mon & Tues) makes a lovely lunchtime halt, serving excellent menus from €13 (lunch only) up to €27.

Rouen

ROUEN, the capital of both the Seine-Maritime *département* and all Upper Normandy, is one of France's most ancient and historic cities. Standing on the site of Rotomagus, built by the Romans at the lowest bridge-able point on the Seine, it was laid out by the Viking Rollo, the first duke of Normandy, in 911. Captured by the English in 1419, after a long siege, it became the stage in 1431 for the trial and execution of Joan of Arc, before returning to French control in 1449.

Bombing during World War II, specifically during the fierce onslaught that preceded the D-Day landings, destroyed all Rouen's bridges, the area between the cathedral and the *quais*, and much of the left bank's industrial quarter. The city has since been almost entirely rebuilt, turning its inner core of streets, a few hundred metres north of the river, into the closest approximation to a medieval city that modern imaginations could conceive. Rouen today can be very seductive, its lively and bustling centre well equipped with impressive churches and museums. Sadly, however, the immediate riverside area has never been adequately restored.

While Rouen proper is home to a population of 110,000, its metropolitan area holds five times that number. The city spreads deep into the loop of the Seine, with its docks and industrial infrastructure stretching endlessly away to the south, and it is increasingly expanding up into the hills to the north as well. As the nearest point that large container ships can get to Paris, this remains the fourth largest port in the country; it's also the biggest exporter of foodstuffs in the European Union, and the biggest in the world for wheat.

Arrival

Rouen is a difficult and unpleasant city to **drive** into. All traffic is funnelled into the hideous multi-lane highways that line either bank of the river, and if you're not familiar with the system it's easy to find yourself repeatedly forced to cross the river and double back on yourself. Many of the central streets, north of the river, have in any case been pedestrianized, so it's best to park as soon as you can – there are plenty of central underground **car parks**, especially near the cathedral and the place du Vieux-Marché – and explore the city on foot.

The main **gare SNCF**, set high above the river at the top end of Rouen's main thoroughfare, rue Jeanne d'Arc, is Gare Rive Droite; Gare Rive Gauche on the south bank only handles goods traffic. Rouen is roughly halfway between Paris and the Channel ports; both **Le Havre** and **Dieppe** are one hour away on different train routes, while the journey to **Paris** takes an hour and a quarter. You can also get trains west to **Lisieux** (1hr 15min) and **Caen** (2hr). To reach the town centre from the *gare SNCF*, walk for ten minutes down rue Jeanne d'Arc.

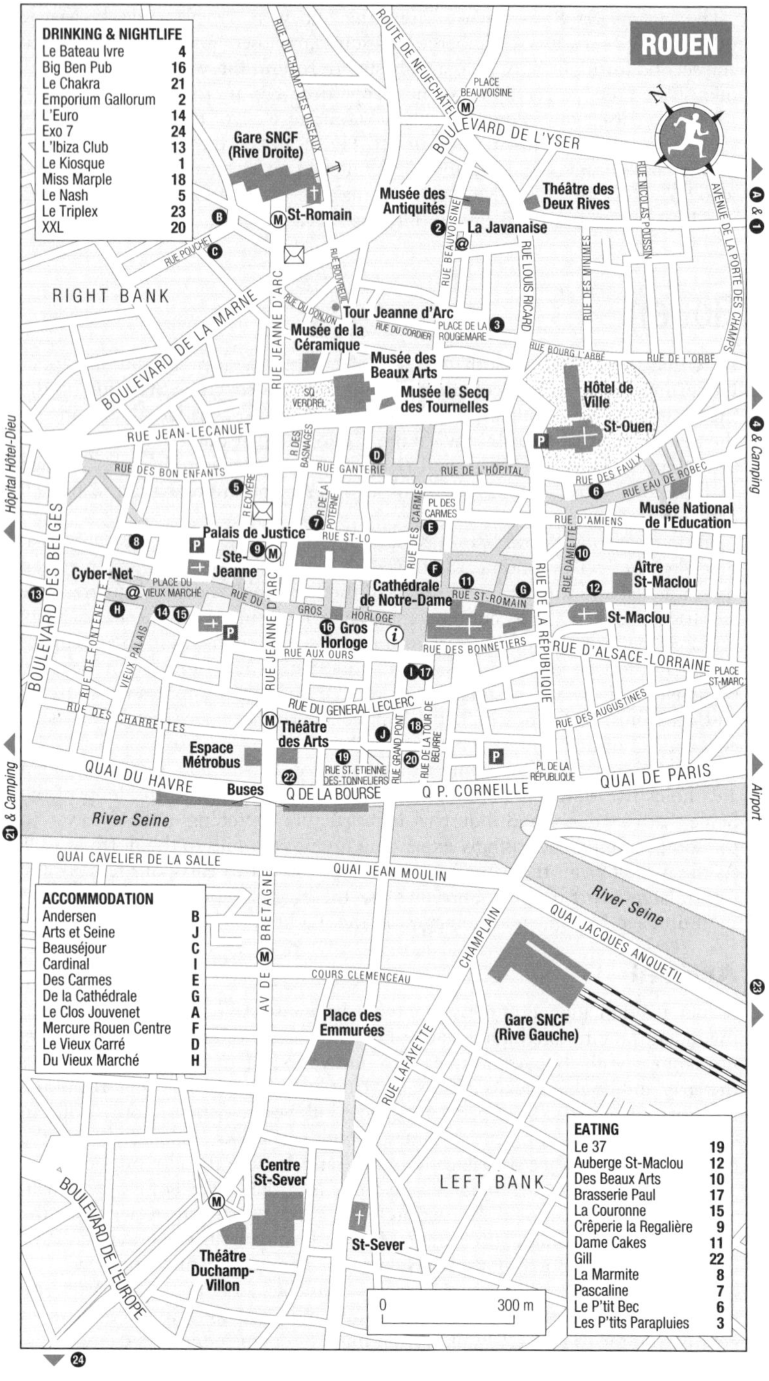
ROUEN
DRINKING & NIGHTLIFE
Le Bateau Ivre 4
Big Ben Pub 16
Le Chakra 21
Emporium Gallorum 2
L'Euro 14
Exo 7 24
L'Ibiza Club 13
Le Kiosque 1
Miss Marple 18
Le Nash 5
Le Triplex 23
XXL 20
ACCOMMODATION
Andersen B
Arts et Seine J
Beauséjour C
Cardinal I
Des Carmes E
De la Cathédrale G
Le Clos Jouvenet A
Mercure Rouen Centre F
Le Vieux Carré D
Du Vieux Marché H
EATING
Le 37 19
Auberge St-Maclou 12
Des Beaux Arts 10
Brasserie Paul 17
La Couronne 15
Crêperie la Regalière 9
Dame Cakes 11
Gill 22
La Marmite 8
Pascaline 7
Le P'tit Bec 6
Les P'tits Parapluies 3
RUE DU CHAMP DES OISEAUX
ROUTE DE NEUFCHÂTEL
PLACE BEAUVOISINE
BOULEVARD DE L'YSER
Gare SNCF (Rive Droite)
St-Romain
Musée des Antiquités
Théâtre des Deux Rives
La Javanaise
RUE NICOLAS POUSSIN
AVENUE DE LA PORTE DES CHAMPS
A & 1
RUE POUCHET
RUE BOUVREUIL
RUE BEAUVOISINE
RUE LOUIS RICARD
RUE DES MINIMES
RIGHT BANK
BOULEVARD DE LA MARNE
RUE JEANNE D'ARC
RUE DU DONJON
Tour Jeanne d'Arc
RUE DU CORDIER
PLACE DE LA ROUGEMARE
Musée de la Céramique
Musée des Beaux Arts
RUE BOURG L'ABBÉ
RUE DE L'ORBE
Hôtel de Ville
SQ VERDREL
Musée le Secq des Tournelles
St-Ouen
4 & Camping
Hôpital Hôtel-Dieu
RUE JEAN-LECANUET
R DES BASNAGES
RUE GANTERIE
RUE DE L'HÔPITAL
RUE DES FAULX
RUE EAU DE ROBEC
RUE DES BON ENFANTS
RECUYÈRE
R DE LA POTERNE
PL DES CARMES
RUE DES CARMES
Musée National de l'Education
RUE D'AMIENS
Palais de Justice
RUE ST-LO
RUE DAMIETTE
Ste-Jeanne
Aître St-Maclou
Cyber-Net
PLACE DU VIEUX MARCHÉ
Cathédrale de Notre-Dame
RUE ST-ROMAIN
RUE DE LA RÉPUBLIQUE
RUE DU GROS HORLOGE
St-Maclou
BOULEVARD DES BELGES
RUE DE FONTENELLE
VIEUX PALAIS
Gros Horloge
RUE AUX OURS
RUE DES BONNETIERS
RUE D'ALSACE-LORRAINE
PLACE ST-MARC
RUE DU GENERAL LECLERC
RUE DES CHARRETTES
Théâtre des Arts
RUE DE LA TOUR DE BEURRE
RUE DES AUGUSTINES
Espace Métrobus
RUE ST. ETIENNE DES-TONNELIERS
RUE GRAND PONT
PL DE LA RÉPUBLIQUE
QUAI DU HAVRE
Buses
Q DE LA BOURSE
Q P. CORNEILLE
QUAI DE PARIS
21 & Camping
Airport
River Seine
QUAI CAVELIER DE LA SALLE
QUAI JEAN MOULIN
AV DE BRETAGNE
River Seine
QUAI JACQUES ANQUETIL
CHAMPLAIN
COURS CLEMENCEAU
23
Place des Emmurées
Gare SNCF (Rive Gauche)
RUE LAFAYETTE
LEFT BANK
Centre St-Sever
BOULEVARD DE L'EUROPE
Théâtre Duchamp-Villon
St-Sever
0 300 m
24

At the bottom end of rue Jeanne d'Arc just before it crosses the Seine, the **gare routière** is located in the Espace Métrobus opposite the Théâtre des Arts, while the buses themselves leave from stops along the quais du Havre and de la Bourse.

Rouen's **airport**, at **Boos** 9km southeast (Ⓣ02.35.79.41.00, Ⓦrouen.aeroport.fr), does not currently receive any flights from the UK.

Information

Rouen's **tourist office**, opposite the cathedral at 25 place de la Cathédrale, stands in the early sixteenth-century "House of the Exchequer" (May–Sept Mon–Sat 9am–7pm, Sun 9.30am–12.30pm & 2–6pm; Oct–April Mon–Sat 9.30am–12.30pm & 1–6pm; Ⓣ02.32.08.32.40, Ⓦwww.rouentourisme.com). They provide audio-guides for self-guided city **walking tours** for €5, while a motorized "**petit train**" makes a forty-minute tour from the tourist office in summer (April–Oct daily 10am, 11am, noon, 2pm, 3pm, 4pm & 5pm; €6.50, ages 3–11 €4.50).

City transport

The city centre of Rouen, north of the Seine, is small enough to stroll around with little effort; the **métro** system is more useful to commuters than tourists. From the Gare-Rue Verte, at the SNCF station, metro trains follow the line of rue Jeanne d'Arc, making two stops before they resurface to cross the river by bridge; thereafter, the tracks dip below and above ground like a rollercoaster. Individual journeys cost €1.40; a book of ten tickets is €11, or you can buy an all-day pass for €4, a two-day one for €6, or a three-day one for €7.50. The same organization runs an efficient local **bus** network. For information on both, visit the **Espace Métrobus** opposite the Théâtre des Arts at 9 rue Jeanne d'Arc (Mon–Sat 7am–7pm; Ⓣ02.35.52.52.52, Ⓦwww.tcar.fr).

Accommodation

With more than three thousand **hotel** rooms in town, there should be no difficulty in finding accommodation in Rouen, even at the busiest times. Few of the city's hotels have restaurants, chiefly because there's such a wide choice of places to eat. Motorists who just want to spend a day or two looking at the sights of Rouen should seriously consider staying beside the river in **La Bouille** (see p.89), or in the woods at **Lyons-la-Forêt** (see p.90).

Hotels

Andersen 4 rue Pouchet Ⓣ02.35.71.88.51, Ⓦwww.hotelandersen.com. Very friendly place with plenty of character, a short walk west of the Gare Rive Droite, and set back beyond a small gravel yard. The exterior is run-down, and the bathrooms a little basic, but the bedrooms are large, light and colourful. ❸

Arts et Seine 6 rue St-Etienne-des-Tonneliers Ⓣ02.35.88.11.44, Ⓦartsetseine.com. Inexpensive, renovated hotel, a block north of the river not far from the cathedral, with friendly owners and clean, well-equipped rooms of varying levels of comfort. ❹

Beauséjour 9 rue Pouchet Ⓣ02.35.71.93.47, Ⓦwww.hotel-beausejour76.com. Good-value, recently revamped hotel close to the station (turn right as you come out). Beyond the orange facade and nice garden courtyard, the rooms themselves are nothing fancy, but they're crisply decorated with large-screen TVs and wi-fi, and there's a cheaper single room without its own shower. Closed second half of July. ❸

Cardinal 1 pl de la Cathédrale Ⓣ02.35.70.24.42, Ⓦwww.cardinal-hotel.fr. Very good-value hotel in a stunning location facing the cathedral. Rooms are spacious and clean, with good en-suite facilities, flat-screen TVs and wi-fi access. Two family rooms available. All have views of the cathedral (the higher ones from balconies). Ample buffet breakfasts for €8. ❹

Des Carmes 33 pl des Carmes Ⓣ02.35.71.92.31, Ⓦwww.hoteldescarmes.com. Twelve-room hotel in a beautiful nineteenth-century house, complete with blue shutters, in a quiet central square a short walk north from the cathedral. The rooms are slightly old-fashioned, but comfortable and cheerfully decorated. Discounts at nearby Hôtel de Ville car park. ❸

De la Cathédrale 12 rue St-Romain ⓣ02.35.71.57.95, ⓦwww.hotel-de-la-cathedrale.fr. Attractive and conveniently located hotel, in a quiet pedestrianized street that's lined with fourteenth-century timber-framed houses, alongside the cathedral. The pleasantly olde-worlde theme even extends to the *toile de jouy* wallpaper, and there's an attractive breakfast room and flower-filled courtyard. Guests pay €5 to use the public car park nearby. Buffet breakfasts €8.50. ❹

Le Clos Jouvenet 42 rue Hyacinthe Langlois ⓣ02.35.89.80.66, ⓦleclosjouvenet.com. Four beautifully decorated, comfortable rooms in an immaculate nineteenth-century house ten minutes' walk east of the train station. Breakfast is served in the conservatory, overlooking the enclosed garden. ❺

Mercure Rouen Centre 7 rue Croix de Fer ⓣ02.35.52.69.52, ⓦwww.mercure.com. Large chain hotel in the heart of the old city. It's a lot more comfortable and stylish than might appear from the outside, though the high room rates mean it's especially popular with business travellers. Extras such as parking (€15.50 in a *very* cramped underground garage) and breakfast (€12) can add considerably to the bill. ❽

Vieux Carré 34 rue Ganterie ⓣ02.35.71.67.70, ⓦwww. vieux-carre.fr. This half-timbered house, set back from a central pedestrianized street, offers very widely assorted rooms, some much larger and nicer than others. There's a peaceful flowery courtyard, and a little tea shop, open in the daytime only, that doubles as the breakfast room. ❹

Du Vieux Marché 15 rue de la Pie ⓣ02.35.71.00.88, ⓦbestwestern-hotel-vieuxmarche.com. Modern place, set around a venerable old courtyard, just a few steps from the place du Vieux-Marché. A high standard of comfort puts it among the most popular upmarket hotels in town. ❼

Campsites

Camping de l'Aubette 23 Vert Buisson in St-Léger du Bourg-Denis ⓣ02.35.08.47.69. Basic site in a more rural, but much less accessible setting than the *Camping Municipal*, 4km east of town on bus route #8.

Camping Municipal rue Jules-Ferry in Déville-lès-Rouen ⓣ02.35.74.07.59. Surprisingly small site, 4km northwest of town, that's geared towards caravans rather than tents; bus #2.

The Town

North of the Seine at any rate, Rouen is a real pleasure to explore. As well as some great sights – the **Cathédrale de Notre Dame**, the **Aître St-Maclou**, all the delightful twisting streets of timbered houses – there's history aplenty too, most notably the links with **Joan of Arc**.

Place du Vieux-Marché

The obvious place to start exploring Rouen is the **place du Vieux-Marché**, where a small plaque and a huge cross, 20m high, adorn the public square in which Joan of Arc was burned to death on May 30, 1431. Louis Arretche designed the adjacent memorial **church** to the saint (daily: April–Oct 10am–noon & 2–6pm; Nov–March 10am–noon & 2–5.30pm). A wacky, spiky-looking thing, said to represent either an upturned boat or the flames that consumed Joan, it was dedicated in 1979. An indisputable triumph, it's part of an ensemble that also incorporates a covered food market, open daily except Monday, and intended less for practical shopping than for show – everything in it does indeed look mouth-wateringly appetizing.

The theme of the church's fish-shaped windows continues in the scaly tiles of its hugely elongated roof, which forms a covered walkway across the square. On the lawns, where a flowerbed marks the precise spot of Joan's martyrdom, the foundations of the church of St-Vincent, destroyed in the war, remain visible. Some sixteenth-century stained glass removed from the vanished church was incorporated into one facade of its replacement. It's now displayed beautifully, even though the windows that hold it are an entirely different shape. The square

Joan of Arc

Joan of Arc stands alone, and must continue to stand alone... There is no one to compare her with, none to measure her by... There have been other young generals, but they were not girls; young generals, but they have been soldiers before they were generals; she began as a general; she commanded the first army she ever saw; she led it from victory to victory, and never lost a battle with it; there have been young commanders-in-chief, but none so young as she: she is the only soldier in history who has held the supreme command of a nation's armies at the age of seventeen.

Mark Twain, *Joan of Arc*

When the 17-year-old peasant girl known to history as **Joan of Arc** arrived at the French court in Chinon early in 1429, the Hundred Years War had already dragged on for over ninety years. Most of northern France was in the grip of an Anglo-Burgundian alliance, whose major strongholds were the châteaux of the Loire. Since 1425, Joan had been hearing voices in her native village of Domrémy, in Lorraine, near France's eastern frontiers. Convinced that she alone could save France, she came to Chinon to present her case to the as-yet-uncrowned Dauphin. Partly through recognizing him despite a simple disguise he wore to fool her at their first meeting, she convinced him of her divine guidance; and after a remarkable three-week examination by a tribunal of the French *parlement*, she went on to secure command of the armies of France. In a whirlwind campaign, which culminated in the raising of the siege of Orléans on May 8, 1429, she broke the English hold on the Loire Valley. She then escorted the Dauphin deep into enemy territory, with town after town rallying to her standard as they advanced, so that in accordance with ancient tradition he could be crowned King Charles VII of France in the cathedral at Reims, on July 17.

Within a year of her greatest triumph, Joan was captured by the Burgundian army at Compiègne in May 1430, and held to ransom. Chivalry dictated that any offer of payment from the vacillating Charles must be accepted, but in the absence of such an offer Joan was handed over to the English for 10,000 ducats. On Christmas Day 1430, she was imprisoned in the château of Philippe-Auguste at Rouen.

Charged with heresy, on account of her "false and diabolical" visions and refusal not to wear men's clothing, Joan was put on trial for her life on February 21, 1431. For three months, a changing panel of 131 assessors – only eight of whom were English-born – heard the evidence against her. Condemned, inevitably, to death, Joan recanted on the scaffold in St-Ouen cemetery on May 24, and her sentence was commuted to life imprisonment. The presiding judge, Bishop Pierre Cauchon of Beauvais, reassured disappointed English representatives that "we will get her yet". The next Sunday, Joan was tricked into breaking her vow and putting on male clothing, and taken to the archbishop's chapel in rue St-Romain to be condemned to death for the second time. On May 30, 1431, she was burned at the stake in the place du Vieux-Marché; her ashes, together with her unburned heart, were thrown into the Seine.

Charles VII finally recaptured Rouen in 1449. Seeing the verdict against Joan as reflecting on the legitimacy of his own claim to the French throne, he instigated a *Procés en Nullité*, which took evidence from all the surviving witnesses, and resulted in a papal declaration of Joan's innocence in 1456. Joan herself passed into legend, until the discovery and publication of the full transcript of her trial in the 1840s. The forebearance and devout humility she displayed throughout her ordeal added to her status as France's greatest religious heroine. She was canonized as recently as 1920, and soon afterwards became the country's patron saint.

itself is surrounded by fine old brown-and-white half-timbered houses; many of those on the south side now serve as restaurants.

Also on the south side of the *place*, the privately owned **Musée Jeanne d'Arc**, in the back of a gift shop at no. 33, displays assorted tawdry waxworks and facsimile manuscripts (daily: mid-April to mid-Sept 9.30am–7pm; mid-Sept to mid-April 10am–noon & 2–6.30pm; €5). Among the bric-a-brac is a page from the records of the Paris *parlement*, dated May 10, 1429, which refers to reports that, on the previous Saturday, the French had trounced the English at Orléans. A sketch in the margin, possibly by a bored clerk, depicts a young woman, with her hair tied back, a banner in one hand and a sword in the other. The only contemporary portrait of the "Maid of Orléans", it was not drawn from life, so it's no more authentic than the museum's movie stills, showing Ingrid Bergman as Joan in both 1948 and 1954, Jean Seberg in the role in 1957, and Milla Jovovich in Luc Besson's 1999 version.

Gros Horloge

From place du Vieux-Marché, rue du Gros-Horloge leads east towards the cathedral. Just across rue Jeanne d'Arc you come to the **Gros Horloge** itself (daily except Mon: April–Oct 10am–1pm & 2–7pm; Nov–March 2–6pm; last admission 1hr before closing; €6). A colourful one-handed clock, it used to be on the adjacent Gothic belfry until it was moved down by popular demand in 1529, so that people could see it better. The lower storey now serves as a museum of the clock's history, and visitors can climb up rather too many steps to see its intricate workings, and enjoy marvellous views of the old city, with its startling array of towers and spires. The bell up there, cast in 1260, still rings what's known as the "Conqueror's Curfew" at 9pm daily.

A block to the north is the Renaissance splendour of the former **Palais de Justice**, which was largely destroyed during World War II, only to be rebuilt as good as new. As it's not open to tourists, you'll have to content yourself with admiring the magnificently ornate exterior.

Cathédrale de Notre Dame

The **Cathédrale de Notre Dame** (mid-March to Oct Mon 2–7pm, Tues–Sat 7.30am–7pm, Sun 8am–6pm; Nov to mid-March Mon 2–6pm, Tues–Sat 7.30am–noon & 2–6pm, Sun 8am–6pm) stands on the site of a Roman place of worship, erected in the third century AD at a major crossroads. Despite the addition of all sorts of towers and spires, it remains at heart the Gothic masterpiece that was built in the twelfth and thirteenth centuries. Later accretions include the flamboyant **Tour du Beurre**, named for the erroneous belief that it was paid for by the granting of dispensations that allowed wealthy churchgoers to eat butter during Lent, and the nineteenth-century iron **spire** of the central lantern tower. Cast in the foundries of Conches, it was built to replace a tower that burned down in 1822, and was at the time, at 151m, the highest in France.

The cathedral has been undergoing extensive **restoration** for several years, an immense task that was rendered more complex when one of the spire's four greenish supports was detached by a hurricane in 1999, and fell, piercing the roof of the cathedral itself and destroying a section of the medieval choir stalls below. Intricately sculpted like the rest of the exterior, the west facade of the cathedral was **Monet's subject** for over thirty studies of changing light, which now hang in the Musée d'Orsay in Paris. Monet might not recognize it now, however – in the last few years it's been scrubbed a gleaming white, free from the centuries of accreted dirt he so carefully recorded. In recent summers, colours inspired by Monet's cathedral paintings have been projected onto the church's façade in a thirty-minute evening light show known as **La Cathédrale de Monet aux Pixels** (daily: July 11pm, Aug 10.30pm; free), transforming it quite magnificently into a series of giant Monet-esque canvases.

Inside the cathedral, the carvings of the misericords in the choir depict fifteenth-century life, in secular scenes, as well as the usual mythical beasts. The chapel dedicated to Joan of Arc, and paid for by an English committee in 1956, contains a statue of Joan at the stake. The **ambulatory** and **crypt** – closed on Sunday mornings and during services – hold the assorted tombs of various recumbent royal figures, stretching back as far as **Duke Rollo**, who died "enfeebled by toil" in 933 AD. Rollo's effigy was destroyed by the bombs of 1944, and has now been replaced by a nineteenth-century copy of someone else's. Both he and **Richard the Lionheart** – whose heart is actually in a lead box in the treasury – have detachable feet, which are occasionally removed for cleaning.

Église St-Maclou and Aître St-Maclou

The intricate wooden panelling in the porch of the fifteenth-century church of **St-Maclou**, a short way east of the cathedral, is the highlight of what is often cited as the most spectacular example of Gothic flamboyant architecture in France (April–Oct Mon & Fri–Sun 10am–noon & 2–6pm; Nov–March Mon & Fri–Sun 10am–noon & 2–5.30pm). The whole building was so badly damaged by bombs on June 4, 1944 that it only reopened in 1980; thankfully, the ornate stone stairway up to the organ inside remains as ethereal as ever. The interior is so light partly because most of its stained glass was destroyed, and the windows are now clear. St Maclou himself – more familiar as St Malo – was a seventh-century missionary from Wales.

Nearby, with its entrance a little hard to find between nos. 184 and 186 rue Martainville, the **Aître St-Maclou** (daily: mid-March to Oct 8am–8pm; Nov to mid-March 8am–7pm; free) was built between 1526 and 1533, in an era of mass plague deaths, as a cemetery and charnel house. The ground floor was used as an open cloister while the bare bones of victims were exposed to view in the rooms above. At first sight it looks very picturesque – a tranquil garden courtyard of half-timbered houses – but look closely at the carvings on the beams of the lower storey and you'll see they bear traces of a macabre **Dance of Death**, everywhere adorned with fading skulls and crossbones. A case to the right of the entrance contains a mummified cat. The buildings are still in use, and still stimulating morbid imaginations, not as a morgue but as Rouen's Fine Arts school. The square outside holds several good antique bookshops and a few art shops.

St-Ouen

Rouen's last great church, **St-Ouen**, stands next to the Hôtel de Ville in a large open square to the north (daily except Mon & Fri: April–Oct 10am–noon & 2–6pm; Nov–March 10am–noon & 2–5.30pm). Larger than the cathedral, it has far less decoration; as a result, its Gothic proportions and the purity of its lines have that instant impact with which nothing built since the Middle Ages can compete. Originally it was a seventh-century Benedictine abbey church, founded before the Viking invasion. The present building was begun in 1318 and completed in the sixteenth century; its main entrance is known as the "Porch of the Marmosets" because its ornate carvings are thought to represent monkeys. Inside, it holds some stunning fourteenth-century stained glass, though much was destroyed during the Revolution – hence the 1960 *Crucifixion* in the choir, by Max Ingrand.

Immediately north of St-Ouen is the city's **Hôtel de Ville**, outside which parades an equestrian statue of Napoleon, weathered to an eerie green and looking like death incarnate.

Rue Eau de Robec

Running east from rue Damiette just south of St-Ouen, **rue Eau de Robec** was described by one of Flaubert's characters as a "degraded little Venice". It's now a textbook example of how Rouen has been restored. Where once a shallow stream flowed beneath the raised doorsteps of venerable half-timbered houses, a thin trickle now makes its way along a stylized cement bed crossed by concrete walkways. It remains an attractive ensemble, if a rather ersatz one, and the houses themselves are now predominantly inhabited by antique dealers, interspersed with the odd café.

In a fine old mansion at no. 185, the **Musée National de l'Éducation** (Mon & Wed–Fri 10am–12.30pm & 1.30–6pm, Sat & Sun 2–6pm; €3) tells the story of the last five centuries of schooling in France, with photos, paintings, ancient textbooks and a mocked-up schoolroom. Unless you read French well, however, it's unlikely to hold your interest.

Tour Jeanne d'Arc

The pencil-thin **Tour Jeanne d'Arc** (April–Sept Mon & Wed–Sat 10am–12.30pm & 2–6pm, Sun 2–6.30pm; Oct–March Mon & Wed–Sat 10am–12.30pm & 2–5pm, Sun 2–5.30pm; €1.50), a short way southeast of the *gare SNCF*, is all that remains of the castle of Philippe-Auguste, built in 1205 and scene of the imprisonment and trial of Joan of Arc. It served as the castle's keep and entranceway, and was itself fully surrounded by a moat. It was not, however, Joan's actual prison – that was the Tour de la Pucelle, demolished in 1809. The trial took place first of all in the castle's St-Romain chapel, and then later in its great central hall, both of which were destroyed in 1590.

Joan came to this building only once, on May 9, 1431, to be confronted with the fearsome torture chamber in its lowest level. Threatened by Bishop Cauchon with the words "There is the rack, and there are its ministers. You will reveal all, now, or be put to the torture", she responded: "I will tell you nothing more than I have told you; no, not even if you tear the limbs from my body. And even if in my pain I did say something otherwise, I would always say afterwards that it was the torture that spoke and not I".

The tall, sharp-pointed tower was bought by public subscription in 1860, and restored to its present state. After seeing a small collection of Joan-related memorabilia, you can climb the steep spiral staircase to the very top, but you can't see out over the city, let alone step outside into the open air.

Musée des Beaux Arts

Rouen's imposing **Musée des Beaux Arts** commands the square Verdrel from just east of the central rue Jeanne d'Arc (daily except Tues 10am–6pm; €4). Even this grand edifice is not quite large enough to display some of its medieval tapestries, which dangle inelegantly from the ceilings to trail along the floor, but the collection as a whole is consistently absorbing. Unexpected highlights include dazzling Russian icons from the sixteenth century onwards, and an entertaining three-dimensional eighteenth-century Nativity from Naples.

Many of the biggest names among the painters – Caravaggio (the centrepiece *Flagellation of Christ*), Velázquez, Rubens – tend to be represented by a single minor work, but there are several Modiglianis and a number of Monets, including *Rouen Cathedral* (1894), the *Vue Générale de Rouen* and *Brume sur la Seine* (1894), as well as canvases by Blanche Hoschedé-Monet, who was both the daughter of Claude Monet's mistress Alice and the wife of his son Jean. The central sculpture court, roofed over but very light, is dominated by a wonderful three-part mural of the course of the Seine from Paris to Le Havre, prepared by Raoul Dufy in 1937 for the Palais de Chaillot in Paris.

Musée de la Céramique

Rouen's history as a centre for *faïencerie*, the manufacture of earthenware pottery, is recorded in the **Musée de la Céramique**, facing the Beaux Arts from rue Faucon to the north (daily except Tues 10am–1pm & 2–6pm; €2.50). A series of beautiful rooms, some of which incorporate sixteenth-century wood panelling rescued from the demolished nunnery of St-Amand, display specimens from the seventeenth century onwards. Until polychrome appeared in 1698, everything was blue; at that time, Rouen's main rivals and influences were the cities of Delft and Nevers, well represented in this collection. Assorted tiles and plates reflect the eighteenth-century craze for chinoiserie, although the genuine Chinese and Japanese pieces nearby possess a sophistication contemporary French craftsmen could only dream of emulating. The mood changes abruptly in the Revolutionary era, as witnessed by a fascinating collection of plates bearing slogans from both sides of the political fence.

Musée Le Secq des Tournelles

Behind the Beaux Arts, housed in the old and barely altered church of St-Laurent on rue Jacques-Villon, stands an interesting and unusual museum of ironmongery, the **Musée Le Secq des Tournelles** (daily except Tues 10am–1pm & 2–6pm; €2.50). It consists of a gloriously eccentric and uncategorizable collection of wrought-iron objects of all dates and descriptions, among them nutcrackers and door knockers, locks and gates, nineteenth-century toys and jewellery, spiral staircases that lead nowhere, and hideous implements of torture.

Musée des Antiquités

The **Musée des Antiquités** (Mon & Wed–Sat 10am–12.15pm & 1.30–5.30pm, Sun 2–6pm; €3), a short walk north of the town centre at the top of rue Beauvoisine, provides a dry but comprehensive run-through of ancient artefacts found in or near Rouen. Starting with an impressive pointed helmet from the Bronze Age and an assortment of early iron tools, it continues with some remarkably complete Roman mosaics from villas unearthed in Lillebonne and the Forêt de Brotonne. Then comes a long gallery filled with woodcarvings rescued from long-lost Rouen houses – including a lovely bas-relief of sheep that served as the sign for a medieval draper's shop – and some fine fifteenth-century tapestries.

The Musée Flaubert et de l'Histoire de la Médicine

For an insight into the Rouen that Flaubert knew, don't go to the **Pavillon Flaubert** at Croisset-Canteleu, 9km from Rouen along the D982 in the direction of Duclair. Like Rouen's two other literary museums – the homes of Pierre Corneille – it only proves the pointlessness of the genre. Visit, instead, the **Musée Flaubert et de l'Histoire de la Médicine**, at the Hôtel-Dieu Hospital (Tues 10am–6pm, Wed–Sat 10am–noon & 2–6pm; €3). This stands on the corner of rue de Lecat and rue du Contrat-Social, a five-minute walk west from the place du Vieux-Marché, and it's infinitely more relevant to Flaubert's writings than the manuscript copies and personal mementos in the Pavillon museum.

Flaubert's father was chief surgeon and director of the medical school, living with his family in this house within the hospital; Gustave himself was born here in 1821. Even during the cholera epidemic when he was 11, the young

Gustave and his sister were not stopped from running around the wards or climbing along the garden wall to look into the autopsy lab. Some of the medical exhibits would certainly have been familiar objects to him – a phrenology model, a childbirth demonstrator resembling a giant ragdoll, and the sets of encyclopedias. There's also one of his stuffed parrots, as featured in Julian Barnes' novel *Flaubert's Parrot*.

Eating

Rouen has a good reputation for **food**, with its most famous dish being *canard rouennais* – prepared by strangling a particular crossbreed of duck from the Seine Valley and cooking it with all its blood, which results in a much meatier taste than usual. Unlike the hotels, which sometimes have cheaper weekend rates, the city's **upmarket restaurants** tend to charge more over weekends, when families eat out.

You can buy fresh fish, fruit and cheese at the daily **food market** in place du Vieux-Marché, while the area just north is full of Tunisian **takeaways**, **crêperies**, and so forth. There are also sumptuous **patisserie** shops everywhere, while if you've had enough of all things continental, the rue du Gros-Horloge holds a half-timbered *McDonald's*.

Le 37 37 rue St-Etienne-des-Tonneliers ⓣ02.35.70.56.65. This classy modern bistro, part of the empire of top Rouennais chef Gilles Tournadre, serves good-value contemporary cuisine in stylishly minimal surroundings, just up from the river. There's an €18 lunch menu, otherwise expect to pay twice that. Closed Sun & Mon.

Auberge St-Maclou 224–226 rue Martainville ⓣ02.35.71.06.67. Half-timbered building in the shadow of St-Maclou church, with tables on the street outside and an old-style ambience inside. The pedestrian street gets crowded in summer, but the traditional French menus are far from overpriced – lunch is €10.50 or €12.50, dinner €19.50 or €23.50. Closed Sun eve (except March–June), Mon, three weeks in Aug & two weeks in Feb.

Des Beaux Arts 34 rue Damiette ⓣ02.35.70.17.15. Very good-value Algerian cuisine, on a pretty pedestrianized street north of St-Maclou church: couscous from €8 or tajine from €10.50, with all kinds of sausages and assorted meats.

Brasserie Paul 1 pl de la Cathédrale ⓣ02.35.71.86.07. The definitive address for Rouen's definitive bistro, an attractive Belle Époque place with seating both indoors and on a terrace in full view of the cathedral. Daily lunch specials, such as the goats' cheese and smoked duck salad that was Simone de Beauvoir's favourite in the 1930s, cost around €12.

La Couronne 31 pl du Vieux-Marché ⓣ02.35.71.40.90. Claims to be the oldest auberge in France, serving food since 1345, a century before Joan of Arc's time. Among the city's finest restaurants, it's definitely the best of the bunch on the place du Vieux-Marché. If you find the interior a little too stuffy and formal, opt for one of a few tables on the square itself. Menus at €25 for lunch and €35 or €48 for dinner.

Crêperie la Regalière 12 rue Massacre ⓣ02.35.15.33.33. This quaint, inexpensive but good-quality crêperie, with some outdoor seating just off the place du Vieux-Marché, is one of central Rouen's best bargains, with menus at €8.50 and €13. Closed Sun.

Dame Cakes 70 rue St Romain ⓣ02.35.07.49.31. Elegant tea room on a quiet street next to the cathedral, tempting the tastebuds with delicious desserts, savoury tarts and salads.

Gill 8–9 quai de la Bourse ⓣ02.35.71.16.14, ⓦgill.fr. Absolutely definitive, stylish and contemporary French restaurant, consistently acclaimed as the best in Normandy, on account of such Gilles Tournadre specialities as lobster grilled with asparagus and pigeon baked in puff pastry. Weekday lunch menus start at around €40 (not bad value considering the quality), while the most expensive dinner menu will set you back €94. Closed Sun & Mon, plus three weeks in Aug.

La Marmite 3 rue de Florence ⓣ02.35.71.75.55, ⓦlamarmiterouen.com. Romantic little place just west of the place du Vieux-Marché, offering beautiful, elegantly presented gourmet dishes on well-priced menus at €28, €38 (featuring hot foie gras) and €55. Closed Sun eve, Mon & Tues lunch.

Pascaline 5 rue de la Poterne ⓣ02.35.89.67.44. Classic bistro, located to the north of the Palais de Justice, near the flower market, with a green wooden enclosure attached to the front of a half-timbered house. As well as set menus at €15, €18 and €28.50, they offer a full list of à la carte specialities and have live jazz on some Thurs.

Le P'tit Bec 182 rue Eau de Robec ⓣ02.35.07.63.33. Friendly brasserie that's Rouen's most popular lunch spot. Two simple menus at €13 and €15.50 include a fish or meat main course, plus plenty of vegetarian options. There's seating both indoors and outside on the pedestrianized street, beside the running water and in view of a fine blue half-timbered mansion next door. Closed Sun, plus Mon & Thurs eves June–Aug, Sun–Thurs eves Sept–May.

Les P'tits Parapluies 46 rue Bourg l'Abbé, pl de la Rougemare ⓣ02.35.88.55.26, ⓦwww.lesptits-parapluies.com. Elegant, secluded half-timbered restaurant not far north of the Hôtel de Ville, on the edge of an attractive little square. Counting your calories (or your pennies) is not really an option; the trio of menus, some of which change weekly, start at €30 and include such delights as foie gras and oysters; €5 extra gets two glasses of wine per person. Closed Sat lunch, Sun eve & Mon.

Nightlife and entertainment

As a city with a strong student population, and one renowned for its (largely rock-oriented) **music scene**, Rouen enjoys a far-from-provincial nightlife. Some of the city's most appealing **bars** lie in the maze of streets between rue Jean-Lecanuet and place du Vieux-Marché. Incoming sailors used to head straight for this area of the city – the small bars are still there, even if the sailors aren't. New **clubs** are springing up all the time, though most are some distance from the centre.

Bars and music venues

Le Bateau Ivre 17 rue des Sapins ⓣ02.35.70.09.05, ⓦbateauivre.rouen.free.fr. Low-key but atmospheric hangout a long way northeast of the centre which puts on a mostly rock-oriented programme of music and performance, with an open-mic night on Tues. Tues & Wed 10pm–2am, Thurs–Sat 10pm–4am. Closed Sun, Mon & all Aug.

Big Ben Pub 95 rue du Gros-Horloge ⓣ02.35.88.44.50. Right under the big clock – hence the name – this busy pub in a splendid half-timbered house has the air of a medieval tavern. There are two floors inside and some tables on the busy street outside – a perfect vantage point for people watching. Mon 6pm–2am, Tues–Sat noon–2am.

Le Chakra 4 bd Ferdinand-de-Lesseps ⓣ02.32.10.12.02, ⓦwww.lechakra.fr. Busy, sweaty club, beside the Seine a couple of kilometres west of the centre, where big-name DJs play house and techno to a predominantly young crowd. Fri 11pm–4am, Sat 5–9pm & 11pm–4am, Sun 5–9pm.

Emporium Gallorum 151 rue Beauvoisine ⓣ02.35.71.76.95. Busy half-timbered bar, a short walk north of the centre, that's especially popular with students; often puts on small-scale gigs and theatrical productions. Tues & Wed 8pm–2am, Thurs–Sat 6pm–4am. Closed Aug.

L'Euro 41 pl du Vieux-Marché ⓣ02.35.07.55.66. Justifiably popular bar occupying a multistorey half-timbered building on the western corner of the place du Vieux-Marché, with lots of outdoor seating. Inside, house music predominates on the ground floor, and music from the 1980s on the first. Daily 10pm–2am.

Exo 7 13 pl des Chartreux ⓣ02.35.03.32.30, ⓦwww.exo7.net. Traditionally the centre of Rouen's heavy-rock scene, a long way south of the centre, the *Exo 7* (pronounced "Exocet") is nowadays a bit more eclectic, with varied gigs and dance nights as well. Fri & Sat 11pm–5am. Closed first three weeks of Aug.

L'Ibiza Club 29 bd des Belges ⓣ02.35.07.76.20, ⓦibiza-club76.com. Despite the name, not an Ibiza-style club, but a three-storey complex, set in a mansion that once belonged to the king of Belgium, and incorporating a restaurant, lots of karaoke rooms, and a basement club where the emphasis is on the Seventies and Eighties. Wed–Sat 8.30pm–3am.

Le Kiosque 43 bd de Verdun ⓣ02.35.88.54.50. Large, lively, late-opening nightclub and bar that's thronged with students dancing to all kinds of music, but also has lots of plush seating for quieter moments. Tues–Sat 11pm–5am.

Miss Marple 35 rue de la Tour du Beurre ⓣ02.35.88.47.32. Small and friendly lesbian bar, where, if you are new, the owner will make a special effort to introduce you to people. If no one captures your interest, there is always the pinball machine, and occasional debates on women's issues. Tues–Sat 6pm–2am.

Le Nash 97 rue Écuyère ⓣ02.35.98.25.24. Relaxed bar popular with locals. The interior has a lounge-like feel with its moody lighting and zebra-striped upholstery, while the outdoor terrace is much more akin to a classic French café, and serves light snacks. Music ranges from ambient to Latin. Mon–Fri 11.30am–2pm & 6pm–2am, Sat 6pm–2am.

Le Triplex 177 rte de Paris, Amfreville-la-Mivoie ⓣ02.35.07.40.30. Mixed but gay-friendly club a few kilometres east of Rouen. Plays host to visiting DJs, with three floors, one devoted to techno, another to "disco-Latino" and another simply playing contemporary hits. Fri & Sat 10pm–4am.

XXL 25–27 rue de la Savonnerie ⓣ02.35.88.84.00. Well-known gay bar near the river, just south of the cathedral, which has regular theme nights and a small dance floor in the basement. Although unambiguously geared to men looking for men, women will not be turned away. Tues & Wed 9pm–2am, Thurs–Sat 9pm–4am, Sun 10pm–2am.

Entertainment

As you would expect in a conurbation of half a million, there's always plenty going on in Rouen, from classical concerts in churches to alternative events in community and commercial centres. The city has several **theatres**, which mainly work to winter seasons. The most highbrow venue for big spectacles is the **Théâtre des Arts**, 7 rue de Dr-Rambert (box office: Tues–Sat 1–8pm; ⓣ08.10.81.11.16, ⓦwww.operaderouen.com), which puts on opera, ballet and concerts. The more adventurous repertory company of the **Théâtre des Deux Rives** (ⓣ02.35.70.22.82, ⓦwww.cdr2rives.com), based opposite the Antiquités museum at the top end of rue Louis-Ricard, presents work by playwrights such as Beaumarchais, Shakespeare, Beckett and Gorky.

Major **concerts** often take place in the **Théâtre Duchamp-Villon** in the St-Sever complex (ⓣ02.32.18.28.10, ⓦwww.theatreduchampvillon.com), accessible by metro (stop "St-Sever"). Also south of the river and on the métro (direction "Georges Braque"), albeit a long way further out, is the **Théâtre Charles Dullin**, allée des Arcades, Grand Quévilly (ⓣ02.35.69.51.18, ⓦwww.theatre-charles-dullin.com).

Shopping

Most of the classier **shops** in Rouen are in the pedestrian streets near, and slightly north of, the cathedral. Rue Jeanne d'Arc and rue du Gros-Horloge is the area to look for fancy foodstuffs, patisserie, chocolates and the like. For **hypermarkets** and cheap clothes, head south of the river to the multistorey St-Sever complex. There's an open-air antiques and bric-a-brac **market** nearby in the place des Émmurées.

Rouen's largest **bookshop**, the all-purpose FNAC, underground in the Espace du Palais mall immediately north of the Palais de Justice (Mon–Sat 10am–7pm), stocks a fine selection of local maps and guides, largely in French, and English-language titles, as well as a wide range of CDs, DVDs and computer paraphernalia. The ABC Bookshop, 11 rue des Faulx (Tues–Sat 10am–6pm; ⓦwww.abc-bookshop.info), near the St-Ouen church, specializes in English titles.

Listings

American Express In the tourist office at 25 pl de la Cathédrale ⓣ02.35.89.48.60 (May–Sept Mon–Sat 9am–1pm & 2–7pm, Sun 9.30am–12.30pm & 2–6pm; Oct–April Mon–Sat 9am–1pm & 2–6pm).

Banks and exchange Most of the major banks are along rue Jeanne d'Arc, such as Société Générale at no. 34 (ⓣ02.35.52.58.00). All have ATMs.

Bike rental The city-sponsored Cy'clic network enables credit-card holders to unlock a simple bike from "stations" scattered along the streets and leave it any other station; journeys of less than thirty minutes are free. Details on ⓦcyclic.rouen.fr.

Cinemas Gaumont, 28 rue de la République ⓣ02.35.07.82.70; Melville, 75 rue du Général-Leclerc ⓣ02.35.76.73.20; UGC CinéCité, Centre Commercial St-Sever ⓣ02.35.73.58.23.

Hospital Hôpital Charles Nicolle – CHRU, 1 rue de Germont ⓣ02.32.88.89.90, ⓦwww.chu-rouen.fr.

Internet access Cyber-Net, 47 place du Vieux-Marché ⓣ02.35.07.73.02, ⓦwww.wifinormandie.fr (Mon–Sat 10am–8pm, Sun 2–7pm; €4 per hr); The Web Cafe, 14–16 rue du Général-Leclerc ⓣ02.35.71.51.93 (€4 per hr).
Pharmacy Grande Pharmacie du Centre, 29 pl de la Cathédrale ⓣ02.35.71.33.17 (Mon 10am–7.30pm, Tues–Fri 9am–7.30pm, Sat 9am–7pm).
Post office 45bis rue Jeanne d'Arc, in the centre of town (post code 76000) ⓣ02.35.15.66.73 (Mon–Fri 8am–7pm, Sat 8.30am–12.30pm).
Swimming pools Centre Sportif Guy Boissière, Île Lacroix ⓣ02.35.07.94.70; Piscine Diderot, 114 bd de l'Europe ⓣ02.35.63.59.14; Piscine du Boulingrin, 37 bd de Verdun ⓣ02.35.98.10.11.

Around Rouen

Pleasant small towns well worth an overnight stop lie within a few minutes of Rouen in either direction along the river – Villequier (see p.73) or Les Andelys (see p.92) spring to mind. On the other hand, a number of places only just outside the city proper make **good day-trips** while you are based in Rouen.

La Bouille

Ten kilometres southwest from central Rouen along the southern riverbank, the small village of **LA BOUILLE** stands near a magnificent sweeping bend in the Seine. Little more than a couple of narrow twisting lanes lined with gnarled half-timbered houses, pressed hard against the steep hillside, it's a complete contrast to the noise and bustle of the city, and makes a perfect place to spend a couple of nights for anyone not dependent on public transport. Not far north, a little *bac* (ferry) crosses the river (14 daily, Mon–Sat) to the small Forêt de Roumare, which makes for a pleasant stroll.

An exquisite **hotel**, the *Bellevue*, 13 quai Hector-Malot (ⓣ02.35.18.05.05, ⓦhotel-le-bellevue.com; ③), overlooks the river across the main road through the village, and has a superb dining room, serving classic French cuisine. Nearby there are two equally fine **restaurants**, the *Maison Blanche*, 1 quai Hector-Malot (ⓣ02.35.18.01.90; closed Sun eve & Mon, plus Wed eve in winter), and the expensive *St-Pierre*, 4 place du Bateau (ⓣ02.35.68.02.01; closed Mon & Tues, plus Sun eve in low season), where dinner menus start at €34.

Clères

Roughly 16km northeast of Rouen – via the D6 if you're driving, or by bus #29 from the *gare routière*, or train – the pretty village of **CLÈRES** has centred since the eleventh century on an imposing **château**, though the stout walls that now remain date back a mere five hundred years. The spacious and beautifully landscaped grounds are home to a popular **zoo**; while not holding a very wide range of species, it displays them in idyllic surroundings (daily: April–Sept 10am–7pm; March & Oct 10am–6.30pm; Feb & Nov 1.30–5pm; €5.50). The whole place is something of a Garden of Eden, in that peacocks, antelope and wallabies can wander at will in the absence of predators; families with pushchairs, however, may well struggle with some of the steeper gravel footpaths. Exotic birds kept in ageing aviaries include emus, rheas and kookaburras, while the château itself plays host to temporary art exhibitions. The infamous French writer Colette made the impenetrable but presumably complimentary remark that "at Clères, in the zoo park, it is easy to lose the melancholy feeling of inevitability".

The Forêt de Lyons

Around 25km east of Rouen, the **Forêt de Lyons** was, a thousand years ago, a favoured hunting ground of William the Conqueror and other dukes of Normandy. Parts of the forest feel as though they have changed little in the intervening millennium – remarkable considering its proximity not only to Rouen but also to Paris. Henry I of England died in the central village of Lyons-la-Forêt in 1135, of a surfeit of lampreys consumed after a late-November hunting expedition. The village itself is a picturesque place, while a few kilometres to the north and south respectively, a château and abbey are worth visiting. Almost any of the little roads through these dense woods rewards exploration by cyclists or walkers.

Lyons-la-Forêt

At the heart of the forest, the little hill village of **LYONS-LA-FORÊT**, actually situated not in Seine-Maritime but the neighbouring *département* of Eure, was the site of William's now completely indiscernible castle, but has retained a superb ensemble of half-timbered Norman houses dating from around 1610. In the centre of the village stand the plain old wooden *halles*, while the roads around abound in splendid rural mansions. One, the house named *Le Fresne* on rue d'Enfer, was much used by the composer Ravel in the 1920s.

Lyons' central **tourist office**, 20 rue de l'Hôtel de Ville (April–Sept Mon–Sat 10am–noon & 2–5.30pm, Sun 10am–noon & 2–4pm; Oct–March Tues–Sat 10am–noon & 2–5pm; Ⓣ02.32.49.31.65, Ⓦwww.paysdelyons.com), has information on the whole forest area. Of the **hotels** in the village, the *Lions de Beauclerc*, near the tourist office at 7 rue de l'Hôtel de Ville, offers six opulent, individually styled en-suite bedrooms (Ⓣ02.32.49.18.90, Ⓦleslionsdebeauclerc.free.fr; ④), has a pleasant little garden and serves good-value meals, while *La Licorne* is an exquisite, expensive alternative at 27 place Bensérade near the *halles* (Ⓣ02.32.48.24.24, Ⓦhotel-licorne.com; ⑤–⑨; closed Tues eve & Wed, plus Feb). That same main square also holds a couple of reasonably priced **restaurants** with outdoor seating.

Abbaye de Mortemer

Half-a-dozen kilometres south of Lyons, clearly signed off a main road, the ruins of the twelfth-century Cistercian **Abbaye de Mortemer** amount to little more than heaps of rubble scattered across gentle lawns, amid a landscape of rolling parklands (park: daily 1.30–6pm; guided tours half-hourly; May–Aug daily 2–6pm; Sept–April Sat & Sun 2–5.30pm; €6 admission, €9 with tour; Ⓦwww.mortemer.fr). Plenty of outbuildings survive, however, including a round stone *pigeonnier*, with a spider's-web tangle of wood inside, and little niches for hundreds of pigeons (bred by the monks for food); a cast-iron pigeon stands permanently on top.

A **museum** in the eighteenth-century château that dominates the grounds displays models of the abbey as it is now, and an audiovisual show of life as it used to be, complete with plenty of tales of hauntings and bumps in the night. Beyond the abbey, which was quarried after the Revolution to build the nearby village of Lisors, a couple of marshy lakes are populated by geese and swans and surrounded by woods and lawns that accommodate free-roaming deer.

Vascoeuil

The small but graceful **Château de Vascoeuil**, on the northwest edge of the forest 12km from Lyons, is known to have existed as early as 1050, and was home during the nineteenth century to the historian Michelet. These days, it's renowned for top-quality temporary **art exhibitions** (April–June & Sept–Nov Wed–Sun 2.30–6pm; July & Aug daily 11am–6.30pm; €8; Ⓣ02.35.23.62.35, Ⓦwww.chateauvascoeuil.com).

Ry

The village of **RY**, 4km northwest of the château, is immortalized in literary history as the real-life home of Flaubert's fictionalized Madame Bovary. A monument in its churchyard commemorates Delphine Couturier, who committed suicide in Ry in 1849 having married a local doctor ten years previously, at the age of 17.

Ry consists of one main street, with green hills rising at either end, and a church to one side with an unusual carved wooden porch. Delphine's husband is buried in the churchyard, and Madame Bovary is evident throughout the village, which seems to have had little else to celebrate for a century or so. The local florist is Emma's, the video shop is Bovary, while the pharmacy was Delphine's real house.

An expensive **Musée des Automates**, appealing largely to young children, though some of its mannequins jerkily act out the less explicit moments of Madame Bovary's career, stands next to a pretty bridge over the River Crevon (May–June & Sept–Oct Sat & Sun 2.30–6pm; July & Aug daily except Mon 2.30–6pm; €5). There are no hotels, but the *Bovary* (Ⓣ02.35.23.61.46) serves reasonable lunches in the town's smartest building, near the church at 14 rue de l'Eglise.

Upstream from Rouen

Upstream from Rouen towards Paris, high cliffs on the north bank of the Seine imitate the coast, looking down on waves of green and scattered river islands. By the time you reach **Les Andelys**, 25km outside Rouen, so accommodation and eating prices tend to be geared towards affluent weekend- and day-trippers. Large country estates abound in this agreeable countryside, while public transport is minimal. Two buses daily run from Rouen to both Petit and Grand Andely, while trains from Rouen call at Vernon, the closest station to **Giverny**, renowned as home to Claude Monet.

Pont St-Pierre

The first point south of Rouen at which the Seine begins to be enticing again is **PONT ST-PIERRE**, where it's joined by the River Andelle. The pink-and-brown *Hostellerie la Bonne Marmite*, 10 rue René Raban (Ⓣ02.32.49.70.24, Ⓦwww.la-bonne-marmite.com; ⑤; closed Sun eve, all Mon & Tues lunch, plus first three weeks in Aug), set around a little courtyard a short way south of the eponymous bridge on the main road, makes for an enjoyable overnight stop. Duck-and-lobster-loaded menus in the restaurant start at €17.50.

The spectacularly sharp **Côte des Deux Amants** soars above the confluence of the two rivers. This sheer escarpment, topped by a high plateau, takes its name from a twelfth-century legend in which a cruel king stipulated that the man who would marry his daughter must first run with her in his arms to the top of this hill. Noble Raoul sprinted up carrying the fair Caliste, then dropped dead; out of sympathy, so did she. That story provides precious little incentive for anyone else to make the climb – but rumour has it that the view from the top does.

Les Andelys

The next town of any size is **LES ANDELYS**, which, as the name implies, consists in fact of two towns, overshadowed by the magnificent Château Gaillard. **Petit Andely**, the birthplace in 1594 of Nicolas Poussin, is a gorgeous little village. Its main street, parallel to the Seine, is lined with ancient half-timbered houses, while from the grassy riverbank itself views stretch north to some imposing white bluffs as well as south to the château. **Grand Andely**, 1.5km inland at the far end of a long boulevard, holds little of interest for tourists, apart from its shops and bars, and Saturday **market**.

Château Gaillard

The single most dramatic sight anywhere along the Seine short of Paris – especially awesome and magical by night – has to be **Château Gaillard**, perched high above Les Andelys. The château was constructed in the space of a single year, 1196–97, under the auspices of Richard the Lionheart. A previous truce had expressly forbidden the construction of a castle here, but Richard went ahead anyway, seizing the rock on which it stands from Archbishop Walter of Rouen, then bribing the pope for permission to build. His object was to deny the king of France access to Rouen by controlling all traffic along the Seine, by both road and river. After Richard's death, Philippe-Auguste managed to capture the château in 1204 (his soldiers gaining access via the latrines). It might well have survived intact, however, had Henry IV not ordered its destruction in 1603. Even then, it would have taken more recent devices to reduce Château Gaillard to rubble. The stout flint walls of its keep, roughly 4m thick, remain reasonably sound, and the outline of most of the rest is still clear, arranged over assorted green and chalky knolls. The castle was originally divided into two separate segments, linked by a bridge across a moat that was never intended to be filled with water – you can still explore the storage caves hidden in its depths.

Visits to the château are permitted between mid-March and mid-November only (daily except Tues 10am–1pm & 2–6pm, €3.15; guided tours at 11am, 3pm & 4.30pm, €5.20). On foot, you can make the steep climb up via a path that leads off rue Richard Coeur-de-Lion in Petit Andely. The only route for motorists is extraordinarily convoluted, following a long-winded one-way system that starts opposite the church in Grand Andely.

Practicalities

The local **tourist office** is below the château at 24 rue Philippe-Auguste in Petit Andely (Mon–Sat 10am–noon & 2–6pm, Sun 10am–1pm; Ⓣ02.32.54.41.93, Ⓦville-andelys.fr).

The nicest places to **stay** have to be two attractive Seine-side hotels in Petit Andely. The fancier of the two is the grand eighteenth-century *Chaîne d'Or*, opposite the thirteenth-century St-Sauveur church at 27 rue Grande (Ⓣ02.32.54.00.31, Ⓦwww.hotel-lachainedor.com; ➏; restaurant closed Mon lunch in Aug, Sun eve & all Mon Sept–July). Those of its gorgeous large modernized rooms that overlook the river are undeniably well priced, but the one drawback is that though the food in its **restaurant** is utterly wonderful, the very cheapest dinner menu costs €45, and even breakfast costs €12. The neighbouring *Normandie*, at 1 rue Grande (Ⓣ02.32.54.10.52, Ⓦhotelnormandie-andelys.com; ➌; restaurant closed Wed eve & Thurs, whole place closed Dec), is just as well situated but significantly cheaper and it too holds a good restaurant, serving menus from €18.50. If you can't get a room at either of those, the *Hôtel de Paris*, further back from the river at 10 av de la République in Grand Andely (Ⓣ02.32.54.00.33, Ⓦhotel-andelys.fr; ➍; restaurant closed Sun eve,

Mon lunch & Wed), is a good alternative, with yet another top-notch dining room. There's also a lovely riverside **campsite**, far below the château, the *L'Île des Trois Rois* (ⓣ02.32.54.23.79, ⓦwww.camping-troisrois.com; closed mid-Nov to mid-March).

Giverny

Had it not caught the eye of Claude Monet from a passing train carriage, the little village of **GIVERNY** might by now have decayed into insignificance; instead, it ranks among the most-visited tourist attractions in Normandy. Standing a few hundred metres from the right bank of the Seine, 20km south of the ancient fortifications of Les Andelys and a mere 40km from Paris, it welcomes a constant stream of traffic in summer. Between November and March, however, when Monet's house and gardens are closed to visitors, everything else seems to close down too. The road south to Giverny from Les Andelys crosses a flat plain dotted with lovely little hamlets. **Port Mort** in particular, where the road is lined by an almost unbroken stone wall, is well worth a stop.

Arrival and accommodation

The closest **train station** to Giverny is at **Vernon** (see p.96), 4km north, across the river and on the Rouen–Paris-St-Lazare line. Either rent a bike for €15 per day at *Café du Chemin de Fer*, directly opposite the *gare SNCF*, or catch the connecting shuttle bus to Monet's gardens (ⓣ02.32.54.57.78; €4). There's free **parking** close to Monet's house; don't be fooled by signs for private car parks elsewhere in Giverny.

Heading right for a hundred metres as you leave Monet's house brings you to Giverny's one **hotel**, the *Musardière*, an imposing village house with spacious well-restored rooms at 123 rue Claude-Monet (ⓣ02.32.21.03.18, ⓦlamusardiere.fr; closed Nov–March; ④). Alternatively, a former café at 1 rue du Colombier, a hundred metres to the right as you leave the Musée d'Art Américain, has been converted into a very friendly **B&B** called *Au Bon Maréchal* (ⓣ02.32.51.39.70, ⓦwww.giverny.fr/au-bon-marechal.html; ③), which has three colourful rooms surrounded by an attractive garden.

Fondation Claude Monet

The former home of Claude Monet is open to visitors as the **Fondation Claude Monet** (April–Oct daily 9.30am–6pm; last ticket sold 5.30pm; €6; ⓣ02.32.51.28.21, ⓦwww.fondation-monet.com). If anything, art lovers who make the pilgrimage here are outnumbered by **garden** enthusiasts. No original Monet paintings are on display – the largest collections are in the Orangerie and Musée d'Orsay in Paris – whereas the gardens that many of his friends considered to be his masterpiece are still lovingly tended in all their glory.

Visits start in the huge **studio**, built in 1915, where Monet painted the last and largest of his many canvases depicting waterlilies (in French, *nymphéas*). It now serves as a well-stocked book and gift shop. A gravel footpath leads from there to the actual **house**, a long two-storey structure facing down to the river, and painted pastel pink with green shutters. Monet's bedroom is bedecked with family photos and paintings by friends and family, while among the washed-out reproductions in his *salon* are a depiction by Renoir of Monet at work in his earlier, less perfect garden at Argenteuil in 1875, and one by Monet himself of his dream closer to realization in the garden at Vétheuil in 1881. All the other main rooms are crammed almost floor-to-ceiling with his collection of Japanese prints, especially works by Hokusai and Hiroshige. Most of the original furnishings are gone, but you do get a real sense of how the dining room used to be,

Claude Monet at Giverny

Claude Monet first rented the Giverny home that now houses the Fondation Claude Monet in 1883. At the age of 43, he was exactly halfway through his life. Born in Paris in 1840, he had grown up in Le Havre, and had spent the previous decade living in Argenteuil, Vétheuil and Poissy. Although his reputation as a painter was already established – the movement known as **Impressionism** had taken its name from a critic's somewhat contemptuous response to his work *Impression, Sunrise*, shown in Paris in April 1874 as part of the First Impressionist Exhibition – his personal and financial circumstances were far from settled.

The Monet ménage, whose houseboat arrived in Giverny on April 29, 1883, consisted of ten people. As well as Claude's two sons by his wife Camille, who had died in 1879, he was now also responsible for the six children of his long-term mistress **Alice Hoschedé**. Her husband Ernest was a former patron of the Impressionists who had fallen on hard times; she finally married Monet after her husband's death in 1891.

Monet was to find both artistic and commercial success in Giverny. In his early years, he continued to travel to paint landscapes not only throughout Normandy but also in Brittany, on the Riviera and in England. As time went by, however, his advancing physical frailty and failing eyesight made extended trips increasingly daunting, while his growing prosperity enabled him to tailor his immediate environment to meet his needs as a painter.

In 1890, Monet began to produce sequences of reworkings and renditions of the same scene, shown at different times of the day or seasons of the year. The first such series consisted of 25 views of the **haystacks** on a neighbouring farm; all were arranged side by side in his studio, to be worked on simultaneously. Designed to be seen en masse, they went on show in Paris early in 1891, and proved hugely popular. The individual paintings sold out quickly, and from then on visiting American collectors – and would-be students – were a constant feature of life at Giverny.

In 1891, Monet painted a sequence showing the poplar trees that stood along the banks of the River Epte, about 1.5km south of his home. By now he was rich enough to buy the trees, for as long as his work was in progress, from a local timber merchant who was due to fell them. Having purchased his house outright, for 22,000F, he went on to buy a further plot of land, across the main road. With permission from the local authorities, he dammed the stream known as the Ru to feed an artificial pond, which he planted with **waterlilies** and spanned with a Japanese footbridge.

A team of gardeners worked to keep different sections of his **flower gardens** in bloom as much of the year as possible, so he would always have a suitable subject on which to work. One man had the full-time responsibility of tending the waterlilies to Monet's specifications, depending, for example, on whether he planned to use square or rectangular canvases. Monet would work outdoors for around six hours each day, avoiding the midday sun, and went on to paint over 250 versions of his waterlilies (*nymphéas*), not to mention the canvases he destroyed in disgust. One set of 48 waterlily pictures is said to have hung in his studio for six years, being constantly reworked, before it was exhibited in 1909.

Photographs of Monet in his later years show him as very much the white-bearded patrician, not only presiding over his studio and household but also playing host to leading painters and politicians. Despite a series of operations on his eyes, he continued to work almost until his death in December 1926. The house at Giverny passed to his son, Jean Monet, who left it in turn to the Académie des Beaux Arts in 1966. After restoration, it reopened as a museum in 1980.

with all its walls and fittings painted a glorious bright yellow; Monet designed his own yellow crockery to harmonize with the surroundings. By contrast, the stairs and upstairs rooms are a pale blue.

More enticing than the house are the colourful flower gardens, with trellised walkways and shady bowers, stretching down from the house. Originally, the main footpath here led straight down to the **waterlily pond**; now, however, visitors have to reach the *jardin d'eau* by burrowing beneath the main road in a dank underpass. Once there, paths around the perimeter of the pond, as well as arching Japanese footbridges of course, offer differing views of the waterlilies themselves, cherished by gardeners in rowing boats. May and June, when the rhododendrons flower, and the wisteria that winds over the Japanese bridge is in bloom, are the best times to visit. Whenever you come, however, you'll have to contend with camera-happy crowds jostling to capture their own impressions of the waterlilies. These same crowds are the cause of long waits to enter the house during the busy summer period.

Musée d'Art Américain

Head left as you leave Monet's house, and walk for a few minutes up the main village street, to reach Giverny's **Musée d'Art Américain** (April–Oct Tues–Sun 10am–6pm; €5.50, free first Sun of each month; Ⓦwww.maag.org). The exterior is far from attractive, but inside you'll find a spacious and well-lit gallery devoted to permanent and temporary exhibitions of works by American artists resident in France between 1865 and 1915, and in particular those who congregated in Giverny from 1887 onwards. Although Monet accepted no formal pupils, some, such as Theodore Robinson, joined his circle of intimates. Some took their admiration to a point that now seems embarrassing, painting many of the same scenes as Monet himself. As well as the waterlilies, for example, John Leslie Brech produced a series of twelve haystacks within a year of Monet's.

Mary Cassatt, who lived in a château at Le Mesnil-Thérebus, is represented by a far more interesting series of woodcuts, heavily influenced by *ukiyo-e* Japanese woodcuts, as well as canvases that focus on the domestic life of women while clearly belonging to the Impressionist movement. John Singer Sargent and Winslow Homer both contribute scenes of Brittany, especially Cancale, while James Henry Whistler's paintings include views of Dieppe and Étretat.

▲ Monet's garden, Giverny

Eating

The *Musardière* (see p.93) serves dinner menus in its **restaurant** from €26, and also offers crêpes and snacks during the day; its terrace, with plenty of shade provided by the surrounding trees, makes a nice spot for lunch. *Les Nymphéas* (Ⓣ02.32.21.20.31; closed Nov–March), a pleasant little tearoom and restaurant serving mainly salads, is located opposite the Fondation Claude Monet, while the restaurant inside the Musée d'Art Américain has a peaceful garden terrace. Otherwise, the charcuterie at 60 rue Claude-Monet, a few doors down from *Au Bon Maréchal*, makes delicious sandwiches. Eating in the grounds of Monet's house or the American art museum is forbidden, and the surrounding countryside is not particularly appealing for picnicking.

Vernon

VERNON straddles the Seine just before it leaves Normandy altogether, with walks laid out along either bank. Were it not for the proximity of Giverny, there'd be no real reason to visit here, let alone stay; as it is, the *gare SNCF*, served by trains between Rouen and Paris, is busy throughout the summer with day-trippers heading for Monet's house (see p.93). The central *Hôtel d'Évreux*, 11 place d'Évreux (Ⓣ02.32.21.16.12; Ⓦwww.hoteldevreux.fr; ➊), has **rooms** at assorted prices – the cheapest with shared bathrooms – and a good restaurant, and you can also eat well at the *Restaurant les Fleurs*, 71 rue Carnot (Ⓣ02.32.51.16.80; closed Sun eve & Mon, plus Tues lunch in low season), where full dinner menus start at €27, but there are cheaper alternatives in the adjoining bistro. Elvis Presley's dad was called Vernon.

Travel details

Trains

Dieppe to: Paris-St-Lazare (19 daily; 2hr 10min) via Rouen (16 daily; 50min).
Fécamp to: Bréauté-Beuzeville (10 daily; 20min) with connections to Le Havre (total journey 1hr) or Rouen (total journey 1hr 30min).
Le Havre to: Paris (11 daily; 2hr 30min); Rouen (15 daily; 50min).
Rouen to: Caen (7 daily; 1hr 30min); Clères (16 daily; 20min); Lisieux (7 daily, 1hr 5min); Paris-St-Lazare (25 daily; 1hr 40min); Vernon (20 daily; 45min); Yvetot (15 daily; 30min) with connecting bus to St-Valery (total 1hr 30min).

Buses

Dieppe to: Fécamp (4 daily; 2hr 20min); Le Tréport (4 daily; 30min); St-Valery (5 daily; 1hr).
Fécamp to: Étretat (10 daily; 40min), with connections to Le Havre (11 daily; 1hr 20min) and Yport (8 daily; 15min).
Le Havre to: Caen (2 daily express services; 1hr 25min); Étretat (11 daily; 40min); Fécamp (11 daily; 1hr 20min); Honfleur (7 daily; 30min).
Rouen to: Clères (6 daily; 45min); Évreux (hourly; 1hr); Le Havre (hourly; 2hr 45min), via Jumièges and Caudebec; Lisieux (2 daily; 2hr 30min).

International ferries

Dieppe to: Newhaven with Transmanche Ferries (1–2 daily; 4hr; Ⓣ08.00.65.01.00, Ⓦwww.transmancheferries.com).
Le Havre to: Portsmouth (1–2 daily; 5hr 30min) with LD Lines (Ⓣ08.25.30.43.04, Ⓦldlines.co.uk). For more details, see Basics.

2

The Lower Normandy Coast

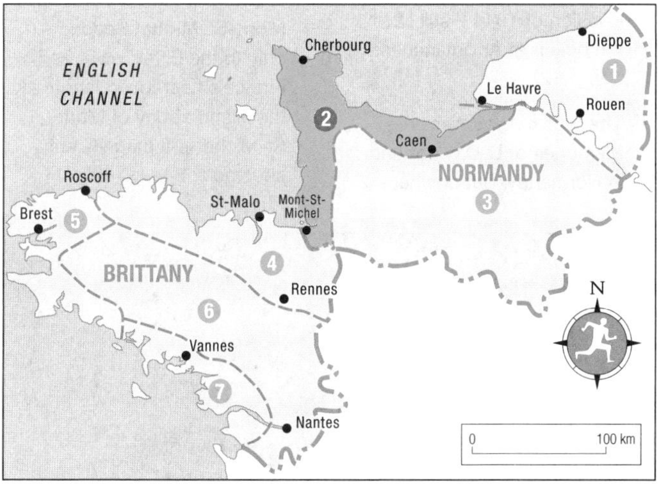

CHAPTER 2

Highlights

* **Les Maisons Satie** Surreal museum devoted to the avant-garde composer in the beautiful harbour town of Honfleur. See p.106

* **The Bayeux Tapestry** An extraordinary historical document, embroidering the saga of William the Conqueror in colourful detail. See p.120

* **Arromanches** The remains of Winston Churchill's Mulberry Harbour – the key to the invasion of 1944 – still litter the beach at Arromanches. See p.127

* **The war cemeteries** Memories of D-Day abound in Normandy, but nowhere more poignantly than in the monumental American cemetery at Colleville-sur-mer. See p.130

* **Le Conquérant** Delightful, inexpensive old hotel in ancient Barfleur, which makes a great stop for ferry passengers. See p.138

* **Croix d'Or** With its fabulous restaurant, this old coaching inn in Avranches makes a great overnight stop near Mont-St-Michel. See p.148

* **Mont-St-Michel** Second only to the Eiffel Tower as France's best-loved landmark, the island abbey of Mont-St-Michel is a magnificent spectacle. See p.148

▲ Mont-St-Michel

2

The Lower Normandy Coast

The **coast of Lower Normandy** changes progressively in character as you move from east to west. Along the **Côte Fleurie**, from Honfleur to Cabourg, it is moneyed and elegant, with the so-called **Norman Riviera**, concentrated on the twin towns of Deauville and Trouville, styling itself as a northern counterpart to the Côte d'Azur. Then, through the much flatter **Côte de Nacre** and into the area known as the **Bessin**, around Caen and Bayeux, the shoreline is much lower key: though the coastal strip remains predominantly built up, few towns amount to more than slender ribbons sandwiched between the broad sandy **Invasion Beaches** used by the Allies in 1944, and the featureless scrub that lies inland. West again, separated from the bulk of the mainland by a series of marshes, is the **Cotentin Peninsula**, with charming harbour villages along its east front, cliffs across the north, and vast dunes and wild beaches to the west. Finally comes the southern bay of **Mont-St-Michel**, where the island abbey is swept by treacherous tides.

The most enjoyable destination along the Côte Fleurie is **Honfleur**, a real gem of a medieval port, familiar from the paintings of Eugène Boudin, Monet and other Impressionists. Many of its neighbours, such as **Trouville**, **Deauville** and **Cabourg**, have become over-priced and rather dull resorts, though they do have a certain nineteenth-century charm.

Thanks to their lack of over-developed resorts, the Côte de Nacre and the Bessin are much more likeable. This region's pivotal role in the **D-Day Landings** is commemorated not only in numerous cemeteries and memorials, but also in the many museums that set out to explain aspects of its wartime history. Successive small-scale seaside towns, all the way from **Ouistreham** to **Grandcamp-Maisy**, make charmingly atmospheric places to spend a few days. Just inland, the venerable cathedral city of **Bayeux** would be a destination to savour even without the bonus of its world-famous **tapestry**, while its much larger neighbour, **Caen** also boasts an abundance of impressive medieval architecture, and rivals Rouen as a centre for contemporary culture.

The main city of the Cotentin Peninsula, **Cherbourg**, may not be a port to linger over, but ferry passengers who arrive here can choose between the lovely little villages that lie to the east, especially **Barfleur**, and the magnificent beaches and dunes of the peninsula's western coastline (popular with

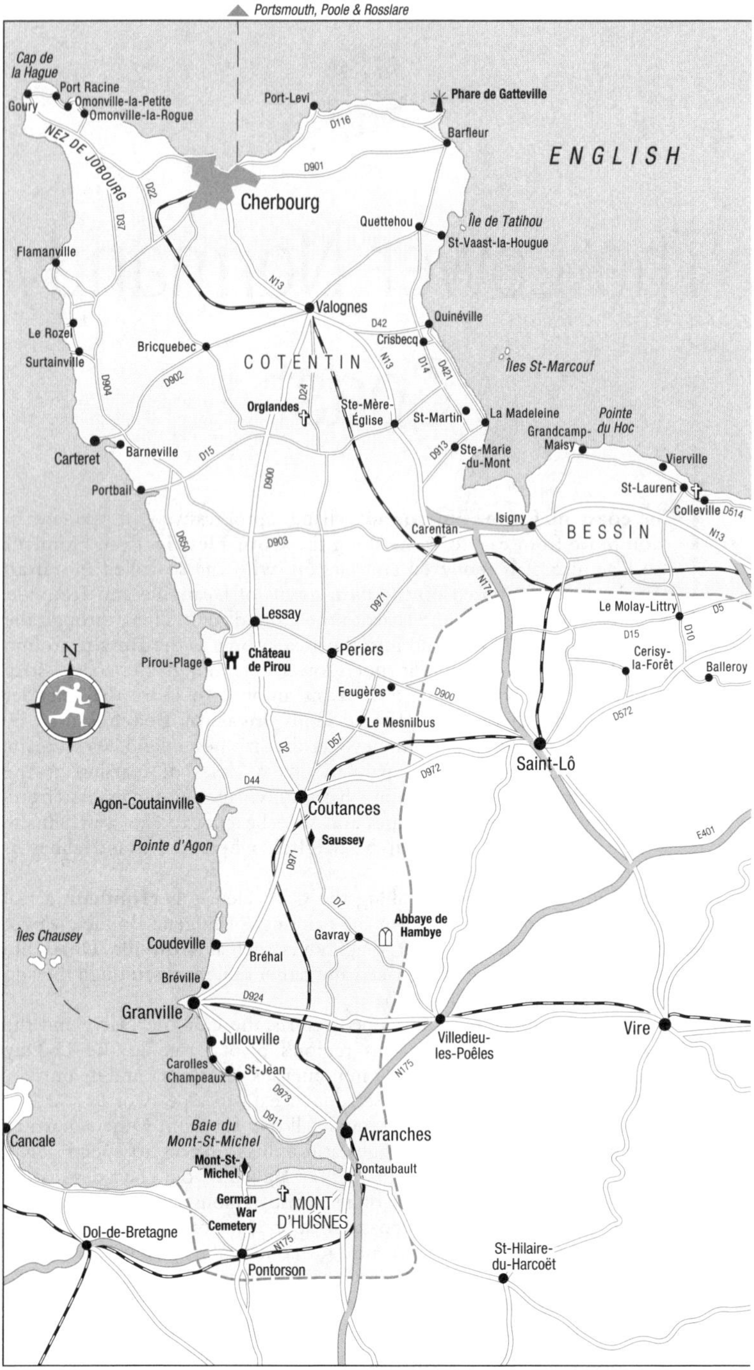

Portsmouth, Poole & Rosslare
Cap de la Hague
Goury
Port Racine
Omonville-la-Petite
Omonville-la-Rogue
NEZ DE JOBOURG
Port-Levi
Phare de Gatteville
Barfleur
ENGLISH
Cherbourg
Quettehou
Île de Tatihou
St-Vaast-la-Hougue
Flamanville
Valognes
Quinéville
Crisbecq
Le Rozel
Surtainville
Bricquebec
COTENTIN
Îles St-Marcouf
Orglandes
Ste-Mère-Église
St-Martin
La Madeleine
Pointe du Hoc
Grandcamp-Maisy
Carteret
Barneville
Ste-Marie-du-Mont
Vierville
Portbail
St-Laurent
Colleville
Isigny
Carentan
BESSIN
Le Molay-Littry
Lessay
Cerisy-la-Forêt
Balleroy
Pirou-Plage
Château de Pirou
Periers
Feugères
Le Mesnilbus
Saint-Lô
Agon-Coutainville
Coutances
Saussey
Pointe d'Agon
Îles Chausey
Gavray
Abbaye de Hambye
Coudeville
Bréhal
Bréville
Granville
Villedieu-les-Poêles
Vire
Jullouville
Carolles
Champeaux
St-Jean
Cancale
Baie du Mont-St-Michel
Avranches
Mont-St-Michel
Pontaubault
German War Cemetery
MONT D'HUISNES
Dol-de-Bretagne
Pontorson
St-Hilaire-du-Harcoët
N
D116
D901
D22
D37
N13
D42
D14
D421
D902
D904
D24
D15
D913
D900
D903
D650
D514
N13
N174
D971
D5
D15
D10
D900
D572
D57
D2
D972
D44
E401
D971
D7
D924
N175
D973
D911
N175

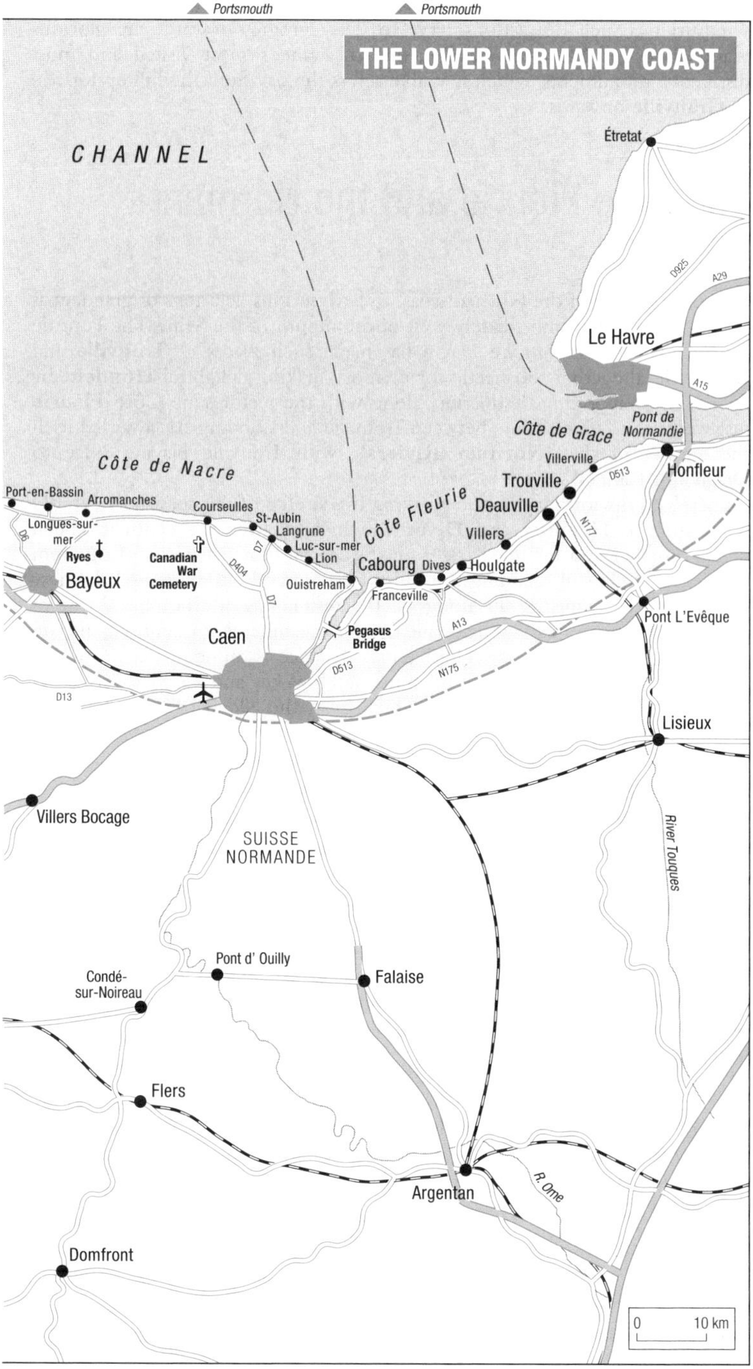
Portsmouth
Portsmouth
THE LOWER NORMANDY COAST
CHANNEL
Étretat
D925
A29
Le Havre
A15
Pont de Normandie
Côte de Grace
Villerville
D513
Honfleur
Trouville
Deauville
N177
Côte de Nacre
Côte Fleurie
Villers
Port-en-Bassin
Arromanches
Longues-sur-mer
D6
Ryes
Courseulles
St-Aubin
Langrune
Luc-sur-mer
Lion
D7
D404
Canadian War Cemetery
Bayeux
Ouistreham
Cabourg
Dives
Houlgate
Franceville
Pont L'Evêque
Pegasus Bridge
Caen
A13
D513
N175
D13
Lisieux
Villers Bocage
SUISSE NORMANDE
River Touques
Pont d' Ouilly
Condé-sur-Noireau
Falaise
Flers
Argentan
R. Orne
Domfront
0
10 km

windsurfers). Such distractions serve to delay progress towards the glorious island abbey of **Mont-St-Michel**, one of France's most visited and most distinctive monuments, which is visible across the bay from the hilltop fortress of **Granville** onwards.

The Côte Fleurie and the Norman Riviera

The only section of the Norman coast to have serious delusions of grandeur is the stretch that lies immediately west of the mouth of the Seine. The Pont de Normandie across from Le Havre has made such places as **Trouville** and **Deauville** altogether too hectic for comfort, making delightful **Honfleur** by far the most appealing destination, along with the picturesque **Côte Fleurie** just west of it. The coastline between Trouville and Cabourg has awarded itself the epithet of the "**Norman Riviera**", with Trouville playing Nice to Deauville's Cannes.

There's an obvious distinction all along this stretch of the coast between old ports such as Honfleur and **Dives** which have, over the centuries, been pushed further and further back from the sea by heavy deposits of silt from the Seine, while still retaining their historic medieval buildings, and the new resorts that have sprung up alongside the resultant sandy beaches. Most of these were unimaginatively laid out during the nineteenth century, and are characterless in the extreme. The happiest balance is found at places such as **Houlgate**, where development has remained low-key and the rocky coastline has stood firm against the river – which gives the added bonus of pleasant corniche drives.

Honfleur

HONFLEUR is the most beautiful of all Normandy's seaside towns, and its best-preserved historic port. All that holds it back from perfection is that it no longer has a beach; with the accumulation of silt from the Seine, the sea has steadily withdrawn, leaving the eighteenth-century waterfront houses of boulevard Charles V stranded and a little surreal. The ancient port, however, still functions – the channel to the beautiful Vieux Bassin is kept open by regular dredging – and though only pleasure craft now use the moorings in the harbour basin, fishing boats continue to tie up alongside the pier nearby. Fish is usually on sale either directly from the boats or from stands on the pier, still run by fishermen's wives.

Honfleur is picturesque enough to have adorned magazine covers the world over, and attracts summer tourists in droves. It has also moved steadily upmarket since the vast **Pont de Normandie**, a toll-bridge spanning the mouth of the Seine, opened in 1995. Despite now being just a few minutes' drive from the city of Le Havre, however, the old port still feels not so very different to the fishing village that appealed so greatly to artists in the second half of the nineteenth century, notably Eugène Boudin, who taught Monet and Cézanne.

Arrival, information and tours

Honfleur's **gare routière**, ten minutes' walk east of the Vieux Bassin, is served by over a dozen direct daily **buses** from Caen (#20), and up to ten services

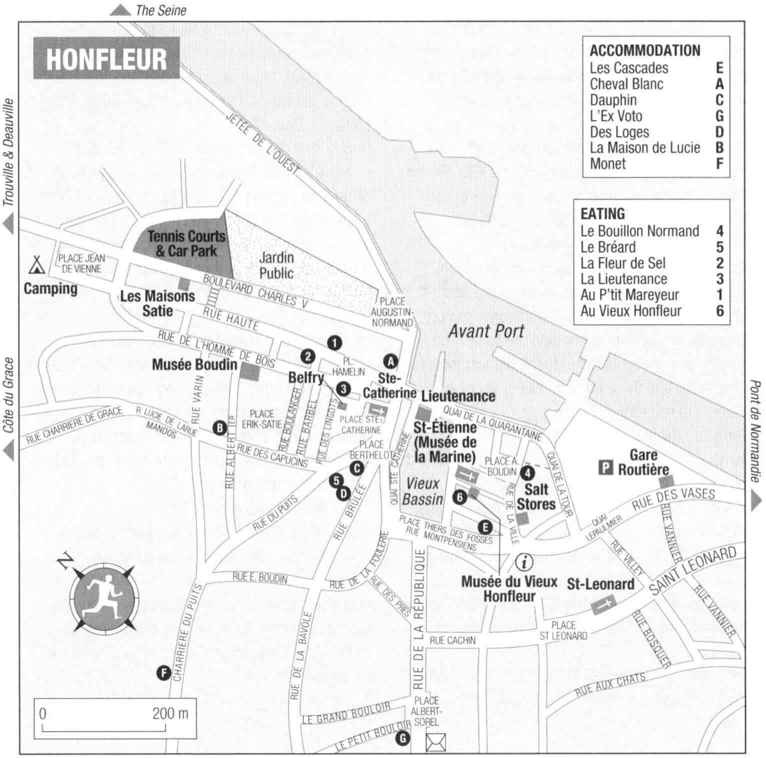

from Le Havre (Bus Verts; ⓣ08.10.21.42.14, ⓦwww.busverts.fr). However, the nearest **train station** is at Pont-l'Évêque (see p.166), connected to Honfleur by the Lisieux bus #50 (20min ride).

The **tourist office**, which also offers cheap **internet access**, adjoins the glass-fronted Mediathèque library on quai Le Paulmier, between the Vieux Bassin and the *gare routière* (Easter–June & Sept Mon–Sat 9.30am–12.30pm & 2–6.30pm, Sun 10am–12.30pm & 2–5pm; July & Aug Mon–Sat 9.30am–7pm, Sun 10am–5pm; Oct–Easter Mon–Sat 10am–12.30pm & 2–6pm; ⓣ02.31.89.23.30, ⓦot-honfleur.fr). During July and August, the tourist office conducts worthwhile evening **guided tours** of the old town. Also in summer, several **cruises** sail upriver each day from either side of the Avant-Port from well-signposted departure points, for a closer look at the Pont de Normandie (45min trip €6, 1hr 30min €8.50; ⓣ02.31.89.07.77).

Accommodation

It's not as easy to live the bohemian life in Honfleur as it used to be. With demand so high, for most of the summer it's hard to find a reasonably priced room, and budget travellers are probably better off simply visiting for the day. No hotels overlook the harbour itself, while motorists will find it all but impossible to park anywhere near most central hotels. There is, however, a two-star **campsite**, the *Camping du Phare* (ⓣ02.31.89.10.26, ⓦwww.campings-plage.com/phare_honfleur; closed Oct–March) at the west end of boulevard Charles V on place Jean-de-Vienne.

Les Cascades 17 pl Thiers Ⓣ02.31.89.05.83, Ⓦlescascades.com. Well priced, seventeen-room hotel-restaurant opening onto both place Thiers and the cobbled rue de la Ville behind. Slightly noisy rooms upstairs, and a good-value if not all that exciting restaurant with outdoor seating on both sides; menus at €13, €24.50 and €32. Closed Mon & Tues in low season, plus mid-Nov to early Feb (hotel and restaurant). 3

Cheval Blanc 2 quai des Passagers Ⓣ02.31.81.65.00, Ⓦwww.hotel-honfleur.com. Large, very central hotel, affiliated to the Best Western chain. Dating from the fifteenth century, it faces the Avant-Port rather than the basin. The rooms have been upgraded to the highest modern standards, and there are a couple of very fancy suites. No restaurant. 6

Dauphin 10 pl Berthelot Ⓣ02.31.89.15.53, Ⓦhoteldudauphin.com. Grey-slate town house just around the corner from Ste-Catherine church, with a wide assortment of generally overpriced rooms, including some larger family rooms; the cheapest ones, in the rather impersonal annexe, are quite plain, while the fanciest ones come with jacuzzis. The creaky floorboards and thin walls are universal, however. Prices drop Mon–Thurs in winter. Closed Jan. 4

L'Ex Voto 8 pl Albert-Sorel Ⓣ02.31.89.19.69. Two clean, well-priced rooms above a friendly family-run bar, a short walk inland along the main road from the Vieux Bassin. Both rooms have a bidet, but share a shower and toilet. Rates include breakfast. Closed Wed Sept–June, plus all Nov & Dec. 3

Des Loges 18 rue Brûlée Ⓣ02.31.89.38.26, Ⓦwww.hoteldesloges.com. Smart, brightly refurbished hotel on a cobbled street just 100m inland from Ste-Catherine church, decked out with flowers, run by helpful staff, and offering a pretty good standard of expensive accommodation, all in a slightly anonymous modern style. Closed Jan. 6

La Maison de Lucie 44 rue des Capucins Ⓣ02.31.14.40.40, Ⓦwww.lamaisondelucie.com. Upscale little hotel, tucked away just seconds from the centre, in a beautiful restored mansion furnished with hints of 1930s-style decadence. As well as four regular rooms, there's a larger suite and a duplex apartment. 8

Monet Charrière du Puits Ⓣ02.31.89.00.90, Ⓦwww.hotel-monet-honfleur.com. This old ivy-covered house, run by very accommodating management and offering plenty of courtyard parking, stands in a very quiet location ten minutes' walk from the centre up a moderately steep hill and offers spruce, modern, en-suite rooms. 3

The Town

Visitors to Honfleur inevitably gravitate towards the old centre, around the **Vieux Bassin**, where slate-fronted houses, each one or two storeys higher than seems possible, harmonize despite their tottering and ill-matched forms. They create a splendid backdrop for the **Lieutenance** at the harbour entrance, the former dwelling of the King's Lieutenant, which has been the gateway to the inner town since at least 1608, when Samuel Champlain sailed from Honfleur to found Québec. Further architectural and historic treasures lie tucked away in the tangled medieval streets and squares to either side of the *bassin*, including several excellent museums and galleries.

The Musée de la Marine and Musée de Vieux Honfleur

Squeezed into the church of **St-Étienne** on the eastern side of the *bassin*, the **Musée de la Marine** combines a collection of model ships with several rooms of antique Norman furnishings (mid-Feb to March & Oct to mid-Nov Tues–Fri 2.30–5.30pm, Sat & Sun 10am–noon; April–Sept daily except Mon 10am–noon & 2–6.30pm; closed mid-Nov to mid-Feb; €3.40, or €4.60 with Musée de Vieux Honfleur).

Alongside on tiny rue de la Prison, a nice little ensemble that once held Honfleur's prison now serves as the **Musée de Vieux Honfleur** (same hours and entrance fee), filling ten rooms with a fascinating assortment of everyday artefacts from old Honfleur. One prize exhibit is a copper bath on wheels, shaped like a clog, that's identical to the one in which Jacobin leader Jean-Paul Marat was assassinated by Charlotte Corday in 1793.

▲ Honfleur

Just behind these two museums on rue de la Ville, two seventeenth-century **salt stores** held the precious commodity during the days of the much-hated *gabelle*, or salt tax, but are now used for art exhibitions.

Musée Eugène Boudin

Honfleur's artistic past, and its present concentration of galleries and painters, owes most to **Eugène Boudin**, forerunner of Impressionism. Born in Honfleur in 1824 – his father worked on the ferries between Honfleur and Le Havre – Boudin continued to paint here throughout his life. He taught the 18-year-old Monet and was joined for various periods by Pissarro, Renoir and Cézanne. Boudin was among the founders of what's now the **Musée Eugène Boudin** (mid-March to Sept daily except Tues 10am–noon & 2–6pm; Oct to mid-March Mon & Wed–Fri 2.30–5pm, Sat & Sun 10am–noon & 2.30–5pm; €4.80), west of the port on place Erik-Satie, and left 53 works to it after his death in 1898. His pastel seascapes and sunsets, some of which are juxtaposed with nineteenth-century photographs of the same scenes, hold an especial resonance in this setting, where panoramic windows on the top floor offer superb views of the Seine estuary and the Pont de Normandie. Several other artists with local connections are also represented, including Dufy, while Fernand Herbo's hellish 1956 vision of workers streaming out of Le Havre's Shell refinery adds a contemporary edge.

Église Ste-Catherine

Honfleur's most remarkable building has to be the church of **Ste-Catherine** (daily: summer 9am–6pm; winter 9am–5.30pm), with its distinctive detached **belfry**, which ranked among Monet's favourite subjects in his younger days (one of his depictions remains in the Eugène Boudin museum). The church was built almost entirely of wood during the Hundred Years War, when stone was reserved for military use; the town's shipbuilders, experienced in working with wood, took responsibility for its construction. All the timbers inside are now exposed to view, having been sheathed in white plaster during the nineteenth century, when an incongruous four-columned porch (long since removed) was added to the front. The changing patterns on its tiles, both along the main body and the belfry, delineate Christian symbols. It all makes a change from the great stone Norman churches, and has the added peculiarity of being divided into twin naves, with one balcony running around both. The belfry itself now holds a fairly random assortment of ethnographic oddities, and visitors are not permitted above ground level (same hours as Eugène Boudin museum; €2 on its own, or free entry with museum ticket).

Les Maisons Satie

The red-timbered former home of composer **Érik Satie**, just down the hill from the Musée Boudin at 67 bd Charles-V, is open to visitors as **Les Maisons Satie** (daily except Tues: May–Sept 10am–7pm; mid-Feb to April & Oct–Dec 11am–6pm; last entry 1hr before closing time; €5.50), From the outside, it looks unchanged since Satie was born here in 1866. Step inside, however, and you'll find yourself in Normandy's most unusual and enjoyable museum. As befits a close associate of the Surrealists, Satie is commemorated by means of all sorts of weird interactive surprises. It would be a shame to give too many of them away here; suffice it to say that you're immediately confronted by a giant pear, bouncing into the air on huge wings to the strains of his best-known piano piece, *Gymnopédies*, and said to represent Satie's soul leaving his body after his death in Paris on July 1, 1925. You also get to see a filmed reconstruction of *Parade*, a ballet on which Satie collaborated with Picasso, Stravinsky and Cocteau, and which created a furore in Paris in 1917.

The Côte de Grace

Satie's home forms part of a row of stately shipbuilders' residences that once lined the Honfleur waterfront; now they look across reclaimed flatlands to the industrial desert of Le Havre's docks in the distance. Over the road, and beyond the public gardens by the place Augustin-Normand, you can follow the **shipping channel** out towards the mouth of the Seine and the sea. A rusty old pipeline runs alongside, inside which you can hear rats and mice scampering to and from the sea. However, it would not occur even to the most hard-nosed mud-caked sewer rat to swim in the sea once it got there – the shore is a slimy grey wasteland, the water foul and sluggish. Nonetheless, it's possible to slip and squirm your way onto the shingle and then walk along the **Côte de Grace**, the name of the stretch of coast immediately to the west of Honfleur before it becomes the Côte Fleurie, with beautiful wooded hills sitting tantalizingly above you. Inland, the grand old houses of ancient aesthetes, and the **Chapelle Notre Dame de Grâce** in Équemauville, beloved of the Impressionists, nestle dry-footed in the forests.

Eating and drinking

With its abundant day-trippers and hotel guests, Honfleur supports an astonishing number of **restaurants**, most naturally specializing in seafood and many very good at it indeed. Surprisingly few restaurants face onto the harbour itself; the narrow buildings around the edge are largely devoted to snack bars, crêperies, cafés and ice-cream parlours. Instead, you'll find extensive arrays both east, along the quai de la Quarantaine, and west, on place Hamelin and rue Haute.

One local speciality, available in October and November, is *crevettes grises* – tiny shrimp eaten with an unsalty bread, *pain brié*. If you're buying your own food, look out for the excellent Panatérie, a **boulangerie** selling granary and wholemeal breads, on the corner of the rue des Prés and rue de la République.

The profusion of restaurants hides the fact that there are very few **bars**. If you fancy a drink without having to order some food, head for the harbour, where on the western side of quai Ste-Catherine, the *Albatros* at no. 32 is the obvious choice for a tea or a coffee, and the *Perroquet Vert*, no. 52 (closed Dec to mid-Jan), for something alcoholic. Both have outdoor seating.

Le Bouillon Normand 7 rue de la Ville ⓣ02.31.89.02.41. Old-fashioned bistro, with indoor and outdoor seating, set just back from the basin behind St-Étienne church. Fish, cider and cheese are prominent on simple, good-value menus at €17 and €25. Closed Wed, Sun eve & Jan.

Le Bréard 7 rue du Puits ⓣ02.31.89.53.49, ⓦwww.restaurant-lebreard.com. Offering a highly creative, contemporary take on classic French cuisine, Fabrice Sébire's new restaurant, just off the church square, has taken Honfleur's culinary scene by storm. Lunch €20 (Thurs & Fri only), dinner menus €28 and €38. July–Sept closed for lunch Mon–Wed; Nov–June closed Mon & Tues, plus lunch Wed; also closed three weeks in Dec.

La Fleur de Sel 17 rue Haute ⓣ02.31.89.01.92. Elegant, formal option, with indoor seating only, offering gourmet menus at €28, €38 and €58 that are equally strong on meat and fish. Closed Tues & Wed, plus all Jan.

La Lieutenance 12 pl Ste-Catherine ⓣ02.31.89.07.52. Not in fact by the Lieutenance, despite the name, but facing both church and belfry on the cobbled pedestrian square, with plenty of outdoor seating. Gourmet dining with a heavy emphasis on oysters; menus start at €24, while a seafood feast for two, consisting of a giant double platter, plus wine and dessert, costs €92. Closed Sun eve in winter.

Au P'tit Mareyeur 4 rue Haute ⓣ02.31.98.84.23. No distance from the centre, but all the seating is indoors and there are no views. Very good fish dishes, such as red crab soup with garlic, plus plenty of creamy *pays d'Auge* sauces and superb desserts. The "Menu Carte" is €27.50, while a bouillabaisse costs €29. Local diners appreciate the restaurant's policy of listing its suppliers of meat, fish, vegetables and even salt. Closed Mon, Tues & Jan.

Au Vieux Honfleur 13 quai St-Étienne ⓣ02.31.89.15.31. The best of the restaurants around the harbour itself, with spacious alfresco dining – in shade at lunchtime – on its pedestrianized eastern side. Simple menus, but the seafood is very good, as befits prices starting at €29. The only other set menu, at €49, offers lobster or turbot.

Villerville

For the 15km **west along the corniche** from Honfleur to Trouville, green fields and fruit trees line the land's edge, and cliffs rise from sandy beaches. The **resorts** aren't cheap, but they're relatively undeveloped, and if you want to stop by the seaside this is the place to do it.

The most conspicuous community is **VILLERVILLE**, 10km west of Honfleur, a coastal village whose narrow twisting streets, filled with old mansions, front onto a huge sandy beach that unfortunately faces straight across the mouth of the Seine to the refineries of Le Havre. The grand old *Bellevue*, dropping down the hillside from the main D513 just east of town at 7 rue Clemenceau (ⓣ02.31.87.20.22, ⓦbellevue-hotel.fr; ❺; closed mid-Jan to mid-Feb), has some very comfortable but rather anonymous **rooms** in its seafront annexe, and cheaper ones in its main building, and serves good fish menus in its sea-view **restaurant** from €26.

Trouville and Deauville

The towns of **Trouville** and **Deauville** lie within a stone's throw of each other to either side of the mouth of the River Touques, sharing many of their amenities, and also their rather exclusive reputations.

Arrival and information

Trouville and Deauville share their **gare SNCF** (served by trains from Paris via Lisieux) and **gare routière** (ⓣ08.10.21.42.14), in between the two just south of the marina. Each day, ten of the hourly buses from Caen continue along the coast to Honfleur.

Deauville's **tourist office** is on place de la Mairie (mid-June to mid-Sept Mon–Sat 9am–7pm, Sun 10am–6pm; mid-Sept to mid-June Mon–Sat 10am–6pm, Sun 10am–1pm & 2–5pm; ⓣ02.31.14.40.00, ⓦdeauville.org). Trouville's equivalent is at 32 quai F. Moureaux (April–June, Sept & Oct Mon–Sat 9.30am–noon & 2–6.30pm, Sun 10am–1pm; July & Aug Mon–Sat 9.30am–7pm, Sun 10am–4pm; Nov–March Mon–Sat 9.30am–noon & 1.30–6.30pm, Sun 10am–1pm; ⓣ02.31.14.60.70, ⓦwww.trouvillesurmer.org).

Accommodation

As you might imagine, **hotels** in Trouville and Deauville tend to be luxurious, or overpriced, or indeed both. For lesser mortals, however, there are a few cheaper options.

Hotels

Flaubert rue Gustave-Flaubert, Trouville ⓣ02.31.88.37.23, ⓦwww.flaubert.fr. If you fancy staying right on the seafront, it's hard to beat this grand faux-timbered mansion, at the start of Trouville's boardwalk. 5

Normandy Barrière 38 rue Jean-Mermoz, Deauville ⓣ02.31.98.66.22, ⓦwww.lucienbarriere.com. Not surprisingly, this enormous, rambling timbered hotel, the fanciest in either town, is where the stars stay during the film festival. 9

Des Sports 27 rue Gambetta, Deauville ⓣ02.31.88.22.67. Nine inexpensive rooms, above a popular café behind Deauville's fish market. Closed Sun in winter, plus March & Nov. 3

Trouville 1 rue Thiers, Trouville ⓣ02.31.98.45.48, ⓦhotelletrouville.com. Trouville's best budget option, just 50m back from the beach, has some cheap single rooms and rents out bicycles. Closed Jan. 4

Campsite

Vallée de Deauville rte de Beaumont-en-Auge, St-Arnoult ⓣ02.31.88.58.17, ⓦwww.camping-deauville.com. The nearest campsite to the twin resorts, 3km from the centre of Deauville. Closed Nov–March.

Trouville

Though **TROUVILLE** retains at least some semblance of a real town, with a constant population and industries other than tourism, it is primarily a resort and has been ever since Napoléon III started bringing his court here for the summer in the 1860s. (His empress, Eugénie, fled France from here in 1870 in the yacht of an English admirer.) A long promenade marks the boundary between the sands and the spectacular villas that line the beach, including the chic former **Hôtel des Roches Noires** (now a private residence), patterned with complex brickwork and topped by ornate turrets; several were painted by Monet during a visit in 1870. Slightly further back, a tangle of busy pedestrian streets are alive with restaurants and hotels. The whole place has a charming Belle Époque feel, and the beach is both enormous and packed with activities for children. The only paying attraction, the **Natur'Aquarium**, is a rather sorry little aquarium that's only accessible from the beachfront boardwalk (daily: Easter–June, Sept & Oct 10am–noon & 2–7pm; July & Aug 10am–7.30pm; Nov–Easter 2–6.30pm; adults €7.50, under-15s €5.50; ⓦnatur-aquarium.com) and also holds assorted tarantulas, stick insects and boa constrictors besides its apathetic sharks.

Deauville

One of Emperor Napoléon's dukes, looking across the river from Trouville, saw not marshlands but money, and lots of it, in the form of a **racecourse**. His vision materialized, and villas appeared between the racecourse and the sea to become **DEAUVILLE**, which likes to style itself as the *21e arrondissement* of

Paris. Now you can lose money on the horses, cross five streets to lose more in the **casino** (formal attire compulsory; temporary membership around €15), where Winston Churchill spent the summer of 1906 gambling every night until 5am, and finally lose yourself in the broad band of private bathing huts that intervene before the *planches*. Beyond this stretch of boardwalk, rows of primary-coloured parasols obscure the sea.

One more congenial reason to visit is the **American Film Festival**, held in Deauville over ten days in early September – a festival that's the antithesis of Cannes, with public admission to a wide selection of previews, but which still attracts big-name stars. For information, visit Ⓦwww.festival-deauville.com.

Eating

A good **place to eat** in Deauville is *Chez Miocque* at 81 rue Eugène-Colas (Ⓣ02.31.88.09.52; closed Tues in winter, plus all Jan), a top-quality Parisian-style bistro where a full meal costs around €40. Trouville also has its fair share of good fish restaurants, including *Les Vapeurs* at 160 bd F. Moureaux (Ⓣ02.31.88.15.24) – one of several lively brasseries opposite the attractive old half-timbered fish market – and *La Petite Auberge*, 7 rue Carnot (Ⓣ02.31.88.11.07; closed Tues all year, plus Wed except in Aug), though both get very crowded at weekends.

Villers-sur-mer

To the west of Deauville, the shoreline at first stays flat, and the main coast road passes through a succession of what are almost suburban resorts – significantly less snobbish than Trouville and Deauville, but equally crowded and equally short of inexpensive hotels.

The largest of these, **VILLERS-SUR-MER**, is noteworthy both for straddling the Greenwich Meridian, and for the giant topiary brontosaurus, complete with calf, which stalks the little roundabout marking the western end of the beach. The venerable *Hôtel Outre-Mer*, nearby at 1 rue du Maréchal-Leclerc (Ⓣ02.31.87.04.64, Ⓦwww.hoteloutremer.com; ⑥), has been entirely refurbished, and each of its bedrooms (some of which have sea-view balconies) decorated in a distinctive, contemporary colour scheme. Downstairs they have a tearoom rather than a restaurant, which stays open until 10.30pm in summer and occasionally features jazz bands. The meridian, incidentally, runs right through the three-star local **campsite**, *Camping de Bellevue* (Ⓣ02.31.87.05.21, Ⓦcamping-bellevue.com; closed Nov–March).

Houlgate

A hundred years ago, **HOULGATE**, 7km west of Villers-sur-mer, was every bit as glamorous and sophisticated as its neighbours. What makes it different today is that it has barely changed since then. Its long straight beach remains lined by a stately procession of ornate Victorian villas, with what few commercial enterprises the town supports confined to the narrow parallel street, the **rue des Bains**, 50m inland. As a result, Houlgate is the most relaxed of the local resorts, ideal if you're looking for a peaceful family break where the only stress is deciding whether to paddle or play mini-golf.

So long as you keep an eye on the tides, it's possible to walk between Villers and Houlgate along the foot of the **Vaches Noires** (Black Cows) cliffs, which force the main road at this point up and away from the sea. However, industrial Le Havre is a bit too visible across the water for it to be an especially picturesque stroll.

Practicalities

Houlgate's **tourist office** is set back from the sea at the eastern end of town, at 10 bd des Belges (Easter–June & Sept Mon–Sat 10am–1pm & 2–6pm, Sun 10.30am–1pm & 2–4pm; July & Aug daily 10am–1pm & 2–6.30pm; Nov–Easter Mon–Sat 10am–1pm & 2–6pm; ⓣ02.31.24.34.79, ⓦwww.ville-houlgate.fr). The *Hostellerie Normande*, just off the rue des Bains at 11 rue E-Deschanel (ⓣ02.31.24.85.50, whotel-houlgate.com; ❹), is a pretty but rather impersonal little **hotel** covered with ivy and creeping flowers, with a €16.50 lunch menu on which you can follow fish soup with *moules frites* or tripe. Nearby, at 17 rue des Bains, rooms at the more formal but friendlier red-brick *Le 1900* (ⓣ02.31.28.77.77, whotel-1900.fr; ❸) offer varying levels of comfort, and dinner menus in the glassed-in Belle É-poque bistro start at €22.

Set well back from the corniche road above the cliffs east of town, *La Ferme Auberge des Aulnettes* (ⓣ02.31.28.00.28, ⓦlafermedesaulnettes.fr; ❸; closed Dec & Jan) is a lovely half-timbered country house in pleasant gardens, where the cheapest rooms have a shower but share a WC, and there's a good restaurant with outdoor seating, serving menus from €18.

Dives

Immediately west of Houlgate, the main D513 is forced to detour away from the open sea when it reaches the mouth of the River Divette. Just 1km along, the venerable little port of **DIVES** was the spot from which William the Conqueror sailed for Hastings, by way of St-Valery; contemporary chronicles tell of vast stockpiles of supplies accumulating on the beach in the days preceding the invasion. Now, like Honfleur, pushed well back from the sea, Dives is older and less commercialized than Cabourg, its haughty aristocratic neighbour across the river.

A lively **Saturday market** focuses around the ancient wooden *halles*, tucked away south of the main through road. The steep tiled roof of the *halles* must be five times the height of its walls, and its venerable weather-beaten timbers are held together by tight metal bands; it's crammed with mouthwatering delicacies and Norman specialities, while more mundane produce and imported jeans are sold in the square alongside and up and down the narrow streets. The town hosts a **puppet festival** in early August.

Dives is home to a large Étap **hotel**, on voie nouvelle de Port-Guillaume (ⓣ08.92.68.08.54, ⓦetaphotel.com; ❷), while the peaceful, attractive *Camping du Golf* (ⓣ02.31.24.73.09, ⓦcampingdugolf.com; closed late Sept to mid-April), is tucked into the woods 2km inland, off the route du Lisieux.

Cabourg

CABOURG is not so much a seaside resort as an exercise in applied geometry, created at much the same time as Deauville for the same elderly clientele. There's an awful lot of town planning, but not really any town.

At the centre of the straightest promenade in France, the **Grand Hôtel**, which once regularly accommodated Marcel Proust (see box opposite) looks out towards the sea, while behind it the crescent that defines the formal **Jardins du Casino** is the first of several concentric crescents, spreading out like ripples and lined with large, placid, undistinguished houses. Cabourg makes an unlikely twin town for the raucous gambling resort of Atlantic City, New Jersey; for example, notices request that you "avoid noise on the beach", where picnicking is forbidden.

Proust at the Grand Hôtel, Cabourg

As both child and adult, between 1881 and 1914, **Marcel Proust** stayed repeatedly at the *Grand Hôtel* in Cabourg. The town is the "Balbec" of *Du Côté de Chez Swann*, and the hotel itself – now officially located on the promenade Marcel-Proust – thrives on its Proustian connection. All guests are served with a *madeleine* for breakfast, and you can even sleep in Proust's own room, meticulously refurbished in line with the author's descriptions. The main dining room, which has a superb sea view, is now called *Le Balbec*. The ambivalent Proust referred to it as "the aquarium"; each night locals would press their faces to its window in wonder at the luxurious life within, "as extraordinary to the poor as the life of strange fishes or molluscs".

Practicalities

Trains run all the way from Paris-Gare-St-Lazare, via Trouville-Deauville, to the **gare SNCF** that Cabourg shares with Dives (see opposite) every day in July and August, and otherwise at weekends only. Cabourg is also on the Caen–Honfleur **bus** route, #20.

Cabourg's **tourist office** is in the Casino gardens (May–June & Sept–Oct Mon–Sat 10am–12.30pm & 2–5.30pm, Sun 10am–noon & 2–4pm; July & Aug daily 9.30am–7pm; Nov–April Mon & Wed–Sat 10am–12.30pm & 2–5.30pm, Sun 10am–noon & 2–4pm; ⓣ02.31.06.20.00, ⓦwww.cabourg.net). The two best-value **hotels**, both set back a few minutes' walk from the sea, are the central, half-timbered *Hôtel de Paris*, on Cabourg's only commercial (semi-pedestrianized) street at 39 av de la Mer (ⓣ02.31.91.31.34, ⓦwww.hotel-de-paris-cabourg.fr; ❹; closed Jan), which has no restaurant, and the quieter *Oie qui Fume*, 18 av de la Brèche-Buhot (ⓣ02.31.91.27.79, ⓦcabourg-hotel.fr; ❺), 100m back from the sea on a peaceful road half a dozen streets west. If money is no object, you can always stay in the famous seafront *Grand Hôtel Mercure*, promenade Marcel-Proust (ⓣ02.31.91.01.79, ⓦmercure.com; ❽), where both the views and the prices are tremendous, and you can even stay in Proust's own room.

Caen

Appropriately enough for a city that has been fought over throughout its long history, the name of **CAEN**, capital and largest city of Basse Normandie, originally came from a Celtic word meaning "battlefield". This site was first fortified in 1060 by **William the Conqueror**, because the navigable River Orne afforded safe access to the Channel. Over the ensuing centuries Caen repeatedly changed hands, and was twice sacked by the English. It was Henry VI of England who founded the university here in 1432, but Caen has been French since Charles VII took it back in 1450.

The modern city began to take shape when a canal to the sea was completed in 1850, running parallel to the heavily silted Orne. At the same time, the Bassin St-Pierre was built, creating a central marina, and the smaller River Odon was covered over. **World War II**, however, devastated the city. It was the prime target of the Allied invasion in June 1944, and historians still argue as to quite why it took so long to capture. The "Battle of Caen" lasted two full months – even once the Canadians had entered the city, four weeks after D-Day, the southern bank of the river remained in enemy hands. Three-quarters of the town had to be destroyed before they were finally dislodged.

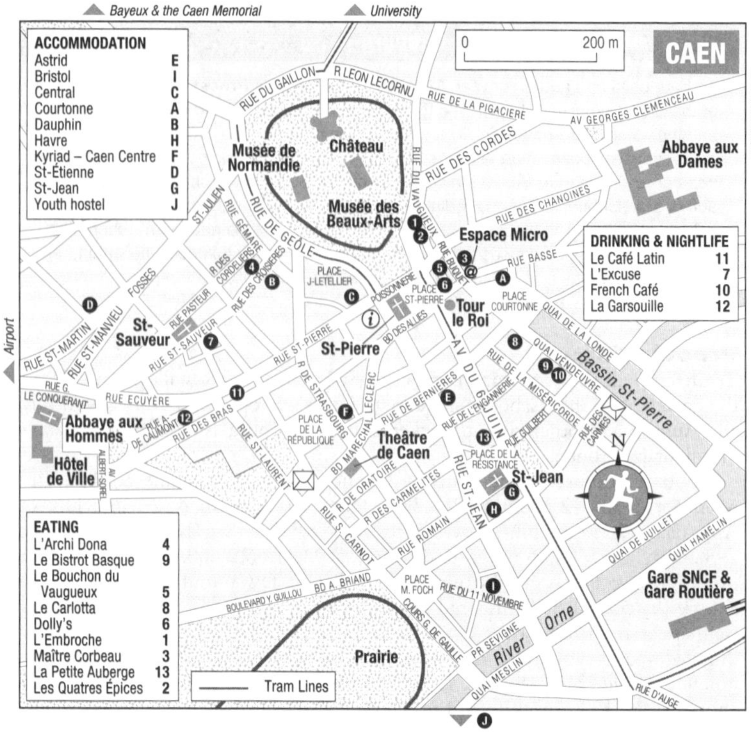

Although few visitors spend much time in Caen – it's the largest city near the Landing Beaches, but there's plenty of accommodation along the coast – it remains in parts highly impressive. Its central feature is a ring of ramparts that no longer has a castle to protect, and, though there are the scattered spires and buttresses of two abbeys and eight old churches, roads and roundabouts fill the wide spaces where prewar houses stood. Approaches are along thunderous highways through industrial suburbs, now prospering thanks to an influx of high-tech newcomers.

Arrival, information and tours

Caen's small **airport** is 7km west on the D9, just outside **Carpiquet** (☎02.31.71.20.10). **Buses** (€1.30) connect with all flights, taking 25 minutes to run to and from the Tour-le-Roi stop in place Courtonne.

The **gare SNCF** is 1km south of the town centre across the river, with the **gare routière** alongside. Local **buses** and **trams** are run by TWISTO (☎02.31.15.55.55, ⓦtwisto.fr), which has ticket and information centres at 15 rue de Geôle (just north of the tourist office), and on boulevard Maréchal-Leclerc. One-way journeys cost €1.20, and a 24-hour pass €3.55. The main tram

The Brittany Ferries service from Portsmouth that's promoted as sailing to Caen in fact docks at **Ouistreham**, 15km north (see p.123). Buses from Caen's *gare routière* connect with each sailing, and Bus Verts' express bus #1 runs the same route.

route connects the southern and northern suburbs, running through the heart of the city from the *gare SNCF* up avenue de 6-Juin to the university and beyond.

Caen's **tourist office** is on place St-Pierre across from the church of St-Pierre (April–June & Sept Mon–Sat 9.30am–6.30pm, Sun 10am–1pm; July & Aug Mon–Sat 9am–6pm, Sun 10am–1pm; Oct–March Mon–Sat 9.30am–1pm & 2–6pm; ⓣ02.31.27.14.14, ⓦwww.tourisme.caen.fr). It's worth dropping in to pick up the *Passe Tourisme*, a booklet filled with discount coupons for sights in and around Caen.

In July and August, the tourist office offers excellent €6 **guided tours**, unfortunately in French only, that focus mainly on William the Conqueror's connections with Caen. Between mid-July and late August, they also put on "dramatized visits", in which actors perform short historical sketches (again in French only) at appropriate locations (Château: Wed, Fri & Sun 5pm; Abbaye aux Dames: Thurs & Sat 9pm; Abbaye aux Hommes: Wed & Fri 9pm; €13).

Accommodation

Caen has a great number of **hotels**, though as so often in Normandy's bomb-damaged cities, few could be called attractive; even those that advertise their antiquity tend to have been totally rebuilt. They're not particularly concentrated in any one area, though you'll find clusters just west of the château and tourist office – convenient for motorists heading to or from the ferry – as well as around the pleasure port, and a handful facing the *gare SNCF*. Charmless motel-type places are also scattered on the ring road around town. Few hotels have their own restaurants.

Hotels

Astrid 39 rue de Bernières ⓣ02.31.85.48.67, ⓦhotel_astrid.club.fr. Recently renovated two-star hotel with spacious rooms but rather compact bathrooms. The friendly staff provide tourist information. ❷

Bristol 31 rue du 11-Novembre ⓣ02.31.84.59.76, ⓦwww.hotelbristolcaen.com. Efficient, spruce, friendly and inexpensive hotel, an easy walk across the river from the train station. ❸

Central 23 pl J. Letellier ⓣ02.31.86.18.52, ⓦwww.centralhotel-caen.com. This budget hotel is not all that quiet, but it's very central. The cheapest rooms have showers but not toilets, while the balconies of the higher ones have good views of the château. ❶

Courtonne 5 rue des Prairies St-Gilles ⓣ02.31.93.47.83, ⓦhotelcourtonne.com. Welcoming, modernized hotel overlooking the place Courtonne and the pleasure port, though the building is so narrow it's easy to miss. All rooms have bath or shower, phone and TV. ❸

Dauphin 29 rue Gémare ⓣ02.31.86.22.26, ⓦwww.le-dauphin-normandie.com. Upmarket Best Western hotel, tucked away behind the tourist office. Part of it was a priory during the eighteenth century, not that you'd guess. The public areas are impressive, while the rooms are comfortable but relatively compact, at least at the lower end of the price scale. Sauna and fitness facilities plus a grand restaurant, with a €16.50 weekday dinner menu; weekend menus €33 and €56 (restaurant closed Sat lunch & Sun all year, and open for dinner only June–Sept). ❺

Havre 11 rue du Havre ⓣ02.31.86.19.80, ⓦwww.hotelduhavre.com. Modern, cosy, welcoming and very good-value budget hotel, a block south of St-Jean church close to the trams, with free parking. ❷

Kyriad – Caen Centre I pl de la République ⓣ02.31.86.55.33, ⓦwww.hotel-caen-centre.com. Large, comfortable, spacious and very central chain hotel, with no restaurant but copious buffet breakfasts. There's an underground car park, but on-street parking is free at weekends. ❹

St-Étienne 2 rue de l'Académie ⓣ02.31.86.35.82, ⓦhotel-saint-etienne.com. Friendly budget hotel housed a venerable stone house in the St-Martin district, not far from the Abbaye des Hommes (room 8 has views). The cheapest rooms share bathrooms; en-suite ones cost little more. ❶

St-Jean 20 rue des Martyrs ⓣ02.31.86.23.35. Simple but well-equipped rooms – all have shower or bath – facing St-Jean church across from the *Petite Auberge* restaurant (see p.117). Free parking. ❷

Hostel

HI hostel Foyer Robert-Remé, 68bis rue E.-Restout, Grâce-de-Dieu ⓣ02.31.52.19.96. Lively and welcoming hostel, situated in an otherwise sleepy area about 500m southwest of the *gare SNCF*. Beds in both four-bed dorms or two-bed private rooms cost €14 per person. Reception open 5–9pm. Open June–Sept.

The City

A virtue was made of the postwar necessity of clearing away the rubble of Caen's medieval houses, which formerly pressed up against its ancient **château ramparts**. The resulting open green space has left those walls fully visible for the first time in centuries. In turn, walking the circuit of the ramparts gives a good overview of the city, with a particularly fine prospect of the reconstructed fourteenth-century facade of the nearby church of **St-Pierre**.

The château and around

Within the castle walls, it's possible to visit the former **Exchequer** – dating from shortly after the Norman Conquest of England, it hosted a banquet thrown by Richard the Lionheart en route to the Crusades – and inspect a garden that has been replanted with the herbs and medicinal plants that would have been cultivated here during the Middle Ages.

Also inside the castle precinct, though in new rather than original structures, are two **museums**. Most visitors will probably prefer the **Beaux Arts**, housed in a light 1960s stone building, kept deliberately low to avoid topping the castle walls (daily except Tues 9.30am–6pm; permanent collection free, special exhibitions €3 or €5). Its upstairs galleries trace a potted history of European art from Renaissance Italy through such Dutch masters as Bruegel the Younger up to grand portraits from eighteenth-century France. Downstairs brings things up to date with a diverse range of twentieth-century and contemporary art – though there are few big-name works – as well as paintings by Monet, Bonnard and Gustave Doré (represented by a spectacular Scottish landscape). The other museum, the **Musée de Normandie** (June–Sept daily 9.30am–6pm, Oct–May daily except Tues 9.30am–6pm; permanent collection free, special exhibitions €3 or €5), provides a surprisingly cursory overview of Norman history, ranging from archeological finds like stone tools from the megalithic period and glass jewellery from Gallo-Roman Rouen to artefacts from the Industrial Revolution. It also hosts two or three temporary exhibitions per year, covering particular themes in much greater detail.

Just north of the château lies the complex of **university** buildings, originally founded in 1432 by Henry VI of England, and now the proud home of the largest nuclear particle accelerator in Europe. The only reason for tourists to pass this way is to see the large-scale **model of Ancient Rome**, as it stood around 300 AD, which has been laid out in the Maison de la Recherche en Sciences Humaines (Sept–June only Mon–Fri 8am–7pm, free; also a 20min "son et lumière" show Mon–Fri 8.30am–12.30pm & 1.30–4pm, €2; ⓦwww.unicaen.fr/rome).

The Abbayes

When William the Conqueror married Mathilda in Eu (see p.59), in 1051, both incurred excommunication. Historians argue as to the precise nature of their offence – they may have been distant cousins – but Pope Nicholas II only agreed to sanction their marriage and readmit them to the church in 1059 upon the solemn vow that each would build an abbey in Caen. William's, the **Abbaye aux Hommes** west of the city centre, is focused on the Romanesque church known as the Abbatiale St-Étienne (Mon–Sat 8.30am–12.30pm &

1.30–7pm, Sun 8.30am–12.30pm & 2.30–7pm; free). The abbey was originally designed to hold William's tomb, but his burial here, in 1087, was hopelessly undignified. The funeral procession first caught fire and was then held to ransom, as various factions squabbled over his rotting corpse for any spoils they could grab. A further interruption came when a man halted the service to object that the grave had been constructed without compensation on the site of his family house, and the assembled nobles had to pay him off before William could finally be laid to rest. His tomb still occupies pride of place in front of the main altar, though as the church was ransacked both by Protestants in 1562 and during the Revolution, it now holds at most a solitary thighbone rescued from the river. Still, the building itself serves as a wonderful monument and is also home to a fine collection of seventeenth- to nineteenth-century paintings. As you explore, look out for the huge wooden clock to the left of the altar. To see the entire complex rather than just the church, you have to join one of the **guided tours** that leave from the **Hôtel de Ville** alongside, which is housed in what used to be its convent buildings (daily 9.30am, 11am, 2.30pm & 4pm; 1hr 15min; €2.40, free on Sun).

William's queen, Mathilda, lies across town in the **Abbaye aux Dames** at the end of rue des Chanoines. She had commissioned the building of the abbey church, La Trinité, well before the Conquest. It's starkly impressive, with a gloomy pillared crypt, superb stained glass behind the altar, and odd sculptural details like the fish curled up in the holy-water stoup (daily 2–5.30pm; guided tours 2.30pm & 4pm; free).

The Pleasure Port

The nineteenth-century **Bassin St-Pierre**, a short walk south of the Abbaye aux Dames, now serves as Caen's **pleasure port**, and marks the end of the canal that links the city to the sea. In summer, when this is one of the liveliest areas in town, a pleasure boat, the *Hastings*, sets off four times daily on **cruises** from the quai Vendeuvre, up to the sea at Ouistreham and back (9am, 12.15pm, 3.15pm & either 7pm or 7.30pm; 2hr 30min; €15, one-way trip €10; ⓣ02.31.34.00.00, ⓦwww.bateau-hastings.com).

▲ The Abbaye aux Hommes, Caen

The Caen Memorial

The **Caen Memorial** (late Jan to mid-Feb & mid-Nov to early Jan daily except Mon 9.30am–6pm; mid-Feb to mid-Nov daily 9am–7pm; closed three weeks in Jan; last entry 1hr 15min before closing time; March–Sept €16.50, Oct–Feb €16; ⓣ02.31.06.06.45, ⓦwww.memorial-caen.fr) is a war museum with a big and welcome difference, in that it proclaims itself to be a "Museum for Peace". Located on a plateau named after General Eisenhower, just north of Caen at the end of avenue Marshal-Montgomery (it's the terminus of bus route #2 from Tour le Roi, and offers plenty of parking), it was funded by the governments of the US, Britain, Canada, Germany, Poland, the former Czechoslovakia and the former USSR, as well as France, and stands immediately above the headquarters used by the German army during June and July 1944. While its brief extends way beyond simply covering the Battle of Normandy, it does organize very detailed tours of the Landing Beaches (see p.123).

All visitors to the ultramodern museum itself have to follow a prescribed route, which, with a slightly heavy-handed literalism, leads on a downwards spiral from World War I and the Treaty of Versailles towards the maelstrom of World War II. Hitler's image recurs with increasing size and frequency on screens beside you as the events of the 1920s and 1930s are recounted.

The war is superbly documented, with a greater emphasis on the minutiae of everyday life in occupied France than on military technology. Nothing is glossed over in the attempt to provide a fully rounded picture of the nation under occupation and at war; the collaborationist Vichy government, for example, is set in its context without being excused. Secret Nazi reports show how Resistance activity in Normandy grew as the war continued, and what reprisals were taken.

Visits to the memorial's **upper section** culminate with two **films** in separate auditoriums. The first, a harrowing account of D-Day and the ensuing battle to liberate Normandy, starts with the screen split in two to show, on one side, the preparations of the Allied forces on the eve of the invasion and, on the other, those of the Germans, then traces the course of the Battle of Normandy. In keeping with the Memorial's theme of peace and reconciliation, the second film, *Espérance* (hope) is a mosaic of the world's problems since World War II. Both films depend on visual stimuli more than words, while most of the captions throughout the museum, though not always the written exhibits themselves, are well translated into English.

The former German bunkers at the foot of the hillside, reached by a short lift ride from the Memorial proper, have been refurbished as the **Nobel Peace Prizewinners' Gallery**. Portraits and short essays commemorate each recipient, and also point out notable omissions from the list, such as Mahatma Gandhi. Outside, formal **gardens** honour the various Allied nations.

All in all, this museum creates something new in a genre which can occasionally seem morally suspect, and the display cannot be recommended too highly for anyone with a serious interest in the war and its lasting legacy. Allow at least two hours for a visit, as the films alone occupy a whole hour. In summer, especially when the weather is not so good, queues can be very long; there's a good-value self-service restaurant upstairs.

Eating

The centre of Caen offers two major areas for **eating**. The attractive pedestrianized **quartier Vaugueux** (around rue du Vaugueux) features cosmopolitan restaurants covering most current world cuisines, from couscous to curry, pizzas to crêpes, and even one from the distant past: *À l'Âge de Pierre* prepares "stone age" food by cooking slabs of horse meat on super-heated stones. Streets such as rue des Croisiers and rue Gémare off **rue de Geôle**, near the western ramparts, on the other hand, house rather more traditional French restaurants.

L'Archi Dona 8 rue des Croisiers ⓣ02.31.85.30.30. This classy and atmospheric restaurant belies its stately setting by serving delightfully fresh Mediterranean-influenced cuisine, ranging from simple entrée-plus-dessert meals at €14 up to the €33 "seduction" menu. Closed Sun, Mon & three weeks in Aug.

Le Bistrot Basque 24 quai Vendeuvre ⓣ02.31.38.21.26, ⓦbistrot-basque.com. Atmospheric restaurant with a bright interior opposite the pleasure port, serving tasty Basque-influenced cooking, such as grilled cod with chorizo, with lunch menus from €14. Closed Sun lunch.

Le Bouchon du Vaugueux 12 rue du Graindorge ⓣ02.31.44.26.26. Intimate little brasserie in the Vaugueux quarter, offering well-prepared French classics on just two menus, at €18 and €26. Closed Mon, Wed & Sun, plus first three weeks of Aug.

Le Carlotta 16 quai Vendeuvre ⓣ02.31.86.68.99, ⓦwww.lecarlotta.fr. Smart, busy, fashionable Paris-style brasserie beside the pleasure port, which serves good Norman cooking both à la carte and on menus at €23 (not Sat), €27 and €36. Closed Sun.

Dolly's 18 av de la Libération ⓣ02.31.94.03.29. Very popular, very central, English-style café, serving not only tea and coffee but good salads, with lots of vegetarian options, and Anglophile snacks like fish'n'chips for €11.50. Closed Mon, plus two weeks in Feb & two weeks in July.

L'Embroche 17 rue Porte au Berger ⓣ02.31.93.71.31. Cosy little place in a busy restaurant district, where the open kitchen whips up simple regional specialities in full view of appreciative diners, with lunch from €19 and dinner from €25. Closed Sat lunch, Sun & Mon lunch.

Maître Corbeau 8 rue Buquet ⓣ02.31.93.93.00. Large, eccentric restaurant with an entirely cheese-related menu featuring fondue, *raclette, tartiflette* to name but a few. The kitsch decor ties in with the theme too – cow print and dairy iconography feature strongly. A typical fondue costs around €14, while non-fondue menus start from €19. Closed Sat lunch, Sun, Mon lunch & three weeks in Aug.

La Petite Auberge 17 rue des Équipes-d'Urgence ⓣ02.31.86.43.30. Simple, attractive restaurant, with a nice view of the St-Jean church from the green-timber gallery at the front. Very well-priced Norman specialities served on a €13.50 menu (daily except Sat eve) that doesn't force you to eat tripe, or a wide-ranging €23 one. Closed Sun, Mon & first three weeks of Aug.

Les Quatres Épices 25 rue Porte-au-Berger ⓣ02.31.93.40.41. Lively West African restaurant, just off rue du Vaugueux. Everything is à la carte – prawns with sweet potato for €19.50, grilled fish with ginger and spices for €16.50, plus plantains and meat galore – and African music plays nonstop.

Nightlife and entertainment

Caen represents your best chance in Lower Normandy of finding something to do of an evening. The pleasure port, and quai Vendeuvre in particular, is absolutely packed with lively **bars**, pubs and clubs, and there's another concentration in the town centre a few hundred metres west. The **Théâtre de Caen**, at 135 bd Maréchal-Leclerc (ⓣ02.31.30.48.00, ⓦwww.theatre.caen.fr; closed July & Aug), offers a complete programme of music, dance and drama, while several **cinemas** show the latest films.

Bars and clubs

Le Café Latin 135 rue St-Pierre ⓣ02.31.85.26.36. Convivial, invariably packed tapas bar in the town centre. Upstairs the theme of the decor is Mexican; downstairs, both inside and on the street terrace, it is much more French. The huge plates of tapas are very good and the music is not so loud as to drown out conversation. Mon–Sat 10am–1am.

L'Excuse 20 rue Vauquelin ⓣ02.31.38.80.89. Tiny bar in a side street next to St-Sauveur church, primarily lesbian, but not off-limits to those of other persuasions. The music tends to be loud, no doubt in an attempt to encourage patrons to grace the small dance floor. Wed–Sat 11pm–3am.

French Café 32 quai Vendeuvre ⓣ02.31.50.10.02. Trendy, antique-filled bar facing the pleasure port alongside the *Carré* nightclub (run by the same management), serving cocktails and reasonable tapas, all you can eat on some evenings. A lot of 1980s music and rock, with the occasional French golden oldie thrown in for good measure. Daily except Mon 7pm–3am.

La Garsouille 11–13 rue Arcisse-de-Caumont ⓣ02.31.86.80.27. Hip, happening bar that also hosts live music and movie nights. Mon–Sat 4pm–1am.

Shopping

Most of central Caen is taken up with busy modern shopping developments and pedestrian precincts, where the cafés are distinguished by such names as *Fast Food Glamour Vault*. The shops are good, possibly the best in Normandy or Brittany, if Parisian style is what you're after. Outlets of the big Parisian **department stores** – and of the aristocrats' grocers, Hédiard, in the Cours des Halles – are here, along with good local rivals. Rue Écuyère has a fine assortment of shops full of unusual and cheap oddments, **antiques**, stuff for collectors and jokes.

The main city **market** takes place on Sunday, filling place Courtonne by the Bassin St-Pierre, while another large one spreads along both sides of Fossés St-Julien every Friday. If you're looking for **books**, **CDs** or **tickets** for local events, call in at the branch of FNAC (closed Sun; ⓣ02.31.02.00.20) in the Centre Paul-Doumer, on the corner of rue Doumer and rue Bras.

Listings

Car rental Avis (ⓣ08.20.61.16.81); Europcar (ⓣ08.25.89.54.70); Hertz (ⓣ02.31.84.64.50) and Sixt (ⓣ02.31.83.70.47) provide car rental both at the airport and in town.

Cinemas Café des Images, 4 square du Théâtre, Hérouville ⓣ02.31.45.34.70 (ⓦwww.cafedes images.fr); Pathé Lumière, 15 bd Maréchal-Leclerc ⓣ08.92.69.66.96; Pathé Malherbe, 55 rue des Jacobins ⓣ08.36.68.22.88; Cinéma Lux, 6 av Ste-Thérèse ⓣ02.31.82.29.87 (ⓦwww .cinemalux.org).

Cycle rental From the tourist office; €1.50 per hour, €10 per day.

Hospitals C.H.U. av Côte de Nacre ⓣ02.31.06.31.06; C.H.R. av Georges-Clemenceau ⓣ02.31.27.27.27.

Internet access *Espace Micro*, a "cyber bistro" on pl Courtonne at 1 rue Basse ⓣ02.31.53.68.68 (Mon–Fri 10am–9pm, Sat 10am–10pm, Sun 10.30am–1.30pm & 3–9pm; €3.20 per hr).

Launderette Lavomatique, rue Écuyère (daily 7am–8pm).

Pharmacie Grande Pharmacie du Progrès, 2 bd des Alliés ⓣ02.31.15.50.94 (Mon–Sat 8am–8pm).

Post office pl Gambetta; ⓣ02.31.39.35.76 (Mon–Fri 8am–7pm, Sat 8.30am–12.30pm).

Swimming pools Chemin Vert, 42 rue Champagne ⓣ02.31.73.08.79; Stade Nautique, av Albert-Sorel ⓣ02.31.30.47.47.

Bayeux

BAYEUX, with its perfectly preserved medieval ensemble, magnificent **cathedral** and world-famous **tapestry**, is 23km west of Caen – a mere twenty-minute train ride. It's a smaller and much more intimate city, and, despite the large crowds of summer tourists, a far more enjoyable place to visit. Just 10km in from the coast, Bayeux was the first French city to be liberated in 1944, the day after the D-Day landings. It was occupied so quickly – before the Germans had got over their surprise – that it escaped serious damage, and briefly became capital of Free France.

Arrival and information

Bayeux's **gare SNCF** is fifteen minutes' walk southeast of the town centre, just outside the "ring road", while **buses** stop both there and on the other side of town, on the north side of place St-Patrice.

The **tourist office** stands in the very centre of town, in what used to be the fish market on the arched pont St-Jean (Jan–March & Nov–Dec Mon–Sat 9.30am–12.30pm & 2–5.30pm; April–May & Sept–Oct daily 9.30am–12.30pm

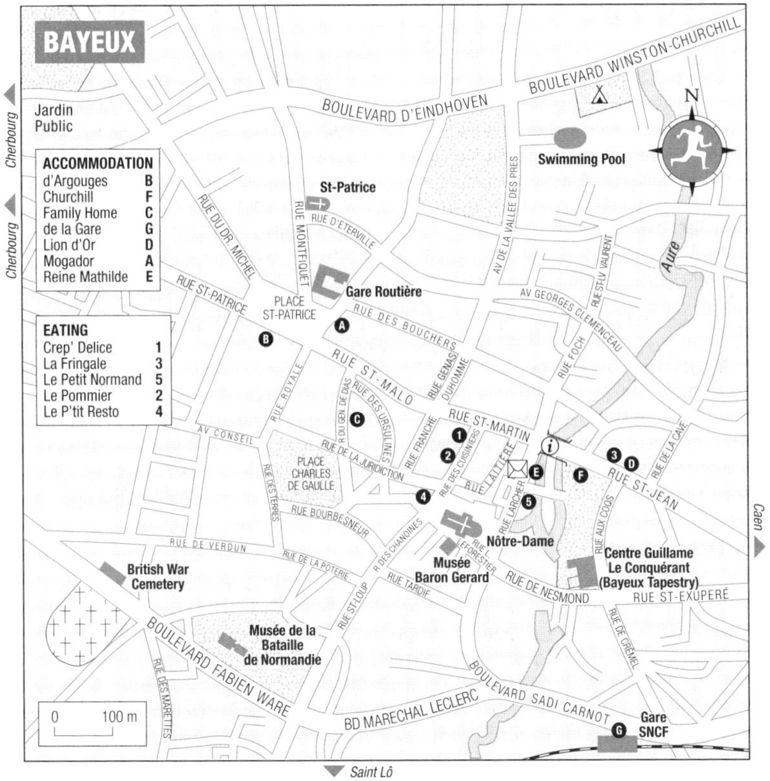

& 2–6pm; June–Aug Mon–Sat 9am–7pm, Sun 9am–1pm & 2–6pm; ⓣ02.31.51.28.28, ⓦbessin-normandie.fr).

Internet access is available at the **post office**, just around the corner at 14 rue Larcher (Mon–Fri 8.15am–6.30pm, Sat 8.15am–noon; ⓣ02.31.51.24.90). **Bicycles** can be rented from the *Family Home* (see below), or Vélos Location, opposite the tourist office (daily 8am–8.30pm; ⓣ02.31.92.89.16).

Accommodation

As one of Normandy's most important tourist destinations, Bayeux is well equipped with accommodation, though it has to be said that its **hotels** tend to be more expensive than elsewhere.

Hotels

d'Argouges 21 rue St-Patrice ⓣ02.31.92.88.86, ⓦhotel-dargouges.com. Quiet, central and very stylish eighteenth-century building, with an imposing courtyard entered via an archway on the west side of place St-Patrice, and a well-kept garden around the back. Several rooms are very grand, with magnificent exposed wooden beams; all have bath plus shower. No restaurant. ⑥

Churchill 14–16 rue St-Jean ⓣ02.31.21.31.80, ⓦhotel-churchill.fr. Perfectly situated in the heart of the town, with its own free parking, this beautifully furnished 32-room hotel has no restaurant, but offers personal and friendly service. Closed Dec–Feb. ⑥

Family Home 39 rue du Général de Dias ⓣ02.31.92.15.22, ⓦbayeux-familyhome.com. Travellers disagree strongly as to the merits of this hostel, in a central seventeenth-century house.

Some are put off by the staff's minimal English, frequent disappearing acts, and cavalier attitude to reservations; others couldn't imagine a friendlier atmosphere. Rates – dorm beds €20, private doubles €30 – include breakfast. Communal dinners, served at 7.30pm nightly, cost €12 per person. They also rent bikes and can find you a bed in their other property, 1km from the centre, if the *Family Home* is full. ❶

de la Gare 26 pl de la Gare ⓣ02.31.92.10.70. Old but perfectly adequate basic hotel, with a simple brasserie, beside the station, on the ring road fifteen minutes' walk from the cathedral. Tours of D-Day beaches arranged through Normandy Tours (see p.123), who are based here but offer tours to guests and non-guests alike. ❶

Lion d'Or 71 rue St-Jean ⓣ02.31.92.06.90, ⓦliondor-bayeux.fr. Grand old coaching inn, dating from 1734 and affiliated to the "Relais du Silence" organization, that's set back behind a courtyard just beyond the pedestrianized section of rue St-Jean. The rooms themselves are brighter and newer than the exterior suggests; the one snag is that there's no parking. Closed mid-Dec to late Jan. Menus from €38, closed for lunch on Mon, Tues & Sat. ❻

Mogodor 20 rue Chartier ⓣ02.31.92.24.58, ⓔhotel.mogador@orange. Friendly little hotel facing Bayeux's main square; the rooms are simple but very presentable, with the quieter ones overlooking the inner courtyard. ❸

Reine Mathilde 23 rue Larcher ⓣ02.31.92.08.13, ⓦhotel-reinemathilde.com. Simple but well-equipped en-suite rooms backing onto the canal, between the tapestry and the cathedral. There's a nice open-air brasserie/crêperie downstairs. Closed Dec–Feb. ❸

Campsite

Camping Municipal bd d'Eindhoven ⓣ02.31.92.08.43. Large, three-star campsite on the northern ring road (RN13) near the river – and the local sewage works. Closed Oct–April.

The Town

The core of Bayeux is surprisingly small. It's basically oriented to either side of one long street, which starts from the place St-Patrice in the west (scene of a Saturday market). As the **rue St-Malo** and **rue St-Martin**, this is lined with the busy little shops of a typical Norman town; it then crosses the attractive canalized River Aure, passing the tourist office and the old watermill, Moulin Crocquevieille, to become **rue St-Jean** (which is pedestrianized in summer) on the east side. Filled with cafés, brasseries, restaurants and souvenir shops, it also becomes the site of a market on Wednesdays.

Both Bayeux's principal attractions lie south of this main thoroughfare. The **Cathédrale Notre Dame** is in an attractive tangle of old streets, best reached along rue des Cuisiniers – look out for the magnificent fourteenth-century half-timbered house that overhangs the street at no. 1, on the corner with rue St-Martin – while the **tapestry** is on the other side of the river.

The Bayeux Tapestry

The extraordinary **Bayeux Tapestry**, also known to the French as the *Tapisserie de la Reine Mathilde*, is housed in an impressive eighteenth-century seminary on rue de Nesmond, remodelled as the **Centre Guillaume le Conquérant** (daily: mid-March to April & Sept to early Nov 9am–6.30pm; May–Aug 9am–7pm; early Nov to mid-March 9.30am–12.30pm & 2–6pm; last admission 45min before closing; €7.80; ⓦtapisserie-bayeux.fr).

Created over nine centuries ago, this seventy-metre strip of linen recounts the story of the Norman Conquest of England. The brilliance of its coloured wools has barely faded, and the tale is enlivened throughout with scenes of medieval life, popular fables and mythical beasts. Technically, it's not really a tapestry at all, but an embroidery; the skill of its draughtsmanship, and the sheer vigour and detail, are stunning. The work is thought to have been carried out by nuns in England, commissioned by Bishop Oddo, William's half-brother, in time for the inauguration of Bayeux Cathedral in 1077.

The tapestry looks, and reads, like a modern comic strip. While it's generally considered to be historically accurate, William's justification for his invasion –

that during an enforced sojourn after he was rescued by William following a shipwreck on the Normandy coast, Harold had sworn to accept him as King of England – remains in dispute. In the tapestry itself, Harold is every inch the villain, with his dastardly little moustache and shifty eyes. At the point when he breaks his oath and seizes the throne, Harold looks extremely pleased with himself; however, his comeuppance swiftly follows, as William crosses the Channel and defeats the English armies at Hastings.

Visits are well planned and highly atmospheric, if somewhat exhausting. You can't linger over the tapestry for long, which is kept for its preservation under very dim light. However, the display is excellent. First you pass along a photographic replica of the tapestry, with detailed commentaries in both French and English that set the expedition in its historical context, as a continuation in a sense of the Viking raids that had created Normandy a century before. Dioramas and models also cover the aftermath of the conquest of England, which is absent from the tapestry itself.

If you feel you know the 1066 story well enough by now, you can skip the film that follows, which goes over much of the same ground. Beyond this, you finally approach the real thing, which has a strong three-dimensional presence you might not expect from all the flat reproductions.

Although the tapestry makes such an effective piece of propaganda that Napoleon exhibited it in Paris – to show that a successful invasion of England was indeed possible – much of the pleasure of viewing it comes from its incidental vignettes of contemporary life. Only the faintest smattering of Latin is required to be able to follow the captions that accompany each major scene, and in any case, audio headsets offer a concise commentary. The saga comes to an abrupt end immediately after the turmoil, carnage and looting of the Battle of Hastings, and of course the death of Harold (who may or may not be the figure with an arrow in his eye).

Cathédrale Notre Dame

The **Cathédrale Notre Dame** (daily: Jan–March 9am–5pm; April–June & Oct–Dec 9am–6pm; July–Sept 9am–7pm), the first home of the tapestry, is a short and very obvious walk away from its latest resting place. Despite such eighteenth-century vandalism as the fungoid baldachin that flanks the pulpit, Bishop Oddo's original Romanesque plan remains intact, for the most part sensitively merged with Gothic additions. The crypt, entirely original, is particularly wonderful, with its frescoes of angels playing trumpets and bagpipes, looking exhausted by their eternal performance. Along the nave is some tremendous twelfth-century sculpture, and you shouldn't miss the beautifully carved wooden choir stalls. The tiled floor of the chapterhouse features a fifteenth-century maze depicting the road to Jerusalem.

The courtyard that adjoins the northern facade of the cathedral is dominated by the **Liberty Tree**, a 200-year-old plane tree planted with much Revolutionary rejoicing in 1797.

Musée Baron Gerard

The grand Hôtel Doyen, on rue Lambert Forestier on the southern side of the cathedral, is home to the **Musée Baron Gerard** (daily: July & Aug 10am–12.30pm & 2–7pm; Sept–June 10am–12.30pm & 2–6pm; €3.50, or free with tapestry ticket). While it's also used for temporary exhibitions, its primary purpose is to display a large collection of beautifully decorated porcelain and intricate lacework. All of it was donated by local families to the archbishops of Bayeux, with the eponymous baron ranking as the most generous patron of them all. The museum also includes a handful of paintings, including works by Eugène Boudin.

The Musée Mémorial de la Bataille de Normandie

Set behind massive guns, next to the ring road on the southwest side of town, Bayeux's **Musée Mémorial de la Bataille de Normandie** (daily: May–Sept 9.30am–6.30pm; Oct–April 10am–12.30pm & 2–6pm; €6.50) provides a readily accessible, visceral and highly visual, overview of the Battle of Normandy. Rather than endless military hardware, it's filled with colour photos, maps and display panels that trace the development of the campaign, with especially good sections on German counter-attacks and the role of the press. It also includes an account of the career of **General de Gaulle**, who until recently had his own museum in Bayeux to commemorate that this was the first place he landed in Free France, on June 14, 1944. That visit was a day-trip undertaken in the face of opposition from the Allied commanders; his arrival was so unexpected that the first two civilians he encountered, two policemen wheeling their bicycles, failed to recognize him.

The understated and touching **British War Cemetery** stands immediately across the road (see box, p.130).

Eating

Several of Bayeux's hotels have acceptable **restaurants** or brasseries. Otherwise, most restaurants are in the rue St-Jean leading east from the river, or near the main door of the cathedral.

Crep' Delice 16 rue des Cuisiniers ☎02.31.51.71.16. Cheap but chic crêperie serving an imaginative range of savoury *galettes* followed by sweet crêpes.

La Fringale 43 rue St-Jean ☎02.31.21.34.40. The nicest of the many pavement restaurants along rue St-Jean, offering lunch menus from €15.50, and also generous salads and snacks, as well as more formal fish dinners. Closed Wed, plus mid-Dec to mid-Feb.

Le Petit Normand 35 rue Larcher ☎02.31.22.88.66. Below the cathedral, offering good traditional cooking, with seafood specialities and local cider. Lunch menus from €13, dinner from €17. Closed Tues & Wed, plus mid-Dec to Jan.

Le Pommier 38–40 rue des Cuisiniers ☎02.31.21.52.10. Ever-expanding traditional restaurant near the cathedral, with a tiny terrace. Meat- and dairy-rich Norman cuisine on menus from €14 (lunch only) up to €28, including a €23.50 vegetarian option. Closed mid-Dec to mid-Jan.

Le P'tit Resto 2 rue Bienvenue ☎02.31.51.85.40. Tiny old place opposite the cathedral, where the "creative cuisine" extends to veal chop fried in wasabi, and rolled monkfish with tandoori stuffing. Menus from €15 at lunch, €20 at dinner. Closed Sun.

The Invasion Beaches

At dawn on **D-Day**, June 6, 1944, Allied troops landed at points along the Norman coast from the mouth of the Orne to the eastern Cotentin Peninsula. For the most part, the shore consists of innocuous beaches backed by gentle dunes, and yet this foothold in Europe was won at the cost of 100,000 lives. The various beaches are still often referred to by their wartime code names. The British and Commonwealth forces landed on **Sword**, **Juno** and **Gold** beaches between Ouistreham and Arromanches; the Americans, further west on **Omaha** and **Utah** beaches.

That the invasion happened here, and not nearer to Germany, was partly due to the failure of the Canadian raid on Dieppe in 1942, which demonstrated the even more appalling casualties that would have resulted from an assault on a

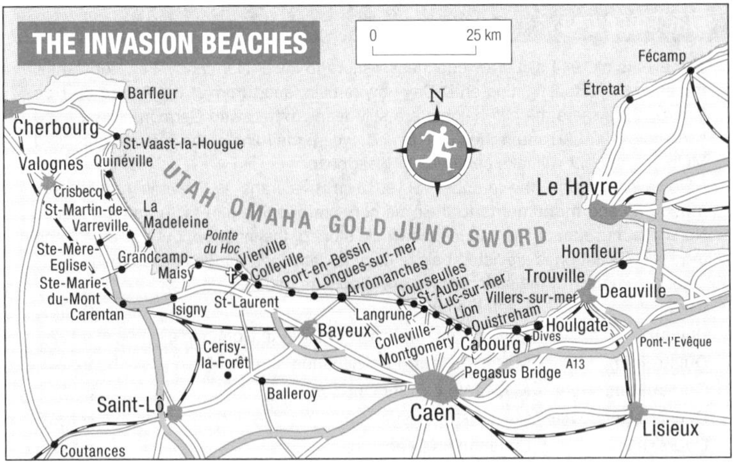

cliff-dominated coastline. The ensuing **Battle of Normandy** killed thousands of civilians and reduced nearly six hundred towns and villages to rubble, but within a week of its eventual conclusion, Paris was liberated.

Even if the events of D-Day are not your primary reason for visiting, the towns and villages offer their own rewards. They are traditional seaside resorts, without the inflated prices or flashiness of the Deauville area – old-fashioned villages, with rows of boarding houses and little wooden bathing huts. And of course the **beaches** themselves are great for young families, though **windsurfing** is better suited to these north-facing resorts than chilly bathing. Attractive individual seaside **hotels** are scattered all along the D-Day coast – typically with simple rooms upstairs above a large glass-fronted sea-view dining room – so ferry passengers have a choice of several Logis de France for a first- or last-night stop.

Bus Verts (Ⓣ08.10.21.42.14, Ⓦwww.busverts.fr) run all along this coast. From Bayeux, bus #75 goes to Arromanches, Courseulles and Ouistreham, and bus #70 to the Pointe du Hoc, the US cemetery at Colleville-sur-mer and Port-en-Bessin. From Caen, bus #30 runs inland to Bayeux, express bus #1 to Ouistreham, and express bus #3 to Courseulles.

The Caen Memorial (see p.116) organizes expensive but informative bilingual **guided tours** of the beaches in small groups of around eight people, with four or five hours on the road and a visit to the Memorial, either at your own pace (€75), or with a guide (€109.50; includes lunch). Other operators offering D-Day **tour**, at prices ranging from €35 for half a day and from €70 for a full day tours, include Normandy Sightseeing Tours (Ⓣ02.31.51.70.52, Ⓦd-daybeaches.com), Victory Tours (Ⓣ02.31.51.98.14, Ⓦvictorytours.com), Battlebus (Ⓣ02.31.22.28.82, Ⓦwww.battlebus.fr), and Normandy Tours (Ⓣ02.31.92.10.70, Ⓦwww.normandy-landing-tour.com).

Ouistreham-Riva Bella

Although **OUISTREHAM-RIVA BELLA**, on the coast 15km north of Caen, has been connected by ferry with Portsmouth, England since 1986, it remains at heart a small seaside village. From the port itself at its eastern end, it's easy to drive straight out of town, on the fast dual carriageway towards Caen.

War Museums

The events of 1944 still draw countless visitors to lower Normandy. Few substantial traces of the actual fighting on D-Day now remain, apart from at the **Pointe du Hoc** (see p.129), where the cliff heights are still deeply pitted with German bunkers and shell-holes, and **Arromanches** (see p.127), where the ruins of the vast prefabricated Mulberry harbour will take centuries to disappear.

However, though the number of surviving veterans is inevitably dwindling, **museums** and **monuments** to their memory are opening at a faster rate than ever. No single museum or site can tell the whole story of the invasion, but the largest and most significant ones are listed below; each is described on the relevant page.

For a summary of the main events, see Contexts, p.395.

Caen	Caen Memorial	p.116
Bayeux	Musée Mémorial de la Bataille de Normandie	p.122
Ouistreham	Musée du Mur de l'Atlantique	p.124
Ouistreham	Musée No 4 Commando	p.124
Ranville-Bénouville	Mémorial Pegasus	p.125
Courseulles	Centre Juno Beach	p.127
Arromanches	Musée du Débarquement	p.127
Arromanches	Arromanches 360	p.127
Longues-sur-mer	La Batterie de Longues-sur-mer	p.128
Port-en-Bessin	Musée des Épaves Sous-Marines du Débarquement	p.128
St-Laurent	Omaha Beach Museum	p.129
Grandcamp-Maisy	Batterie de Maisy	p.131
Grandcamp-Maisy	Musée des Rangers	p.131
Ste-Marie-du-Mont	Musée du Débarquement d'Utah-Beach	p.131
Quinéville	Mémorial de la Liberté Retrouvé	p.131
Crisbecq	Musée de la Batterie de Crisbecq	p.132
Ste-Mère-Église	Musée Airborne	p.132
Cherbourg	Musée de la Libération	p.135

Head west instead from the place de Gaulle, immediately outside the terminal, and you'll soon come to the handful of charming old streets at the heart of the old town. The sea itself lies a couple of hundred metres north of here, along the semi-pedestrianized **Avenue de la Mer**, home to several inexpensive snack bars and restaurants. Strictly speaking, the waterfront, backing a long straight beach, is a separate community known as **Riva Bella**. Its large central **casino**, on place Alfred-Thomas, has been remodelled as a 1930s passenger liner, housing an expensive restaurant and cocktail bar, while gloriously old-fashioned bathing huts face onto the sands.

Nearby on avenue 6-Juin, the **Musée du Mur de l'Atlantique** (daily: Feb, March & Oct–Dec 10am–6pm; April–Sept 9am–7pm; closed Jan; €7; Ⓦwww.musee-grand-bunker.com) is housed in a lofty bunker – hence its alternative name, the Grand Bunker. This was the headquarters of the several German batteries that defended the mouth of the River Orne; after brief resistance, it fell to Allied forces on June 9, 1944. Inside the heavily restored bunker, displays re-create living conditions, with newspapers, cutlery and packets of cigarettes adding a welcome human touch to the moderately interesting explanations of the workings of the generators, gas filters and radio room.

Even closer to the casino, the **Musée No 4 Commando** (daily mid-March to late Oct 10.30am–6pm; €4.50; Ⓦmusee-4commando.org) details the story of the 117 Free-French commandos who landed at what's now Colleville-Montgomery on June 6, 1944; a documentary film covers their training as well as the actual invasion.

Arrival and Information

Brittany Ferries (Ⓣ08.25.82.88.28, Ⓦbrittanyferries.com) services from Portsmouth (2–4 daily) are detailed in Basics (see p.21). The **tourist office**, alongside the casino (April–June & Sept daily 10am–12.30pm & 2–6.30pm; July & Aug daily 10am–1pm & 2–7pm; Oct–March Mon–Sat 10am–12.30pm & 2.30–6pm, Sun 2.30–5.30pm; Ⓣ02.31.97.18.63, Ⓦville-ouistreham.fr), provides cheap **internet access**. The Cyclorama on the seafront (Ⓣ06.77.56.79.55), rents **bikes** as well as family-sized pedal cars for group excursions. If you're **cycling**, the obvious direction to take for a gentle start to your holiday is west along the coast, but if you head south towards Caen, the designated cycle path that follows the canal all the way to Caen city centre is far more pleasant than the main road.

Accommodation and eating

Ouistreham makes a perfectly pleasant place to spend a night before or after a ferry crossing, with hotels concentrated close to the ferry terminal as well as nearer the beach in Riva Bella.

Broche d'Argent pl de Gaulle Ⓣ02.31.97.12.16, Ⓔlabrochedargent.ludo@free.fr. Very inexpensive rooms, and a reasonable restaurant too, right on the square by the ferry port. ❶

Le Normandie 71 av Michel-Cabieu Ⓣ02.31.97.19.57, Ⓦlenormandie.com. Smart hotel, just around the corner from place de Gaulle near the ferry terminal, offering pleasant, quiet rooms, some of them in the *Chalut* annex opposite, and good menus at €21 and €33.50. Closed Jan, plus Sun eve & Mon Nov–March. ❹

De la Plage 39–41 av Pasteur Ⓣ02.31.96.85.16, Ⓦhotel-plage-ouistreham.com. Good value rooms in an imposing red-brick mansion, in a peaceful location barely 100m from the casino near the Commando museum. No restaurant. Closed Dec to mid-Feb. ❸

St-Georges 51 av Andry Ⓣ02.31.97.18.79, Ⓦwww.hotel-le-saint-georges.com. Spacious, well-equipped rooms near the casino, many with great sea views, and good food on menus from €22. Closed three weeks in Jan; ❹

Pegasus Bridge

Five kilometres south of Ouistreham, the main road towards Caen passes close by the site now known as **Pegasus Bridge**. Just after midnight on the night before D-Day, the twin bridges here that cross the Caen canal and the River Orne were the target of a daring **glider assault**. Seizing them intact was a crucial Allied objective, because it both enabled the invaders to advance east along the coast and blocked potential German reinforcements. Three of the six Horsa gliders launched from the *Halifax*, six miles offshore, landed close enough for what was then Bénouville Bridge to be captured within half an hour, although Lieutenant Brotheridge, leading the charge, became the first British casualty of D-Day in the process.

The original bridge, which was replaced in 1994, now spans a hole in the lawns outside the **Mémorial Pegasus** immediately to the east (daily: Feb, March, Oct & Nov 10am–1pm & 2–5pm; April–Sept 9.30am–6.30pm; €6; Ⓦwww.memorial-pegasus.org). This vaguely glider-shaped museum holds the expected array of helmets, goggles, medals and other memorabilia, most captioned in English, as well as various model bridges used in planning the attack, and a replica glider.

Sword and Juno beaches

The coastline west of Ouistreham, along Sword and Juno beaches, is also known to the French as the **Côte de Nacre**. Although the landscape is predominantly flat and featureless, the towns themselves are welcoming. A long promenade curves by the sea all the way from Ouistreham to Lion – it's built up, though always in a low-key way, and makes a pleasant walk straight from the ferry. **Colleville-Montgomery**, the first village after the port, is one of the few "Montgomeries" in the area to be named after the British general rather than his Norman ancestors. It's not otherwise distinguished.

Luc-sur-mer

If you're looking for atmosphere – albeit sedate – **LUC-SUR-MER**, 11km from Ouistreham, has much to recommend it. It's a gentle resort with a small wooden pier, neon-lit crêpe-stands, and tearooms along the pedestrian promenade that runs parallel to its long straight beach. The skeleton of a forty-ton whale that caused a sensation when it was washed up here in 1885 is displayed in the park in the heart of town; alongside, the **Maison de la Baleine** ("house of the whale") tells the whole story and provides copious information on whales in general (April, May & Sept Sat & Sun 2.30–6pm; June daily 2.30–6pm; July & Aug daily 10am–noon & 2–7pm; free).

Luc has its own summer-only **tourist office** on the main drag, rue Docteur Charcot (mid-June to mid-Sept daily 9.30am–12.30pm & 2–7pm; ⓣ02.31.97.33.25, ⓦluc-sur-mer.fr). In its most reasonably priced **hotel**, the *Beau Rivage*, splendidly sited right on the seafront at 1 rue Docteur Charcot (ⓣ02.31.96.49.51, ⓦwww.hotel-beaurivage-lucsurmer.fr; ④; closed mid-Dec to mid-Jan), the rooms are comfortable enough, even if they aren't decorated in the most modern of styles. Dinner menus range from €23 to €33. A couple of hundred metres further west along the seafront, several rooms at the newer and much grander *Hôtel des Thermes et du Casino*, at 3 rue Guynemer (ⓣ02.31.97.32.37, ⓦwww.hotelresto-lesthermes.com; ⑥; closed Nov to mid-March), have large sea-view balconies, and there's a heated pool around the back. There's also a huge four-star **campsite** near the beach, *La Capricieuse* (ⓣ02.31.97.34.43, ⓦcampinglacapricieuse.com; closed Oct–March).

Langrune and St-Aubin-sur-mer

The *Hôtel de la Mer*, virtually on the beach on the boulevard Aristide-Briand in **LANGRUNE** (ⓣ02.31.96.03.37, ⓦhoteldelamer.fr; closed Dec; ③), has eleven simple, good-value rooms and decent if unexceptional food.

Further west, in **ST-AUBIN-SUR-MER**, the large but extremely peaceful, ivy-covered *Clos Normand* stretches from the main road all the way to the pedestrian beachside promenade (ⓣ02.31.97.30.47, ⓦclosnormandhotel.com; ④; closed Dec to mid-March), and has nicely renovated rooms. Its **restaurant** has a seafront terrace and offers three- to eight-course menus priced from €24 to €67.

Courseulles and Juno Beach

COURSEULLES, 3km west of St-Aubin, is a bit more of a town, with an enjoyable Friday **market** in an old square set back from the sea, and, allegedly, the best oysters in Normandy. Rather too many holiday apartments have been constructed in recent years, but the seafront remains recognizable as **Juno Beach**. This section of Norman coast was allocated to the 14,000 Canadian soldiers who took part in the D-Day landings; within ten days of its capture, Winston Churchill and King George VI visited the beach on morale-boosting excursions.

The **Centre Juno Beach**, next to the beach (daily: April–Sept 9.30am–7pm; March & Oct 10am–6pm; Feb, Nov & Dec 10am–1pm & 2–5pm; closed Jan; €6.50; Ⓦjunobeach.org), commemorates the Canadian contribution to World War II, focusing not so much on what happened at Juno itself as on all matters Canadian. In summer, the Centre also conducts tours of the ruins of the Atlantic Wall, down on the actual beach (April, May, Sept & Oct, daily 11am & 3pm; June–Aug daily 10am, 11am, noon, 2pm, 3pm & 4pm; €5, or €10 with museum admission). The beautiful **Canadian Cemetery**, which holds many of the 359 Canadians who died on D-Day, is 3km inland at Bény-sur-mer, on flat ground from which you can see the sea.

Courseulles' main function these days is as a yachting port. Of its small array of **hotels**, the *Crémaillère-Le-Gytan*, 23–25 av de la Combattante (Ⓣ02.31.37.46.73, Ⓦwww.la-cremaillere.com; ❸), has the best sea views, plus a good restaurant with menus from €19.50.

Arromanches

While basically a little seaside village, **ARROMANCHES**, 13km west of Courseulles and a total of 31km from Ouistreham, has the strongest identity of all the resorts along this stretch of shoreline. That's partly because it's given a clear geographical definition by the cliffs that rise to either side, finally breaking the monotonous flatness of the Côte de Nacre. However, the real reason that it's become the centre of the D-Day tourism industry is that this was the location of the artificial **Mulberry harbour**, "Port Winston", that facilitated the landings of two and a half million men and half a million vehicles during the Invasion. Two of these prefab concrete constructions were built in segments in Britain, while "doodlebugs" blitzed overhead, then submerged in rivers away from the prying eyes of German aircraft, and finally towed across the Channel at 6kph as the invasion began. Meanwhile, the British 47 Royal Marine Commando were storming Arromanches itself to clear the way.

The seafront **Musée du Débarquement**, in Arromanches's main square (daily: Feb, Nov & Dec 10am–12.30pm & 1.30–5pm; March & Oct 9.30am–12.30pm & 1.30–5.30pm; April 9am–12.30pm & 1.30–6pm; May–Aug 9am–7pm; Sept 9am–6pm; closed Jan; €6.50; Ⓦnormandy1944.com), recounts the whole story by means of models, machinery and movies – and the evidence of your own eyes. A huge picture window stares straight out to where the bulky remains of the harbour stretch away along the coast, making a strange intrusion on the beach and shallow seabed. Its sheer scale is impossible to appreciate at this distance; for three months after D-Day, this was the largest port in the world. (The other such harbour, slightly further west on Omaha Beach, was broken up within two weeks by a huge storm, but this one was repairable.)

Several other war memorials are scattered throughout Arromanches, including a crucifix and a statue of the Virgin Mary, high up on the cliffs above the invasion site (parking €4). Alongside, a steel dome contains **Arromanches 360** (daily: Feb, March, Nov & Dec 10.10am–5.10pm; April, May, Sept & Oct 10.10am–5.40pm; June–Aug 9.40am–6.40pm; closed Jan; shows at 10 and 40 minutes past each hour; €4.20; Ⓦarromanches360.com), a wraparound cinema which at half-hourly intervals, under the slogan of "eighteen minutes of total emotion", plunges viewers into the heart of the fighting. Despite there being little contemporary footage, the effect, with the action running simultaneously on separate screens, is undeniably impressive.

Practicalities

Arromanches is quite a cheerful place to stay, with a lively pedestrian street of bars and brasseries, and a long expanse of sand where you can rent windsurf boards. Its **tourist office** is just back from the sea at 2 rue Maréchal-Joffre (daily: July & Aug 9am–6pm; Sept–June 10am–noon & 2–5pm; Ⓣ02.31.22.36.45, Ⓦwww.arromanches.com).

La Marine, 1 quai Canada (Ⓣ02.31.22.34.19, Ⓦhotel-de-la-marine.fr; ❹), is a slightly expensive **hotel**, with well-appointed rooms – many of which enjoy superb sea views – and an excellent restaurant serving fish menus from €22; there's also a cheaper brasserie, the *Winston*, alongside. Across the main square, the *Arromanches*, 2 rue du Colonel René Michel (Ⓣ02.31.22.36.26, Ⓦhoteldarromanches.fr; closed Jan, plus Tues & Wed in low season; ❹), is less well situated but just as comfortable; here, the *Pappagall* restaurant has reasonable menus. The town's spacious three-star municipal **campsite** is located 200m back from the seafront (Ⓣ02.31.22.36.78; closed Nov–March).

Omaha Beach

West of Arromanches, and especially beyond Port-en-Bessin, the coastline becomes steadily hillier. As **Omaha Beach** it presented a stiff challenge to the American forces on D-Day. Stark reminders of the task they faced remain visible at the **Pointe du Hoc**, while the US cemetery at **Colleville-sur-mer** holds over nine thousand American dead.

Longues-sur-mer

Six kilometres west of Arromanches, a minor road leads 1.5km north of the village of **LONGUES-SUR-MER** to the best-preserved German defensive post to survive the war. **La Batterie de Longues-sur-mer** consists of four concrete Nazi pillboxes, from which mighty gun barrels still point out across the Channel. Visitors are free to wander in and over the bunkers, and there are guided tours in English, French and German in summer (April–Sept daily 10am–6pm; €5).

Port-en-Bessin

PORT-EN-BESSIN, 11km west of Arromanches, and the nearest point on the coast to Bayeux (on the #70 bus route), has a thriving fishing industry and – rare on this coast – a sheltered, enclosed site. The fish, caught off Devon and Cornwall, are auctioned three times a week. Despite lacking a beach, it's a nice enough place, with an intriguing round watchtower at its eastern end. A kilometre back from the sea towards Bayeux, the **Musée des Épaves Sous-Marines du Débarquement** (May Sat & Sun 10am–noon & 2–6pm; June–Sept daily 10am–noon & 2–6pm; €6) displays miscellaneous artefacts salvaged from D-Day shipwrecks; film and photos explain how they were brought back to the surface.

Port-en-Bessin doesn't make an obvious base for visitors, but the *de la Marine* (Ⓣ02.31.21.70.08; Ⓦwww.hoteldelamarine.pretexx.fr; ❸; closed second fortnight in Nov, plus three weeks in Feb) is a classic seaside **hotel** on quai Letourneur, with menus from €17.

Colleville-sur-mer and St-Laurent

The clifftop village of **COLLEVILLE-SUR-MER**, 10km along, marks the start of the long approach road to the larger of the two **American war cemeteries**, a sombre place, described in the box on p.130. Unlike the British and Commonwealth forces, the Americans repatriated over half of their dead.

▲ Cemetery at Colleville-sur-mer

At the next point where road access to the sea becomes possible – **ST-LAURENT**, 2.5km further on – a colossal flat beach stretches away beneath the cliffs. An abstract but evocative stainless-steel sculpture by French artist Anilore Banon, erected in 2004 and named *Les Braves*, emerges from the sandes at its centre. The small **Omaha Beach Museum** (daily: mid-Feb to mid-March 10am–12.30pm & 2.30–6pm; mid-March to mid-May & mid-Sept to mid-Nov 9.30am–6.30pm; mid-May to June & first fortnight of Sept 9.30am–7pm; July & Aug 9.30am–7.30pm; €5.80; Ⓦmusee-memorial-omaha.com), 100m uphill from the seafront, displays a fine assortment of photos taken on D-Day itself, but few artefacts of any interest.

Overlooking the beach from the foot of the road, the *D-Day House* (Ⓣ02.31.92.66.49, Ⓦd-dayhouse.com; ❹) offers fourteen comfortable rooms, many with sea-view balconies, a pool and a terrace restaurant with menus from €14.

Vierville

Just beyond St-Laurent, **VIERVILLE**, like Arromanches (see p.127), was chosen as a site for the building of an artificial harbour. Codenamed "Gooseberry" to Arromanches' "Mulberry", it lasted just thirteen days before breaking up in an unprecedented storm. A memorial to the US National Guard stands atop a ruined German pillbox where the road from the village proper drops down to the sea; at the foot of the cliff, a Logis de France, the *Hôtel du Casino* (Ⓣ02.31.22.41.02; ❹), surveys the scene.

Pointe du Hoc

The most dramatic American landings took place along the cliff heights of the **POINTE DU HOC**, 6km west of Vierville, and still today deeply pitted with German bunkers and shell-holes. Standing amid the scarred earth and rusty barbed wire, looking down to the rocks at the base of the cliff, it seems inconceivable that the first US sergeant was at the top five minutes after landing, and

The war cemeteries

The World War II **cemeteries** that dot the Norman countryside are filled with foreigners; most of the French dead are buried in the churchyards of their home towns. After the war, some felt that the soldiers should remain in the makeshift graves that were dug where they fell. Instead, commissions gathered the remains into purpose-built cemeteries devoted to the separate warring nations. In total, over 140,000 young men were disinterred; more than half of the 31,744 US casualties were repatriated.

The 27 **British** and **Commonwealth** cemeteries are magnificently maintained, and open in every sense. They tend not to be screened off with hedges or walls, or to consist of endless expanses of manicured lawn, but are instead intimate, punctuated with bright flowers. The family of each soldier was invited to suggest an inscription for his tomb, making each grave very personal, and yet part of a common attempt to bring meaning to the carnage. Some epitaphs are questioning – "One day we will understand"; some are accepting – "Our lad at rest"; some matter-of-fact, simply giving the home address. Interspersed among them all is the chilling refrain of the anonymous: "A soldier... known unto God". Thus the cemetery outside **Ryes**, northeast of Bayeux, where so many of the graves bear the date of D-Day, and so many of the victims are under 20, remains immediate and accessible – each grave clearly contains a unique individual. Even the monumental sculpture is subdued, a very British sort of fumbling for the decent thing to say (to reach it, head 2km southeast of the village on the D87 towards Bazenville). The understatement of the memorial at **Bayeux**, with its contrived Latin epigram commemorating the return as liberators of "those whom William conquered", conveys deep humility and sadness.

What the **German** cemeteries, filled with soldiers who died for a cause that largely precludes talk of "nobility" or "sacrifice", might have been like had the Nazis won doesn't bear contemplation. As it is, they are sombre places, inconspicuous in order to minimize the bitterness they still arouse. At **Orglandes**, 10km south of Valognes (see p.140) on the Cotentin Peninsula, ten thousand lie buried, three to each of the plain headstones set in the long flat lawn, almost hidden behind an anonymous wall. There are no noble slogans and the plain entrance is without a dedicatory monument. At the superb site of **Mont d'Huisnes**, 6km east of Mont-St-Michel, ten thousand more are filed away in the cold concrete tiers of a circular mausoleum. There is no attempt to defend the indefensible, and yet one feels an overpowering sense of sorrow – that there is nothing to be said in such a place bitterly underlines the sheer waste.

The largest **American** cemetery, at **Colleville-sur-mer** near the Pointe du Hoc, may already be familiar from the opening sequences of *Saving Private Ryan*. Neat rows of crosses cover the tranquil clifftop lawns, with no individual epitaphs, just gold lettering for a few exceptional warriors. At one end, a muscular giant dominates a huge array of battlefield plans and diagrams, covered with surging arrows and pincer movements. Barack Obama is the latest of many US presidents to have paid his respects here; one president's son, General Theodore Roosevelt Jr, is among those buried.

Companies that offer guided tours of the D-Day beaches and cemeteries are detailed on p.123.

the whole complex taken within another quarter of an hour. There's a small visitor centre next to the large car park, set well back from the cliffs (April–Oct daily 10am–1pm & 2–6pm, Nov–March Fri–Mon 9am–1pm & 2–5pm), but access to the site, which now legally belongs to the US, is free and unrestricted.

Grandcamp-Maisy

GRANDCAMP-MAISY, 3km west of Pointe du Hoc, was extensively damaged in the war. Centring on a compact fishing harbour, rebuilt in severe grey stone, it makes fewer concessions to tourism than its neighbours, but that somehow lends it a perverse, austere appeal. It's home to two **war museums**: the **Musée des Rangers** (mid-Feb to April daily except Mon 1–6pm; May–Oct Mon 2.30–6.30pm, Tues–Sun 9.30am–1pm & 2.30–6.30pm; €4; Ⓦmaisybattery.com), tells the story of the American landings at the Pointe du Hoc; while the **Batterie de Maisy**, just off the D514 towards Isigny (daily: mid-Feb to April & Oct to mid-Nov 10am–4pm; May–Sept 10am–6pm; €5.50; Ⓦmaisybattery.com), is a secret German gun emplacement that has only recently been unearthed.

Grandcamp-Maisy holds a couple of reasonably priced **hotels**: the *Duguesclin*, just east of the port at 4 quai Crampon (Ⓣ02.31.22.64.22; ❸; closed Mon in winter, plus all Jan), which has a panoramic sea-view dining room serving menus from €13, though most of the accommodation is in the annexe behind, and *Au Petit Mareyeur*, a long way back from the sea on avenue Marcel Destors (Ⓣ02.31.22.65.91, Ⓔhayetlamali@hotmail.com; ❸), also with menus from €13. There's a good seafront **campsite**, *du Joncal* (Ⓣ02.31.22.61.44, Ⓦcampingdujoncal.com; closed Oct–March), immediately west of the harbour. Facing the port at 5 quai Henri-Charon, *La Marée* (Ⓣ02.31.21.41.00; closed Jan to mid-Feb) is a nice **restaurant** with some outside tables, and a recommended €25 menu.

Utah Beach

The westernmost of the Invasion Beaches, **Utah Beach** stretches up the eastern shore of the Cotentin Peninsula, running 30km north towards St-Vaast (see p.139). Operations here on D-Day started at 4.30am, with the capture of the uninhabited **Îles St-Marcouf**, clearly visible 6km offshore; from 6.30am onwards, 23,000 men and 1700 vehicles landed on the beach itself. A minor coast road, the D421, traces the edge of the dunes and enables visitors to follow the course of the fighting, though in truth there's precious little to see these days. Ships that were deliberately sunk to create artificial breakwaters are still visible at low tide, while markers along the seafront commemorate individual fallen heroes.

Ste-Marie-du-Mont and St-Martin-de-Varreville

The single best opportunity to learn about the Utah Beach landings comes at the southern end of the D421, in **STE-MARIE-DU-MONT**. Built over a former German bunker, the **Musée du Débarquement d'Utah-Beach** (daily: Feb, March & Nov 10am–5.30pm; April, May & Oct 10am–6pm; June–Sept 9.30am–7pm; last admission 45min before closing; closed Dec & Jan; €6; Ⓦutah-beach.com) explains operations in exhaustive detail, with huge sea-view windows to lend immediacy to its copious models, maps, films and diagrams.Visitors can sit in a genuine landing vehicle, while the foaming surf is at high tide just a few metres away.

At **ST-MARTIN-DE-VARREVILLE,** 4km north of Ste-Marie, a monument honours the French General Leclerc, who landed here with his 2nd Armoured Division on August 1, 1944; see also p.178.

Quinéville

At the northern end of the D421, in **QUINÉVILLE**, the **Mémorial de la Liberté Retrouvée** (late March to mid-Nov daily 10am–7pm; €6; Ⓦwww.memorial-quineville.com) is a museum that focuses on the everyday life of Normandy under Nazi occupation. Its central reconstruction of a village street is adorned with German posters announcing the strict nightly curfew, or offering a 30,000-franc reward for anyone turning in a saboteur. Displays covering their American liberators include some fine shots of aircrews sporting Mohican haircuts.

A short way back from the beach here, the *Hôtel de la Plage*, at 7 av de la Plage (ⓣ02.33.21.43.54; closed Mon in winter; ❷), offers six pleasant guest **rooms** and serves well-priced menus from €12.

Head inland from the coast road towards **Crisbecq**, 4km south of Quinéville, and you'll soon come to the **Musée de la Batterie de Crisbecq** (daily: April, Oct & Nov 2–6pm; May, June & Sept 10am–6pm; July & Aug 10am–9pm; closed Dec–March; €6; ⓦbatterie-marcouf.com), where you can visit a complex of German bunkhouses, connected by trenches and now inhabited by mannequins.

Ste-Mère-Église

The church of the market town of **STE-MÈRE-ÉGLISE**, a short way inland from Utah Beach on the main road between Valognes and Carentan, was immortalized in the film *The Longest Day*, thanks to scenes of an unfortunate US paratrooper dangling from its steeple during the heavy fighting. That incident was based on fact, and the man in question, John Steele, used to return occasionally to re-enact and commemorate his ordeal. He's now dead, but a uniformed mannequin is permanently entangled on the roof in his stead. The new stained glass above the main door of the church also depicts American parachutists, surrounding the Virgin with Child.

Ste-Mère these days seems to attract more D-Day tourists than any other town. Just behind the church, Ste-Mère's approximately parachute-shaped **Musée Airborne** (Airborne Troops Museum) tells the story of the landings, complete with tanks, jeeps, and even a troop-carrying plane (daily: Feb, March, Oct & Nov 9.30am–noon & 2–6pm; April–Sept 9am–6.45pm; closed Dec & Jan; €7; ⓦmusee-airborne.com).

The **tourist office** in Ste-Mère-Église, facing the church, offers internet access (Mon–Sat 9am–1pm & 2–6pm; April–Sept also Sun 9am–6.45pm; ⓣ02.33.21.00.33, ⓦwww.sainte-mere-eglise.info), while the adjoining, English-owned *C-47* **café** organizes its own D-Day tours (ⓣ02.33.94.44.13). There are three **hotels**. The ivy-covered *Auberge John Steele*, just north of the church at 4 rue du Cap de Laine (ⓣ02.33.41.41.16, ⓦaubergejohnsteele.com; ❷; closed Sun eve & all Mon, except July–Sept), offers simple rooms and meals. Not far away, this time behind the church, the *Hôtel du Six Juin*, 11 rue des Clarons (ⓣ02.33.21.07.18, ⓦhotel-du-6-juin.com; ❸; closed Nov–Jan), is a plain alternative with no restaurant, while the ugly modern *logis Le Ste-Mère*, south of the centre at the intersection of the main street with N13 (ⓣ02.33.21.00.30, ⓦhotel-sainte-mere.com; ❸; closed Fri eve, Sat lunch & Sun), serves cheap buffet dinners.

The Cotentin Peninsula

Hard against the frontier with Brittany, and cut off from the rest of Normandy by difficult marshy terrain, the **Cotentin Peninsula** has traditionally been seen as something of a backwater, far removed from the French mainstream. The local *patois* has a special pejorative word for "stranger", applied indiscriminately to foreigners, Parisians and southern Cotentins alike, while official disdain for the region might explain why the Cap de la Hague, the peninsula's westernmost tip, was chosen as the site for a controversial nuclear reprocessing plant. The Cotentin nonetheless makes a surprisingly rewarding goal for travellers, and one that by sea at least is very easily accessible. Ferries from England and Ireland still dock at the peninsula's major port, **Cherbourg**, with a plethora of attractive little villages nestled amid the hills to both east and west.

Geographically, this is an area of transition. Little ports such as **Barfleur** and **St-Vaast** on the indented northern headland presage the rocky Breton coast, while inland the meadows resemble the farmlands of the Bocage and the Bessin. The long western flank with its flat beaches serves as a prelude to **Mont-St-Michel**, with hill towns such as **Coutances** and **Avranches** cherishing architectural and historical relics associated with the abbey. Halfway down, the approaches to the Baie du Mont-St-Michel are guarded by the walled port of **Granville**, an extremely popular destination with French holiday-makers and a sort of small-scale mirror-image of Brittany's St-Malo.

Cherbourg

Though its heyday as one of the great transatlantic passenger ports is now long in the past, the sizeable town of **CHERBOURG** still makes an appealing place to arrive in France. Despite the town's busy network of pedestrian streets lined with attractive stone facades, the labyrinth of alleyways known as *boëls*, some lively bars, and an impressive **maritime museum** in a converted Art Deco ferry terminal, many visitors head straight out and on, lured in part by the truly delightful little villages that lie within a few kilometres to either side. Napoleon inaugurated the transformation of what had been a rather poor, but perfectly situated, natural harbour into a major port, by means of massive artificial breakwaters. An equestrian statue commemorates his boast that in Cherbourg he would "re-create the wonders of Egypt". As yet, however, there are no pyramids nearer than the Louvre in Paris.

Arrival and information

Cross-Channel **ferries** still sail into Cherbourg's *gare maritime*, not far east of the town centre. Brittany Ferries (ⓣ08.03.82.88.28, ⓦbrittany-ferries.com) operate services from both **Portsmouth** (1–2 daily; May–Oct high-speed 3hr, otherwise 5–7hr) and **Poole** (1–3 daily; some high-speed in summer, 2hr 15min, otherwise 4hr 15min–5hr 30min). Both Irish Ferries (ⓣ02.33.23.44.44, ⓦirishferries.com) and LD Lines (ⓦldlines.co.uk) also sail to Cherbourg, from Rosslare. Regular €1.20 shuttle buses connect the terminal with the tourist office and **gare SNCF**.

The **gare SNCF**, on avenue François-Millet/place Jean-Jaurès, is served by regular trains to Paris, Bayeux and Caen. Tourisme Verney (ⓣ02.33.44.32.22) run **buses** to Barfleur, Valognes, Coutances, St-Lô, Granville and other destinations from the **gare routière** opposite.

Cherbourg's **tourist office** is at 2 quai Alexandre III (June Mon–Sat 9am–12.30pm & 2–6.30pm; July & Aug Mon–Sat 9am–6.30pm, Sun 10am–12.30pm; Sept–May Mon–Fri 9am–noon & 2–6pm Sat 9am–12.30pm & 2–6pm; ⓣ02.33.93.52.02, ⓦot-Cherbourg-cotentin.fr). An information kiosk at the ferry terminal is open to coincide with sailings (ⓣ02.33.44.39.92). The **post office** is at 1 rue d'Ancien Quai (Mon–Fri 8am–7pm, Sat 8.30am–noon), while the Forum Espace Culture, on place Centrale, is a large book and record shop that also offers **internet** access (Mon 2–7pm, Tues–Sat 10am–7pm; €5 per hr; ⓣ02.33.78.19.30), as does Archesys, 16 rue de l'Union (ⓣ02.33.53.04.93, ⓦarchesys.com).

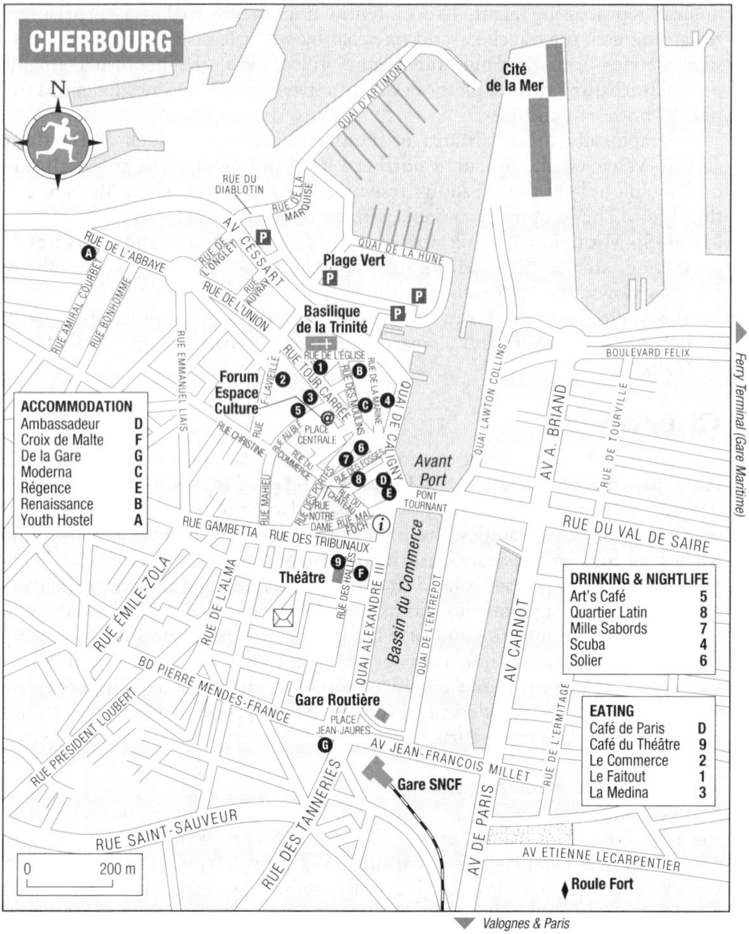

Accommodation

By the standards of the rest of Normandy, **room** rates in Cherbourg are very reasonable. It makes a lively enough place to pass an evening – though the crowds and traffic can get a bit much, and the lack of daytime parking space is a problem for motorists. Few of the hotels maintain their own restaurants.

Hotels

Ambassadeur 22 quai de Caligny ⓣ02.33.43.10.00, ⓦambassadeurhotel.com. Inexpensive, good-value central hotel, poised at corner of the quayside and holding four storeys of en-suite rooms (there's a lift). ❷

Croix de Malte 5 rue des Halles ⓣ02.33.43.19.16, ⓦhotelcroixmalte.com. Simple hotel on three upstairs floors, one block back from the harbour and around the corner from the theatre. Clean renovated rooms – all have TV and at least a shower – with the cheapest rates being for the perfectly acceptable, windowless ones in the attic. ❶

De la Gare 10 pl Jean-Jaurès ⓣ02.33.43.06.81, ⓔluc-fleury@orange.fr. Renovated hotel that's very convenient for the *gares SNCF* and *routière*, if not exactly stunning in itself. All rooms are en suite. ❷

Moderna 28 rue de la Marine ⓣ02.33.43.05.30, ⓦmoderna-hotel.com. Friendly small hotel with reasonable, very well-priced en-suite rooms, slightly back from the harbour. ❷

Régence 42–44 quai de Caligny ⓣ02.33.43.05.16, ⓦlaregence.com. Slightly more upmarket than Cherbourg's other offerings, this Logis de France has small, neat rooms overlooking the harbour. The dining room downstairs starts with a reasonable €20 menu, and ranges up to €35; it's not the best restaurant along the *quai*, but there's something to be said for eating where you sleep. ❹

Renaissance 4 rue de l'Église ⓣ02.33.43.23.90, ⓦhotel-renaissance-cherbourg.com. Nicely refurbished rooms, all with either shower or bath and some with sea views, in a friendly hotel facing the port in the most appealing quarter of town. The "Église" of the address is the attractive Trinité. ❸

Hostel

HI Hostel 55 rue de l'Abbaye ⓣ02.33.78.15.15, ⓦfuaj.org/Cherbourg-Octeville. Well-equipped red-brick hostel, fifteen minutes' walk west of the centre, offering dorm beds for €17.30 (members) or €20.50 (non-members), including breakfast. Two bedrooms are designed for visitors with limited mobility. Check-in 9am–1pm & 6–11pm, closed Jan.

The Town

Cherbourg's **old town**, immediately west of the quayside, is an intriguing maze of pedestrian alleys that abounds in shops and restaurants. The tempting array of small shops and boutiques clustered round the place Centrale includes a place to buy the city's most famous product, the genuine **Cherbourg umbrella**, at 30 rue des Portes, while the excellent Thursday **market** is held on and off rue des Halles, near the majestic theatre with its Belle Époque facade. A pleasant stroll north of the commercial zone leads to the Basilique de la Trinité and the former town beach, now grassed over to form the "Plage Vert".

Southeast of the centre, you can climb up to **Roule Fort** for a view of the whole port. The fort itself contains the **Musée de la Libération**, which, with the usual dry maps and diagrams but plenty of contemporary newsreel – much of it, for once, in English – commemorates the period in 1944 when, despite the massive destruction wrought by the Nazis before they surrendered, Cherbourg briefly became the busiest port in the world (May–Sept Mon & Sun 2–6pm, Tues–Sat 10am–noon & 2–6pm; Oct–April Wed–Sun 2–6pm; €3).

La Cité de la Mer

Across from the pleasure port, **La Cité de la Mer** combines a large aquarium with a visitable nuclear submarine (daily: May, June & Sept 9.30am–6pm; July & Aug 9.30am–7pm; Oct–Dec & Feb–April 10am–6pm, with irregular closures on certain Mon, and additional variations depending on school hols; closed Jan; last entry 1hr before closing; April–Sept €18, Oct–March €15.50; ⓦcitedelamer.com). Though from the outside the complex looks as though it centres on the grand former Transatlantic ferry terminal, in fact that simply houses its ticket offices. Instead, displays in a new building behind tell the story of underwater exploration in history and fiction, starting with an image of Alexander the Great in 352 BC descending into the Bay of Bengal in the first diving bell, then moving swiftly via Jules Verne and H.P. Lovecraft to Jacques Cousteau, pictured with his diving saucer "shaped like a giant lentil" in 1959. Separate fish tanks hold species such as jellyfish, seahorses, and large (though sadly not giant) squid, while walkways enable you to peer into a vast cylindrical aquarium at ever greater depths. In a dry dock alongside, the *Redoutable* was France's first ballistic missile submarine. With an audio commentary from its former captain, visitors can scramble through its labyrinth of tube-like walkways and control rooms, though as the nuclear generator that once powered it has been removed, there's a cavernous empty space at its heart. The cramped crew quarters will feel very familiar if you've just shared a cabin on an overnight ferry crossing, while the plush carpeting and moulded chairs in the living room are remarkably reminiscent of Elvis's Graceland.

The Kearsarge and the Alabama

In June 1864, Cherbourg played host to one of the most extraordinary incidents of the **US Civil War** – a pitched **naval battle** between two rival warships, the Union *Kearsarge* and the Confederate *Alabama*.

The **Alabama** had been cruising the Atlantic for a year, harassing ships carrying supplies to the northern United States. By the time it docked at Cherbourg, to allow its crew some shore leave and the boat itself a refit, it had captured, destroyed or held to ransom over eighty Yankee merchant vessels. The **Kearsarge**, meanwhile, had been prowling the coasts of Europe in pursuit; **Captain John A. Winslow** heard of the *Alabama*'s arrival while in Amsterdam, and was anchored off Cherbourg within two days.

Both vessels then spent several days preparing for the inevitable duel. **Captain Raphael Semmes** of the *Alabama* – known as "Old Beeswax" on account of his huge pointed moustache – noted in his diary that "the combat will no doubt be contested and obstinate, but the two ships are so evenly matched that I do not feel at liberty to decline it". Cherbourg buzzed with excitement: its hotels filled with eager spectators brought by special trains from Paris, and hundreds more camped along the quaysides.

Sunday being Semmes' lucky day, he ordered the *Alabama* out of the harbour on the morning of Sunday June 12. At first, the *Kearsarge* seemed to retreat; then it turned, and charged the *Alabama* at full steam. The *Alabama* was the first to fire its guns. One shell lodged in the sternpost of the *Kearsarge*, but it failed to explode. Instead, a slow, steady barrage from the *Kearsarge* began to pound the *Alabama* to pieces.

To Captain Semmes' bewilderment, the *Alabama*'s shells kept bouncing off the *Kearsarge*. When it later transpired that the *Kearsarge* was lined below the water level with iron chains, he furiously expostulated that "It was the same thing as if two men were to go out and fight a duel, and one of them, unknown to the other, were to put on a suit of mail under his own garment".

Eventually, the doomed *Alabama* attempted to flee. Its escape was cut off, but Semmes himself managed to get away. As his ship went down, he whirled his sword above his head and flung it into the Channel, then leaped into the sea. Together with several members of his crew, he was picked up by a British holiday-maker who had watched the battle from his yacht, and taken to Southampton. Hailed by *The Times* as a "set of first-rate fellows", the defeated Confederates in due course managed to return home.

Captain Winslow – whose ship had suffered just three casualties, as opposed to the *Alabama*'s 43 – brought the *Kearsarge* into Cherbourg harbour after the battle. Their previous Confederate sympathies conveniently forgotten, the local citizens hailed him as a hero, before he made his way to a celebration banquet arranged by the American community in Paris.

The separate "Walking into the Depths" section of the Cité de la Mer is aimed primarily at children, although they do a good job of keeping exactly what it entails under wraps. Entry is by timed admission, and once inside, visitors are divided into teams; be sure to ask staff for a headset with an English commentary. An over-long film explaining your "mission", to help an underwater explorer in his latest expedition, is followed by some rather silly "training" exercises, and a ride in a submarine simulator. The whole experience is pretty long at around 45 minutes, but the final "surprise" is undeniably amusing.

Eating

Restaurant options in Cherbourg divide readily into the glass-fronted seafood places along the quai de Caligny, each with its copious *assiette de fruits de mer*, and the more varied and less expensive little places tucked away in the pedestrianized streets and alleyways of the old town.

If you want to stock up on food, your best bets for large-scale shopping are the Auchan **hypermarket** at the junction of RN13 and N13, south of town, or the Carrefour, on the southeast corner of the Bassin du Commerce.

Café de Paris 40 quai de Caligny ☎02.33.43.12.36. Work your way up through the ranks of *assiettes de fruits de mer*, from the €18.50 *Matelot* to the *Corsaire* at €55 for two; there's also a selection of menus from €21.50–36.50, featuring a few meat dishes along with the predominately fishy selection. Closed Sun, plus Mon lunch.

Café du Théâtre 8 pl de Gaulle ☎02.33.43.01.49. Attractive setup adjoining the theatre, with a café behind plate-glass windows on the ground floor and a full-scale brasserie upstairs. It's a place used by the community as a whole rather than a typical tourist restaurant. The varied menus, from €14, offer more than just seafood. Closed Sun.

Le Commerce 42 rue François-la-Vieille ☎02.33.53.18.20. If you're tired of white tablecloths and over-attentive service, this in-town brasserie, much larger than it looks from the outside, serves huge portions of good food from 11am until late, with cheap menus from €14 and plenty of à la carte options. The home-made pâté is recommended. Closed Sun.

Le Faitout 25 rue Tour-Carrée ☎02.33.04.25.04. Stylish, faux-rustic fishing-themed restaurant in the shopping-district that offers traditional French cuisine, including mussels prepared with celery, apples and the like for around €12.50, and has good menus at €19 and €29. It's so popular in summer that you may have to reserve. Closed Sun, plus Mon lunch.

La Medina 54 rue Tour-Carrée ☎02.33.93.25.01. Smart, attractive Tunisian restaurant, decked out with little mosaic tables, and serving meaty couscous dishes from €12 or tajines for €13, plus Tunisian wine. Closed Sun, plus lunch on Sat, Mon & Tues.

Drinking and nightlife

While the **bars and cafés** on place Centrale itself are not overly appealing, several more promising establishments lie on the small streets around it, most notably rue des Fosses, where you will find the cosy *Quartier Latin*, the nautically themed *Mille Sabords*, and a decent pub in the *Solier* (the main entrance is at 55 Grande Rue). The *Art's Café*, at 69 rue au Blé (closed Sun), is a hip little bar that regularly puts on live music.

East from Cherbourg: the Val de Saire

East from Cherbourg, the D901, which switchbacks through a series of pretty valleys, is the most direct route to the old ports of **Barfleur** and **St-Vaast**. Following the D116 along the coast, however – signposted throughout as the **Route du Val de Saire** – takes you past a succession of stunning viewpoints and some really lovely quasi-fortified villages, shielded from the sea winds by stout stone walls.

Abundant footpaths make this a great area for walking; one particularly appealing stroll leads five kilometres from the magnificent crescent bay of **L'Anse du Brick** to the stark but pretty little harbour of **Port-Levi**, near Fermanville.

Barfleur

Seven centuries ago, the pleasant little harbour village of **BARFLEUR**, 25km east of Cherbourg, was the biggest port in Normandy. The population has since dwindled from nine thousand to around six hundred, and fortunes have diminished alongside. It's now a low-key place, whose grey granite quayside and formal main street retain an appealing elegance that if anything is boosted by their relative austerity. Although the broad, sweeping crescent of the main harbour sees little tourist activity, clusters of tiny fishing vessels tie up alongside, and fresh fish is often for sale.

At the far left-hand end of the harbour, the stocky church of **St-Nicolas** stands in a tiny walled enclosure; it's worth looking inside to admire its chief treasure, a sixteenth-century *pietà*. A lichen-covered rock on the shoreline nearby commemorates the fact that, when William the Conqueror embarked for southern England in 1066, it was in a ship constructed at Barfleur – the *Mora* – and piloted by a Barfleurais, Étienne. On November 25, 1120, William's descendant – also called William – set out from here to return home after a visit to France. He was travelling in a separate vessel to his father, Henry I of England. According to a contemporary account, the *Blanche Nef* "flew swifter than the winged arrow…but the carelessness of the intoxicated crew drove her onto a rock, which rose above the waves not far from the shore". William reached the safety of a small lifeboat, but turned back to sea upon hearing the cries of his sister, and was drowned together with three hundred of his companions, leaving the desolate Henry I without a male heir, and thus precipitated strife over the succession.

Since 1834, the rock upon which William came to grief, north of Barfleur, has been guarded by the **Gatteville lighthouse**. A pleasant footpath leads there in thirty minutes from town, starting beside what was in 1865 the first lifeboat station to be built in France. At 75m, the lighthouse is the second tallest in both France and Europe – the tallest is near L'Aber-Wrac'h in Brittany – with a beam that in reaching 50km overlaps with that of its opposite number on the Isle of Wight. Energetic visitors can climb the 365 steps to the top (daily: Feb, first two weeks in Nov & last two weeks in Dec 10am–noon & 2–4pm; March & Oct 10am–noon & 2–5pm; April & Sept 10am–noon & 2–6pm; May–Aug 10am–noon & 2–7pm; closed mid-Nov to mid-Dec & all Jan; €2; Ⓦpharede-gatteville.com).

Practicalities

Barfleur's small **tourist office** is next to the church (April–June & Sept Mon–Sat 9.30am–12.30pm & 2.30–6.30pm, Sun 10am–12.30pm & 2.30–7pm; July & Aug daily 10am–2.30pm & 2.30–7pm; Ⓣ02.33.54.02.48, Ⓦville-barfleur.fr).

The better of the village's two **hotels**, *Le Conquérant*, is a short way back from the sea at 16–18 rue St-Thomas-à-Becket (Ⓣ02.33.54.00.82, Ⓦhotel-leconquerant.com; ❹; closed mid-Nov to mid-March); behind its stern stone facade lies a gorgeous, rambling and very welcoming old town house, where the nicest rooms face onto a lovely garden courtyard, and there's a summer-only crêperie. Accommodation at *Le Moderne*, tucked away south of the main road at 1 place de Gaulle (Ⓣ02.33.23.12.44; ❸; closed Tues eve & Wed mid-Sept to mid-July, plus all Jan to mid-Feb), is not quite as appealing, but the **restaurant** is quite superb, with the €28 menu including the house speciality, oysters – stuffed or raw. A nice, albeit basic **campsite** stands a couple of kilometres north of town in Le Crabec. *La Ferme du Bord du Mer* (Ⓣ02.33.54.01.77) is exactly what its name suggests, a farm beside the sea, where grassy meadows hold donkeys as well as tents and caravans, and there's a scruffy flat beach.

Though few businesses of any kind face Barfleur harbour itself, there are a couple of top-notch restaurants on the waterfront. As well as its outdoor tables, the friendly and very charming *Comptoir de la Presqu'île*, 30 quai Henri Chardon (Ⓣ02.33.20.37.51; closed Sun eve & Mon), has an upstairs dining room with good views of the port. The cuisine is mostly fishy, with a good menu at €14, and main courses like the deliciously simple whole grilled bream costing €8.60–15. Closer to the church at 12 quai Henri Chardon, the *Café de France* (Ⓣ02.33.54.00.38) makes a fine alternative, with menus at €15.50 and

€20. For a lighter snack, *Chez Buck*, at 1 rue St-Thomas-à-Becket where the main road meets the port (Ⓣ02.33.54.02.16; closed mid-Nov to mid-Jan), is a cosy, busy little crêperie that also serves conventional menus from €13.

St-Vaast

ST-VAAST-LA-HOUGUE, 11km south of Barfleur, is more of a resort, with lots of tiny Channel-crossing yachts moored in the bay where Edward III landed on his way to Crécy. It's still a fishing port as well, though, its quayside busy with men in oilskins washing down gleaming boatloads of squid and mussels.

The narrow spit of sand called **La Hougue**, south of the centre, holds various sporting facilities, such as tennis courts and a diving club, although the tip itself is a sealed-off military installation; the fortifications are graceful, courtesy (as ever) of the celebrated seventeenth-century military architect Vauban. The whole area is at its best at high tide; low tide reveals, especially on the sheltered inland side, bleak muddy flats dotted with some of the country's best-loved **oyster beds**.

Practicalities

St-Vaast has a **tourist office** at the southern end of the seafront quai Vauban (April–Sept Mon–Sat 9.30am–noon & 2.30–6pm, Sun 2.30–6pm; Oct–March Mon–Sat 10am–noon & 3–6pm; Ⓣ02.33.23.19.32, Ⓦsaint-vaast-reville.com). The **hotel** *de France*, a couple of hundred metres back from the sea at 20 rue du Maréchal Foch (Ⓣ02.33.54.42.26, Ⓦwww.france-fuchsias.com; ❸–❼; closed Jan–Feb, plus Mon in winter), with its splendid gardens, is an ideal stopover for ferry passengers – in fact both it and the annexe at the end of the garden are packed throughout the season with British visitors. Its **restaurant**, *Les Fuchsias*, is also excellent, with dinner menus from €20 on weekdays, and €28.50 at weekends; it has tables outside in fine weather. If you can't get a room there, *La Granitière*, down the road at 74 rue du Maréchal Foch (Ⓣ02.33.54.58.99, Ⓦhotel-la-granitiere.com; ❸; closed mid-Dec to mid-March) is an appealing alternative, with attractive gardens, while at the harbourside *Nelson*, attached to the *Café du Port*, 5 quai Vauban (Ⓣ02.33.23.42.42; ❸; closed mid-Nov to mid-Dec), all five rooms have en-suite facilities and sea views.

Île Tatihou

In 1692, a French and Irish army gathered at St-Vaast and set sail for Britain in an attempt to restore the deposed Stuart King James II to the English throne. However, the fleet was destroyed by a combined Anglo-Dutch force, before it could get any further than La Hougue. The battle took place just off the sandy flat island of **TATIHOU**, very close to the mainland, which now doubles as a bird sanctuary and the location of an ecologically minded Musée Maritime (daily 10am–12.45pm & 1.30–5.30pm; €4.60, or €7.80 with ferry).

A limited number of visitors each day are carried across to Tatihou by amphibious mud-wallowing "**ferries**" from St-Vaast; the exact schedule is determined by the state of the tides, and tickets are only available from the *Accueil Tatihou* office on St-Vaast's quai Vauban (April–June & Sept daily 10am–4pm; July & Aug daily 10am–7pm; March & Oct Sat & Sun 2–5pm; Nov & Feb only during school hols; €4.60 return; Ⓣ02.33.23.19.92, Ⓦwww.tatihou.com). It's also possible to **walk** to Tatihou when the tide is low enough; check at the same office for current advice.

Tatihou hosts a four-day **folk-music festival** in mid-August each year. Between February and mid-November, visitors can stay overnight in comfortable rooms on the island (same phone and website as ferry; rates include meals; ❹). In addition, the *Restaurant du Fort Carré* serves simple food (Ⓣ02.33.54.07.20).

Valognes

VALOGNES, around 18km through the woods from St-Vaast on the main road south from Cherbourg, is described in tourist handouts, with a dose perhaps of wishful thinking, as "the Versailles of Normandy". The tag might have had some meaning before the war, when the region was full of aristocratic mansions, but thanks to the bombing that preceded D-Day, only a scattering of fine old houses remain, along with the very scant ruins of a Gallo-Roman settlement called Alauna.

All Valognes has to show for itself is a **cider museum** housed in an old watermill (April–June & Sept Mon & Wed–Sat 10am–noon & 2–6pm, Sun 2–6pm; July & Aug Mon–Sat 10am–noon & 2–6pm, Sun 2–6pm; Oct–March groups by appointment; €4; ⓣ02.33.40.22.73), crammed with bizarre old wooden implements and ancient warped barrels – including a particularly obscene example upstairs – a little public garden, and a big empty square, enlivened only for the Friday **market**. But it's a quiet, convenient alternative to waiting around in Cherbourg, and the surrounding country lanes make for a pleasant stroll.

The rambling, ivy-coated *Hôtel du Agriculture* at 16–18 rue L-Delisle (ⓣ02.33.95.02.02, ⓦhotel-agriculture.com; ❸; closed Sun eve & Mon eve) is the best of several inexpensive **hotels**. All the rooms are en suite, and its restaurant serves top-quality food on menus that start at €17.

West from Cherbourg: the Cap de le Hague

The stretch of coast immediately west of Cherbourg is similar to that to the east, although it holds no harbour town to compare with Barfleur or St-Vaast. The main goal for most visitors is the windswept **Cap de la Hague** at its westernmost tip. However, the old villages of **Omonville-la-Petite** and **Omonville-la-Rogue**, 20km out of Cherbourg, are lovely places to stroll around, and all the way along you'll find wild and isolated countryside where you can lean against the wind, watch waves smashing against rocks or sunbathe in a spring profusion of wild flowers, while a whole range of activities are on offer.

The real drawback of the area around **Cap de la Hague** is that the discharges of "low-level" radioactive wastes from the **nuclear reprocessing plant** may discourage you from swimming. In 1980, the Greenpeace vessel *Rainbow Warrior* chased a ship bringing spent Japanese fuel into Cherbourg harbour. The *Rainbow Warrior's* crew were arrested, but all charges were dropped when three thousand Cherbourg dockers threatened to strike in their support. In the spring of 1985, the French secret service finally took their revenge on the *Rainbow Warrior* by sinking it in Auckland harbour, killing a member of the crew in the process. As detailed in Contexts (see p.398), controversy continues to surround the plant, which has no longer welcomed visitors since September 11, 2001.

The main road, the D901, continues a couple of kilometres beyond the plant to **GOURY**, where the fields finally roll down to a craggy pebble coastline, a splendidly windswept spot. Here the **restaurant** *Auberge de Goury* (ⓣ02.33.52.77.01; closed Mon), facing the octagonal lifeboat station and looking out towards a slate-grey lighthouse, serves fresh seafood on menus ranging from €15.50 to €57.

From the cape of **La Hague** itself, the northern tip of the peninsula, bracken-covered hills and narrow valleys run south to the cliffs of the **Nez de Jobourg**, claimed in wild local optimism to be the highest in Europe. South of that, a great curve of sand – some of it military training ground – takes the land's edge to **Flamanville** and another nuclear installation. Halfway along, in the picturesque village of **VAUVILLE**, the tropical-looking garden at the **Château de Vauville** is famed for its huge palm-grove, a sure sign of the area's mild microclimate (April–Sept daily 2–6pm; Oct Wed & Fri–Sun 2–6pm; €6; Ⓦwww.jardin-vauville.fr).

The area's main tourist office, at 45 rue Jallot in **Beaumont-Hague**, can supply details of suggested walks (June Mon–Sat 9am–12.30pm & 2–6.30pm; July & Aug Mon–Sat 9am–6.30pm, Sun 10am–12.30pm; Sept–May Mon–Sat 9am–12.30pm & 2–6pm; Ⓣ02.33.52.74.94, Ⓦlahague.org).

Barneville and Carteret

The next two sweeps of beach down to Carteret, backed by sand dunes like miniature mountain ranges, are among the best **beaches** in Normandy – if you have transport and want solitude. **CARTERET** itself, sheltered by a rocky headland, is the nearest harbour to the English-speaking island of **Jersey**, just 25km away across seas made treacherous by the fast Alderney current. **Ferry** services from the harbour to both Jersey and Guernsey are operated to very erratic schedules by Manche Îles Express (day return €50 in high season; Ⓣ02.33.61.08.88, Ⓦwww.manche-iles-express.com).

Carteret's old port area is not especially attractive, but does have several seafront **hotels**, including the elegant, very tastefully restored *Hôtel des Ormes*, quai Barbey d'Aurévilly (Ⓣ02.33.52.23.50, Ⓦhoteldesormes.fr; ❼; closed Jan), which has a good restaurant, *Le Rivage* (closed in low season on Sun eve plus all Mon & Tues), and the cheaper *Hôtel du Cap* on promenade A. Lebouteiller (Ⓣ02.33.53.85.89; ❸), which also serves decent food.

Visitors who prefer to be beside a beach should head instead for Carteret's twin community of **BARNEVILLE**, directly across the mouth of the bay but a few kilometres away by road. Here an endless (and quite exposed) stretch of clean, firm sand is backed by a long row of weather-beaten villas and the odd hotel, including the *Hôtel des Isles* near the northern end at 9 boulevard Maritime (Ⓣ02.33.04.90.76, Ⓦwww.hoteldesisles.com; ❼; closed Feb), which has a heated outdoor swimming pool and a superb **restaurant** that offers views clear to the Channel Islands on fine evenings. Menus range from €16 to €29 and include oysters stewed in *pommeau*. There are **tourist offices** in both Barneville, at 10 rue des Écoles (Mon–Sat 9am–12.30pm & 2–6pm; Ⓣ02.33.04.90.58, Ⓦbarneville-carteret.net), and Carteret, on place Flandres-Dunkerque (July & Aug daily 10am–12.30pm & 3–7pm; Ⓣ02.33.04.94.54).

Two **campsites** are located in the dunes north of town: the two-star *Le Ranch* at **Le Rozel** (Ⓣ02.33.10.07.10, Ⓦcamping-leranch.com; closed Oct–March), and the three-star *Les Mielles* at **Surtainville** (Ⓣ02.33.04.31.04, Ⓦsurtainville.new.fr).

Portbail

Five kilometres further down the coast from Barneville, the dunes are interrupted once again by the broad estuary of the Ollonde River. Set slightly back from the sea, **PORTBAIL** is a delightful village with a tiny Romanesque church that is now deconsecrated and hosts temporary art exhibitions in summer. Its streets are thronged on summer Tuesdays with a bustling **market**, where, as well as buying spit-roasted chickens and fresh oysters, you can pick up a dining table or have your chairs re-upholstered. Access to two fine beaches is by way of an old stone bridge, beneath which crowds of fishermen wade thigh-deep in the river.

Good-value **rooms** are available above *Aux XIII Arches* (Ⓣ02.33.04.87.90; ③), an attractive café-restaurant close to the bridge that serves mussels from €11. The similar *Au Rendezvous des Pêcheurs* opposite also makes a pleasant spot to sit and watch the world go by.

The first French beach that **Charles Lindbergh** crossed as he completed the first solo transatlantic flight in 1927, just south of Portbail, is now called plage Lindbergh.

Lessay

Heading south from Carteret, the road around the headland joins the main D900 at **LESSAY**, where an important Romanesque **monastery** stands right in the heart of town. Until the war it was one of the few early Norman churches still intact. When it had to be rebuilt from scratch afterwards, guided by photographs, the job was done using not only the original stone but also authentic tools and methods.

The square central tower of Lessay is similar to that which collapsed centuries ago on Mont-St-Michel. The abbey hosts a series of evening concerts, under the umbrella title **Heures Musicales**, in July and August (for details call Ⓣ02.33.46.90.27), while its monks sing Gregorian chants each Sunday. They're also very much in evidence at the **Holy Cross Fair** in the first half of September, which celebrates cattle and other animals (Ⓦwww.canton-lessay.com).

Pirou

Off the main coastal road, the D650, roughly 2km south of the junction for Lessay, turns inland for a few hundred metres to reach the **Château de Pirou** (daily except Tues: Feb, March & mid-Oct to Nov 10am–noon & 2–5pm; April–Sept 10am–noon & 2–6.30pm; July & Aug daily 10am–noon & 2–6.30pm; closed Dec, Jan and first half of Oct; €5; Ⓦchateau-pirou.org). Although you see nothing from the road, once you've passed through its three successive fortified gateways you are confronted by a ravishing little castle. Some historians have suggested that this is the oldest castle in Normandy, dating back to the earliest Viking raids; it's thought to have taken its current form around the twelfth century.

Considering that it was converted into a farm, and then for centuries forgotten and all but submerged in ivy, it remains remarkably complete. Originally built of wood, on the coast, it was later remodelled in stone and now stands encircled by a broad moat, its towers rising sheer from the water. At your own risk, you can pick your way up to the top of the keep and look out over the surrounding fields. Between mid-June and September, a modern tapestry depicting the 1091 Norman invasion of Sicily, embroidered in the style of the Bayeux Tapestry, is displayed in a barn opposite the drawbridge.

Heading towards the sea instead of inland, at the turn-off for the Château de Pirou, brings you to a dead end in a couple of hundred metres at the tiny community of **PIROU-PLAGE**. When the tide is low, you can see the *buchôts*, poles used in the cultivation of shellfish, poking up from the six-kilometre strip of endless flat sand that stretches away to either side. To sample the local produce, call in at the seafront **restaurant** *De la Mer*, 2 rue Ferdinand Desplanques, where menus start at €20 (Ⓣ02.33.46.43.36; lunch daily except Wed, dinner Fri & Sat only; closed Jan).

Coutances

The old hill town of **COUTANCES**, 65km south of Cherbourg and confined by its site to just one main street, has on its summit a landmark for all the surrounding countryside – the **Cathédrale de Notre Dame**, whose twin towers stand in magnificent silhouette against the sky. Essentially Gothic, it is very Norman in its unconventional blending of architectural traditions; Louis XIV's master architect Vauban said the lantern tower must be "the work of a madman".

Walk the length of the main square that faces the cathedral, then head to the right and slightly downhill, to reach the fountained **Jardins Publiques**, highly formal gardens with smooth rolling lawns, a well of flowers, a fountain of obelisks and an odd pyramid of hedges. Pleasantly illuminated (and left open) on summer nights, they enclose a small **Musée Municipal** (July & Aug Mon & Wed–Sat 10am–noon & 2–6pm, Sun 2–6pm; Sept–June Mon & Wed–Sat 10am–noon & 2–5pm, Sun 2–5pm; €2.50), which has a rather dull collection of permanent paintings but a nice line in pretentious temporary art exhibitions.

Practicalities

Coutances's **gare SNCF**, at the bottom of the hill 1.5km southeast of the centre, also serves as the stop for all **buses**. The **tourist office** is housed behind the Hôtel de Ville in place Georges-Leclerc (July & Aug Mon–Fri 9.30am–6pm, Sat 10am–12.30pm & 2–6pm, Sun 10am–1pm; Sept–June Mon–Fri 9.30am–12.30pm & 2–6pm, Sat 10am–12.30pm & 2–5pm; ⓣ02.33.19.08.10, ⓦville-coutances.fr).

Central Coutances is very short of **hotels**. In the cathedral square, the *Hôtel du Parvis* (ⓣ02.33.45.13.55; ❷; restaurant closed Sun), has unexciting but adequate rooms, above a reasonable brasserie. A more comfortable alternative is the large *Cositel* (ⓣ02.33.19.15.00, ⓦcositel.fr; ❹), a Logis de France with 55 modern rooms, in spacious gardens halfway up the hill west of town that's climbed by the D44 towards Agon. Next to it is an excellent year-round municipal **campsite**, *Les Vignettes* (ⓣ02.33.45.43.13).

Agon-Coutainville

AGON-COUTAINVILLE, 10km west of Coutances and its nearest resort, is crammed in summer with visitors. This is an utterly nondescript stretch of coast, where the open sea batters against an endless, featureless beach. Huge tides expose massive sandflats, while behind the line of dunes dull holiday homes are punctuated by the occasional snack bar, campsite or motel.

A long walk south from town, fighting against the wind, brings you after three or four kilometres to the **Pointe d'Agon**, where a lighthouse commands a view of the dune environment at its most ecologically unspoiled.

Les Fresques, 100m back from the sea in town at 9 rue de l'Amiral-Tourville (ⓣ02.33.47.05.77, ⓦhotellesfresques.fr; ❹), is a simple **hotel** with no restaurant, and there are several shorefront **campsites** on boulevard Lebel Jehenne, including two municipal ones, the three-star *Marais* (ⓣ02.33.47.05.20, ⓦpagesperso-orange.fr/campings.martinetmarais; July & Aug only) and the two-star *Martinet* (same contact details; closed Nov–March).

Abbaye de Hambye

What's left of the **Abbaye de Hambye** stands in a very sylvan setting 20km southeast of Coutances and 10km northwest of Villedieu, with little lawns laid out in front, an orchard alongside, and cows grazing in the adjacent meadows

(April–June & Sept daily except Tues 10am–noon & 2–6pm; July & Aug daily 10am–noon & 2–6pm; Oct daily except Tues 10am–noon & 2–5pm; €2.70 unguided, €4 guided).

Very reminiscent of such Yorkshire abbeys as Rievaulx, the abbey was constructed as a Cistercian monastery in the second half of the twelfth century, just as builders were about to abandon the Romanesque tradition in favour of the new Gothic style. Much of the structure was quarried for stone and left in ruins after the Revolution; nineteenth-century prints show the walls drowning in rampant ivy. However, the central tower still stands foursquare above the high narrow walls of the nave, and a few delicate buttresses remain in place, the whole ensemble crammed in tight against a wooded hillside and inhabited mostly by crows. To explore the ruins themselves, beyond the little exhibition in the entrance room above the ancient gateway, you have to join a guided tour.

The *Auberge de l'Abbaye*, a luxurious but very well priced rural **hotel**, stands 100m from the abbey at the turning off the D51 (Ⓣ02.33.61.42.19, Ⓔauberge.abbaye@orange.fr; ❸; closed Mon, plus second half of Feb & first half of Oct; restaurant also closed Sun eve). There being few alternative ways to pass an evening here, its restaurant serves up extravagant and expensive gourmet **dinners** (€26–€65).

Granville

The striking fortified coastal town of **GRANVILLE** is in many ways the Norman equivalent to Brittany's St-Malo, with a similar history of piracy and an imposing, severely elegant citadel – the **haute ville** – guarding the approaches to the bay of Mont-St-Michel across from Cancale. Here however the fortress was originally built by the English, early in the fifteenth century, as the springboard for an attack on Mont-St-Michel that never came to fruition.

Granville these days has become a deservedly popular destination for tourists. Thanks in part to the long beach that stretches away north of town, which disappears almost completely at high tide, it's the most popular resort in the area. Traffic in the maze-like new town, down below the headland, can be nightmarish, but the beaches are excellent, with facilities for watersports of all kind, while the *haute ville* makes a fascinating and much more peaceful refuge. Riotous four-day **carnival** celebrations take over the town at Mardi Gras each year.

Granville had an unexpected brush with destiny on March 9, 1945, when it was overrun for an hour and a half by German commandos from Jersey, long after the invading Allied forces had swept on to Germany.

Arrival and information

Trains between Paris and Cherbourg arrive well to the east of the town centre at the **gare SNCF** on avenue Maréchal-Leclerc, which doubles as the **gare routière** (Ⓣ02.33.50.77.89). **Ferry** services from the harbour to Jersey are operated by Manche Îles Express (day return €50 in high season; Ⓣ02.33.61.08.88, Ⓦwww.manche-iles-express.com), and to the Îles Chausey (see p.146) by Jolie France (Ⓣ02.33.50.31.81, Ⓦvedettejoliefrance.com). The **tourist office** is down below the citadel at 4 cours Jonville (July & Aug Mon–Sat 9am–1pm & 2–7pm, Sun 10am–1pm & 3–6pm; May, June & Sept Mon–Sat 9am–12.30pm & 2–6pm, Sun 10am–1pm & 3–6pm; Oct–April Mon–Sat 9am–noon & 2–6pm; Ⓣ02.33.91.30.03, Ⓦgranville-tourisme.fr).

Bikes can be rented from Gérard Marchand Cycles, 35 av Maréchal-Leclerc (☎02.33.61.53.62).

Accommodation

With so many visitors in summer, it's well worth booking **accommodation** in advance. There are no hotels in the *haute ville*; most of the possibilities are concentrated in the new town, either beneath the walls near the casino on the seaward side, or near the station.

Centre Régional de Nautisme bd des Amiraux ☎02.33.91.22.62, Ⓦcrng.fr. The modern, ocean-front hostel 1km south of the station and just south of the town centre. Dorm beds cost from €15.85, and there are also private singles (€25.50) and doubles (€41.50); they also offer sailing lessons. closed Sat & Sun Nov–Feb. ❶–❷

Logis du Roc 13 rue St-Michel ☎06.18.35.87.42, Ⓦlelogisduroc.com. This nicely furnished B&B, in a grey-granite town house above a former butcher's shop, offers the only opportunity to stay in the peace and elegance of the *haute ville*, It has three en-suite rooms; the owner speaks very good English and will even pick up guests from the *gare SNCF*. ❸

de la Mer 74 rue du Port ☎02.33.50.01.86, Ⓔhotel-de-la-mer-granville@orange.fr. Simple hotel in front of the piles of rusting ironmongery of the commercial port, a short walk from the town centre. Restaurant reviewed on p.146. Closed Mon, plus Tues in low season, & last three weeks of Dec. ❸

Michelet 5 rue Jules-Michelet ☎02.33.50.06.55, Ⓦhotel-michelet-granville.com. Cream-fronted hotel, very near the sea and facing towards the high crags of the old town. It offers reasonably well-equipped but rather characterless rooms, the very cheapest of which lack en-suite facilities, and there's no restaurant. Closed Sun. ❶

Terminus 5 pl de la Gare ☎02.33.50.02.05, Ⓦwww.hotel-granville-france.com. Simple, inexpensive hotel, immediately across from the station, where those of its reasonably pleasant bedrooms that have en-suite facilities cost just €6 more than those that don't, and there's no restaurant. ❶

The Town

The great difference between Granville and St-Malo is that Granville's walled, fortified **citadel** stands separate from the modern town, and remains resolutely uncommercialized. Although – or rather, because – it holds only a handful of shops and restaurants, and no hotels – it's an intriguing enclave, well worth a couple of hours of your time. Sheltered behind a rocky outcrop that juts out into the Channel, it's reached by steep stairs from alongside the beach and casino, or circuitous climbing roads from the port. Once up there, you'll find three or four long narrow parallel streets of grey-granite eighteenth-century houses – some forbidding and aloof, some adorned with brightly painted shutters – that lead to the church of Notre Dame. The views up and down the coast, across to Mont-St-Michel and out to the Îles Chausey, are dramatic. Ornamental gardens close to the headland boast a statue of the city's best-known pirate, **Georges Pléville le Pellay**, splendidly complete with peg leg and cutlass.

Set into the citadel walls directly above the port, the **Musée du Vieux Granville**, 2 rue le Carpentier (April–Sept daily except Tues 10am–noon & 2–6pm; Oct–March Wed, Sat & Sun 2–6pm; €1.70), holds three floors of rather dry displays on local history. The main feature downstairs, amid old postcards and paintings, is a model of Granville as it appeared in 1912; higher up, antique coiffes and costumes jostle for space with hefty wooden Norman furniture, while the top level is devoted to the history of the Newfoundland cod fisheries.

In pride of place at the inland end of the *haute ville*, the **Musée d'Art Moderne Richard Anacréon** (April–Sept daily except Mon 11am–6pm; Oct–March Wed–Sun 2–6pm; €2.60) houses art accumulated by the eponymous M. Anacréon, who was born in Granville in 1907 and opened his L'Originale bookshop in Paris in 1940. Filled with sketches and autographs from the likes of Jean Cocteau and André Derain – and one or two Picasso *eau-fortes* – it's not all that compelling, but the gallery itself is impressive and hosts interesting temporary exhibitions.

The family home of a more famous Granvillais contemporary of Anacréon, the couturier **Christian Dior**, who was responsible for the "New Look", overlooks the beach a few hundred metres northeast of the citadel. A striking orange-and-pink-painted Belle Époque mansion, it can be reached along a coastal footpath that continues another 6.5km to St-Martin de Bréhal. Its tranquil, flower-filled gardens enjoy sweeping views, while the interior of the actual house has been stripped bare and is refitted each summer for changing annual exhibitions on aspects of twentieth-century fashion, focusing on Dior in particular (May to late Sept daily 10am–6.30pm; €6; ⓦwww.musee-dior-granville.com).

Eating

Granville's best **restaurants** are of the seafood variety, situated hard below the citadel walls with waterfront views – albeit of a gritty commercial port rather than a delightful harbour.

La Citadelle 34 rue du Port ⓣ02.33.50.34.10, ⓦrestaurant-la-citadelle.com. The closest to the town centre of the port's top-notch seafood places. Dinner menus from €23, with a sumptuous €28.50 option featuring veal or fried sea bass. Closed Wed, plus Tues in winter, four weeks around Christmas, and second half of March.

L'Échauguette 24 rue St-Jean ⓣ02.33.50.51.87. Cosy, stone-walled old-town crêperie, which serves good simple meals, grilled over an open fire. *Galettes* cost under €8, meat main courses more like €14, and there's a menu at €19.

de la Mer 74 rue du Port ⓣ02.33.50.01.86. Seafood restaurant attached to a small hotel (see p.145) in the port. The restaurant has a dull €17 menu, but gets interesting at €26; it's best to sit upstairs to get a view. Closed Mon, plus Tues in low season, & last three weeks of Dec.

Restaurant du Port 19 rue du Port ⓣ02.33.50.00.55. Top-quality seafood place in the small-boat harbour, with a mouth-watering assortment of very fishy menus, and an unbelievably garlicky fish soup as its speciality. Menus range from €16.50 up to €31.50; the good-value €27 menu features nine stuffed oysters and a delicious parcel of duck in Camembert sauce. Closed Sun eve, plus Mon in low season, and last three weeks of Jan.

The Îles Chausey

Nowadays visited for their long beaches of fine sand, the myriad low-lying **Îles Chausey** were the site of the quarries that provided the granite that built Mont-St-Michel. They originally formed part of the ancient Forest of Scissy, until exceptional tides at the spring equinox of 709 AD, combined with strong north winds, flooded the entire region.

The only inhabited island, the **Grand Île**, which as the name suggests is by far the largest of the archipelago, holds the one (summer-only) **hotel**. The lonely *Hôtel du Fort et Îles* (ⓣ02.33.50.25.02, ⓦhotel-chausey.com; *demi-pension* ❼; closed late Sept to mid-April, restaurant closed Mon), has eight simple rooms and only accepts guests on at least a *demi-pension* basis. Other accommodation is available in either private or municipal *gîtes*, the latter run by the tourist office in Granville (see p.144). Apart from the hotel, the only other place to eat on the island is a modest crêperie, the *Bellevue* (ⓣ02.33.51.80.30).

Ferries out to the islands from Granville's *gare maritime* are operated by Jolie France II (April–Sept up to 5 daily, Oct–March 1–5 weekly; ⓣ02.33.50.31.81, ⓦvedettejoliefrance.com). Precise timings and frequencies depend on the tides; the trip takes just under an hour each way, and day returns cost €21.30.

Around Granville

If you prefer to base yourself out of town, the coastal countryside is best to the **north**, although the villages tend to be nonevents. As well as windsurfers, the huge flat sands attract hordes of sand-yachters. Among **accommodation** possibilities, **Coudeville** has a good campsite on its long beach, the two-star *Dunes* (Ⓣ02.33.51.76.07; closed Nov–March).

Eight kilometres south of Granville, **Jullouville** is geared more towards young families. Its main through road, a block inland from the sea, is lined with generally downmarket snack bars, but the seafront promenade makes for a very pleasant stroll, while the *Promenade*, in the former casino building, is a delightful old-style **restaurant** (Ⓣ02.33.90.80.20; closed Mon & Tues, plus Sun eve).

Carolles has a good beach, but little more; its one hotel is uninviting. However, in the clifftop village of **Champeaux**, a short steep climb further on from Carolles, the *Hôtel les Hermelles* at 25 rte des Falaises (Ⓣ02.33.61.85.94, Ⓦwww.hotel-leshermelles.com; ❸; closed Tues eve & Wed, plus mid-Dec to March), enjoys truly spectacular views out across the bay; guests check in at its run-of-the-mill restaurant, the *Marquis de Tombelaine*, on the other side of the road.

Another kilometre downhill, at **St-Jean-Le-Thomas** – which promotes itself as "le Petit Nice de la Manche", but is remarkably unlike Nice in that it consists of a single street leading up to a beach – the sea retreats so far at low tide that it's possible to walk across to Mont-St-Michel. However, this is not a walk to take on impulse; only do it with a licensed guide (see p.150).

Avranches

Perched high above the bay on an abrupt granite outcrop, **AVRANCHES** is the nearest large town to Mont-St-Michel. It has always had close connections with the abbey. The Mont's original church was founded by an eighth-century bishop of Avranches, spurred on by the Archangel Michael, who supposedly became so impatient with the lack of progress that he prodded a hole in the bishop's skull. Subsequently gold-plated, that skull now forms part of the *trésor* of Avranches's St-Gervais basilica. Robert of Torigny, a later abbot of St-Michel, played host in the town on several occasions to Henry II of England, the most memorable being when Henry – bare-footed and bare-headed – did public penance for the murder of Thomas à Becket, on May 22, 1172. Henry's act of contrition took place in **Avranches Cathedral**. Designed by Robert himself, though without expertise, it eventually "crumbled and fell for want of proper support"; all that now marks the site of Henry's humbling is a fenced-off platform.

A more vivid evocation of the area's medieval splendours comes from the illuminated manuscripts, mostly created on the Mont, on display in a state-of-the-art museum in the place d'Estouteville, the **Scriptorial d'Avranches** (Feb–April & Oct–Dec Tues–Fri 10am–12.30pm & 2–5pm, Sat & Sun 10am–12.30pm & 2–6pm; May, June & Sept daily except Mon 10am–6pm; July & Aug daily 10–7pm; closed Jan; €7; Ⓦscriptorial.fr). Additional exhibits trace the history of Avranches, and bring the story up to date by covering modern book-production techniques. All that rather overshadows the long-established **municipal museum**, housed in what was once the bishop's palace, which concentrates on local costumes and popular traditions (June–Sept daily 10am–12.30pm & 2–6pm; €1.50, or free with Scriptorial).

The ruins of Avranches' old **castle** dominate the entire central area of the town; the highest point of all is the former keep, which, together with the vestiges of a small section of ramparts, has been landscaped into a small garden.

From the very top, you get long views over Avranches itself, and the Mont away to the west. The terrace of Avranches's large formal public gardens, the **Jardin des Plantes** across town, is another good vantage point for the Mont.

A monument to **General George Patton**, southeast of the town centre, commemorates the spot where he stayed the night before his crucial Avranches breakthrough, at the end of July 1944. This small plot of land was ceded to the USA, so technically the statue stands on US soil – and it does literally as well, earth having been brought across the Atlantic to create a memorial garden.

Practicalities

Avranches' **gare SNCF** is a long way below the town centre; the walk up is enough to discourage most rail travellers from stopping here at all. The **tourist office** is located in the central square – scene of a lively market on Saturday mornings – at 2 place Général-de-Gaulle (July & Aug Mon–Sat 9.30am–12.30pm & 2–7pm, Sun 9.30am–12.30pm & 2–6pm; Sept–June Mon–Fri 9.30am–12.30pm & 2–6pm, Sat 10am–12.30pm & 2.30–5pm; ⓣ02.33.58.00.22, ⓦwww.ot-avranches.com). In high summer, one **bus** per day runs to Mont-St-Michel from right outside.

The nicest **hotel** has to be the gloriously old-fashioned *Croix d'Or*, a former coaching inn at 83 rue de la Constitution (ⓣ02.33.58.04.88, ⓦhoteldelacroixdor.fr; ④; closed Jan, plus Sun eve in winter), which boasts lovely rooms, beautiful hydrangea-filled gardens and a truly outstanding **restaurant**, serving a magnificent €25 dinner menu with a delicious array of cheese and desserts. Reasonable alternatives include *Le Jardin des Plantes*, a large Logis de France near the eponymous gardens at 10 place Carnot (ⓣ02.33.58.03.68, ⓦle-jardin-des-plantes.fr; ④), though its restaurant is frankly poor. A better option for a quick meal is the unassuming but always busy *Littré*, at 8 rue du Dr-Gilbert (ⓣ02.33.58.01.66; closed Sun & Mon), where there's a brasserie and a coffee shop as well as a fully-fledged restaurant that serves a great-value €17 *menu du jour*.

If you're **camping**, the two-star, English-owned *Vallée de la Sélune* site (ⓣ02.33.60.39.00; closed mid-Oct to March) at **Pontaubault**, 7km south, makes a better base for the Mont than Avranches.

Mont-St-Michel

The island at the very frontier of Normandy and Brittany, which for over a millennium has housed – indeed, all but consisted of – the stupendous abbey of **MONT-ST-MICHEL**, was once known as "the Mount in Peril from the Sea". Many were the pilgrims in medieval times who were drowned or sucked under by quicksand while trying to cross the bay to this eighty-metre-high rocky outcrop. The Archangel Michael was its vigorous protector, the most militant spirit of the Church Militant, with a marked tendency to leap from rock to rock in titanic struggles against Paganism and Evil.

The abbey dates back to the eighth century, when the archangel appeared to a bishop of Avranches, Aubert, who duly founded a monastery on the island poking out of the Baie du Mont-St-Michel. Since the eleventh century – when work on the sturdy church at the peak commenced – new buildings have been grafted onto the island to produce a fortified hotchpotch of Romanesque and Gothic buildings, piled one on top of the other and clambering to the pinnacle of the graceful church, to form the most recognizable silhouette in France after the Eiffel Tower.

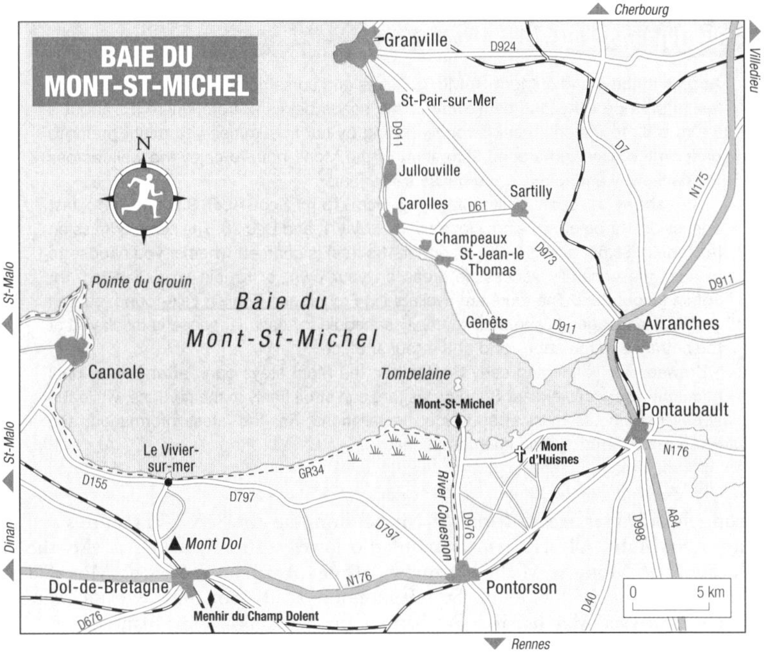

Over the course of its long history, the island has been besieged many times. However, unlike all the rest of northern France, it was never captured, not even during the 27 years, from 1423 to 1450, when the English had a permanent fort on nearby Tombelaine. Although the abbey was a fortress town, home to a large community, even at its twelfth-century peak it never housed more than sixty monks, who said Mass for pilgrims and ran their own school of art. The Revolution ultimately closed the monastery down, and converted it into a prison, renaming the island "Free Mount". In 1966, exactly a thousand years after Duke Richard the First originally brought the order to the Mont, the Benedictines were invited to return, but they departed again in 2001, having found that the present-day island does not exactly lend itself to a life of quiet contemplation. In their place, a dozen nuns and monks from the Monastic Fraternity of Jerusalem now maintain a presence.

For many years, the Mont has not, strictly speaking, been an island – the causeway (*digue*) that leads to it is never submerged, and is continuing to silt up to either side. Current plans envisage that the causeway will soon be cut away and replaced by a bridge, with a tram service to spare visitors the two-kilometre walk from the mainland. Currently scheduled for completion in 2014, this should not only make tourist numbers easier to control but also enable the sea to wash away much of the accumulated silt. For the latest news on the project, drop in at the temporary visitor centre at the mainland end of the causeway, or see Ⓦwww.projetmontsaintmichel.fr.

Arrival and information

In addition to the regular **bus** service from the nearest *gare SNCF* at Pontorson (see p.142), Keolis Emeraude (Ⓣ02.99.19.70.80, Ⓦwww.keolis-emeraude.com)

Visiting Mont-St-Michel

Access to the island of Mont-St-Michel is free and unrestricted, although there's a €4 fee to park on either the causeway or the sands below it, from where it's about a 500m walk to the entrance. If you're visiting by car in summer, you might prefer to park on the mainland around 2km short of the Mont, both to enjoy the walk across the causeway and to avoid the dense traffic jams.

The **abbey** is open daily: May–Aug 9am–7pm; Sept–April 9.30am–6pm; last admission 1hr before closing; closed Jan 1, May 1, and Dec 25. The same admission fee (adults €8.50, ages 18–25 €5, under-18s free) is charged whether you choose to wander the generally accessible areas on your own, or to join an expert-led 1hr 15min guided tour. The tours are available in French and English year-round, as well as other languages in summer; the daily schedule for each language is displayed at the entrance to the abbey and at the tourist office.

Between early July and early September, the Mont stays open **after hours**, until midnight, every day except Sunday. Visitors can stroll freely in the gardens, while the abbey itself hosts musical and video installations. For the latest information, see Ⓦmont-saint-michel.monuments-nationaux.fr.

run scheduled services to Mont-St-Michel from the *gare SNCF* in **Rennes** and from **St-Malo**. All arrive in front of the lowest gateway, which is also the location of Mont-St-Michel's **tourist office** (April–June & Sept Mon–Sat 9am–12.30pm & 2–6.30pm, Sun 9am–noon & 2–6pm; July & Aug daily 9am–7pm; Oct–March Mon–Sat 9am–noon & 2–6pm, Sun 10am–noon & 2–5pm; Ⓣ02.33.60.14.30, Ⓦwww.ot-montsaintmichel.com), and **post office** (Mon–Fri 7am–5.30pm, Sat 9am–4pm). There's an **ATM** next door.

Tours

Walking tours across the bay to Mont-St-Michel set off from **Genêts** on a schedule that varies according to the tides. Quite how far you go, and how much time you spend once you get there, changes daily. With Chemins de la Baie (Ⓣ02.33.89.80.88, Ⓦwww.cheminsdelabaie.com), the standard guided trip, from the beach at Genêts to the Mont and back (a total of 13km), takes 4hr 30min and costs €5.80 without a commentary; for a shorter walk, though pretty much the same total time, you can make the return trip by bus (€10.30). The same walk with a commentary costs €9.80, while narrated themed tours, aimed at explaining various aspects of the Mont's history or wildlife, are available in English, and can take anything up to ten hours and cost up to €14.80.

Other walking-tour operators include Dans Les Pas Du Guide (Ⓣ02.33.58.44.82, Ⓦlespasduguide.com; no under-13s), Didier Lavadoux (Ⓣ02.33.70.84.19, Ⓦtraversee-baie.com), and La Maison du Guide (Ⓣ02.33.70.83.49, Ⓦdecouvertebaie.com).

Accommodation

Grande Rue, the island's one "street", holds a surprising number of **hotels**, but nothing like enough to cope with the sheer number of visitors. Most are predictably expensive, and all charge extra if you want a view of the sea, though higher up the Mont, room prices fall to more realistic levels. The main approach road to the island, the D976, is lined shortly before the causeway by around a dozen large and virtually indistinguishable hotels and motels. For accommodation in nearby Pontorson, see p.142.

On the island

Croix Blanche Grande Rue ⓣ02.33.60.14.04, ⓦhotel-la-croix-blanche.com. This little hotel is the nicest option on Mont-St-Michel, with nine sprucely decorated rooms, but there's a hefty premium for a sea view. Closed mid-Nov to mid-Feb. 6

Du Guesclin Grande Rue ⓣ02.33.60.14.10, ⓦhotelduguesclin.com. The cheapest option on the island, a Logis de France where all the rooms have been reasonably spruced up, and five have sea views. Closed mid-Nov to March. 4

La Mère Poulard Grande Rue ⓣ02.33.89.68.68, ⓦwww.mere-poulard.com. Mont-St-Michel's most famous hotel uses the time-honoured legend of its fluffy omelettes, as enjoyed by Leon Trotsky and Margaret Thatcher (not simultaneously), to justify extortionate charges. 8

Mouton Blanc Grande Rue ⓣ02.33.60.14.08, ⓦwww.lemoutonblanc.com. Wood-panelled fourteenth-century house, now a hotel with fifteen small and somewhat plain rooms, and a large old-fashioned restaurant. 5

On the mainland

Camping du Mont-St-Michel rte de Mont-St-Michel ⓣ02.33.60.22.10, ⓦcamping-montsaint michel.com. Three-star, 350-pitch campsite, on the mainland just short of the causeway. Closed mid-Nov to early Feb.

De la Digue rte de Mont-St-Michel ⓣ02.33.60.14.02, ⓦladigue.eu. Logis de France hotel, with 35 spacious rooms and a terrace restaurant with views towards the Mont. 4

Formule Verte rte de Mont-St-Michel ⓣ02.33.60.14.13, ⓦle-mont-saint-michel.com. Sprawling inexpensive motel/restaurant, on the approach road just short of the island. Closed mid-Nov to early Feb. 3

Vert rte de Mont-St-Michel ⓣ02.33.60.09.33, ⓦhotelvert-montsaintmichel.com. Low-slung, anonymous but perfectly adequate motel, with *Rôtisserie* restaurant and bar. Closed mid-Nov to early Feb. 3

The Island

The base of Mont-St-Michel rests on a primeval slime of sand and mud. Just above that, you pass through the heavily fortified **Porte du Roi** onto the narrow **Grande Rue**, climbing steadily around the base of the rock, and lined with medieval gabled houses and a jumble of postcard and souvenir shops. A plaque near the main staircase records that Jacques Cartier was presented to King François I here on May 8, 1532, and charged with exploring the shores of Canada.

The rather dry **Musée Maritime** offers an insight into the island's ties with the sea, while the Archangel Michael manages in just fifteen minutes to lead visitors on a voyage through space and time in the **Archéoscope**, with the full majestic panoply of multimedia trickery. Further along the Grande Rue and up the steps towards the abbey church, next door to the eleventh-century **church of St-Pierre**, the absurd **Musée Grévin** contains such edifying specimens as a wax model of a woman drowning in a sea of mud (all open Feb to mid-Nov daily 9am–6pm; €18 for all, or €9 each one).

Large crowds gather each day at the **North Tower** to watch the tide sweep in across the bay. During the high tides of the equinoxes (March & Sept), the waters are alleged to rush in like a foaming galloping horse. Seagulls wheel away in alarm, and those foolish enough to be wandering too late on the sands toward Tombelaine have to sprint to safety.

Amazingly enough, less than a third of the three million visitors who come to Mont-St-Michel each year climb up to visit the abbey itself, so the higher you go the more the crowds thin out. If you're impatient to escape all the jostling, you can duck through St-Pierre church to reach the **gardens**. From the various footpaths here, popular with picnickers, you can see the giant ramp up the side of the hill, up which prisoners used to haul supplies for the abbey by walking around a treadmill at the top.

The Abbey

The **abbey** (for hours and prices, see p.150), an architectural ensemble incorporating the high-spired archangel-topped church and the magnificent Gothic buildings known since 1228 as the **Merveille** ("The Marvel") – which in turn includes the entire north face, with the cloister, Knights' Hall, Refectory, Guest Hall and cellars – is visible from all around the bay, but it becomes if anything more awe-inspiring the closer you approach. In Maupassant's words:

> I reached the huge pile of rocks which bears the little city dominated by the great church. Climbing the steep narrow street, I entered the most wonderful Gothic building ever made for God on this earth, a building as vast as a town, full of low rooms under oppressive ceilings and lofty galleries supported by frail pillars. I entered that gigantic granite jewel, which is as delicate as a piece of lacework, thronged with towers and slender belfries which thrust into the blue sky of day and the black sky of night their strange heads bristling with chimeras, devils, fantastic beasts and monstrous flowers, and which are linked together by carved arches of intricate design.

The Mont's rock comes to a sharp point just below what is now the transept of the **church**, a building where the transition from Romanesque to Gothic is only too evident in the vaulting of the nave. In order to lay out the church's ground plan in the traditional shape of the cross, supporting crypts had to be built up from the surrounding hillside, and in all construction work the Chausey granite has had to be sculpted to match the exact contours of the hill. Space was always limited, and yet the building has grown through the centuries, with an architectural ingenuity that constantly surprises in its geometry – witness the shock of emerging into the light of the **cloisters** from the sombre Great Hall. The statue of St Francis of Assisi here commemorates the fact that 1228, when the cloisters were completed, was the same year that Francis was canonized.

Not surprisingly, the building of the monastery was no smooth progression; the original church, choir, nave and tower all had to be replaced after collapsing. The style of decoration has varied, too, along with the architecture. That you now walk through halls of plain grey stones is a reflection of modern taste. In the Middle Ages, the walls of public areas such as the refectory would have been festooned with tapestries and frescoes, while the original coloured tiles of the cloisters have long since been stripped away to reveal bare walls.

All visitors exit the abbey on its north side; as you follow the circling footpath back to the mayhem below, you pass beneath what Victor Hugo described as "the most beautiful wall in Europe".

To get a clearer sense of the abbey's historical development, be sure to take a look at the intriguing scale models in the reception area, which depict it during four different epochs.

Eating

Sadly, the **restaurants** on Mont-St-Michel, both independent and in the hotels, are consistently worse than almost anywhere in France. It's impossible to make any confident recommendations, other than that ideally you should aim to eat elsewhere – for example, Cancale (see p.213), which has a fabulous selection of restaurants.

Pontorson

Many visitors to Mont-St-Michel find themselves lodging either at Avranches or **PONTORSON**, 6km inland. The latter has the nearest **gare SNCF**, connected to the Mont by regular buses. Nothing much about Pontorson itself is worth staying for, although the café attached to the station isn't bad.

The **hotels** are not especially interesting, but both the *Montgomery*, in a fine old ivy-covered mansion at 13 rue du Couesnon (Ⓣ02.33.60.00.09, Ⓦhotel-montgomery.com; ❹; closed last two weeks in Nov), and the *Bretagne*, just along the main road at 59 rue du Couesnon (Ⓣ02.33.60.10.55, Ⓦlebretagnepontorson.com; ❷; closed Feb), have distinguished **restaurants**. The *Tour Brette*, at the western end of the central drag at 8 rue de Couesnon (Ⓣ02.33.60.10.69, Ⓦlatourbrette.fr.st; ❷; restaurant closed Wed Oct–June), is a friendly and inexpensive Logis with good lunch menus from €11.30. A huge and rather forbidding **hostel** stands near the cathedral, 1km west of the station, in the *Centre Duguesclin* at 21 rue du Général-Patton (Ⓣ02.33.60.18.65, Ⓔaj@ville-pontorson.fr; dorm beds €11.30 members, €13.50 nonmembers; closed Oct–March).

Along the bay

The most direct **route from Pontorson to the Mont** runs alongside the River Couesnon, which marks the Normandy–Brittany border. The sands at the mouth of the Couesnon are those from which Harold can be seen rescuing two floundering soldiers in the Bayeux Tapestry, in the days when he and William were still getting on. The sheep that graze on the scrubby pastures of the marshes at the sea's edge provide meat for the local delicacy, *mouton pré-salé*.

A more roundabout road to the abbey can take you to the **German war cemetery** at **MONT D'HUISNES**, a grim and unforgettable concrete mausoleum on a tiny hill (see p.130).

Travel details

Trains

Caen to: Cherbourg (10 daily; 1hr 15min), via Bayeux (20min) and Valognes (1hr); Le Mans (5 daily; 2hr), via Argentan (45min) and Alençon (1hr 15min); Lisieux (21 daily; 30min); Paris-St-Lazare (11 daily; 2hr 10min); Rennes (4 daily; 3hr), via Bayeux (20min), St-Lô (50min), Coutances (1hr 15min) and Pontorson (2hr); Rouen (6 daily; 2hr); Tours (1 daily; 3hr).
Cherbourg to: Lison (12 daily; 45min), with connections to St-Lô (total 1hr 5min), and Coutances (1hr 40min); Paris (8 daily; 3hr) via Valognes (15min) and Caen (1hr 15min).
Coutances to: Caen (6 daily; 1hr 15min) with connections to Paris.
Dives-Cabourg to: Trouville-Deauville (July & Aug 6 daily, rest of year 2 daily Sat, Sun & national hols only; 30min) via Houlgate (6min) and Villers (20min).
Granville to: Coutances (7 daily; 30min).
Trouville-Deauville to: Lisieux (6 daily in winter, much more frequently in summer; 20min); Paris (6 daily in winter, much more frequently in summer; 2hr).

Buses

Bayeux to: Arromanches (4 daily; 30min); Courseulles (4 daily; 40min); Grandcamp-Maisy (6 daily; 1hr); Ouistreham (3 daily; 1hr 15min); Port-en-Bessin (5 daily; 20min).
Caen to: Arromanches (1 daily; 1hr 10min); Bayeux (3 daily; 50min); Clécy (4 daily; 50min); Falaise (7 daily; 1hr); Honfleur (13 daily; 2hr) via Cabourg (50min), Houlgate (1hr) and Deauville (1hr 15min), of which 5 continue to Le Havre (2hr 30min); Le Havre (3 daily express services; 1hr 40min) via Honfleur (1hr); Luc-sur-mer (12 daily; 40min); Ouistreham (20 daily; 30min); Pont-L'Évêque (3 daily; 1hr 10min); Thury-Harcourt (5 daily; 40min); Vire (connections for Brittany; 3 daily; 1hr 30min).
Cherbourg to: Barneville-Carteret (3–4 daily; 1hr 10min); Coutances (2 daily; 1hr 20min); St-Lô (3 daily; 1hr 45min) via Valognes (30min) and Carentan (1hr); St-Vaast (3–4 daily; 1hr 10min) via Barfleur (1hr).

Coutances to: Agon-Coutainville (1–2 daily; 20min). **Mont-St-Michel** to: Pontorson (11 daily; 20min); St-Malo (4 daily; 1hr 30min); Rennes (5 daily; 1hr 20min).

Ferries

Caen (Ouistreham) to: Portsmouth (2–4 daily; 3hr 30min–6hr) with Brittany Ferries (ⓣ08.03.82.88.28, ⓦbrittany-ferries.com). **Cherbourg** to: Portsmouth (1–2 daily; May–Oct high-speed 3hr, otherwise 5–7hr) and Poole (1–3 daily; 2hr 15min–5hr), with Brittany Ferries; Rosslare, with Irish Ferries (ⓣ02.33.23.44.44, ⓦwww.irishferries.com; 3–4 weekly; 18hr 30min) and LD Lines (ⓦwww.ldlines.co.uk; 0–6 weekly; 17hr). **Granville** to: Jersey (1–2 daily; 1hr–1hr 50min) with Manche Îles Express (ⓣ02.33.61.08.88, ⓦwww.manche-iles-express.com), and to the Îles Chausey with Jolie France II (April–Sept up to 5 daily, Oct–March 1–5 weekly; ⓣ02.33.50.31.81, ⓦvedettejoliefrance.com).

3

Inland Normandy

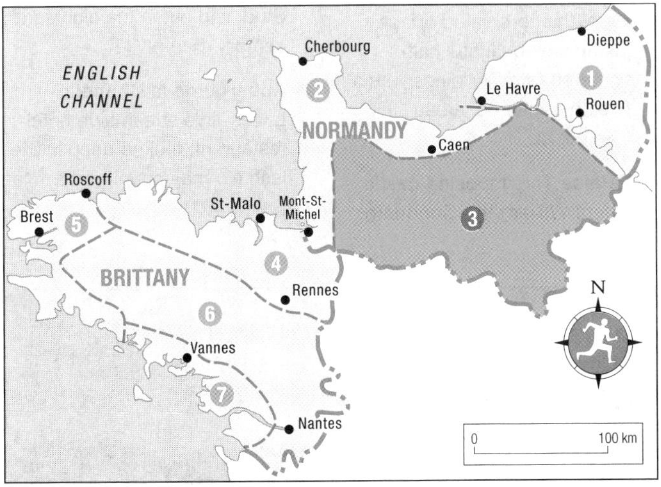

CHAPTER 3

Highlights

* **Château de la Ferté-Fresnel** Gorgeous stately château that's now run as a memorable and very affordable B&B. See p.162
* **Abbaye de Bec-Hellouin** One of the most venerable monasteries in Christendom sets the tone for an idyllic rural valley. See p.164
* **Crévecoeur-en-Auge** Evoking the Middle Ages as they never were, this re-created village juxtaposes beautiful half-timbered farm buildings with a twelfth-century château. See p.170
* **Falaise** The imposing castle where William the Conqueror was born is now a top-class exhibition centre. See p.173
* **Camembert** See the cows that eat the grass that make the milk that makes the cheese that made the name of Normandy. See p.175
* **Le Pin-au-Haras** If you love horses, you won't be able to resist the French National Stud, laid out in the eighteenth century. See p.177
* **Auberge de la Chapelle** Lovely little streamside hotel-restaurant, tucked deep in the lush Norman countryside. See p.187

▲ Crévecoeur-en-Auge

3

Inland Normandy

When you're exploring **inland Normandy**, seeking out specific highlights is not really the point. The pleasure of a visit lies not so much in show-stopping sights, or individual towns, as in the feel of the landscape – the lush meadows, orchards and forests of the Norman countryside. On top of that, of course, there's the **food**, a major attraction in these rich dairy regions. To the French, the **Pays d'Auge**, **Calvados** and the **Suisse Normande** are synonymous with cheeses, cream, apple and pear brandies, and ciders.

Other sensory pursuits can also be indulged. There are spas, forests, rivers and lakes for lazing or stretching the muscles in, and, everywhere, classic half-timbered houses and farm buildings. If you are staying on the Norman coast, trips inland – even just ten to twenty kilometres – will pay dividends, while if you arrive at a Norman port intending to head straight for Brittany or southern France you may well find yourself tempted to linger.

Travelling from **east to west**, you pass through a succession of distinct regions. **South of the Seine**, and natural targets from Le Havre, Dieppe or Rouen, lie the **river valleys** of the **Eure**, **Risle** and **Charentonne**. While certain areas – especially along the Charentonne – have been disfigured by industrial development, the valleys remain for the most part rural and verdant. The occasional château, castle ruin or abbey provides a focus, most memorably at **Bec-Hellouin**, near Brionne, and at the country town of **Conches**. Further south lie the wooded hills and valleys of **the Perche**, home of the mighty Percheron horse and also of the original Trappists (see p.167).

Following the rivers northwest, on the other hand, as they flow towards the sea near Honfleur or Cabourg, brings you into the classic cheese and cider country of the **Pays d'Auge**, all rolling pastoral hills, grazing meadows and orchards. **Livarot**, **Pont-l'Évêque** and **Camembert** here are renowned throughout the world for their cheeses, while **Lisieux**, as the home little more than a century ago of Saint Thérèse, has become one of the major pilgrimage towns of France.

To the **south** of the Pays d'Auge extend the forests of the **Parc Naturel Régional de Normandie-Maine**, with the sedate and famous spa at **Bagnoles** and the national stud at **Le Pin**, as well as the historic towns of **Argentan** and **Alençon**.

Further west, on the routes inland from either Caen or Cherbourg and the Cotentin, comes something of a shift. Around Thury-Harcourt and stretching south to Pont d'Ouilly and Putanges lies the area dubbed the **Suisse Normande**, for its "alpine" valleys and thick woods; fine walking country, if not genuinely mountainous. To its west, the **Bocage** begins with grim

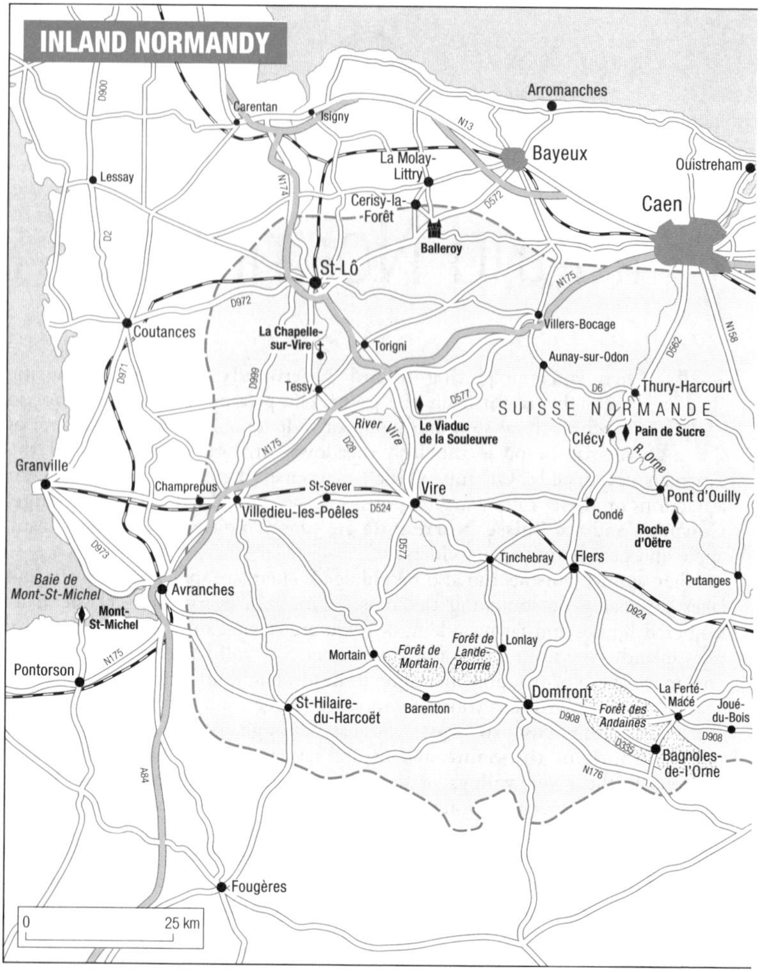

memories of war around **St-Lô** – this was the main 1944 invasion route – but subsides into a pastoral scene once more as you hit the gastronomic centres of the **Vire**.

South from the Seine

South across the Seine from Rouen lies the long and featureless **Neubourg plain** – intensive agricultural land where the crumbling barns, Tudor-style houses and occasional grazing horses look oddly out of place. The first sizeable town you come to, war-ravaged **Évreux**, provides little incentive to stop, so most visitors choose instead to press on as far as the attractive medieval communities of **Conches**, tucked snugly into the forest, and **Verneuil**.

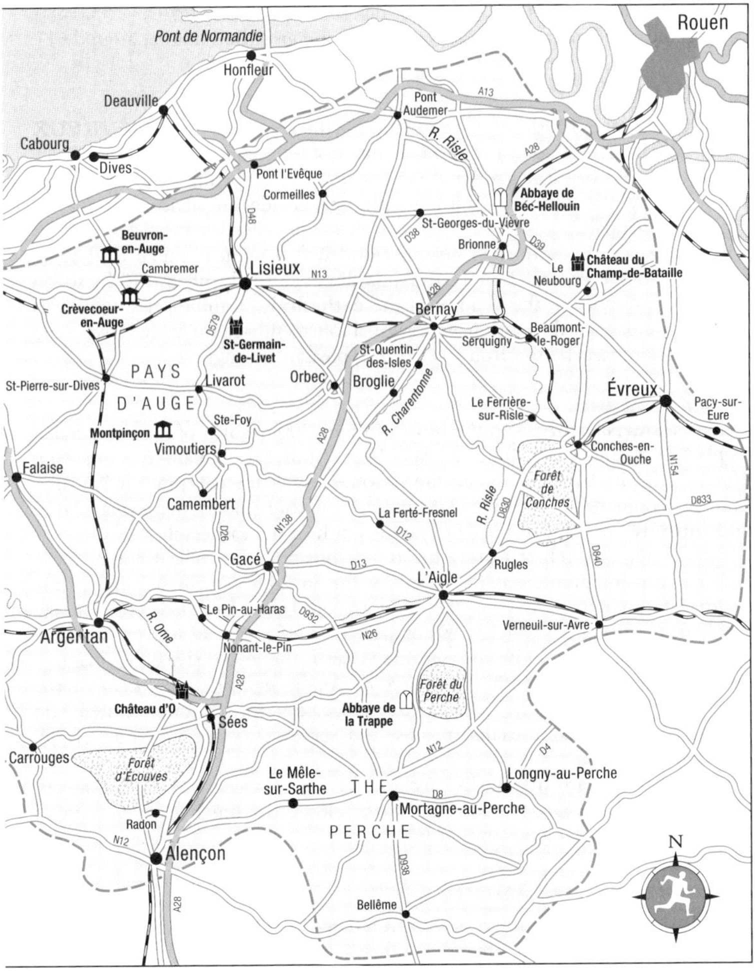

Le Neubourg

Five kilometres northwest of the only significant town on the Neubourg plain, **LE NEUBOURG** itself, the enormous seventeenth-century **Château du Champ-de-Bataille** stands just off the D39 (gardens: Easter–April & Oct Sat & Sun 2–6pm; May, June & Sept daily 2–6pm; July & Aug daily 10am–6pm; château: Easter–June, Sept & Oct Sat & Sun 3.30–5.30pm; July & Aug daily 3.30–5.30pm; gardens €12, château & gardens €24; Ⓦchateauduchampdebataille.com). Since the early 1990s, as a colossal labour of love, interior designer Jacques Garcia has re-vamped both the château itself, which has been meticulously kitted out with period furnishings, and, more playfully and imaginatively, its extensive gardens, which now feature contemporary flourishes like a topiary chess board.

Le Neubourg holds a couple of good, central **hotel-restaurants**, the *Le Soleil d'Or*, place du Château (Ⓣ02.32.35.00.52, Ⓦhotel-lesoleildor.fr; ❸), and the

Logis *Au Grand St-Martin*, 68 rue de la République (Ⓣ02.32.35.04.80, Ⓦau-grand-saint-martin.com; ❸). Sumptuous menus at both start at around €17.

Évreux

Twenty kilometres southeast of Le Neubourg, the venerable town of **ÉVREUX** is the capital of the Eure *département*, despite not being on the Eure River itself. Throughout history, it has suffered violent reversals of fortune – as early as the fifth century, its affluent Gaulish community made an inviting target for rampaging Vandals.

Bombing raids by both sides during World War II reduced much of the city to rubble, however, and Évreux today is disconcertingly lifeless. Even so, an afternoon's wander in the vicinity of the **cathedral** – a minor classic with its flamboyant exterior decoration and original fourteenth-century windows – and along the ramparts by the Iton riverbank is pleasant enough.

Practicalities

Évreux's **tourist office** is in the heart of town, 300m north of the cathedral at 1 placede Gaulle (late June to late Sept Mon–Sat 9.30am–6.30pm, Sun 10am–12.30pm; late Sept to late June Mon–Fri 9.30am–6.15pm, Sat 9.30am–1pm & 2–6pm; Ⓣ02.32.24.04.43, Ⓦgrandevreuxtourisme.fr); the **gares SNCF** and **routière** are side by side, 400 metres south of the cathedral.

Sadly, Evreux's loveliest **hotel**, the strange but splendid Belle Époque *Biche*, at 9 rue Ste-Joséphine, was destroyed by fire in 2008. The best-value in the centre of town these days is the modernized *Hôtel de l'Orme*, 13 rue des Lombards (Ⓣ02.32.39.34.12, Ⓦhotel-de-lorme.fr; ❹). However, a more enticing prospect would be to continue as far as the lovely riverside village of **PACY-SUR-EURE**, 13km east, where the traditional *Hôtel de l'Étape*, 1 rue Isambard (Ⓣ02.32.36.12.77, Ⓦetapedelavallee.com; ❹; restaurant closed Sun eve & Mon), has comfortable rooms, and serves tasty menus from €18.50 lunch, €28.50 dinner.

The finest **restaurant** in Évreux itself is *La Gazette*, 7 rue St-Sauveur (Ⓣ02.32.33.43.40, Ⓦrestaurant-lagazette.fr; closed Sat lunch, Sun & most of Aug), where dinner menus start at €20.

Conches-en-Ouche

The classic old Norman town of **CONCHES-EN-OUCHE**, which can have changed little since the nineteenth century, stands above the River Rouloir on a spur so narrow and abrupt that the railway line is forced to tunnel right beneath its centre. Arriving by train, you're barely aware that the place exists at all; all you see is the cutting, deep into the hill.

On the highest point of the spur, in the middle of a row of medieval houses on the main rue Ste-Foy, the **church of Ste-Foy** is topped by a cast-iron spire. Conches was formerly renowned for its metal foundries, which were responsible for the iron spire added to Rouen Cathedral in 1876. The windows of the church hold a sequence of Renaissance stained glass. Venture into the gift shop opposite, and you'll find an unlikely secret; the stone spiral staircase in the back room leads to a labyrinth of eleventh-century cellars that extends under most of its neighbours.

Behind the church, in the gardens of the **Hôtel de Ville**, a robust, if anatomically odd, stone boar gazes proudly out over a spectacular view, raising its eyes to the horizon far beyond the sewage works. Next to the Hôtel de Ville, you can scramble up the slippery steps of the ruined twelfth-century **castle**, though it's too dangerous to go inside. Twice captured by the English during the Hundred Years War, this was one of the many haunts of the ubiquitous Bertrand du Guesclin (see p.391). Such sights ensure that Conches remains firmly rooted in the past, but the town is given an added contemporary flavour, too, by the pieces of modern sculpture that you come upon around seemingly every corner.

On the other side of the main road from the castle, you'll find a long **park**, with parallel avenues of trees, a large ornamental lake and fountain. On Thursdays, both this and the main street are taken up by a **market**.

Practicalities

Conches' **tourist office**, close to the castle 200m south of the church in place Aristide-Briand (Tues–Sat 10am–12.30pm & 2–6pm, plus Sun 10am–noon in July & Aug only; ⓣ02.32.30.76.42, ⓦconches-en-ouche.fr), rents out mountain **bikes** by the hour or day. The best **accommodation** option is *Le Cygne*, a Logis de France at 2 rue Paul Guilbaud at the north end of town (ⓣ02.32.30.20.60, ⓦlecygne.fr; ❷; closed Sun eve & Mon), where menus start at €18. The *Grand'Mare* is a classy **restaurant** in a green and quiet location beside the park at 13 av Croix de Fer (ⓣ02.32.30.23.30, closed Sun eve, Tues eve & all Mon), serving a €22 menu that's rich in local flavours; the *Bistro* in the same building is a less formal place to have lunch.

The Forêt de Conches

The wild and open woodland of the **Forêt de Conches**, which stretches southwest of Conches, is very popular with hikers and **horse-riders**. The Village Equestre de Conches (ⓣ02.32.30.22.56, ⓦwww.conches.fr), which caters specifically for young riders up to the age of eighteen, is based in the hamlet of Le Fresne, 1km east of town.

The village of **LA FERRIÈRE-SUR-RISLE**, 14km west of Conches, consists of a stately array of old buildings around a spacious central square that holds both a beautiful **church**, with a garish altar but some fine wooden statues, and a restored fourteenth-century covered **market hall**. Paddocks and meadows lead down to the river, while on the quiet square itself you'll find a small and inviting **hotel**, the *Vieux-Marché* (ⓣ02.32.30.25.93; ❷), with a daily set menu at €11.

Verneuil-sur-Avre

Southwest of Conches, the towns of Rugles and L'Aigle are both industrial and uninteresting. However, 25km due south on the D840 you come to the pretty little hilltop town of **VERNEUIL-SUR-AVRE**. While now marking nothing more significant than the transition from the Ouche to the Perche, this was, during the Hundred Years War, a crucial fortified outpost between (English-held) Normandy and France proper. Traces of its former ramparts and deep moat can still be seen along boulevard Casati on the west side of town, while the three main streets and numerous alleyways are lined with venerable half-timbered houses.

As you approach along the arrow-straight D840 from the north, the solid bell tower of **La Madeleine** is perfectly framed for several kilometres' distance by the avenue of trees. The actual church of La Madeleine, to which it is somewhat inelegantly attached, stands in the main square, completely dwarfed by the belfry, which opens for occasional visits (first Sun of each month, April–Sept, 3.30pm; €1.10).

Following the pedestrian lanes that lead away from the square will bring you out at the **Notre Dame** church in the southeast, built of crude red agglomerate stone in the twelfth century, or to the sixteenth-century **Tour St-Jean** to the southwest, a former church spire separated by wartime bombing from its Gothic porch.

Practicalities

Verneuil's **gare SNCF**, five minutes' walk north of the centre, is served by four daily trains from Paris. The local **tourist office** is at no. 129 on the main place de la Madeleine (June–Sept Mon 2–6pm, Tues–Fri 10am–noon & 2–6pm, Sat 10am–noon & 2.30–6pm, Sun 10.30am–noon & 3–6pm; Oct–May Mon–Fri same hours, Sat 10am–noon; ⓣ02.32.32.17.17, ⓦwww.verneuil-sur-avre.fr).

Virtually next door to the tourist office, the cream-coloured **hotel** *Le Saumon*, 89 place de la Madeleine (ⓣ02.32.32.02.36, ⓦhoteldusaumon.fr; ❸; closed mid-Dec to mid-Jan, plus Sun eve Nov–March), which glows an inviting pink at sunset, offers well-equipped and comfortable rooms, all en suite, at very reasonable rates. A tankful of live lobsters nervously await patrons of the more expensive menus; in midweek especially, the lower-priced menus are very good value, though you need to spend at least €31 to be sure of avoiding a surfeit of innards. The *Hostellerie Le Clos*, 98 rue de la Ferté-Vidame (ⓣ02.32.32.21.81, ⓦhostellerieduclos.fr; ❽; closed mid-Jan to mid-Feb; restaurant closed Tues lunch and all Mon), a bizarre little château near the Notre Dame church, has an even better restaurant and phenomenally expensive rooms.

Nine kilometres southwest of Verneuil is the glass-covered dome of a family holiday complex, *Les Bois-Francs*, run by **Center Parcs** (ⓣ08.25.80.28.04, ⓦwww.centerparcs.com), which insists on a three-night minimum booking.

The Charentonne and the Risle

The **River Risle** drains down from the Ouche region, north of the Perche, and passes initially through traditional and now very faded ironworking towns such as L'Aigle. Roughly 30km northwest of Conches, it's joined by a fast-flowing tributary, the **Charentonne**. In the area to either side of the confluence, and from then on northwards as the newly strengthened Risle heads towards the sea near Honfleur, several small riverside towns are worth visiting.

La Ferté-Fresnel

The little hamlet of **LA FERTÉ-FRESNEL**, in the southern reaches of the Charentonne valley 12km northwest of L'Aigle (or 17km northeast of Gacé; see p.176), is noteworthy as the site of one of Normandy's most unusual, and magnificent, **B&Bs**. The neat and very charming little nineteenth-century *Château de la Ferté-Fresnel* makes an absolutely delightful overnight stop (ⓣ02.33.24.23.23, ⓦchateau.fertefresnel.free.fr; ❺). The château itself stands at the end of a majestic avenue of trees, and is set in superb formal grounds, while the huge, high-ceilinged guest rooms are reached via a graceful curving double staircase.

Broglie

The southernmost town of any size along the Charentonne is **BROGLIE**, pronounced "Broy", 12km east of Orbec (see p.171). The impressive private **château** that stands on the brow of the hill above Broglie is the ancestral home of the de Broglie family. Its last but one owner, Prince Louis, won the Nobel

Physics Prize for demonstrating that matter, like light, has wavelike properties. His work – to "seek the last hiding places of reality", as he put it – subsequently formed the foundation of the whole discipline of quantum mechanics. Originally a medieval historian, Louis was attracted to his great theory "purely on the grounds of intellectual beauty".

Across Broglie's charming little central square, the place des Trois Maréchaux, from the half-Roman, half-Gothic church of **St-Martin**, the local **tourist office** (May to mid-Oct Tues–Fri 3–6pm, Sat 10.30am–12.30pm & 3–6pm, Sun 9.30am–12.30pm; Ⓣ02.32.46.27.52, Ⓦwww.cc-broglie.fr) can offer several useful maps and brochures detailing cycling and sightseeing tours of the region. The town does not, however, currently have either a hotel or a campsite.

Downstream from Broglie

Immediately downstream from Broglie, the Charentonne sprawls between its banks on a wide flood plain. It is classic inland Normandy, uneventful and totally scenic; the one flaw in the whole thing is the unseemly preponderance of porcelain donkeys in people's front gardens.

Not far short of Bernay, a couple of kilometres north of **ST-QUENTIN-DES-ISLES** on the D33, the sixteenth-century riverside windmill *Moulin Fouret* (Ⓣ02.32.43.19.95, Ⓦmoulin-fouret.com; ③; closed Sun eve & Mon), is primarily a **restaurant**, serving menus at €28, €41 and €56, with some lovely outdoor seating in summer, but it also has a few **rooms**, making it the nicest place to stay in the vicinity.

Bernay

As you approach **BERNAY**, 11km northeast of Broglie, factories and warehouses line both sides of the river. The town itself, however, has a few humpback footbridges and picturesque half-timbered old streets, and one of those churches typical of the region with a spire that looks like a stack of inverted octagonal ice-cream cones. An impressive Romanesque twelfth-century **abbey church** forms part of the town museum (daily except Mon: mid-June to mid-Sept 10am–noon & 2–7pm; mid-Sept to mid-June 2–5.30pm; €3.60).

Bernay has few claims to renown, though Edith Piaf lived here as a child, and a local baker found fame for **running** each stage of the Tour de France during the night before the cyclists raced over it. The local **tourist office** is very central, at 29 rue Thiers (mid-June to mid-Sept Mon–Sat 9.30am–6pm, Sun 10am–1pm; mid-Sept to mid-June Mon–Sat 9.30am–noon & 2–5.30pm; Ⓣ02.32.43.32.08, Ⓦville-bernay27.fr). There's a conventional, good-quality **hotel-restaurant** nearby, the *Lion d'Or*, 48 rue Général-de-Gaulle (Ⓣ02.32.43.12.06, Ⓦhotel-liondor-bernay.com; ③), while the municipal **campsite** is a short way southwest (Ⓣ02.32.43.30.47, Ⓦville-bernay27.fr; closed Oct–April).

Beaumont-le-Roger

BEAUMONT-LE-ROGER is set beside the Risle 25km northwest of Conches and 17km east of Bernay, shortly before the Risle meets the Charentonne. Its ruined thirteenth-century priory **church** is gradually crumbling to the ground, the slow restoration of one or two arches unable to keep pace. Little happens in the village beyond the hourly hammering of the church bell – next door to the abbey – by a nodding musketeer; and with each passing hour, the ruins crumble a little more.

Beaumont-le-Roger is home to a sixteenth-century **coaching inn** with some quiet courtyard rooms – again called the *Lion d'Or*, 91 rue St-Nicolas (Ⓣ02.32.46.54.24, Ⓦhostellerieduliondor.com; ❸; restaurant closed Sun eve & Mon) – and also a top-quality and very friendly **restaurant**, *La Calèche*, nearby at 54 rue St-Nicolas (Ⓣ02.32.45.25.99, Ⓦlacaleche27.com; closed Tues & Wed, plus three weeks in July), which offers menus from €22.

Brionne

The small town of **BRIONNE**, 15km north of Beaumont-le-Roger and the first stop on the rail line to Rouen, plays host to large regional **markets** on Tuesday and Sunday. The fish hall is on the left bank; the rest by the church on the right bank. Above them both, with panoramic views, is a **donjon**, or old castle keep, spotlit by the setting sun. Should you decide to climb up the hill to reach it, you'll find a *table d'orientation* with arrows pointing out local landmarks.

Brionne holds two good **hotels** that also contain excellent restaurants: the lovely old half-timbered *Auberge du Vieux Donjon*, facing the marketplace at 19 rue de la Soie (Ⓣ02.32.44.80.62, Ⓦaubergeduvieuxdonjon.com; ❸; closed Mon, plus Sun eve & Thurs eve Oct–May), where the food, on menus from €15, is significantly better than the accommodation – watch out for sagging mattresses – and the much more modern *Logis de Brionne*, close to the *gare SNCF* but a long way west of the centre at 1 place St-Denis (Ⓣ02.32.44.81.73; ❺; closed second half of Feb & first half of Aug).

The Abbaye de Bec-Hellouin

Following the Risle on towards Honfleur and the sea, the **D39** is lined with perfect timbered farmhouses. Four kilometres from Brionne, the size and tranquil setting of the **ABBAYE DE BEC-HELLOUIN** lend a monastic feel to the whole valley. Bells echo between the hills and white-robed monks go soberly about their business. From the eleventh century onwards, the abbey was one of the most important centres of intellectual learning in the Christian world; an intimate association with the court of William the Conqueror meant that three of its early abbots – Lanfranc, the philosopher Anselm, and Theobald – became archbishops of Canterbury. Recent archbishops of Canterbury have maintained tradition by coming here on retreat.

Owing to the Revolution, most of the monastery buildings are relatively new – the monks only returned in 1948 – but some have survived amid the appealing clusters of stone ruins, while fragments of medieval lettering are still visible on the solitary tower, topped by a beehive spire. Visitors are welcome to wander through the grounds for no charge (daily 8am–9pm); to get a better sense of what you're seeing, join a **guided tour** (Mon & Wed–Sat 10.30am, 3pm & 4pm, plus extra tour at 5pm June–Sept only; Sun & hols noon, 3pm & 4pm; €5; Ⓦabbayedubec.com).

The tiny and rather twee adjacent village of **BEC-HELLOUIN** holds a pretty, half-timbered **hotel**, the *Auberge de l'Abbaye* (Ⓣ02.32.44.86.02, Ⓦauberge-abbaye-bec-hellouin.com; ❺; closed Tues, plus all Dec & Jan, & Wed Oct–March), and also a nice **restaurant**, the ivy-covered *Canterbury* (Ⓣ02.32.44.14.59; closed Sun eve, Tues eve, Wed & all Feb), which serves regional specialities on menus from €19 up to €39. At the local **riding stables**, the Centre Equestre du Bec-Hellouin, horses can be booked by the hour or the day (Ⓣ02.32.44.86.31).

▲ Abbaye de Bec-Hellouin

Pont-Audemer

At the northernmost major crossing point over the Risle, **PONT-AUDEMER**, medieval houses lean out at alarming angles over the crisscrossing roads, rivers and canals. It's an attractive little place, the scene of busy markets on Mondays and Fridays. Set in a grand nineteenth-century mansion on an island in the river, amid gorgeous grounds, the *Belle-Isle-sur-Risle*, 112 rue de Rouen (Ⓣ02.32.56.96.22, Ⓦbellile.com; ❼–❾; closed mid-Nov to mid-March), is a luxurious **hotel** with an especially opulent glassed-in dining room, serving menus from €30 at lunchtime and €39 in the evening. Much cheaper rooms are usually available at the basic but welcoming riverside *Hôtel de l'Agriculture* at 84 rue de la République (Ⓣ02.32.41.01.23; ❷; closed Sun eve in winter), which has a lunch-only café. Across the river from there, the *Erawan*, 4 rue de la Seule (Ⓣ02.32.41.12.03; closed Wed & Aug), must be Normandy's only traditional half-timbered Thai **restaurant**, with a €20 set menu.

From Pont-Audemer you have the choice of making for the sea at **Honfleur** (see p.102), passing some tottering Giacometti-style barns on the way to St-Georges-du-Vièvre 15km or so to the south along the thickly wooded valleys of the D38, or going on towards the **Seine**. If you plan to cycle north across the Forêt de Brotonne towards Caudebec, follow a map, not the road signs; to discourage motorists from spoiling the nicest part of the forest, the signs direct you the long way round, via La Mailleraye.

Pont-l'Évêque

There was little left after the war of the old **PONT-L'ÉVÊQUE**, 35km west of Pont-Audemer and technically the northernmost town of the Pays d'Auge (see p.168). One or two ancient houses remain, most notably along rue St-Michel where some have been repainted in the bright colours of the Middle Ages, and the whole place comes alive on **market** day, Monday. However, for most of the time it's too much of a turmoil of major roads to linger in for too long.

A couple of kilometres south of town on the D48, an impressive medieval barn at the twelfth-century Château de Betteville is home to a **vintage car museum**, while there's a karting circuit laid out in the grounds (daily: April–June & Sept 10am–12.30pm & 1.30–6pm; July & Aug 10am–6pm; Oct to mid-Nov 2–6pm; €8). Immediately opposite, the *Hôtel-Restaurant Eden Park* (Ⓣ02.31.64.64.00, Ⓦedenparkhotel.com; ❹), is a large Logis de France, housed in a sprawling complex of buildings beside its own lake, that makes an ideal overnight stop for families.

Cormeilles

The village of **CORMEILLES**, 17km southeast of Pont-l'Évêque, makes a more appealing destination for a day out, having been left relatively unscathed by fighting. Each Friday sees a **market** in its tiny centre, and there are several half-timbered restaurants scattered around.

On the southern edge of town, the *Auberge du Président*, 70 rue de l'Abbaye (Ⓣ02.32.57.80.37, Ⓦhotel-cormeilles.com; ❸; closed Sun eve & Mon lunch, plus Mon eve in low season, & three weeks in Jan), is an efficient hybrid, featuring motel-style rooms around the back and a very traditional, formal and good plush-velvet restaurant in the old building facing the street, with menus from €19. The very best restaurant in town, however, has to be *Gourmandises*, at the other end of the main street in what used to be a cheese shop at 29 rue de l'Abbaye (Ⓣ02.32.42.10.96; closed Mon–Wed), where you can watch a formerly Michelin-starred chef from Paris hard at work in the open kitchen whipping up ultra-fresh Normandy specialities, served à la carte only at reasonable prices.

The Perche

All roads south of Verneuil start to undulate alarmingly as you enter the region known as the **Perche**, which lies within the *département* of Orne. This offers some of Normandy's most bucolically appealing countryside, with green valleys nestled between heavily forested hills. Despite its apparent fertility, however, it has never been a particularly rich area. It's well known for the mighty **Percheron horses**, the strongest workhorses in the world, while its remoteness and seclusion made it an ideal home for the first **Trappist** monks, who took their name from the Forêt de la Trappe.

The Trappists

The **Abbaye de la Trappe** is set in open rolling fields on the fringes of the Forêt de la Trappe – a minor western appendage of the Forêt du Perche – just beyond a popular fishing lake and 10km north of Mortagne, outside Soligny-la-Trappe. This was the original home of one of the world's most famous – yet deliberately self-effacing, and consistently misunderstood – Christian monastic orders. Although the abbey was founded in the thirteenth century, and suffered the vicissitudes of the Hundred Years War, it was not until the reforms instigated by the **Abbé Rancé** in 1664 that its monks began to follow the principles for which the Trappists are known today. The Abbé reacted against the excesses of his time by setting out to re-create the lives of the **"Desert Fathers"** of the first few centuries after Christ, who lived in contemplative isolation in the Sinai, and to follow St Benedict's precept that true monks should live by the labour of their own hands.

The monks were driven out by the Revolution, successively to Switzerland, Poland, Russia and as far as the United States, but succeeded in returning to their utterly devastated abbey in 1815, still under the leadership of Dom Augustin l'Estrange – which made them the only order of monks in France not to be wiped out.

The abbey as it exists today is a nineteenth-century creation. The monks live communally – they don't have individual cells – and not in the absolute silence of popular myth, but speaking only for the necessities of work and community life and spending the rest of their time in quiet reflection. Tourists are not encouraged to disturb them, but you can watch a video in a reception room beside the entrance. There's also an unusual **shop** (Mon–Sat 10.30am–noon & 3–5.30pm, Sun after 10am Mass until noon & 3–5.30pm; Ⓣ02.33.84.17.00, Ⓦlatrappe.fr) which sells all things monk-made: herbal teas, muesli, shampoo, furniture wax – even local *boudin* (pork blood sausage) and coffee grown in Cameroon (by different monks).

Mortagne-au-Perche

MORTAGNE-AU-PERCHE, the largest town of the Perche region, stands on a hill set in the heart of the forests. Although it has lost virtually all of its fortifications, it remains an appealing country town, with a pleasant ensemble of stone town houses. The one part of the ramparts to survive is the **Porte St-Denis**, a fifteenth-century arch topped in the sixteenth century by two ordinary storeys of rooms that now contain an exhibition about Percheron horses (mid–June to mid–Sept Tues–Sat 3–6pm; free).

In Mortagne's liveliest square, the **place de Gaulle**, the nineteenth-century market hall has been imaginatively converted into a cinema, with some postmodern spiral staircases attached to either side. Nearby stands an unusual modern fountain, looking like an open mummy case made of copper. If you cross from here through the main gates of the Hôtel de Ville to reach the flower-filled gardens around the back, which are filled with sculpture old and new, you can enjoy fine views over the Perche hills.

During the seventeenth century, times in the Perche were hard enough for much of the population to emigrate to **Canada**, or New France. That story is told by the **Musée de l'Emigration** in the small town of **TOUROUVRE**, 10km northeast of Mortagne (mid-Feb to May & Oct–Dec Wed–Sun 2–6pm; June–Sept daily except Mon 11am–6pm; €5; Ⓦwww.musealesdetourouvre.com).

Practicalities

Mortagne's former market hall, described above, is also the site of the local **tourist office** (mid-May to Sept Tues–Sat 9.30am–12.30pm & 2.30–6pm; Oct to mid-May Tues–Sat 10am–12.30pm & 3–6pm; Ⓣ02.33.85.11.18,

Ⓦot-mortagneauperche.fr). The nicest **hotel** in town has to be the *Hôtel du Tribunal*, a *logis* on the sleepy little tree-lined place du Palais (Ⓣ02.33.25.04.77, Ⓦhotel-tribunal.fr; ❸), which consists of two or three old stone buildings with a few exposed timbers, crammed together on the corner of an alleyway leading to Porte St-Denis. This is where Yves Montand chose to stay when filming locally; the comfortable bedrooms are in an annexe at the back, while menus in the **restaurant** at the front, which has some outdoor seating, start at €25. Alternatively, the *Genty-Home*, just off place de la République at 4 rue Notre-Dame (Ⓣ02.33.25.11.53; ❸; closed Sun eve), has a handful of very plush rooms upstairs and a couple of restaurants. The most famous local dish is the black *boudin noir*, a crumbly black pudding or blood sausage with a healthy dose of fat and tripe thrown in.

By far the nicest **campsite** in the vicinity is the year-round *Camping Monaco Parc* (Ⓣ02.33.73.59.59, Ⓦcampingmonacoparc.com), in a gorgeous wooded valley outside **Longny-au-Perche**, roughly 15km east of Mortagne, which has a huge, opulent swimming pool.

Bellême

Tiny **BELLÊME**, 17km due south of Mortagne on the switchback D938, is actually the capital of the Perche despite being very much smaller. In many ways it's more attractive, too, crammed so tightly onto the top of a sharp hill that the views are consistently superb. Like Mortagne, hardly anything survives of the fortifications that once ringed the very crest of the hill. The one exception is the forbiddingly thick **Porche** – now the home of the local library, but still equipped to take a portcullis if things turn bad – reached by an alleyway leading off from a corner of the place de la République near the St-Sauveur church.

Practicalities

Behind its grand façade, Bellême's best **hotel**, the *Relais St-Louis*, 1 bd Bansard des Bois (Ⓣ02.33.73.12.21, Ⓦwww.relais-st-louis.com; ❹; closed Sun eve & Mon), is an elegant place, and its seven guest rooms are even spacious enough to boast proper armchairs. The light dining room downstairs, serving menus from €19 to €49, looks out on one side to a flowery garden, and across the town's diminutive ring road on the other to a small vestige of moat overlooked by an imposing eighteenth-century mansion. There's also a tiny two-star municipal **campsite**, *Le Val*, on the edge of town (Ⓣ02.33.85.31.00, Ⓦlepaysbellemois.com; closed mid-Oct to mid-April).

The local **tourist office** (Mon & Sun 2–6.30pm, Tues–Sat 9.30am–12.30pm & 2–6.30pm; Ⓣ02.33.73.09.69, Ⓦlepaysbellemois.com), all but next door to the *Relais St-Louis*, doubles appealingly as the headquarters of the adjoining miniature golf course. It can also provide details of Bellême's annual five-day **Mycology Festival** (Ⓦmycologiades.com), held at the start of each October to celebrate the more obscure mushrooms of the surrounding forests.

The Pays d'Auge

The pastures of the **Pays d'Auge**, the region that extends south from the ancient cathedral city of **Lisieux** – itself now almost entirely preoccupied with the cult of Ste Thérèse – are the lushest in all of Normandy, renowned for producing the world-famous cheeses of Camembert, Livarot and Pont-l'Évêque. Its rolling hills and green twisting valleys are scattered with magnificent **half-timbered manor houses**. Each sprawling farm is liable to consist of a succession of such treasures, each family house, as it becomes too dilapidated to live in, being converted for use as a barn, and replaced by a new one built alongside. In addition to grazing land, the area has acres of orchards, which yield the best of Norman ciders, both apple and pear (*poiré*), as well as Calvados apple brandy.

Much of the appeal lies in the scope just to wander, and it's easy to fill the days following signs down the back roads to farms where you can sample home-made **ciders** and **cheeses**. In addition, the manor houses of **Beuvron-en-Auge**, **Crèvecoeur-en-Auge** and **Montpinçon** are well worth finding, while at **Cambremer**, 20km west of Lisieux, there is a special crafts market on Sunday mornings in July and August.

Lisieux

LISIEUX, the main town of the Pays d'Auge, was a regional capital successively under the Gauls, the Romans and the Franks. However, it was obliterated by barbarians in 275 AD, and again by the Allies in 1944, with the result that what had once been a beautiful market town is now for the most part nondescript. Although it still boasts a Norman Gothic cathedral built in 1170, which holds a chapel erected by Pierre Cauchon, the judge who sentenced Joan of Arc to death, these days Lisieux's identity is thoroughly wrapped up in the life and death of **Ste Thérèse**.

Pilgrims come to Lisieux in considerable numbers, and even a casual visitor will find the Thérèse cult inescapable. The garish and gigantic **Basilique de Ste-Thérèse**, crowning a slope southwest of the centre, was modelled on the Sacré-Coeur in Paris. Completed in 1954, it was the last major religious building in France to be erected solely by public subscription. Thérèse is in fact buried in the chapel of the Carmelite convent roughly opposite the tourist office on rue du Carmel, though her presence in the Basilica is ensured by selected bones from her right arm and by countless photographs, Thérèse being one of the very few saints to have lived since the invention of the camera. The

Sainte Thérèse

Born at Alenćon in 1873, **Thérèse Martin** lived for the last nine years of her short life in the Carmelite convent in Lisieux, until she died of TB at the age of 24. She had felt the call to take holy orders when only 9, but it took a pilgrimage to Rome and a special dispensation from the pope before she was allowed into the convent at the age of 15. The prioress said then that "a soul of such quality should not be treated as a child".

Thérèse owes her fame to her book *Story of a Soul*, in which she describes the approach to life she called her "Little Way" – a belief that all personal suffering, thankless work and quiet faith is made holy and worthwhile as an offering to God. Her reflections proved astonishingly popular after her death, particularly in trying to make sense of the vast suffering of World War I, and Thérèse was rapidly beatified. In 1945, she was declared France's second patron saint, after her heroine Joan of Arc. In fact, Thérèse wrote several poems to Joan, and there are even photographs of her dressed as the imprisoned saint chained to a wall. Her continuing relevance to Catholics was celebrated by the late Pope John Paul II, who not only made his own pilgrimage to Lisieux but also declared Thérèse in 1997 to be the 33rd "Doctor of the Church". This highest of theological honours had only previously been conferred on two women, Catherine of Siena and Theresa of Avila. Her relics regularly tour the world, and attracted crowds of devotees in Britain in 2009.

huge modern mosaics that decorate the nave are undeniably impressive, but the overall impression is of a quasi-medieval hagiography.

In summer, a white, flag-bedecked funfair "train" runs forty-minute tours around the holiest sites, chugging through the open, wide streets and squares, and past the delightful flower-filled park, raised above street level behind the restrained and sober Cathédrale St-Pierre (departures from the Basilica: mid-June to Aug daily 10am, 11am, 2pm, 3pm, 4pm, 5pm & 6pm; May to mid-June & Sept Sat & Sun same times; €6).

To get a glimpse of Lisieux's former glories, take a look at the fading photos in the **Musée d'Art et d'Histoire**, 38 bd Pasteur (daily except Tues 2–6pm; €3.50).

Practicalities

Lisieux is 35 minutes by train from Caen, en route to Paris or Rouen; the **gare SNCF** is on the south side of town, below the Basilica. Its **tourist office** is at 11 rue d'Alençon (mid-June to Sept Mon–Sat 8.30am–6.30pm, Sun 10am–12.30pm & 2–5pm; Oct to mid-June Mon–Sat 8.30am–noon & 1.30–6pm; Ⓣ02.31.48.18.10, Ⓦlisieux-tourisme.com).

The number of pilgrims means that Lisieux is full of good-value places to stay. Among its **hotels** are the *Terrasse*, a Logis de France up on the hill near the Basilica at 25 av Ste-Thérèse (Ⓣ02.31.62.17.65, Ⓦlaterrassehotel.com; ❷; closed mid-Jan to mid-Feb, plus Mon in winter), which serves good menus from €18 on its pleasant terrace, and the smart, central *Azur Hôtel*, just north of the Église St-Jacques at 15 rue au Char (Ⓣ02.31.62.09.14, Ⓦazur-hotel.com; ❹; closed mid-Dec to mid-Jan). There is also a large two-star **campsite**, *de la Vallée* (Ⓣ02.31.62.00.40; closed early Oct to early April), but campers would probably be better off somewhere more rural, such as Livarot or Orbec.

Most of the hotels are equipped with tempting **restaurants**, but the best stand-alone place to eat, assuming you can put up with its twee pastel decor, is the *Aux Acacias*, 13 rue de la Résistance (Ⓣ02.31.62.10.95; closed Sun eve & Mon), where menus start at €18. If Thérèse isn't your prime motivation, Saturday is the best day to visit, for the large **street market**, stacked with Pays d'Auge cheeses.

Crèvecoeur-en-Auge

While it's always fun simply to stumble across dilapidated old half-timbered farms in the Pays d'Auge, here and there it's possible to visit prime specimens that have been beautifully restored and preserved. An especially fine ensemble has been gathered just west of **CRÈVECOEUR-EN-AUGE**, 17km west of Lisieux on the N14, in the grounds of a small twelfth-century **château** (April–June & Sept daily 11am–6pm; July & Aug daily 11am–7pm; Oct Sun 2–6pm; guided tours July & Aug Sun 2.30–4.30pm; €6; Ⓦchateau-de-crevecoeur.com). Around the pristine lawns of a re-created village green, circled by a shallow moat, this photogenic group of golden adobe structures includes a manor house, a barn and a tall thin dovecote that date from the fifteenth century. They were brought here by the Schlumbergers, a local family of German origin, who made their fortune from the 1920s onward by pioneering the use of electricity in prospecting for petroleum. That process is described in exhaustive detail in the barn, while the manor house explains exactly what's involved in restoring these kinds of buildings.

By far the most interesting displays are in the little twelfth-century chapel that adjoins the château, which holds a fascinating exhibition on the music and instruments of the Middle Ages. Unfortunately, almost all the explanatory captions are in French. For eight days starting on the first Sunday of each

August, volunteers re-create the life of a medieval village in the château grounds, complete with a daily mystery for children to solve.

For **accommodation**, at 44 rue de St-Pierre-sur-Dives in the actual village of Crèvecoeur-en-Auge, the five-room *Auberge du Cheval Blanc* (Ⓣ02.31.63.03.28, Ⓔaubchevalblanc@aol.com; ❸; hotel closed mid-Jan to mid-Feb, restaurant closed Mon & Tues lunch), is a welcoming hotel that serves fine regional food.

Beuvron-en-Auge

Few villages anywhere can be as pretty as **BEUVRON-EN-AUGE**, 7km north of the N13 halfway between Lisieux and Caen, which consists of an oval central *place*, ringed by a glorious ensemble of multicoloured half-timbered houses. The largest of these, the yellow-and-brown sixteenth-century **Vieux Manoir** at the south end of the village, backs onto a stream and open fields. The beams around its first storey bear weather-beaten carvings, including one of a Norman soldier. A map in the main square details suggested **walking routes** through the countryside nearby, while if you step off the square into the alleyway known as **rue de la Catouillette**, opposite the Vieux Manoir, you'll find another set of lovely half-timbered structures clustered around a tiny courtyard.

Beuvron-en-Auge stages its own **Cider Festival**, with a huge local market in the square, on the last Sunday in October each year.

Practicalities

The only **accommodation** in Beuvron-en-Auge is in *chambres d'hotes* (B&Bs). Monique Hamelin runs a friendly and comfortable two-room option in a former farmhouse opposite the Vieux Manoir (Ⓣ02.31.39.00.62, Ⓔhamelin monique@orange.fr; ❸; closed Nov–Easter), while the top-notch *Pavé d'Auge* **restaurant,** in the very centre of the *place* (Ⓣ02.31.79.26.71, Ⓦpavedauge.com; closed Mon, plus Tues Sept–June) – where regularly changing menus start at €36 – offers four rooms in the separate, but also half-timbered *Pavé d'Hôtes* (same contact details; ❺).

St-Germain-de-Livet

Around 7km south of Lisieux, off the D579, the **château** of **ST-GERMAIN-DE-LIVET** (guided tours only, Feb–Sept & mid-Oct to Nov daily except Tues 11am–6pm; closed first half of Oct, plus Dec & Jan; €6.60, under-18s free) is an appealing blend of fifteenth- and sixteenth-century architectural elements. From the main gate, its half-timbered older wing – home to some stirring military frescoes – is largely concealed by the more imposing later addition, with its cheerful checked facade of coloured stones and brick. The whole edifice is topped by classic pointed grey-slate turrets, circled by a moat, and surrounded by immaculate lawns.

If you want to explore some of the surrounding countryside, you can do so by horse-drawn **carriage rides** operated by the farm next to the château (€30 per hr for four people, €5 per extra person up to a maximum of eight; Ⓣ02.31.31.08.68). When not in use, the carriage is housed in an amazing tumbledown barn next door.

Orbec

The most attractive of the larger Pays d'Auge towns, **ORBEC** lies just a few kilometres along a valley from the source of its river, the Orbiquet, 19km southeast of Lisieux. Consisting of little more than its main road, the rue

Grande, with the huge tower of Notre Dame church at its southern end, it epitomizes the simple pleasures of the region.

Along the Rue Grande, you'll see several houses in which the gaps between the timbers are filled with intricate patterns of coloured tiles and bricks. Debussy composed *Jardin sous la Pluie* in one of these, and the oldest and prettiest of the lot – a tanner's house dating back to 1568, and called the **Vieux Manoir** – holds a museum of local history (April Sat & Sun 10am–12.30pm & 3–6pm; May–Sept Wed–Sun 10am–12.30pm & 3–6pm; €1.50). On the whole, though, it's more fun just to walk down behind the church to the river, and its watermill and paddocks.

Practicalities

In the absence of any **hotels** in Orbec, check the list of *chambres d'hôtes* at the tourist office, at 6 rue Grande (July & Aug Mon–Sat 9.30am–12.30pm & 2–7pm, Sun 10am–12.30pm; Sept–June Mon–Fri 9.30am–12.30pm & 2–5.30pm, Sat 10am–12.30pm & 3–5.30pm; ⓣ02.31.32.56.68, ⓦtourisme-normandie.fr). Prime among them is the *Côte Jardin*, which focuses on a central mansion at 62 rue Grande (ⓣ02.31.32.77.79, ⓦwww.cotejardin-france.be; ④), and offers five bedrooms set in lovely gardens. The best **restaurant** in town is nearby at the narrowest point of rue Grande, where *Le Caneton* (ⓣ02.31.32.73.32; closed first two weeks of both Sept & Jan, plus Sun eve & Mon) in the half-timbered house at no. 32 serves top-quality menus from €23. Orbec also has a two-star municipal **campsite**, *Les Capucins* (ⓣ02.31.32.76.22; closed early Sept to late May).

Livarot

The centre of the cheese country is the old crossroads village of **LIVAROT**, 18km south of Lisieux, where the **Fromagerie Graindorge** on the route de Vimoutiers (Mon–Fri 9.30am–noon & 1.30–5pm, Sat 9.30am–noon; free; ⓦwww.graindorge.fr), gives you a closer look at how Livarot's eponymous cheese is made, with free samples doled out at the end of each visit. For the best

The cheese of the Pays d'Auge

The tradition of cheesemaking in the Pays d'Auge started in monasteries during the Dark Ages, and the characteristics of the local product became fairly standard by the eleventh century. At first, it was variously known as either *Augelot* or *Angelot*; the *Roman de la Rose* in 1236 referred to *Angelot* cheese, which was identified with a small coin depicting a young angel killing a dragon. This cheese was the forerunner of the principal modern varieties, which began to emerge in the seventeenth century – **Pont-l'Évêque**, which is square, with a washed crust, and is soft but not runny, and **Livarot**, which is round, thick and firm, with a stronger flavour.

Although Marie Herel is generally credited with having invented **Camembert** in the 1790s, a smaller and stodgier version of that cheese had already existed for some time. Apparently, one Abbé Gobert, a priest fleeing the Revolutionary Terror at Meaux, stayed in Mme Herel's farmhouse at Camembert and watched the methods she used for making cheese. He suggested modifications in line with the techniques he'd seen employed to produce Brie de Meaux – a slower process, gentler on the curd and with more thorough drainage. The rich full cheese thus created was an instant success in the market at Vimoutiers, and the development of the railways (and the invention of the chipboard cheesebox in 1880) helped to give it a worldwide popularity.

views of the valley, climb up to the thirteenth-century church of **St-Michel de Livet**, just above the town.

Practicalities

Livarot's **tourist office** is at 1 place Georges-Bisson (Mon 2–6pm, Tues–Sat 9.30am–12.30pm & 2–6pm; Ⓣ02.31.63.47.39, Ⓦwww.paysdelivarot.fr). The village's one, simple **hotel** is at the north end: the *De La France* in the place de la Gare (Ⓣ02.31.31.59.35; ❶), while there's also a tiny one-star municipal **campsite** (Ⓣ02.31.32.01.18; closed Sept–April). The local **cheese fair** falls on the first weekend of August.

St-Pierre-sur-Dives

ST-PIERRE-SUR-DIVES, 16km west of Livarot, is noteworthy for two fine old architectural treasures, both of which date back to the twelfth century. The wooden *halles* in its vast open marketplace – which still plays host to a large traditional **market** every Monday, and an antiques market on the first Sunday of each month – were burned to the ground in 1944, but had been rebuilt by 1949. Only traditional techniques were used, so there's not a single nail or screw in the place – the timber frame rests on low stone walls and is held together by chestnut pegs alone.

Just across the central street stands a Gothic-Romanesque **church**, whose windows depict the history of the town. The Benedictine abbey of which it forms part is progressively being restored, and its former convent buildings now house a slightly academic complement to the practical-minded *fromagerie* at Livarot (see opposite), the **Musée des Techniques Fromagères** (mid-April to mid-Oct Mon–Fri 9.30am–12.30pm & 1.30–6pm, Sat 10am–noon & 2.30–5pm; mid-Oct to mid-April Mon–Fri 9.30am–12.30pm & 1.30–5.30pm; free).

Practicalities

St-Pierre's **tourist office** shares the convent on rue St-Benoist with its cheesy neighbours (same hours; Ⓣ02.31.20.97.90, Ⓦwww.mairie-saint-pierre-sur-dives.fr). The best bet for both **accommodation** and **food** is *Les Agriculteurs*, a ten-room Logis de France at 118 rue de Falaise (Ⓣ02.31.20.72.78, Ⓦlesagriculteurs.com; ❷; restaurant closed Sun eve), where menus start at €17.50.

Falaise

William the Conqueror, or William the Bastard as he is more familiarly known to Normans, was born in **FALAISE**, 40km southwest of Lisieux. His mother, Arlette, a laundress and daughter of a tanner, was spotted by his father, Duke Robert of Normandy, at the washing place below the mighty **château** that remains the town's major feature. A shrewd woman, she scorned secrecy in her eventual assignation by riding publicly through the main entrance to meet him. During her pregnancy, she dreamed of bearing a mighty tree that cast its shade over Normandy and England.

From a distance, the sheer wall of the **castle keep**, firmly planted on the massive rocks of the cliff (*falaise*) that gave the town its name, and towering over the **Fontaine d'Arlette** down by the river, looks all but impregnable. Nonetheless, it was so heavily damaged during the war that it took over fifty years to reopen the castle for regular visits (Feb–June & Sept–Dec daily 10am–6pm; July & Aug daily 10am–7pm; closed Jan; English-language tours daily 11.30am, with another at 3.30pm in July & Aug; €7; Ⓦchateau-guillaume-leconquerant.fr). Huge resources have been lavished on restoring the central *donjon* – reminiscent of the Tower of London, with its cream-coloured Caen stone – in accordance with cutting-edge contemporary concepts. A guiding principle was to avoid any possible confusion between what is original and what is new. Steel slabs, concrete blocks, glass floors and tent-like canvas awnings have been slapped down atop the bare ruins, and metal staircases even squeezed into the wall cavities. The raw structure of the keep, down to its very foundations, lies exposed to view, while the new rooms are used for changing exhibitions that focus on the castle's fascinating past. Add the superb views of the town and surroundings from the battlements, and you have one of Normandy's most rewarding historical sites.

The whole of Falaise was devastated during the struggle to close the "Falaise Gap" in August 1944 – the climax of the Battle of Normandy, as the Allied armies sought to encircle the Germans and cut off their retreat. By the time the Canadians entered the town on August 17, they could no longer tell where the roads had been and had to bulldoze a new four-metre strip straight through the middle. The full bloody story is told in horrific detail at the **Musée Août 44**, beyond the château on the Chemin des Rochers, in a former cheese factory that resembles nothing so much as a giant cheesebox (early April to May & Sept to mid-Nov daily except Tues 10am–noon & 2–6pm; June–Aug daily 10am–noon & 2–6pm; €6; Ⓦwww.normandie-museeaout44.com).

Opposite the tourist office (see opposite), the **Musée des Automates**, also known as "Automates Avenue", preserves mechanical window displays that graced the department stores of Paris between the 1920s and 1950s (April–June & Sept daily 10am–12.30pm & 1.30–6pm; July & Aug daily 10am–6pm; Oct–March Sat, Sun & hols 10am–12.30pm & 1.30–6pm; €6; Ⓦwww.automates-avenue.fr). The highlight is a mock-up of a real-life collision that took place in a tiny village between the cyclists of the Tour de France and a herd of pigs.

▲ The château at Falaise

Practicalities

Falaise's modern, well-stocked **tourist office** is located in the Forum, on the boulevard de la Libération (May to mid-June Mon–Sat 9.30am–12.30pm & 1.30–6.30pm; mid-June to mid-Sept same hours plus Sun 10am–12.30pm & 2–4pm; mid-Sept to April Mon–Sat 9.30am–12.30pm & 1.30–5.30pm; ⓣ02.31.90.17.26, ⓦfalaise-tourisme.com).

Now that central Falaise is bypassed by the motorway, it's generally a quiet place to spend the night. The best-value **hotel** is the *Poste*, not far from the tourist office at 38 rue Georges-Clémenceau (ⓣ02.31.90.13.14, ⓔhotel.delaposte@orange.fr; ❸; hotel closed Jan, restaurant closed Fri eve, Sun eve & Mon), which serves good food on menus from €16. The three-star municipal **campsite**, *Camping du Château* (ⓣ02.31.90.16.55; closed Oct–April), is in a great location, next to Arlette's fountain and the local swimming pool.

Vimoutiers

The pretty little town of **VIMOUTIERS**, 10km south of Livarot, contains a quirky **cheese museum** at 10 av Général-de-Gaulle (March–Oct only, Mon & Thurs–Sun 2–5.30pm; €3), featuring a glorious collection not to be missed by tyrosemiophiles – cheese-label collectors (they do exist) – who will find Camembert stickers ranging from remote Chilean dairies to Marks & Spencer. Most of the cheese on display, however, turns out to be polystyrene.

A statue in the main square honours **Marie Harel**, who, at the nearby village of **Camembert**, developed the original cheese early in the nineteenth century, promoting it with a skilful campaign that included sending free samples to Napoleon. There's a photo in the museum of the statue with its head blown off after a US air raid in June 1944; its replacement was donated by the cheese-makers of Ohio. Marie is confronted across the main street by what might be called the statue of the Unknown Cow.

Practicalities

Vimoutiers hosts a **market** on Monday afternoons. Its **tourist office**, 21 place de Mackau (June–Sept Mon 2–6pm, Tues–Sat 9.30am–12.30pm & 2–6pm, Sun 10am–12.30pm & 2–6pm; Oct–May Mon 2–5.30pm, Tues–Sat 10am–12.30pm & 2–5.30pm; ⓣ02.33.67.49.42, ⓦwww.vimoutiers.fr), has piles of information on local cheese-related attractions. *La Couronne*, 9 rue du 8 Mai (ⓣ02.33.67.21.49, ⓦhotelrestaurantlacouronne.fr; ❷), the better of the two central **hotels**, has a reasonable restaurant.

A short way south of Vimoutiers, en route to Camembert, the beautifully sited lake known as the **Escale du Vitou** offers everything you need for windsurfing, swimming and horse-riding, as well as its own comfortable rural waterfront hotel, *L'Escale du Vitou* (ⓣ02.33.39.12.04, ⓦdomainedelescaleduvitou.com; ❸), which has some separate guest cottages, rented at lower rates for weekends or entire weeks. There's also a clean and very cheap **campsite** nearby on boulevard Docteur-Dentu, the two-star *La Campière* (ⓣ02.33.39.18.86, ⓦwww.vimoutiers.fr; closed Oct–April).

Camembert

CAMEMBERT itself, 3km southeast of Vimoutiers, is tiny, hilly and very rural, home to far more cows than humans. On one side of its little central square, the largest local cheese producers, **La Ferme Président**, run their own, surprisingly amateurish, museum (April–Oct Mon 2–6pm, Tues–Sat 9am-noon & 2–6pm, Sun 10am–noon & 2.30–6pm; €3; ⓦwww.fermepresident.com), which whirls through the history of the cheese and the methods, both traditional and modern, used to make it. Afterwards comes a cheese tasting at **Le Maison du Camembert** on the other side of the square, which also serves as an information centre and café (Feb–April & Sept Wed–Sun 10am–6pm, May–Aug daily 10am–6pm; Ⓦwww.maisonducamembert.com).

The **Fromagerie Durand**, below Camembert on the road towards Trun (Ferme de la Hérronière; Mon–Sat 9.30am–12.30pm & 3–6pm; free), offers an alternative experience: a visit to the last farm in the region that makes Camembert in the traditional way, using unpasteurised milk. An interesting film explains – you've guessed it – the cheese production process, while four windows allow visitors to view the cheese at various stages in its life, and you're also likely to catch a glimpse of the artisan at work. The end product and other local produce are on sale in the shop.

Gacé

The **D26** runs along the **valley of the Vie** south of Vimoutiers – a route that is something of a microcosm of Norman vernacular architecture, lined with ramshackle old barns, outhouses and farm buildings. Faded orange clay crumbles from between the weathered wooden beams of these flower-covered beauties.

Although **GACÉ** itself, just off the A28 motorway 18km from Vimoutiers, is not wildly exciting, this area has a certain renown as being the original home of Alphonsine Plessis, a celebrated courtesan whose lovers included Alexandre Dumas and Franz Liszt. Born in **Nonant-le-Pin**, 12km south of Gacé, in 1824, she was only 23 when she died, but served as the inspiration for Dumas' *La Dame aux Camélias* and Verdi's *La Traviata*. A museum is devoted to her in Gacé's château, and she's also remembered in its finest **hotel**, the nineteenth-century *Manoir des Camélias*, set in spacious gardens on the route d'Alençon south of the centre (Ⓣ02.33.35.67.43, Ⓦmanoirdescamelias.com; ④; restaurant closed Wed).

Argentan and around

Although the small town of **ARGENTAN** has a long and venerable history, it was so comprehensively obliterated in August 1944, during General Patton's bid to close the "Falaise pocket", that there's virtually nothing for modern visitors to see. Its sole landmark is the **church of St-Germain**, which dominates all approaches, and took well over fifty years to restore.

You won't find it unless you look hard, but the crest of a hill that overlooks the central place du Marché holds the vestiges of a **ruined castle**. This was where Henry II of England received the news on New Year's Day 1171 that four of his knights had taken him at his word and murdered Thomas à Becket.

Although Argentan makes an enjoyable enough halt when its Tuesday **market** is in full swing, or for boat trips on the River Orne, the main reason anyone comes here is not monuments but **horses**. Outside the town are numerous equestrian centres, with riding schools, stables, racetracks and studs.

Practicalities

The local **tourist office** is in the old chapel St-Nicolas at 6 place du Marché (July & Aug Mon 9am–1pm & 2–6.30pm, Tues–Sat 9am–6.30pm; Sept–June Mon–Fri 9.30am–12.30pm & 2–6pm, Sat 9.30am–12.30pm & 1.30–5.30pm; Ⓣ02.33.67.12.48, Ⓦwww.argentan.fr). Trains to Argentan pull in at the **gare**

Feasting in northern France

If you enjoy France's world-famous food, you're certain to love Brittany and Normandy. In ports like Dieppe, Honfleur, St-Malo, Roscoff and Quiberon in Brittany, fresh-caught fish and shellfish dominate almost every menu. Away from the sea, every Norman village seems to hold a high-class restaurant. The emphasis here is on rich dairy produce, from meat prepared in thick creamy sauces, to signature cheeses like Camembert, Livarot, and Pont l'Evêque.

A seafood galette ▲ Oyster beds, Cancale ▼

Brittany

Brittany's proudest addition to world cuisine has to be the crêpe, or pancake. Strictly speaking, a crêpe is the sweet version, made with white flour, and served perhaps with sugar, fruit or chocolate; its savoury equivalent, made with buckwheat and considerably more substantial, is a galette, which can be filled with ham, cheese, eggs or indeed almost anything. Either or both make a great inexpensive lunch, whether served formally in a crêperie, or as a take-away snack from a market stall.

However, few people plan holidays around eating pancakes. Gourmets are more likely to be enticed to Brittany by its magnificent seafood, and above all its shellfish. Certain seaside towns even depend on a single mollusc for their livelihood, like Cancale, renowned for its oysters (*huîtres*), and Erquy, with its scallops (*coquilles St-Jacques*).

Although not uniquely Breton, two appetizers feature on every menu: moules marinières, giant bowls of succulent orange mussels steamed in white wine, shallots and parsley, and soupe de poissons, served with the garlicky mayonnaise known as *rouille* and a bowl of croûtons.

Paying a little extra in a restaurant brings you into the realm of the assiette de fruits de mer, a mountainous heap of langoustines, crabs, oysters, mussels, clams, whelks and cockles, most of them raw. Main courses tend to be plainer than in Normandy, with fresh fish prepared in simple sauces. Skate served with capers, or salmon baked with mustard or cheese, are typical dishes, while even the cotriade stew is distinctly less rich than the Mediterranean bouillabaisse.

Practicalities

Alençon's **gare routière** and **gare SNCF** are both northeast of the centre, with the train station slightly the further out of the two. If you arrive by **car**, on the other hand, watch out for the town's abysmal one-way system. The **tourist office** is housed in the dramatic fifteenth-century Maison d'Ozé on the central place La Magdeleine (July & Aug Mon–Sat 9.30am–7pm, Sun 10am–12.30pm & 2.30–5pm; Sept–June Mon–Sat 9.30am–12.30pm & 1.30–6pm; ⓣ02.33.80.66.33, ⓦpaysdalencontourisme.com). Free **internet access** is available a short walk west, in the town hall annexe at 6–8 rue des Filles-Notre-Dame (Mon–Sat 8.30am–7pm; ⓣ02.33.32.40.43).

Alençon's most inexpensive **hotel**, the *Hôtel de Paris*, is above a bar facing the *gare SNCF* at 26 rue de Denis-Papin (ⓣ02.33.29.01.64; ❶); even its en-suite rooms cost under €40. *Le Chapeau Rouge*, just across the river west of the centre at 3 bd Duchamp (ⓣ02.33.26.00.51, ⓦlechapeaurouge.fr; ❷; restaurant closed Sat lunch & Sun), has large comfortable rooms and offers decent meals in its adjoining restaurant.

Good **restaurants**, cafés and shops are scattered through the handful of pedestrianized streets in the town centre. For a well-priced meal, drop into *Le Hangar*, near the lace museum at 12 place a l'Avoine (ⓣ02.33.82.04.27; closed Sat & Sun), where the daily menu costs around €15. High spots on the thriving **bar** scene include *La Caves Aux Boeufs*, spreading across the pedestrian rue de la Caves Aux Boeufs (ⓣ02.33.82.99.45), which also serves a simple brasserie menu.

The Forêt d'Écouves

The **Forêt d'Écouves**, easily reached (under your own steam) from Alençon or Sées, is the centrepiece of the Parc Régional Normandie-Maine, an amorphous area that stretches from Mortain in the west to within a few kilometres of Mortagne-au-Perche in the east. A dense mixture of old spruce, pine, oak and beech, set on high hills a few kilometres north of Alençon, the Écouves forest is one of the most attractive in Normandy. These commanding heights were bitterly fought over during the war, and a Free French tank still guards the **Croix-de-Médavy** at their very apex.

Unfortunately, the forest is now a favoured spot of the military – and, in autumn, of deerhunters too. To avoid risking life and limb, check with the park's offices to find the safe routes. You can usually ramble freely along the cool paths, happening on wild mushrooms and even the odd wild boar. The nearest accommodation is in either Alençon or Sées.

Carrouges

One alternative base at the western end of the Forêt d'Écouves is the appealing little hilltop town of **CARROUGES**, 28km northwest of Alençon. Down below the centre, at the foot of the hill, a fine fourteenth-century **château** commands spacious landscaped grounds (daily: April to mid-June & Sept 10am–noon & 2–6pm; mid-June to Aug 9.30am–noon & 2–6.30pm; Oct–March 10am–noon & 2–5pm; €7; ⓦcarrouges.monuments-nationaux.fr). Its two highlights are a superb restored brick staircase, and a room in which hang portraits of fourteen successive generations of the Le Veneur family, an extraordinary illustration of the processes of heredity. Local craftsmen sell their work in the **Maison de Métiers**, the former castle chapel.

On the narrow rue Ste-Marguerite that runs through the heart of Carrouges – a noisier location than it might look – the *Hôtel du Nord* (ⓣ02.33.27.20.14; ❷; closed mid-Dec to mid-Jan, plus Fri & Sun eve Sept–June) is a Logis de France that offers a handful of reasonably large en-suite rooms at low rates, and delicious local cuisine on menus that start at €17.

Bagnoles de l'Orne

The spa town of **BAGNOLES DE L'ORNE**, 17km west of Carrouges, lies at the heart of a long, narrow wood, the Forêt des Andaines. Broad avenues radiate into the forest from the town centre, where a forbidding nineteenth-century building holds the town's famed thermal baths. Bagnoles attracts the sick from all over France; its springs are such big business that they maintain a booking office next to the Pompidou Centre in Paris. Treatments start at €50, but can easily run into hundreds of euros (Ⓦwww.thermes-bagnoles.com); the tourist office can arrange all-inclusive packages.

Although life in the town is conducted at a phenomenally slow pace, it is all surprisingly jolly – redolent with aged flirtations and gallantry. The lakeside gardens are the big scene, with pedalos, horse-drawn *calèches* and an enormous casino. Innumerable cultural **events**, concerts and stage shows take place throughout the summer; the ostensible high spot, the annual *Spectacle* in July – a tedious mock-historical pageant – is one of the less enthralling

Away from its main roads, the **Forêt des Andaines** is pleasant, with scattered and unspoilt villages, such as Juvigny and St-Michel, and the secluded, private **Château de Couterne**, a visual delight even from the gates, with its lake and long grass-floored avenue approach.

Practicalities

Bagnoles' **tourist office** is on place du Marché (April–Oct Mon–Sat 9.30am–12.30pm & 2–6pm, Sun 10am–12.30pm & 2.30–6.30pm; Nov–March Mon–Sat 9.30am–12.30pm & 2–6pm; Ⓣ02.33.37.85.66, Ⓦbagnolesdelorne.com). Note that the town as a whole operates to a season that lasts roughly from early April to the end of October; arrive in winter, and you may find everything shut.

The numerous **hotels** are sedate places, in which it's possible to be too late for dinner at 7pm and locked out altogether at 9pm. The nicest of the bunch, *Ô Gayot*, by the tourist office at 2 av de la Ferté Macé (Ⓣ02.33.38.44.01, Ⓦogayot.com; ❷–❺), offers a contemporary take on the spa experience with its minimalist rooms, and has a pleasant **restaurant** with outdoor seating. More traditional alternatives include the neighbouring, recently revamped *Bagnôles Hôtel*, at 6 place de la République (Ⓣ02.33.37.86.79, Ⓦbagnoles-hotel.com; ❸; closed Nov–March), which has its own bistro. The three-star **campsite**, *de la Vée* (Ⓣ02.33.37.87.45; closed Nov to mid-March), south of town, is rather forlorn.

Domfront

The road **west through the forest** from Bagnoles, the D335 and then the D908 climbs above the lush woodlands and progressively narrows to a hog's back before entering **DOMFRONT**, 22km on. Less happens here than at Bagnoles, but the countryside is prettier.

A public park, near the long-abandoned former train station, leads up to some redoubtable **castle ruins** perched on an isolated rock. Henry II and his queen, Eleanor of Aquitaine, often visited this castle; their daughter, also called Eleanor, was born here in October 1162. Thomas à Becket came to stay for Christmas 1166, saying Mass in the Notre-Dame-sur-l'Eau church down by the river, which has sadly been ruined by vandals. The views from the flower-filled gardens that surround the mangled keep are spectacular, including a very graphic panorama of the ascent you've made to get up.

A slender footbridge connects the castle with the narrow little **village** itself, which boasts an abundance of half-timbered houses. Near its sweet little central square, the modern **St-Julien** church, constructed out of concrete segments during the 1920s, is bursting with exciting Byzantine-style mosaics, which culminate in the vast *Christ in Majesty* above the altar. From the outside, it's an odd-looking building, especially when its belfry is swathed in green netting to catch loose stones, which seems to be pretty much all the time.

Practicalities

The **tourist office** is beside the castle at 12 place de la Roirie (Tues–Sat 10am–12.30pm & 2–6pm; ⓣ02.33.38.53.97, ⓦdomfront.com). On two summer afternoons a week (July & Aug Tues & Thurs 4.30pm), they run **guided tours** of old Domfront.

A couple of pleasant and very similar Logis de France **hotels** stand side by side at the foot of the hill below the old town, though sadly that means they're exposed to the noise of passing traffic rather than enjoying the tranquility higher up. The *Relais St-Michel*, 5 rue du Mont-St-Michel (ⓣ02.33.38.64.99, ⓦhotellerelaisstmichel.com; ❶–❸; closed Fri & Sun eve), has rooms with and without en-suite facilities, at varying prices, plus menus from €19, while the *France*, 7 rue du Mont-St-Michel (ⓣ02.33.38.51.44, ⓦhoteldefrance-fr.com; ❷), has a nice bar and garden as well as a restaurant. Campers should take note that the two-star local **campsite**, *du Champs Passais* (ⓣ02.33.37.37.66, ⓦdomfront.com; closed mid-Oct to March), is exceptionally small.

The Suisse Normande

The area known as the **Suisse Normande** starts roughly 25km south of Caen, stretching along the gorge of the River **Orne** between **Thury-Harcourt** and **Putanges**. While the name, with its allusion to the Alps, may be a little far-fetched – there are certainly no mountains – it's a distinctive and highly attractive region, with cliffs and crags and wooded hills at every turn. The energetic race along the Orne in canoes and kayaks, their lazier counterparts contenting themselves with pedalos or a bizarre species of inflatable rubber tractor, while high above them climbers dangle from thin ropes and claw desperately at the sheer rock face. For mere walkers, the Orne can be frustrating: footpaths along the river are few and far between, whatever maps may say, and often entirely overgrown with brambles. At least one road sign in the area warns of unexploded mines from World War II, so tread carefully.

The Suisse Normande is most usually approached from Caen or Falaise, and contrasts dramatically with the prairie-like expanse of wheatfields en route. **Bus** Verts #34 can take you to Thury-Harcourt or Clécy on its way from Caen to Flers, and **SNCF** run occasional special summer train excursions from Caen. If you're **cycling** head out of Caen via the village of Ifs, following signs for Falaise. The least stressful approach is to follow the D212, cruising across the flatlands to Thury-Harcourt, though swooping down the D23 from Bretteville, with thick woods to either side, is exhilarating. **Touring** the Suisse Normande on a bike, however, is an exhausting business: the minor roads do not follow the gorge floor, but undulate endlessly over the surrounding slopes.

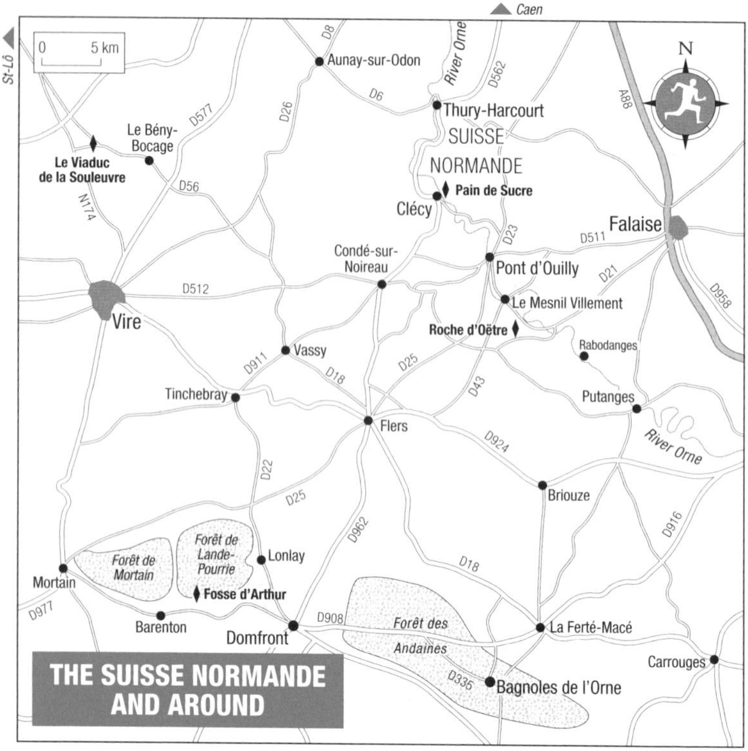

Thury-Harcourt

THURY-HARCOURT is really two separate towns: a little village around a bridge across the Orne, and a larger market town on the hill that overlooks it. In summer, the grounds of the local manor house are open to visitors, providing access to the immediate riverside (March–April & Oct Sun 2.30–6.30pm; May–Sept daily 2.30–6.30pm; €4.30).

The **tourist office**, 2 place St-Sauveur (May, June & Sept Tues–Sat 10am–12.30pm & 2.30–6.30pm, Sun 10am–12.30pm; July & Aug same hours plus Mon 10am–12.30pm; Oct–April Mon 2.30–5pm, Tues–Fri 10am–12.30pm & 2.30–5pm, Sat 10am–12.30pm; ⓣ02.31.79.70.45, ⓦwww.ot-suisse-normande.com), can suggest walks, rides and *gîtes d'étape* throughout the Suisse Normande. Kayak Club Thury-Harcourt at the waterfront Base de Canoe (ⓣ02.31.79.40.59, ⓦkcth.fr) rent out both bikes and canoes.

Thury-Harcourt is home to a Logis de France **hotel**, the *Relais de la Poste* (ⓣ02.31.79.72.12, ⓦwww.hotel-relaisdelaposte.com; ❹; closed March, plus Fri lunch in summer, all Fri and Sat lunch in winter), and also an attractive four-star **campsite**, the *Vallée du Traspy* (ⓣ02.31.79.61.80, ⓦcampingtraspy.com; closed Oct–March), beside the river on the rue du Pont-Benoit.

Aunay-sur-Odon

AUNAY-SUR-ODON, 14km west of Thury-Harcourt and the river, is no one's idea of a holiday destination; all but obliterated during the war, it was rebuilt from scratch in functional concrete. In summer, however, when all the **accommodation** possibilities in the Suisse Normande proper tend to be wildly over-subscribed, you may well be glad of finding a room in either the *Hôtel de la Place*, 10 rue du 12-Juin-1944 (Ⓣ02.31.77.60.73, Ⓦhotel-place-aunay-odon.federal-hotel.com; ❷; restaurant closed Sun eve mid-Nov to March), where the excellent €25 menu includes crayfish and sea bass, or the *Hôtel St-Michel*, 6–8 rue de Caen (Ⓣ02.31.77.63.16; ❷; closed Nov & Jan, plus all Mon & Sun eve Sept–June, Mon eve only July & Aug).

Clécy

The small village of **CLÉCY**, 10km south of Thury-Harcourt, is perched on a hill about 1km up from the point where the D133A crosses the River Orne by means of the Pont du Vey. On the way up, the Parc des Loisirs holds a **Musée du Chemin de Fer Miniature** (March–Easter, Oct & Nov Sun 2–5.30pm; Easter–June & first half Sept daily except Mon 10am–noon & 2–6pm; July & Aug daily 10am–6pm; second half Sept daily except Mon 2–6pm; €5.50; Ⓦchemin-fer-miniature-clecy.com), featuring a gigantic model railway certain to appeal to children.

Practicalities

For advice on accommodation and the wide variety of holiday activities available, head for the **tourist office** (May, June & first half of Sept Tues–Sat 10am–12.30pm & 2.30–6.30pm, Sun 10am–12.30pm; July & Aug Mon–Sat 10am–12.30pm & 2.30–6.30pm, Sun 10am–12.30pm; second half of Sept Tues–Fri 10am–12.30pm, Sat 10am–12.30pm & 2.30–5pm; Ⓣ02.31.69.79.95, Ⓦwww.suisse-normande.com), which is tucked in behind the church.

Clécy is a better bet than Thury-Harcourt for finding a **room**, although its visitors outnumber residents in high season and the whole area can get much too crowded for comfort. The *logis* facing the church, *Au Site Normand*, 2 rue des Châtelets (Ⓣ02.31.69.71.05, Ⓦausitenormand.com; ❷; closed mid-Dec to

▲ Cows near Clécy in the Suisse Normande

mid-Feb), consists of a main timber-framed building, where menus in the old-fashioned and good-value dining room start at €19, and a cluster of newer units open onto a courtyard around the back. They also have bikes for rent.

Down the hill, the *Moulin du Vey* (02.31.69.71.08, moulinduvey.com; 5; hotel closed Dec, restaurant closed Sun in winter), set in spacious grounds on the far bank of the river, is a luxury hotel that takes its name from the restored watermill right by the bridge, which is itself, confusingly, now a restaurant. The western riverbank continues in a brief splurge of restaurants, takeaways and snack bars as far as the two-star municipal **campsite**, *Les Rochers des Parcs* (02.31.69.70.36, www.ocampings.com/campingclecy; closed Oct–March).

The Pain de Sucre

Across from Clécy, the **east bank** of the Orne is dominated by the exposed rock face of the giant **Pain de Sucre**, or Sugarloaf, looming above the river. Small footpaths, and the tortuous Route des Crêtes, wind up to its flat top, making for some fabulously enjoyable walks. Picnic sites and parking places along the crest hold orientation maps so weather-beaten as to be almost abstract, but the views down to the flat fields of the Orne Valley are stupendous. This is a prime site for **hang-gliders**; disconcertingly, at two points paved concrete ramps, built to facilitate launches, lead right to the edge of the precipice.

Pont d'Ouilly

If you're planning to walk, or cycle, **PONT D'OUILLY**, a dozen or so kilometres upriver from Clécy, where the main road from Vire to Falaise crosses the river, makes a good central base. It's just a village, with a few basic shops, an old covered market hall and a promenade (with bar) slightly upstream alongside the weir. Canoes, kayaks and mountain bikes can be rented by the hour or the day at the Base de Plein Air by the river (02.31.69.86.02, pontdouilly-loisirs.com). Alternatively, a pleasant walk leads for 3.5km south along the riverside to the pretty little village of **Le Mesnil Villement**. A Grand Pardon de St-Roch takes place along the river on the third Sunday in August.

Practicalities

Pont d'Ouilly has a summer-only **tourist office** in the market square (June & first three weeks of Sept, Sat & Sun 2–6pm; July & Aug Mon–Fri 2–6pm, Sat & Sun 10am–1pm & 2–6pm; 02.31.90.17.26, falaise-tourisme.com). As well as its **campsite**, overlooking the river (02.31.69.46.12; closed Oct–Easter), there's an attractive **hotel**, the *Relais du Commerce* (02.31.69.80.16, www.relaisducommerce.fr; 4; closed Sun eve & Mon). Unfortunately though, while the rooms are undeniably comfortable, and the outdoor terrace is a great spot to enjoy fine cuisine on menus that start at €25, recent modernizations are a little bland.

About 1km north of Pont d'Ouilly, the *Auberge St-Christophe*, covered with ivy and geraniums, offers seven en-suite rooms in a beautiful setting on the right bank of the Orne (02.31.69.81.23; 3; closed Sun eve, Mon & three weeks in Feb–March). The cheapest of its imaginative menus costs €25, while the *Menu Gastronomique* is €55.

The Roche d'Oëtre

A short way south of Pont d'Ouilly, the high rock known as the **Roche d'Oëtre** affords a tremendous view, not over the Orne but into the deep and totally wooded gorge of the Rouvre. The rock itself is private property, though you're under no obligation to visit the café there.

The river widens soon afterwards into the **Lac du Rabodanges**, formed by the many-arched Rabodanges Dam. It's a popular spot, where grassy picnic slopes lead down to the water's edge, and the occasional bather risks a swim among the waterskiers, speedboats, windsurfers, canoes and kayaks. The imposing Rabodanges château, higher up the hillside, is now a stud farm.

Putanges

Further climbing roads bring you to **PUTANGES**, another possible place to stay, with a well-priced **hotel**, the *Lion Verd* (ⓣ02.33.35.01.86, ⓦwww.hotel-restaurant-lion-verd.com; ❶; closed Sun eve & Mon, plus all Jan), very near the river, and a small **campsite**, the *Val d'Orne* (ⓣ02.33.35.00.25, ⓦoffice-tourisme-putanges.com; closed Oct–March). The town lies somewhat south of the main attractions of the region, but nevertheless it's a pleasant stop, with a few bars and pavement cafés and, just upstream from the bridge, the weirs over which the Orne appears from its source a short way south.

The Bocage

The region that centres on **St-Lô**, west of Caen and just south of the Cotentin, is known as the **Bocage Normande**. The word *bocage* refers to a type of cultivated countryside common in the west of France, in which fields are delineated by tight hedgerows rooted into walls of earth well over a metre high.

An effective form of smallhold farming, at least in pre-industrial days, the *bocage* also proved to be a perfect system of anti-tank barricades. When the Allied troops tried to advance through the region in 1944, it was almost impenetrable – certainly bearing no resemblance to the East Anglian plains where they had trained. The war here was hand-to-hand, inch-by-inch slaughter; the destruction of villages often wholesale.

St-Lô

The city of **ST-LÔ**, a transport junction 60km south of Cherbourg and 36km southwest of Bayeux, was crucial in the war to the Allied breakout of the Cotentin, and is still known as the "Capital of the Ruins". Black-and-white postcards of the wartime devastation are on sale everywhere, and you come across memorial sites at every turn. In the main square, the gate of the old prison commemorates Resistance members executed by the Nazis, citizens deported east to the concentration camps, and soldiers killed in action. When the bombardment of St-Lô was at its fiercest, the Germans refused to take any measures to protect the prisoners; the gate was all that survived. In similar vein, behind the cathedral, a monument to the dead of World War I is pitted with shrapnel from World War II. Less depressingly, at the foot of the rock under the castle you can see the entrance to caves where locals sheltered from the onslaught, while somewhere far below lie great vaults used by the German command. In Studs Terkel's book, *The Good War*, a GI reminisces about the huge party thrown there after the Americans found vast stockpiles of champagne; Thomas Pynchon's *Gravity's Rainbow* has a crazed drinking scene based on the tale. Samuel Beckett was here during the battle and after, working for the Irish Red Cross as interpreter, driver and provision-seeker – for such items as rat poison for the maternity hospitals. He said he took away with him a "time-honoured conception of humanity in ruins".

The newness of so much in St-Lô reveals the scale of fighting. It took sixty years for the canalized channel of the Vire, running in between the *gare SNCF* and the castle rock, to be extensively re-landscaped, Now known as **Port-St-Lô**, it's become an attractive area to walk around, and pedalos are even available for rent. But the most visible – and brilliant – reconstruction is the **Cathédrale de Notre Dame**. The main body of this, with its strange southward-veering nave, has been conventionally repaired and rebuilt. Between the shattered west front and base of the collapsed north tower, however, a startling sheer wall of icy green stone makes no attempt to mask the destruction.

By way of contrast, a lighthouse-like 1950s folly spirals to nowhere on the main square, place Général-de-Gaulle. Should you feel the urge to climb its 157 steps, make your way into the labyrinth of glass at its feet, which houses St-Lô's tourist office (for hours, see below), and pay the €1.50 admission fee. More compelling, around the back of the Mairie, is a **Musée des Beaux Arts** (Wed–Sun 2–6pm; €2). This is full of treasures: a Boudin sunset; a Lurçat tapestry of his dog Nadir and the Pirates; works by Corot, van Loo, Moreau; a Léger watercolour; and a fine series of sixteenth-century Flemish tapestries.

Practicalities

St-Lô makes an interesting pause, but it's virtually abandoned at night. Full information on what it has to offer can be obtained from the **tourist office** in place Général-de-Gaulle, described above (July & Aug Mon–Fri 9.30am–6.30pm, Sat 10am–1pm; Sept–June Mon 2–6pm, Tues–Fri 10am–12.30pm & 2–6pm, Sat 10am–1pm; ⓣ02.33.77.60.35, ⓦwww.mairie-saint-lo.fr). The **gare routière** is on the rue des 80e and 136e, a short way south.

St-Lô's largest and most prominent **hotel**, the *Mercure Saint-Lô*, stands just across the river beside the **gare SNCF**, ranged along the brow of a ridge at 1 av Briovère (ⓣ02.33.05.10.84; ❺); it's home to the *Tocqueville* **restaurant** (dinner only; closed Sun) which serves menus from €16. If you'd rather be up in town, *La Crémaillère*, at 8 rue de la Chancellerie (ⓣ02.33.57.14.68; ❷; closed Fri eve & Sat in low season), also has a good restaurant, where all the menus, which start at €9.50 for lunch and €13.50 for dinner, include a buffet of hors d'oeuvres.

Northeast from St-Lô

Travellers heading **northeast from St-Lô**, towards Bayeux, pass close to two remarkable buildings: the **Abbaye de Cerisy-la-Forêt** and the **Château de Balleroy**. Neither is easy to get to without transport, but if you have a bike or car they shouldn't be missed.

Cerisy-la-Forêt

The village of **CERISY-LA-FORÊT** stands at the edge of its forest 6km west of the D572 and a total of 20km northeast of St-Lô. Its eleventh-century Romanesque **abbey of St-Vigor** (access to church: April–June & Sept to mid-Nov daily except Mon 10.30am–6.30pm; July & Aug daily 10.30am–6.30pm; €3; guided tours: April–Sept daily except Mon 10.30am–12.30pm & 2.30–6.30pm; Oct Sat & Sun 10.30am–noon & 2.30–6pm; €4; ⓦabbayes-normandes.com) was founded by William the Conqueror's father on the site of an already venerable monastery. Set on a hill, overlooking an attractive pond just east of Cerisy itself, its triple tiers of windows and arches, lapping light onto its cream stone, can make you sigh in wonder at the skills of medieval Norman masons.

Balleroy

At **BALLEROY**, 8.5km east of Cerisy across the D572, you switch to an era when architects ruled over craftsmen. The main street of the village leads straight to the **château** (mid-March to June & Sept to mid-Oct daily except Tues, château 10am–noon & 2–6pm, museum 10am–6pm; July & Aug château and museum daily 10am–6pm; mid-Oct to mid-March, château and museum Mon & Wed–Fri 10am–noon & 1.30–5pm; château €6.50, museum €4.50, both €8; Ⓦchateau-balleroy.com), masterpiece of the celebrated seventeenth-century architect François Mansard. The formal gardens were laid out by André le Nôtre, also responsible for those at Versailles. In keeping with its ostentatious past, its most recent purchaser was the late American press magnate Malcolm S. Forbes (1919–90), pal of presidents Nixon, Ford and Reagan, not to mention Elizabeth Taylor. You can tour the house to see its eclectic furnishings, pieces of modern sculpture and an original *salon*, which holds superb royal portraits by Mignard.

Forbes was responsible for creating the museum at Balleroy that's devoted to his principal passion, **ballooning**. The history exhibits are truly fascinating, even if there is rather too much emphasis on Forbes himself.

The Vire Valley

Once St-Lô was taken in the Battle of Normandy, the armies moved speedily on to their next confrontation. Consequently, the **Vire Valley**, trailing south from St-Lô, saw little action – and indeed its towns and villages have rarely been touched by any historic or cultural mainstream. The motivation in coming to this landscape of rolling hills, occasional gorges, and orchards of apples and pears, is essentially to consume the region's cider, Calvados and butter-rich fruit pastries.

Between St-Lô and Vire

The finest section of the Vire is the valley that stretches south from St-Lô through the Roches de Ham to Tessy-sur-Vire. A pair of sheer rocky promontories high above the river, known as the **Roches de Ham**, are promoted as a "viewing table", though the pleasure lies as much in the walk up, through lanes lined with blackberries, hazelnuts and rich orchards.

Just downstream from the Roches, the tiny village of **LA CHAPELLE-SUR-VIRE** makes a perfect spot for a rural stopover. Its church, towering majestically above the river, has been an object of pilgrimage since the twelfth century, though in its current incarnation it dates from 1886. There's a weir nearby and a scattering of grassy islands. Next to the bridge on the lower road in a traditional village cottage, the *Auberge de la Chapelle* (Ⓣ02.33.56.32.83; ❷) is a good **restaurant** that also offers a few cheap **rooms** (where rates include breakfast). Menus are priced at €22 and €28, and feature plenty of fresh river fish.

An alternative base for the Roches, 5km northeast of La Chapelle, **TORIGNI-SUR-VIRE** was home to the Grimaldi family before they achieved quasi-royal status upon moving on to the principality of Monaco. A spacious country town, it boasts a few grand buildings and an attractive **campsite**, *Le Lac des Charmilles* (Ⓣ02.33.56.91.74, Ⓦwww.camping-lacdescharmilles.com; closed Nov–Feb).

At the eastern end of the sinuous Vire gorge, 10km north of Vire and 6km west of Le Bény-Bocage, stands the former railway viaduct of **Le Viaduc de la Souleuvre**, designed by Gustave Eiffel. Only the six supporting granite pillars of Eiffel's original structure remain – the railway closed down in 1970 – but in 1990 a wooden boardwalk was relaid across half the span of the bridge, on which visitors can cross to the deepest part of the gorge. Once there, 61m up, they are expected to jump off – this is A.J. Hackett's **bungy-jumping** centre (hours vary, but July & Aug open daily; June & Sept daily except Tues & Wed; mid-April to May & Oct to mid-Nov Sat, Sun & hols only; reservations essential Ⓣ02.31.66.31.66, Ⓦwww.ajhackett.fr). Jumpers have to be aged at least 13, and for up to three people to make a single jump each costs €89 per person; you also have to pay €3 to park in the adjacent field. Less intrepid souls can walk down to the meadows immediately beneath the viaduct and watch the plummeting from there.

Vire

The pride and joy of the people of the hill town of **VIRE** are their *andouilles*, the highly spiced sausages known in English as chitterlings. If you can avoid these hideous parcels of pigs' intestines, and the assortment of abattoirs that produce them, it's possible to have a good time; in fact, Vire is worth visiting specifically for its food.

The only problem is what to do when you're not eating. As testified by a memorial in the **belfry** that stands alone in the town centre, the town was all but destroyed on D-Day, at a cost of five hundred lives. That stunted tower houses temporary exhibitions each summer (July & Aug Mon–Thurs 2–6pm, Fri & Sat 10am–noon & 2–6pm; free), while down the hill towards the river, the **Museum of Vire** in the place Ste-Anne holds furniture, costumes and paintings by regional artists (May, June & Sept–Nov Wed–Fri 2–6pm, Sat & Sun 10am–12.30pm & 2–6pm; July & Aug Wed–Sun 10am–12.30pm & 2–6pm; €3). Nearby, you can wander by the little scrap of **canal**, equipped with twee floating houses for the ducks, which lies just below the one stark finger that survives of the castle. The only action is at the Friday **market**, again obsessively dedicated to food.

For some exercise, head 6km south along the D76 to **Lac de la Dathée**. Set in open country, the lake is circled by footpaths; in summer it sometimes dries up completely, but when it's wet it can also be crossed by rented sailing boat, kayak or windsurf board (daily June–Sept; Ⓣ02.31.66.01.58).

Incidentally, the small industrial area immediately north of Vire, where the Vire and Varenne valleys meet, holds a remarkable place in the history of popular music. As the **Vaux de Vire**, this became a centre during the fifteenth century for the manufacture of cloth. The drinking songs composed by one of the textile workers, Olivier Basselin, acquired such popularity throughout medieval Europe that the district gave its name to a new kind of entertainment – **vaudeville**.

Practicalities

Vire's **tourist office** is in the square de la Résistance at the heart of town (July & Aug Mon–Sat 9.30am–1pm & 1.45–6.30pm; Sept–June Mon–Sat 9.30am–12.15pm & 1.45–6pm; Ⓣ02.31.66.28.50, Ⓦwww.vire-tourisme.com). **Hotels** with good dining rooms include the central *Hôtel de France*, within sight of the tourist office at 4 rue d'Aignaux (Ⓣ02.31.68.00.35, Ⓦhoteldefrancevire.com; ❸; closed mid-Dec to mid-Jan, plus Sun eve & Mon lunch), which serves several separate menus; the €33 *menu Virois* is packed with local specialities, including *andouilles*, but no one's going to make you eat it if you don't want to – there's always *tripes a là mode de Caen* instead. Otherwise, *Au Vrai Normand*, 14 rue Armand-Gasté (Ⓣ02.31.67.90.99; closed Wed, plus Tues eve & Sun eve), is the best stand-alone **restaurant**, with lunch from €15 and a €20 dinner menu that includes a *Montgolfière de pêcheur*, a sort of fish stew covered with pastry.

West and south from Vire

Once past Vire, the roads towards Brittany present you with the choice either of heading southwest for the frontier towns of **Fougères** and **Vitré** (see p.224 & p.226), or directly to the coast and making the magnificent **Mont-St-Michel** (see p.148) your last port of call in Normandy.

West from Vire, the road to Villedieu passes through the village of **ST-SEVER**, which is backed by a dark and magical **forest** holding a dolmen, an abbey and a scattering of good picnic spots marked by signs showing a champagne bottle in a hamper.

Villedieu-les-Poêles

VILLEDIEU-LES-POÊLES – literally "City of God the Frying Pans" – is a lively place, usually busy with tourists, 28km west of Vire. Much of this ancient town still retains significant elements of its medieval appearance, especially in its backstreets, where perfectly preserved old courtyards are tucked away behind unprepossessing wooden gateways. Ever since the twelfth century, Villedieu has been a centre for metalworking, despite the fact that with no mines in Normandy the only source of copper came from melting down unwanted artefacts. To this day, copper souvenirs and kitchen utensils gleam from its rows of shops, and the tourist office can provide lists of dozens of local ateliers for more direct purchases.

Displays at the **Musée de la Poeslerie**, in a pretty little courtyard at 25 rue Général-Huard (April to mid-Nov Tues & alternate Sun 2–6.30pm, Wed–Sat 10am–12.30pm & 2–6.30pm; €4), illustrate the historical development of Villedieu's copperware; the same ticket also gets you into the **Musée de la Dentelle** (lace) in the same building – while paying an extra €1 entitles you to admission to the **Musée du Meuble Normand** (Norman furniture) down the street in the place du Pussoir Fidèle (same hours as the Poeslerie; €4 on its own). On the road between the museums, you can also watch copper craftsmen at work, and buy the results, in the **Atelier du Cuivre** at 54 rue Général-Huard (July & Aug Mon–Fri 9am–noon & 1.30–6pm, Sat 9am–noon & 2–6pm; Sept–June Mon–Fri 9am–noon & 1.30–5.30pm, Sat 9am–noon & 2–5.30pm; €5; Ⓦwww.atelierducuivre.com).

Even if all this emphasis on copper pots and pans is starting to seem obsessive, it's well worth making time to visit the **Fonderie de Cloches** at 13 rue du Pont-Chignon, one of the twelve remaining **bell foundries** in Europe. Work here is only part-time due to limited demand, but you may find the forge lit nonetheless (mid-Feb to early July & Sept to mid-Nov Tues–Sat 10am–12.30pm & 2–6pm; early July to Aug daily 9am–6pm; €4.90; Ⓦcornille-havard.com). Expert craftsmen will show you the moulds, composed of an unpleasant-looking combination of clay, goats' hair and horse manure.

Practicalities

Villedieu's **tourist office** is at 43 place de la République (July & Aug daily 9am–6pm; Sept–June Mon–Sat 9am–noon & 2–5.30pm; Ⓣ02.33.61.05.69,

Ⓦot-villedieu.fr). If you're charmed into **staying**, the very welcoming Logis *Hôtel St-Pierre et St-Michel*, in the heart of the main street at 12 place de la République (Ⓣ02.33.61.00.11, Ⓦwww.st-pierre-hotel.com; ❸; closed mid-Jan to mid-Feb), houses a stylish restaurant, where the €35 menu is seriously gastronomic. The *Fruitier*, on place Costils (Ⓣ02.33.90.51.00, Ⓦwww.le-fruitier.com; ❸; closed Christmas to mid-Jan), also serves good food, and there's a three-star **campsite** by the river, *des Chevaliers* (Ⓣ02.33.61.02.44, Ⓦwww.camping-deschevaliers.com; closed Nov–March). *Le Triskell*, just below the main street at no. 2 on the pedestrian place du Pussoir Fidèle (Ⓣ02.33.51.94.58; closed Mon Oct–May) is part brasserie, part pizzeria, and part pub, and serves a € 9.50 lunch menu.

Champrepus

Eight kilometres west of Villedieu at **CHAMPREPUS**, an arch across the D924 serves as both a sign announcing, and a bridge between the two sections of, Normandy's finest **zoo** (Feb to mid-March daily 1.30–6pm; second half of March Sat & Sun 1.30–6pm; April–Sept daily 10am–7pm; first three weeks of Oct Sat & Sun 11am–7pm; late Oct to early Nov daily 11am–7pm; €12.80; Ⓣ02.33.61.30.74, Ⓦwww.zoo-champrepus.com). It displays a vast array of species in remarkably natural surroundings, starting a little disappointingly with domestic and farm animals such as bunnies and donkeys, but swiftly moving on to tigers and chimps, ostriches and otters, and even giraffes. In this typically pastoral Norman landscape, it's oddly shocking to encounter zebras grazing in the meadows, wallabies hopping around the orchards, and lions making their homes amid dolmens. In the most unusual section, visitors are free to stroll among large groups of sleepy-eyed lemurs, with nothing to stop you touching them apart from their prominently bared canine teeth. Children are invited to milk an artificial cow or bounce on an inflatable elephant, and there's a little grill restaurant on site.

Mortain and the Forêt de Lande-Pourrie

South from Vire, anyone heading for Fougères (see p.224) or Domfront (see p.180) passes through the **Forêt de Mortain** and its continuation, the **Forêt de Lande-Pourrie**. The **Fosse d'Arthur**, a remote spot in the forest east of Mortain, is one of many unlikely claimants to King Arthur's death scene. A couple of waterfalls disappear into deep limestone caverns, but there's little to see.

The war-ravaged town of **MORTAIN** itself perches high above the very deep gorge of the Cance, 24km south of Vire. It's not a place to linger very long, but the views, especially from the south end of the main street, are spectacular. A short walk west out of town leads into some lovely countryside, with two **waterfalls** – known as the Grande Cascade and the Petite Cascade – interrupting the river itself. Head up the high rocky bluff to the east, on the other hand, and from the tiny chapel at the top the neighbouring province of Maine spreads before you. On a clear day, you can even see Mont-St-Michel.

If you want a **place to stay** in Mortain, the *Hôtel de la Poste*, 1 place des Arcades (Ⓣ02.33.59.00.05, Ⓦhoteldelaposte.fr; ❸; restaurant closed Mon & Tues), is the best option, with the restaurant serving good menus from €19.

St-Hilaire-du-Harcoët

The thriving (Wed) market town of **ST-HILAIRE-DU-HARCOËT**, 28km north of Fougères, amounts to little more than a crossroads near the big market square. It does, however, hold a few restaurants and **hotels**, such as *Le Cygne et*

Résidence, on the main road into town from Fougères at 99 rue Waldeck-Rousseau (Ⓣ02.33.49.11.84, Ⓦhotel-le-cygne.fr; ❹; closed Sun eve & Fri eve Oct–March), a comfortable modern *logis* with a swimming pool in the garden and an appealing set of menus from €14 up to €70.

Travel details

Trains

Alençon to: Caen (8 daily; 1hr 10min) via Sées (12min) and Argentan (30min); Le Mans (11 daily; 40min); Tours (4 daily; 1hr 50min).
Argentan to: Granville (7 daily; 1hr 20min) via Vire (50min) and Villedieu (1hr 5min).
Bagnoles to: Briouze (3 daily; 40min) for Argentan (1hr 15min) and Paris (3hr).
Lisieux to: Caen (20 daily; 30min); Paris (11 daily; 1hr 40min); Rouen (8 daily; 1hr 5min) via Bernay (20min) and Brionne (35min).
St-Lô to: Caen (12 daily; 45min) via Bayeux (25min); Rennes (4 daily; 2hr 10min) via Coutances (20min) and Pontorson (1hr 15min).
Vire to: Granville (6 daily; 35min) via Villedieu (15min); Paris (5 daily; 2hr 45min) via Argentan (50min) and L'Aigle (1hr 30min).

Buses

The main inland bus networks are operated by **Bus Verts**, who cover Calvados in particular (Ⓣ08.01.21.42.14; Ⓦwww.busverts.fr), and **STAO**, whose routes extend across most of the Orne region further south (Alençon Ⓣ02.33.26.06.35; Argentan Ⓣ02.33.80.09.09; Mortagne Ⓣ02.33.25.19.11).
Alençon to: Bagnoles (3 daily; 1hr); Bellême (1–2 daily; 1hr); Évreux (1 daily; 2hr), via L'Aigle (1hr 40min); Mortagne (1–3 daily; 1hr); Vimoutiers (1–3 daily; 1hr 30min) via Sées (30min).
Argentan to: Alençon (1–2 daily; 1hr 15min) via Sées (40min); Carrouges (1–3 daily; 45min); Domfront (1–3 daily; 1hr 50min) via Bagnoles (1hr).
Caen to: Falaise (7 daily; 1hr); Flers (4 daily; 1hr 20min) via Thury-Harcourt (40min) and Clécy (50min); Pont-L'Évêque (3 daily; 1hr 10min); Vire (3 daily; 1hr 30min) via Aunay-sur-Odon (1hr).
Lisieux to: Le Havre (2 daily; 1hr 30min); Orbec (6 daily; 35min); Pont-l'Évêque (4 daily; 25min) and on to Honfleur (50min); Vimoutiers (4 daily; 40min) via Livarot (30min).
Mortagne to: Bellême (1–4 daily; 20min).
St-Lô to: Bayeux (8 daily; 30min); Cherbourg (3 daily; 1hr 40min); Coutances (5 daily; 50min); Villedieu-les-Poêles (4 daily; 1hr 10min).
Vire to: Avranches (5 daily; 45min); Condé-sur-Noireau (2 daily; 30min); Fougères (4 daily; 1hr 30min); St-Hilaire-du-Harcoët (4 daily; 1hr).

4

The North Coast and Rennes

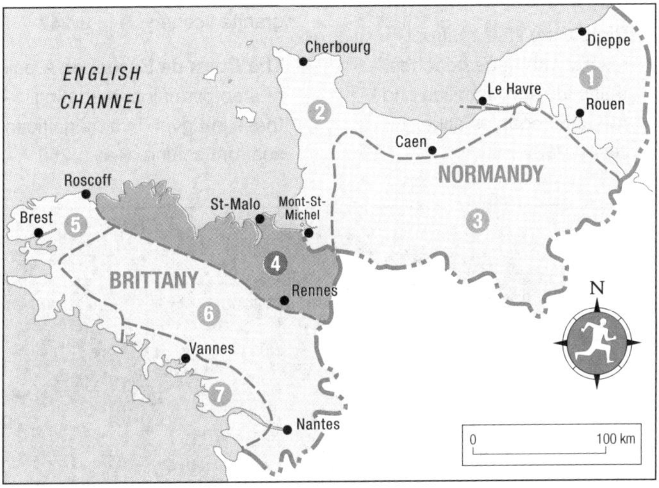

CHAPTER 4 # Highlights

* **St-Malo** St-Malo's walled citadelle still feels like the romantic haunt of pirates and explorers. See p.197

* **Dinan** With its imposing walls and delightful lanes, Dinan is one of France's f inest medieval towns. See p.209

* **Cancale** Cancale is thronged with seafood lovers; picnic on oysters from a harbourfront stall, or dine at a fine restaurant without breaking the bank. See p.213

* **Binic** Cute little seafront resort, with huge beaches, that's ideal for families and romantic couples alike. See p.236

* **Île de Bréhat** Even in high summer, a boat trip to this beautiful island enables you to escape the traffic and crowds. See p.240

* **Manoir de Troazel Vras** Delightful rural *chambre d'hôte*, in a converted farm set back from a gorgeous stretch of coast. See p.243

* **The Sentier des Douaniers** The spectacular coastal footpath between Perros-Guirec and Ploumanac'h passes extraordinary pink-granite scenery. See p.247

* **The Cairn de Barnenez** A pair of step pyramids, predating those in Egypt, in a magnificent seafront setting. See p.250

▲ A coastal footpath along the Côte de Granit Rose

4

The North Coast and Rennes

The northern coast of Brittany is varied in the extreme. Long sections, open to the full force of the Atlantic, are spectacular but much too dangerous for swimming; others shelter superb natural harbours and peaceful resorts. The old citadelle port of St-Malo makes an attractive point of arrival, with plenty of nearby sights and diversions.

The best of the **resorts** are concentrated along two separate stretches of coastline, the Côte d'Émeraude and the Côte de Granit Rose. As green as its name suggests, the **Côte d'Émeraude** remains largely unspoiled, at its wildest on the heather-covered headlands of Cap Fréhel. Thanks to gorgeous beaches, seaside towns such as **Erquy** and **Le Val-André** hold plenty of hotels and restaurants, while it's always possible to find a secluded campsite for a night or two's stopover.

Further west, beyond the placid **Baie de St-Brieuc**, the coastline erupts into a garish labyrinth of pink granite boulders, the famed **Côte de Granit Rose**. This harsher territory was once, at **Paimpol** and elsewhere, the home of cod and whaling fleets that ranged right across the Atlantic. Today it's reliant on tourism, especially at the attractive twin resorts of **Perros-Guirec** and **Ploumanac'h.** There are also plenty of smaller places where you can avoid the crowds, such as **Loguivy** on the mainland, and, just offshore, the **Île de Bréhat** – among the most beautiful of all northern French islands.

The first 20km of the route **inland** from St-Malo take you alongside the delightful **Rance estuary**. Frequent boats connect both St-Malo and Dinard with **Dinan**, a medieval fortress town *par excellence* that, like most of this region, owes its prosperity to an epic saga of trading and piracy on the high seas. Beyond it, south of the more ancient community of **Dol**, lies a patchwork of waterways and woodlands, while further **east**, the redoubtable **citadelles** of **Fougères** and **Vitré** still guard the frontier with Normandy.

At the heart of the *département* of Ille-et-Vilaine, the city of **Rennes** has after centuries of rivalry with Nantes finally established itself as the indisputable capital of Brittany. Rennes may not be the prettiest town in the province, but it is without doubt the liveliest. It hosts an important university and most of the major Breton political and cultural organizations; it's also renowned for **festivals**, devoting itself to ten days of theatre and music each July during the **Tombées de la Nuit**, and celebrating the **Transmusicales** rock festival in December.

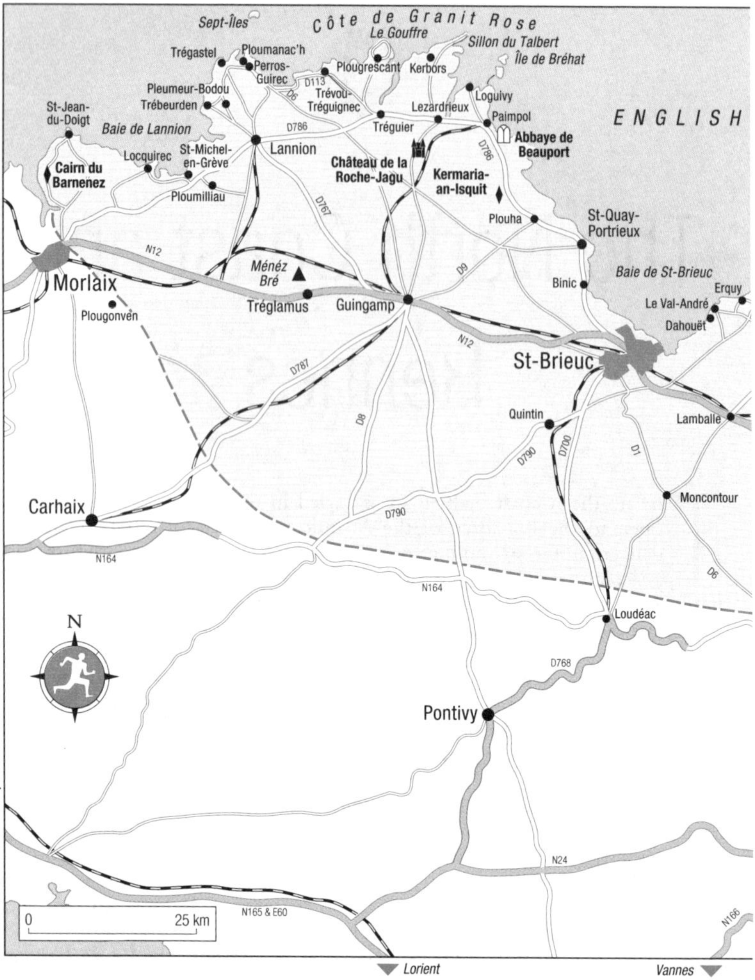

East: the Rance and Rennes

Whether you approach across the Channel by ferry, or along the coast from Mont-St-Michel in Normandy, the wide estuary of the **River Rance** serves as a spectacular introduction to Brittany. The towns of **St-Malo** and **Dinard**, each with its own distinct ambience, stand to either side of its mouth, while **Dinan** guards the head of the river itself 20km upstream. From those few places where it's possible to cross the Rance (most notably, along the top of the tidal power dam known as the **Barrage de la Rance**), you can enjoy magnificent views of its sheltered banks – rich, fertile and repeatedly pierced by tributaries.

East of the river spreads the **Baie du Mont-St-Michel**, dominated by the pinnacle of the Mont itself (see p.148), and swept by extraordinary tides that

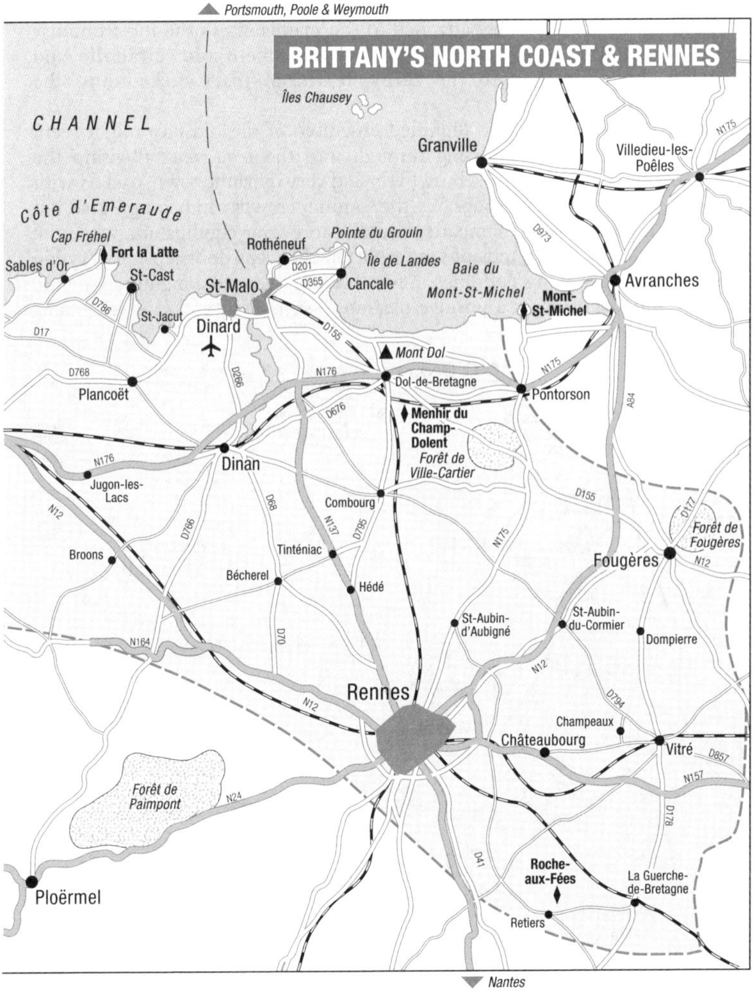

render swimming out of the question. **Cancale**, the most sheltered point along the Breton side of the bay, is a good spot from which to appreciate it all, ideally as you sample the town's famous oysters. Inland, all roads either curve eventually to **Rennes**, or head out east towards Normandy, via the medieval fortress towns of **Fougères** and **Vitré**.

St-Malo

The elegant, ancient, and beautifully positioned city of **ST-MALO** makes an essential stop on any tour of Brittany. Walled and built with the same grey granite stone as Mont-St-Michel, St-Malo was originally a fortified island at the mouth of the Rance, controlling not only the estuary but also the open sea beyond. Now inseparably attached to the mainland, it's the most popular destination in the region, thanks more to its superb **old citadelle** and sprawling **beaches** than to the **ferry terminal** that's tucked into the harbour behind.

From outside the walls, the dignified ensemble of the old city might seem stern and forbidding, but passing through into the *intra-muros* ("within the walls") streets brings you into a busy, lively and very dynamic town, packed with hotels, restaurants, bars and shops. Yes, the summer crowds can be oppressive, but even then a stroll atop the ramparts should restore your equilibrium, while the presence of vast, clean strands of sand right on the city's doorstep is a very big bonus if you're travelling with kids in tow. Having to spend a night here before or after a ferry crossing is a positive pleasure – so long as you reserve accommodation in advance.

A, B, C, D, Rothéneuf, ▲ Courtoisville, Camping & Paramé

Grande Plage

Bassin Duguay-Trouin

Gare SNCF

Château/Musée

Gare Routière

Porte St-Vincent

Cyber'Com @
ST-MALO

Grand Bé

CITADELLE

Bassin Jaques-Cartier

Bassin de Vauban

Quai Dinan

Moving Bridges

Moving Bridge

Bassin Bouvet

Terminal Ferry du Naye

QUAI DE TRICHET

ST-SERVAN

Môle des Noires

see 'St Malo: Intra-Muros' map for detail

Port de Plaisance

Grand Aquarium

Fort

Camping d'Alet

CITÉ D'ALETH

Port Solidor

Tour Solidor

Dinard

ACCOMMODATION

Le Beaufort	A
Centre Patrick Varangot	D
De l'Europe	E
Hostel	C
Le Mont-Fleury	B
La Rance	F

0 250 m

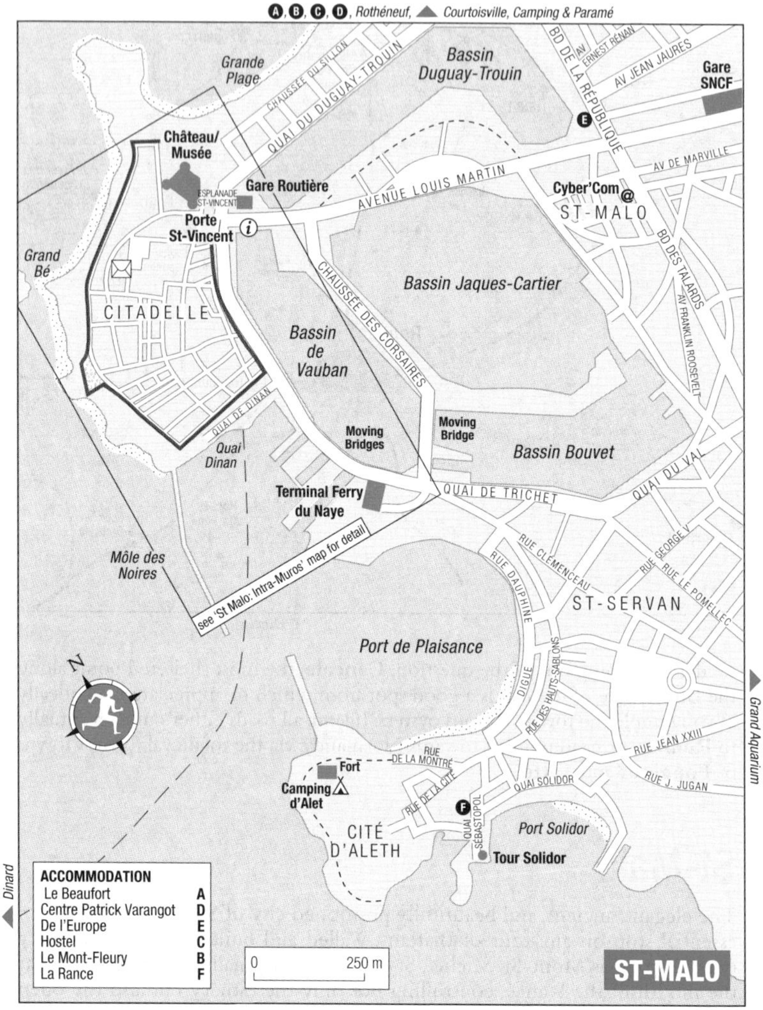

While the promontory fort of Alet, south of the modern centre in what's now **St-Servan**, commanded approaches to the Rance even before the arrival of the Romans, modern St-Malo traces its origins to a monastic community founded by saints Aaron and Brendan early in the sixth century. From 550 AD onwards the settlement was identified with the Celtic St Maclou (or possibly MacLow), and in later centuries it became notorious as the home of a fierce breed of **pirate-mariners**. These adventurers were never quite under anybody's control but their own; for four years from 1590, St-Malo even declared itself to be an independent republic, under the motto "*Ni Français, Ni Bretons, Malouins Suis*". Over a period of centuries, the *corsaires* of St-Malo not only forced English ships passing up the Channel to pay tribute, but also brought wealth from further afield. **Jacques Cartier**, who founded the earliest French colony in Canada, lived in and sailed from St-Malo, as did the first colonists to settle the Falklands – hence the islands' Argentinian name, Las Malvinas. Even when the Duke of Marlborough landed 15,000 men just up the coast near Cancale in 1758, and attempted to take the city by land, St-Malo's defences proved too formidable.

Arrival and city transport

St-Malo is always busy with **boats**. From the **Terminal Ferry du Naye**, Brittany Ferries (Ⓣ02.99.40.64.41, Ⓦbrittany-ferries.com) sails to Portsmouth, while Condor Ferries (Ⓣ02.99.40.78.10, Ⓦcondorferries.co.uk) connect with Weymouth and Poole (via Jersey or Guernsey) during spring and summer. Between April and early November, regular passenger **ferries to Dinard** operate from the **quai Dinan**, just outside the westernmost point of the ramparts in front of the port (Compagnie Corsaire; €4.20 one-way, €6.50 return; under-13s €2.70/€4.20; bikes €2 one-way, €3 return; Ⓣ08.25.13.80.35, Ⓦcompagniecorsaire.com); the trip across the estuary takes an all-too-short ten minutes. Compagnie Corsaire also conduct excursions up the river to Dinan (see p.209), and cruises along the Brittany coast to Cap Fréhel, St-Cast and the Île Cézembre, and out to Jersey and the Îles Chausey (see p.146).

St-Malo's **gare SNCF** is 2km out from the citadelle, set back from square Jean Coquelin, and convenient neither for the old town nor the ferry. All trains to and from St-Malo pass through Dol. Most continue through to Rennes, so if you're heading west towards Dinan and St-Brieuc, or northeast into Normandy, you'll probably have to change at Dol.

Though almost all St-Malo buses – whether local or long distance – also call at the *gare SNCF*, the **gare routière** – not a building, just an expanse of concrete – is officially located on the esplanade St-Vincent next to the tourist office. Illenoo (Ⓣ02.99.82.26.26, Ⓦillenoo.fr) run services to Dinard, Cancale, Dol, Rennes and, in summer, Mont-St-Michel; Kéolis Emeraude (Ⓣ02.99.19.70.80, Ⓦwww.keolis-emeraude.com) run express services to Mont-St-Michel; and Tibus (Ⓣ08.10.22.22.22, Ⓦwww.tibus.fr) serve Dinan, Dinard and St-Cast.

River cruises

Le Chateaubriand (Ⓣ02.99.46.44.40, Ⓦwww.chateaubriand.com) offers **sightseeing cruises** through the year in the Baie du Mont-St-Michel and up the Rance, starting from the Gare Maritime du Barrage de la Rance, at the Dinard end of the barrage (90min trip €16, 3hr €25). Gastronomic cruises, which include a full meal, cost €48–70.

St-Malo has traditionally had far too few **car parks** to cope with the sheer level of its summer traffic; the problem may have been alleviated to some extent by the time you read this, thanks to the construction of a massive **underground** car park beneath the esplanade St-Vincent. Even if that is indeed the case, if you're driving in to catch a ferry, keep well clear of the old town; the **Chaussée des Corsaires**, which links the citadelle with the ferry terminal, can be closed for long periods while its moveable bridge is opened to let boats out of the Bassin Jacques-Cartier.

Information

St-Malo's helpful **tourist office** (April–June & Sept Mon–Sat 9am–12.30pm & 1.30–6.30pm, Sun 10am–12.30pm & 2.30–6pm; July & Aug Mon–Sat 9am–7.30pm, Sun 10am–6pm; Oct–March Mon–Sat 9am–12.30pm & 1.30–6pm; ⓣ08.25.13.52.00, ⓦsaint-malo-tourisme.com) is housed in a single-storey building on the Esplanade St-Vincent, right in front of the city walls, in between the Bassin de Vauban and the Bassin Duguay-Trouin in the **Port des Yachts**. As well as good detailed city maps, it can provide information on annual festivals such as the **Étonnants Voyageurs** (Amazing Travellers; ⓦwww.etonnants-voyageurs.com), dedicated to the film and literature of travel and adventure, which takes place for three days in late May and/or early June.

Accommodation

St-Malo boasts over a hundred **hotels**, including the traditional seaside boarding houses located just off the beach, as well as several **campsites** and one of the busiest **hostels** in France.

In high season, St-Malo needs every one of its hotel rooms: the demand is phenomenal. Motorists intending to stay the night before catching a summer ferry sailing should make reservations well in advance; if you don't have a reservation, don't demoralize yourself hunting around, and settle for spending the night somewhere else along the coast or nearby. Apart from the obvious alternatives of Dinard and Dinan, it's worth considering peaceful smaller towns such as Combourg, Cancale, Jugon-les-Lacs, St-Jacut or Erquy.

Hotels in the citadelle

The thirty or so of St-Malo's **hotels** that stand **within the city walls** charge premium rates. Those *intra-muros* hotels with their own restaurants tend to take advantage of high summer demand by insisting that all guests eat in, and most also charge **parking** fees of around €10.

Bristol Union 4 pl de la Poissonnerie ⓣ02.99.40.83.36, ⓦhotel-bristol-union.com. Tall, somewhat upscale hotel, equipped with a lift, in a relatively quiet little square facing the former fish market, just off the Grande Rue, which offers unexciting but acceptable modernized rooms, some very small. Buffet breakfast €9. ④

Le Croiseur 2 pl de la Poissonnerie ⓣ02.99.40.80.40, ⓦwww.hotel-le-croiseur.com. A new, contemporary-style hotel overlooking the fish market, with sleek and spotless rooms, wi-fi throughout and a great bar and terrace on the ground floor. Friendly and very good value. ③

Elizabeth 2 rue des Cordiers ⓣ02.99.56.24.98, ⓦst-malo-hotel-elizabeth.com. Seventeenth-century mansion, grandly furnished to a Far Eastern theme, set just back from the walls. Its ten guest rooms are spacious but have rather small bathrooms, and there are also cheaper but very modern and comfortable additional rooms in "the Skippers", an annexe 100m away. Breakfast is €11. ⑦, Skippers ④

de France et de Chateaubriand pl Chateaubriand ⓣ02.99.56.66.52, ⓦwww.hotel-fr-chateaubriand.com. Elegant rooms at surprisingly reasonable prices in the imposing birthplace of the writer Chateaubriand, approached via a courtyard from the main square. Higher rooms have sea views; breakfast is €11 and parking €12. 5

Louvre 2 rue des Marins ⓣ02.99.40.86.62, ⓦhoteldulouvre-saintmalo.com. Pleasant, upmarket place just off Grande Rue, between the Grande Porte and Cathédrale St-Vincent, with fifty refurbished rooms – some suitable for disabled visitors – and good €12 buffet breakfasts. 7

Le Nautilus 9 rue de la Corne de Cerf ⓣ02.99.40.42.27, ⓦlenautilus.com. This colourfully refitted, totally non-smoking hotel (with a lift), not far in from the Porte St-Vincent, offers small but good-value and bright rooms, all with shower and WC. Friendly and helpful staff ensure it's hugely popular with younger travellers especially. Bar but no restaurant. Closed mid-Nov to mid-Dec. 3

Pomme d'Or 4 pl du Poids-du-Roi ⓣ02.99.40.90.24, ⓦwww.la-pomme-dor.fr. Twelve modernized rooms in a fine old building, just inside the citadelle near the ramparts – take a sharp left after entering through the Grande Porte. Conventional menus start at €17, while the breakfast buffet spread is €7.50. Closed Jan to mid-Feb. 3

Porte St-Pierre 2 pl du Guet ⓣ02.99.40.91.27, ⓦhotel-portestpierre.com. Comfortable Logis de France, peeping out to sea over the walls of the citadelle, near the small Porte St-Pierre and very handy for the plage de Bon Secours. Predominantly fish-based dinner menus, in the separate restaurant across the alley (closed Tues, plus Thurs lunch & Sun eve), run from €29 upwards. Closed mid-Nov to Feb. 4

Quic en Groigne 8 rue d'Estrées ⓣ02.99.20.22.20, ⓦquic-en-groigne.com. Friendly little hotel at the far end of the citadelle, with attractive en-suite rooms. 3

San Pédro 1 rue Ste-Anne ⓣ02.99.40.88.57, ⓦsanpedro-hotel.com. Twelve compact but tastefully and stylishly refurbished rooms in a nice quiet setting, just inside the walls in the north of the citadelle, near the Porte des Bés. The bubbly owner makes great breakfasts and is thrilled to offer advice. Rooms on the higher floors (reached via a minuscule lift) enjoy sea views, and cost around €12 extra. No smoking. Closed mid-Nov to Feb. 3

l'Univers 10 pl Chateaubriand ⓣ02.99.40.89.52, ⓦhotel-univers-saintmalo.com. One of the grand hotels that face you immediately upon entering the Porte St-Vincent. Some guests revel in the classic French atmosphere and furnishings, others find the place a little stuffy. 5

Hotels outside the walls

Although most visitors spend almost all their time in the citadelle, there are two significant advantages to staying in a hotel outside St-Malo's city walls: prices are generally cheaper, and access is easier, whether you're travelling by train or car – especially an issue if you have heavy luggage. On the other hand, most of the after-dark activity takes place inside the walls, and getting there from any of the surrounding suburbs requires a fair walk in through the docks. There are also a handful of very nice **beach** hotels, in suburban Coutoisville and Paramé to the east.

Le Beaufort 25 chaussée du Sillon, Coutoisville ⓣ02.99.40.99.99, ⓦwww.hotel-beaufort.com. Grand sea-view hotel – ideal for a bracing morning dip – 30min walk along the beach from the citadelle. Beautifully restored rooms – some with lovely balconies – and a good restaurant. 7

De l'Europe 44 bd de la République ⓣ02.99.56.13.42, ⓦhoteldeleurope-saintmalo.com. Year-round cheap but clean rooms (the cheaper ones don't have en-suite facilities) in a genuinely friendly, if noisy, hotel near the *gare SNCF*, with a cosy café. Some rooms can accommodate up to seven people; for groups of four or more, it works out cheaper than the hostel. 1

Le Mont-Fleury 2 rue du Mont-Fleury ⓣ02.23.52.28.85, ⓦlemontfleury.com. Bed and breakfast in a beautiful seventeenth-century house and park couched in the suburbs of Paramé. There's a big fire in the living room and the owner, a former pilot, has decorated the four rooms in travelling themes from Oriental to American. 4

La Rance 15 quai Sébastopol, St-Servan ⓣ02.99.81.78.63, ⓦlarancehotel.com. Small, tasteful and airy option in sight of the Tour Solidor, with eleven spacious rooms and a much more tranquil atmosphere than St-Malo itself. 4

Hostel

Centre Patrick Varangot 37 av du Père-Umbricht, Paramé ⓣ02.99.40.29.80, ⓦcentrevarangot.com. Dominated as a rule by lively young travellers, this is one of France's busiest hostels, 2km northeast of the *gare SNCF* in the suburb of Paramé, not far from the beach. Dorm beds at €17.10 in a room with just a washbasin, €19.30 with en-suite facilities; pay €15 extra for a private room; hostelling association membership required. Rates include breakfast, and there's also a cut-price cafeteria, as well as kitchen facilities and tennis courts. No curfew, open all year.

Campsites

All four of St-Malo's municipal **campsites** tend to be full in July and August, so you may have to travel inland to find space; there are several private sites in the vicinity.

d'Alet Allée Gaston Buy, St-Servan ⓣ02.99.81.60.91, ⓦwww.ville-saint-malo.fr/campings. The nicest local campsite is also by far the nearest to the citadelle, a municipally run gem in a dramatic location on the headland southwest of St-Malo, overlooking the city from within the wartime German fortified stronghold. Take bus #1 from the *gare SNCF* or Porte St-Vincent. Closed Oct–April.

Les Ilôts av de la Guimorais, Rothéneuf ⓣ02.99.56.98.72, ⓦwww.ville-saint-malo.fr/campings. Green little municipal site, located 5min walk inland from either of two crescent beaches, roughly 5km east of the citadelle. Closed Sept–June.

Du Nicet av de la Varde, Rothéneuf ⓣ02.99.40.26.32, ⓦwww.ville-saint-malo.fr/campings. Municipal site, right on the coast, by the Pointe de Nicet, just beyond the headland that marks the eastern limit of Paramé. Reservations essential. Closed Sept–June.

Les Nielles av John Kennedy, Paramé ⓣ02.99.40.26.35, ⓦwww.ville-saint-malo.fr/campings. Another municipal site on the beach at the smaller of Paramé's strands, the plage du Minhic, just a short walk from the town's facilities. Closed Sept–June.

La Ville Huchet rte de la Passagère ⓣ02.99.81.11.83, ⓦlavillehuchet.com. Four-star campsite in the grounds of a château, south of St-Malo on the road to Rennes, with an aquatic park, pool and bike rental. Closed mid-Sept to mid-April.

The Town

The **citadelle** of St-Malo, very much the prime destination for visitors, was for many years joined to the mainland only by a long causeway, before the original line of the coast was hidden forever by the construction of the harbour basin. Although its cobbled streets of restored seventeenth-and eighteenth-century houses can be packed to the point of absurdity in summer (and the cobbles present quite a challenge to parents pushing buggies), away from the more popular thoroughfares random exploration is fun.

Due to space limitations on this tiny peninsula, the buildings tend to be a little more high-rise than you might expect. Venerable as they may look, they are almost entirely reconstructed – photographs of the damage suffered in 1944, when General Patton bombarded the city for two weeks before the Germans surrendered, show barely a stone left in place. Eighty percent of the city had to be lovingly and precisely rebuilt, stone by stone. Beneath grey skies, the narrow lanes can appear sombre, even grim, but in high summer or at sunset they take on a different, softer hue, much more in keeping with the citadelle's romantic atmosphere. In any case, you can always surface to the sunlight on the **ramparts** – first erected in the fourteenth century, and redesigned by the master builder Vauban four hundred years later – to enjoy wonderful views all round, especially to the west as the sun sets over the sea.

The main gate of the citadelle as you approach by road is the **Porte St-Vincent**, constructed in 1709. Until 1770, the whole town was sealed off by

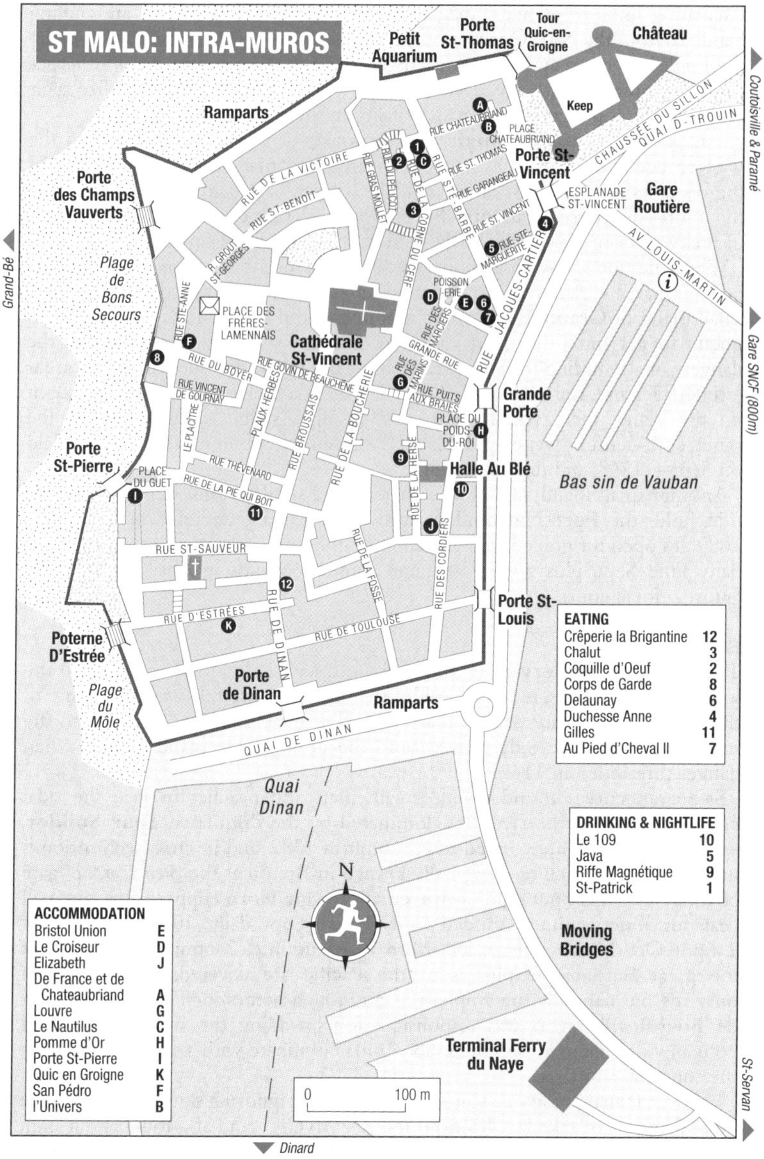

a 10pm curfew; as you walk through the gateway, you pass the small room where latecomers were obliged to spend the night. To the right, as you pass through the gate, you'll see the forbidding stone walls of the **castle**, which houses the **Musée d'Histoire de la Ville** (daily 10am–noon & 2–6pm; closed Mon mid-Nov to March; €5.20), something of a paean to the "prodigious prosperity" enjoyed by St-Malo during its days of piracy, colonialism and slave-trading. Climbing the 169 steps of the castle keep – whose walls are up to 7m thick – you pass a fascinating mixture of maps, diagrams and exhibits. Among them are chilling handbills from the Nazi Occupation, accounts of the "infernal machine" used by the English to blow up the port in 1693, and savage four-pronged *chaussetrappes*, thrown by pirates onto the decks of ships being boarded to immobilize their crews. At the top a gull's-eye prospect takes in the whole citadelle.

It is possible to pass **through the ramparts** at a couple of points on the western side of the peninsula, where there are some small, sheltered **beaches**. On the open shore to the east of the citadelle, a huge beach stretches away beyond the resort-suburbs of **Courtoisville** and **Paramé**. Out to sea stands a procession of rocky islets, many of which still hold traces of medieval fortifications.

When the tide is low, an easy short walk across the sands of the Plage du Bons Secours, past a seawater swimming pool refreshed by each high tide, leads to the small island of **Grand-Bé**. It's such a popular stroll that you may even need to queue to get onto the short causeway. Solemn warnings are posted of the dangers of attempting to return from the island when the tide has risen too far – timetables are displayed by the Porte St-Pierre and elsewhere. If you're caught on the island, there you have to stay. Its one "sight" is the **tomb** of the nineteenth-century writer-politician Chateaubriand (who was born in St-Malo on Sept 4, 1768, and died in 1848).

Another small island, just off the château and similarly only accessible at low tide, holds the **Fort National**, a sturdy little fortress designed by Vauban in 1689. It's open for guided tours in summer only (precise hours depend on tides: daily June–Sept, plus school hols and some weekends in April in May; €5; Ⓦfortnational.com).

St-Servan

The district of **St-Servan**, within walking distance along the corniche to the south of the citadelle, is actually older than St-Malo itself. It was on the site of the Gallo-Roman city of Alet that St Maclou established his church, and the seat of the bishopric only moved onto the impregnable island fortress when danger threatened in 1142.

St-Servan curves round several small inlets and beaches to face the tidal power dam across the river. It's dominated by the distinctive **Tour Solidor**, which consists of three linked towers built in 1382, and in cross-section looks just like the ace of clubs. Originally known in Breton as the *Steir Dor*, or "gate of the river", this now holds a **museum** of Cape Horn clipper ships, open all year for ninety-minute guided visits (April–Sept daily 10am–12.30pm & 2–6pm; Oct–March daily except Mon 10am–noon & 2–6pm; €5.40). Most of the great European explorers of the Pacific are covered, from Magellan onwards, but naturally the emphasis is on French heroes such as Louis Antoine de Bougainville, who was responsible for spreading the brightly coloured bougainvillea plant around the globe. Tours culminate with a superb view from the topmost ramparts.

Follow the main road due south from St-Servan, ignoring signs for the Barrage de la Rance – or take bus #5 from the *gare SNCF* – and at a roundabout high above town you'll come to the **Grand Aquarium** (daily: April–June & Sept 10am–7pm; first two weeks in July & second two weeks in Aug 9.30am–8pm; mid-July to mid-Aug 9.30am–10pm; Oct–March 10am–6pm as a rule, but wide variations day by day, with some closures Nov–Jan; last admission one hour before closing; €15.50, under-15s €9.50; Ⓣ02.99.21.19.00, Ⓦaquarium-st-malo.com). This postmodern structure can be a bit bewildering at first, but once you get the hang of it it's an entertaining place, where you can either learn interesting facts about slimy monsters of the deep or simply pull faces back at them. Its eight distinct fish tanks, which hold fish from all over the world, include one shaped like a Polo mint, where dizzy visitors stand in the hole in the middle as myriad fish whirl around them.

The Barrage de la Rance

The road from St-Malo to Dinard crosses the Rance along the top of the world's first **tidal power dam**. Built in 1966, the Barrage de la Rance alas failed to set a non-nuclear example to the rest of the province, where a century ago there were five thousand working windmills. If you choose to cover the 4km between the centre of St-Malo and the *barrage* on foot or bicycle, try to make your way on the small roads through St-Servan, following the line of the estuary southwards, rather than the signposted (circuitous) inland route used by motorists.

Rothéneuf

Just inside the eastern end of St-Malo's city limits, as the D201 winds towards Cancale, signs direct visitors away from the central streets of suburban **Rothéneuf** to the **Roches Sculptées**, or "sculpted rocks" (daily: Easter–Sept 9am–9pm; Oct–Easter 10am–5pm; €3). The hermit priest Abbé Fouré spent 25 years, from the 1870s onwards, carving these jumbled boulders into the forms of dragons, giants and assorted sea monsters. Perched on a rocky promontory high above the water line, they're quite weathered now, and not all that compelling in themselves, but with the town well out of sight this makes an appealing spot to stop and admire the coastline. The gardens of the site also hold a small, sheltered café, and a shop that sells Breton pottery.

Eating

Even more **restaurants** than hotels are crammed into *intra-muros* St-Malo, with a long crescent lining the inside of the ramparts between the Porte St-Vincent and the Grande Porte. In recent years, there's been a trend for gourmet seafood restaurants to be replaced by crêperies and snack bars, but prices are still probably higher than anywhere else in Brittany, especially on the open café terraces. If you just fancy an **ice cream**, call in at *Glacier Sanchez*, 9 rue de la Vieille-Boucherie (☎02.99.56.67.17; closed Wed in low season). There are **markets** in the Halle au Blé within the walls of St-Malo on Tuesdays and Fridays, in St-Servan on Mondays and Fridays, and in Paramé on Wednesdays and Saturdays. All the restaurants listed below are in the citadelle.

Chalut 8 rue de la Corne de Cerf ☎02.99.56.71.58. Quite an exclusive dining room, in a stylish blue-painted bistro a short way in from the Porte St-Vincent. All the menus offer a limited choice, with perhaps one or two exclusively fishy main courses, and the odd meaty appetizer. The €25 menu centres on the catch of the day; otherwise you can pay €39 or €55 for a gourmet fish dinner, designed to be not quite as rich as the traditional norm, or €70 for a three-course menu consisting entirely of lobster. Reservations preferred. Closed Mon & Tues.

Coquille d'Oeuf 20 rue de la Corne de Cerf ☎02.99.40.92.62. This stylish restaurant prides itself on serving "slow food" from its open kitchen. The decor may be whimsical but the food is seriously good; €21 lets you choose from the simple daily menu, with fish or meat for each course. Lunch Sat & Sun only, dinner nightly except Mon.

Corps de Garde 3 montée Notre Dame ☎02.99.40.91.46. The only restaurant that's right up on St-Malo's ramparts is just an ordinary crêperie, serving standard €2.20–8.90 crêpes. However, the views from its large open-air terrace (covered when necessary) are sensational, looking out over the beach to the myriad little islets. Closed mid-Nov to mid-Feb.

Crêperie la Brigantine 13 rue de Dinan ☎02.99.56.82.82. Sweet and savoury pancakes at very reasonable prices – the seafood fillings are exceptional. An individual crêpe can cost under €2, and there's a full menu for €10, with a strong emphasis on organic ingredients. Closed Tues & Wed in low season.

Delaunay 6 rue Ste-Barbe ⓣ02.99.40.92.46. Located between the Porte St-Vincent and Cathédrale St-Vincent, and serving high-quality traditional French cooking. There's one set menu, at €32, but otherwise you can order à la carte, with the most expensive courses €32 for fish and €30 for meat. Dinner only; closed Sun.

Duchesse Anne 5–7 pl Guy-la-Chambre ⓣ02.99.40.85.33. Situated right next to the Porte St-Vincent, the best known of St-Malo's upmarket restaurants continues to work hard to keep up its reputation – and its prices. The only set menu is a €78 lobster option; you might manage to get a lunch for under €25, but dinner will cost well over twice that. Whole baked fish is the main speciality. Closed Mon & Wed lunch, Sun eve in low season, plus all Dec & Jan.

Gilles 2 rue de la Pie-qui-Boit ⓣ02.99.40.97.25. Bright, modern, good-value restaurant, just off the central pedestrian axis. The basic €20.80 menu is fine; alternatively, €24.50 brings you oysters or mussel soup and a rabbit *cuissot* with cider. Closed late Nov to mid-Dec, plus Wed & Thurs in winter.

Au Pied d'Cheval II 6 rue Jacques Cartier ⓣ02.99.40.98.18, ⓦau-pied-de-cheval.com. The *Pied d'Cheval*, a superb little harbourfront seafood joint in nearby Cancale – see p.215 – has done well enough to open this citified offshoot. Though less rough'n'ready, and more of a place to linger, it serves exactly the same well-priced menu, heavy on oysters and mussels for under €10, with a delicious *assiette de fruits de mer* for two at €44.

Nightlife

Along with the multitude of restaurants *intra-muros*, you'll also find a few decent places to have a **drink**.

Le 109 3 rue des Cordiers ⓣ02.99.56.81.09, ⓦle-109.com. Flashy club, decked out in fiery reds and yellows and open until 3am.

Java 3 rue Ste-Barbe ⓣ02.99.56.41.90, ⓦwww.lajavacafe.com. An entertaining and unique cider bar, with swings at the bar, old dolls on the wall, and an elevator door into the toilet.

Riffe Magnétique 20 rue de la Herse ⓣ02.99.40.85.70, ⓦleriffmagnetique.com. Lively, friendly bar, with a fine choice of wines plus regular café-concerts, and DJs at the weekend. Closed Sun & Mon.

St-Patrick 24 rue Ste-Barbe ⓣ02.99.56.66.90. Cosy Irish pub, tucked away not far from the château.

Listings

Bicycle rental Les Vélos Bleus, 19 rue Alphonse Thébault ⓣ02.99.40.31.63, ⓦvelos-bleus.fr; Espace Nicole, 11–13 rue R-Schuman, Paramé ⓣ02.99.56.11.06, ⓦwww.cyclesnicole.com.

Car rental Most of the major car-rental companies are represented in town; both Avis (ⓣ02.99.40.58.68) and National (ⓣ02.23.18.00.00) have offices at the ferry terminal and *gare SNCF*.

Hypermarkets Carrefour, Centre Commercial La Madeleine ⓣ02.99.21.10.10 (closed Sun); Centre Leclerc, 55 bd des Déportés, Paramé ⓣ02.99.19.97.97 (closed Sun).

Internet access Cyber' Com, just west of the *gare SNCF* at 29bis bd des Talards (Mon 2–6pm, Tues, Wed & Fri 9am–noon & 2–6pm, Thurs 2–9pm, Sat 9am–noon & 2–5.30pm; €4; ⓣ02.99.56.05.83, ⓦwww.cybermalo.com); also in the tourist office.

Post office The most convenient post office for visitors is within the walls at 4 pl des Frères Lamennais (Mon–Fri 8.45am–12.15pm & 1.30–5.45pm, Sat 8.45am–noon).

Sailing St-Malo's Station Nautique can provide full information on all aspects of sailing in the vicinity, from lessons to rentals and cruises; the tourist office has advisers in summer (ⓣ02.99.56.18.88, ⓦnautisme-saint-malo.fr).

Scuba diving St-Malo Plongée Émeraude, Centre Bleu Émeraude, Terre Plein du Naye, St-Servan ⓣ02.99.19.90.36, ⓦsaintmaloplongee.com.

Surfing and windsurfing Boards are available for rental from Surf School, 2 av de la Hoguette (ⓣ02.99.40.07.47, ⓦsurfschool.org), or the Société Nautique de la Baie de St-Malo, quai de Bons Secours (ⓣ02.99.40.11.45, ⓦsnbsm.com). Most surfers make for the beaches further along the coast towards Cancale, the plage du Verger and the larger Anse du Guesclin.

Dinard

Formerly a fishing village, now a smart little resort blessed with several lovely beaches, **DINARD** sprawls around the western approaches to the Rance estuary, just across the water from St-Malo but a good twenty minutes' drive away. With its casino, spacious shaded villas and social calendar of regattas and ballet, it might not feel out of place on the Côte d'Azur. The nineteenth-century metamorphosis of Dinard was largely thanks to the tastes of affluent English and Americans. Although Dinard is a hilly town, undulating over a succession of pretty little coastal inlets, it attracts great numbers of older visitors; as a result, prices tend to be high, and pleasures sedate.

Arrival and information

Dinard's small **airport**, 4km southeast of the centre, off the D168 near Pleurtuit, is served by Ryanair flights from London Stansted (Ⓣ02.99.16.00.66, Ⓦryanair.com; see p.21), and Aurigny Air Services from Guernsey (Ⓣ02.99.46.18.46, Ⓦaurigny.com). **Rental cars** are available in the terminal, while Illenoo bus #990 runs via Dinard's tourist office to St-Malo (€4 flat fare).

Many visitors to Dinard simply come over for the day on the regular **boats** from St-Malo; tickets can be bought in Dinard, a ten-minute walk east of the tourist office on promenade du Clair de Lune, directly above the pleasure port where the ferries actually come in (April to early Nov only; €4.20 one-way, €6.50 return; under-13s €2.70/€4.20; bikes €2 one-way, €3 return; Ⓣ08.25.13.81.30, Ⓦcompagniecorsaire.com). If the ten-minute crossing only serves to whet your appetite, you can also take a trip down the Rance to Dinan (see p.209).

Local **buses** run regularly between Dinard and St-Malo, across the dam, while long-distance buses go from the former *gare SNCF* and "Le Gallic" stop (near the tourist office) to Dinan, Rennes, Cancale and St-Brieuc, run by Illenoo (Ⓣ02.99.82.26.26, Ⓦillenoo.fr) and Tibus (Ⓣ08.10.22.22.22, Ⓦwww.tibus.fr).

Dinard's **tourist office** is close to the seafront in the heart of town at 2 bd Féart (July & Aug Mon–Sat 9.30am–1pm & 2–7pm, Sun 10am–12.15pm & 2–6.30pm; Sept–June Mon–Sat 9.30am–12.30pm & 2–6.30pm, Sun 10am–12.15pm & 2.15–6pm; Ⓣ02.99.46.94.12, Ⓦot-dinard.com). **Cycles** are available for rental from Cycles Duval, 53 rue Gardiner (Ⓣ02.99.46.19.63).

Accommodation

On the whole, Dinard is an expensive place to stay, but it does at least have a wide selection of **hotels** (many are listed on Ⓦdinard-hotel-plus.com). The best positioned of its several **campsites** is the municipal *Port Blanc*, over 1km west of the centre on rue Sergent-Boulanger, and offering shady pitches right by the plage du Port-Blanc (Ⓣ02.99.46.10.74, Ⓦcamping-port-blanc.com; closed Oct–March).

Didier Méril 1 pl du Général-de-Gaulle Ⓣ02.99.46.95.74, Ⓦrestaurant-didier-meril.com. Having firmly established its reputation as a gourmet restaurant, named for its go-getting young chef (and featuring menus from €22), the next step for this establishment was to add luxurious designer bedrooms, a couple of which have baths right in the actual sleeping area, so you can enjoy amazing sea views as you bathe. They'll even pick you up from the station in a London taxi. ❻

les Mouettes 64 av Georges V Ⓣ02.99.46.10.64, Ⓦhotel-les-mouettes.com. Inexpensive, twelve-room family-oriented hotel, a short walk from the sea, above a traditional bar; the rooms are far from fancy, but they're clean, and great value. ❷

Parc des Tourelles 20 av Édouard VII Ⓣ02.99.46.11.39, Ⓦhotelduparc.org. Friendly, somewhat basic but well maintained and extremely good-value little hotel, on a busy (and steep) street a short way west of the place de la

République. Good buffet breakfasts. Closed mid-Nov to mid-Jan ❹

Printania 5 av Georges V ⓣ02.99.46.13.07, ⓦwww.printaniahotel.com. Good-value place around 250m east of the centre, on a relatively quiet seafront street near the Port de Plaisance; sea-view rooms cost significantly extra. Menus in the magnificent terrace restaurant, looking over to St-Malo, start at €23, featuring *moules marinières* and sole. Closed mid-Nov to mid-March. ❹

La Vallée 6 av Georges V ⓣ02.99.46.94.00, ⓦhoteldelavallee.com. Attractive Logis de France, down at sea level in the pleasure port, but unfortunately facing the wrong way for views of St-Malo. The most basic rooms look straight onto a bare cliff face, but in principle this is a nice spot, and the restaurant is good too. ❺

The Town

Central Dinard faces north to the open sea, across the curving bay that holds the attractive **plage de l'Écluse**. As so often in Breton resorts, the buildings that line the waterfront are, with the exception of the casino in the middle, venerable Victorian villas rather than hotels or shops, and so the beach itself has a relatively low-key atmosphere, despite the summer crowds. Rows of delightful, blue-and-white-striped, tent-like sunshelters, which cost €15 to rent for the afternoon, add colour to the sands below. Few casual visitors realize that some of **Pablo Picasso**'s most famous images, such as *Deux Femmes Courants sur la Plage* and *Baigneuses sur la Plage* – both of which look quintessentially Mediterranean with their blue skies and golden sands – were painted on the main **beach** at Dinard during the artist's annual summer visits in the 1920s.

Other unlikely visitors to Dinard have included Lawrence of Arabia, who lived here as a child. Though local claims that **Alfred Hitchcock** based the house in *Psycho* on a solitary villa high above the plage de l'Écluse are not generally accepted, a statue of the director long dominated its main access point. Depicting Hitchcock standing on a giant egg with a ferocious-looking bird perched on each shoulder, it was toppled by a storm in 2003, but a replacement is promised in the near future. The idea is to commemorate the town's annual festival of English-language films, held in early October (ⓦfestivaldufilm-dinard.com).

▲ Dinard

Enjoyable **coastal footpaths** lead off in either direction from the beach. The path heading east – which is floodlit each evening between July and early October – leads up to the Pointe du Moulinet for views over to St-Malo, and then (as the **promenade du Clair de Lune**) continues past the tiny and now exclusive port, and down to the estuary beach, the plage du Prieuré. Setting off west, on the other hand, takes you around more rocky outcrops to the secluded strand at neighbouring **St-Énogat**, where windsurfing equipment and kayaks are available for rent in summer (Ⓣ02.99.46.83.99, Ⓦwindschool.fr).

Eating

Several of the hotels listed on p.207 – particularly *Didier Méril* – have top-quality **restaurants**. Good alternatives include the busy *Brasserie Le Cancaven*, whose outdoor tables take up most of the central place de la République (Ⓣ02.99.46.15.45), and *La Gonelle*, a lovely waterfront seafood option on the promenade du Clair du Lune (Ⓣ02.99.16.40.47, Ⓦlagonelle.com; closed Oct to mid-April, plus Tues & Wed except in July & Aug).

Dinan

The wonderful citadel of **DINAN** has preserved almost intact its three-kilometre encirclement of protective masonry, along with street upon colourful street of late medieval houses. However, despite its slightly unreal perfection (it would make the ideal film set for *The Three Musketeers*), it's seldom overrun with tourists. There are no essential museums, the most memorable architecture is vernacular rather than monumental, and time is most easily spent wandering from crêperie to café and down to the pretty port, admiring the overhanging half-timbered houses along the way.

Arrival and information

Both the Art Deco **gare SNCF** and the **gare routière** are in Dinan's modern quarter (a rather gloomy exile from the rest of the town), on place du 11 Novembre, ten minutes' walk west of the main entrance of the walled town on Grande Rue.

Between May and October, **boats** along the Rance sail between the port downstream and Dinard and St-Malo. The trip takes 2 hours 45 minutes, with the exact schedule varying according to the tides (adults €23, under-13s €14). It's only possible to do a day return by boat (adults €29, under-13s €17.50) if you start from St-Malo or Dinard; starting from Dinan, you'd have to come back by bus or train. For details, contact Compagnie Corsaire on the quai de la Rance (Ⓣ08.25.13.81.20, Ⓦcompagniecorsaire.com).

Dinan's modern **tourist office**, at the southwest corner of the place du Guesclin near the Tour Coëtquen, at 9 rue du Château (July & Aug Mon–Sat 9am–7pm, Sun 10am–12.30pm & 2.30–6pm; Sept–June Mon–Sat 9am–12.30pm & 2–6pm; Ⓣ02.96.87.69.76, Ⓦwww.dinan-tourisme.com), offers **internet access**. The **post office** is on place Duclos (Mon–Fri 8am–6.30pm, Sat 9am–12.30pm; Ⓣ02.96.85.83.68).

Accommodation

Many of Dinan's **hotels** lie within the walled town or down by the pretty port. Both locations are convenient if you're on foot, but motorists should note that

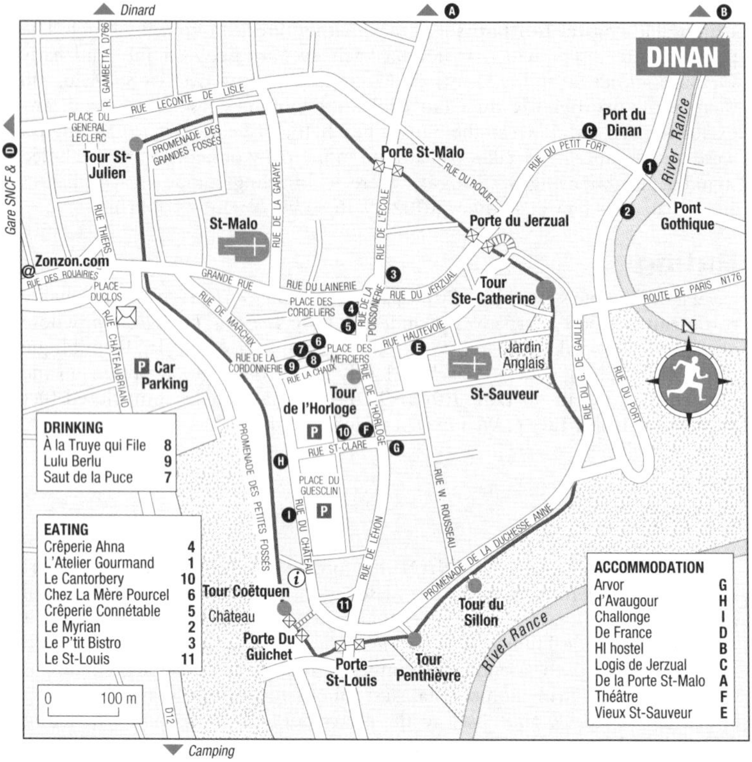

finding parking spaces during summer can be difficult. Most hotels are in the mid-range price category, with only a couple of genuine budget options.

Hotels

Arvor 5 rue Pavie ⓣ02.96.39.21.22, ⓦhotelarvordinan.com. Renovated eighteenth-century town house in the heart of town, with some surviving traces of the convent that previously occupied the site. Smart, well-equipped rooms, and free parking. ❸

d'Avaugour 1 pl du Champ ⓣ02.96.39.07.49, ⓦavaugourhotel.com. Smart, elegant hotel, entered from the main square but backing onto the ramparts, with very tasteful renovated rooms and lovely gardens. Closed Nov to mid-Feb. ❼

Le Challonge 29 pl du Guesclin ⓣ02.96.87.16.30, ⓦ hotel-dinan.fr. The modern, spotless rooms feature slightly busy decor, but many have balconies, and they're above a good brasserie overlooking Dinan's main square. ❺

De France 7 pl du 11 Novembre ⓣ02.96.39.22.56, ⓦhoteldefrance-dinan.com. An excellent *logis* opposite the *gare SNCF*, with fourteen renovated and well-equipped rooms, the top ones with attractive wooden floors. Friendly, English-speaking management and a good restaurant where dinner menus start at €17. ❸

Logis de Jerzual 25–27 rue du Petit Fort ⓣ02.96.85.46.54, ⓦwww.logis-du-jerzual.com. *Chambres d'hôtes* halfway up the exquisite little lane that leads from the port. The five rooms have wonderful character, with four-poster beds, modern bathrooms and romantic views over the rooftops. The house is surrounded by a lovely garden terrace and the friendly owner serves tasty breakfasts (included in rates). ❹

De la Porte St-Malo 35 rue St-Malo ⓣ02.96.39.19.76, ⓦhotelportemalo.com. Simple but very comfortable rooms in a welcoming and tasteful small hotel just outside the walls, beyond the Porte St-Malo, with a little courtyard where you can escape the bustle of the centre. ❸

Théâtre 2 rue Ste-Claire ⓣ02.96.39.06.91. Nine basic rooms above a friendly bar, right by the Théâtre des Jacobins; the cheapest come only with a sink, but even those with en-suite bathrooms still cost under €30, which is amazing for such a central location. Run by the same efficient management as the nearby *Restaurant Cantorbery* (see p.212). ❶

Du Vieux St-Sauveur 21 pl St-Sauveur ⓣ02.96.85.30.20, ⓦhotelpubsaintsauveur.com. Ancient edifice facing the St-Sauveur church, which has a slightly noisy bar/brasserie downstairs, but six basic but well equipped and good-value en-suite rooms upstairs, including a three-person family room. ❷

Hostel and campsite

Camping Municipal 103 rue Châteaubriand ⓣ02.96.39.11.96. In a quiet spot just outside the western ramparts, with just fifty pitches. Closed late Sept to late May.

HI hostel Moulin de Méen, Vallée de la Fontaine-des-Eaux ⓣ02.96.39.10.83, ⓦfuaj.org/Dinan. Attractive, rural former watermill, set right next to the river in green fields below the town centre. Unfortunately it's not on any bus route: to walk there, follow the quay downstream from the port on the town side. After a few hundred metres you'll see a small sign to the left – from there it's another 500m. Dorm bed €12.60, double room same price per person, breakfast €3; in addition, camping is permitted in the grounds. Closed Jan.

The Town

Like St-Malo, Dinan is best seen when arriving by boat up the Rance. By the time the ferries get to the lovely **port du Dinan**, down below the thirteenth-century ramparts, the river has narrowed sufficiently to be spanned by a small but majestic old stone bridge. High above it towers the former railway viaduct now used by the N176. The steep, cobbled **rue du Petit-Fort** twists up from the artisans' shops and restaurants along the quay. Taking advantage of its many stone benches to catch your breath, it makes a wonderful climb, passing ancient flower-festooned edifices of wood and stone, as well as several crêperies and even a half-timbered poodle parlour, before it enters the city through the **Porte du Jerzual**.

Above that imposing gateway, **St-Sauveur** church sends the skyline even higher. It's a real hotchpotch, with a Romanesque porch and an eighteenth-century steeple. Even its nine Gothic chapels feature five different patterns of vaulting in no symmetrical order; the most complex pair, in the centre, would make any spider proud. By contrast, a very plain cenotaph on the left contains the heart of **Bertrand du Guesclin**, the fourteenth-century Breton warrior (and later Constable of France) who fought and won a single combat with the English knight Thomas of Canterbury, in what is now place du Guesclin, to settle the outcome of the siege of Dinan in 1364. Relics of his life and battles are scattered all over Brittany and Normandy; in death, he spread himself between four separate burial places for four different parts of his body (the French kings restricted themselves to three burial sites).

The large **place du Guesclin** holds an equestrian statue of du Guesclin himself, looking remarkably like an armour-clad Winston Churchill. The square, but sadly not the statue, comes alive on Thursdays, when together with the adjoining place du Champ Clos it's the scene of a large **market**; for the rest of the week, it serves as the main central car park. The true heart of town consists of two much smaller squares, the **place des Merciers** and the **place des Cordeliers**. These hold Dinan's finest assortment of medieval wood-framed houses, painted in lively hues and with their upper storeys perching precariously on splintering wooden pillars that appear to buckle beneath the weight.

Unfortunately, you can only walk along one small stretch of the **ramparts**, from the Jardin Anglais behind St-Sauveur church to a point just short of Tour Sillon overlooking the river. You can, however, get a good general overview from the wooden balcony of the central **Tour de l'Horloge**, which dates from the end of the fifteenth century (daily: April, May & Sept 2–6pm; June–Aug

10am–6.30pm; €2.95). A small and uninteresting shopping mall has been created around the foot of the belfry's stout stone walls.

As you might guess from its blending of two separate towers, the fourteenth-century keep that once protected the town's southern approach, towering above the Porte du Guichet, was built by Estienne Le Tour, architect of St-Malo's Tour Solidor (see p.204). Now collectively known as the **Château de Duchesse Anne** it offers visitors access to both towers (daily: June–Sept 10am–6.30pm; Oct–Dec & Feb–May 1.30–5.30pm; €4.50). The keep itself, or *donjon*, consists of four storeys, each of which holds an unexpected hotchpotch of items, including two big old looms and assorted Greek and Etruscan perfume jars; at ground level, well below the walls, there's a slender, closed drawbridge. Nearby, the ancient **Tour Coëtquen** is all but empty, though if you descend the spiral staircase to its water-logged bottom floor, you'll find a group of stone fifteenth-century notables resembling some medieval time capsule, about to depetrify at any moment.

On the third weekend of July, every other (even-numbered) year, the **Fête des Remparts** is celebrated with medieval-style jousting, banquets, fairs and processions, culminating in an immense fireworks display (Ⓦ fete-remparts-dinan.com).

Eating and drinking

All sorts of specialist **restaurants**, including several ethnic alternatives, are tucked away in the old streets of Dinan. Stroll through the town and down to the port, and you'll pass at least twenty places, most of which offer better value for money than Brittany's seaside resorts.

Once you've eaten, sample the **bars** in the tiny alleyways between place des Merciers and rue de Marchix. Along rue de la Cordonnerie, the busiest of the lot, the various hangouts define themselves by their taste in music: *À la Truye qui File* at no. 14 is a contemporary folky Breton dive, while *Lulu Berlu*, next door at no. 12 (closed Sun & Mon), and *Saut de la Puce* opposite, are considerably more raucous.

L'Atelier Gourmand 4 rue de Quai Ⓣ 02.96.85.14.18. A delightful spot, right beside the river on the corner of the bridge, with indoor and outdoor seating, and serving a well-priced menu of *tartines* (€9), *moules* (€10–12), and assorted main courses (€11–14). Closed Sun eve & all Mon in low season.

Le Cantorbery 6 rue Ste-Claire Ⓣ 02.96.39.02.52. High-class food served in an old stone house with rafters, a spiral staircase and a real wood fire. Lunch from €13, while traditional dinner menus start with a good €25 option that includes fish soup and veal kidneys. Closed Sun eve & Wed in low season.

Chez La Mère Pourcel 3 pl des Merciers Ⓣ 02.96.39.03.80, Ⓦ chezlamerepourcel.com. Beautiful half-timbered fifteenth-century house in the central square. Good à la carte options are served all day, while the dinner menus, ranging at €18–33, are gourmet class. Closed Sun eve & Mon in low season.

Crêperie Ahna 7 rue de la Poissonnerie Ⓣ 02.96.39.09.13. Smart central crêperie, with limited outdoor seating, that's very popular with lunching locals. Savoury pancakes cost €3.50–9.25, and they also serve potato blinis and grilled meats – even ostrich. Closed Sun in low season.

Crêperie Connétable 1 rue de l'Apport Ⓣ 02.96.39.06.74. Magnificent old house diagonally opposite the *Mère Pourcel* beside the place des Merciers. Sit at the pavement tables, and enjoy crêpes and espresso. Perfect for people watching.

Le Myrian 3 rue du Port Ⓣ 02.96.87.93.36. Attractive and inexpensive pizzeria in a waterfront cottage down by the port, serving €7–14 pizzas, plus assorted salads and wine by the carafe, on its shady terrace immediately next to the river. Closed Thurs eve and all Wed in low season.

Le P'tit Bistro 4 rue de l'École Ⓣ 02.96.39.76.77. Friendly, central bistro/pub, serving inexpensive *tartines* (€8) and fruit tarts at wooden tables on its pavement deck, and hosting local music evenings on Fri.

Le St-Louis 9–11 rue de Léhon Ⓣ 02.96.39.89.50. Good-value restaurant, just inside the Porte St-Louis, which specializes in buffets; both the €18 and €22 menus include extensive buffets of *hors d'oeuvres* and desserts, with a conventional main course in between. Closed Wed eve & Sat lunch.

Around the Baie du Mont-St-Michel

The **coastal road** D201 runs east from St-Malo to **Cancale**, past a succession of coves and beaches, where lines of dunes attempt to hang on against the battering from the sea. At the **Pointe du Grouin** – a perilous and windy height that also overlooks the bird sanctuary of the **Île de Landes** to the east – the line of cliffs turns sharply back on itself at one extremity of the **Baie du Mont-St-Michel**. This is a huge flat expanse of mud and sand, over which the tide can race faster than a galloping horse. It's dangerous to wander out too far, quite apart from the risk of quicksands, and, in the Breton part of the bay at least, the beaches have little appeal for bathers.

The course of the **River Couesnon**, which marks the border between Brittany and Normandy, has shifted repeatedly over the centuries. So too has the shoreline of the bay, in which traces of long-drowned villages can be seen when the tide is out. Bretons like to say that it is just an accident that the river now runs west of Mont-St-Michel; be that as it may, the Mont and Pontorson, the nearest town to it, are both in Normandy (see p.148). The pinnacle of *La Merveille*, however, remains clearly visible from every vantage point along the coast.

Cancale

The delightful harbour village of **CANCALE**, just south of the Pointe du Grouin less than 15km east of St-Malo, is not so much a one-horse as a one-mollusc town – the whole place is obsessed with the **oyster**, and with "*ostréiculture*". Its current population is, at around five thousand, less than it was a century ago, but thanks to all the visitors attracted by its edible hinged bivalves, it looks bigger than that would suggest.

Arrival and information

The best place to **park** in Cancale is down by the port. **Buses** come here from St-Malo (Illenoo: ⓣ02.99.82.26.26, ⓦillenoo.fr), but there's no train service. The **tourist office** is near the church square, at the top of the hill well above the port, at 44 rue du Port (July & Aug Mon–Sat 9am–7pm, Sun 9.30am–1pm; Sept–June Mon–Sat 9.30am–1pm & 2.30–6pm, Sun 9am–12.30pm; ⓣ02.99.89.63.72, ⓦwww.cancale-tourisme.fr), but there's also a convenient summer-only kiosk on the waterfront (July & Aug Mon–Sat 10am–noon & 4–7pm, Sun 4–7pm; ⓣ02.99.89.74.80).

Accommodation

A long row of **hotels** lines the quayside down in the port of Cancale. Most insist that you eat if you want to stay, but that's no great problem considering all the restaurants are good.

Le Grand Large 4 quai Jacques-Cartier ⓣ02.99.89.82.90, ⓦhotel-restaurant.hotellegrandlarge.com. Comfortable rooms in an ivy-covered house at the quieter southern end of the port, well away from most of the action but with its own good restaurant (see opposite). Closed Jan. ❸

La Houle 18 quai Gambetta ⓣ02.99.89.62.38, ⓦhotellahoule.fr. Very nice, inexpensive option in the middle of the port, and distinct from the restaurant of the same name; the cheapest rooms lack en-suite facilities, but paying a little more gets you an excellent bathroom, and more still a sea-view balcony. ❶

Le Phare 6 quai Thomas ⓣ02.99.89.60.24, ⓦlephare-cancale.com. Appealing *logis* towards the far end of the harbour, offering good rooms above its top-notch restaurant (see p.215). Restaurant closed Wed, plus Thurs in low season. Closed Dec & Jan. ❸

La Pointe du Grouin ⓣ02.99.89.60.55, ⓦwww.hotelpointedugrouin.com. Splendidly isolated *logis*, 5km north of town and very close to the spectacular

Pointe du Grouin. All the rooms have great views, and the restaurant (closed all Tues, plus Thurs eve in low season) serves menus from €24 to €77. Closed mid-Nov to March. ⑥

Hostel and campsite

HI hostel Port Picain ⓣ02.99.89.62.62, ⓦfuaj.org/Cancale-Baie-de-Saint-Michel. Attractive modern hostel, just a few metres from the beach 2km north of town, with kayaking and windsurfing among the sports on offer. Coastal buses to St-Malo stop here in summer. Dorm bed €13.50, and there's also camping. Closed Dec & Jan.

Pointe du Grouin Port Picain ⓣ02.99.89.63.79. By far the best campsite in the vicinity, perched beside the sea just beyond the hostel north of town, and enjoying sensational views. Closed Nov–March.

The Town

Cancale is divided into two distinct halves: the old town up on the hill, and the port area of **La Houle** down below, now very pretty and smart. Glass-fronted hotels and restaurants stretch the length of the waterfront, always busy with visitors, while fishing boats bob in the harbour itself. At its northern end, demarcated by a stone jetty, local women sell fresh oysters by the dozen from stalls with bright striped canvas awnings.

When the sea recedes at low tide, it exposes the **parcs** where the oysters are grown. There used to be an annual event, *La Caravanne*, when a huge flotilla of sailing vessels dragged nets along the bottom of the sea for wild oysters; now they are farmed like any other crop. The seabed is divided into countless segments of different sizes, each having an individual owner who has the right to sell what it produces. The oysters are cultivated from year-old "spat" bought in from elsewhere. Behind, the rocks of the cliff are streaked and shiny like mother-of-pearl; underfoot, the beach is littered with countless generations of empty shells.

Follow the corniche road out of Cancale to the southwest, and you'll soon come to the **Ferme Marine**, a working *parc* where the entire oyster-raising process is described on enjoyable guided tours (mid-Feb to June & mid-Sept to Oct Mon–Fri at 3pm; July to mid-Sept daily at 11am, 3pm & 5pm, with an English-language tour at 2pm; €6.80; ⓣ02.99.89.69.99, ⓦferme-marine.com).

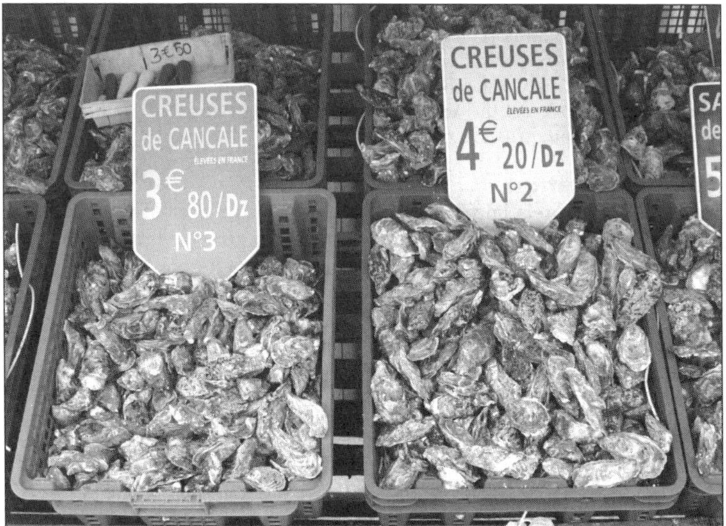

▲ Oysters for sale in Cancale

Back in town, the old church of **St-Méen** at the top of the hill holds a small **Musée des Arts et Traditions Populaires**, documenting Cancale's oyster obsession with meticulous precision (May Sat & Sun 2.30–6.30pm; June & Sept Mon & Fri–Sun 2.30–6.30pm; July & Aug Mon 2.30–6.30pm, Tues–Sun 10am–noon & 2.30–6.30pm; €4). Cancale oysters have been found in the camps of Julius Caesar, were taken daily to Versailles for Louis XIV, and even accompanied Napoleon on the march to Moscow. The most famous symbol of the town – and its oyster cultivation – is the stark rocky pinnacle known as the **Rocher du Cancale** just offshore; the museum lists all the *Rochers du Cancale* restaurants that have ever existed, including ones in Shanghai and Phnom Penh, and one in Moscow that closed in the 1830s.

Cancale has a **market** on Sunday in the streets behind the main church, the rue de la Marine and the rue Cocar.

Eating

Cancale offers a fabulous range of **restaurants** for seafood-lovers; there's no great reason to recommend any one of them above the rest. All serve enticing seafood spreads, with twenty or so options. **Oysters** cost as little as €2 per dozen from takeaway stalls; just grab a plate and have a picnic by the sea.

Le Grand Large 4 quai Jacques-Cartier ⓣ02.99.89.82.90. This spacious restaurant at the southern end of the port comes into its own in the summer, when its large wedge-shaped wooden terrace makes a great spot for an evening meal. It also offers a change from all that seafood, with lots of meaty couscous options.

L'Huîtrière 14 quai Gambetta ⓣ02.99.89.94.35. Very classy seafood specialist with a €12 menu of a dozen oysters followed by salmon or mussels, while the lovely €24 menu includes skate.

Le Phare 6 quai Thomas ⓣ02.99.89.60.24. Another good choice for oysters, seafood platters and lobster, with menus starting at €15.50 for lunch and €19.50 for dinner, plus a heated outdoor terrace for end-of-season alfresco dining. Closed Wed & Thurs in low season.

Au Pied d'Cheval 10 quai Gambetta ⓣ02.99.89.76.95. Once a little seafront shack, this is now a casual, always crowded seafront restaurant that works out a bit more expensive than many of its neighbours because it doesn't have any set menus. The fresh seafood remains beyond reproach; they'll dish up a dozen oysters from the huge baskets that weigh down their wooden quayside tables for just €6, or prepare a massive *fruits de mer* plate for two people for €44.

Dol-de-Bretagne

The foundation of **DOL-DE-BRETAGNE**, 30km west of Mont-St-Michel, is attributed to St Samson, one of the many Celtic evangelists who flooded into Brittany around the sixth century. The Breton hero King Nominoë appointed its first official bishop during the ninth century, and the city remained an important bishopric throughout the Middle Ages.

Dol is no longer large enough to merit its own bishop, but Samson's name lives on in the fortified thirteenth-century **Cathédrale St-Samson**, with its strange, squat, tiled towers and ornate porches. Housed in a former school in the cathedral square, the highly ambitious **Médiévalys** (April–Oct daily 10am–7pm; €7.50; ⓦwww.medievalys.com) is a modern museum that has just changed its name from the similarly impenetrable "Cathédraloscope", to mark that its focus has expanded from merely cathedrals to cover medieval life in general. For all its high-tech presentation and flair, however, non-French speakers may find it heavy going.

An appealing handful of Dol's older streets are still packed with venerable buildings, most notably the pretty **Grande Rue des Stuarts**, just south of the cathedral, where one Romanesque edifice dates back as far as the eleventh century, an assortment of five hundred-year-old half-timbered houses look down on the bustle of shoppers below, and a laundry claims to have been visited by Victor Hugo in 1836.

Practicalities

Dol's **tourist office** is at 3 Grande Rue des Stuarts (June & Sept Mon–Sat 10am–12.30pm & 2–6pm, Sun 2.30–6pm; July & Aug Mon–Fri 9.30am–7pm, Sat & Sun 9.30am–1pm & 2–7pm; Oct–May Mon 2–6pm, Tues–Fri 10am–12.30pm & 2–6pm, Sat 10am–12.30pm; ⓣ02.99.48.15.37, ⓦpays-de-dol.com). The **hotel** *Bretagne*, next to the market at 17 place Chateaubriand (ⓣ02.99.48.02.03; ❸; closed Feb), east of Grande Rue des Stuarts has rooms to suit all budgets – those at the back look out across a vestige of ramparts towards Mont Dol – and menus from €10 to €32.

Good **campsites** nearby include the four-star *Vieux Chêne* (ⓣ02.99.48.09.55, ⓦcamping-vieuxchene.fr; closed Oct–March), 3km east towards Baguer-Pican on N176, where the main pool has four waterslides, and the phenomenally luxurious *Castel Camping des Ormes* (ⓣ02.99.73.53.00, ⓦwww.lesormes.com; closed Oct–April), set around a lake in the grounds of a château 6km south towards Combourg on the N795, which arranges **horseriding** for its guests, and boasts its own golf course and even a cricket pitch.

La Grabotais, a nice **fish restaurant** in an ancient house at 4 rue Ceinte, between Grande Rue des Stuarts and the cathedral (ⓣ02.99.48.19.89; closed Mon, plus Sun eve in low season), serves menus from €18. After you eat, the *Katédral* **bar**, at the other end of rue Ceinte between the church and museum, is worth a brief pause.

Mont Dol

All approaches to Dol from the bay are watched over by the former island of **Mont Dol**. This abrupt granite outcrop, now eight rather marshy kilometres in from the sea and looking mountainous beyond its size on such a flat plain, was the legendary site of a battle between the Archangel Michael and the Devil. The site has been occupied since prehistoric times – flint implements have been unearthed alongside the bones of mammoths, sabre-toothed tigers and even rhinoceroses. Later on, it appears to have been used for worship by the druids, before becoming, like Mont-St-Michel, an island monastery. Traces of the abbey have long vanished, though the mythic battle may recall its foundation, with Christianity driving out the old religion.

It's possible to drive up a steep narrow road to the top of Mont Dol, from the attractive little village at the foot of the hill. Alternatively, it makes a pleasant climb on foot, via a footpath that winds up among the chestnuts and beeches. Just below the summit, the lawns of a crêperie-cum-bar hold crowds of summer day-trippers. A little further up, there's a tiny chapel, while the peak itself is crowned by a granite tower topped by a white statue of the Madonna and Child. Ascending the 55 tight little spiral steps within brings you to a viewing platform commanding immense views across the surrounding pancake-flat plains.

If you fancy an extended hike, Dol and Mont Dol are in fact located on the long-distance **GR34** trail, which leads east to Mont-St-Michel (reckoned as an eight-hour stroll), and west along the coast way beyond St-Malo.

The Menhir du Champ-Dolent

A short way out of Dol to the south, a small picnic area fenced off among the fields contains the **Menhir du Champ-Dolent**. According to one legend, this

9.6-metre standing stone dropped from the sky to separate two brothers who were on the point of mutual fratricide. Another has it that the menhir is inching its way into the soil, and the world will end when it disappears altogether. It has to be said, this would not be a particularly interesting spot on which to experience the end of the world – the unadorned stone, big though it is in its banal setting, has little of the romance or mystery of the megalithic sites of the Morbihan and elsewhere.

The Forêt de Ville-Cartier

The *Circuit Touristique* signposted from Dol continues beyond the menhir and the village of Trans to the **Forêt de Ville-Cartier**. The pines and beech of the dense forest sweep down to a lake in which it is possible – in fact almost irresistible – to swim. Keeping to the *circuit*, along the D155, would lead eventually to Fougères (see p.224).

Inland to Rennes

Much the most direct route inland from the north coast to Rennes is the **D137**, which takes barely half an hour to drive from St-Malo. The D795 south from Dol however makes an appealing alternative, passing through the castle town of **Combourg**. The twin canalside towns of **Hédé** and **Tinténiac** also merit a brief detour.

Combourg

As well as being a pleasant little town in its own right, **COMBOURG**, 17km south of Dol, has two chief attractions. Perched on a hill and dominating magnificent landscaped gardens, the **Château de Combourg** was the childhood home of the writer Chateaubriand (now buried at St-Mal; see p.204), and remains in the hands of his descendants (château guided tour only: April–June & Sept daily except Sat 2–5.30pm; July & Aug daily 10.30–11.15am & 2–5.30pm; Oct daily except Sat 2–5pm; gardens: April–June & Sept daily except Sat 9.30am–12.30pm & 2–6pm; July & Aug daily 9.30am–12.30pm & 2–6pm; Oct daily except Sat 10am–noon & 2–5pm; €6 for gardens & château; Ⓦwww.combourg.net). The castle's Tour du Chat is supposedly haunted by a ghost taking the form of a cat; Chateaubriand himself claimed it was haunted by the ghost of the **wooden leg** of a former lord – and that the cat was merely an acquaintance of this phantasmal limb. The entrance to the château is not where you expect it to be: turn right at the end of Combourg's main square instead of continuing straight towards the keep, and it's a short way up on the left.

Below both the château and town, the tranquil cypress-lined **lake** is, if anything, more appealing than the château itself. Misty and quiet early in the morning, busy only with anglers, it provides a welcome opportunity for leisurely countryside walks.

Practicalities

Combourg maintains a small **tourist office** in the Maison de la Lanterne, at 23 place Albert-Parent (April–Sept Mon–Sat 10am–1pm & 2.30–6.30pm, Sun 10am–12.30pm; Oct–March Tues–Sat 10am–1pm & 2–6pm; Ⓣ02.99.73.13.93, Ⓦwww.combourg.org). Two superb if somewhat expensive (and not very imaginatively named) **hotels** square off against each other across place Chateaubriand, which squeezes in between château and lake. While the

Hôtel du Château at no. 1 (Ⓣ02.99.73.00.38, Ⓦhotelduchateau.com; ❺; closed Mon lunch, Sat lunch, Sun eve in low season, plus mid-Dec to mid-Jan) is faultlessly correct, the *Hôtel du Lac* at no. 2 (Ⓣ02.99.73.05.65, Ⓦhotel-restaurant-du-lac.com; ❹; closed Fri eve & Sun eve in low season, plus all Feb) just has the edge, with lake views from most rooms, as well as from the restaurant, where dinner menus start at €25.

Beside the canal: Hédé and Tinténiac

The D795 south from Combourg meets the D137 roughly 20km north of Rennes, close to the particularly pleasant stretch of the **Canal d'Ille-et-Vilaine** that connects the two old towns of **HÉDÉ** and **TINTÉNIAC**. There are tempting places to collapse in the sun between the many locks and lock-keepers' cottages, although the towpath isn't consistent enough to follow for any distance on foot, let alone bike.

Both Hédé and Tinténiac are set on hills to the west of the canal. The one **hotel** in the area is situated on the main road just north of Hédé, where the *Hostellerie du Vieux Moulin* (Ⓣ02.99.45.45.70; ❸; closed Sun eve & Mon, plus the first three weeks in Jan & the last two weeks in Oct), a Logis de France, stands in a lovely rural setting below the ruined ramparts of the town castle; the guest rooms are pretty minimal for the price, but the restaurant is magnificent, with menus starting at €23.

In addition, a flower-festooned stone cottage just off the highway between Tinténiac and Hédé, a couple of hundred metres north of the *Vieux Moulin*, holds the inexpensive but high-quality *Restaurant le Genty-Home* (Ⓣ02.99.45.46.07; closed Sun eve, Tues eve & Wed), whose enthusiastic chef prepares traditional meats and fish on menus from €25 and up.

Rennes

For a city that has been the capital and power centre of Brittany ever since it was united with France in 1532, **RENNES** is – outwardly at least – uncharacteristic of the province, with its Neoclassical layout and grandiose major buildings. Much of its potential to be a picturesque tourist destination was destroyed in 1720, when a drunken carpenter managed to set light to virtually the whole city. The fire lasted a week, razing 33 streets and nine hundred houses. Only sections of the area known as **Les Lices**, at the junction of the canalized Ile-et-Rance and the River Vilaine, were left undamaged; fortunately, it was even then the oldest part of Rennes, so some traces of the medieval town survive.

The subsequent remodelling of the rest of the city left it, on the north side of the river at any rate, as something of a patchwork quilt, consisting of grand eighteenth-century public squares interspersed with intimate little alleys of half-timbered houses. It's a lively enough place though, with over forty thousand **students** at the local university, based on a huge campus to the east, to help stimulate its political and cultural activity, and a couple of major annual **festivals**, the Tombées de la Nuit and the Transmusicales, to lure in outsiders.

Rennes was first laid out by the **Romans**, at a convenient ford in the Vilaine that was already home to the Celtic community of Condate; over thirty thousand Roman coins have been found in the riverbed, it being traditional for travellers to toss in an offering whenever they crossed water. Although it was ravaged by barbarian invaders in 276 AD, the city subsequently enjoyed over a thousand years of independence before it was captured by Charles VIII of

France in 1491. That defeat obliged Duchess Anne to marry Charles, and led to the union of Brittany and France.

Arrival, city transport and information

For drivers, it's best to park as soon as you reach the city centre; the most convenient **car parks** are the underground one beneath the place des Lices, and between the *quais* Duguay Trouin and Lamennais.

Rennes' modern **gare SNCF** (Ⓣ08.36.35.35.35) is south of the Vilaine, around twenty minutes' walk from the tourist office and a little more from the medieval quarter. As well as direct TGV trains to and from Paris – which take just over two hours – it also has connections east to Brest, north to Dol and south towards Nantes. The fast, efficient and ultra-clean **Métro** system runs from La Poterie in the southeast to J.F. Kennedy in the northwest; the most useful stops for tourists are at the *gare SNCF*, the place de la République, and the place Ste-Anne. Any one-way journey costs just €1.20 (including any bus transfers within 1hr), or you can ride all day for €3.50 (Mon–Sat 5am–12.45am, Sun 7.15am–12.45am). In addition to the métro, a vast system of **local buses** (run by STAR; Ⓣ02.99.79.37.37, Ⓦwww.star.fr) covers all points of the city; the same tickets are valid.

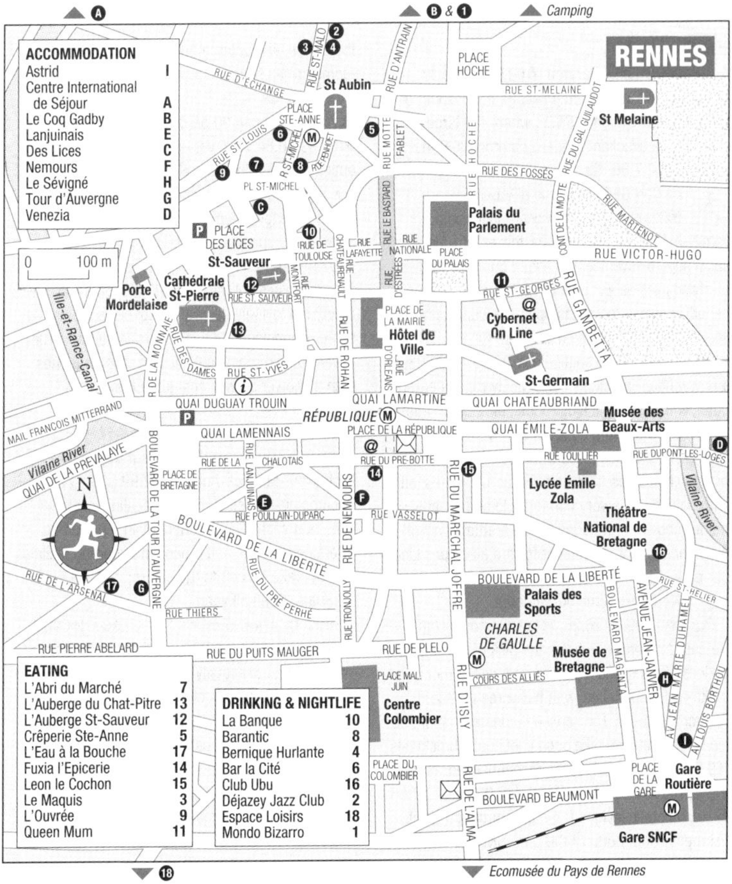

The city's **gare routière** (closed Sun; T02.99.30.87.80) stands immediately east of the *gare SNCF* on boulevard Solferino, but most local buses start and finish by the canal in the heart of town, on or near place de la République. Rennes is a busy junction, with direct services to St-Malo (Illenoo: T02.99.82.26.26, Willenoo.fr), and Mont-St-Michel (Keolis Emeraude: T02.99.19.70.80, Wwww.keolis-emeraude.com).

The **tourist office** stands in a disused medieval church, the Chapelle St-Yves, just north of the river at 11 rue St-Yves (April–Sept Mon–Sat 9am–7pm, Sun 11am–1pm & 2–6pm; Oct–March Mon 1–6pm, Tues–Sat 10am–6pm, Sun 11am–1pm & 2–6pm; T02.99.67.11.11, Wwww.tourisme-rennes.com). It's a larger complex than is immediately obvious, with information on the whole of Brittany and beyond; the main body of the church contains models and other displays that show how the city has grown.

Accommodation

There are surprisingly few **hotels** in the old part of Rennes – and those that there are can be hard to find. If you arrive by train or bus, it's easier to settle for staying south of the river, near the *gares SNCF* and *routière*. Rennes' hotels stay open all year round.

Hotels

Astrid 32 av Louis Barthou T02.99.30.82.38, Whotel-astrid-rennes.eu. Peaceful hotel, south of the river near the *gare SNCF*, where the large rooms have excellent modern bathrooms. Buffet breakfasts € 7.50. ③

Le Coq Gadby 156 rue d'Antrain T02.99.38.05.55, Wlecoq-gadby.com. Family-run for four generations, this exceptional hotel, set in superb seventeenth-century buildings, has re-styled itself as an "urban resort", with luxurious period-furnished rooms, an open-fire lounge, on-site spa and Michelin-starred restaurant. ⑧

Lanjuinais 11 rue Lanjuinais T02.99.79.02.03, Wwww.hotel-lanjuinais.com. Nicely renovated hotel, with light, spacious rooms, on a quiet little street less than 50m south of the river. ③

Des Lices 7 pl des Lices T02.99.79.14.81, Wwww.hotel-des-lices.com. Forty-five rooms, all with balcony, in a very comfortable and friendly modern hotel on the edge of the prettiest part of old Rennes, very convenient for the place des Lices car park. ④

Nemours 5 rue de Nemours T02.99.78.26.26, Whotelnemours.com. Re-cast as a boutique hotel, the pick of the central options offers spotless, stylish and well-lit rooms in white and green tones, with flat-screen TVs and comfortable beds. The service is friendly and professional and you can take good continental breakfasts (€9.50) in bed. Reservations recommended. ④

Le Sévigné 47 av Jean-Janvier T02.99.67.27.55, Wwww.hotellesevigne.fr. Smart, upmarket establishment 100m north of the *gare SNCF* en route to the centre, with a large brasserie next door. All rooms are en suite, with satellite TV; discounts at weekends. ④

Tour d'Auvergne 20 bd de la Tour-d'Auvergne T02.99.30.84.16. A very simple but welcoming option between the *gare SNCF* and the river. Some low-priced rooms have en-suite shower facilities, but the cheapest come only with a sink. ①

Venezia 27 rue Dupont-les-Loges T02.99.30.36.56, Ehotel.venezia@orange.fr. The friendly hostess of this budget hotel offers slightly musty but lovingly decorated, spacious rooms, some overlooking the canalized Vilaine River. The lowest-priced rooms only have a toilet, but ones with a shower as well cost just €6 extra. ②

Hostel and campsite

Camping Municipal des Gayeulles rue de Professeur-Maurice-Audin T02.99.36.91.22, Wcamping-rennes.com. An appealingly verdant site, 1km east of central Rennes in a park that offers good shade and a pool and sporting facilities nearby. Take bus #3 to the centre; last bus runs at 12.30am. Open all year.

Centre International de Séjour 10–12 Canal St-Martin T02.99.33.22.33, Wfuaj.org/rennes. Welcoming, attractively positioned HI hostel, 3km north of the centre beside the Canal d'Ille et Rance. Charging €18.30 per person per night for a dorm bed, it has a cafeteria and a laundry, and operates a 1am curfew; membership of a hostelling association is compulsory. Bus #18 runs there from the place Ste-Anne métro station, direction "St-Gregoire". Open all year.

The City

Rennes' original **medieval core** – the "ville rouge", bordered by the canal to the west and the river to the south – is known to have been enclosed by walls well before 1422. Those walls were enlarged in 1440, when the **Porte Mordelaise** was constructed to serve as the ceremonial entrance to the city. While the gateway itself is now hidden away in a sleepy back alleyway, the old quarter remains the liveliest part of town, and it stays up late, particularly in the area around St-Aubin church and along rue St-Michel and rue de Penhöet.

Just northeast of the *porte*, the **place des Lices**, now dominated by two usually empty market halls, comes alive every Saturday for one of France's largest **street markets**. The place was originally the venue for jousting tournaments, and on this spot in 1337 the hitherto unknown **Bertrand du Guesclin**, then aged 17, fought and defeated several older opponents. This set him on his career as a soldier, during which he was later to save Rennes during an English siege. However, after the Bretons were defeated at Auray in 1364, he fought for the French and twice invaded Brittany.

The magnificent medieval-style town houses that overlook the place des Lices are not as old as they look: most were built in the late seventeenth century to house Brittany's parliamentarians. The streets immediately northeast offer a more genuine glimpse of ancient Rennes. Wander around the back of the excellent crêperie at 5 place Ste-Anne (see p.223), through an archway beside no. 7 rue Motte-Fablet, and you'll find an extraordinary specimen of medieval high-rise housing.

The one central building to escape the 1720 fire, the **Palais du Parlement** on rue Hoche downtown, was all but destroyed by a major conflagration in 1994, sparked by a flare set off during a demonstration by Breton fishermen. Now rebuilt and restored, it's once more topped by an impressive array of gleaming gilded statues. Inside, its lobby stages temporary exhibitions.

The **Vilaine River** flows through the centre of Rennes, narrowly confined into a steep-sided channel, and even forced underground at one point. The city districts on its **south bank** are every bit as busy as those on the north. Just west of the *gare SNCF*, the vast **Centre Colombier** is packed with shops of all kinds, plus cafés and snack bars, and featuring a crystal model of itself in its main entrance hall. Slightly nearer the river, **rue Vasselot** has its own array of half-timbered old houses.

The **Lycée Émile Zola**, just south of the Beaux Arts museum at the corner of avenue Jean-Janvier and rue Toullier, was the scene in 1899 of the retrial of **Captain Alfred Dreyfus**. It had taken three years – and Émile Zola's famous letter "J'accuse" – to secure him the retrial following his wrongful conviction of treason in 1896. The notorious saga is commemorated by a modern steel statue, *La Dégradation de Dreyfus*, by Igael Tumurkin. Public opinion in Rennes at the time, incidentally, was strongly against Dreyfus, and the city witnessed violent anti-Semitic demonstrations.

The museums

An imposing former university building at 20 quai Émile-Zola on the south bank of the Vilaine houses Rennes' **Musée des Beaux Arts** (Tues 10am–6pm, Wed–Sun 10am–noon & 2–6pm; €5.60; Ⓦwww.mbar.org). Its collection reaches back several millennia, as far as mummified Egyptian cats and Etruscan urns as well as Greek and Roman statues and ceramics. Many of its finest artworks – which include drawings by Leonardo da Vinci, Botticelli, Fra Lippo Lippi and Dürer – are, however, not usually on public display. Instead you'll find a number of indifferent Impressionist views of Normandy by the likes of

Boudin and Sisley, interspersed with the odd treasure such as Pieter Boel's contemporary-looking seventeenth-century animal studies, Veronese's depiction of a flying *Perseus Rescuing Andromeda*, and Pierre-Paul Ruben's *Tiger Hunt*. Only a few of its many canvases by lesser-known Breton artists tend to be on show at any one time, but if you're lucky they'll include the haunting landscapes of Théodore Caruelle d'Aligny, painted in the 1850s but suffused with a delicate Maxfield-Parrish-style glow. Picasso also makes a cameo appearance, with a nude from 1923, a simple *Baigneuse à Dinard* from 1928, and a very late and surprisingly Cubist canvas from 1970.

A high-tech overview of Breton history and culture, the **Musée de Bretagne**, is housed in a state-of-the-art edifice known as Les Champs Libres, 500m south on the Cours des Alliés (Tues noon–9pm, Wed–Fri noon–7pm, Sat & Sun 2–7pm; €4, or €7 for museum and Éspace des Sciences; ⓦwww.musee-bretagne.fr). Displays start (up on the second floor) at the very beginning, with a hearth used by humans in a Finistère sea cave half a million years ago that ranks among the oldest signs of fire in the world. Then follows an entertaining skate through regional history, covering the dolmens and menhirs of the megalith builders, some magnificent jadeite axes and Bronze Age swords, and the arrival of first the Celts, next the Romans, and later still the spread of Christianity from the fifth century onwards. With labels in English as well as French and Breton, it makes a good introduction to the region, but unless some compelling temporary exhibition is on it's not really unmissable.

Under the same roof, and sharing the same hours and entrance fees, the **Éspace des Sciences** is a peculiar sort of scaly volcano that contains two floors of rather dry scientific displays, this time with no English captions. One storey, the Salle Eureka, is devoted to time, from the formation of the universe and development of the first ancient calendars; the other, the Salle de la Terre, outlines the geology of Brittany.

For a more distinctly Breton take on the past, head out to the **Ecomusée du Pays de Rennes** (April–Sept Tues–Fri 9am–6pm, Sat 2–6pm, Sun 2–7pm; Oct–March Tues–Fri 9am–noon & 2–6pm, Sat 2–6pm, Sun 2–7pm; €4.60; ⓦwww.ecomusee-rennes-metropole.fr), south of the centre on the route Chatillon sur Seiche (reached on city bus #15 from the place de la République, getting off at the "Tage" stop, or by métro – stop "Triangle"). This former farmhouse, the Ferme de la Bintinais, has been preserved as a monument to local rural history. Recounting the minutiae of five centuries of daily life, it shows the vital role Rennes has played in the evolution of Breton agriculture; living exhibits range from dairy cattle to honey bees.

Eating

Most of Rennes' more interesting **restaurants** lie along the streets just south of the place Ste-Anne, towards the place des Lices, with rues St-Michel and Penhoët – each with a fine assemblage of ancient wooden buildings – at the epicentre. Ethnic alternatives, including African, Lebanese, Greek and Indian options, are concentrated along rue St-Malo just north, and rue St-Georges near the place du Palais. Rue Vasselot is the nearest equivalent south of the river. There are also plenty of brasseries, restaurants and bars in the *gare SNCF* complex and the surrounding streets.

L'Abri du Marché 9 pl des Lices ⓣ02.99.79.73.87. Nothing but the Breton staples of *moules* (€9–10) and *galettes* (€3–9) are served at this local favourite, which sources fresh market produce every morning and serves it in a pleasant dining room smothered in old Breton trinkets.

L'Auberge du Chat-Pitre 18 rue du Chapitre ⓣ02.99.30.36.36. Enjoyable re-creation of medieval dining, seated at long communal tables in a very pretty red half-timbered mansion close by the cathedral, and interrupted by the odd jester. Hearty stews and roasts predominate; there's a €24 menu, or starters cost around €7, main courses €13–19. Dinner only. Closed Sun.

L'Auberge St-Sauveur 6 rue St-Sauveur ⓣ02.99.79.32.56. Classy, romantic restaurant, in an attractive medieval house near the cathedral, with light lunches for €12.50 and richer, meaty dinner menus at €19 and €28. Closed for lunch on Sat & Mon, plus all day Sun.

Crêperie Ste-Anne 5 pl Ste-Anne ⓣ02.99.79.22.72. Appealing crêperie nicely situated on the place Ste-Anne opposite the church, with plenty of outdoor seating and a good selection of *galettes* for €5–8. Closed Sun.

L'Eau à la Bouche 12 rue de l'Arsenal ⓣ02.23.40.27.95. Exquisite little restaurant serving a modern take on classic French cuisine on ever-changing menus that range €16–34.Closed Sun, Mon & Sat lunch.

Fuxia l'Epicerie 2 rue Jules Simon ⓣ02.99.79.44.78. Stylish, modern Italian trattoria/deli, with some pavement seating, serving zesty pasta, risottos and salads for lunch (set menu €11.50) and dinner daily.

Leon le Cochon 1 rue Maréchal-Joffre ⓣ02.99.79.37.54. Tasteful, contemporary but classically French restaurant, where the simple lunch menu costs just €12.50 including wine, but it's best to reserve to enjoy dinner menus that start at €26. Closed Sun in July & Aug.

Le Maquis 13 rue St-Malo ⓣ02.99.63.83.06. Very lively, friendly African restaurant, serving lots of Senegalese marinated chicken and fish dishes for around €10, plus a €18.50 vegetarian set menu. Closed Sun & Mon.

L'Ouvrée 18 pl des Lices ⓣ02.99.30.16.38, ⓦwww.louvree.com. Formal but very friendly gourmet restaurant, spread through two dining rooms decorated in rich, warm reds and yellows. Menus range from €14.80 to €33.20, and feature small but very tasty portions with an emphasis on fish, as for example with the *flan de langoustines*, plus wonderful desserts. Closed Sat lunch, Sun eve & Mon.

Queen Mum 11 rue St-Georges ⓣ02.23.20.09.83. Despite the quirky name, this is a smart little traditional restaurant, with a few tables out on the street. Weekday lunches for €10.50, dinner menus range €18–28. Closed Sun.

Nightlife and entertainment

As with restaurants, the prime area for **bars** and **nightlife** is around the place Ste-Anne. Leading off the south side of the square, rue St-Michel boasts half a dozen bars within spitting distance, while the rue St-Malo to the north is if anything even rowdier, and stays up later.

Rennes is seen at its best during the first ten days of July, when the **Festival des Tombées de la Nuit** takes over the whole city to celebrate Breton culture with music, theatre, film, mime and poetry in joyful rejection of the influences of both Paris and Hollywood (ⓣ02.99.32.56.56, ⓦlestombeesdelanuit.com). A pocket version of the same festival is also held in the week between Christmas and New Year. In the first week of December, the **Transmusicales** rock festival attracts big-name acts from all over France and the world at large, though still with a Breton emphasis (ⓣ02.99.31.12.10, ⓦlestrans.com).

The **Théâtre National de Bretagne**, 1 rue St-Helier (TNB; ⓣ02.99.31.12.31, ⓦwww.t-n-b.fr), puts on varied events throughout the year, except in August. All year round, in a different auditorium on the same premises, *Club Ubu* (ⓣ02.99.31.12.10, ⓦubu-rennes.com) is the venue for large-scale rock concerts. The TNB also has a good **cinema** showing films other than Hollywood blockbusters, often in their original languages.

Bars and clubs

La Banque 5 allée Rallier du Baty. Just south of the place St-Michel, this labyrinthine Irish pub is on the first floor of an intriguing medieval building that once served as Rennes' prison, and also holds a restaurant, a cocktail bar and a club.

Barantic 4 rue St-Michel. One of the city's favourite bars, putting on occasional live music for a mixed crowd of Breton nationalists and boisterous students; if it's too full, there are half a dozen similar alternatives within spitting distance.

Bernique Hurlante 40 rue St-Malo ⓣ02.99.38.70.09. Rendezvous for local artists and activists, as well as being one of Rennes' more gay-friendly bars. Closed Mon.

Bar la Cité 5 rue St-Louis. This great little bar, with art on the walls and friendly staff and clientele, is the ideal place for a cider, or some of their stronger house brews (€2). They host live music to suit a range of tastes on Saturday nights, and the staff favour electro on the stereo. Open until 2am.

Déjazey Jazz Club 54 rue St-Malo ⓣ02.99.38.70.72. Good quality live jazz and other gigs take place twice weekly here and the late closing makes it the popular "after" spot, despite somewhat steep prices (€7 for a large beer on tap). Open until 5am, closed Sun.

Espace Loisirs 45 bd de la Tour d'Auvergne. Rennes' best club plays thumping electro-house music and r'n'b, and attracts a mixed straight and gay crowd.

Mondo Bizarro 264 av Général-Patton ⓣ02.99.87.22.00, ⓦmondobizarro.free.fr. Rock, metal and especially punk club, 1km northeast of the centre on bus line #15, and kept busy most nights with local bands and international punk stalwarts, plus a leavening of tribute bands, ska, reggae and jazz.

Listings

Bookshops Co-op Breizh, 17 rue Penhoët ⓣ02.99.79.01.87, ⓦwww.gwalarn.org, stocks Breton and Celtic CDs along with books and posters; FNAC, Centre Commercial Colombier ⓣ02.99.67.10.10.

Bicycle rental A free bike rental system is based at the *gare SNCF*. This is a separate scheme to the one open only to city residents, under which locals are given special identity cards to unlock the free white bicycles you'll see parked all over town.

Car rental Most of the main agencies have offices at the *gare SNCF*, including Avis ⓣ02.23.42.14.14, Hertz ⓣ02.23.42.17.01 and Budget ⓣ02.99.65.41.76.

Cinemas Schedules for all Rennes' cinemas are on ⓦcine35.com. Cinemas include the Gaumont, 8 quai Duguay-Trouin; L'Arvor, 29 rue d'Antrain, which shows films in English, and Ciné TNB, 1 rue St-Hélier.

Hospital Hôtel Dieu, 2 rue de l'Hôtel Dieu ⓣ02.99.28.43.21.

Internet access Cybernet On Line, 22 rue St-Georges ⓣ02.99.36.37.41 (Mon 2–8pm, Tues–Sat 10.30am–1pm & 2–8pm; €4 per hr; ⓦcybernetonline.com); France Telecom shop, next to the post office on the place de la République (Mon–Sat 9am–7pm; €1 per 20min).

Pharmacy Pharmacie Colombia, Centre Commercial Colombier ⓣ02.99.65.08.08 (Mon–Sat 9am–8pm).

Post office Palais du Commerce in the heart of town on the place de la République ⓣ02.99.79.50.71 (Mon–Fri 8am–7pm, Sat 8.30am–12.30pm); 27 bd du Colombier, just west of the *gare SNCF* ⓣ02.99.31.42.72 (Mon–Fri 8am–7pm, Sat 8am–noon).

Fougères

FOUGÈRES, 50km east of Rennes on the main road into Brittany from Caen, promotes itself as the "*ville au joli nom*", *fougères* being the French for "fern". While, name apart, it's not actually all that pretty, it does boast a magnificent medieval **castle** that's worth going a long way out of your way to see.

Thanks to its split-level site, the topography of the town is almost impossible to grasp from a map. Streets that look a few metres long turn out to be precipitous plunges down escarpments, and lanes collapse into flights of steps; the only efficient way to get around is on foot.

Perhaps the oddest feature is the positioning of the **château**, sited in pre-artillery days well below the main part of the town, on a low spit of land that separates two mighty rock faces towering above. The massive structure was laid out in 1166 to replace a wooden fort destroyed by English invaders. Shielded by great curtain-walls, and circled by a hacked-out moat full of weirs and waterfalls, it was also protected in its heyday by the River Nançon. None of this, however, prevented it being captured several times by medieval adventurers such as du Guesclin. Today it remains a spectacular sight; the moat is still filled with water, while every crevice of the surrounding buildings seems to erupt with bright geraniums.

The large area that lies within the castle walls was being extensively restored as this book went to press. Several grand towers, and especially the main keep, will hold multi-media displays on the history of both castle and town, while the majestic lawns, once occupied by a heavily populated settlement, will continue as tranquil havens for picnickers and sunbathers. Many nooks and crannies still lie in ruins, often overgrown with colourful wild flowers. Vistors can explore by themselves, pick up an audioguide, or join a guided tour for no extra charge (daily: Feb–April & Oct–Dec 10am–12.30pm & 2–5.30pm; May, June & Sept 10am–1pm & 2–7pm; July & Aug 10am–7pm; closed Jan, plus some Mon in low season; €7.50; Ⓦchateau-fougeres.com).

The best approach to the castle is from **place des Arbres** beside St-Léonard's church off rue Nationale, the main street of the old fortified town. Footpaths, ramps and stairways drop down through successive tiers of formal public gardens, offering magnificent views of the ramparts and towers along the way, to reach the water meadows of the River Nançon. You cross the river itself beside a little cluster of medieval houses – the sculpted doorway at 6 rue de Lusignan is particularly attractive.

Up in the town, at 51 rue Nationale, the **Musée de la Villéon** (mid-June to mid-Sept daily 10am–12.30pm & 2.30–6pm; mid-Sept to mid-June Wed–Sun 10am–noon & 2–5pm; free), commemorates the Impressionist Emmanuel de la Villéon. Born in Fougères in 1858, he painted numerous memorable Breton landscapes.

Practicalities

Several **car parks** lie around the perimeter of the castle; parking in the town centre higher up is much harder. The only public transport to serve Fougères are **buses** to and from Vitré and Rennes (Ⓣ08.10.35.10.35, Ⓦillenoo.fr). The **tourist office** is at 2 rue Nationale in the upper town (Easter–June, Sept & Oct Mon–Sat 9.30am–12.30pm & 2–6pm; July & Aug Mon–Sat 9am–7pm, Sun 10am–noon & 2–4pm; Nov–Easter Mon 2–6pm, Tues–Sat 10am–12.30pm & 2–6pm; Ⓣ02.99.94.12.20, Ⓦwww.ot-fougeres.fr).

Nearby, on the main road, the renovated *Hôtel les Voyageurs*, 10 place Gambetta (Ⓣ02.99.99.08.20, Ⓦwww.hotel-fougeres.fr; ③; closed the second two weeks in Aug), is a particularly nice **place to stay** – ask for one of the quieter rooms at the back. The excellent **restaurant** downstairs (closed Sat lunch & Sun eve) is run by different management, despite having the same name as the hotel; dinner menus start at €35, but you can get a good à la carte meal for much less. A central alternative is the *Hôtel Balzac*, in a grey granite town house at 15 rue Nationale (Ⓣ02.99.99.42.46, Ⓦbalzachotel.fr; ③), with pleasant rooms, while the *Buffet*, down the street at no. 53bis (Ⓣ02.99.94.35.76; closed Wed eve & Sun, plus first two weeks in Aug), serves great-value food from €11.20, including all-you-can-eat buffets of *hors d'oeuvres*, cheeses and desserts.

There are no hotels in the immediate vicinity of the château, but the squares on all sides are crammed with an abundance of appealing **bars** and **crêperies**. At *Le Mediéval*, 2 place Raoul-II (Ⓣ02.99.94.92.59), which has lots of outdoor seating beside the moat, you can snack on *moules frites* or crêpes, or get a full dinner from €19.

The Forêt de Fougères

Northeast of Fougères, the **Forêt de Fougères**, stretching for roughly 8km on either side of the D177, which heads towards Vire (see p.188), is one of the most enjoyable in the province. The beech woods are spacious and light, with various megaliths and trails of old stones scattered among the chestnut and spruce. It's quite a contrast to their normal bleak and windswept haunts to see dolmens in such verdant surroundings. A good walk is to start at **Landéan**, about 8km northeast of Fougères on the D177, and walk west through the forest for another 8km or so as far as **Le Chatellier**, a village set high in thick woods.

For a **horseback tour** of the Forêt de Fougères, contact the Centre d'Activitiés et Loisirs de Chénedet in **Chénedet**, 2.5km south of Landéan. (Ⓣ02.99.97.35.46, Ⓦwww.chenedet-loisirs.com).

Vitré

VITRÉ, just north of the Le Mans–Rennes motorway, 30km east of Rennes, is a lesser rival to Dinan as the best-preserved **medieval town** in Brittany. Occupation of the site dates right back to the Romans, when a certain Vitrius owned a villa here. While its thirteenth-century walls are no longer quite complete, their effect is enhanced by the fact that what lies outside them has changed so little. To the north are stark wooded slopes, while into the western hillside beneath the castle burrow thickets of stone cottages that must once have been Vitré's medieval slums.

In best fairy-tale fashion, the towers of the **castle** itself (May–Sept daily except Tues 10am–12.45pm & 2–6pm; Oct–April Mon & Wed–Sat 10am–12.15pm & 2–5.30pm, Sun 2–5.30pm; €4), which dominates the western end of the ramparts, have pointed slate-grey roofs that look like freshly sharpened pencils. First erected in 1060, the castle was remodelled to its present appearance two hundred years later. Unfortunately, the **museum** inside throws little light on the town's eventful past; instead, it's a ragbag of pretty much anything some nineteenth-century curator could get his hands on. The highlight amid all the seashells, birds and bugs is a collection of tatty **stuffed frogs** doing amusing things, such as fighting duels and playing billiards.

The admission fee for the castle also includes entry to three other, mediocre museums in the general vicinity (same opening hours). The **Musée St-Nicholas**, on the western outskirts of town, occupies the huge former chapel of a fifteenth-century hospital, with a sober collection of medieval reliquaries and religious paraphernalia; the attractive seventeenth-century manor house of the **Musée de la Faucillonnaie**, 3km northwest of the centre in Montreuil-sous-Pérouse, is more of a draw than the general mishmash of secular artefacts within; and the **Château des Rochers Sévigné**, 10km southeast, is a place of pilgrimage for French devotees of the seventeenth-century society letter-writer Madame de Sévigné, and holds little interest for anyone not familiar with her work.

Vitré is a market town, with its principal **market** held on Mondays in the square in front of Notre Dame church. The old city is full of twisting streets of half-timbered houses, a good proportion of which are bars. The **rue de la Baudrairie**, between the church and the castle, and formerly the town's leather-working quarter, is the most picturesque of the streets, but the **rue d'en Bas**, which climbs up from Rachapt to the castle, has the best selection of bars; the *Aston* at no. 7 is a nice place to spend an evening.

▲ The castle at Vitré

Practicalities

Vitré's candy-striped **gare SNCF** is on the southern edge of the centre, where the ramparts disappear and the town imperceptibly blends into its newer sectors. Left of the station, on place Général de Gaulle, you'll find the **tourist office** (July & Aug Mon–Sat 9.30am–12.30pm & 2–6.30pm, Sun 10am–12.30pm & 3–6pm; Sept–June Mon 2.30–6pm, Tues–Fri 9.30am–12.30pm & 2.30–6pm, Sat 10am–12.30pm & 3–5pm; Ⓣ02.99.75.04.46, Ⓦot-vitre.fr), which runs an intricate schedule of guided tours in summer.

Most of the **hotels**, too, are near the *gare SNCF*. The *Petit Billot*, 5bis place du Général-Leclerc (Ⓣ02.99.75.02.10, Ⓦpetit-billot.com; ❷), is good value, and has the excellent *Potager* restaurant downstairs, while rooms on the higher floors of the *Hôtel du Château*, 5 rue Rallon (Ⓣ02.99.74.58.59, Ⓦperso.orange.fr/hotel-du-chateau; ❷; closed Sun in low season) on a quiet road just below the castle, have views of the ramparts. In the heart of town, the *Minotel*, 47 rue Poterie (Ⓣ02.99.75.11.11, Ⓦwww.leminotel.fr; ❷), might sound like a chain motel, but it's actually a nice little place above a bar, featuring for some reason golf-themed decor.

Of the **restaurants**, *La Soupe aux Choux*, 32 rue Notre-Dame (Ⓣ02.99.75.10.86; closed Sat lunch, plus Sun in low season), prepares simple but classic French food, with the occasional eccentricity like kangaroo cooked in cider (€14) thrown in.

Around Vitré

There are several interesting smaller towns in the area. **CHAMPEAUX**, 8km west of Vitré, consists of a central paved square, surrounded by stone houses, with an ornate well in the centre. Its fifteenth-century collegiate **church** contains a superb stained-glass *Crucifixion* by Gilles de la Croix-Vallée, the ornate tombs of its founding family, and some fine carved choir stalls. **CHÂTEAUBOURG**, halfway between Vitré and Rennes, has a wonderful but expensive **hotel**, the *Ar Milin* (Ⓣ02.99.00.30.91, Ⓦwww.armilin.com; ❻;

restaurant closed Tues lunch & Sat lunch, plus Mon in summer), straddling the River Vilaine in huge gardens at 30 rue de Paris. Breakfast, at €12, includes an enormous buffet of fresh pastries.

The Roche-aux-Fées

About 15km south of Châteaubourg, not far from the road just off the D341 near Retiers, the **ROCHE-AUX-FÉES** is the least-visited of the major megalithic monuments of Brittany. The "fairy rock" is a twenty-metre-long covered alleyway of purplish stones, with no apparent funerary purpose or, indeed, any evidence that it was ever buried. It's set on a high and exposed spot, guarded by just a few venerable trees, and it's thought the slabs had to be dragged a good 45km to get here. There's no admission charge. Tradition has it that engaged couples should come to the Roche-aux-Fées on the night of a full moon and separately count the stones; if they agree on the total, things are looking good.

West along the coast

West of the Rance, beyond Dinard, stretches the green of the **Côte d'Émeraude**. While this region has its fair share of developed family resorts, such as **St-Jacut**, **Erquy** and **Le Val-André**, it also offers wonderful camping, at its best around the heather-surrounded beaches near **Cap Fréhel**. Further west, the coast becomes wilder and harsher. Beyond **St-Brieuc**, the seaside towns tend to be crammed into narrow rocky inlets or set well back in river estuaries, and only a few beaches manage to break out from the rocks. Once past **Paimpol**, the shoreline is known as the **Côte de Granit Rose** – a literal description of its primeval tangle of vast pink-granite boulders. Much of this magnificent landscape remains relatively untroubled by tourists, though a prime attraction does lie just offshore – the verdant island of **Bréhat**, accessible only by ferry.

The Côte d'Émeraude

The splendidly attractive coast immediately **west of Dinard** is one of Brittany's most traditional family resort areas, with old-fashioned holiday towns, safe sandy beaches and a plethora of well-organized campsites. None of the towns is of any significant size, and paying attractions or entertainments suitable for whiling away rainy afternoons are almost nonexistent. If you're lucky enough to be here on a fine summer's day, however, **St-Jacut**, **St-Cast**, **Erquy** and **Le Val-André** all make idyllically lazy seaside destinations, while **Cap Fréhel** offers a fine, if bracing, coastal walk.

St-Jacut-de-la-mer

ST-JACUT, which takes up most of the tip of a narrow peninsula roughly 16km west of St-Malo, was founded over a thousand years ago by an itinerant Irish monk. The general shape, and many of the buildings, of the old fishing village are still there, though that's now mingled with the fine villas and promenades added when St-Jacut became a classic nineteenth-century bathing resort. A peaceful little spot, it has everything young children could want – good sand, rocky pools to clamber about, and woods nearby to scramble in.

St-Jacut also boasts one of Brittany's most distinctive **hotels**, atop the central spine of the peninsula. As the *Hôtel le Vieux Moulin*, 22 rue du Moulin (ⓣ02.96.27.71.02, ⓦhotel-le-vieux-moulin.com; ❸; closed Nov–Feb), centres on a fifteenth-century windmill, two of its guest rooms are completely round and offer sea views in two directions. It also serves good, if eccentric, food, with generous portions on changing dinner menus, priced at €22 and €30, that are apt to include home-made crisps as a vegetable. The *Municipal* **campsite** is beside the plage de la Manchette (ⓣ02.96.27.70.33; closed Oct–March).

St-Cast-le-Guildo

The pleasant seaside community of **ST-CAST**, on the next promontory along, is a thirty-kilometre drive from St-Malo, and connected by SNCF buses with the nearest train station, at Lamballe (see p.232). Most of its commercial activity takes place in the rather uninspiring **Bourg**, set back from the water, but the seaside area down below is very nice, with a large swathe of **beach** popular with families running parallel to rue du Duc d'Auguillon – the main through road, holding plenty of restaurants – and a quiet, picturesque **port** north of the beach as you approach the headland. There are also good walks along the coast to the headland.

The **tourist office** on place Charles-de-Gaulle (July & Aug Mon–Sat 9am–7pm, Sun 10am–12.30pm & 3–6.30pm; Sept–June Mon–Sat 9am–noon & 2–6pm; ⓣ02.96.41.81.52, ⓦwww.ot-st-cast-le-guildo.fr) sells tickets for summer-only **cruises** along the coast, to St-Malo, Dinard and Cap Fréhel (Thurs only in recent years; see ⓦcompagniecorsaire.com for timetable).

Among medium-price **hotels** in St-Cast is the attractive *Hôtel des Mielles*, 3 rue du Duc d'Auguillon (ⓣ02.96.41.80.95, ⓦwww.hotels-saint-cast.com; ❸; closed mid-Oct to mid-March, plus, in low season, Sun eve & Mon), just a few metres from the beach. Local **campsites** include the four-star *Châtelet* beside the bay on rue des Nouettes (ⓣ02.96.41.96.33, ⓦwww.lechatelet.com; closed mid-Sept to April). The most popular of St-Cast's **restaurants** is *Le Bonheur est dans le Blé*, 17 rue du Duc d'Auguillon (ⓣ02.96.81.03.99; closed Tues & Wed Sept–June), a crêperie known for its generous portions and imaginative fillings; reserve in advance during summer.

Cap Fréhel

While the entire Côte d'Émeraude is ravishingly beautiful, the **Cap Fréhel**, a high, warm expanse of heath, cliffs and heather 9km north of the main D786, and a total drive of 24km west of St-Cast, is exceptional. The unspoiled headland itself lies 400m walk from the road (parking €2), with no more than a few ruins of old buildings and a small "tearoom" nearby. The rocks sixty metres down at the foot of the cliffs, busy with puffins and guillemots, officially constitute the Fauconnière **seabird sanctuary**. Offshore, the heather-covered islands are grand to look at, although too tiny to visit; the view from the cape's **lighthouse** (July & Aug daily 2–6pm; free) can extend as far as Jersey and the Île de Bréhat.

The nearest place to **camp** is the ideal, isolated *Camping des Grèves d'En Bas* at Pléherel (ⓣ02.96.41.43.34, ⓔmairie.cap.frehel@orange.fr; closed Sept to late June).

Fort la Latte

The fourteenth-century **Fort la Latte**, at the tip of a lesser headland 2km southeast of Cap Fréhel, is reached along a few hundred metres of hedge-lined footpath from its free car park. At the far end, as you re-emerge onto open heathland, the fortified castle is a gorgeous little gem, restored by private owners in the 1930s. Visitors enter the enclosure across two drawbridges; outbuildings scattered within include a cannonball factory, and there's also a medieval herb garden, but the highlight is the keep, which contains historical exhibits. Precarious walkways climb to its very summit, for superb coastal views (early July to late Aug daily 10am–7pm; April to early July, and late Aug to Sept daily 10am–12.30pm & 2–6pm; Oct–March Sat, Sun & hols 2–6pm; €4.90; Ⓦcastlelalatte.com).

A lovely little open-air bar alongside the car park sells coffee and ice cream in summer. Nearby, the newly restored **hotel** *Bellevue* (Ⓣ02.96.41.41.61, Ⓦhotel-bellevue-ushuaia.fr), offers seven tastefully furnished bedrooms, some with sea views, and has its own crêperie.

Erquy

The delightful little family resort of **ERQUY** nestles into a vast natural bay around 20km west of Cap Fréhel, with a perfect crescent beach that curves through more than 180 degrees. At low tide, the sea disappears way beyond the harbour entrance, leaving gentle ripples of paddling sand. Adventurers equipped with suitable boots could walk right across its mouth, from the grassy wooded headland on the left side over to the picturesque little lighthouse at the end of the jetty on the right. The town has its own schools of **sailing**, **kayaking** and **windsurfing** (all Ⓣ02.96.72.32.62, Ⓦeverquy.org), and also **diving** (Ⓣ02.96.72.49.67, Ⓦhistoiredeauplongee.com).

Between April and September, to a very irregular schedule, roughly once a week, Les Vedettes de Bréhat operate **boat trips** from either Erquy or nearby Dahouët out to the **Île de Bréhat** (see p.240; departures 8.30am or 9am; €30.50; Ⓣ02.96.55.79.50, Ⓦvedettesdebrehat.com).

Practicalities

Erquy's **tourist office** is at 3 rue du 19 Mars (April–June Mon–Sat 9.30am–12.30pm & 2–6pm, Sun 10am–12.30pm; July & Aug Mon–Sat 9.30am–1pm & 2–7pm, Sun 10am–1pm & 4–6pm; first fortnight of Sept Mon–Sat 9.30am–12.30pm & 2–6pm; mid-Sept to March Mon–Sat 9.30am–12.30pm & 2–5pm; Ⓣ02.96.72.30.12, Ⓦerquy-tourisme.com). **Bus** #2 (Tibus; Ⓦwww.tibus.fr) from St Brieuc to Fréhel, which also calls at the TGV station in Lamballe, stops in Erquy at the place du Centre.

The *Hôtel Beauséjour*, grandly poised above the southern end of the beach at 21 rue de la Corniche (Ⓣ02.96.72.30.39, Ⓦbeausejour-erquy.com; ❸; closed Sun eve, plus Mon & Thurs eve in low season), is Erquy at its most quirky. Its kitsch decor ranges from dungaree-wearing teddies to pastel-painted pebbles, but the guest rooms are really nice and cosy, and the **restaurant**, which has a great view of the bay, is truly excellent, with sumptuous fish dinners from €20. There's also some top-notch and very tasteful **B&B** accommodation in a grand nineteenth-century villa nearby, *La Villa Nazado*, 2 rue des Patriotes (Ⓣ02.96.63.67.14, Ⓦvillanazado.com; ❸). On the other side of the harbour, the *Relais* at 60 rue du Port (Ⓣ02.96.72.32.60, Ⓦlerelais-erquy.chez-alice.fr; ❷) has cheaper sea-view rooms and another good restaurant (closed Thurs), while the *Reflet de la Mer*, 18 rue du Port (Ⓣ02.96.72.00.95; closed Oct–March), is a jaunty little crêperie.

Several **campsites** lie along the promontory (dotted with tiny coves) that leads to the Cap d'Erquy north of town, including the three-star *St-Pabu* (Ⓣ02.96.72.24.65, Ⓦwww.saintpabu.com; closed mid-Nov to March) right beside the sea.

Le Val-André

The beach in the broader bay of **LE VAL-ANDRÉ**, another 11km down the coast, is on a slightly larger scale than that of Erquy, and composed of finer sand. The pedestrian promenade that stretches along the seafront consists solely of huge old holiday villas undisturbed by shops or bars. However, Le Val-André is definitely more of a commercial town than Erquy, and rue A-Charner, running parallel to the sea one street back, is lively with holiday-makers in summer.

For an enjoyable scenic **walk**, follow the 2km-long footpath around the headland to the small, secluded lagoon of **Dahouët** (see p.240 for details of summer sailings to the Île de Bréhat). The construction of a large yachting marina here has obliterated all significant traces of its past, but this lagoon is known to have been used by Viking raiders over a thousand years ago.

Le Val-André's helpful **tourist office** (Mon–Sat 9am–12.30pm & 2.30–6pm; May–Sept only also Sun 10.30am–1pm & 3–5pm; Ⓣ02.96.72.20.55, Ⓦval-andre.org) is located in the modern casino at the very centre of the waterfront. Of its **hotels**, the tastefully refurbished *Hôtel de la Mer*, 63 rue A-Charner (Ⓣ02.96.72.20.44, Ⓦwww.hotel-de-la-mer.com; ❷; closed mid-Nov to mid-Feb), serves magnificent food, including a €25 "Menu de Luxe". En-suite rooms cost extra, and more again for a sea view. The same management operate the characterless *Nuit et Jour* motel nearby for guests without reservations.

PLÉNEUF, the *bourg* associated with Le Val-André, 1.5km up the hill from the sea, also has a few hotels. The *Hôtel de France*, in its main church square at 4 rue Pasteur (Ⓣ02.96.72.22.52, Ⓦpleneuf-hoteldefrance.com; ❷), has an eccentric block of cheap rooms out the back, all accessed from open balconies and marine-themed with knots, canvas and navy-blue trimmings. It also has a good restaurant hidden away, with a recommended €20 menu.

Back down close to the beach, the *Biniou*, 121 rue Clemenceau (Ⓣ02.96.72.24.35; closed Tues eve & Wed in low season, plus all Feb), is the best of several adjacent seafood **restaurants** just back from the casino; in addition to the usual choices, its €26 menu features various fish in original sauces such as mussel and ginger.

The inland route: west to Morlaix

While following the coast from Dinard and Dinan is by far the most scenic route westwards across Brittany, it can also be pretty slow. Travellers in a hurry to reach Morlaix and Finistère can choose instead to head **inland**, either by branching onto the D768 just south of St-Jacut if coming from Dinard, or following first the N176, and then the N12 motorways west from Dinan. Both routes pass the occasional time-forgotten little town or village; few have tourist facilities, but all make pleasant opportunities to stretch your legs.

Jugon-les-Lacs

Tiny old **JUGON-LES-LACS**, 20km west of Dinan, is poised at one end of its own artificial lake – the *grand étang* – which was originally created for defensive purposes during the twelfth century. Peculiarly, the central place du Martray – scene of a market each Friday – is well below the water level, and you have to climb uphill to reach the massive cobblestone dyke that shields it from inundation. At the opposite end of town, the N176 crosses high above the valley on a viaduct. Jugon, nestled cosily between the two, has no room to expand even if it wanted to – it's a subdued but atmospheric place, whose few streets are almost deserted in the evenings.

For most of the way around the **lake**, there's no approach road or footpath, only meadows and trees sweeping down to the water. However, just out of town at the campsite (see below), there's a small beach from which you can go swimming.

The local **tourist office** is on the main square (May–Sept Mon 10am–12.30pm & 2–5.30pm, Tues–Sat 10am–12.30pm & 2–6pm, Sun 10.30am–1pm; Oct–April Mon–Fri 10am–noon & 2–5pm; ⓣ02.96.31.70.75, ⓦjugon-les-lacs.com). The attractive Logis **hotel**, *La Grande Fontaine*, 7 rue Penthièvre (ⓣ02.96.31.61.29; ❸), a couple of hundred metres east of the centre on the main road towards Dinan, has a lively bar with a roadside terrace, and menus at €20 and €30.50. *The Auberge de l'Ecu* is a charming, old-fashioned flower-festooned **bar/restaurant** with seating on the main square (ⓣ02.96.31.61.41; closed Mon & Tues), serving menus from €11.80 up to €35.50.

Out of town along the D52 towards Mégrit, the *Au Bocage du Lac* **campsite** (ⓣ02.96.31.60.16, ⓦcampingjugon.fr; closed late Sept to early April) is very much a family campsite; it has a heated swimming pool, and a mini-golf course. Boats and **windsurf boards** are available for rent from the nearby École de Voile (ⓣ02.96.31.64.58).

Lamballe

The fine old market town of **LAMBALLE**, 20km west of Jugon, is crammed into a narrow valley beside a broad river, dominated by a church high up on battlement walls. Its most famous former citizen was the princess of Lamballe, a lady-in-waiting to Marie Antoinette, who was guillotined in 1792.

Lamballe's picturesque main square, the **place du Martray**, holds a handful of impressive fourteenth-century half-timbered buildings, the grandest of which is the **Maison du Bourreau**. Formerly home to the town's public executioner, it now houses not only the tourist office, but also the tiny **Musée Mathurin Méheut** (April Mon–Sat 10am–noon & 2.30–5pm; May & Oct–Dec Wed, Fri & Sat 2.30–5pm; June–Sept Mon–Sat 10am–noon & 2.30–6pm; €3). Half the museum explores the town's history, and features a fascinating model of Lamballe as it looked in 1417; the rest focuses on the paintings of local-born Mathurin Méheut (1882–1958), which range from Breton landscapes to illustrations for children's books.

A branch of the **national stud** (the *haras national*) all but adjoins the main square, in an imposing ensemble in the very heart of town. Though not quite on the same scale as Le Nôtre's dramatic park near Argentan (see p.177), and specializing in any case more in sturdy Breton workhorses than glossy thoroughbreds, it will still delight any horse-lover (guided tours only: mid-June to mid-Sept daily 10am–5.30pm, with tours at half-hourly intervals; July & Aug tours in English daily 2.30pm & 3.30pm; mid-Sept to mid-June daily except Mon at 3pm only; €5.50). It's the focus of a big **horse festival** on the first weekend after August 15.

Lamballe's **tourist office** is in the Maison du Bourreau in the main square (July & Aug daily 10am–6pm; Sept–June Mon 1.30–5.30pm, Tues–Sat 10am–noon & 1.30–5.30pm; ⓣ02.96.31.05.38, ⓦlamballe-tourisme.com). The best central **hotel-restaurant** is the *Tour des Arc'hants*, a Logis de France at no. 2 on rue Dr-Lavagne, the road that becomes the D102 as it leaves town (Ⓣ02.96.31.01.37, Ⓔlatourdesarchants@orange.fr; ❸; closed Sat in low season). *Au Boeuf d'Or*, just beyond the tourist office at 12 rue du Dr-Calmette (Ⓣ02.96.31.31.31), is a nice little restaurant that serves lunch daily but dinner at weekends only; look out for the frogs' legs on the €16 menu.

Moncontour

The attractive little hill town of **MONCONTOUR**, 18km southwest of Lamballe and 23km southeast of St-Brieuc, prospered during the Middle Ages, thanks to its hemp industry. Having been under no pressure to grow since then, it remains largely enclosed by its medieval fortifications – not that you get much impression of them once you're actually in the town, as the houses all face inwards onto the narrow streets.

Moncontour centres on the pretty, triangular **place du Penthièvre**. Here, the Romanesque tower of the church of St-Mathurin gained a delightfully eccentric new belfry with wooden eaves and grey-slate domes in 1902, and now constitutes the highest point on the hill.

Moncontour's **tourist office** is at 4 place de la Carrière, a short way south of place du Penthièvre (July & Aug daily 10am–12.30pm & 2–6pm; Sept–June Tues, Wed, Fri & Sat 10am–12.30pm & 2–5pm, Thurs 2–5pm; Ⓣ02.96.73.49.57, Ⓦtourisme-moncontour.com). The village lacks hotels, but there's a beautifully situated **B&B**, the four-room *à la Garde Ducale*, in a sixteenth-century house at 10 place Penthièvre (Ⓣ02.96.73.52.18, Ⓦwww.gitesdarmor.com/a-la-garde-ducale; ❸). Near the tourist office, the *Chaudron Magique* (Ⓣ02.96.73.40.34; closed Mon Oct–May) is a medieval-theme **restaurant** where liveried waiters can serve you a decent meal for €20 and upwards. On the final Sunday of August, Moncontour echoes its days of glory by hosting a hectic "medieval fair".

Quintin

QUINTIN, 20km southwest of St-Brieuc, is in the official jargon "a little city of character", still readily recognizable as a seventeenth-century weaving village. Work on the grand **Château de Quintin** began in 1640, and was never completed, but you can tour a few of the rooms (June and first three weeks of Sept daily 2–5.30pm; July & Aug daily 10.30am–noon & 2–6pm; late Sept to Nov daily 2.30–5pm; Dec–May Sun 2.30–5pm; €5). The château is at its most imposing, however, when seen from the River Gouët below.

A twenty-minute stroll up from the river can show you the best of Quintin. Follow the rue du Vau-du-Gouët from the east, and climb a stone staircase up through the vestiges of the old town walls, which are overshadowed by the round **Tour des Archives**, covered with creeping wild flowers. At the top is the late nineteenth-century **Basilique Notre Dame**. Beyond that, you enter the central place 1830, with the rue Grande stretching ahead. Most of its houses are made of elegant grey stone, but a few of their half-timbered predecessors still remain.

Quintin's **tourist office** is at no. 6 on the main place 1830 (July & Aug Mon–Sat 9.30am–12.30pm & 2–6pm, Sun 10.30am–12.30pm & 2.30–4.30pm; Sept–June Tues–Sat 9.30am–noon & 2–5pm; Ⓣ02.96.74.01.51, Ⓦwww.pays-de-quintin.com). The ivy-coated *Commerce*, on the western fringes of the centre at 2 rue Rochenen (Ⓣ02.96.74.94.67, Ⓦwww.hotelducommerce-quintin.com; ❹; closed Fri eve, Sun eve & all day Mon), is a classic little village **hotel**, tasteful if far from fancy. Its solemn but attractive dining room serves good meals from €15 upwards.

Guingamp

The only town of any size along the N12 motorway, as it heads west towards Finistère across the centre of the northern peninsula, is the old weaving centre of **GUINGAMP** – its name possibly the source of the striped or checked fabric "gingham". It's an attractive place of cobbled streets, but there's not much to see beyond the main square – where a fountain bedecked in griffins and gargoyles is overlooked by a splendid pair of lopsided old timber-frame houses propping each other up – and the Black Virgin in the thirteenth-century **basilica**. A big *pardon*, featuring a night procession to the basilica, is held on the first Saturday in July, while a ten-day **Festival de la Danse Bretonne** enlivens the middle of August.

Guingamp's main claim to fame these days is the local **football** team, En Avant de Guingamp, which for a community of eight thousand inhabitants has enjoyed phenomenal success; past players include Didier Drogba. Although two recent sojourns in the French First Division ended in relegation, En Avant won the Coupe de France in 2009, beating Rennes in an all-Breton final, and thereby secured a place in the Europa league. The Roudourou stadium is a short way northwest of the town centre; for fixtures and tickets, which start at €10.60 for regular league games, visit Ⓦeaguingamp.com.

The **tourist office** is in the central place Champ-au-Roy (Tues–Sat 10.15am–noon & 2.15–6pm; Ⓣ02.96.43.73.89, Ⓦwww.ot-guingamp.org), near the **gare routière**, while the **gare SNCF** is 500m southeast.

The white-painted, modernized *d'Armor*, near the station at 44–46 bd Clemenceau (Ⓣ02.96.43.76.16, Ⓦarmor-hotel.com; ❸), is the best-value local **hotel**, and has a nice garden around the back. The finest **restaurant** in town is the *Boissière*, in a park northwest of the centre at 90 rue de l'Yser (Ⓣ02.96.21.06.35; closed Sat eve, Sun lunch & Mon, plus mid-Aug to early Sept), where traditional dinner menus start at €23.

The Ménéz Bré

A dozen kilometres west of Guingamp towards Morlaix, the "mountain" of the **Ménéz Bré** is a rounded and exposed monolith that may be just 302m tall but nonetheless seems a spectacular height amid these plains. In the mid-nineteenth century, the local rector was often observed to climb, laden with books, to the mountain's peak on stormy nights, accompanied only by a donkey. For all his exemplary piety, his parishioners suspected him of sorcery and witchcraft; he was in fact doing early research into electrical forces. Modern visitors hike to the top for dramatic views towards the sea to the north and the rolling hills inland. A footpath leads to the Ménéz Bré from the village of **Tréglamus**, 8km west of Guingamp just off the N12; the round-trip walk is 10km.

The Baie de St-Brieuc

St-Brieuc itself may be more of an obstacle to be avoided than an appealing destination, but it serves as a gateway to the series of attractive little resorts that dot its eponymous bay. It also marks the point at which many visitors become aware that Brittany really does amount to something more than just another stretch of French coastline, and has its own very distinct culture and traditions.

As you move northwest from St-Brieuc along the edge of the V-shaped bay towards Paimpol, the countryside becomes especially rich – it's called the **Goëlo** – while the coast itself grows wilder and harsher. The seaside towns tend to be crammed into narrow rocky inlets or set well back in river estuaries.

St-Brieuc

The major city on the Côte d'Émeraude, **ST-BRIEUC**, is far too busy being the industrial centre of the north to concern itself with entertaining tourists. It's an odd-looking city, with two very deep wooded valleys spanned by viaducts at its core. The streets are hectic, with the centre cut in two by a motorway, unrelieved by any public parks, and not much improved either by a mega-shopping complex. Motorists and cyclists, unfortunately, have little choice but to plough straight through rather than attempting to negotiate the back roads and steep hills around.

At the end of May or start of June, St-Brieuc hosts the **Art Rock Festival** (Ⓣ02.96.52.59.59, Ⓦwww.artrock.org). The Comité Départmentale de Tourisme at 7 rue St-Benoît (Ⓣ02.96.62.72.00, Ⓦwww.cotesdarmor.com) arrange one-day **tours** in summer to visit **craft workshops** of every variety – taxidermists, bakers, farmers and makers of furniture and of cider.

Practicalities

Trains between Paris and Brest stop at the **gare SNCF**, 1km south of the centre, and regular **buses** run to the nearby resorts. The **tourist office** is in the centre, by the cathedral at 7 rue St-Gouéno (July & Aug Mon–Sat 9.30am–7pm, Sun 10am–1pm; Sept–June Mon–Sat 9.30am–12.30pm & 1.30–6pm; Ⓣ02.96.33.32.50, Ⓦwww.baiedesaintbrieuc.com).

The two best central **places to stay** are the *Champ-de-Mars*, 13 rue du Général-Leclerc (Ⓣ02.96.33.60.99, Ⓦhotel-saint-brieuc.fr; ❸), where the old-fashioned green-painted brasserie downstairs, *Le Grand Café*, serves inexpensive pizzas and salads, and the *Duguesclin*, a *Best Western* at 2 place Duguesclin (Ⓣ02.96.33.11.58, Ⓦhotel-duguesclin.com; ❺). St-Brieuc also has a **hostel**, 2km northwest of the place du Champ-de-Mars, in the magnificent fifteenth-century Manoir de la Ville-Guyomard (Ⓣ02.96.78.70.70, Ⓦfuaj.org/saint-brieuc; €17.30 including breakfast); served by bus #3 from the Champ-de-Mars (direction "C.Com. Les Villages"), it also offers bicycles and canoes for rent.

Nice **eating** options in the old quarter, behind the cathedral, include *La Cuisine du Marché*, 4–6 rue des Trois-Frères-Merlin (Ⓣ02.96.61.70.94),

Brittany's sulphurous seaweed

During the summer of 2009, alarming reports spread around the world of the contamination of Brittany's beaches by **toxic seaweed**. The culprit, *ulva lactuca* – commonly known as sea lettuce – grows offshore in vast quantities, fed by the massive amount of nitrates released into the water system by Breton farmers. Once it dies, it washes ashore in unsightly green swathes, to leave beaches lined with thousands of tons of decaying vegetation. As if that weren't bad enough, it produces poisonous hydrogen sulphide as it rots, which builds up beneath a crust then emerges as rotten-egg fumes when the surface is disturbed.

Although almost a hundred Breton beaches were affected, all the way from the Baie du Mont-St-Michel to La Baule, the situation was at its worst on the north coast. At Saint-Michel-en-Grève, a horse died after its rider was overcome by fumes, while a council worker was killed in a lorry crash when he passed out after loading up with seaweed at Binic.

While insisting that the problem is not actually all that widespread, and is by no means unique to Brittany, local councils have – under intense pressure from the French government – promised to instigate comprehensive clear-up procedures. According to campaigners, however, only extensive restrictions on Breton agricultural practices will eliminate the threat altogether.

a friendly bistro serving impeccable classic French dishes, with a €10 lunch time *plat* and dinner menus at €19 and €25. *Youpala*, 5 rue Palasne-de-Champeaux (Ⓣ02.96.94.50.74; closed Sun eve, Mon & Tues, plus first fortnights of June, Sept & Jan), is a more upscale contemporary restaurant.

Binic

BINIC is probably the nicest place to stay on the Baie de St-Brieuc. The whole place is on an appealingly small scale with sandy beaches, a narrow pleasure port crammed with yachts, a jazzed-up little central shopping and dining district, a paved promenade along the seafront, and to either side Devon-like meadows that roll down to the sea. In the mid-nineteenth century, Binic was one of the busiest ports in all France; these days it's simply a minor but attractive tourist resort, with a lucrative sideline of selling mud from the River Ic for fertilizer.

The main beach at Binic, the **Plage de la Banche**, stretches away east of the road as you come into town from St-Brieuc. Spacious even at high tide, packed in summer with families, swimmers, children's clubs and groups playing pétanque, at low tide it becomes absolutely vast (though this was one of the beaches worst affected by 2009's toxic seaweed problem; see p.235). On the far side of town, well away from the through highway and out of sight even from the dead-end little road around the harbour, there's another large but much more secluded beach, the **Plage de l'Avant Port**.

During July and August, Les Vedettes de Bréhat (generally Tues and/or Thurs; departs 8am; €27.50; Ⓣ02.96.55.79.50, Ⓦvedettesdebrehat.com) run **day-trips** from Binic to the **Île de Bréhat** (see p.240).

Practicalities

Binic's **tourist office** is well back from the sea on avenue du Général-de-Gaulle (April–June, Sept & Oct Mon–Fri 9.30am–12.30pm & 2–6pm, Sat 10am–12.30pm & 2–5pm; July & Aug Mon–Sat 9.30am–12.30pm & 2–7pm, Sun 10am–12.30pm & 2–6pm; Nov–March Mon–Fri 9.30am–noon & 2–5.30pm, Sat 10am–noon & 2–5pm; Ⓣ02.96.73.60.12, Ⓦwww.ville-binic.fr).

The only sea-view **accommodation** in town is at the very pleasant *Hôtel Benhuyc*, on the north side of the port at 1 quai Jean-Bart (Ⓣ02.96.73.39.00, Ⓦbenhuyc.com; ⑤). The adjoining *Grand Large* restaurant (Ⓣ02.96.65.25.68), is highly recommended, with menus from €24 up to €42. Less expensive rooms, all en suite, are available above a bar/brasserie immediately across the street (despite the address), in *Le Neptune*, on place de l'Église (Ⓣ02.96.73.61.02; ③).

Also on the north side of the port, the quai du Courcy is lined with **restaurants** and **crêperies**. *La Batelière* (Ⓣ02.96.73.36.26) is a busy, friendly **brasserie** with pizzas and salads at €7–12. Of the many local **campsites**, the best is the secluded three-star *Les Madières* to the south (Ⓣ02.96.79.02.48, Ⓦwww.campinglesmadieres.com; closed mid-Nov to early April), 3km from Binic off the main road near the village of **Pordic**. Set back slightly from the sea, it also has a swimming pool.

St-Quay-Portrieux

ST-QUAY, 5km north of Binic, is considerably more upmarket and a bit soulless, though its sister town of **PORTRIEUX** has at least been livened up by the construction of a yacht marina to replace its crumbling old fishing harbour. The two towns share no less than seven **beaches**: the Plage du Casino in St-Quay and the fine sandy beach next to the port in Portrieux are both

Into the Breton heartland

Plouha, a short way along the D786 from St-Quay, marks the traditional boundary between French-speaking "Upper Brittany" and Breton-speaking "Lower Brittany". As a general indication, you can tell which language used to be spoken in a particular area by its place names. From here on west a preponderance of names begin with the Breton "PLOU" (meaning parish), "TREZ" (sand or beach), "KER" (town) or "PENN" (head). See p.422 for a comprehensive glossary of Breton words.

popular with families; while for more seclusion head for the Grève d'Isnain and the Grève de Fontenay, both in small bays surrounded by cliffs.

During July and August, Les Vedettes de Bréhat (generally Tues and/or Thurs; departs 8.30am; €27.50; ⓣ02.96.55.79.50, ⓦvedettesdebrehat.com) run **day-trips** from Binic to the **Île de Bréhat** (see p.240).

The **tourist office** for St-Quay-Portrieux is at 17bis rue Jeanne-d'Arc (July & Aug Mon–Sat 9am–7pm, Sun 10.30am–12.30pm & 3.30–6pm; Sept–Nov & Feb–June Mon–Sat 9am–12.30pm & 2–6.30pm; Dec & Jan Mon–Sat 9am–12.30pm & 2–6pm; ⓣ02.96.70.40.64, ⓦwww.saintquayportrieux.com). In St-Quay itself, the *Gerbot d'Avoine*, 2 bd de Littoral, near the Plage du Casino (ⓣ02.96.70.40.09, ⓦgerbotdavoine.com; ❸; closed Jan to mid-Feb, restaurant closed in low season on Sun eve, Mon & Tues), is a welcoming, modernized **Logis** worth staying at for its good food. The *Hôtel le Commerce*, 4 rue Georges-Clemenceau (ⓣ02.96.70.41.53; ❷; closed Tues in low season, plus three weeks in Jan), is a cheaper, much plainer alternative, convenient for the beach in Portrieux.

Kermaria-an-Isquit

The little village of **KERMARIA-AN-ISQUIT** is not easy to find, especially if you're coming from the north; the best signposted of its approaches is along the D21 from Plouha. Nonetheless, a fairly constant trickle of visitors make their way here in summer to see the village's **chapel** and its extraordinary **Dance of Death**, one of the most striking of all French medieval images (Easter–Sept Mon–Sat 10am–noon & 2–6pm, Sun 3–6pm; donation).

This huge series of frescoes – depicting Ankou, the skeletal death-figure, leading representatives of all social classes in a *Danse Macabre* – covers the arcades all round the chapel. Painted at the end of the plague-fearing fifteenth century, they were subsequently whitewashed over, not to be rediscovered until 1856. Since then, much of the work has vanished altogether, especially on the ceiling, while in what survives the original colours have faded, and the figures are often no more than silhouettes. However, the fresco has lost little of its power to shock.

In yellow, on a red background, the skeleton alternates with such living characters as a King, a Knight, a Bishop and a Peasant. In verses below, each person pleads for life and laments death, while Ankou insists that all must in the end come to him. A wall to the left of the altar holds a barely discernible representation of the classic medieval theme of the encounter between the *Trois Vifs*, three finely apparelled noblemen out hunting, with the *Trois Morts*, three corpses reflecting in a cemetery on the transience of all things human.

The chapel originally belonged to the lords of the manor of Noë Vert, and is said to be linked by a tunnel, long since flooded, to their manor house 5km away. It was known in Breton as "*Itron Varia An Iskuit*", meaning "Our Lady Who Helps". A small display case behind the altar contains the skull of one of the lords – Jean de Lannion, who died in 1658 – while a couple of grotesque heart-shaped boxes hold the hearts of another and his wife. Just in front of the altar, to the left, a unique statue shows the infant Jesus refusing milk from the Virgin's proffered breast, symbolizing the choice of celestial over terrestrial food.

Abbaye de Beauport

As the D786 north of Kermaria and Binic meanders back towards the shoreline, a couple of kilometres short of Paimpol it passes the substantial ruins of the **Abbaye de Beauport** (daily: mid-June to mid-Sept 10am–7pm, with regular 1hr 30min guided tours; mid-Sept to mid-June 10am–noon & 2–5pm; €5.50; Ⓦwww.abbaye-beauport.com). In summer, the abbey reopens for late-night visits, with imaginative lighting effects (July & Aug, Wed & Sun 10pm–1am; €6), and also hosts weekly Breton music concerts (mid-July to mid-Aug Thurs 9pm; €13).

The abbey of Bellus Portus was established halfway between St-Brieuc and Tréguier in 1202 by Count Alain de Goëlo, as a way station for English pilgrims en route to Santiago de Compostela. Much of its income was drawn from thirteen parishes in Lincolnshire, and it never recovered from the Reformation in England. A merchant from Paimpol bought the entire estate after the Revolution, and his family owned it until 1992.

The abbey is currently being restored, but the main appeal for visitors is the sheer romance of its setting and semi-dilapidated condition. Its stone walls are covered with wild flowers and ivy, the central cloisters are engulfed by a huge tree, and birds flutter about everywhere. The Norman Gothic **chapterhouse** is the most noteworthy building to survive, but wandering through and over the roofless halls you may spot architectural relics from all eras. The monks' refectory looks out across the **salt meadows** where they raised their sheep, and planted orchards on land reclaimed from the sea with an intricate network of dams. Footpaths lead all the way down to the sea, offering the same superb views of the hilltop abbey that must have been appreciated by generations of arriving pilgrims.

Paimpol

An appealing old fishing port that has re-invented itself as a pleasure harbour, **PAIMPOL** focuses on a tangle of cobbled alleyways lined with fine grey-granite houses. During the nineteenth century, it was home to a fifty-strong cod and whaling fleet that sailed for the fisheries of Iceland each February, sent off with a ceremony marked by a famous *pardon*. From then until August or September, the town would be empty of all young men.

The central **place du Martray** is lined with an impressive array of sixteenth-century houses. Cobbled streets lead from here down to the port through the peaceful **quartier latin**, an area once filled with bars and cabarets relieving returning fishermen of their money and frustrations. Thanks to naval shipyards and the like, the open sea is not visible from Paimpol; a maze of waterways leads to its two separate harbours. Both are usually filled with the high masts of yachts, but still also used by the fishing boats that keep a fish market and a plethora of *poissonneries* busy. The tiny port has been very much rebuilt and is rather plain, though it's always lively in summer.

The best **beach** in town, La Tossen, is a short way east of the port, but there are better seaside resorts elsewhere along this stretch of coast, and with its plentiful accommodation Paimpol is more often used as a base for visits to the Île de Bréhat (see p.240).

Arrival and information

Paimpol's **tourist office** is 100m from the pleasure port on place de la République (July & Aug Mon–Sat 9.30am–7.30pm, Sun 10am–1.30pm; Sept–June

Mon–Fri 9.30am–12.30pm & 1.30–6.30pm, Sat 9.30am–12.30pm & 1.30–6.30pm; ⓣ02.96.20.83.16, ⓦpaimpol-goelo.com). The **gare SNCF** and **gare routière** are also near the pleasure port, next to each other on avenue du Général-de-Gaulle.

Between early May and late September, the restored **steam train** known as **La Vapeur de Trieux** chugs its way on regular excursions from the *gare SNCF* through the Trieux Valley between Paimpol and Pontrieux to the southwest, passing within view of the Château de la Roche-Jagu. The schedule is extremely intricate, with no trains on Mondays, and none on Tuesdays except in the height of summer, but on most other days there's a departure from Paimpol at either 10.15am or 11.15am, and between mid-July and August there's often a 3.40pm departure as well (reservations essential; €22 return; ⓣ08.92.39.14.27, ⓦwww.vapeurdutrieux.com).

Accommodation

Most of the nicest of Paimpol's many **hotels** are clustered together on the northern side of the port, either right on the waterfront or in the network of semi-pedestrianized little alleyways just behind.

Berthelot 1 rue du Port ⓣ02.96.20.88.66. Small, somewhat kitsch but very hospitable family-run hotel, offering a dozen simple rooms – some en suite, some not, with one of the latter suitable for four people – set slightly back from the pleasure port. ❶

Le Goëlo 4 quai Duguay-Trouin ⓣ02.96.20.82.74, ⓦlegoelo.com. Modern, double-glazed hotel (equipped with a lift) in the ugly new block that lines the inland side of the fishing harbour; some of the rather plain rooms overlook the port. ❸

K'Loys 21 quai Morand ⓣ02.96.20.40.01, ⓦk-loys.com. Imposing, very comfortable harbourside mansion, where sea-view rooms cost significantly extra. There's also a little pavement crêperie-bistro. ❺–❻

Origano 7bis rue du Quai ⓣ02.96.22.05.49. Somewhat plain, but very comfortable hotel, on a quiet cobbled street opposite the *Berthelot*. Closed mid-Nov to March. ❷

Eating and drinking

Enticing **restaurants** stand on all sides of the port, as well as in the backstreets of the town proper, near the marketplace. The *Corto Maltese* **bar** at 11 rue du Quai, very near the *Berthelot* and *Origano* hotels, serves a fine selection of British and other beers.

La Cotriade quai Armand-Dayot ⓣ02.96.20.81.08, ⓦla-cotriade.com. Uncompromising gourmet restaurant on the far side of the harbour to the town centre, that's a great bet for authentic fish dishes. Menus from €25, bursting with crab, prawns and scallops. Dinner nightly in summer, plus lunch on Tues, Thurs, Fri & Sun; otherwise closed all day Mon, Wed eve & Sat lunch.

Crêperie-Restaurant Ty Krampoul 11 pl du Martray ⓣ02.96.20.86.34. Cavernous place just a few steps from the port in the main square in the heart of town, that's popular with locals not only for its inexpensive €4–10 *galettes*, but also for its good-value daily bistro specials and large *terrasse* on the square. Closed Sun.

La Vieille Tour 13 rue de l'Église ⓣ02.96.20.83.18. Cosy but sophisticated upstairs dining room, tucked away from the port in the cobbled pedestrian area, and offering top-quality seafood on a quartet of constantly changing menus; the €29 one is usually good enough, but you can pay up to €50. Closed Sun eve & all Mon, plus Wed in low season.

Loguivy-sur-mer

If Paimpol is too crowded for you, it's well worth continuing a few kilometres further across the headland to reach the tiny fishing hamlet of **LOGUIVY**. All of the long river inlets along this northern coast tend to conceal tiny coves – at Loguivy a working harbour manages to squeeze into one such gap in the rocks, with alluring footpaths disappearing up the cliffs to either side. **Lenin** holed up here for his summer holidays for two months in 1902, straight from three years of forced labour in Siberia.

Loguivy's one **hotel** is right on the waterfront, looking out towards Bréhat: *Le Grand Large* (Ⓣ02.96.20.90.18, Ⓦhotelrestaurantaugrandlarge.com; ❸; closed Jan, restaurant closed Sun eve & Mon in low season) has nice sea-view rooms, serves superb fish dinners from €17 – look out for the chef's speciality, a salad of seared scallops – and has a nice little outdoor terrace. Just back from the sea, *Chez Gaud Café du Port* is a funky, folk-art-decorated little café.

The Île de Bréhat

Two kilometres off the coast at Pointe de l'Arcouest, 6km northwest of Paimpol, the **ÎLE DE BRÉHAT** gives the appearance of spanning great latitudes. In reality, there are two islands, joined by a tiny slip of a bridge. On the north side lie windswept meadows of hemlock and yarrow, sloping down to chaotic erosions of rock; on the south, you're in the midst of palm trees, mimosa and eucalyptus. All around is a multitude of little islets – some accessible at low tide, others *propriété privée*, most just pink-orange rocks. All in all, this has to be one of the most beautiful places in Brittany, renowned as a sanctuary not only for rare species of **wild flowers**, but also for **birds** of all kinds. Individual private gardens are also meticulously tended, so you can always anticipate a magnificent display of colour, for example in summer from the erupting blue acanthus.

A high proportion of the homes on this island paradise belong to summer-only visitors from Paris and beyond. In winter, the remaining three hundred or so natives have the place to themselves, without even a *gendarme*; the summer sees two imported from the mainland, along with upwards of three thousand temporary residents and a hundred times as many day-trippers.

Information and accommodation

Bréhat's **tourist office** is in the old Mairie in the main square in Le Bourg (July & Aug Mon–Sat 10am–1pm & 2–5pm, Sun 10am–1pm; March–June & Sept

Getting to Bréhat

Bréhat is connected by regular **ferry** from the Pointe de l'Arcouest, 6km northwest of Paimpol; buses run frequently in summer from Paimpol's *gare SNCF* to the Pointe de l'Arcouest. Sailings, with Les Vedettes de Bréhat (Ⓣ02.96.55.79.50, Ⓦvedettesdebrehat.com), are roughly hourly between April and September, with a couple of extra sailings in July and August, and every 1 hour 30 minutes for the rest of the year; the first boat out to Bréhat is at 8.15am in summer, and the last boat back at 7.45pm. The return trip costs €8.50, whether for a day-trip or a longer stay, while bringing your own bike costs an additional €15; to bring a bike in summer, you have to catch a ferry before 9.30am, and leave the island before 4pm. You can purchase tickets at the tourist office in Paimpol (see p.238) as well as at the Pointe de l'Arcouest.

The same company also operates guided **boat tours** around the island from the Pointe de l'Arcouest (April to mid-July & Sept 6 daily; mid-July to Aug 11 daily; Oct–March 1 daily at 2.30pm, depending on weather and tides; 45min; €13), and summer-only trips from Erquy, Dahouët, Binic and St-Quay-Portrieux.

To a varying schedule, a restored **sailing boat**, once part of the sardine fleet, takes day-trips from Paimpol to around Bréhat (Ⓣ02.96.55.99.99, Ⓦwww.eulalie-paimpol.com; €42).

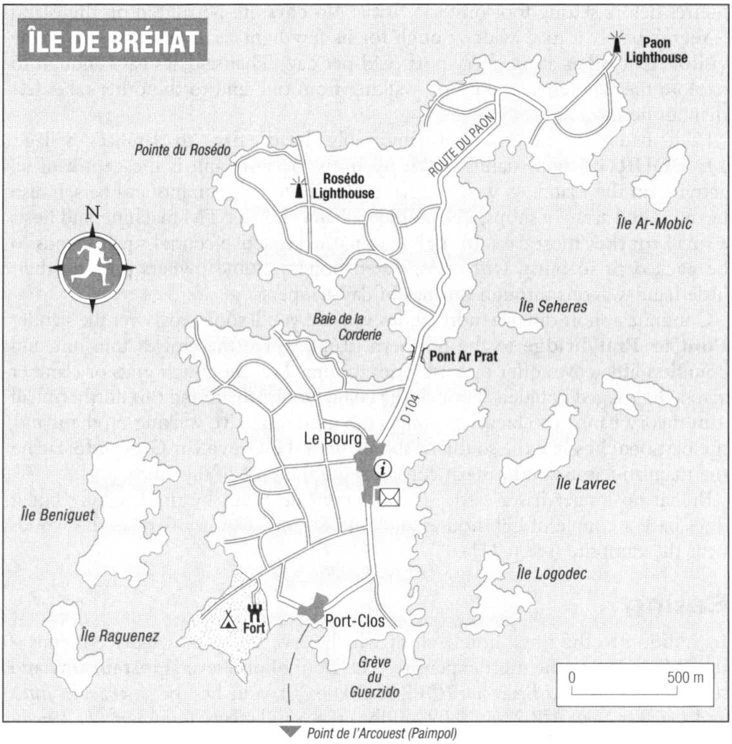

Mon, Tues & Thurs–Sat 10am–12.30pm & 1.30–4.30pm; Oct–Feb Mon & Thurs–Sat 10am–12.30pm & 1.30–4.30pm; ⓣ02.96.20.04.15, ⓦbrehat-infos.fr).

All three of the island's **hotels** tend to be permanently booked through the summer, and closed for at least part of the winter. There's also a wonderful municipal **campsite**, in the woods high above the sea west of the port (ⓣ02.96.20.02.36; closed mid-Sept to mid-June); when it's closed, you can pitch your tent almost anywhere.

Bellevue Port-Clos ⓣ02.96.20.00.05, ⓦhotel-bellevue-brehat.fr. Imposing, white-painted mansion, right by the *embarcadère* in Port-Clos, where several of the crisp, bright bedrooms enjoy wonderful sea views. *Demi-pension* only in high season Closed mid-Nov to mid-Feb. 6

Men-Joliguet Port-Clos ⓣ02.96.20.08.29, ⓦlocations-brehat.net. Bréhat's best value; this village house beside the *Bellevue* has been modernized to hold bright, sleek B&B rooms, and has a lovely sea-view garden. Closed Nov–Easter. 4

Aux Pêcheurs Le Bourg ⓣ02.96.20.00.14. Small hotel on the main square in Le Bourg, with a nice little garden terrace. *Demi-pension* compulsory for stays of longer than two nights in high season. Closed Jan. 3

Vieille Auberge Le Bourg ⓣ02.96.20.00.24, ⓦwww.brehat-vieilleauberge.eu. Eighteenth-century privateer's house, on your left as you enter Le Bourg, with fifteen simple but very light rooms. *Demi-pension* only in high season. Closed Dec–Easter. 6

Around the island

All boats to Bréhat arrive at the small harbour of **PORT-CLOS**, though depending on the level of the tide passengers may have to walk several hundred metres before setting foot on terra firma. No **cars** are permitted on the island – there's barely a road wide enough for its few light farm vehicles – so many visitors rent **bikes** at the ferry port (€15 per day). That said, it's easy enough to explore the whole place on foot; walking from one end to the other takes less than an hour.

Each batch of new arrivals invariably heads first to Bréhat's village, **LE BOURG**, which stands 500m up from the port and is the centre of all activity on the island. As well as a handful of hotels, restaurants and bars, it also has a limited array of shops, a post office, a bank and an ATM machine, and hosts a small **market** most days. In high season, the attractive central square tends to be packed fit to burst, with exasperated holiday-home owners pushing their little hand-wagons through throngs of day-trippers.

Continue a short distance north, however, and you'll soon cross over the slender **Pont ar Prat bridge** to the northern island, where the crowds thin out, and countless little coves offer opportunities to sprawl on the tough grass or clamber across the rugged boulders. Though the coastal footpath around this northern half – in theory, banned to bicycles – offers the most attractive walking on the island, the best **beaches** line the southern shores, with the **Grève du Guerzido**, facing the mainland at its southeastern corner, being the pick of the crop.

Bréhat no longer has a castle (it was blown up twice by the English), but it does have a couple of lighthouses and a nineteenth-century **fort**, in the woods near the campsite (see p.241).

Eating

In addition to the three hotels, all of which serve the usual set-price menus – the *Bellevue* being the most expensive – Le Bourg holds several **restaurants** and snack places, like *La Brazérade* (☎02.96.20.06.30), your best bet for *moules frites*, and *Les Blés Noirs* (☎02.96.20.09.44) for crêpes and salads. Elsewhere, *Le Paradis Rose*, just short of the Paon Lighthouse on the north island (☎02.96.20.03.89; closed mid-Sept to Easter), is in reality no more than a crêpe and hot-dog stand, but is set in such a ravishing garden that it makes an ideal lunch-time halt for round-island walkers.

The Côte de Granit Rose

The whole of the northernmost stretch of the Breton coast, from Bréhat to Trégastel, is loosely known as the **Côte de Granit Rose**. Great granite boulders are scattered in the sea around the island of Bréhat, and at the various headlands to the west, but the most memorable stretch lies around **Perros-Guirec**, where the pink granite rocks are eroded into fantastic shapes.

Pink granite, glittering sharply but wearing smooth and soft, is an absolutely gorgeous stone – which is just as well, for everything in this area seems to be made of it. The houses are faced with granite blocks, and the streets paved with them; the breakwaters in the sea are granite, and the polished pillars of the banks are granite; the hotels even have overgrown granite mini-golfs with little pink granite megaliths as obstacles; and the markets claim to sell *granit-smith* apples.

The Sillon du Talbert

The D786 turns west from Paimpol, crossing a bridge over a green *ria* after 5km to reach the little town of **LÉZARDRIEUX**. Few visitors take the time to explore the peninsula that stretches off to the north from here. Though known as the Presqu'Île Sauvage, in truth it's dotted with sleepy villages and holiday homes and while it's certainly pretty, it's no more wild than anywhere else in these parts. However, at its northeastern tip, 10km out from Lézardrieux, it does hold one unusual feature.

The **Sillon du Talbert** is a narrow, windswept, curving spit of sand and shingle that reaches out 3.5km into the ocean, and makes for a splendid bracing walk with great opportunities for watching seabirds. At its far end stands the 45m **lighthouse** of Héaux, while at its start, *Bigouden Blues* (Ⓣ02.96.22.94.97, Ⓦbigouden.blues.free.fr) serves lobster and chips on its sea-view terrace for €18, or the more usual *moules frites* for €10.

Outside **KERBORS**, on the peninsula halfway between the Sillon and Tréguier, the *Manoir de Troezel Vras* is an irresistibly tranquil rural **B&B**, set in an old farmhouse that has been sensitively converted to a very high standard (Ⓣ02.96.22.89.68, Ⓦtroezel-vras.com; ❹; no credit cards; closed mid-Oct to March). The five large guest rooms are splendidly furnished, and the friendly hosts serve an excellent nightly dinner for €21; there's no menu, you just get what you're given.

Tréguier

Ten kilometres west of Lézardrieux, another bridge, this time across the mouth of the Jaudy River, leads into the lovely old town of **TRÉGUIER**. One of the very few hill-towns in Brittany, set at the confluence of the Jaudy with the Guindy river, it was rebuilt on this fortified elevation in 848 AD after an earlier monastery was destroyed by Norman raiders. It does however spread down to include a small commercial and pleasure port by the Jaudy.

The central unmissable feature of Tréguier is the **Cathédrale de St-Tugdual**, whose geometric Gothic spire, dotted with holes, contrasts sharply with its earlier Romanesque "Hastings" tower. Inside, the masonry blocks are appealingly crude, and dripping with damp that has somehow spared the wooden stalls. The most elaborate of several recumbent tombs is that of **St Yves**, a native of the town who died in 1303 and – for his incorruptibility – became the patron saint of lawyers. Attempts to bribe him continue to this day; his tomb is surrounded by marble plaques and an inferno of candles invoking his aid. An annual *pardon* of St Yves is held on the Sunday closest to his feast day, May 19.

The half-timbered houses of the pretty square outside look down on a portly, seated statue of the writer and philosopher **Ernest Renan**, born here in 1823, whose work formed part of the great nineteenth-century attempt to reinterpret traditional religious faith in the light of scientific discoveries. Worthy Catholics were so incensed at the erection of this memorial in 1903 that they soon built their own "Calvary of Reparation" on the quayside.

Practicalities

Tréguier's **tourist office** is at 67 rue Ernest-Renan, opposite the commercial port (mid-June to mid-Sept Mon–Sat 9am–7pm, Sun 10am–1pm & 2–6pm; mid-Sept to mid-June Tues–Sat 10am–1pm & 2–6pm; Ⓣ02.96.92.22.33, Ⓦpaysdetreguier.com). Down by the port, you'll find two **hotels**: the fancy *Aigue-Marine*, close to the bridge, which has a swimming pool and jacuzzi (Ⓣ02.96.92.97.00, Ⓦwww.aiguemarine.fr; ❺; restaurant closed Sun & Mon in low season), or the much more basic *d'Estuaire* (Ⓣ06.15.08.77.03; ❶), which has great views from its upstairs dining room and serves a reasonable €13 menu, with *moules* followed by fish of the day and dessert. Up in town, the *St-Yves*, at

4 rue Colvestre near the cathedral, is equally cheap, and charges very little extra for en-suite facilities (☎02.96.92.33.49; ❶; closed Thurs).

The upper town holds a fine array of places to **eat**. The *Poissonnerie Moulinet*, above a fish shop just below the cathedral at 2 rue Ernest-Renan (☎02.96.92.30.27), is a sort of tasting room where you can buy superb seafood platters at low prices, perhaps to take away and eat in the square. For a more formal sit-down meal, *Le Canotier*, opposite at 5 rue Ernest-Renan (☎02.96.92.41.70; closed Sat lunch, plus Wed eve in winter), serves several full fish menus, from €14.

During Tréguier's Wednesday **market**, clothes and so on are spread out in the square up by the cathedral, with food and fresh fish further down by the port. The cafés and delis of the main square save their best displays for that day.

Plougrescant

Perhaps the best-known photographic image of Brittany is of a small seafront cottage somehow squeezed between two mighty pink-granite boulders. Surprisingly few visitors, however, manage to see the house in real life. It stands 10km north of Tréguier, close to the tip of another under-explored peninsula, and just 2km out from the village of **PLOUGRESCANT**. The precise spot tends to be marked on regional maps as either **Le Gouffre** or Le Gouffre du Castel-Meur, and is signposted off the coastal road a short way west of the Pointe du Château. Although you can't visit the cottage itself, which actually faces inland, across a small sheltered bay with its back to the open sea, the shoreline nearby offers superb short walks, and there's a little summer-only café selling snacks and ice creams. The owners of the cottage recently won a large financial settlement against advertisers who used its image without permission, so perhaps it will be less ubiquitous in years to come.

There's a lovely seafront **hotel** in **TRÉVOU-TRÉGUIGNEC**, 8km west. The *Kerbugalic* is set in large gardens, overlooking the bay of Trestel (☎02.96.23.72.15, ⓦwww.kerbugalic.fr; ❹; closed Jan); its larger rooms have gorgeous sea-view terraces, and dinner menus in its panoramic **restaurant** start with a vegetarian option at €21 (closed Tues & Wed; lunch Fri–Sun only).

Château de la Roche-Jagu

About 10km inland from Tréguier and Lézardrieux, the fifteenth-century **Château de la Roche-Jagu** (daily: Feb–Easter & Nov 2–5pm; Easter–June & mid-Sept to Oct 10am–noon & 2–6pm; July to mid-Sept 10am–7pm; park access free, château €4, or more during special exhibitions; ⓦcotesdarmor.fr/larochejagu) stands on a heavily wooded slope above the meanders of the Trieux River, just as it starts to widen. It's a really gorgeous building, a harmonious combination of fortress and home. The central solid facade is composed of irregular reddish-granite boulders, cemented together, and incorporating one venerable turreted tower at the front and one at the back.

The château plays host to lavish **annual exhibitions**, usually on some sort of Celtic theme. The rooms within are bare, but it's well worth climbing right up to the top of the building. Here you can admire the beautiful woodwork of the restored eaves, and walk the two long indoor galleries, one of wood and one of stone, to enjoy tremendous views over the river. Outside, the modern landscaped park is traced through by several **hiking trails**.

The *Restaurant de la Château de la Roche-Jagu* (☎02.96.95.16.08), in the castle gateway, offers lunch menus on the lawns from €15.

The seabird sanctuary of Sept-Îles

The seven craggy islands that constitute the **bird sanctuary of Sept-Îles** were originally set aside in 1912 to protect puffins – whose population had dropped in the space of twenty years from an estimated fifteen thousand breeding couples to a mere four hundred couples. The new sanctuary was, however, rapidly "discovered" by other seabirds, and thirteen different species now nest here for all or part of the year. The puffins take up residence between March and July; other visitors include storm petrels (April–Sept), gannets (Jan–Sept), kittiwakes (March–July), and guillemots (Feb–July).

Between February and November each year, **boat trips** out to the islands leave from the *gare maritime* on the Plage de Trestraou in Perros-Guirec (Ⓣ02.96.91.10.00, Ⓦwww.armor-decouverte.fr). Trips vary from 75-minute excursions to the two easternmost islands, Île Malban and Île Rouzic (€14), a two-hour trip which adds on Île Bono and Île aux Moines (€16), and a two-and-a-half-hour trip that includes a brief landfall on Île aux Moines, the one island that permits human visitors (€19). Precisely what's available on any particular day depends on the tides, and in high season there are additional departures from Ploumanac'h and Trégastel (Ⓣ02.96.15.31.00).

Perros-Guirec

PERROS-GUIREC is the most popular resort along this coast, if not perhaps the most exciting. It has a reputation that seems to attract the retired – its tourist brochures list places where you can get a game of bridge or Scrabble – and an array of shops intended to match: antiques, bric-a-brac and pottery with a big line in granite guillemots and puffins. Perros is also a lot less city-like than it looks on the maps: most of its roads turn out to be tree-lined avenues of suburban villas.

The commercial streets of the centre (up the hill from the port) hold little of interest, and are often jammed solid with traffic in summer. Much more enjoyable is to take a walk around the headland to see the magnificent view from the **Table d'Orientation** at the sharp curve of the boulevard Clemenceau. The best beach is the **Plage de Trestraou**, on the opposite side of town to the port, a long curve of sand speckled with bars, snack bars and crazy-golf courses.

Practicalities

Perros-Guirec's extremely efficient **tourist office** is at 21 place de l'Hôtel-de-Ville (July & Aug Mon–Sat 9am–7.30pm, Sun 10am–12.30pm & 4–7pm; Sept–June Mon–Sat 9am–12.30pm & 2–6.30pm; Ⓣ02.96.23.21.15, Ⓦwww.perros-guirec.com). Ask for their schedule of **guided walks** in the vicinity.

What few **buses** serve Perros-Guirec arrive at and leave from the Bassin du Lin Kin in the port, a few hundred metres down from the town centre. **Bikes** and **kayaks** can be rented from TS Loisirs, 61 bd des Traouïéro (Ⓣ02.96.91.66.61). It's also possible to **surf** here; for lessons, contact the École de Surf de Bretagne, 2 rue Maréchal-Joffre (Ⓣ02.96.23.18.38, Ⓦwww.ecole-surf-bretagne.fr).

Good **hotels** include two places with tremendous sea views, the *Gulf Stream*, perched high on the hillside at 26 rue des Sept-Îles (Ⓣ02.96.23.21.86, Ⓦgulf-stream-hotel-bretagne.com; ③), which serves dinner to guests only for €25, and the *Hôtel du Port*, facing the pleasure port (Ⓣ02.96.23.21.79, Ⓦperros-hotel.com; ③), where several of the rather plain, modern rooms enjoy superb panoramas, and there's no restaurant. An attractive **campsite**, *du Trestraou*, 89 av du Casino (Ⓣ02.96.23.08.11, Ⓦtrestraou-camping.com; closed Oct–April), is just across Trestraou beach.

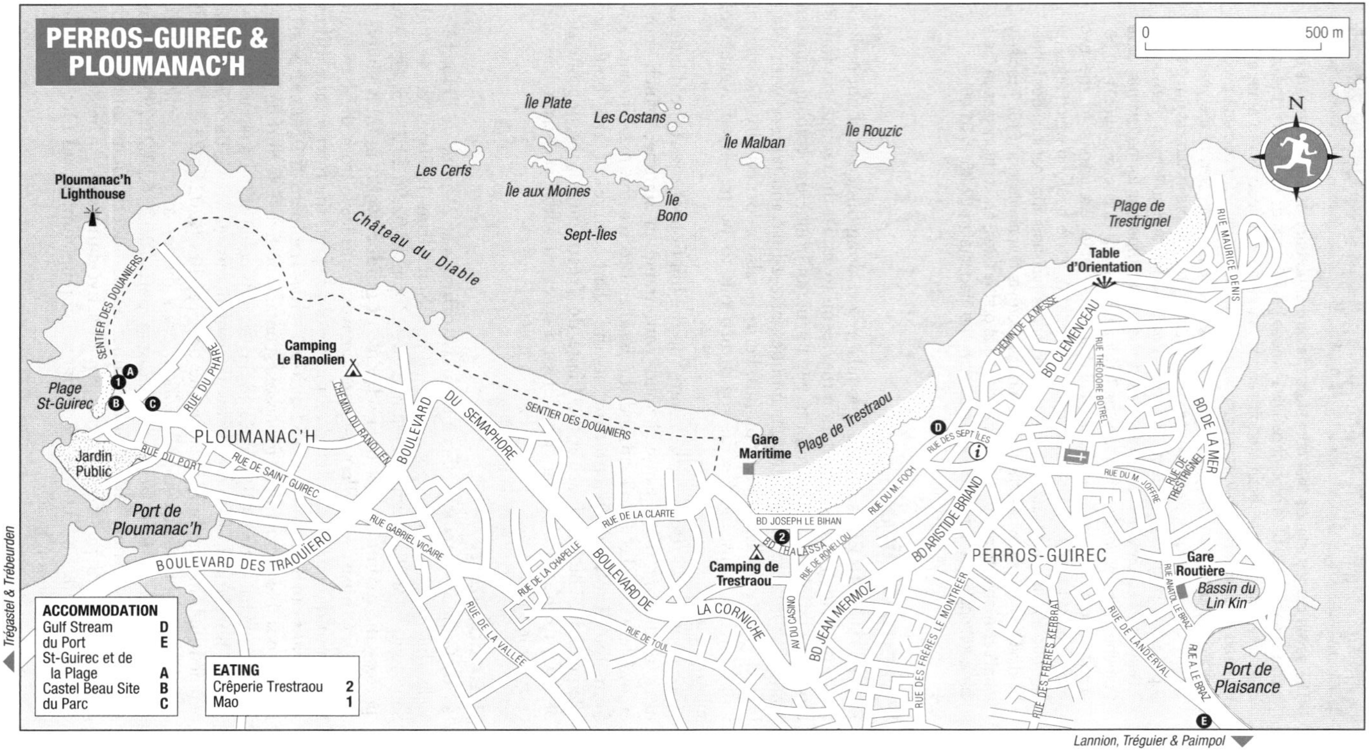
PERROS-GUIREC & PLOUMANAC'H
0
500 m
N
Île Plate
Les Costans
Île Malban
Île Rouzic
Les Cerfs
Île aux Moines
Île Bono
Sept-Îles
Château du Diable
Ploumanac'h Lighthouse
Plage de Trestrignel
Table d'Orientation
SENTIER DES DOUANIERS
Camping Le Ranolien
Plage St-Guirec
RUE DU PHARE
CHEMIN DU RANOLIEN
BOULEVARD DU SEMAPHORE
PLOUMANAC'H
Jardin Public
RUE DU PORT
RUE DE SAINT GUIREC
Port de Ploumanac'h
RUE GABRIEL VICAIRE
BOULEVARD DES TRAOUÏERO
Gare Maritime
Plage de Trestraou
RUE DE LA CLARTE
BD JOSEPH LE BIHAN
BD THALASSA
RUE DE ROHELLOU
Camping de Trestraou
RUE DE LA CHAPELLE
BOULEVARD DE LA CORNICHE
RUE DE LA VALLÉE
RUE DE TOUL
AV DU CASINO
BD JEAN MERMOZ
RUE DES FRÈRES LE MONTREER
RUE DU M. FOCH
RUE DES SEPT ÎLES
BD ARISTIDE BRIAND
PERROS-GUIREC
CHEMIN DE LA MESSE
BD CLEMENCEAU
RUE THÉODORE BOTREL
RUE MAURICE DENIS
BD DE LA MER
RUE DU M. JOFFRE
RUE DE TRESTRIGNEL
Gare Routière
RUE ANATOL LE BRAZ
Bassin du Lin Kin
RUE DES FRÈRES KERBRAT
RUE DE LANDERVAL
RUE A. LE BRAZ
Port de Plaisance
Trégastel & Trébeurden
Lannion, Tréguier & Paimpol
ACCOMMODATION
Gulf Stream D
du Port E
St-Guirec et de la Plage A
Castel Beau Site B
du Parc C
EATING
Crêperie Trestraou 2
Mao 1

As for **eating**, it's fun to have lunch in one of the countless sea-view places down by the Plage du Trestraou, like the *Crêperie Trestraou*, 20 bd Thalassa (ⓣ02.96.23.04.34; closed Wed & Thurs off season).

The Sentier des Douaniers

Perros-Guirec's Trestraou beach is made of ordinary sand; the pink granite coast proper starts just beyond its western end. One of the finest coastal walks in Brittany, the **Sentier des Douaniers** pathway, winds round the clifftops to **Ploumanac'h** past an astonishing succession of deformed and water-sculpted rocks. Allow around an hour to walk its full length one-way, assuming you take the time to enjoy the many splendours en route. Birds wheel overhead towards the sanctuary, and battered boats shelter in the narrow inlets or bob uncontrollably out on the waves. There are patches and brief causeways of grass, clumps of purple heather and yellow gorse. Occasionally the rocks have crumbled into a sort of granite grit to make up a tiny beach.

Ploumanac'h

Although it's much smaller than Perros-Guirec, the village of **PLOUMANAC'H**, 2km west, is a more active resort, largely because the dominant clientele here is families with youngish children. In fact, few places on earth can offer quite such enchantment for energetic kids, who love to scramble around the surreal sandscape revealed when the long tides draw out. Around the delightful crescent **beach**, glinting pink granite boulders, fringed with green seaweed, erupt from the depths, and rock pools bursting with crabs and other mysteries just wait to be explored. The most obvious focal point is the tiny **Château du Diable**, framing the horizon on one of the countless little islands in the bay – which was where the novel *Quo Vadis* was written around the end of the nineteenth century. When the tide is in, head instead for the pleasantly wild **municipal park** that separates the two halves of Ploumanac'h, the Bourg and the Plage.

In summer, half-day **boat trips** out to the Sept-Îles (see box, p.245) also run from the little port in Ploumanac'h, south around the headland from the beach; call ⓣ02.96.91.44.40 for schedules.

Practicalities

The road into Ploumanac'h comes to a dead end at the beach. A beautifully situated and good-value **hotel**, the *St-Guirec et de la Plage* (ⓣ02.96.91.40.89, ⓦhotelsaint-guirec.com), commands the prime beachfront spot; both it and its restaurant were however being totally renovated as this book went to press, so you'll have to contact it directly to see its current rates. Immediately across the road, with a similarly superb prospect of the beach, the imposing *Castel Beau Site*, plage du St-Guirec (ⓣ02.96.91.40.87, ⓦcastelbeausite.com; ❻), has traditionally been a much more lavish alternative, with a more expensive restaurant into the bargain.

Just short of the beach, the small lively rue St-Guirec leads to the little square that serves as the main local car park. The *Mao*, at 147 rue St-Guirec (ⓣ02.96.91.40.92; closed Mon, plus Oct–March), is a former snack bar that has expanded to take over several adjacent buildings, including a Polynesian-style thatched hut; it offers bargain menus from €10 (even less for crêpes) and, like most places in Ploumanac'h, it has special cheap menus for children. The *Hôtel du Parc*, on the square itself at 175 place St-Guirec (ⓣ02.96.91.40.80, ⓦwww.www-hotelduparc.com; ❸; closed mid-Nov to March), has reasonably priced if unspectacular rooms, and serves good seafood menus as well as lavish buffet breakfasts.

A nice place to **camp** is the four-star *Le Ranolien* (ⓣ02.96.91.65.65, ⓦleranolien.fr; closed mid-Sept to March), which backs onto the Sentier des Douaniers (see p.247) near a little beach about halfway round; it's also directly accessible on the other side by road, and has its own swimming pools and waterslides.

Trégastel-Plage

Three kilometres west of Ploumanac'h along a pretty coastal road, **TRÉGASTEL-PLAGE** boasts a delightful sheltered beach with a couple of huge lumps of pink granite slap in the middle. Sadly, however, the village itself is an ugly stretch of concrete, centring on the seafront **Forum**, a swimming pool and leisure complex. A little way back from the seafront, a small **aquarium** is all but crushed beneath another massive pile of boulders (April–June & Sept Mon, Sat & Sun 2–6pm, Tues–Fri 10am–6pm; July & Aug daily 10am–7pm; Oct & March daily except Mon 2–5pm; €7; ⓦwww.aquarium-tregastel.com).

Of Trégastel's three **hotels**, the *Beau Séjour*, 5 plage du Coz-Pors (ⓣ02.96.23.88.02, ⓦbeausejoursarl.com; ❹; closed mid-Jan to mid-Feb & mid-Nov to mid-Dec), has the best sea views, especially from the terrace of its restaurant, *Le Roof* (closed Mon). **Campsites** include the three-star *Tourony* by the beach (ⓣ02.96.23.86.61, ⓦcamping-tourony.com; closed late Sept to March).

Trébeurden

Outbreaks of bizarre red rocks have all but petered out by the time you reach **TRÉBEURDEN**, another 11km southwest along the coast from Trégastel, but you do at least come to one more long curving sandy beach, much less developed than most in these parts. A Logis de France **hotel**, *Ker An Nod* is splendidly situated on a bluff above the sea, with fabulous views, on rue de Pors-Termen (ⓣ02.96.23.50.21, ⓦwww.kerannod.com; ❸; closed mid-Nov to March), and serves menus from €24. There's also a lovely **hostel**, *Le Toëno*, 2km north of town at 60 rue de la Corniche (ⓣ02.96.23.52.22, ⓦfuaj.org/trebeurden; dorm beds €12.10; closed Nov–Feb).

Pleumeur-Bodou

Head inland from Trégastel on the **route de Calvaire**, rather than along the coast, and you'll come in a few kilometres to a spectacle stranger than anything the erosions can manage: an old stone saint halfway up a high calvary raising his arm to bless or harangue the gleaming white discs and puffball dome of the **Pleumeur-Bodou Telecommunications Centre**. A new pink granite "dolmen" commemorates its opening in 1962, when it was the first receiving station to pick up signals from the American Telstar satellite. No longer operational, the centre has been remodelled as a **Museum of Telecommunications**, also known as **Cosmopolis** (April & Sept Mon–Fri 10am–6pm, Sat & Sun 2–6pm; May & June daily 10am–6pm; July & Aug daily 10am–7pm; Oct–March school hols only Mon–Fri 10am–6pm, Sun 2–6pm; €7; ⓦwww.leradome.com). Inside the golf ball itself, the **Radôme**, spectacular *son-et-lumière* shows explain the history of the whole ensemble, and there's also a smaller **planetarium** alongside.

A final incongruous note is struck by the reconstructed **Gaulish village** nearby (April–June & Sept Mon–Fri & Sun 2–6pm; July & Aug daily 10.30am–7pm; €4.50; ⓦlevillagegaulois.org), which is designed to raise money for a French charity working in Africa, and thus incorporates some traditional huts from Togo.

The Bay of Lannion

Despite being located significantly back from the sea on the estuary of the River Léguer, **Lannion** gives its name to the next bay west along the Breton coast – and it's the bay rather than the town that is most likely to impress visitors. One enormous beach stretches from **St-Michel-en-Grève**, which is little more than a bend in the road, as far as **Locquirec**; at low tide you can walk hundreds of metres out on the sands.

Lannion

Set amid plummeting hills and stairways, **LANNION** is a historic city with streets of medieval housing, and a couple of interesting old churches. As a hi-tech telecommunications centre, it's also one of modern Brittany's real success stories – hence its rather self-satisfied nickname, *ville heureuse* or "happy town".

In addition to admiring the half-timbered houses around the place de Général-Leclerc and along rue des Chapeliers (look out for nos. 3 and 4), it's well worth climbing from the town up the 142 granite steps that lead to the twelfth-century Templar **Église de Brélévenez**. This church was remodelled three hundred years later to incorporate a granite bell tower, and the views from its terrace are quite stupendous.

Lannion's **tourist office** is on the quai d'Aguillon (July & Aug Mon–Sat 9am–7pm, Sun 10am–1pm; Sept–June Mon–Sat 9.30am–12.30pm & 2–6pm; Ⓣ02.96.46.41.00, Ⓦwww.ot-lannion.fr). The **gare SNCF** is on the far side of the river, across an attractive little bridge,

The only central **accommodation** – the *Ibis*, opposite the station at 30 av de Général-de-Gaulle (Ⓣ02.96.37.03.67, Ⓦwww.ibishotel.com; ④) – has modern rooms, but no restaurant; the *Tire-Bouchon* is a good traditional **restaurant** in the heart of town at 8 rue de Keriavily (Ⓣ02.96.37.10.43; closed Sun, Sat lunch & Mon lunch). There's also a year-round **hostel**, *Les Korrigans*, handily near the station and the town centre at 6 rue du 73e Territorial (Ⓣ02.96.37.91.28, Ⓦfuaj.org/lannion-les-korrigans; dorm beds €17.30 including breakfast). Its friendly management do not operate a curfew, and they arrange birdwatching and similar expeditions, and rent out bikes – not that you'll necessarily relish cycling around Lannion itself, with its gruelling hills.

Ploumilliau

At the trim little inland village of **PLOUMILLIAU**, 10km southwest of Lannion, the weathered granite parish **church** stands surrounded by beds of colourful flowers. Dating from the early seventeenth century, it contains a beautiful pulpit and sculpted wooden panelling, but is really worth a visit for its unique white-painted wooden representation of **Ankou**, the skeletal symbol of death (daily 2–6pm). The statue, carrying a scythe to catch the living and a spade to bury them, was once carried in local processions.

In a magnificent setting at the northern end of the enormous beach at St-Michel-en-Grève, 4km west of Ploumilliau – another spot plagued by toxic seaweed in 2009 (see p.235) – the *Hotel de la Plage* (Ⓣ02.96.35.74.43,

Ⓦhoteldelaplage.be; ❶) makes a great overnight stop. En-suite rooms cost a little extra, and dinner menus start at €18.

Locquirec

Further huge and very inviting beaches lie to both sides of the peninsula that's tipped by the perfect little village of **LOCQUIREC**, across the bay from Lannion and officially just within the *département* of Finistère. Around the main port, smart houses stand in sloping gardens, looking very southern English with their whitewashed stone panels, grey-slate roofs and jutting turreted windows. The small beach here is said to be the only one facing south along the entire northern coastline of Brittany, which prompts some brave souls to test the waters as early as Easter. On the last Sunday in July, Locquirec holds a combined *pardon de St-Jacques* and Festival of the Sea.

Locquirec's *Grand Hôtel des Bains*, 15bis rue de l'Église (Ⓣ02.98.67.41.02, Ⓦgrand-hotel-des-bains.com; ❾), is an elegant and very expensive hotel in an unbeatable location, with an indoor heated swimming pool, jacuzzi and gym. It became widely known in France when it was used as the location for *Hôtel de la Plage*, a coming-of-age movie about youngsters summering in Brittany. The municipal **campsite**, the *Toul ar Goue*, 1km south along the corniche (Ⓣ02.98.67.40.85, Ⓦmairie-locquirec.fr; closed Oct–March), is beautifully positioned, too.

The Cairn de Barnenez

In a glorious location at the mouth of the Morlaix estuary, 6km north of Plouézoch and a total of 13km north of Morlaix, the prehistoric stone **Cairn**

▲ The Cairn de Barnenez

de Barnenez overlooks the waters from the summit of a hill (May–Aug daily 10am–6.30pm; Sept–April Tues–Sun 10am–12.30pm & 2–5.30pm; €5; Ⓦbarnenez.monuments-nationaux.fr). As on the island of Gavrinis in the Morbihan (see p.368), its ancient masonry has been laid bare by excavations, and provides a stunning sense of the architectural prowess of the megalith builders. Dated back by radiocarbon testing to 4500 BC, this is one of the oldest large monuments in the world; André Malraux called it "the Breton Parthenon". It remained in continuous use for around 2500 years, and was probably used repeatedly as a place of burial, then sealed off and abandoned.

The ensemble consists of two distinct **stepped pyramids**, the older one constructed of local dolerite stone, and the other of grey granite from the nearby Île de Sterec. Each rises in successive tiers, built of large flat stones chinked with pebbles (but no mortar); the second was added onto the side of the first, and the two are encircled by terraces and ramps. Both were long ago buried under an eighty-metre-long earthen mound. The whole thing measures roughly 70m long by 15m to 25m wide; the current height of 6m is thought to be smaller than that of the original structure.

While the actual cairns are completely exposed to view, most of the passages and chambers that lie within them are sealed off. Visitors cannot in any case enter the structure, but simply walk around it to admire it from all angles. The two minor corridors that are open simply cut through the edifice from one side to the other, and were exposed by twentieth-century quarrying – which inadvertently provided a good insight into the construction methods, though nothing much was found inside. Each is covered with great slabs of rock; in fact most of the familiar dolmens seen all over Brittany and elsewhere are thought to be the vestiges of similarly complex structures. Local tradition has it that one tunnel runs right through this "home of the fairies", and continues out deep under the sea.

Travel details

Trains

Lannion to: St-Brieuc (4 daily; 1hr) via Plouaret (15min) and Guingamp (35min).
Paimpol to: Guingamp (2–5 daily; 45min).
Rennes to: Brest (8 daily; 2hr 15min); Caen (4 daily; 3hr) via Dol (35min) and Pontorson (1hr); Morlaix (10 daily; 1hr 45min) via Lamballe (40min), St- Brieuc (50min), Guingamp (1hr 10min) and Plouaret (1hr 25min); Nantes (8 daily; 1hr 15min); Paris-Montparnasse (9 TGVs daily; 2hr 10min); Quimper (10 daily; 2hr 15min); Vannes (10 daily; 1hr 10min); Vitré (5 daily; 22min).
St-Malo to: Rennes (14 daily; 1hr; connections for Paris on TGV). All trains pass through Dol (15min).

Buses

Dinan to: St-Cast (3 daily; 1hr 5min); St-Jacut (3 daily; 45min).
Dinard to: Cancale (2 daily; 1hr 30min); Dinan (6 daily; 40min); St-Brieuc (8 daily; 25min).
Fougères to: Vitré (2 daily; 35min).
Lannion to: Locquirec (4 daily; 30min) and Morlaix (4 daily; 1hr 20min); Paimpol (3 daily, 1hr); Perros-Guirec (7 daily; 20min) and Trégastel (7 daily; 40min); .
Rennes to: Dinan (6 daily; 1hr 20min); Dinard (5 daily; 1hr 40min); Fougères (10 daily; 1hr); Mont St-Michel (5 daily; 1hr 20min).
St-Brieuc to: Cap Fréhel (2 daily, 1hr 25min) via Le Val-André (50min) and Erquy (1hr 10min); Carhaix (1 daily; 3hr); Dinan (4 daily; 1hr); Lamballe (3 daily; 1hr 10min) with connections to St-Cast (4 daily; 40min); Lannion (3 daily; 1hr 40min) via Guingamp (45min); Moncontour (4 daily; 1hr); Paimpol (8 daily; 1hr 30min); St-Malo (2 daily; 2hr); Vannes (2 daily; 2hr).
St-Malo to: Cancale (6 daily; 45min); Combourg (2 daily; 1hr); Dinan (6 daily; 45min); Dinard

(10 daily; 30min); Fougères (3 daily; 2hr 15min); Mont St-Michel (4 daily; 1hr 30min); Pontorson (4 daily; 1hr 15min); Rennes (3 daily; 1hr 30min); St-Cast (2 daily; 1hr) via St-Jacut (35min).

Ferries

St-Malo to: Brittany Ferries to Portsmouth (1 daily; 10hr 45min); Condor Ferries to Jersey and Guernsey (varies from 1 or 2 weekly in winter up to 3 daily in summer) with connections to Weymouth, Poole, and Portsmouth; Dinan (mid-April to late Sept; 2hr 45min); Dinard (April to early Nov; 10min); Jersey (2 daily; 1hr 10min).

Flights

Dinard to: Guernsey by Aurigny Air Services (ⓣ02.99.46.18.46; ⓦaurigny.com; 1–2 daily; 20min); London Stansted with Ryanair (ⓦryanair.com; daily; 1hr 5min).

5

Finistère

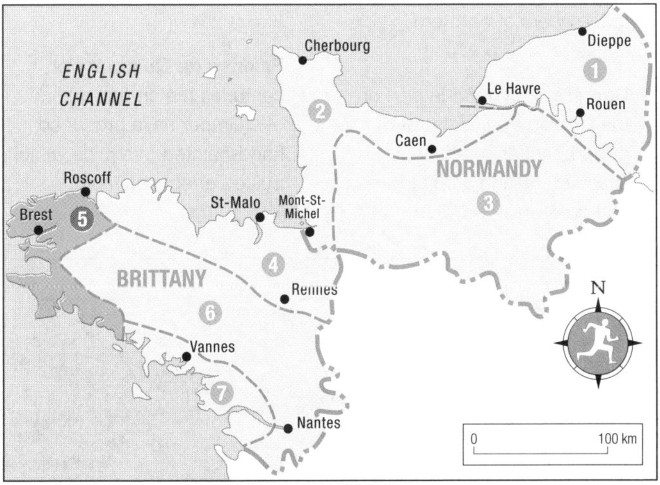
ENGLISH CHANNEL
Cherbourg
Dieppe
Le Havre
Rouen
Caen
NORMANDY
Roscoff
Brest
St-Malo
Mont-St-Michel
BRITTANY
Rennes
Vannes
Nantes
N
0
100 km
1
2
3
4
5
6
7

CHAPTER 5

Highlights

- **Île de Batz** Small, car-free island, a perfect family destination only a few hundred metres offshore from the attractive ferry port of Roscoff. See p.259
- **Guimiliau** One of the finest parish closes – a remarkable medieval church in a pretty rural village. See p.266
- **Hôtel la Baie des Anges** Gorgeous, peaceful seafront hotel, just outside L'Aber-Wrac'h, a pleasant little resort in the *abers* of northern Finistère. See p.270
- **Camaret** Picturesque port on the Crozon Peninsula, with good beaches, prehistoric sites, interesting architecture and great seafood. See p.284
- **Locronan** Jewel-like hilltop village that has hardly changed in five centuries. See p.287
- **Hôtel de la Baie des Trépassés** Romantic land's-end hotel, facing its own colossal beach in splendid isolation. See p.291
- **Île de Sein** Barely rising from the Atlantic, this misty and mysterious island makes a romantic day-trip from Audierne in western Finistère. See p.291
- **Faïence de Quimper** For centuries the craftsworkers of Quimper have produced hand-painted ceramics, which make perfect souvenirs. See p.299

▲ Le Conquet

5

Finistère

The *département* of **Finistère** has always been isolated from the French (and even Breton) mainstream: its name literally means "the end of the world". This remote rural landscape was the last refuge of the Druids from encroaching Christianity, and its mysterious forests and elaborate parish closes testify to its role as the province's spiritual heartland. Today, Roscoff has reopened the old maritime links with England, high-speed TGV trains mean that Brest is just four hours from Paris, and the motorway loops around the end of the peninsula. Yet Finistère remains only sporadically touched by modern industry; agriculture and low-key tourism are the mainstays of the economy. Breton survives as a spoken language here more than anywhere else, and traditional costumes are still worn in reverence of culture not tourism at many a Breton festival.

Memories of the days when Brittany was "Petite Bretagne", as opposed to "Grande Bretagne" across the water, linger in the names of Finistère's two main areas. Both the northern peninsula – **Léon**, once Lyonesse – and its southern neighbour – **Cornouaille**, the same word as "Cornwall" – feature prominently in Arthurian legend.

A succession of jagged **estuaries** corkscrew deeply into Brittany's wild and dramatic northwestern coastline. Known both as *abers* (as in Welsh place names) and as *rias* (as in Spanish Galicia), each shelters its own tiny harbour and countless tiny deserted coves. Rarely are conditions as bleak as you might expect; possible stopping places, interspersed with vast beaches and dunes, punctuate the route all the way west from the delightful old port of **Roscoff** to the picturesque working fishing village of **Le Conquet**. A notoriously treacherous stretch of ocean separates the mainland at this point from **Ouessant** and **Molène**, which can make for an uncomfortable ferry ride, yet those two islands have the mildest winter climate in all France. The one coastal destination you might prefer to avoid is the regional capital, and lone big city, of **Brest**, the base of the French Atlantic fleet. Inland, the **parish closes** lie strung across sleepy little villages southwest of **Morlaix**, each ornate church and its associated ensemble still perpetuating a fierce medieval rivalry.

In the south, Cornouaille's capital, lively **Quimper**, is one of the most pleasant, and least-known, little cities in France, with plenty to see and a vibrant atmosphere, while thriving resorts such as **Bénodet**, **Loctudy** and **Pont-Aven** (the last made famous by Gauguin) line the south coast. There are surprises everywhere – take the perfectly preserved medieval village of **Locronan**, or the extraordinary world apart that is the tiny **Île de Sein**.

Finistère's most popular region for holiday-makers, the **Crozon peninsula**, juts into the sea beneath the **Menez-Hom** mountain as a distinct entity

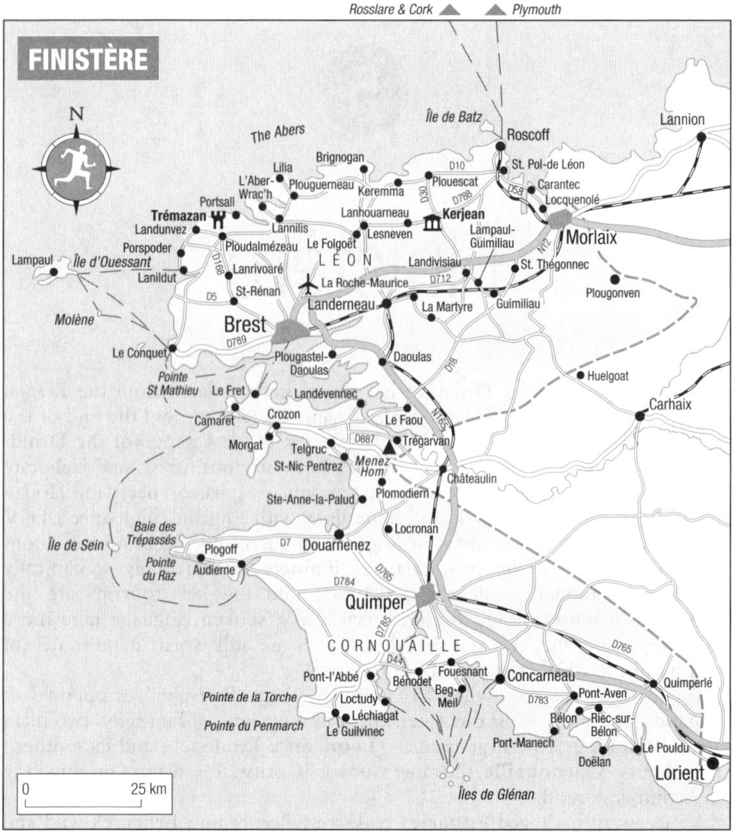

between the two ancient realms. **Morgat** and **Camaret** here are both ideal for long and leisurely seaside stays, and all around there are opportunities for secluded camping.

Roscoff

ROSCOFF has long been a significant port – Mary Queen of Scots landed here in 1548 on her way to Paris to be engaged to the son of Henri II of France, and so too did Bonnie Prince Charlie in 1746, after his defeat at Culloden. The opening of its deep-water harbour in 1973, and the instigation of a **ferry** service to England, had especial significance in the general revitalization of the Breton economy. The town itself, however, has remained delightfully small and unspoiled, on a different scale to other Channel ports. Almost all activity is confined to the pedestrianized medieval lanes around **rue Gambetta** and the **old port** – the rest of the roads are residential backstreets full of retirement homes and stern institutions. The preservation of its old character is helped by the fact that both the ferry port and *gare SNCF* are some way from the town centre.

Arrival and information

Boats from Plymouth, Cork and Rosslare dock not in Roscoff's original natural harbour, but at the Port de Bloscon, a couple of kilometres east (and just out of sight) of the town. In summer, direct **buses** to Morlaix and Quimper leave from the ferry terminal (daily 8.05am; Penn-ar-Bed; ⓣ08.10.81.00.29, ⓦviaoo29.fr). To reach the town centre, either walk, in around twenty minutes, or call a taxi (ⓣ02.98.69.74.38). From the **gare SNCF**, a few hundred metres south of the town proper, a restricted rail service (often replaced by buses) runs to Morlaix, with connections beyond. Most **local buses** also go from here, including a direct service to Brest (ⓣ02.98.83.45.80, ⓦbihan.fr).

The helpful **tourist office** is on the quayside in town, at 46 rue Gambetta (July & Aug Mon–Sat 9am–12.30pm & 1.30–7pm, Sun 10am–12.30pm & 2–7pm; Sept–June Mon–Sat 9am–noon & 2–6pm; ⓣ02.98.61.12.13, ⓦwww.roscoff-tourisme.com).

Bikes and **kayaks** can be rented in summer in the central car park by the jetty, from Escapades Légendes (ⓣ02.72.10.25.71, ⓦescapadeslegendes.fr).

Accommodation

For a small town, Roscoff is well equipped with **hotels**, which are accustomed to late-night arrivals from the ferries. However, most are relatively expensive and close for some or all of the winter. There's also a **hostel** on the Île de Batz (see p.260), and a two-star **campsite**, the beachfront *Aux Quatres Saisons*, 2km west in Perharidy, just off the route de Santec (ⓣ02.98.69.70.86, ⓦcamping-aux4saisons.com; closed Nov–March).

Les Arcades 15 rue Amiral-Réveillère ⓣ02.98.69.70.45, ⓦwww.hotel-les-arcades-roscoff.com. Sixteenth-century building with superb views from some of its modernized rooms and from the restaurant, which despite being slightly overrun by tourists, has economical menus at €11, with a particularly good €26.90 option. En-suite facilities cost around €12 extra. Closed mid-Nov to mid-Feb. ❷

Bellevue rue Jeanne-d'Arc ⓣ02.98.61.23.38, ⓦhotel-bellevue-roscoff.fr. Seafront hotel with well-appointed, en-suite rooms, on the opposite side of the pleasure harbour to the town centre, and thus somewhat nearer the ferry terminal. Despite having no restaurant – just a lively bar – it's a Logis de France. Closed mid-Nov to mid-March. ❹

du Centre 5 rue Gambetta ⓣ02.98.61.24.25, ⓦchezjanie.com. Family hotel above the café-bar *Chez Janie*, entered via the main street but looking out on the port. The rooms are modern and tastefully furnished; those with sea views cost €25 extra. Closed mid-Nov to mid-Feb. ❹

les Chardons Bleus 4 rue Amiral-Réveillère ⓣ02.98.69.72.03, ⓦchardonsbleus.fr.st. Very friendly and helpful hotel in the heart of the old town, with a good restaurant (closed Thurs & Sun eve Sept–June) where dinner menus start at €20. Closed three weeks in Feb. ❸

Chez Lucie Quéméneur 27B rue Le Mat ⓣ02.98.69.71.36. Good-value B&B with fine and clean en-suite rooms, plus a lovely garden and very friendly owner. ❷

Grand Hôtel Talabardon 27 pl Lacaze-Duthiers ⓣ02.98.61.24.95, ⓦwww.talabardon.fr. Imposing old stone building in the main square, facing the church on the inland side but with big sea-view balconies attached to several rooms. Seafood menus in the attractive dining room €27–49. Affiliated to Best Western. Closed mid-Nov to mid-Feb. ❻

Regina 1 rue Ropartz-Morvan ⓣ02.98.61.23.55, ⓦwww.hotel-regina.fr. Very comfortable rooms, but relatively expensive considering the location, some distance from the sea next to the *gare SNCF*. Closed Nov–Feb. ❹

Aux Tamaris 49 rue É-Corbière ⓣ02.98.61.22.99, ⓦhotel-aux-tamaris.com. Renovated, comfortably furnished rooms, several with lovely sea views towards the Île de Batz, and some that sleep four. Closed mid-Nov to mid-Feb. ❹

Le Temps de Vivre 19 pl Lacaze-Duthiers ⓣ02.98.19.33.19, ⓦwww.letempsdevivre.net, This ultra-stylish contemporary hotel, in an old mansion near the Notre-Dame church in the heart of town, offers luxuriously spacious rooms with designer bathrooms, and wonderful sea views. Off-season rates are at least €60 lower. ❽

The Town

The old **harbour** is very much the liveliest part of Roscoff. Two long stone jetties enclose the fishing port – the local economy is still heavily based on the sea – while pleasure boats bob in the bay behind. Tourists gather all through the day to watch the fishermen at work, and to join the low-key pleasure trips to the **Île de Batz**. The island looks almost walkable; a narrow pier stretches over 400m towards it before abruptly plunging into deep rocky waters. The Pointe de Bloscon and the white fisherman's chapel, the Chapelle Ste-Barbe, make a good vantage point, particularly when the tide is in. Below the headland are the *viviers*, where you can see trout, salmon, lobsters and crabs being reared for the pot.

In addition to the island ferries, detailed on p.260, the Compagnie Maritime Armein (Ⓣ02.98.61.77.75) operate two-and-a-half-hour cruises from here around the **Bay of Morlaix** (July to mid-Sept daily 2.30pm; €13).

Like so many other Breton ports, Roscoff used to make most of its money from piracy. Along **rue Gambetta**, which becomes rue Amiral-Réveillère, and runs parallel to the old harbour a short way inland, the charming, ornate and playfully embellished grey granite houses serve as reminders of that wealth. At the end of the street, in place de l'Église, the sculpted ships and protruding stone cannons of the Renaissance belfry that tops the sixteenth-century town church, **Notre Dame de Croas Batz**, also recall seafaring days. From the side, rows of bells can be seen hanging in galleries, one above the other, like a tall narrow wedding cake created by the young Walt Disney.

More recently, the town earned a more respectable living from exporting **onions**. That trade started in 1828, when Henri Ollivier chartered a barge and took the first Roscoff onions over to England, and flourished until the 1930s; older locals remember travelling as children with their fathers as far afield as Glasgow to sell their produce. At one time, 1500 "Johnnies" – that classic French image of men in black berets with strings of onions hanging over the handlebars of their bicycles – would set off each year. These days, around twenty still do. The whole story is told by way of hour-long guided tours at

Alexis Gourvennec and Brittany Ferries

Few British holiday-makers sailing to France with **Brittany Ferries** will realize the significance of the company's original ideology. The ferry services from Roscoff to Plymouth and to Cork were started not simply to bring tourists, but also to revive the traditional trading links between the Celtic nations of Brittany, Ireland and southwest England – links which were suppressed for centuries as an act of French state policy after the union of Brittany with France in 1532.

Until the 1960s, no direct ferries crossed the Channel to Brittany, and all the cross-Channel operators were British-owned. Brittany Ferries is the creation of **Alexis Gourvennec** (1936–2007), who in 1961, at 24, was the militant leader of a Breton farmers' cooperative. Frustrated by the lack of French government support, the farmers decided to start their own shipping line to find new markets for their produce – the immediate region of Roscoff and Morlaix being particularly noted for its artichokes and cauliflowers. Ferries between Plymouth and Roscoff started operation in 1973, at first for freight only but swiftly carrying passengers as well.

The company's financial success has allowed it to expand, running services from Britain to St-Malo and the Norman ports of Cherbourg and Caen, as well as to Spain. Above all, however, Brittany Ferries has been an important factor in a resurgence of Breton fortunes, with as much cultural as commercial significance.

La Maison des Johnnies et de l'Oignon Rosé de Roscoff, 48 rue Brizeux, near the *gare SNCF* (mid-June to mid-Sept Mon–Fri 11am, 3pm & 5pm, Sun 3pm & 5pm; mid-Feb to mid-June & mid-Sept to Dec Mon 10.30am, Thurs 3pm; €4). The town stages an **onion festival** at the end of August, with such amusements as onion cart-making contests, a vintage tractor parade and onion soup tasting.

A couple of hundred metres west along the coast from the town centre, the **Thalassotherapy Institute** of Rock Roum is a luxury residential spa specializing in seawater cures (Ⓣ08.25.00.20.99, Ⓦthalasso-roscoff.com; ⑨). Having opened in 1899 as the first such establishment in France, it's still thriving over a century later. A kilometre further on, you come to Roscoff's best **beach**, at Laber, surrounded by expensive hotels and apartments.

In the opposite direction, a short walk south along the coast from the ferry terminal leads to the **Jardin Exotique** – tropical garden – at Rock Hievec (daily: March & Nov 2–5pm; April–June, Sept & Oct 10.30am–12.30pm & 2–6pm; July & Aug 10am–7pm; €5; Ⓦjardinexotiqueroscoff.com). In this slightly surreal enclave, cacti, palm trees and flowers of South America and the Pacific flourish in the mild Gulf-Stream climate.

Eating

While the obvious places to **eat** in Roscoff are the hotel dining rooms, there are also a few specialist **restaurants** as well, plus a bunch of appealing crêperies around the old harbour. If you arrive on an evening ferry out of season, it can be difficult to find a restaurant still serving any later than 9.15pm.

Crêperie de la Poste 12 rue Gambetta Ⓣ02.98.69.72.81, Ⓦcreperiedelaposte.fr. Cosy old stone house, just back from the port in the heart of town, offering inexpensive à la carte meals of sweet and savoury pancakes; more exotic seafood crêpes cost up to €8.20. They also serve fish soup, mussels and other simple meals. Daily 11.30am until late; closed mid-Nov to mid-Jan, plus Wed Sept–June, Tues July & Aug.

L'Écume des Jours quai d'Auxerre Ⓣ02.98.61.22.83, Ⓦwww.ecume-roscoff.fr. Romantic restaurant in a grand old house facing the port, offering good-value set lunches for €12.50 on weekdays, plus dinner menus from €21, featuring such delights as braised oysters or scallops with local pink onions. Closed mid-Dec to Jan & Tues, plus Wed lunch in summer, all Wed in low season.

Le Temps de Vivre pl de l'Église Ⓣ02.98.61.27.28. Long-standing gourmet restaurant, with sea views, on the main church square – next to but separate from the hotel of the same name – serving rich French cuisine with a modern twist. Almost the only deviations from the chef's recommendations on menus ranging from €39 (not Sat lunch) to €99 are to accommodate oyster *refuseniks*. Try the milk-raised lamb; its pale meat melts in the mouth. Closed two weeks in both March & Oct plus Mon, Sun eve and Tues lunch.

The Île de Batz

The long, narrow, and very lovely **ÎLE DE BATZ** (pronounced "ba") forms a sort of mirror image of Roscoff across the water, separated from it by a sea channel that's barely 200m wide at low tide, but perhaps five times that when the tide is high. Appearances from the mainland are somewhat deceptive, however; the island's old town, home to a thousand or so farmers and fishermen, may fill much of its southern shoreline, but those parts of Batz that aren't visible from Roscoff are much wilder and more windswept. With no cars permitted, and some great expanses of sandy beach, it makes a wonderfully quiet retreat for families in particular, whether you're camping or staying in its hotels, hostel or B&Bs.

The island's first recorded inhabitant, a "laidly worm", was a dragon that infested the place in the sixth century. Such dragons normally symbolize pre-Christian religions, in this case perhaps a Druidic serpent cult. Allegorical or not, when St Pol arrived to found a monastery he wrapped a Byzantine stole around the unfortunate creature's neck and cast it into the sea. These days, there are no dragons; there are hardly even any trees, just an awful lot of seaweed, which is collected and sold for fertilizer.

There's a nice small beach near where the ferry docks, along the edge of the harbour, though the sea withdraws so far at low tide that the entire port turns into a morass of seaweed. All arriving passengers make the obvious 500m walk towards the town, ranged enticingly along the quayside. Once there, there's nothing particularly to see, but strolling among the beautiful little houses and their radiant gardens is a real joy.

Turning left when you get to the town church will bring you to the hostel (see below), and the 44-metre **lighthouse** that stands on the island's peak, all of 23m above sea level (second half of June & first half of Sept Thurs–Tues 2–5pm; July & Aug daily 1–5.30pm; €2). Turning right at the church, on the other hand, leads you towards the island's best beach, the white-sand **Grève Blanche** at its eastern end, which you may well have spotted already from the boat. Nearby, the **Jardin Exotique Georges-Delaselle** (April–June, Sept & Oct daily except Tues 2–6pm; July & Aug daily 1–6.30pm; € 4.50) is a 75-year-old garden that takes advantage of the temperate Batz microclimate to sustain its palm trees and other out-of-context flora.

Practicalities

Three separate **ferry** companies make the ten-minute crossing from Roscoff to Batz (10min; €7.50 return; bikes €7); in summer only, they work together and your ticket will be valid on any ferry. Compagnie Maritime Armein (ⓣ02.98.61.77.75), Compagnie Finistèrienne or CFTM (ⓣ02.98.61.78.87, ⓦvedettes-ile-de-batz.com), and Armor Excursions (ⓣ02.98.61.79.66, ⓦvedettes.armor.ile.de.batz.fr) have ticket booths at the landward end of Roscoff's long pier. At low tide, the boats sail from the far end of the pier, a good five minutes' walk further on. Between late June and mid-September, the service is pretty much nonstop between 8am and 8pm daily; for the rest of the year, each company runs eight to ten trips daily between 8.30am and 7pm.

Ferries arrive in Batz at the quayside of the old town. The nicer of the island's two **hotels**, the *Grand Hôtel Morvan* at the centre of the harbour (ⓣ02.98.61.78.06; ❸; closed Dec & Jan), serves good meals on its large seafront terraces. Alongside the ferry landing, the more casual, but friendly and good-value *Roch Ar Mor* (ⓣ02.98.61.78.28, ⓦrocharmor.net; ❸; closed mid-Oct to March), makes a slightly cheaper alternative, with menus from €13.50. The best **B&B** is *Ti Va Zadou* near the church (ⓣ02.98.61.76.91; ❸), with comfortable rooms, a good view, cycles for rent and big breakfasts. For budget travellers, there's also a **hostel** in a beautiful setting by the beach at the evocatively named Creach ar Bolloc'h, which has its own restaurant (ⓣ02.98.61.77.69, ⓦaj-iledebatz.org; €15.50; closed Nov–March).

As for **eating** and **drinking**, a quirky little **crêperie-restaurant**, *Les Couleurs du Temps* (ⓣ02.98.61.75.75, closed Oct–Easter), near the ferries, sells sweet and savoury pancakes named after assorted islands, from Wight to Man, for €5–7, prepares the Breton speciality *kig ha farz*, a kind of seafood stew topped by a crêpe, and also stocks herb teas. Nearby, the *Bigorneau Langoureux* (ⓣ02.98.61.74.50) is a very pleasant bar to be languorous over a bottle from the good selection of Basque wines.

South from Roscoff

The main road south from Roscoff, the D58, swiftly emerges into a heavily agricultural landscape, abounding in fields of the famous Breton artichokes. Motorists soon find themselves, however, entangled in a phenomenally intricate network of bypasses and roundabouts, all designed to keep traffic away from the attractive old village of **St-Pol-de-Léon**.

Cyclists in particular would do well to get onto the minor roads to the east. That way, you can call in at the appealing little resort of **Carantec**, and then follow the D73 southeast, along a narrowing estuary which at **Locquenolé** becomes the mouth of the River Morlaix. The beautiful deep valley south from here has promenades and gardens along its stone-reinforced banks, and views across to isolated villages such as Dourduff on the other side.

St-Pol-de-Léon

ST-POL-DE-LÉON, 6km south of Roscoff, holds two churches that merit a pause. Its **cathedral**, in the main square, was rebuilt towards the end of the thirteenth century along the lines of Coutances – a quiet classic of unified Norman architecture. The remains of St Pol are inside, alongside a large bell, rung over the heads of pilgrims during his *pardon* on March 12 in the unlikely hope of curing headaches and ear diseases.

Just downhill, the **Kreisker Chapel** is notable for its sharp-pointed soaring granite belfry, now coated in yellow moss. It was originally modelled on the Norman spire of St-Pierre at Caen, which was destroyed in the last war (see p.114); as an elegant improvement on its Norman counterpart, it was itself much copied, and similar "Kreisker" spires are dotted all over rural Brittany. The dramatic view to be seen if you climb this spire (daily 10–11.30am & 2–6pm; free), out across the **Bay of Morlaix**, should be enough to persuade you to follow the road along the shore.

Rooms at the *Hôtel de France*, 29 rue des Minimes (Ⓣ02.98.29.14.14, Ⓦwww.hoteldefrancebretagne.com; ❸), are slightly more comfortable than the cheaper *Passiflore*, near the station at 28 rue Pen-ar-Pont (Ⓣ02.98.69.00.52, Ⓦwww.hotel-restaurant-lepassiflore.fr; ❷; closed Sun eve). Both are central, open all year and have reasonable restaurants.

Carantec

From St-Pol, if you take the foliage-covered lane down to join the D58, you can cross the pont de la Corde to reach the resort and peninsula of **CARANTEC**, studded with small coves and secluded beaches. The nicest of all the local beaches, the **plage du Kelenn**, is the first to the east of the slightly drab town itself. The **Île de Callot**, an enticing hour's walk from Carantec at low tide, is the scene of a *pardon* and blessing of the sea on the Sunday after August 15 – a rather dour occasion, as are most of the religious festivals around Finistère.

Practicalities

The Carentec, 20 rue de Kelenn (Ⓣ02.98.67.00.47, Ⓦhoteldecarantec.com; ❾; closed Jan), is a stylish and very expensive beachfront **hotel**, where five of the luxurious rooms have terraces with magnificent views of the sea. This stretch of coast comes alive in summer with a scattering of seasonal **campsites**, among them the excellent four-star *Les Mouettes* (Ⓣ02.98.67.02.46, Ⓦles-mouettes.com; closed early Sept to mid-May), where you pay over the usual odds for the benefit of having a supermarket, a pool complex with three impressive water slides, a bar and a club on site.

Right on the waterfront in town, the *Cabestan* **restaurant** (ⓣ02.98.67.01.87; closed Mon all year, plus Tues in low season) provides the focus of Carantec's nightlife, serving great seafood, but also putting on live music. Several snack bars with spacious open-air terraces also face the plage du Kelenn, including the *Restaurant Les Îles* (ⓣ02.98.67.05.24; lunch daily, dinner Fri & Sat only, closed Dec–Feb), which serves *moules frites* for around €10. For the finest seafood, the *Maison de l'Huître*, in a gorgeous and very clearly signposted waterfront spot east of the centre, sells prize **oysters** from the beds at Prat-Ar-Coum in western Finistère (July & Aug Mon–Sat 9.30am–1pm & 3–7pm, Sun 10am–noon; Sept–June Mon–Fri 10am–noon & 3–6pm, Sat 9.30am–12.30pm & 2.30–7pm, Sun 10am–noon; ⓣ02.98.78.30.68, ⓦprat-ar-coum.com).

The Château de Taureau

Occupying the whole of a tiny island, the fortified **Château de Taureau** guards the entrance to Morlaix Bay, a short way east of Carantec and 12km north of Morlaix itself. It was built after a succession of skirmishes that began in 1522 when Morlaix pirates raided and looted Bristol. Henry VIII's pride was hurt and, seeking revenge, he sent a sizeable fleet to storm Morlaix. The citizens were absent at a neighbouring festival when the English arrived; when they returned, they found the English drunk in their wine cellars. Once the Bretons had routed their enemies, they built the château to forestall further attacks from the sea. Until the nineteenth century, it also served as a prison. Meanwhile, Morlaix adopted the motto which it keeps to this day: "If they bite you, bite them back."

To get a close-up view of the château, you have to venture onto the water. Boat trips out to it, which include an hour to explore the actual structure, depart from Carantec and Plougasnou in summer, to a very complicated tide-dependent schedule (round trip €13; ⓣ02.98.62.29.73, ⓦwww.chateaudutaureau.com), and also from Roscoff.

The best vantage point on the mainland is at the tip of the **Pointe de Pen-al-Lann**, 2km east of Carantec. A steep footpath from the car park here leads 300m down to one of the most delightful – and quiet – **beaches** in this region.

Morlaix

During the "Golden Period" of the late Middle Ages, **MORLAIX**, 25km southeast of Roscoff, was one of the great Breton ports, thriving – in between wars – on trade with England. Set where the Queffleuth and Jarlot rivers join to flow together into broad Morlaix Bay, it now seems too far from the open sea to attract many long-stay visitors. Many attractive buildings still survive from its medieval heyday, but it's a strange-looking place, literally overshadowed by a massive nineteenth-century railway viaduct.

Morlaix's sober stone houses, climbing both sides of a steep valley, were originally protected by an eleventh-century castle and a circuit of walls. Little is left of either, but the old centre remains in part medieval, with its cobbled streets and half-timbered houses. Later, the town grew still more prosperous on piracy and the tobacco trade (both legal and illegal), and spread north, down the valley, towards the port.

Arrival and information

The **gare SNCF** is on rue Armand-Rousseau, high above the town at the western end of its railway viaduct. It was originally supposed to be linked to town by a funicular railway, but as this was never built you still have to reach it on foot, climbing the steep steps of the Venelle de la Roche. All **buses** conveniently depart from place Cornic, right under the viaduct.

Morlaix's **tourist office** is also all but beneath the viaduct, in place des Otages (July & Aug Mon–Sat 9am–12.30pm & 1.30–7pm, Sun 10.30am–12.30pm; Sept–June Mon–Sat 9am–12.30pm & 2–6pm; ⓣ02.98.62.14.94, ⓦtourisme.morlaix.fr).

Accommodation

A few **hotels** are dotted around Morlaix's old quarter. As the budget options seem to be giving up the ghost, those that survive tend to be of a relatively high standard.

de l'Europe 1 rue d'Aiguillon ⓣ02.98.62.11.99, ⓦhotel-europe-com.fr. Slightly eccentric but very central old place, near the Jacobin convent. The public spaces, furnished in assorted styles, are much more flamboyant than the rather plain modern rooms, many of which have somewhat rudimentary bathrooms. The on-site brasserie serves simple but good menus featuring a *plat du jour* from €12–15. ❺

de la Gare 25 pl St-Martin ⓣ02.98.88.03.29, ⓦhotelgare29.com. Reasonable value en-suite rooms above a cosy bar with a small terrace, close to the *gare SNCF* at the top of the hill. ❸

du Port 3 quai de Léon ⓣ02.98.88.07.54, ⓦlhotelduport.com. Bright, simple hotel in a converted tobacco warehouse, overlooking the port from the left bank. All rooms are en-suite, most have views of the port. ❹

The Town

Morlaix is dominated by its pink granite **railway viaduct**, built high above the valley in the 1860s to carry trains en route between Paris and Brest. Despite all Allied attempts during World War II to bomb it, it still looms 60m above the central **place des Otages**, and as you enter the town today by road from the north your first view is of shiny yacht masts in the pleasure harbour paralleling its slender pillars. The first level of the viaduct is intermittently open to visitors, usually (but not always) from 11am until 7pm each day. There are few actual sights in town, but it's a pleasure to roam the length of the steep stairways that lead up from the places des Otages and Cornic, or walk up to the viaduct from the top of Venelle aux Prêtres, along an almost rural overgrown path lined with brambles.

On her way from Roscoff to Paris in 1548, Mary Queen of Scots stayed at Morlaix's **Jacobin convent**. A contemporary account records that the crush to catch a glimpse of the 5-year-old was so great that the inner town's "gates were thrown off their hinges and the chains from all the bridges were broken down". The convent, on place des Jacobins, has long housed the **Musée de Morlaix**, which hosts two temporary exhibitions per year (April, May & Sept Mon & Wed–Sat 10am–noon & 2–6pm, Sun 2–6pm; July & Aug daily 10am–12.30pm & 2–6.30pm; Oct–March & June Mon & Wed–Sat 10am–noon & 2–5pm; €4). The same ticket entitles you to a guided tour of the **Maison à Pondalez**, at 9 Grand-Rue (same hours), a fabulously restored sixteenth-century house that takes its name from the Breton word for the sculpted wooden internal gallery that dominates the ground floor.

The austere church of **St-Mathieu**, off rue de Paris a short walk southeast of the convent, contains a sombre and curious statue of the Madonna and Child, made in Cologne around 1400 AD. Mary's breast was apparently lopped off by a prudish former priest, to leave the babe suckling at nothing. The whole statue stands open down the middle, to reveal a separate figure of God the Father, clutching a crucifix.

Duchess Anne of Brittany visited Morlaix in 1506, by which time she had become queen of France. She is reputed to have stayed at the **Maison de la Duchesse Anne**, not far west of St-Mathieu church at 33 rue du Mur (May & June Mon–Sat 11am–6pm; July & Aug Mon–Sat 11am–6.30pm; Sept Mon–Sat 11am–5pm; €1.60), which, although much restored, does indeed date from the sixteenth century. Its intricate external carvings, and the lantern roof and splendid Renaissance staircase inside, make it the most beautiful of the town's ancient houses, each of its storeys overhanging the square below by a few more centimetres.

Eating and drinking

The best area for **restaurants** in Morlaix is between St-Mélaine church and place des Jacobins, but plenty of other options are tucked away on the backstreets. As for **bars**, the venerable half-timbered *Ty Coz*, 10 Venelle au Beurre, near place Allende, has boisterous Bretons playing darts, and locally-brewed draught Coreff beer, while the lively *Tempo Café* faces the port on quai de Tréguier and puts on occasional concerts.

Les Bains Douches 45 allée du Poan-Ben ☎02.98.63.83.83. Small bistro that doesn't quite live up to its unusual location – set in the former public baths, and reached via a little footbridge across a canal – but makes an attractive spot for a light €13 lunch. Closed Sat lunch, all Sun & Mon eve.

La Dolce Vita 3 rue Ange-de-Guernisac ☎02.98.63.37.67. Italian place at the foot of a pretty central alley, with pizzas mostly priced at €8–10, plus pasta, salads and traditional Italian dishes such as *osso bucco*. Closed Mon, plus three weeks in Feb and two weeks in Oct.

La Marée Bleue 3 rampe St-Mélaine ☎02.98.63.24.21. Well-respected seafood restaurant, a minute's walk up from the tourist office. The €14 menu is a bit limited, but €26 ensures you a superb *assiette de fruits de mer*, and €36.50 buys a five-course feast. Closed Oct, plus Sun eve & Mon Sept–June.

The parish closes

A few kilometres west of Morlaix, bounded by the valleys of the Elorn and the Penzé rivers, lies an area remarkable for the wealth and distinction of its church architecture. This region holds the best-known examples of what the French call *enclos paroissiaux* – a phrase that translates into English as "**parish closes**", and describes a walled churchyard which in addition to the church itself incorporates a trinity of further elements: a cemetery, a calvary and an ossuary.

The **ossuaries** – which now tend to contain nothing more alarming than a few rows of postcards – were originally charnel houses, used to store the exhumed bones of less recent burials. They are the most striking features of the closes, making explicit a peculiarly Breton proximity and continuity between the living and the dead. Parishioners would go to pray, with the informality of making a family visit, in the ossuary chapels where the dead bones of their families were on display. The relationship may have originated with the builders of the megalithic passage graves, which were believed to serve as doorways between our world and the netherworld.

The **cemeteries** tend to be small, and in many cases have disappeared altogether, while the **calvaries** that complete the ensemble are tenuously based on the hill of Calvary. Each is, therefore, in theory surmounted by a Crucifixion, but the definition is loose enough to take in any cluster of religious statuary, not necessarily even limited to biblical scenes, standing on a single base.

That there are so many fine *enclos* in such a small area is thanks to intense inter-village rivalry during the sixteenth and seventeenth centuries, when each parish competed to outdo the next in the complexity and ornament of its village church. It's no coincidence that most such Breton churches date from the two centuries to either side of the union with France in 1532 – Brittany's wealthiest period. A clearly signposted **route** leading past the most famous churches – St-Thégonnec, Guimiliau and Lampaul-Guimiliau – can be joined by leaving the N12 between Morlaix and Landivisiau at St-Thégonnec. Public transport is poor.

St-Thégonnec

At the **ST-THÉGONNEC** *enclos*, just off the N12 10km southwest of Morlaix, the church **pulpit**, carved by two brothers in 1683, is the acknowledged masterpiece, albeit so swamped with detail – symbolic saints, sibyls and arcane figures – as to be almost too intricate to take in. The painted oak **entombment** in the crypt under the ossuary has more immediate effect. Complete with a stunning life-size figure of Mary Magdalene, it was sculpted by Jacques Laispagnol of Morlaix in 1702. The entire east wall of the church is a carved and painted altarpiece, with saints in niches.

The upmarket *Auberge de St-Thégonnec*, 6 place de la Mairie (Ⓣ02.98.79.61.18, Ⓦaubergesaintthegonnec.com; ⑤; closed Sun Sept–March, plus mid-Dec to mid-Jan), is a surprisingly smart **hotel** for such a small village. Its main building houses a superb **restaurant**, where menus start at €21 and rise to €45 for the gourmet option featuring lobster, crab, sea bass and the like, carefully prepared in original and delicious sauces. The *Restaurant du Commerce* at 1 rue de Paris (Ⓣ02.98.79.61.07; lunch only, Mon–Fri; closed Sat, Sun & Aug), very near the church, serves more basic, good-value lunches from €11, while the *Crêperie Steredden*, nearby at 6 rue de la Gare (Ⓣ02.98.79.43.34;

▲ Detail of the calvary at Guimiliau

closed Mon & Tues), is a friendly village crêperie that offers numerous speciality pancakes, with set menus costing around €10.

Guimiliau

The showpiece at the pretty flower-filled village of **GUIMILIAU**, 6km southwest of St-Thégonnec, is its **calvary**. This incredible ensemble holds over two hundred granite figures, depicting scenes from the life of Christ and rendered all the more dramatic by being covered with "secular lichen". A uniquely Breton illustration, just above the Last Supper, depicts the unfortunate Katell Gollet – a figure from local myth who stole consecrated wafers to give to her lover, who naturally turned out to be the Devil – being torn to shreds by demons.

Inside the church, years of patient restoration have turned the seventeenth-century organ from a tangle of mangled wood back into its original harmonious condition.

Lampaul-Guimiliau

The third of the major parish closes, **LAMPAUL-GUIMILIAU**, is a few kilometres northwest from Guimiliau. Here the painted oak **baptistry**, the dragons on the beams and the appropriately wicked faces of the robbers on the **calvary** are the key components. An unusual stoup depicts a couple of devils squirming as they're doused with holy water.

Landivisiau

LANDIVISIAU, just south of the N12 20km west of Morlaix, makes a good alternative to Morlaix as a base from which to tour the nearby parish closes. There's not much to the town itself, but the **tourist office** at 14 av Foch (July & Aug Mon–Fri 9am–noon & 2–6pm, Sat 10am–noon & 2–5pm; Sept–June Mon–Fri 9am–noon & 2–5pm; ⓣ02.98.68.33.33, ⓦwww.ot-paysdelandivisiau.com) can recommend bike routes, while coach tours operate regularly from the main square. There's also a choice of cheap **hotels**, the best value of which are *Le Terminus*, 94 av Foch (ⓣ02.98.68.02.00; ❶; restaurant closed Sat lunch, Fri eve & Sun eve), which serves excellent meals, and *Hôtel de l'Avenue*, 16 av de Coatmeur (ⓣ02.98.68.11.67, ⓦwww.avenue-hotel-landivisiau.com; ❷; closed mid-Sept to mid-Oct).

La Roche-Maurice

West of Landivisiau, the N12 races towards Brest, but the lesser D712 and the railway follow a far more pleasant route, along the banks of the pretty Elorn River. After about 12km – not far beyond the chapel of **Pont-Christ**, beside a broad waterfall – the village of **LA ROCHE-MAURICE** occupies a steep high bluff above a curve in the river.

Only the solemn ivy-covered keep now remains of the **castle** that has occupied this site since the eleventh century, and was once supposedly home to Katell Gollet. It was abandoned at the end of the seventeenth century, and its stones used to build the houses that now surround it. Visitors are free to climb the wooden stairway that's rather clumsily attached to the outside, but not to ascend any further inside the ruin itself.

Nearby stands another large **parish close**, notable mainly for its rendition of the death-figure **Ankou** (see p.249). This time he's carved above the holy-water stoup on the wall of the ossuary, facing the church, beneath the warning

"I kill you all". The interior of the church is gorgeous, the nave divided in two by a lovely green-and-red rood screen, which shows the Twelve Apostles propped up by grotesque animals. Ringed by older carvings, the blue ceiling holds a celestial choir of angels. In summer, the ossuary houses local information and an exhibition on local history.

La Roche-Maurice has no hotels, but the *Auberge du Vieux Château* (ⓣ02.98.20.40.52; closed eve Mon–Thurs), in the square immediately below the castle, serves excellent **food**, with menus starting at €14.

La Martyre

The oldest parish close of all, built in 1460, stands at the heart of **LA MARTYRE**, 7km south of La Roche-Maurice on the road to Sizun (see p.315). This is the most attractive of all the local villages, with stones of its complete parish close seamlessly integrated into the walls of its main street. Ankou clutches a severed head above the stoup in the peculiarly lopsided entrance porch, watched over not only by a carved red-ochre Virgin, giving birth, but also a nest of house martins. Inside, the church is damp and somewhat faded, but it does have an attractive gilt altar.

Landerneau

The delightful town of **LANDERNEAU**, 20km east of Brest at the mouth of the Elorn estuary, was once a major port, but it's attractive enough to have re-invented itself as a tourist showpiece. The **pont de Rohan** in the middle of town is said to be, along with the Ponte Vecchio in Florence, one of the last **inhabited bridges** in Europe; as a plaque proudly boasts, it was *re*-constructed in 1510. The bridge itself holds no fewer than four crêperies, along with assorted shops, bars and houses, while streets of fine old mansions climb away to either side of the river.

Landerneau's **tourist office** is not far north of the bridge, in a particularly splendid town house at 9 place de Gaulle (June, Sept & Oct Tues–Sat 10am–1pm & 2–6pm; July & Aug Mon–Sat 10am–7pm, Sun 10am–1pm & 2–6pm; Nov–May Tues–Sat 10am–noon & 2–5pm; ⓣ02.98.85.13.09, ⓦwww.tourisme-landerneau-daoulas.fr). *Le Clos du Pontic*, south of the river at 3 rue du Pontic (ⓣ02.98.21.50.91, ⓦclos-pontic.com; ❹; restaurant closed Mon lunch, Sat lunch & Sun eve Sept–June), and the cheaper *l'Amandier*, 53–55 rue de Brest (ⓣ02.98.85.10.89; ❸; restaurant closed Sun eve & Mon), are comfortable old-style **hotels** with good restaurants.

Plougastel-Daoulas

West of Landerneau, the Elorn broadens dramatically as it enters the Rade de Brest. The city of Brest (see p.276) sprawls along its northern banks at this point, but the southern side holds one final village associated with the parish closes. While the church in **PLOUGASTEL-DAOULAS** was built in 1870, and is far from interesting, the **calvary** just outside it ranks among the finest in Brittany.

This extraordinarily elaborate affair was completed in 1604 to celebrate the passing of an outbreak of the plague – hence the bumps on the shaft of the main cross, designed to recall the sores on the bodies of the victims. Carvings on each side of the base depict scenes from the life of Christ. Sadly, the rest of the village has not been restored so sensitively after the bombing of World War II. A weird shopping mall now overlooks the calvary, equipped with a giant Scrabble board for local senior citizens and a truly awful mural recounting the history of cinema.

Between the parish closes and the sea

The swathe of land north of the parish closes on your way to Finistère's rugged northern coastline holds relatively few tourist attractions, the notable exception being the Renaissance château of **Kerjean**. Also worth a stop is the village of **Le Folgoët**, whose pretty church compares favourably with those in the parish closes.

Kerjean

If not quite the "Versailles of Brittany", as it is promoted, **Kerjean** is for this remote corner of France a surprisingly classic **château** (Feb, March, Nov & Dec Wed & Sun 2–5pm; April & May daily except Tues 2–6pm; June & Sept daily except Tues 1–6pm; July & Aug daily 10am–7pm; Oct daily except Tues 2–5pm; closed Jan; €5; Ⓣ02.98.69.93.69, Ⓦwww.chateau-de-kerjean.com). Despite being little more than 15km from Roscoff, it's not that easy to find, standing 500m west of the D30, halfway between Landivisiau and Plouescat.

This moated Renaissance château, set in its own park, was built in the sixteenth century by the lords of Kerjean, with the express intention of overshadowing the mansion of their former feudal overlord, the Carman of Lanhouarneau, who, under some archaic quirk of fealty, made them take an egg, in a cart, each year and cook it in front of him.

Now state property and extensively restored, the building hosts annual exhibitions focusing on some aspect of medieval life. In recent years, it has also put on open-air musical and theatrical performances in summer.

Le Folgoët

Centring on a well-kept and rather English-looking green, the appealing village of **LE FOLGOËT** stands a couple of kilometres southwest of the slightly larger town of **LESNEVEN**, itself 15km west of Kerjean. Both its **Notre Dame** church, and its name, which means "Fool's Wood", stem from a fourteenth-century simpleton called Solomon. After an unappreciated lifetime repeating the four Breton words for "O Lady Virgin Mary", he found fame in death by growing a white lily out of his mouth.

Erected on the site of Solomon's favourite spring, the church is quite lovely, colourfully garnished with orange moss and clinging verdure (a sign of the penetrating damp inside), and with a bumpy and stubbly approximation of a "Kreisker" spire. It has been restored bit by bit since the damage of the Revolution, and an unusual amount of statuary has been placed on the many low niches all around the outside. On September 8 or the preceding Sunday, it holds a *pardon*, and there's also another *pardon* of St Christopher on the fourth Sunday of July, which involves a blessing of cars that non-motorists may find verging on the blasphemous. A summer-only **museum** facing the main entrance holds more delicate pieces (mid-June to mid-Sept Mon–Sat 10am–12.30pm & 2.30–6.30pm, Sun 2.30–6.30pm; €3).

The nearest reasonable **accommodation** is *Le Week-End*, at pont du Châtel near **PLOUIDER**, 5km northeast of Lesneven (Ⓣ02.98.25.40.57, Ⓦwww.hotelrestaurantweekend.com; ❷; restaurant closed Mon lunch July & Aug, Sun eve & all day Mon Sept–June), a quiet little Logis de France that also provides good-value food.

The abers

Some of the most dramatic shoreline in Brittany lies to the west of Roscoff, a jagged series of **abers** – narrow estuaries, neither as deep nor as steep-sided as the Norwegian fjords with which they are occasionally compared – in the midst of which are clustered small, isolated **resorts**, heavy on modern holiday homes but relatively short on hotels and other amenities. All these resorts have adequate beaches, but the coastal scenery is the real attraction. It's a little on the bracing side, especially if you're making use of the numerous **campsites**, but in summer, at least, the temperatures are mild enough, and there's more shelter as you move towards Le Conquet and Brest.

Plouescat

The first real resort to the west of Roscoff, **PLOUESCAT**, is not quite on the sea itself, but there are **campsites** nearby on each of three adjacent beaches, the nicest being *La Baie du Kernic* (ⓣ02.98.69.86.60, ⓦwww.village-center.com/bretagne; closed mid-Sept to early April). In the town, you'll find a high-roofed old wooden market hall for picnic provisions, and an unexpected, slightly surreal statue of a seahorse with a yin and yang symbol in its tail. Of the **hotels**, the best value is the little *Roc'h-Ar-Mor*, 18 rue Ar Mor (ⓣ02.98.69.63.01, ⓔroch.ar.mor@orange.fr; ❷; closed Oct–Easter); though it's right on the beach at Porsmeur, none of its rooms actually give sea views. Roscoff to Brest **buses** stop at Plouescat before turning inland.

At the village of **Keremma**, inland from the sea on the way between Plouescat and Brignogan, there's another lovely little **campsite** (ⓣ02.98.61.62.79; closed early Sept to mid-June), set along a green avenue lined with meadows of purple-and-yellow flowers.

Brignogan-Plage

Pretty little **BRIGNOGAN-PLAGE**, on the next *aber*, is blessed with a small natural harbour. Once the lair of wreckers, it has beaches and weather-beaten rocks to either side, as well as its own menhir. As the tide here recedes way out towards the mouth of the bay, surreal clumps of seaweed-coated stone bulge up among the stranded boats. The *Café du Port* makes a perfect vantage point. The **plage de Ménéham**, 2km west of town, is a gem of a beach.

Brignogan town centre, 1km inland, is more of a traffic intersection than a destination in its own right – particularly now that its last **hotel** has closed down – but it does hold a very helpful **tourist office**, on the main road at 7 av de Gaulle, where staff are happy to book accommodation (July & Aug Mon 10am–1pm & 4–7pm, Tues–Sat 9.30am–1pm & 4–7pm, Sun 10am–1pm; Sept–June Tues–Fri 10am–noon & 2–4.30pm, Sat 10am–noon; ⓣ02.98.83.41.08, ⓦwww.ot-brignogan-plage.fr). Both local **campsites** are by good beaches, and have two stars: *Camping de la Côte des Legendes* (ⓣ02.98.83.41.65, ⓦcampingcotedeslegendes.com; closed Nov–Easter), the central municipal site at Keravézan, on the western side of the bay, north of the centre and 50m from the sailing school; and *Camping du Phare*, east of Brignogan (ⓣ02.98.83.45.06, ⓦcamping-du-phare.com; closed Oct–March).

Lilia and Grouannec

LILIA is a dramatic waterfront community at the tip of a headland 5km northwest of the inland village of **PLOUGUERNEAU**, a total of 21km west of Brignogan. In summer, pleasure boats from here take a short cruise out to bob at the foot of the shaft of the **Vierge lighthouse** – at 82.5m it's said to be the tallest in Europe (April–Oct; standard cruise €16; visits to the lighthouse itself €2.50; schedules on ⓣ02.98.04.74.94 or ⓦvedettes-des-abers.com). The harbour makes a perfect setting for the low-slung modern **hotel** *Castel Ac'h* (ⓣ02.98.37.16.16; ❹), where an excellent seafood **restaurant** serves what amounts to a Breton version of sushi.

Plouguerneau is also near to an unexpected pleasure, the church of **Notre Dame de Grouannec**, a small but complete parish close ensemble about 4km further inland. It has been extensively restored, and looks all the better for it, with its fountain, ossuary, mini-cloister and profusion of gargoyles.

L'Aber-Wrac'h

The *aber* between Plouguerneau and the yachting port of **L'ABER-WRAC'H** has a stepping-stone crossing just upstream from the bridge at Lannilis, built in Gallo-Roman times, where long cut stones still cross the three channels of water (access off the D28 signposted "Rascoll", and continue past farm buildings to the right).

L'Aber-Wrac'h itself – which you may well also see referred to as "Landeda" – is a promising place to spend a little time. An attractive, modest-sized resort, it lies within easy reach of a whole range of sandy **beaches** and a couple of worthwhile excursions. Beyond the tiny fishing port, which is home to a busy sailing school, the Baie des Anges stretches away towards the Atlantic, with the only sound the cry of seagulls feasting on the oyster beds. The coastal waters nearby are prime territory for **divers**; boat trips can be arranged through Aber Benoît Plongée (ⓣ02.98.89.75.66, ⓦaberbenoitplongee.com).

At the start of the bay, a couple of hundred metres past the town's little strip of bars and restaurants, the irresistible *Hôtel la Baie des Anges*, 350 rte des Anges (ⓣ02.98.04.90.04, ⓦbaie-des-anges.com; ❻; closed Feb), commands stunning views out to sea from the start of its vast curve; part of the *Châteaux & Hôtels de France* organization, it's a peaceful and exceptionally comfortable place to **stay**, featuring a spacious bar with a small waterfront terrace, for the use of guests only. The municipal **campsite**, the three-star *Camping des Abers* (ⓣ02.98.04.93.35, ⓦcamping-des-abers.com; closed Oct–April), nestles amid the dunes at the very tip of the headland.

The best **restaurant** in L'Aber-Wrac'h, *Le Brennig* (ⓣ02.98.04.81.12, ⓦrestaurant.brennig.free.fr; closed Tues & Nov–Feb), is back at the other end of the main strip, and prepares fine menus from €24.50. However, you're surer of getting a table at the *Cap'tain* in the port proper (ⓣ02.98.04.82.03; closed Mon in low season, plus Nov–Feb), a busy but friendly crêperie that offers continuous service not only of crêpes but also any seafood speciality you care to name.

Clearly signposted 4km west of L'Aber-Wrac'h, on the right side of the next inlet along, L'Aber-Benoît, the **oyster beds** of **Prat-Ar-Coum** (ⓣ02.98.04.00.12, ⓦprat-ar-coum.fr) are renowned for producing the best oysters in western Brittany. A quayside stall sells them year round, and a small restaurant is open in July and August only (closed Mon eve & all Sun; menus from €25).

Portsall

At the small harbour of **PORTSALL**, 5km along the coast from L'Aber-Benoît, the **Espace Amoco Cadiz** (July & Aug daily except Mon 2.30–6.30pm;

Sept–June Sat & Sun 2.30–6.30pm; free) commemorates a defining moment in local history: on March 17, 1978, the sinking of the *Amoco Cadiz* supertanker resulted in an **oil spill** that devastated 350km of the Breton coastline, and threatened to ruin the local economy. Displays and films document not only the immense task of cleaning up the mess, but also the long legal battle to obtain compensation from the "multinational monster" responsible. The French government eventually obtained 1045 million francs in 1992, of which 100 million were passed on to local councils and communities. The ship's huge **anchor** now stands in the car park across from the hall, while the wreck itself, 1100m offshore, has become a popular dive site.

Trémazan and around

Once past Portsall, the coast becomes a glorious succession of dunes and open spaces, with long beaches stretching at low tide way out towards tiny islands. Each little inlet here seems to shelter a treasure of a beach, ideal for family swimming, while bracing walks lead through the heather-covered headlands that abut the open sea. One especially romantic spot comes just 5km beyond Portsall, where the crumbling walls of the *Sleeping Beauty*-style **castle** of **Trémazan** look down on a magnificent beach. The fleeing Tristan and Iseult are said to have made their first landing in Brittany here, and the cracked ivy-covered keep still stands proud, pierced by a large heart-shaped hole. The castle is not formally open to the public; it's totally overgrown, and to reach it you have to scramble your way through the brambles that fill its former moat. Once you're here, however, it's a real haven for a summer afternoon.

In the nearby nondescript village of **KERSAINT LANDUNVEZ**, the *Hostellerie du Castel* (ⓣ02.98.48.63.35, ⓦhostellerie-du-castel.com; ❸; restaurant closed Sun eve & Mon, hotel closed Oct–March except for advance reservations), makes an ideal overnight stop, with very comfortable and moderately priced en-suite rooms, and a good restaurant. If you are continuing west to Porspoder, pause to look at the exquisite wooden seaside **chapel of St Samson** on the way.

Porspoder

PORSPODER is a sleepy little resort, but does serve as a centre for the many campers who set themselves up on the dunes of the **Presqu'île St-Laurent** which lies opposite. It's an attractive place to be, looking out over the ocean, and relatively busy in season, but rather bleak in winter when many of the surrounding houses are unoccupied. There's a cheap **hotel**, the *Pen Ar Bed* (ⓣ02.98.89.90.38; ❷; closed Oct–March), on the long seafront rue de l'Europe.

Le Conquet and around

LE CONQUET, the southernmost of the *abers* resorts, at the far western tip of Brittany 24km beyond Brest, makes the best holiday base in the region. A wonderful place, scarcely developed, it is flanked by a long **beach** of clean white sand, protected from the winds by the narrow spit of the Kermorvan peninsula, and has ferry access to the islands of Ouessant and Molène. It is very much a working fishing village, the grey-stone houses leading down to the stone jetties of a cramped harbour, which occasionally floods, to the intense amusement of the locals, the waves washing over the cars left by tourists making the trip to Ouessant – so leave your car slightly inland while visiting the island.

The **coast** around Le Conquet is low-lying, not the rocky confrontation that one might expect, and Kermorvan, across the estuary, seems to glide into the sea – its shallow cliffs topped by a strip of turf. Apart from the lighthouse at the end, the peninsula is just grassland, bare of buildings and a lovely place to walk in the evening across the footbridge from Le Conquet.

A good walk 5km south of Le Conquet brings you to the lighthouse at **Pointe St-Mathieu**, looking out to the islands of Ouessant and Molène from its site among the ruins of the Benedictine **Abbaye de St-Mathieu**. A small exhibition (April–June Wed, Sat & Sun 2.30–6.30pm; July–Sept Mon 10am–12.30pm & 2–3pm, Tues–Sat 3–7pm, Sun 2–7pm; Oct–March Wed & Sat 2.30–6.30pm; €1.50) explains the abbey's history, including the legend that it holds the skull of St Matthew, brought here from Ethiopia by local seafarers.

Practicalities

Buses from Brest drop passengers at various points in Le Conquet; only one daily express services goes all the way to the harbour, nestled below the tip of the promontory, from which boats depart for Ouessant. In addition to the island **ferries**, detailed opposite, **Finist'Mer** run three or four daily **cruises** in the Molène archipelago, offering activities such as dolphin-spotting and birdwatching (no fixed schedules; €39–50; Ⓣ08.25.13.52.35, Ⓦwww.finist-mer.fr).

Right by the jetty, the *Relais du Vieux Port*, 1 quai Drellac'h (Ⓣ02.98.89.15.91; ❸; closed Jan), offers a handful of inexpensive but attractive rooms, and has a simple crêperie. There's also a well-equipped, two-star **campsite** over on the Kermorvan peninsula, *Les Blancs Sablon* (Ⓣ02.98.89.06.90, Ⓦlescledelles.com; closed Oct–March). **Market** day in Le Conquet is Tuesday.

The *Hostellerie de la Pointe St-Mathieu*, housed in a thirteenth-century stone structure opposite the abbey entrance at Pointe St-Mathieu (Ⓣ02.98.89.00.19, Ⓦpointe-saint-mathieu.com; ❺; closed Feb & Sun eve in low season), is a top-quality **hotel**, with a modern wing of tasteful ocean-view rooms, an indoor swimming pool and a sauna. Its **restaurant** offers menus from €25 to €78 featuring foie gras, *pot au feu* (a vegetable and beef stew), and blue lobster.

Ouessant and Molène

The island of **Ouessant** (Ushant in English), 30km northwest of Le Conquet, was first described by the geographer Pytheas as early as 325 BC, under the name of Uxisama, which means something along the lines of "the most remote". Standing at the outermost end of a chain of smaller islands and half-submerged granite rocks, its lighthouse at Creac'h is regarded as the entrance to the English Channel. Most of the archipelago is uninhabited, save perhaps for a few rabbits, but **Molène**, midway between Le Conquet and Ouessant, has a village and can also be visited.

Ouessant

The ride to **OUESSANT** is generally a tranquil affair, though the ferry has to pick its way from buoy to buoy, through a sea which is liable suddenly to become choppy and dangerous. Of the many wrecks among the reefs, the most famous was the *Drummond Castle*, which foundered as the finale to a concert celebrating the end of its voyage from Cape Town to England in June 1896, with the loss of 234 lives. Despite its storms, though, the climate is mild – Ouessant even records the highest mean temperatures in France in January and February.

Getting to Ouessant and Molène

Both islands are served by at least one **ferry** each day from Le Conquet and Brest; however, it is not practicable to visit both in a single day. Ferries can be very crowded in summer, so book your **tickets** in advance if at all possible.

Penn Ar Bed (Ⓣ02.98.80.80.80, Ⓦpennarbed.fr) sail to Ouessant and Molène all year, with one to six daily departures from **Le Conquet**, and one to three daily from **Brest**, of which only one stops at Molène. The timetables are extremely intricate, but broadly speaking the first sailing from Le Conquet is at 8am early July to late August, at 9am in the spring and autumn, and at 9.45am in winter. Corresponding times from Brest are half an hour earlier. Between early July and early September, they also depart from **Camaret** to Ouessant at 8.15am daily except Sundays, with some additional 11am sailings, while between early April and early July, and from early September until late September they sail from Camaret at 8.15am on Thursdays only. Only on Fridays between early July and late August is it possible to sail from Camaret to Molène, again at 8.15am. In every instance, whether you leave from Brest, Le Conquet or Camaret, and whichever island you go to, the round-trip **fare** is the same (June–Sept €30.20, Oct–May Mon–Fri €18.40, Sat & Sun €20.40).

Finist'Mer, whose sightseeing **cruises** in the archipelago are detailed opposite, also offer an on-demand, high-speed "taxi" service out to the islands (Ⓣ08.25.13.52.35, Ⓦwww.finist-mer.fr)

In addition, you can **fly** to Ouessant in just fifteen minutes from Brest's Guipavas airport with **Finist'Air** (Mon–Sat 8.30am & 4.45pm, Sun 9am & 4.45pm; one-way €64, return, not on same day, €93; Ⓣ02.98.84.64.87, Ⓦwww.finistair.fr).

Information and accommodation

General information on Ouessant is available from the **tourist office** in the main square in Lampaul (mid-July to Aug Mon–Sat 9am–1pm & 1.30–7pm, Sun 9.30am–1pm; Sept to mid-July Mon–Sat 10am–noon & 2–5pm, Sun 10am–noon; Ⓣ02.98.48.85.83, Ⓦwww.ot-ouessant.fr).

Lampaul holds three **hotels**, as well as a hostel and campsite. You could, in fact, camp almost anywhere on the island, making arrangements with the nearest farmhouse (which may well let out rooms, too).

Hotels

Fromveur Lampaul Ⓣ02.98.48.81.30. Hotel set a short walk back from the sea, just up the street near the church. The rooms have been reasonably renovated, and the traditional island cooking is pretty good, even if much of it does consist of attempting to render seaweed and mutton as palatable as possible. Expect to pay around €20 for a set lunch. Closed mid-Nov to Jan. ❸

Roch Ar Mor Lampaul Ⓣ02.98.48.80.19, Ⓦpagesperso-orange.fr/rocharmor. This attractive hotel is the only one on Ouessant to offer sea views, though not from all rooms. Its restaurant too enjoys a fine prospect of the beach, but its food is more expensive and less tasty than at the *Fromveur*. Closed Jan to mid-Feb & mid-Nov to mid-Dec. ❸

Ti Jan Ar C'Hafé Lampaul Ⓣ02.98.48.82.64, Ⓦpagesperso-orange.fr/rocharmor. A newcomer to the scene, this restored village house offers eight tastefully decorated rooms but no restaurant. Closed Jan to mid-March & mid-Nov to mid-Dec. ❹

Hostel and campsite

Camping Penn ar Bed Lampaul Ⓣ02.98.48.84.65. Small official campsite, in a walled enclosure on the eastern edge of town, beside the road in from the port. Closed Oct–March.

La Croix Rouge Lampaul Ⓣ02.98.48.84.53, Ⓔajouessant@club-internet.fr. Little hostel, north of the centre towards Niou, where a dorm bed plus breakfast costs €15. Closed Jan.

Around the island

Ferries arrive on Ouessant at the modern **harbour** in the ominous-sounding Baie du Stiff. There's a scattering of houses here, and a small snack bar, but the

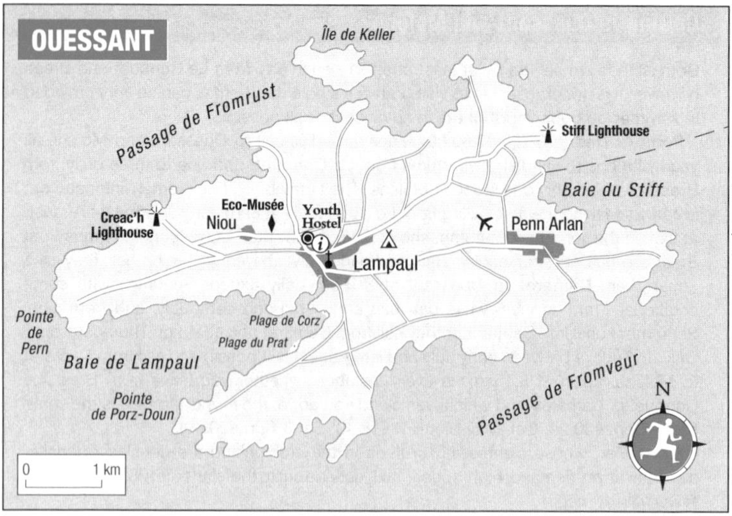

only town (with the only hotels and restaurants) is 4km distant at **LAMPAUL**. Everyone from the boat heads there, either by the bus that meets each arriving ferry (€3.50 return to Lampaul, €12 for a full island tour), by bike, or in a long walking procession that straggles along the one road. **Bicycle** rental (€10–15 per day; operators wait at the port) is the most convenient option, as the island is really too big to explore on foot; many local tracks are uneven, so it's worth going for a (more expensive) mountain bike, but be warned that you're forbidden to cycle on the coastal footpaths.

As well as its more mundane facilities, Lampaul has Ouessant's best **beaches** sprawled around its bay. There are few specific sights, but the town **cemetery** is worth visiting, with its war memorial listing all the ships in which the townsfolk were lost, and its graves of unknown sailors washed ashore. A unique Ouessant tradition is also on show in the cemetery chapel – an array of wax *proëlla* crosses, which were used during the funerals of those islanders who never returned from the sea, to symbolize their absent remains.

At **NIOU**, 1km northwest, the **Maisons du Niou** – two houses and a few outbuildings – jointly form the **Éco-Musée d'Ouessant** (April–Sept daily 11am–6pm in school hols, 11am–5pm otherwise; Oct–March daily except Mon 1.30–5.30pm; €3.50, or €7 for combined admission with the Musée des Phares et Balises). One house contains a museum of island history, detailing how boys from the age of eleven used to embark on sea voyages of up to three years' duration, while the women were responsible for growing crops back home. The other is a reconstruction of a traditional island house, almost entirely filled by massive "box-beds", one of which was for the parents and the other for the children.

Another kilometre west, the **Creac'h lighthouse** was when this, its third incarnation, opened in 1939 the most powerful in the world, with a 500-million-candlepower beam capable of being seen from England's Cape Lizard. You can't visit the lighthouse tower itself, but the complex at its base holds the **Musée des Phares et Balises** (same hours as the Éco-Musée; €4.30 or €7 for both museums), a large museum about lighthouses and buoys. As well as providing a history of lighthouses from the Pharos of Alexandria and Roman examples, it's crammed with assorted lenses and mirrors, and has detailed displays on shipwrecks in the vicinity. None of the information is in English, however, and photography is not permitted.

The Creac'h lighthouse makes a good starting point from which to set out along the barren and exposed rocks of the north coast. Particularly in September and other migratory seasons, it's a remarkable spot for birdwatching, frequented by puffins, storm petrels and cormorants. The star-shaped formations of crumbling walls you can see were built so that the sheep – peculiarly tame here – could shelter from the strong winds.

Molène

MOLÈNE is quite well populated for a sparse strip of sand. The port itself being better protected than that of Ouessant, more fishermen are based here. The island's inhabitants derive their income from seaweed collection and drying – and to an extent from crabs and crayfish, which they gather on foot, canoe and even tractor at low tide. The tides are more than usually dramatic, halving or doubling the island's territory at a stroke and giving the island its name, which comes from the Breton for "the bald isle".

There are no real sights here, so walking the rocks and the coast is the basic activity, though, as on Ouessant, the island **cemetery** is poignant and interesting. The concentration of babies' graves from a typhoid epidemic in the nineteenth century illustrates life in such a small community; marked by silver crosses, they're repainted each November 1.

Few visitors come for longer than an afternoon, but it's possible to stay in the **rooms** – very chilly in winter – at *Kastell An Doal* (ⓣ02.98.07.39.11; ❸; closed mid-Jan to mid-Feb), one of the old buildings by the port. You can also **camp**, on a rugged municipal site (ⓣ02.98.07.39.05), or arrange to stay in a private house (for details, call the town hall on the same number).

▲ Creac'h, Ouessant

Brest

Set in a magnificent natural harbour, known as the Rade de Brest, the city of **BREST** is doubly sheltered from ocean storms by both the bulk of Léon to the north, and by the Crozon peninsula to the south. The Rade (or roadstead) is entered by the narrow deep-water channel of the Goulet de Brest, 5km long and 1.5km wide, with steep banks on both sides.

As one of the finest natural harbours in Europe, Brest has always played an important role in war, as well as in trade whenever peace allowed. All the great names in French strategic planning – including Richelieu, Colbert, Vauban and Napoleon – have been instrumental in developing the port, which is today the base of the French Atlantic Fleet. Its dry dock can accommodate ships of up to 500,000 tonnes, and as a ship-repair centre it ranks sixth in the world.

During World War II, Brest was relentlessly bombed to prevent the Germans from using it as a submarine base. When the Americans liberated it on September 18, 1944, after a six-week siege, they found the city devastated

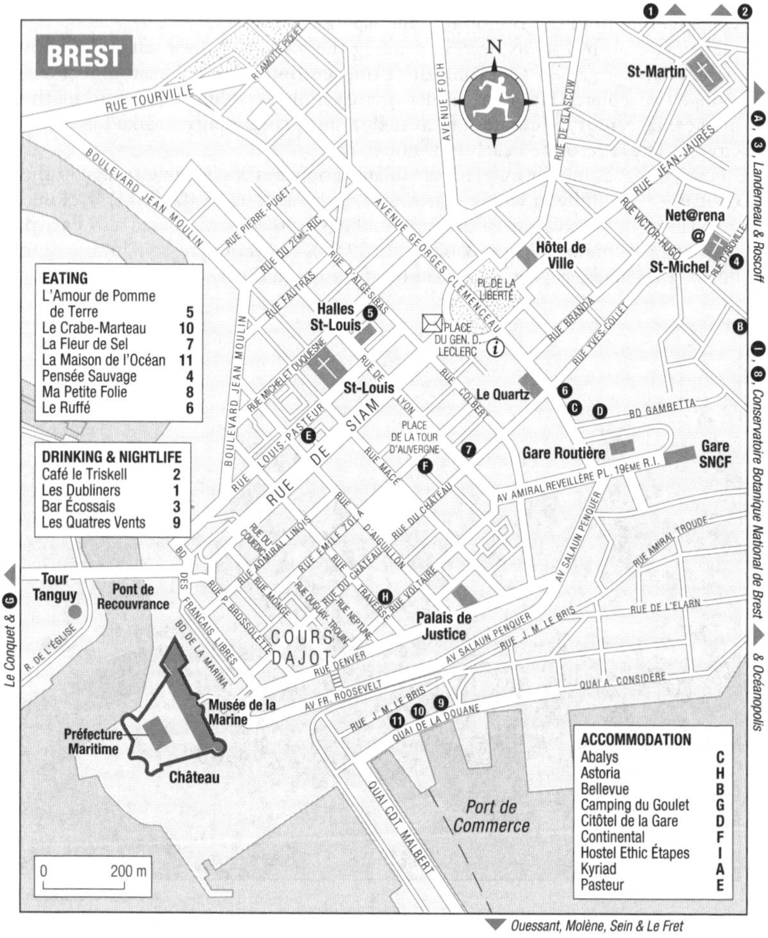

beyond recognition. To help normal life resume as soon as possible, rebuilding was rushed at the expense of restoration, and the architecture of the postwar town is raw and bleak, echoing Le Havre in its preponderance of concrete. Beautification efforts have additionally been hampered by the fact that, despite the heaviest rainfall in France, Brest is a bit too windswept for flora to flourish.

While Brest is a reasonably lively city, and its hilly site offers great sea views, it's not a place where many visitors linger. The most rational reason to come would probably be for the **bagpipe festival**, held here for three days every August, or its spectacular four-yearly **maritime festival** (next due in 2012).

Arrival and information

The **gare SNCF** and **gare routière** stand shoulder-to-shoulder in place du 19ème RI at the bottom of avenue Clemenceau. Though right at the end of the railway system, Brest is just four hours from Paris by TGV (which follows the northern route, via Morlaix and Rennes; the journey via Quimper takes much longer).

Brest's **airport**, at Guipavas 9km northeast (Ⓦwww.brest.aeroport.fr), is served by flights from London Luton on Ryanair (Ⓦryanair.com), and from Birmingham and Southampton on British European (Ⓦflybe.com), and also offers local connections to Ouessant (see p.273). An **airport shuttle** bus runs from the *gare SNCF* and the tourist office (6–12 daily; 25min; Ⓣ02.98.32.86.00; €4.60 one-way). All the major **car rental** chains have desks at the airport.

Brest's helpful **tourist office**, on avenue Clemenceau facing place de la Liberté, runs an excellent website (July & Aug Mon–Sat 9.30am–7pm, Sun 10am–noon; Sept–June Mon–Sat 9.30am–6pm; Ⓣ02.98.44.24.96, Ⓦbrest-metropole-tourisme.fr). The main **post office** is on place Général-Leclerc (Mon–Fri 8am–7pm, Sat 8am–noon). **Internet access** is available at Net@rena, 30 rue Yves Collet (Mon–Thurs noon–1am, Fri & Sat noon–4am, Sun 2–11pm).

Ferries and cruises

As well as the sailings to Ouessant, detailed on p.273, in summer **boats** make the 25-minute crossing from Brest's Port de Commerce to **Le Fret** (see p.286) on the Crozon peninsula (April–June & Sept 3 sailings daily except Mon; July & Aug 3 sailings daily; €17 return; Ⓣ02.98.41.46.23, Ⓦazenor.com). The same company also sails from both the port and Océanopolis to **Camaret** (July & Aug 3 sailings daily except Sat; €17 return), and offers excursions, along with other operators, around the harbour and the Rade de Brest, (1hr 30min; usually around €15.50).

Accommodation

Used more by business travellers than tourists, the vast majority of Brest's **hotels** remain open throughout the year, and many offer discounted **weekend** rates. Only a few, however, maintain their own restaurants. Several lie within easy walking distance of the stations, near the central place de la Liberté.

Hotels

Abalys 7 av Clemenceau Ⓣ02.98.44.21.86, Ⓦabalys.com. Small but very good-value accommodation (especially with weekend reductions) in a spruce little hotel above a bar near the stations. Not all rooms have en-suite facilities, and even in those that do the bathrooms can be tiny. ❶

Astoria 9 rue Traverse Ⓣ02.98.80.19.10, Ⓦhotel-astoria-brest.com. Behind its very plain exterior, this peaceful central hotel, not far up from the port, has a cheerful ambience and decor. Some rooms have sea views, while the four cheapest only have sinks. Closed three weeks Dec–Jan. ❶

Bellevue 53 rue Victor-Hugo ⓣ02.98.80.51.78, ⓦwww.hotelbellevue.fr. Six-storey building, equipped with a lift and bright, modern but not very fancy rooms. A short walk from the *gare SNCF* and well on the way to the lively St-Martin area, near the St-Michel church. Distant sea views. ❸

Citôtel de la Gare 4 bd Gambetta ⓣ02.98.44.47.01, ⓦhotelgare.com. Convenient, good-value option very near the stations. The cheapest rooms have a shower but no WC, while for a bit extra you can get a magnificent view of the Rade de Brest from the upper storeys. ❸

Continental pl de la Tour d'Auvergne ⓣ02.98.80.50.40, ⓦoceaniahotels.com. Despite the usual dull concrete facade, this grand luxury hotel, not far from the tourist office, has some fine Art Deco features, and is very popular with business travellers. Spotlessly clean and thankfully now no-smoking rooms; several on the fourth floor have large balconies. Good weekend rates. ❻

Kyriad 157 rue Jean-Jaurès ⓣ02.98.43.58.58, ⓦwww.kyriad-brest.com. Although the rooms are on the sterile and small side, this hotel enjoys a good location near the town's nightlife, has good buffet breakfasts (€8) and is close to a free public car park. ❸

Pasteur 29 rue Louis-Pasteur ⓣ02.98.46.08.73. Clean, good-value budget hotel, offering plain if potentially noisy en-suite rooms above a bar, a couple of blocks south of the St-Louis church. ❷

Hostel and campsite

Camping du Goulet Ste-Anne du Portzic ⓣ02.98.45.86.84, ⓦwww.campingdugoulet.com. This leafy and green, two-star, year-round campsite is pretty hard to find, on a headland close to the sea on the outskirts of Brest 8km from the centre, across the Pont de Recouvrance and then to the left of the Le Conquet road (D789) – take bus #7 or #14 from the *gares*.

Hostel Ethic Étapes 5 rue de Kerbriant, Port de Plaisance du Moulin-Blanc ⓣ02.98.41.90.41, ⓦaj-brest.org. Brest's year-round hostel, set in a wooded park, is modern, clean and serves inexpensive meals. It's 3km east of the *gare SNCF*, by the beach and Océanopolis – take bus #7 or #15. Dorm beds €17 including breakfast. ❶

The Town

The one major site in Brest's city centre is its fifteenth-century **château**, perched on a headland above the point where the Penfeld River meets the bay, and offering a tremendous panorama of both the busy port and the roadstead. This site has been continuously occupied since at least the third century AD, when it held the fortified Roman camp of Osismis. Not quite as much of the castle survives as its impressive facade might suggest, though new buildings in the grounds still house the French naval headquarters.

Three still-standing medieval towers of the château, however, house Brest's portion of the **Musée National de la Marine** (daily: Feb, March & Oct–Dec 1.30–6pm; April–Sept 10am–6.30pm; closed Jan; €5; ⓦwww.musee-marine.fr). Collections include some ornate carved figureheads and models, as well as a German "pocket submarine" that was based in Brest during World War II, and visitors can also stroll the parapets to enjoy the views. For motorists, there's also the boon of free parking right outside.

Down on the opposite bank of the Penfeld, and reached via the largest drawbridge in Europe, the **Pont de Recouvrance**, stands the fourteenth-century **Tour Tanguy** topped by a conical slate roof. It's now a museum of local history, where dioramas convey a vivid impression of just how attractive a city Brest used to be (June–Sept daily 10am–noon & 2–7pm; Oct–May Wed & Thurs 2–5pm, Sat & Sun 2–6pm; free).

The **Conservatoire Botanique National de Brest**, a short distance north of Océanopolis in the Parc du Vallon de Stang-Alar beyond the football stadium, claims to be second in Europe only to Kew Gardens (gardens daily: July to mid-Sept 9am–8pm; spring and autumn 9am–7pm; winter 9am–6pm; free; greenhouses: Easter–June & mid-Sept to Oct Wed & Sun 2–5.30pm; July to mid-Sept daily except Sat 2–5.30pm; €4.50; buses #3, #17, #25 or #27, stop "Palaren"; ⓦwww.cbnbrest.fr).

Océanopolis

A state-of-the-art complex of **aquariums** and related attractions, Brest's futuristic and ever-growing **Océanopolis** sprawls a couple of kilometres east of the city centre, beside the Port de Plaisance du Moulin-Blanc (mid-Jan to April and mid-Sept to Dec Tues–Fri 10am–5pm, Sat & Sun 10am–6pm; May, June and first half of Sept daily 9am–6pm; July & Aug daily 9am–7pm; Ⓦwww.oceanopolis.com bus #3; adults €16.20, under-18s €11), Its original white dome, now known as the **Temperate Pavilion**, focuses on the Breton littoral and Finistère's fishing industry, with its half-million gallons of water holding all kinds of fish, seals, molluscs, seaweed and sea anemones. The emphasis is very much on the edible, with displays on the life-cycle of a scallop, for example, culminating in a detailed recipe.

To that has been added a **Tropical Pavilion**, with a tankful of ferocious-looking sharks plus a myriad of rainbow-hued smaller fish that populate a highly convincing coral reef; a **Polar Pavilion**, complete with polar bears and penguins; and a **3-D cinema**. Everything's very high-tech, and perhaps a little too earnest for some visitors' tastes, but it's quite possible to spend a whole entertaining day on site – especially if you take the assorted restaurants, snack bars and gift stores into consideration.

Eating

As well as a concentration of low-priced places in the immediate area of the stations, Brest also offers a wider assortment of **restaurants**. Rue Jean-Jaurès, which climbs up east from the place de la Liberté, holds plenty of bistros and bars, and there are several good seafood places down by the port.

L'Amour de Pomme de Terre 23 rue des Halles Ⓣ02.98.43.48.51. The name says it all: this central restaurant, facing the market *halles*, specializes not merely in potatoes, but in one single kind of potato, the "samba". The most basic dish is simply a baked potato topped with cheese or sausage, but the eccentric owner has also invented all kinds of strange treatments and concoctions, typically costing just under €20, and there are also some tasty Breton stews. Daily until late.

Le Crabe-Marteau 8 quai de la Douane Ⓣ02.98.33.38.57. Once again, it's all in the name; take one crab, add one hammer, and there's your meal, costing something under €20; they also serve oysters and lobsters by way of variety. Closed Sun & Mon.

La Fleur de Sel 15bis rue de Lyon Ⓣ02.98.44.38.65, Ⓦwww.lafleurdesel.com. Brest's finest restaurant serves largely traditional cuisine in highly sophisticated and flavourful combinations. Lunch menu €21, dinner €27–40. Closed Sat lunch, Sun & first three weeks in Aug.

La Maison de l'Océan 2 quai de la Douane Ⓣ02.98.80.44.84. Blue-hued fish restaurant down by the port, with a terrace facing across to the island ferries. Open daily for lunch and dinner, and serving wonderful seafood on menus from €16 to €38.

Pensée Sauvage 13 rue d'Aboville Ⓣ02.98.46.36.65. Popular and informal neighbourhood budget restaurant in the St-Martin district, which offers a bargain €8 lunch special and inexpensive meat or fish dinners from €12. Closed Sat Lunch, plus all Sun & Mon.

Ma Petite Folie plage du Moulin-Blanc Ⓣ02.98.42.44.42. Converted fishing boat, moored in the pleasure port, which serves a wonderfully fishy €22 set menu and also offers a wide range of à la carte dishes and daily specials.

Le Ruffé 1bis rue Yves-Collet Ⓣ02.98.46.07.70. Simple restaurant between the *gare SNCF* and the tourist office, entirely indoors and staying open late, that prides itself on good, traditional French seafood dishes, served on menus costing €13.50–33, with a good-value wine list. Closed Sun eve & Mon.

Drinking, nightlife and entertainment

As well as enjoying a stimulating cultural life, Brest is unusual by Breton standards in having plenty of lively **bars**. The basic choice lies between hanging out with the sailors and fishermen in the busy scene down by the port, with the business community around the place de la Liberté, or with the seriously trendy student population in the St-Martin quarter, high up on and around Jean-Jaurès. Every **Thursday** from mid-July until the end of August is party night at the port, with free music and other performances on three stages along the quai de la Douane.

Bar Écossais 241 rue Jean-Jaurès. An unlikely spectacle, way up at the top of the hill and positively festooned with Scottish memorabilia, which attracts an exuberant Celtic crowd.
Café le Triskell 31 rue Massillon. Pub-style place with wooden tables, where students and Breton activists come to drink and listen to the odd bit of music (literally).
Les Dubliners 28 rue Mathieu-Donnart. Lively Irish pub in the St-Martin district, about 10min walk from St-Martin church. Open daily from mid-afternoon until late, with Irish dancing on Mon and live music on Thurs & Sun.
Le Quartz 2–4 av Clemenceau ⓣ02.98.33.70.70, ⓦlequartz.com. This prestigious national performance space, in the heart of the city, welcomes touring dance, theatre and musical companies.
Les Quatres Vents 18 quai de la Douane. Busy, friendly portside café-bar, with a nautical-themed interior, which also doubles as a brasserie.

From Brest to the Crozon Peninsula

Heading south from Brest, cyclists and pedestrians can cut straight over to the Crozon Peninsula by **ferry** to Le Fret (see p.286). The ferry doesn't, however, carry cars, so **drivers** have a longer and more circuitous route, crossing the Elorn River over the vast spans of the **Pont Albert-Louppe** (42m high and almost 1km long) and then skirting the estuaries of the **Plougastel peninsula**.

Plougastel-Daoulas, just across the bridge, is at the edge of the main parish closes region (see p.267).

Daoulas

Ten kilometres beyond Plougastel-Daoulas, the former site of the **abbey** at **DAOULAS** holds Brittany's only Romanesque cloister. The abbey itself was comprehensively destroyed during the Revolution, leaving only the vestiges of its cloisters, now standing beautiful and isolated at the edge of cool monastery gardens. The abbey gardens make a welcome oasis on a hot summer's day, and also hold a new **museum** building, which each year stages a temporary but large-scale exhibition on some historical or archeological theme (only open during exhibition, usually May–Dec, daily 10.30am–6.30pm; €6 for abbey, gardens and exhibition; ⓣ02.98.25.84.39, ⓦabbaye-daoulas.com).

In the pretty little village of Daoulas itself, immediately below the abbey, a charming B&B, *Ar Baradoz Bihan*, 12 rue de l'Église (ⓣ02.98.85.04.87, ⓦmembres.lycos.fr/baradozbihan; ❸; closed Nov–March), serves a €20 evening meal, and there's also a crêperie and a restaurant.

Le Faou

From Daoulas, the motorway and railway cut down to Châteaulin and Quimper. For Crozon, you'll need to veer west at **LE FAOU**, a tiny medieval port that has retained some of its sixteenth-century gabled houses and is set on its own estuary. From beside the pretty little village **church** – whose porch contains some intriguing carved apostles – a sheltered corniche follows the river to the sea, where there are sailing and windsurfing facilities.

Le Faou has two good and very similar Logis de France **hotels**, both with top-class restaurants – the *Relais de la Place*, 7 place aux Foires (ⓣ02.98.81.91.19; ❸;

closed Sat & all of Jan), which serves menus from €13.20 with a particularly good €26.50 *Menu du Terroir*, and the *Beauvoir* (Ⓣ02.98.81.90.31, Ⓦhotel-beauvoir.com; ④; closed Mon lunch & Sun eve), where menus in the adjoining *Vieille Renommée* range €16–60. The one snag is that they're not in the most attractive part of town, near the river, but a few hundred metres south in the newer and much noisier main square place aux Foires.

The Crozon Peninsula

Though the spectacular **Crozon Peninsula**, thrusting out into the Atlantic between Léon and Cornouaille, is almost entirely given over to tourism, its wild beaches and craggy cliffs remain remarkably unspoiled, and it's hard to beat as a family destination. This whole dramatic promontory forms part of the **Parc Naturel Régional d'Armorique**, a protected natural landscape area that stretches from the forest of Huelgoat to the island of Ouessant.

Even though the western, oceanward end of the peninsula holds its largest towns and the lion's share of its tourist facilities, nowhere is overrun, and the atmosphere remains essentially peaceful. **Crozon** is the largest town, but it makes sense to head straight on either to the classic traditional resort of **Morgat**, arrayed along a splendid curve of golden sand, or **Camaret**, a historic port with a sideline in superlative seafood restaurants.

The **tourist office** for the whole peninsula is at Crozon (see p.283) and there are smaller tourist offices at Camaret and Morgat. At the end of July and/or the start of August, the Festival du Bout du Monde, a **world music festival**, takes place on the Prairie de Landaoudec immediately north of Crozon (Ⓦfestivalduboutdumonde.com).

Public transport around the peninsula is limited to routes between the main towns and tourist resorts: the Brest–Camaret bus stops at Crozon and Morgat,

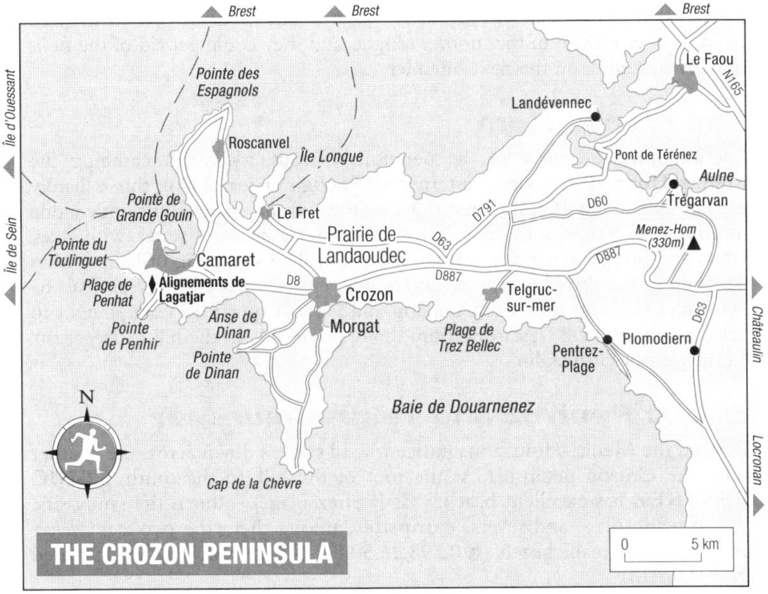

while Quimper–Camaret buses stop at Locronan, St-Nic Pentrez, Telgruc-sur-mer and Crozon.

Landévennec

Nine kilometres west of Le Faou, by way of a beautiful shoreline road, the **Pont de Térénez** spans the Aulne – outlet for the Nantes–Brest canal – to the Crozon peninsula. Doubling back to the right as soon as you cross the bridge brings you after a further 5km to **LANDÉVENNEC**, where archeologists are uncovering the outline of what may be Brittany's oldest **abbey** (mid-Feb to March, Oct & Nov Sun 10am–5pm; April–June daily except Sat 2–6pm; July & Aug daily 10am–7pm; Sept daily 10am–6pm; €4; Ⓦ musee-abbaye-landevennec .fr). Nothing survives above ground of the original thatched hut, constructed in a forest clearing by St Gwennolé around 485 AD. After the abbey had been pillaged by raiding Normans in 913 AD, however, it was rebuilt in stone. Those foundations can now be seen, together with displays on monastic history and facsimile manuscripts.

There's a small but attractive **hotel** in the heart of Landévennec, *Le St-Patrick* (Ⓣ 02.98.27.70.83, Ⓦ le-saint-patrick.fr; ❶; closed mid-Sept to March).

Trégarvan

Still inland from the peninsula, at a solitary crossroads outside the village of **TRÉGARVAN** roughly 3km north of the Menez-Hom, the **Musée de l'École Rurale** provides a fascinating glimpse of rural educational life in the last century (mid-Feb to June daily except Sat 2–6pm; July & Aug daily 10.30am–7pm; Sept daily 2–6pm; Oct & Nov daily except Sat 2–5pm; Dec to mid-Feb Mon–Fri 2–5pm; €4; Ⓦ musee-ecole.fr). It's housed in what used to be the local secondary school, which closed due to lack of numbers in 1974, then reopened a decade later as a re-creation of a Breton classroom circa 1920. At that time, all the kids would have spoken Breton at home – but they were forbidden to speak it here. The teacher gave a little wooden cow to the first child to utter a word in the mother tongue, and they could get rid of the *vache* only by squealing on the next offender.

The Menez-Hom

For an initial overview of the peninsula's layout, it's worth climbing the **Menez-Hom** at its inland, eastern end. Though at just 330m, this is hardly the "mountain" its Breton name suggests, the summit stands sufficiently alone to command tremendous views across Crozon – a chaos of water, with lakes, rivers and bridges wherever you look, and usually a scattering of hang-gliders dangling in the sky. The exposed and windswept viewing table reveals it to be 300 miles (483km) from both London and Paris. A spur road leads straight to the top from the D887, starting from the opposite side of the hill to Trégarvan, 12km west of Châteaulin.

St-Nic Pentrez and Telgruc-sur-mer

Beyond the Menez-Hom, a magnificent road sweeps down across the heather onto the Crozon peninsula. At the foot of the hill, to the south, **ST-NIC PENTREZ** has excellent beaches (at Pentrez Plage) – this is the sandy side of the peninsula – and several **campsites**, among them the two-star *Menez Bichen* on the main beach (Ⓣ 02.98.26.50.82, Ⓦ menezbichen.free.fr; closed Nov–March).

Further round towards Crozon, the village of **TELGRUC-SUR-MER** is poised well above the sea, leaving the gorgeous **Trez Bellec** beach below remarkably pristine for most of the year, though in high summer countless caravans seem to fill the meadows just behind it. A two-star **campsite**, the *Pen Bellec* (Ⓣ02.98.27.31.87, Ⓦcamping-telgruc.fr; closed Oct–May), stands at the eastern end of the beach, while the four-star *Panoramic* (Ⓣ02.98.27.78.41, Ⓦcamping-panoramic.com; closed Oct–April), perches a few hundred metres above its western end.

Some of the smaller towns inland hold **hotels**, such as the *Hôtel-Crêperie de Pors Morvan* (Ⓣ02.98.81.53.23; ❸; closed Jan & Feb), 3km outside **Plomodiern**.

Crozon

The main town on the peninsula proper, **CROZON**, has a nice little stone-built core that serves as the commercial hub for all the surrounding communities, and plays host to a large-scale **market** on the second and fourth Wednesday of each month. As it's also, unfortunately, a traffic hub, its one-way traffic system ever busy distributing tourists among the various resorts, and in any case it's set back from the sea, it's more of a place to pass through than to linger. If you're staying anywhere nearby, however, you'll probably drop in to shop and while away an hour or two in its bars and cafés.

The peninsula's main **tourist office** is a little west of the centre in the *gare routière*, which keeps a constantly updated list of which hotels have rooms available, and also houses an SNCF ticket office (July & Aug Mon–Sat 9.38am–1pm & 2–7pm, Sun 10am–1pm; Sept–June Mon–Sat 9.15am–noon & 2–5.30pm; Ⓣ02.98.27.07.92, Ⓦcrozon.com).

Morgat

MORGAT, just down the hill from Crozon without any noticeable intervening gap, makes a more enticing base than its larger neighbour. It has a long

▲ Seagulls on the beach, the Crozon Peninsula

and very sandy crescent **beach**, much loved by windsurfers, which ends beneath a pine slope, and a well-sheltered harbour that's filled with pleasure boats raced down from England and Ireland.

Other than swimming and sunbathing, the main attractions are **boat trips** around the various headlands, such as the Cap de la Chèvre, which is also a good clifftop walk if you'd rather make your own way. Most popular of all is the 45-minute tour of the **Grottes** with Vedettes Rosmeur (daily April to late Sept, timetables dependent on tides; €10; ⓣ06.85.95.55.49, ⓦgrottes-morgat .com). From these multicoloured caves in the cliffs, accessible only by sea but with steep "chimneys" up to the clifftops, saints would allegedly emerge in bygone days to rescue the shipwrecked. Even though the trips run every quarter of an hour in high season, they often leave full, so it's worth booking a few hours in advance.

Arrival and information

Morgat's summer-only **tourist office** is in the resort's main square, place d'Ys (July & Aug Mon–Sat 10am–1pm & 3–7pm, Sun 4–6.30pm; ⓣ02.98.27.29.49, ⓦcrozon.com). **Bikes** and **kayaks** can be rented from the splendidly named Crapato Bicyclo, next to the tourist office on the boulevard de la Plage (mid-June to mid-Sept daily 9am–7pm; ⓣ06.88.71.72.22; bike €10 per day, kayak €20 per day). If you fancy formal instruction, the Centre Nautique de Crozon-Morgat (ⓣ02.98.16.00.00, ⓦcncm.fr) offers summer classes in sailing, kayaking and surfing, and rents all the relevant equipment.

Accommodation and eating

Morgat holds a handful of appealing **hotels**, while with around nine hundred pitches available, **campers** are spoilt for choice. Away from the hotels, the best place to **eat** is the central *Restaurant Saveurs et Marée*, across from the tourist office at 52 bd de la Plage (ⓣ02.98.26.23.18), which serves great seafood, and has the bonus of outdoor seating.

Hotels

de la Baie 46 bd de la Plage ⓣ02.98.27.07.51, ⓦpresquile-crozon.com/hotel-de-la-baie. This cream-and-blue hotel, in the heart of town, has no restaurant, but offers some very cheap rooms with shared bathrooms, more expensive en-suites, and a couple of family rooms capable of sleeping two adults and two children for around €70. ❷

Grand Hôtel de la Mer bd de la Plage ⓣ02.98.27.02.09, ⓦwww.belambra-vvf.fr. This imposing 1930s structure, set in neat little gardens at the eastern end of the beach, is run as a "holiday club". Guests have to take either half or full board, and in July & Aug you have to stay for a week. Closed early Oct to early April. ❻

Julia 43 rue de Tréflez ⓣ02.98.27.05.89, ⓦhoteljulia.fr. Neat, quiet hotel in a townhouse set 300m back from the beach, with a good restaurant. Closed Jan & Feb. ❸

Campsites

Les Pins rte de Dinan ⓣ02.98.26.23.16, ⓦcamping-crozon-lespins.com. Well-shaded three-star site, well up from the sea above town, with a covered heated swimming pool. Closed Nov–Easter.

Plage de Goulien Goulien, Crozon ⓣ02.98.26.23.16, ⓦcamping-crozon -laplagedegoulien.com. Green-field, three-star campsite, 100m from the southern end of the white-sand Anse de Dinan. Closed mid-Sept to May.

Camaret

One of the loveliest seaside towns in all Brittany, the sheltered port of **CAMARET**, nestles at the western tip of the peninsula. A long jetty runs parallel to the main town waterfront, sheltering it from the open sea. Beyond the quay at the far end of the harbour, assorted headlands offer pretty **beaches** and fine clifftop hiking, while the heathland to the south boasts some haunting **megalithic alignments**.

Arrival and information

Camaret's **tourist office** is at 15 quai Kléber in the port (Mon–Sat 9am–noon & 2–6pm; ⓣ02.98.27.93.60, ⓦcamaret-sur-mer.com).

In summer Penn Ar Bed (ⓣ02.98.80.80.80, ⓦpennarbed.fr) operates an irregular **ferry** service from Camaret to the islands of Ouessant and Sein (both €30.20 return), as detailed on p.273. In July and August, Société Azénor (ⓣ02.98.41.46.23, ⓦazenor.com) runs **cruises** around the bay (daily except Sat 2pm; €15.50), and a ferry service to **Brest** (see p.277), which includes the possibility of day-trips to **Océanopolis** (daily except Sat 10am; €31.50 including admission).

Accommodation

Camaret holds a row of excellent **hotels**, lined up along the quai du Styvel at the far end of the town, close to the start of the protective jetty, while **campsites** are dotted around the heathlands nearby.

Hotels

Du Styvel 2 quai du Styvel ⓣ02.98.27.92.74, ⓔhotelstyvel@orange.fr. Inviting seaside hotel, with comfortable sea-view rooms and a good restaurant; the €17 menu offers *moules à la Ouessane*, the €34 menu oysters, scallops and salmon. Closed Jan. ❷

Thalassa 6 quai du Styvel ⓣ02.98.27.86.44, ⓦhotel-thalassa.com. Upmarket but still good-value hotel, with heated seawater swimming pool and jacuzzi. Paying a little extra will get you a room with a sea-view balcony. Closed Oct–March. ❹

Vauban 4 quai du Styvel ⓣ02.98.27.91.36. Exceptionally hospitable hotel, where the modern, pleasant and very good-value rooms, above a friendly bar, have great views across the port. Closed Dec & Jan. ❷

Campsites

Grand Large Lambézen ⓣ02.98.27.91.41, ⓦwww.campinglegrandlarge.com. Four-star site, with pool and waterslide, near a beach 2km east of Camaret. Closed Oct–March.

Lannic rue du Grouannoc'h ⓣ02.98.27.91.31, ⓦcamaret-sur-mer.com. High-quality, two-star municipal campsite, set back from the sea up the hill in town. Closed Nov–March.

The Town

Foursquare at its far end of the jetty, directly across from the port, the prominent, pink-orange **château de Vauban** was built in 1689 to guard the approaches to Brest. Walled, moated, and accessible via a little gatehouse reached by means of a drawbridge, it now guards no more than a picturesque assortment of decaying half-submerged fishing boats, abandoned to rot beside the jetty.

In 1801, an American, Robert Fulton, tested the first **submarine** off Camaret. The *Nautilus* was a stuffy, leaking, oar-powered wooden craft, whose five-man crew spent some time scuttling about beneath the waves in the hope of sinking a British frigate. Fulton was denied his glory, though, when the frigate chose to sail away, ignorant of the heavy-breathing peril that was so frantically seeking it out.

The largest and most attractive **beach** near Camaret is a couple of kilometres east, beside the main D8 from Crozon, in the low-lying (and rather marshy) Anse de Dinan. Much closer to town, the small sandy **plage du Correjou**, popular with families, starts on the seaward side of the jetty and stretches west. A network of wonderful **coastal footpaths** leads on from here, winding over and/or around successive headlands. The scenery is utterly magnificent, with craggy rocks and sea arches standing just off the heather-topped cliffs, though the dramatic **Plage de Penhat**, just west of the Pointe du Toulinguet, is much too exposed to the ocean to be safe for swimming. Immediately inland, the **Manoir de St Pol Roux** was built by Symbolist poet Pierre Paul Roux in 1904, and subsequently smashed into photogenic ruins by the elements.

The round-trip walk from the port past the headlands and back into Camaret takes between one and two hours, though a six-hour version continues out to the Pointe du Penhir and back (see below). Just across a minor road from the *manoir*, on the southern fringes of Camaret beside the D8 stand the megalithic **Alignements de Lagatjar**. Two centuries ago, six hundred standing stones were counted here. Only 65 of those remain, and many of those are now little more than weather-beaten stumps, jutting out amid the brilliant purples and yellows of the heathland. They're still impressive here at the end of the world, however, and starkly beautiful. Their name means "eye of the chicken", and comes from the Breton name for the Pleiades constellation. Archeologists say they were originally arranged in four distinct lines rather than a circle, and suggest that the open area in the middle was used for rituals or even games.

Eating

Camaret boasts a considerable number of top-class **restaurants**, with fish not surprisingly as the main speciality. The best place to start browsing is the quayside in the centre of town, the quai Toudouze. Options include *Les Frères de la Côte* at no. 11 (Ⓣ02.98.27.95.42; closed late Sept to April), which is à la carte only and serves a succulent *cotriade* fish stew for €15.70, and the *Côté Mer* at no. 12 (Ⓣ02.98.27.93.79; closed Wed & Thurs in low season), which has all-day brasserie service and a good €27 set menu.

The Pointe du Penhir

At the **Pointe du Penhir**, 3km south of Camaret, footpaths lace around the various exposed and windy headlands, frequented mainly by binocular-toting twitchers eyeing up the guillemots and other seabirds that swoop on the **Tas de Pois** rock stacks, scattered out in the sea. Even crazier individuals abseil their way down similar rock stacks still attached to the mainland; here and there, a few paths pick their way down the sheer cliffs, but most peter out in the little natural amphitheatre that faces the Tas de Pois. A monument to the Breton Resistance stands nearby, while an intricate set of wartime German bunkers, marked by a row of black anchors, serves as a memorial to the role of merchant ships in the Battle of the Atlantic.

The Pointe des Espagnols

Heading north from Camaret or Morgat brings you to the **Pointe des Espagnols**, where a viewing point signals the northern tip of the peninsula. Brest is very close and very visible – without being any the more enticing. Around the cape are several forbidden military installations and abandoned wartime bunkers. You're not allowed to leave the road, and neither are you encouraged to turn the provided telescope towards the nuclear submarine base on the Île Longue.

Le Fret

The delightful port village of **LE FRET**, on the northern shore of the peninsula 5km east of Camaret and 5km north of Crozon, is noteworthy mainly for its seasonal **ferry** service to Brest's Port du Commerce, detailed on p.277, and also day-trips to Océanopolis (April–June & Sept 2 sailings daily except Mon; July & Aug 2 sailings daily; €31.50 including admission; Ⓣ02.98.41.46.23, Ⓦazenor.com).

Le Fret only has the tiniest of beaches, though the lagoon nearby is much frequented by birdwatchers. Its pretty quayside holds a fine **hotel**, the *Hostellerie* *de la Mer* (⛹ ⓣ02.98.27.61.90, ⓦhotel.hostelleriedelamer.com; ❸; closed Jan), with a restaurant serving menus from €25.

Locronan

LOCRONAN, a short way from the sea on the minor road that leads down to Quimper from the Crozon peninsula, and enjoying long countryside views from its hilltop eminence, is a prime example of a Breton town that has remained frozen in its ancient form thanks to economic decline.

Each year on the second Sunday in July the town hosts a **pardon** at St-Ronan church; the procession, known as the *petit Tromenie*, expands to a week-long festival, the *grand Tromenie*, every sixth year (2013, 2019 and so on). The processions follow a time-hallowed route said by some to be St Ronan's favourite Sunday walk, and by others, to be the outline of a long-vanished Benedictine abbey. It could even be a pre-Christian circuit of megalithic sites.

Arrival and information

Motorists visiting Locronan are directed to large car parks on the outskirts. Once you've walked to the centre, you'll find the **tourist office** next to the museum (same hours as museum; ⓣ02.98.91.70.14, ⓦlocronan.org).

Accommodation

The only **hotel** in the town proper, *du Prieuré*, at 11 rue du Prieuré on the main approach street (ⓣ02.98.91.70.89, ⓦhotel-le-prieure.com; ❹; closed mid-Nov to mid-March), is normally fully booked well in advance. Though not particularly attractive in itself, it's lovely and quiet in the evenings when the day-trippers have gone, and offers well-equipped rooms, including some suitable for families. It also has a good restaurant with menus from €19 upwards. An alternative, *L'Hostellerie du Bois du Névet*, is set in extensive wooded gardens another 1km out, but lacks its own restaurant (ⓣ02.98.91.70.87, ⓦhostellerie-bois-nevet.com; ❹; closed Nov–Easter). The municipal **campsite** (ⓣ02.98.91.87.76, ⓦcamping-locronan.fr; closed Nov–May) is in a pleasant wooded position not far away.

The Town

From 1469 through to the seventeenth century, Locronan was a hugely successful centre for woven linen, supplying sails to the French, English and Spanish navies. It was first rivalled by Vitré and Rennes, before suffering the "agony and ruin" of the nineteenth century so graphically described in its small **museum** (Feb–June & Sept Mon–Fri 10am–noon & 2–6pm; July & Aug Mon–Sat 10am–1pm & 2–6pm, Sun 2–7pm; €2), just off the main square. The consequence of that ruin has been that the rich medieval houses of the town centre have never been superseded or surrounded by modern development. Film directors love its authenticity, even if Roman Polanski, to film *Tess*, deemed it necessary to change all the porches, put new windows on the Renaissance houses, and bury the main square in mud to make it all look a bit more English.

Today Locronan is once more thriving, thanks to a steady throng of tourists. The town itself is genuinely remarkable, its narrow lanes, lined gorgeous old cottages bedecked in flowers, radiating away from the cobbled square, complete with medieval well, in front of its focal **Église St-Ronan**. Be sure to take the time to walk 300m down the hill of the **rue Moal**, where the lovely little stone chapel of Notre Dame de Bonne Nouvelle holds some surprising modern stained glass, as well as a wooden statue of a depressed-looking Jesus, sitting alone cross-legged.

Eating

Crêperies and snack bars in and around the main square include the good-value *Crêperie Ty Coz* facing the church (ⓣ02.98.91.70.79; closed Nov–Easter), while the *Restaurant Au Coin de Feu*, across from the hotel, (ⓣ02.98.51.82.44; closed Sun, Mon & Tues), serves more substantial menus starting at €19, with views from its glassed-in terrace that reach all the way (just) to the sea.

Douarnenez

Sufficient quantities of tuna, sardines and assorted crustaceans are still landed at the port of **DOUARNENEZ**, in the superbly sheltered Baie du Douarnenez, south of the Crozon peninsula, to keep the largest fish canneries in Europe busy. However, the catch has been declining ever since 1923, when eight hundred fishing boats brought in a hundred million sardines during the six-month season. Over the past twenty years or so, Douarnenez has therefore redefined itself – at phenomenal expense, the subject of considerable local controversy – as a living museum of all matters maritime.

The whole area of **Port-Rhû**, on the west side of town, has become the **Port-Musée**, with its entire waterfront taken up with fishing and other vessels gathered from throughout northern Europe. Its centrepiece, the **Musée du Bateau** in place de l'Enfer (Boat Museum: April–June & Sept to early Nov daily except Mon 10am–12.30pm & 2–6pm; July & Aug daily 10am–7pm;

▲ Surfing at Douarnenez

€6.20; Ⓦwww.port-musee.org) houses slightly smaller vessels than those found in the port, including a *moliceiro* from Portugal and coracles from Wales and Ireland, with exhaustive explanations on construction techniques and a strong emphasis on fishing.

The most appealing part of the Port-Musée, however, is back at the waterfront, where you can roam in and out of five of the boats moored in the port and peer into their oily metallic-smelling engine rooms and cramped sleeping quarters (same opening hours and ticket as the museum).

Of the three separate harbour areas still in operation in Douarnenez, by far the most appealing is the rough-and-ready **port du Rosmeur**, on the east side, which is nominally the fishing port used by the smaller local craft. Its quayside – which is far from totally commercialized, but holds a reasonable number of cafés and restaurants – curves between a pristine wooded promontory to the right and the fish canneries to the left, which continue around the north of the headland. You can buy fresh fish at the waterfront, or go on a sea-fishing excursion yourself, or a tour of the bay.

Although the various **beaches** around town look pretty enough, the sea here is dangerous for swimming. They have, however, become very popular with **surfers** in recent years.

The seaside village of **Ste-Anne-la-Palud**, north of Douarnenez, holds one of the best-known *pardons* in Brittany on the last Sunday in August.

Practicalities

Douarnenez's **tourist office** is at 1 rue du Dr-Mével (April–June Mon–Sat 10am–12.30pm & 2–6pm, Sun 10.45am–12.45pm; July & Aug Mon–Sat 10am–7pm, Sun 10am–1pm & 4–6.30pm; Sept Mon–Sat 10am–12.30pm & 2–6pm; Oct–March Mon–Sat 10am–12.30pm & 2–5.30pm; Ⓣ02.98.92.13.35, Ⓦdouarnenez-tourisme.com), a short walk up from the Port-Musée. Among good-value **hotels** are *Le Bretagne*, nearby at 23 rue Duguay-Trouin (Ⓣ02.98.92.30.44, Ⓦle-bretagne.fr; ③), above a reasonable restaurant, and the more upmarket *De France*, also nearby, on the main street at 4 rue Jean Jaurès (Ⓣ02.98.92.00.02, Ⓦlafrance-dz.com; ④; closed Mon, Sat lunch & Sun eve), where menus in the good restaurant start at €25. Close by on the bay, at Tréboul/Les Sables Blancs, there's a two-star **campsite**, *Croas Men* (Ⓣ02.98.74.00.18, Ⓦcroas-men.com; closed Oct–Easter).

In addition to the hotel **restaurants**, *Le Bigorneau Amoureux*, 2 bd Richepin (Ⓣ02.98.92.35.55, Ⓦbigorneau-amoureux.com; closed Mon), is a good seafood place with a terrace overlooking the plage des Dames. Next to the Musée du Bateau on quai de Port-Rhû, the *Pourquoi Pas* **bar** serves local beers and occasionally hosts live Breton music.

Audierne and around

Though the exposed southwestern extremities of Brittany are not areas you'd normally associate with a classic summer sun-and-sand holiday, **AUDIERNE**, 25km west of Douarnenez on the Bay of Audierne, is something of an exception. An active fishing port, specializing in prawns and crayfish, it squeezes into the narrow inlet of the Goyen estuary, a short way back from the Atlantic. From out to sea, you'd hardly know there was a town here.

At the inland end of town, an **aquarium** called L'Aquashow (April–Sept daily 10am–7pm; Oct daily 2–6pm; Nov–March school hols only, 2–6pm; €13.80;

Ⓦaquarium.fr) holds tankfuls of mostly local fish, captioned as ever with the stress on gastronomy – "the flesh is firm and much enjoyed", or "its flesh is really tasteful". You'll also learn that an octopus can squeeze through a hole as small as its eye, while under-14s can take the "La Tempête" thrill-ride. There's no great point watching the fifteen-minute, commentary-free film show of tropical fish in some unspecified South Seas location, but do make a point of sticking around for one of the regular shows in the open-air riverfront arena, in which captive cormorants and gulls, joined occasionally by their wild brethren, put on aerobatic displays in return for dead sprats. An on-site snack bar serves simple meals on a pleasant terrace, and there's plenty of open space for picnics just outside.

From the town centre, the road continues just over 1km to the long, curving and surprisingly sheltered **beach** of **Ste-Evette**, which has its own crop of hotels and grand homes. Its southern end, 1km further on and close to the open ocean, is the departure point for boats to the Île de Sein (see p.291).

Practicalities

Audierne's **tourist office** is on the main square in the heart of town, at 8 rue Victor-Hugo (July & Aug Mon–Sat 10am–1pm & 2–7pm, Sun 10am–1pm; Sept–June Mon–Fri 9am–noon & 2–5pm, Sat 9am–1pm; Ⓣ02.98.70.12.20, Ⓦaudierne-tourisme.com). One of the few buildings on the seaward side of the road out, in a superb position facing the mouth of the estuary at the very start of Ste-Evette beach, is the **hotel** *Au Roi Gradlon*, 3 bd Manu-Brusq (Ⓣ02.98.70.04.51, Ⓦauroigradlon.com; ❺; closed mid-Dec to Jan). Its unusual design means that the street-level dining room – where the €19 dinner menu offers changing daily specials – is in fact on the top storey, with several further floors, concealed from the road, dropping down below it to the beach. The same management is also responsible for running the significantly larger *L'Horizon*, slightly nearer the town proper at 41 rue J-J-Rousseau (Ⓣ02.98.70.09.91; ❹; closed mid-Oct to March), where rooms are a little cheaper, and identical menus are served. Alternative options nearby include the aptly named *Hôtel de la Plage*, a Logis de France facing the middle of the beach at 21 av Manu-Brusq (Ⓣ02.98.70.01.07, Ⓦhotel-finistere.com; ❹; closed Nov–March), where many of the more expensive sea-view rooms have balconies.

The Pointe du Raz

The **Pointe du Raz** – the Land's End of both Finistère and France, a slow drive 17km west of Audierne – is a "Grand Site National", and makes a magnificent spectacle. Don't come in summer expecting to get the place to yourself; it attracts a million visitors every year, and they've had to build a huge car park roughly 1km short of the actual headland (€6 cars, €3 motorcycles). Alongside stands a welcome and **information** complex that in summer seems always to be thronged with visitors (April–June & Sept daily 10.30am–6pm; July & Aug daily 9.30am–7pm; Ⓣ02.98.70.67.18, Ⓦwww.pointeduraz.com). A couple of **cafés** here sell adequate simple meals, but there's no accommodation or camping.

To reach the *pointe*, either catch one of the frequent free shuttle buses (and check the time of the last one back); walk the most direct route, along an undulating, arrow-straight, track; or take a longer stroll along the footpath that skirts the top of the cliffs. However you get there, you'll be glad of strong-gripping shoes as you teeter above the plummeting fissures of the *pointe*, filling and draining with a deafening surf-roar. The winds are often as fierce as the waves, buffeting the thousands of seabirds that make this their home.

The Baie des Trépassés

The **Baie des Trépassés** (Bay of the Dead), just north of the Pointe du Raz, gets its grim name from the shipwrecked bodies that were once washed up here, and is a possible site of the sunken city of Ys (see p.294). However, it's actually a very attractive spot; green meadows, too exposed to support trees, end abruptly on the low cliffs to either side, there's a huge expanse of flat sand (in fact little else at low tide), and out in the crashing waves surfers and windsurfers get thrashed to within an inch of their lives. Beyond them, you can usually make out the white-painted houses along the harbour on the Île de Sein, while the uninhabited rocks in between hold a veritable forest of lighthouses.

In total, less than half a dozen scattered buildings intrude upon the emptiness. There are no facilities for casual visitors on the beach, but the car park just back from the dunes is usually filled with camper vans from all over Europe.

There are also two **hotels**, both with tremendous views. Right in the middle is the pink *Hôtel de la Baie des Trépassés* (ⓣ02.98.70.61.34, ⓦbaiedestrepasses.com; ❶–❹; closed mid-Nov to mid-Feb; restaurant closed Mon in low season), where some rooms sleep up to four guests, and menus of wonderfully fresh seafood cost from €21. The larger *Relais de la Pointe du Van*, run by the same management, is slightly higher up, to the right (ⓣ02.98.70.62.79, same website; ❸; closed Oct–March).

The Île de Sein

Of all the Breton islands, the tiny **Île de Sein**, just 8km off the end of the Pointe du Raz, has to be the most extraordinary. Nowhere does it rise more than six metres above the surrounding ocean, and for much of its 2.5km length it's barely broader than the breakwater wall of bricks that serves as its central spine. Its very grip on existence seems so tenuous that it's hard to believe anyone could truly survive here. However, the island has in fact been inhabited since prehistoric times. Roman sources tell of a shrine served by nine virgin priestesses, and it was reputed to have been the very last refuge of the Druids in Brittany, who held out there long after the rest of the region was Christianized. It also became famous during World War II, when its entire male population, a total of 140 men, answered General de Gaulle's call to join him in exile in England. During his first muster of the Free French army, de Gaulle observed that Sein appeared to constitute a quarter of France. He subsequently awarded the island the Ordre de la Libération, and came here in 1960 to unveil a monument to its bravery. Over three hundred islanders continue to make their living from the sea, gathering rainwater and seaweed and fishing for scallops, lobster and crayfish.

According to a traditional saying, "Who sees Sein, sees his death", though that's more because it happens to rhyme in French ("*qui voit Sein, voit sa fin*") than because it holds any particular evil. Setting off to reach the island on a misty morning, however, feels as though you're sailing off the edge of the world; in fact, it's so notoriously inconspicuous that it was described by the French Admiral Tourville as the most dangerous reef in the world.

Depending on tide levels, island **ferries** pull in at one or other of the two adjoining harbours that constitute Sein's one tightknit village. There are no cars on the island, its few streets being far too narrow for them to squeeze through, and even bicycles are not permitted. A little **beach** appears in front of the village at low tide, and there's also a **museum** of local history (June & Sept daily

10am–noon & 2–4pm; July & Aug daily 10am–noon & 2–6pm; €2.50), packed with black-and-white photos and press clippings, and displaying a long list of shipwrecks from 1476 onwards. The basic activity for visitors, however, is to take a bracing walk to enjoy some absolutely ravishing coastal scenery.

The **eastern tip** of the island, barely connected to the rest when high tides eat away at the slender natural causeway, was in days gone by laboriously cleared to create scores of tiny agricultural terraces. These have long been overgrown with sparse yellow broom and left to the rabbits, however, so if you fancy picking your way through the rock pools you'll have the place to yourself.

Heading **west** from town, a somewhat longer walk leads past the Free French Monument and a couple of sandy little bays to the island's main **lighthouse**, the Phare de Goulenez.

Practicalities

The principal departure point for **boats** to Sein is Ste-Evette beach, just outside **Audierne** (see p.289); the crossing takes around an hour. Services are operated by Penn Ar Bed (daily: early July to late Aug 3–5 sailings daily, with first at 8.45am; late Aug to early July 1–2 daily, with first at 9.30am; ⓣ02.98.70.70.70, ⓦpennarbed.fr). On Sundays from late June to early September, Penn Ar Bed also run trips to Sein from **Brest** (departs 9am; 1hr 30min) via **Camaret** (9.30am; 1hr). The round-trip **fare** on every route is the same (June–Sept €30.20, Oct–May Mon–Fri €18.40, Sat & Sun €20.40)

Sein is hardly bursting with facilities for tourists, but it does have two **hotels**. The nicest, the *Hôtel-Restaurant d'Armen* (ⓣ02.98.70.90.77, ⓦhotel-armen.net; ❸), is the very last building you come to as you walk west out of town, which makes it the last restaurant in Europe. All its simple but lovely rooms face the sea, as there's ocean on both sides, while its restaurant has seating outside when weather permits, and serves an excellent €20 dinner menu featuring mussels in cider, skate and delicious home-baked bread. Back in town, looking out over the beach from the middle of the port, the *Trois Dauphins*, 16 quai des Paimpolais (ⓣ02.98.70.92.09, ⓦhoteliledesein.com; ❷), offers cosy and attractive rooms, completely fashioned and furnished in wood, but not all en suite or with sea views. It doesn't have a restaurant, but the bar downstairs sells sandwiches.

Of the other **restaurants**, *Le Men Brial*, right by the picturesque little Men Brial lighthouse (ⓣ02.98.70.90.87), offers crêpes, *moules frites* for €10, and a €20 menu; *Chez Brigitte*, facing the beach at 14 quai des Paimpolais (ⓣ02.98.70.91.83; closed Sun eve & Mon, plus mid-Oct to Nov), serves a simple brasserie menu; and the bright blue *Casa de Tom*, nearby on quai des Paimpolais (ⓣ02.98.70.93.12), is a crêperie with a very pleasant terrace.

The Penmarch peninsula

At one time the **Penmarch peninsula** – the southwestern corner of Finistère, which stretches south of Audierne and southwest of Quimper – was one of the richest areas of Brittany. That was before it was plundered by the pirate La Fontenelle in 1597, who led three hundred ships in raids on the local peasantry from his base on the island of La Tristan in the Bay of Douarnenez, and also before the cod, staple of the fishing industry, stopped coming.

Now, in the local tourist literature, the region is known as the **Pays de Bigouden**, *bigouden* being the name of the traditional and very elaborate lace headgear that you may see still worn by the women in many of the villages around Pont l'Abbé. Often as much as a foot high, these are sometimes supported by half-tubes of cardboard, sometimes just very stiffly starched. The white of the *coiffes* swaying in the wind provides one of the memorable colours of the area, along with the red fields of poppies and verges of purple foxgloves.

Pont l'Abbé

PONT L'ABBÉ, the principal town of the peninsula, has a Bigouden museum, spread over three storeys of the keep of its fourteenth-century **château** (Easter–May Mon–Sat 10am–noon & 2–5pm; June–Sept daily 10am–12.30pm & 2–6.30pm; €3.50). As it's almost entirely devoted to local costumes, as described above, you'd need to share that interest to sustain much of a visit. More accessible pleasures lie in a stroll through the woods along the banks of its estuary. The *Tour d'Auvergne*, in the small place Gambetta (Ⓣ02.98.87.00.47, Ⓦtourdauvergne.fr; ❷; restaurant closed Sun & Mon), is a good-value **hotel**, with a fine restaurant and nice outdoor bar seating, under the trees. There are also several decent crêperies around, including the *Quatres Saisons*, at 2 rue Burdeau (Ⓣ02.98.87.06.05; closed Sun in low season).

Le Guilvinec and around

West of Pont L'Abbé, the world **windsurfing** championships have frequently been held at **Pointe de la Torche**, and at any time there are likely to be aficionados of the sport twirling effortlessly about on the dangerous water. For equipment rental or lessons, contact the Twenty Nine **surf shop** in Plomeur (Ⓣ02.98.82.46.33, Ⓦtwenty-nine.com). The coast only becomes swimmable, however, as you round the Pointe de Penmarch towards Loctudy.

The first village you come to, **LE GUILVINEC**, is a not especially attractive, but surprisingly busy, fishing port, sheltered in the mouth of a little river, that's home to the fourth largest fish auction (*criée*) in France. It's also playing a pioneering role in a government initiative to turn fishing into a tourist spectacle. To that end, the second storey of the long harbourfront buildings where the fish are landed and sold has been converted to become **Haliotika**, a sort of museum of the fishing industry that combines exhaustive displays on all aspects of the whole messy business with an open-air terrace offering ringside views as the fleet return each afternoon, from around 4pm, after which there's an early-evening fish auction (early April to early July & Sept Mon–Fri 10am–12.30pm & 2.30–6.30pm; early July to Aug Mon–Fri 9.30am–7pm, Sat & Sun 3–6.30pm; Oct to early Nov Mon–Fri 3–6pm; €5.50, or €6.50 including guided visit to the auction; Ⓣ02.98.58.28.38, Ⓦhaliotika.com). It's also possible to arrange a trip out to sea on a working fishing boat. Le Guilvinec's other main attraction is its small but very pleasant **beach**, facing onto the open sea.

The best **hotel** in Le Guilvinec, the stylish, contemporary *Poisson d'Avril* at 19–21 rue de Men-Meur (Ⓣ02.98.58.23.83, Ⓔlepoisson-d-avril@wanadoo.fr; ❹; closed Jan, restaurant closed Mon in low season), also has a good sea-view **restaurant**.

Loctudy

LOCTUDY, 8km east of Le Guilvinec and 6km south of Pont l'Abbé, is well located for boat trips along the River Odet and out to the nearby islands, and also has its own attractive beaches, while at the same time being relatively uncommercial and laid-back. **Campsites** along its main beach include the two-star *Hortensias*, 38 rue des Tulipes (Ⓣ02.98.87.46.64, Ⓦleshortensias.chez-alice.fr; closed Oct–March) and the three-star *Mouettes*, 6 rue de Pen Hador

(Ⓣ02.98.87.43.51, Ⓦcampingdesmouettes.com; closed mid-Aug to mid-June), as well as some good-value **hotels**, such as the nicely refurbished *Porte des Glénan*, 19 rue du Port (Ⓣ02.98.87.40.21, Ⓦlaportedesglenan.com; ❸).

The Îles de Glénan

The **Îles de Glénan** are a string of islands 16km off the mainland, surrounded by a lagoon with surprisingly clear water and a few pleasant sandy beaches. There are a couple of basic restaurants on the main island, **St-Nicholas**, but they lack the facilities, and the potential activities, for anyone to visit as more than a day-trip. In theory, boat trips depart daily during the summer, though you need to check whether they're running on any particular day; services are cancelled in bad weather or simply if not enough people show up.

Vedettes de l'Odet (all trips €30 return; Ⓣ02.98.57.00.58, Ⓦvedettes-odet.com) **ferries** go to the islands from Loctudy (mid-June to mid-July & first fortnight of Sept Thurs 2pm; mid-July to Aug Tues–Sat 10.15am & 2pm); Bénodet (April Tues & Wed 1.30pm; May to mid-July & first fortnight of Sept daily except Mon & Fri 1.30pm, plus irregular 10am departures; mid-July to Aug Mon & Sun 10am & 1.30pm Tues–Sat 10am, 11am & 1.30pm; second fortnight of Sept Tues, Thurs & Sun 1.30pm); La Forêt-Fouesnant (mid-July to Aug Mon–Fri 10am & 1pm, Sat & Sun 10am); Beg-Meil (April Thurs 2pm; mid-July to Aug Mon–Fri 10.30am & 2pm, Sat & Sun 1.30pm); and Concarneau (mid-July to Aug daily 11am & 2pm).

Between April and mid-September, Vedettes Glénn (€25 return; Ⓣ02.98.97.10.31, Ⓦvedettes-glenn.fr) also run trips from Concarneau; schedules vary enormously, though between early July and late August there are daily sailings at 10am & 2.15pm.

Quimper

Pretty, historic, laid-back **QUIMPER** ranks high among the most attractive cities in Brittany. Still "the charming little place" known to Flaubert, it takes at most half an hour to cross it on foot. Though relaxed, it's active enough to have the bars and atmosphere to make it worth going out café-crawling. The word *kemper* denotes the junction of the two rivers, the Steir and the Odet, around which lie the cobbled streets (now mainly pedestrianized) of the medieval quarter, dominated by the cathedral towering nearby.

The drowned city of Ys

Legend has it that **King Gradlon** built the city of **Ys** in the Baie de Douarnenez, protected from the water by gates and locks to which only he and his daughter had keys. She sounds like a pleasant sort, providing all the citizens with pet sea-dragons to do their errands, but **Saint Corentin** saw decadence and suspected evil. He was proved right: at the urging of the Devil, the princess used her key to open the floodgates, the city was flooded, and Gradlon escaped only by obeying Corentin and throwing his daughter into the sea. Back on dry land, and in need of a new capital, Gradlon founded Quimper. Ys remains on the sea floor, but will rise again when Paris ("*Par-Ys*", "equal to Ys") sinks. According to tradition, on feast days sailors can still hear church bells and hymns under the water.

Boats from Quimper

Between June and September you can **cruise** from Quimper down the Odet to Bénodet, which takes about 1 hour 15 minutes each way, on Vedettes de l'Odet (€25 return; ⓣ02.98.57.00.58, ⓦvedettes-odet.com). Both the schedules and the precise departure point from Quimper vary according to the tide; the river in the town centre is too shallow, so the boats always moor at least a short distance downstream. Between one and four boats sail every day (except Sun in July & Aug); check with the tourist office, who also sell tickets. The same company also sails between Quimper and the **Îles de Glénan** (see p.294).

As the Odet curves from east to southwest, it is crossed by numerous low flat bridges, bedecked with geraniums, and chrysanthemums in the autumn. You can stroll along the boulevards on both banks of the river, where several ultra-modern edifices blend in an oddly harmonious way with their ancient – and attractive – surroundings. Overlooking all is tree-covered **Mont Frugy** (all of 87m above the river), which you can climb for good views over the city. There is no great pressure in Quimper to rush around monuments or museums, and the most enjoyable option may be to take a boat and drift down the Odet "the prettiest river in France" to the open sea at Bénodet.

Capital of the ancient diocese, kingdom and later duchy of Cornouaille, Quimper is the oldest Breton city. According to the only source – legend – its first bishop, St Corentin, came with the first Bretons across the English Channel to Brittany, the place they named Little Britain, some time between the fourth and seventh centuries. He lived by eating a regenerating and immortal fish all his life, and was made bishop by one King Gradlon, whose life he later saved when the sea-bed city of Ys was destroyed (see box opposite).

Arrival, information and city transport

Finding a **parking** space in the centre of Quimper can be difficult; if there's no room in the paying car park beside the river, near the tourist office, head for the free, thousand-place Parking de la Providence, a ten-minute walk north of the centre.

The **gare SNCF** and **gare routière** are next to each other on avenue de la Gare, 1km east of the town centre on bus route #6. If you want to get to the coast using public transport, the **bus** is your only option. The most useful operator is CAT, 10 rue Jules Verne (ⓣ02.98.90.68.40, ⓦcat29.fr). **Bikes** are available for rent from Torch VTT, 58 rue de la Providence (ⓣ02.98.53.84.41, ⓦmonsite.orange.fr/torchvttquimper; closed Sun).

The **tourist office**, which organizes a complex schedule of **guided tours** in season, is on the south bank of the Odet at 7 rue de la Déesse, place de la Résistance (April & May Mon–Sat 9.30am–12.30pm & 1.30–6.30pm; June & Sept Mon–Sat 9.30am–12.30pm & 1.30–6.30pm, Sun 10am–12.45pm; July & Aug Mon–Sat 9am–7pm, Sun 10am–12.45pm; Oct–March Mon–Sat 9am–12.30pm & 1.30–6pm; ⓣ02.98.53.04.05, ⓦwww.quimper-tourisme.com). For **internet** access, call in at *Wok Café*, 53 bd de Kerguélen (ⓣ02.98.64.40.07, ⓦwokcafe.fr).

Accommodation

There are remarkably few **hotels** in the old streets in the centre of Quimper, though several can be found near the station. Rooms can be especially difficult to find in late July or early August, when reservations are advisable.

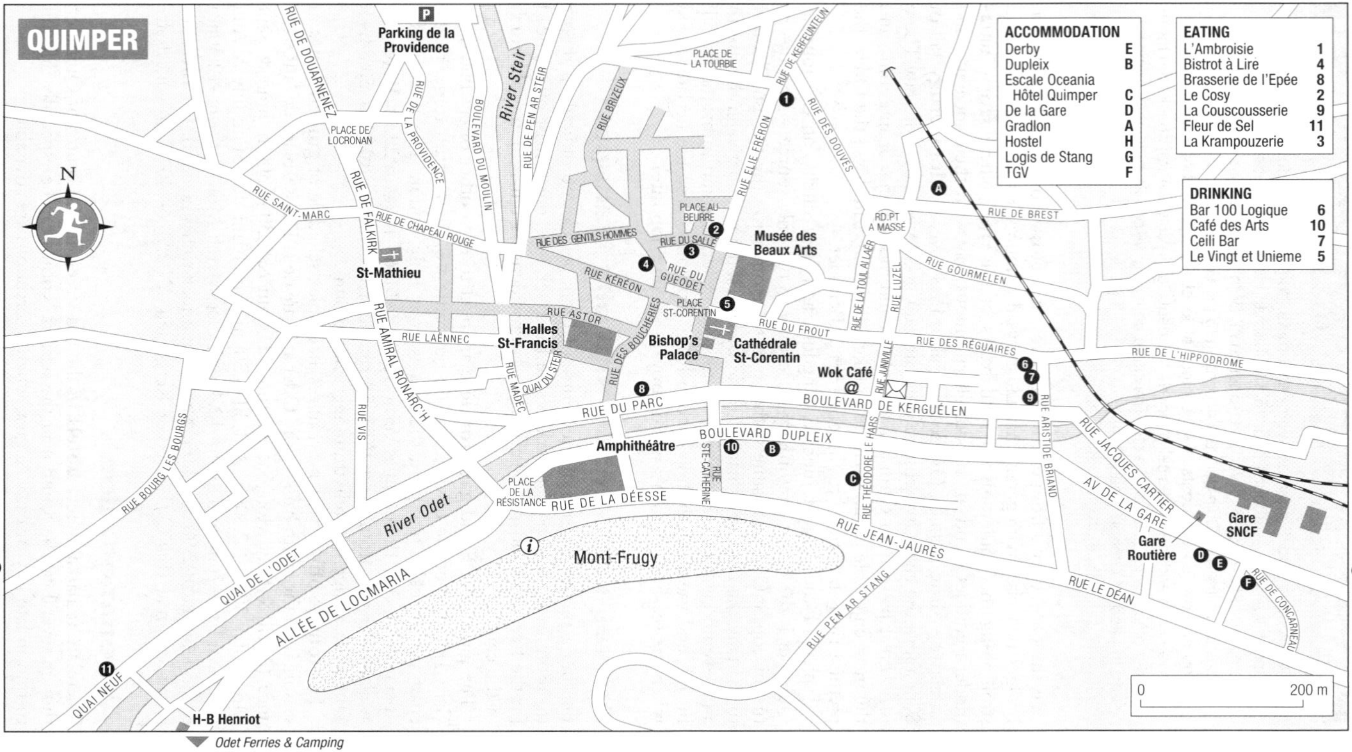
QUIMPER
ACCOMMODATION
Derby E
Dupleix B
Escale Oceania Hôtel Quimper C
De la Gare D
Gradlon A
Hostel H
Logis de Stang G
TGV F
EATING
L'Ambroisie 1
Bistrot à Lire 4
Brasserie de l'Epée 8
Le Cosy 2
La Couscousserie 9
Fleur de Sel 11
La Krampouzerie 3
DRINKING
Bar 100 Logique 6
Café des Arts 10
Ceili Bar 7
Le Vingt et Unieme 5
Parking de la Providence
St-Mathieu
Halles St-Francis
Bishop's Palace
Cathédrale St-Corentin
Musée des Beaux Arts
Wok Café
Amphithéâtre
Mont-Frugy
River Steir
River Odet
Gare SNCF
Gare Routière
H-B Henriot
Odet Ferries & Camping
RUE DE DOUARNENEZ
PLACE DE LOCRONAN
RUE DE LA PROVIDENCE
BOULEVARD DU MOULIN
RUE DE PEN AR STEIR
RUE BRIZEUX
PLACE DE LA TOURBIE
RUE DE KERFEUNTEUN
RUE DES DOUVES
RUE ELIE FRÉRON
PLACE AU BEURRE
RUE DU SALLE
RUE DES GENTILS HOMMES
RUE KÉRÉON
RUE DU GUEODET
PLACE ST-CORENTIN
RUE ASTOR
RUE DES BOUCHERIES
RUE SAINT-MARC
RUE DE FALKIRK
RUE DE CHAPEAU ROUGE
RUE LAËNNEC
RUE AMIRAL RONARC'H
RUE VIS
RUE MADEC
QUAI DU STEIR
RUE DU PARC
RUE BOURG LES BOURGS
QUAI DE L'ODET
QUAI NEUF
ALLÉE DE LOCMARIA
PLACE DE LA RÉSISTANCE
RUE DE LA DÉESSE
RUE STE-CATHERINE
BOULEVARD DUPLEIX
BOULEVARD DE KERGUÉLEN
RUE DU FROUT
RUE DE LA TOUL AL LAER
RUE LUZEL
RUE JUNIVILLE
RUE DES RÉGUAIRES
RD.PT A MASSÉ
RUE DE BREST
RUE GOURMELEN
RUE DE L'HIPPODROME
RUE THÉODORE LE HARS
RUE ARISTIDE BRIAND
RUE JACQUES CARTIER
AV DE LA GARE
RUE JEAN-JAURÈS
RUE PEN AR STANG
RUE LE DÉAN
RUE DE CONCARNEAU
0 200 m

Hotels and B&Bs

Derby 13 av de la Gare ⓣ02.98.52.06.91, ⓦwww.hotel-le-derby.fr. Inexpensive, surprisingly quiet option above a corner bar facing the station. ❷

Dupleix 34 bd Dupleix ⓣ02.98.90.53.35, ⓦwww.hotel-dupleix.com. Modern concrete hotel, not very attractive from the outside but airy and bright within, in a good central location overlooking the Odet, with fine views across the river to the cathedral. Some rooms have balconies. The free private garage is a major advantage in this part of town. ❺

Escale Oceania Hôtel Quimper 6 rue Théodore Le Hars ⓣ02.98.53.37.37, ⓦoceaniahotels.com. Comfortable and centrally located hotel, next to a parking garage, that offers slightly characterless, but reliably clean and quiet rooms, very helpful and polite service and €9 buffet breakfasts. ❺

De la Gare 17 av de la Gare ⓣ02.98.90.00.81, ⓦhoteldelagarequimper.com. Simple en-suite rooms arranged around a floral patio and above a no-nonsense snack bar across from the station. ❷

Gradlon 30 rue du Brest ⓣ02.98.95.04.39, ⓦwww.hotel-gradlon.com. Central but quiet, this exceptionally friendly hotel is an ideal city base, and has a pleasant garden. The rooms may not be cheap, but they're very tastefully decorated. There's also a good bar, focusing around an open fire in the cooler months. ❻

Logis de Stang Allée du Stang-Youen ⓣ02.98.52.00.55, ⓦwww.logis-du-stang.com. Delightful B&B, set away east of the bustle of the centre in a nineteenth-century house, with five well-furnished en-suite rooms at a great price and a hortensia-filled garden. ❺

TGV 4 rue de Concarneau ⓣ02.98.90.54.00, ⓦhoteltgv.com. Another cheap option opposite the station, this time offering plain but clean rooms with shower and TV at bargain rates. Steer clear of the first floor ones; they get a bit noisy. ❶

Hostel and camping

Hostel 6 av des Oiseaux, Bois de Seminaire ⓣ02.98.64.97.97, ⓦfuaj.org/quimper. Unremarkable but clean hostel, 2km west of the centre on bus route #1. Guests have use of a kitchen, there's a quiet garden, and bikes are available for rent. The €12.50 price for a dorm bed includes sheets, but breakfast is €3 extra. Closed Oct–March.

Orangerie de Lanniron rte de Bénodet ⓣ02.98.90.62.02, ⓦwww.lanniron.com. Four-star campsite, 4km south of the centre in the grounds of a château, with swimming pool and tennis court, and also chalets and stone cottages for rent. Closed mid-Sept to mid-May.

The Town

Quimper's focal point, the enormous **Cathédrale St-Corentin** is said to be the most complete Gothic cathedral in Brittany, though its neo-Gothic spires date from 1856, and several years of elbow grease have turned it a sparkling white. When the nave was being added to the old chancel in the fifteenth century, the extension would either have hit existing buildings or the swampy edge of the (then) unchannelled river. The masons eventually found a solution and placed the nave at a slight angle – a peculiarity which, once noticed, makes it hard to concentrate on the other Gothic splendours within.

The exterior, however, gives no hint of the deviation, with King Gradlon now mounted in perfect symmetry between the spires. Before the Revolution, each St Cecilia's Day a climber would ascend to give the king a drink, and there was a prize of 100 *écus* for whoever could catch the glass, thrown down afterwards. During the sixteenth century, fifteen hundred refugees died of plague inside the building.

Alongside the cathedral, the quirky-looking **Bishop's Palace** nestles against one of the few remaining fragments of the old city walls. Inside you'll find a wonderful staircase, and the beautifully laid out **Musée Départemental Breton** (June–Sept daily 9am–6pm; Oct–May Tues–Sat 9am–noon & 2–5pm, Sun 2–5pm; €4). Its collections start with Bronze Age spear- and axe-heads and prehistoric golden jewellery, move rapidly through Roman and medieval statues, and culminate with a remarkable assortment of Breton oddments and *objets d'art*. The highlights are the sixteenth-century statues of polychromed wood, some of which stood originally in the cathedral, but upstairs you'll also find prized examples of regional costumes, furniture including an ornate nineteenth-century *lit clos* (enclosed bed) and ceramics.

Even more compelling is the **Musée des Beaux Arts**, alongside the Hôtel de Ville at 40 place St-Corentin (April–June, Sept & Oct daily except Tues 10am–noon & 2–6pm; July & Aug daily 10am–7pm; Nov–March Mon & Wed–Sat 10am–noon & 2–6pm, Sun 2–6pm; €4.50; Ⓦmusee-beauxarts.quimper.fr). Refurbished to very classy effect, with new floors and suspended walkways, it focuses especially on an amazing assemblage of drawings by Max Jacob – who was born in Quimper – and his contemporaries. Jean-Julien Lemordant's vibrant murals of Breton scenes, commissioned in 1907 for Quimper's *Hôtel de l'Epée* (which closed in 1974) get a room to themselves, and there's also quite a selection of nineteenth- and twentieth-century paintings from the Pont-Aven school, though you'd hardly notice the only Gauguin, a goose he painted on the door of Marie Henry's inn in Pont-Aven itself.

The heart of **old Quimper** lies in and to the west of place St-Corentin, in front of the cathedral. This is where you'll find the liveliest shops and cafés, housed in the old half-timbered buildings, such as the Breton Keltia-Musique record shop at 1 place au Beurre (Ⓣ02.98.95.42.65, Ⓦkeltiamusique.com), and the Celtic shop, Ar Bed Keltiek, between the cathedral and the river at 2 rue du Roi-Gradlon (Ⓣ02.98.95.42.82, Ⓦarbedkeltiek.com). The old market hall was burned down in 1976, but the light and spacious **Halles St-Francis**, built to replace it on rue Astor, is quite a delight, not just for the food, but for the view past the upturned boat rafters through the roof to the cathedral's twin spires. It's open from Monday to Saturday, with an extra-large market spreading into the surrounding streets on Saturdays.

Eating

Although the pedestrian streets west of the cathedral are unexpectedly short on places to eat, there are quite a few **restaurants** further east on the north side of the river, en route to the *gare SNCF*. For crêperies, place au Beurre, a short walk northwest of the cathedral, is a good bet.

L'Ambroisie 49 rue Élie-Fréron Ⓣ02.98.95.00.02. Upmarket French restaurant a short climb north from the cathedral, featuring lots of fine seafood (including tuna) and meat dishes on menus from €23. Closed Mon, plus Sun eve in winter.

Bistrot à Lire 18 rue des Boucheries Ⓣ02.98.95.30.86. This café specializes in two things: desserts and detective thrillers. The fruit crumbles are an excellent choice for the former; you can pick the latter off the bookshelves and read while you eat. Lunchtime *plats du jour* at lunch for €7.50. Tues–Sat 9am–7.30pm.

Brasserie de l'Epée 14 rue du Parc Ⓣ02.98.95.28.97. Lovely Art Nouveau brasserie, facing the river not far from the cathedral, which serves good-value menus (dinner is €25 or €35) or *moules frites* for €13, and stays open late – you can still get a meal at 11pm, which is rare indeed for Brittany. Closed Sun & Mon.

Le Cosy 2 rue du Sallé Ⓣ02.98.95.23.65. Pretty little bistro just north of the cathedral, where the menu proudly insists they serve *pas de crêpes, pas de frîtes*; instead savoury *tartines* or daily *plats* cost €10.50–14. Closed Sun & Mon.

La Couscousserie 1 bd de Kerguélen Ⓣ02.98.95.46.50. Plush, enjoyable Middle Eastern restaurant by the river, serving couscous platters at €12–24, and tagines for around €17, in two Arabian Nights-themed rooms decked out with hookahs and the like. Closed Aug.

Fleur de Sel 1 quai Neuf Ⓣ02.98.55.04.71, Ⓦfleur-de-sel-quimper.com. Gourmet French cooking not far west of the town centre opposite the atelier H-B Henriot on the north bank of the river, with largely fish menus (dinner €27 or €38). Closed lunch on both Sat & Sun.

La Krampouzerie 9 rue du Sallé Ⓣ02.98.95.13.08. One of the best of Quimper's many crêperies, with some outdoor seating on the pl au Beurre. Most crêpes, such as the one with Roscoff onions and seaweed, cost around €3.80, though a wholewheat *galette* with smoked salmon and cream cheese is €5.50. Closed Sun, plus Mon in winter.

The faïenceries of Quimper

Faïence – tin-glazed earthenware – was first popularized by the city of Faenza in Italy in the sixteenth century. Its production was subsequently taken up by Delft in Holland, Majolica in Spain, and then, from 1690 onwards, in Quimper. Around 1875, just as the coming of the railways brought the first influx of tourists in search of authentic souvenirs, some unknown Breton artisan hit on the idea of painting ceramic ware with naive "folk" designs. Little has changed in the local pottery business since.

As you walk through Quimper, it is impossible to ignore faïence – you are invited to look and to buy on every corner. It's also possible to take a tour in either French or English of the major atelier **H-B Henriot**, which under American ownership continues to produce hand-painted pottery in the allée de Locmaria a few hundred metres west of the tourist office (July & Aug Mon–Sat 9.15–11.15am & 1.30–4.15pm; Sept–June Mon–Fri 10.15–11.15am & 2–4.15pm; ⓣ02.98.90.09.36, ⓦhb-henriot.com; €5). H-B Henriot maintain a bright, modern **gift shop** alongside; the prices, even for the seconds, are similar to those on offer everywhere else, but the selection is superb (Mon–Sat 9.30am–7pm).

Drinking and entertainment

Quimper is a youthful and, by Breton standards, exuberant city, with enough **cafés** and **bars** dotted around the centre to keep you well entertained of an evening.

Quimper's **Festival de Cornouaille** started in 1923, and is still going from strength to strength. This great jamboree of Breton music, costumes, theatre and dance is held in the week before the fourth Sunday in July, attracting guest performers from the other Celtic countries and a scattering of other, sometimes highly unusual, ethnic-cultural ensembles. The whole thing culminates in an incredible Sunday parade through the town. The official programme does not appear until July, but you can get provisional details in advance from the tourist office or at ⓦwww.festival-cornouaille.com. Accommodation is at a premium during the festival.

Not so widely known are the **Semaines Musicales**, which follow in the first three weeks of August (ⓦwww.semaines-musicales-quimper.org). The music is predominantly classical, and tends to favour French composers such as Berlioz, Debussy, Bizet and Poulenc. Founded in 1978, the event serves to bring the rather stuffy nineteenth-century theatre on boulevard Dupleix alive each year.

Bars

Bar 100 Logique 9 rue des Réguaires ⓣ02.98.95.44.69. Classy little bar that makes the most of being Quimper's only gay and lesbian hangout. Closed Mon.

Café des Arts 4 rue Ste-Catherine ⓣ02.98.90.32.06. Young, sociable café on the south bank of the river, which holds debates on the first Friday of every month, where patrons are encouraged to speak out on subjects such as "Men and Women" or "War and Peace".

Ceili Bar 4 rue Aristide Briand ⓣ02.98.95.17.61. This lively and convivial bar is the place to go for all things Breton: beer and opinionated conversation, plus live traditional Celtic bands and occasionally jazz on Sunday nights. Open until 1am.

Le Vingt et Unieme 38 pl St-Corentin ⓣ02.98.95.92.34. Very central bar/brasserie with contemporary decor, including stainless steel walls, and a loungy atmosphere enjoyed by a young, fashionable crowd. Salads and dishes of the day for under €10, plus a good terrace for an evening glass of wine. Closed Sun in low season.

Bénodet

Once out of its city channel, the Odet takes on the anarchic shape of most Breton inlets, spreading out to lake proportions then turning narrow corners between gorges. The resort of **BÉNODET** at the mouth of the river (reachable by boat from Quimper) has a long sheltered beach on the ocean side. The town is a little overdeveloped but the sands are undeniably good, especially for kids, for whom there's a lot laid on – including windsurfing and "beach club" crèches (Club Mickey is highly recommended). During its less busy periods, such as spring or autumn, Bénodet is one of the finest spots for a family holiday in the whole of Brittany.

Across the rivermouth, the equally attractive town of **Ste-Marine** is served by regular pedestrian-only ferries. You can also drive there in a matter of minutes over the graceful **Pont de Cornouaille**, 1km upstream, which offers spectacular views of the estuary.

Practicalities

Ferries between Bénodet and Quimper are detailed on p.295, while trips out to the Îles de Glénan are covered on p.295. The local **tourist office** is at 29 av de la Mer (April to mid-June & last two weeks of Sept Mon–Sat 9.30am–noon & 1.30–6pm; mid-June to mid-Sept Mon–Sat 9am–7pm, Sun 10am–6pm; Oct–March Mon–Sat 9.30am–noon & 2–5pm; ⓣ02.98.57.00.14, ⓦwww.benodet.fr). **Bicycles** can be rented from Cycletty, 5 av de la Mer (ⓣ02.98.57.12.49, ⓦwww.cycletty.com).

Les Bains de Mer, 11 rue du Kerguélen (ⓣ02.98.57.03.41, ⓦlesbainsdemer.com; ❹; closed Jan), is a nice *logis* **hotel** that has comfortable rooms, is close to the port and beach, and has the added attraction of an outdoor heated swimming pool, while the nearby *Ker Vennaïk*, 45 av de la Plage (ⓣ02.98.57.15.40, ⓦhotel-benodet.com; ❸; closed Nov–Easter), is a reasonable lower-priced alternative, where some rooms have balconies. Bénodet also has several large **campsites**, including uniformly comfortable and well-equipped four-star ones such as the enormous *Camping du Letty*, southeast of the village next to the plage du Letty, on rue du Canvez (ⓣ02.98.57.04.69, ⓦcampingduletty.com; closed early Sept to mid-June); the *Camping de la Pointe St-Gilles* nearby (ⓣ02.98.57.05.37, ⓦstgilles.fr; closed late Sept to May); and the *Camping du Port de Plaisance* near the pleasure port (ⓣ02.98.57.02.38, ⓦcampingbenodet.fr; closed late Sept to March), which has its own covered water park.

Recommended **restaurants** include *Le Spi*, at 3 av de la Plage (ⓣ02.98.57.19.50), which serves a fantastic €25 menu, and the restaurant at *Hôtel du Bac* at 19 rue Bac across the rivermouth (ⓣ02.98.51.33.33, ⓦwww.hotelsaintemarine.com; ❻; closed mid-Nov to mid-Dec, plus Mon in low season), though in summer the *Hôtel du Bac* tends to be too full to feed non-guests.

Along the south coast

The final, rocky stretch of the Finistère coast that lies east of Bénodet, cut repeatedly by deep valleys, holds some of the region's most ruggedly attractive scenery. Every little indent and inlet seems to harbour its own gorgeous pocket **beach**, around which resorts such as **Fouesnant** have developed, becoming especially popular for family holidays, and there are also a couple of more substantial communities to attract day-trippers: the walled town of **Concarneau**, and the artists' haven of **Pont-Aven**. The inland town of **Quimperlé** and **Le Pouldu** on the coast are the final two stops of any note before you leave Finistère and enter Morbihan. Trains between Quimper and Lorient run well inland from the sea, so only Quimperlé has a rail service, while Concarneau is the only town it's at all practicable to reach by bus.

Fouesnant and around

Not so much a town as a loose conglomeration of villages, **FOUESNANT**, 9km east of Bénodet, is coming to rival its neighbour as a prime destination for family holidays. While Fouesnant itself is renowned for its cider-makers, and holds a pretty little Romanesque church, most local tourist amenities are gathered in its sister community of **LA FORÊT-FOUESNANT**, 3km further east. Clustered along the waterfront at the foot of a hill so steep that caravans are banned from even approaching, it holds an assortment of attractive **hotels** such as the *Hôtel de l'Espérance*, place de l'Église (Ⓣ02.98.56.96.58, Ⓦwww.hotel-esperance.org; ❸), and the *du Port*, 4 corniche de la Cale (Ⓣ02.98.56.97.33, Ⓦwww.hotelduport.fr; ❸; closed Dec–March; restaurant closed Mon, plus Sun eve & all Tues in low season).

The small resort of **BEG-MEIL**, perched at the headland 3km south of Fouesnant but still under its overall aegis, barely survived the hurricane of 1987, with just a handful of trees to protect its vast expanse of dunes. However, as well as boasting the **hotel** *Thalamot*, just back from the seafront at 4–6 le Chemin-Creux (Ⓣ02.98.94.97.38, Ⓦhotel-thalamot.com; ❹; closed Oct–Easter), it makes an ideal spot for campers. Four-star **campsites** include *La Roche Percée* (Ⓣ02.98.94.94.15, Ⓦwww.camping-larochepercee.com; closed Oct–March), which has two pools and a waterslide, and the seafront *Kervastard* (Ⓣ02.98.94.91.52, Ⓦwww.campinglekervastard.com; closed Oct to late May). Seasonal **ferry** services to the Îles de Glénan are detailed on p.294; in July and August, ferries also connect Beg-Meil with Concarneau across the bay (Mon & Wed only; Ⓣ02.98.97.10.31, Ⓦvedettes-glenn.fr; €13 return).

Concarneau

The historic town of **CONCARNEAU**, on the far side of Fouesnant's Baie de la Forêt 20km east of Bénodet, ranks as the third most important fishing port in France. Nonetheless, it does a reasonable job of passing itself off as a holiday resort. Its greatest asset is its walled medieval **Ville Close**, the small and very well-fortified old city located a few metres offshore on an irregular rocky island in the bay.

Arrival and information

Concarneau's **tourist office** (May, June & first fortnight of Sept Mon–Sat 9am–12.30pm & 1.45–6.30pm, Sun 10am–1pm; July & Aug daily 9am–7pm; mid-Sept to April Mon–Sat 9am–noon & 2–6pm; Ⓣ02.98.97.01.44, Ⓦwww.tourismeconcarneau.fr) is just outside the Ville Close on the quai d'Aiguillon. Long-distance **buses** stop near the tourist office; there's no rail service, but SNCF buses connect with Quimper and Rosporden. **Bikes** can be rented from Cycles Gloanec, 65 av Alain le Lay (Ⓣ02.98.97.09.77).

In summer, Vedettes Glénn (Ⓣ02.98.97.10.31, Ⓦvedettes-glenn.fr) run **ferries** up the Odet to Quimper (early July to end Aug Tues, Thurs & Sun 2.15pm; mid-June to early July & first two weeks of Sept Wed 2.15pm; €27 return); across to Beg-Meil (see p.301); and out to the Îles de Glénan (see p.294). Vedettes de l'Odet also sail to the Îles de Glénan in high season.

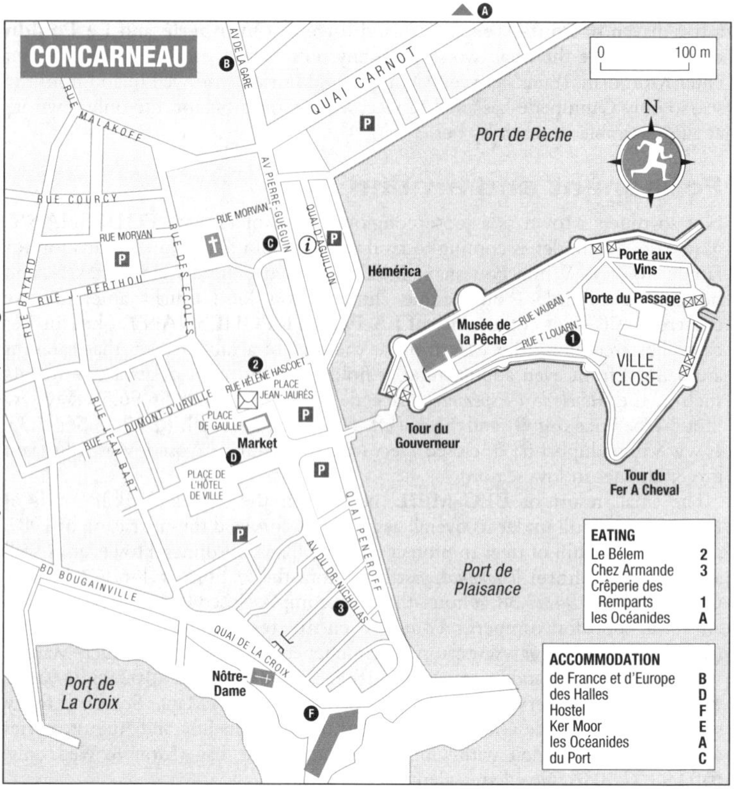

Accommodation

The Ville Close is almost completely devoid of **hotels**, so most of Concarneau's accommodation options are located in the backstreets of the mainland. What's more, the steady flow of tourists keeps them full throughout much of the summer, so it's highly advisable to reserve in advance. As well as an excellent **hostel**, there are also some lovely **campsites**, close to the Sables-Blancs beach.

Hotels

de France et d'Europe 9 av de la Gare ⓣ02.98.97.00.64, ⓦwww.hotel-france-europe.com. Bright, modernized and very central hotel near the main bus stop, which has a small gym. Closed Sat in winter. ❸

des Halles pl de l'Hôtel de Ville ⓣ02.98.97.11.41, ⓦwww.hoteldeshalles.com. Spruce pastel-orange hotel near the fish market, across from the entrance to the Ville Close, offering well-equipped rooms at reasonable rates. ❸

Ker Moor plage les Sables-Blancs ⓣ02.98.97.02.96, ⓦhotel-kermor.com. Classic, beautifully restored seafront hotel, nautically themed throughout, right on the beach 2km west round the headland from town. All the rooms have some view of the sea, but you can pay extra for a full-on balcony. ❻

les Océanides 3 & 10 rue du Lin ⓣ02.98.97.08.61, ⓦlesoceanides.free.fr. Good-value place a couple of streets up from the sea, above the fishing port, with a highly recommended and reasonably priced restaurant (see p.304). Some of the fancier rooms are in the nominally distinct *Petites Océanides* across the street. ❸

du Port 11b av Pierre Guéguin ⓣ02.98.97.31.52, ⓦhotelduport-concarneau.fr. Simple, reasonably priced rooms just outside the Ville Close, above a bar immediately across from the tourist office. ❷

Hostel and campsite

Hostel pl de la croix ⓣ02.98.97.03.47, ⓦajconcarneau.com. Budget travellers will like this very central hostel, which enjoys magnificent ocean views just around the south tip of the headland from the town centre, and has a windsurfing shop nearby. Dorm beds €15 including breakfast.

Prés Verts Kernous plage ⓣ02.98.97.09.74, ⓦpresverts.com. This spacious and utterly irresistible four-star campsite spreads through verdant fields at Kernous beach at the far western end of town. Closed late Sept to April.

The Town

Even if it can get too crowded for comfort in the height of summer, Concarneau's **Ville Close** is a real delight. You reach it by crossing a narrow bridge and then passing through two successive gateways, marked by a little clocktower and a sundial. Like those of the citadelle at Le Palais on Belle-Île, the ramparts were completed by Vauban in the seventeenth century. The island itself, however, had been inhabited for at least a thousand years before that, and is first recorded as the site of a priory founded by King Gradlon of Quimper.

Concarneau boasts that it is a *ville fleurie*, and the flowers are at their most evident inside the walls, where climbing roses and clematis swarm all over the various gift shops, restaurants, ice cream shops and crêperies. Walk the central pedestrianized street to the far end, and you can pass through a gateway to the shoreline to watch the fishing boats go by, or catch a little *bac* (ferry) across the river mouth. The best views of all come from the promenade on top of the **ramparts**; you can't stroll all the way round to make a complete circuit of the walls, but here and there you can climb up for short stretches.

By exploring the history and practice of fishing all over the world, from prehistoric times onwards, the **Musée de la Pêche**, immediately inside the Ville Close (daily: July & Aug 9.30am–8pm; June & Sept 10am–6pm; Oct–May 10am–noon & 2–6pm; €6), provides an insight into the traditional life Concarneau shared with so many other Breton ports. The four rooms around its central quadrangle illuminate four specific aspects of fishing. The whaling room contains model boats and a genuine open boat from the Azores; the tuna room shows boats dragging nets the size of central Paris; and there's also a herring room and a model of a sardine cannery (which this building once was). Passing through the city walls at the rear of the museum, you can tour a genuine trawler moored alongside, the *Hémerica*. Also on show are a three-thousand-year-old anchor from Crete, and further oddities collected by fishermen; the swords of swordfish and the saws of sawfish; a Japanese giant crab; photos of old lifeboatmen with fading beards; cases full of sardine and tuna cans; and a live aquarium. A small diorama illustrates the story of local man Jean-Marie Le Bris who apparently in 1856 became the first man to fly, in a sort of winged boat drawn by a horse and cart, on the beach at Tréfeuntec. Back in the museum shop, you can buy diagrams and models of ships, and stock up on tinned sardines and mackerel.

Eating

To complete the experience of visiting Concarneau with an atmospheric **meal**, your best bet is to choose from any of the restaurants along the main street that runs through the Ville Close, or explore the little lanes that lead off it. There are, however, plenty of cheaper places, where the food is just as good if not better, back in town.

The main **market** is held in front of the Ville Close on Friday, with a smaller one on Monday; the covered market *halles* on the far side of the square are open every morning, and hold plenty of snack stalls.

Le Bélem 2 rue Hélène Hascoët ⓣ02.98.97.02.78. Pretty little indoor restaurant, next to the market on the mainland, serving mussels for €9.60 and good seafood menus from €20. Closed Wed, plus Thurs eve & Sun eve in low season.

Chez Armande 15 av du Dr-Nicholas ⓣ02.98.97.00.76. Excellent seafood not far south of the market on the mainland, on menus starting from €12.65 at lunch, €18 in the evening. Closed Wed & Tues in winter.

Crêperie des Remparts 31 rue Théophile Luarn ⓣ02.98.50.65.66. Good inexpensive crêpes, slightly off the beaten track behind the main street in the walled city, served either indoors or on a nice terrace. There's also a good €12 lunch menu. Closed Mon & Nov–Easter.

les Océanides 3 rue du Lin ⓣ02.98.97.08.61. One of the better hotel restaurants, again specializing in seafood, with menus up to €32; the €17 option has scallops as a starter and the fish of the day as the main course.

Pont-Aven

PONT-AVEN, 14km east of Concarneau and just inland from the tip of the Aven estuary, is a small port village that's packed with tourists and art galleries. This was where **Paul Gauguin** came to paint in the 1880s, before he left for Tahiti in search of a South Seas idyll. By all accounts Gauguin was a rude and arrogant man who lorded it over the local population (who were already well used to posing in "peasant attire" for visiting artists). As a painter and printmaker, however, he produced some of his finest work in Pont-Aven, and his influence was such that the **Pont-Aven School** of fellow artists developed here. He spent some years working closely with these – the best known of whom was Émile Bernard – and they in turn helped to revitalize his own approach.

For all the local hype, however, the town has no permanent collection of Gauguin's work. The **Musée Municipal** (daily: Feb, March, Nov & Dec 10am–12.30pm & 2–6pm; April–June, Sept & Oct 10am–12.30pm & 2–6.30pm; July & Aug 10am–7pm; €4.50), in the Mairie, holds changing exhibitions of the numerous members of the school, and other artists active in Brittany during the same period, but you can't count on paintings by the man himself.

Gauguin aside, Pont-Aven is pleasant in its own right, with countless galleries making it easy to while away an afternoon, and the small neat pleasure port boasting a watermill and the odd leaping salmon. Just upstream of the little granite bridge at the heart of town – home to perhaps the world's prettiest public toilet – the **promenade Xavier-Grall** crisscrosses the tiny river itself on landscaped walkways, offering glimpses of the backs of venerable mansions, dripping with red ivy, and a little "chaos" of rocks in the stream itself. A longer walk – allow an hour – leads into the **Bois d'Amour**, wooded gardens which have long provided inspiration to visiting painters – and a fair tally, too, of poets and musicians.

If you can't afford to take a souvenir canvas home with you, the town's other speciality is more affordable, and tastes better too. Pont-Aven is the home of two manufacturers of **galettes** – which here means "butter biscuits" rather than "pancakes" – and their products are on sale everywhere.

Practicalities

Pont-Aven's **tourist office** is at 5 place de l'Hôtel de Ville (April–June & Sept Mon–Sat 10am–12.30pm & 2–6pm, Sun 3–6pm; July & Aug Mon–Sat 9.30am–7pm, Sun 10am–1pm & 3–6.30pm; Oct–March Mon–Sat 10am–12.30pm & 2–6pm; ⓣ02.98.06.04.70, ⓦpontaven.com).

Once the day-trippers have gone home, Pont-Aven makes a tranquil place to spend a night. Much the best of the town's three relatively expensive **hotels** is the central *Ajoncs d'Or*, 1 place de l'Hôtel de Ville (ⓣ02.98.06.02.06, ⓦajoncsdor-pontaven.com; ❸; closed Jan, plus Mon & Sun eve in low season),

Megaliths and monuments

Both Brittany and Normandy boast ancient sites and monuments out of all proportion to their size, testament to the dramatic impact each has had on the history of Europe. Brittany can trace its heritage back to the dawn of human civilization – its megalithic monuments are the oldest stone structures on the continent. The heyday of Normandy came later, when its warriors conquered territories from England to Sicily, and its architects erected magnificent cathedrals, castles and monasteries. Gothic and Romanesque masterpieces still dominate the landscape, with the majestic island abbey of Mont-St-Michel as the sublime apex.

Menhirs near Carnac ▲ Cairn du Barnenez ▼

Interior of a dolmen, Locmariaquer ▼

Brittany's megaliths

From solitary stones on windswept hillsides to intricate alignments marching across the meadows, from mysterious tombs to multi-chambered pyramids, megaliths are a defining feature of the Breton landscape. Their sheer age is mind-boggling: the earliest monuments are almost eight thousand years old.

The words used to describe the megaliths are largely Breton. Thus a single standing stone is a **menhir**, from the Breton for "long stone", while a pi-shaped structure is a **dolmen** ("stone table"), and a ring of stones is a **cromlech** ("stone circle").

That certain megalithic structures are aligned with astronomical phenomena may simply show their builders knew about astronomy, not that that was the purpose of their monuments. What's more, how we see them today may bear little resemblance to how they originally looked, surrounded by wooden huts or temples, daubed with ochre or lit by fire, or festooned with pelts and trophies.

The pre-eminent Breton site, **Carnac**, holds an extraordinary profusion of *menhirs*, laid out in groups of a thousand or more. Neighbouring **Locmariaquer** is home to a single enormous *menhir* that once stood more than twenty metres tall, but now lies in pieces alongside the intriguing Table des Marchand, a *dolmen* whose dark inner chamber is adorned with enigmatic carvings. The tumulus of **Gavrinis**, on a tiny island nearby, resembles an Egyptian step-pyramid, with the rounded central chamber at its heart reached by a long tunnel. The even more impressive **Cairn du Barnenez** on Brittany's rugged north coast, consists of two separate pyramids, riddled with passageways of impenetrable purpose.

6

Inland Brittany: The Nantes–Brest Canal

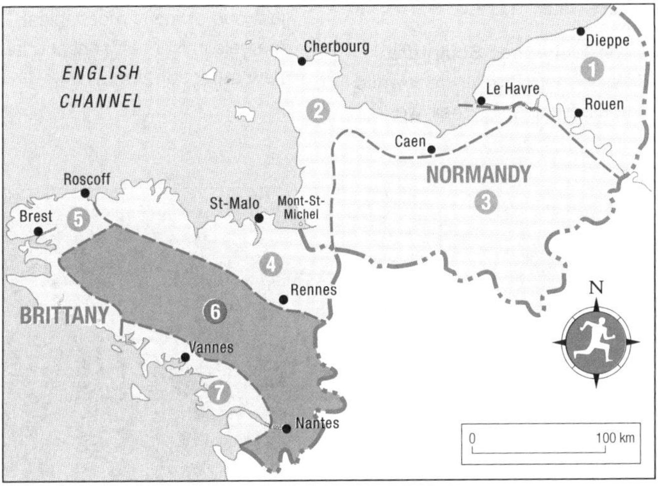

CHAPTER 5

Highlights

* **Huelgoat** A tangled ancient forest, concealing mysterious ruins and deep caverns, all but surrounds an archetypal Breton village. See p.315

* **Jardins de l'Abbaye** Gorgeous little hotel, tucked into the outbuildings of a ruined medieval monastery in a beautiful waterfront setting near Lac de Guerlédan. See p.318

* **Venus de Quinipily** An ancient statue, possibly of Egyptian origin, still draws curious pilgrims to the country backwater of Baud. See p.320

* **Kerguéhennec Sculpture Park** Internationally renowned sculptors display their works in the surreal setting of the grounds of an eighteenth-century château – and you can see them all for free. See p.322

* **Malestroit** The central square in this quiet medieval town holds fascinating vernacular carvings and sculptures. See p.326

* **Redon** Sizeable and likeably lively town at the junction of several major roads and waterways. See p.329

* **Les Machines de l'Île** The majestic Grand Elephant is just one of many mechanical marvels in Nantes' sensational new attraction. See p.335

▲ The Nantes–Brest Canal

6

Inland Brittany: The Nantes–Brest Canal

The meandering chain of waterways known as the **Nantes–Brest canal**, which interweaves natural rivers with purpose-built stretches of canal, runs all the way from Finistère to the Loire. En route it passes through medieval riverside towns, such as **Josselin** and **Malestroit**, which long predate its construction; commercial ports and junctions – **Pontivy**, most notably – that developed along its path during the nineteenth century; the old port of **Redon**, where the canal crosses the River Vilaine; and a succession of scenic splendours, including the string of lakes around the **Barrage de Guerlédan** dam near Mur-de-Bretagne. The canal ends by meeting the Loire River at the major city of **Nantes**, which is currently experiencing a huge revitalization focused especially on the stunning **Machines de l'Île** project.

The canal is ideal as a focus for exploring **inland Brittany**, perhaps cutting in to the towpaths along the more easily accessible stretches, and then heading out to the towns and sights around. Enjoyable detours include the **sculpture park** at Kerguéhennec, near Josselin, and the village of **La Gacilly** near Malestroit.

According to legend, this area was covered in the distant past by one vast forest, the *Argoat*. Vestiges of ancient woodland still remain in several areas, like the forests of **Huelgoat**, with its boulder-strewn waterfalls, and **Paimpont,** said in Arthurian legend to have concealed the Holy Grail.

Although for much of the route described in this chapter no road runs adjacent to the canal, the **towpath** is normally clear enough for walking, and it's usually possible to cycle alongside as well. The best way to explore is to rent a **boat**, **barge** or even a **houseboat** along the navigable stretches.

The canal in Finistère

Although the westernmost section of the canal, passing through Finistère, is now one of its least used stretches, it does hold a number of interesting towns and villages, including peaceful **Châteaulin**, and dynamic **Carhaix**, home to France's largest rock festival.

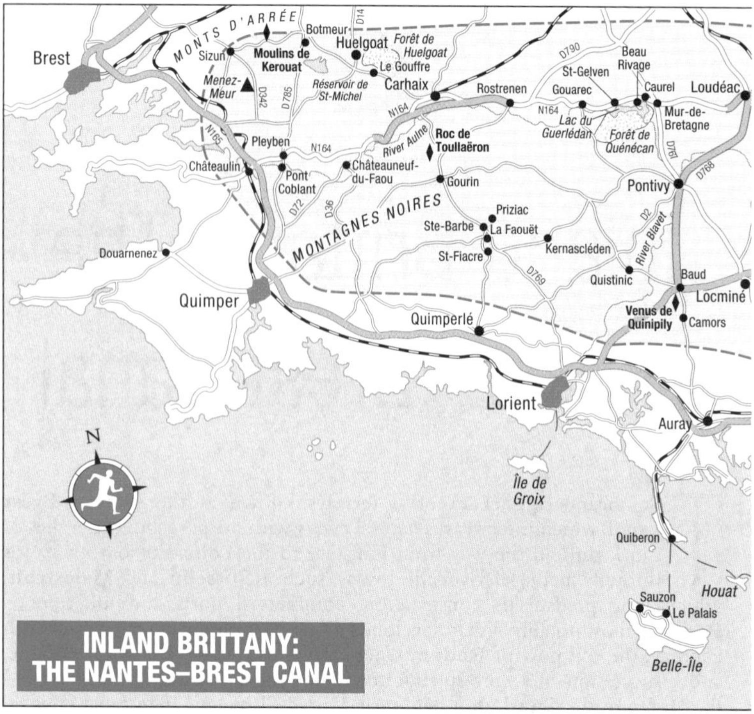

Châteaulin

CHÂTEAULIN, the first real town on the canal route, amounts to little more than a brief, picturesque waterside strip, overlooked by the pretty little chapel of Notre Dame. It's a quiet place, where the main reason to stay is the River Aulne itself. Enticingly rural, the river is renowned for salmon and trout **fishing**; if you're interested, most bars sell permits (as do angling shops, some of which rent tackle). You might also be drawn here by **cycling**: regional championships are held each September on a circuit that races through the centre, and on occasion it's used for the French professional championship.

Along the **riverbank**, a statue commemorates **Jean Moulin**, the Resistance leader of whose murder SS officer Klaus Barbie was found guilty in Lyon in 1987. Moulin was *sous-préfet* in Châteaulin from 1930 to 1933; the inscription reads "mourir sans parler" ("to die without speaking").

Within a couple of minutes' walk upstream from the statue, and the town centre, you're on towpaths overhung by trees full of birds, with rabbits and squirrels running ahead of you on the path. For the first couple of kilometres, diagrams of corpulent yet energetic figures incite you to join them in unspeakable exercises – if you can resist that temptation, you'll soon find yourself ambling in peace past the locks and weirs that climb towards the Montagnes Noires.

Practicalities

Châteaulin's **tourist office** is beside the river on quai Cosmao (April–Sept Mon–Sat 9.30am–12.30pm & 2–7pm, Sun 9.30am–12.30pm; ⓣ02.98.86.02.11,

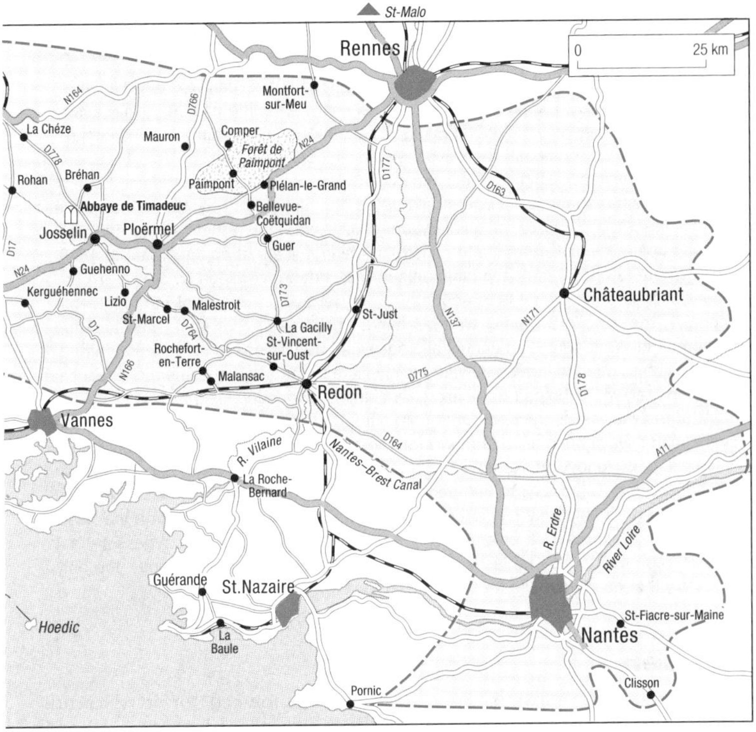

ⓦchateaulin.fr). You should have little difficulty finding a room in any of the town's three or four modest **hotels**. The best value of them is *Le Chrismas* at 33 Grande-Rue (ⓣ02.98.86.01.24, ⓔle-chrismas@orange.fr; ❸; closed Sat eve & Sun in low season), a Logis de France a short walk up the road that climbs east of the town centre towards Pleyben, which has a good **restaurant**.

The two-star municipal **campsite**, *Rodaven* (ⓣ02.98.86.32.93, ⓦcampingderodaven.fr; closed Oct–April), is very attractively situated beside the river.

Pont Coblant

If you set out to walk the canal from Châteaulin, the small village of **PONT COBLANT** may look just 10km distant on the map, but be warned, the meanders make it a hike of several hours. Pick your side of the water, too, as there are no bridges between Châteaulin and Pont Coblant – if you stay on the north side, it's easier to take a short cut back by road if you're getting tired.

It's possible to rent **kayaks** and **canoes** at the Centre Nautique de Pleyben in Pont Coblant, which also offers dormitory accommodation at €13 per person, primarily for school groups (ⓣ02.98.73.34.69, ⓦcnpleyben.neuf.fr; ❶). The village also has a tiny, six-room **hotel**, the *Auberge du Poisson Blanc* (ⓣ02.98.73.35.95; ❸; restaurant closed Mon eve), and a two-star **campsite** (ⓣ02.98.73.31.22; closed mid-Sept to mid-June).

The canal

The idea of connecting the inland waterways of Brittany dates back to 1627. However, nothing was done to implement the scheme until it became a **military necessity** during the Napoleonic wars, when English fleets began to threaten the ships circumnavigating the Breton coast. To relieve the virtual blockade of Brest in 1810, Napoleon authorized the construction of a canal network to link it with both Nantes and Lorient.

In the event, economic disasters held up its completion, but by 1836 a navigable path was cut and the canal officially opened. It was not an immediate success. Having cost sixty million francs to construct, the first years of operation, up to 1850, raised a mere 70,000 francs in tariffs. It survived, however, helped by a navy experiment of transporting coal cross-country to its ports. By the end of the nineteenth century, the canal's business was booming: in the years between 1890 and the outbreak of World War I, an annual average of 35,000 tonnes of cargo were carried. In addition to coal, the cargoes were mainly slate from the quarries near Châteaulin, and fertilizer, which helped to develop agricultural production inland.

After the war, motor transport and more effective roads brought swift **decline**. The canal had always been used primarily for short journeys at either end – from Brest to Carhaix and Pontivy to Nantes – and in 1928 the building of a dam at Lac de Guerlédan cut it forever into two sections, with the stretch from Carhaix to Pontivy becoming navigable only by canoe. Plans for the dam were approved on the basis that either a hydraulic lift, or a side channel, would enable barges to bypass it – but neither was ever built. The last barge arrived at Châteaulin in 1945; today, the only industry that has much use for the canal is tourism.

Pleyben

PLEYBEN, 4km north of Pont Coblant, is renowned for its sixteenth-century **parish close** (see p.264). On its four sides the calvary traces the life of Jesus, combining great detail with an appealing naivety. The well-scrubbed church of St-Germain itself – twin-towered, with a huge ornate spire dwarfing its domed Renaissance neighbour – features an altarpiece that's blackened and buckled by age.

A summer-only **tourist office** (mid-June to early Sept Mon–Fri 10.15am–12.15pm & 2.30–6.15pm, Sat 10.15am–12.15pm & 2–6.15pm; Ⓣ02.98.26.71.05, Ⓦmairiepleyben.fr/~tourisme) stands in the spacious and grandiose main square, the place de Gaulle, across from one of the village's few **restaurants**, *La Blanche Hermine* (Ⓣ02.98.26.61.29, Ⓦla-blanche-hermine.com; closed Wed & all Jan), which serves various à la carte Breton specialities from around €10 and up. The nearest hotel is in Pont Coblant (see p.311).

On the N164 between Châteaulin and Pleyben, the *Run Ar Puns* (Ⓣ02.98.86.27.95, Ⓦrunarpuns.com; closed Sun & Mon) is a lively **music club** and bar, housed in old farm buildings, serving a wide selection of beers and specializing in Breton music. Rock bands from further afield also play here, but there are no concerts in summer.

Châteauneuf-du-Faou

CHÂTEAUNEUF-DU-FAOU, a little way south of the N164, 25km east of Châteaulin, is much the same sort of low-key destination as Châteaulin and Pleyben, sloping down to the tree-lined river. It's a little more developed, though, with a riverside **tourist complex**, the *Penn ar Pont* (Ⓣ02.98.81.81.25, Ⓦbretagnenet.com/penn_ar_pont; closed early Nov to early April), which boasts a swimming pool, *gîtes* and camping, as well as cycle and boat rental.

The **canal proper** separates off from the Aulne a few kilometres to the east at Pont Triffen, making its own way past Carhaix, and out of Finistère.

Carhaix

CARHAIX, a further 25km east from Châteauneuf, is a road junction that dates back to pre-Roman times, when it marked the headquarters of the Osisme tribe. As Vorgium, from the third century AD onwards, it became the most important Roman town in Brittany. Two lengthy but largely subterranean aqueducts, vestiges of which can still be seen on clearly marked walking trails, were built to provide it with fresh water. Behind the most striking building in the modern town – the granite Renaissance **Maison de Sénéchal** on rue Brizeux, which houses the tourist office – Carhaix's spacious Roman street plan remains readily apparent, though it now holds nothing more interesting than a few cafés and shops to replenish supplies. During the third weekend of July each year, however, Carhaix hosts France's biggest **rock festival**, the massive four-day **Vieilles Charrues** (Ⓦvieillescharrues.asso.fr); recent headliners have included Bruce Springsteen.

East of Carhaix, the canal – as far as Pontivy – is navigable only by canoe. If that's not how you're travelling, it probably makes more sense to loop round to the south, through the **Montagnes Noires**, Le Faouët and Kernascléden, before rejoining the canal at the **Lac de Guerlédan**. Alternatively, to the north – assuming you resisted the detour from Morlaix – you could explore the **Forêt de Huelgoat** and the **Monts d'Arrée**. These routes are covered in the next two sections.

Practicalities

Carhaix's **tourist office** is in the town centre on rue Brizeux (July & Aug Mon–Sat 9am–12.30pm & 1.30–7pm, Sun 10am–1pm; June & Sept Mon–Sat 9am–noon & 2–6pm; Oct–May Mon 2–6pm, Wed–Sat 10am–noon & 2–5.30pm; Ⓣ02.98.93.04.42, Ⓦwww.poher.com).

The modern **hotel** *Noz Vad* at 12 bd de la République, near the church (Ⓣ02.98.99.12.12, Ⓦnozvad.com; ❸), makes a comfortable place to spend the night, as well as being the venue for live concerts in the spring, and regular exhibitions of art, sculpture and photography. Its close neighbour, *Le Paradis* at 2 bd de la République, also near the church (Ⓣ02.98.83.39.75; ❶), is a simpler but still perfectly adequate alternative.

The Montagnes Noires

South of Châteauneuf, the **Montagnes Noires** delineate the southern borders of Finistère. Despite the name, they are really no more than escarpments, though bleak and imposing nonetheless in a harsh, exposed landscape at odds with the gentle canal path. From their highest point – the stark, slate, 318-metre **Roc de Toullaëron**, between Pont Triffen and Gourin – you can look west and north over kilometres of what seems like totally deserted countryside.

Le Faouët

The D769 beyond Gourin offers access to the twin churches of St-Fiacre and Kernascléden, built simultaneously, according to legend, with the aid of an angelic bridge. En route is the secluded town of **LE FAOUËT**, served neither by buses nor trains, and distinguished mainly by its large old market hall. Above a floor of mud and straw, still used by local traders on market days on the first and third Wednesday of every month, rises an intricate latticework of ancient wood, propped on granite pillars and topped by a little clock tower.

Practicalities

Two similar and highly recommended **hotels** in the immediate area of Le Faouët both offer good food. The *Croix d'Or*, opposite the old market in the heart of town at 9 place Bellanger (Ⓣ03.44.54.00.04, Ⓦlacroixdor.net; ❺; closed mid-Dec to mid-Jan, plus Sun eve & Mon in low season), has a €33 menu that changes according to the season, but can feature the likes of snail ravioli and skate's wing with thyme. The *Cheval Blanc*, 5 rue Albert St-Jalmes (Ⓣ02.97.34.61.15, Ⓦhotelrest-cheval-blanc.com; ❸), stands by a lake a few kilometres east in **PRIZIAC**, reached along the pleasant (but steep) D132. Le Faouët also has its own three-star riverside municipal **campsite**, the *Beg-er-Roch* (Ⓣ02.97.23.15.11; closed Oct to early March).

St-Fiacre

The church at **ST-FIACRE**, 2km south of Le Faouët, is notable for its rood screen, brightly polychromed and carved as intricately as lace. The original purpose of a rood screen was to separate the chancel from the congregation – the decorations of this 1480 masterpiece go rather further than that. They depict scenes from the Old and New Testaments as well as a dramatic series on the wages of sin. Drunkenness is demonstrated by a man somehow vomiting a fox; theft, by a peasant stealing apples.

Ste-Barbe

The fifteenth-century chapel of **Ste-Barbe** (slightly out of the village of the same name) perches on a rocky outcrop a couple of kilometres east of Le Faouët. Accessible only along a very poor road that crosses a bridge over the main D769, it commands views of the deep wooded ravine of the Ellé River. Visitors traditionally ring a large bell in the crude bell tower on the hilltop, before descending a steep stone staircase to the chapel itself.

Kernascléden

At the ornate and gargoyle-coated church at **KERNASCLÉDEN**, 15km southeast of Le Faouët along the D782, the focus turns from carving to frescoes. The themes, however, contemporary with St-Fiacre, are equally gruesome. On the damp-infested walls of a side chapel, horned devils stoke the fires beneath a vast cauldron filled with the souls of the damned, while alongside you should be able to discern the outlines of a Dance of Death, a faded cousin to that at Kermaria (see p.237). The ceiling above the main altar holds better-preserved but less bloodthirsty scenes.

The Monts d'Arrée

A broad swathe of the more desolate regions of Finistère, stretching east from the Crozon peninsula right to the edge of the *département*, is designated as the **Parc Régional d'Armorique**. The park, in theory at least, is an area dedicated to conservation and rural regeneration along traditional lines; in reality, lack of funding ensures that it creates rather less impact. The **Monts d'Arrée**, however, which cut northeast across Finistère from the Aulne estuary, are something of a nature sanctuary; kestrels circle high above the bleak hilltops, sharing the skies with pipits, curlews and great black crows.

Over to the east, the ancient woods of the **Forêt de Huelgoat** can offer an atmospheric afternoon's walking, with the lakeside village of Huelgoat itself making an attractive base if you have the time to linger.

Menez-Meur and Sizun

The most obvious place to pick up information on the Parc d'Armorique is at **MENEZ-MEUR**, off the D342 near the Forêt de Cranou – just inland from the Brest–Quimper motorway. Menez is an official **animal reserve**, with wild boar and deer roaming free, and a museum of Breton horses (March, April, Oct & Nov Wed, Sun & hols 1.30–5.30pm; May, June & Sept daily 10am–6pm; July & Aug daily 10am–7pm; Dec–Feb Wed, Sun & hols 1–5pm; €4). Rangers at the reserve gate can provide a wealth of detail on the park and all its various activities (Ⓣ02.98.68.81.71, Ⓦarc-naturel-armorique.fr).

Ten kilometres north, at **SIZUN**, a research station, **aquarium** and fishing exhibition, known collectively as the **Maison de la Rivière**, sets out to increase public awareness of the significance of Brittany's rivers and inland waterways (July & Aug daily 10.30am–6.30pm; Sept–June Mon–Fri 10am–noon & 2–5.30pm; €4; Ⓣ02.98.68.86.33, Ⓦmaison-de-la-riviere.fr).

The Moulins de Kerouat

Another 3km east of Sizun, along the D764 to Commana, the abandoned hamlet of **MOULINS DE KEROUAT** (*Milin-Kerroc'h* in Breton) has been restored as an **Eco-Musée** (Feb hols & Christmas hols Mon–Fri 10am–5pm; mid-March to May, Sept & Oct Mon–Fri 10am–6pm, Sun 2–6pm; June Mon–Fri 10am–6pm, Sat & Sun 2–6pm; July & Aug daily 11am–7pm; €4.50). After Kerouat's last inhabitant died in 1967, it might have crumbled into indiscernible ruins. However, one of its water mills has been restored to motion, and its houses repaired and refurnished as part of the museum. The largest belonged in the nineteenth century to the mayor of Commana, who also controlled the mills, and its furnishings are, therefore, those of a rich family.

The Forêt de Huelgoat

The **FORÊT DE HUELGOAT** spreads out to the north and east of the village of Huelgoat, the halfway point between Morlaix and Carhaix on the minor road D769, and is served by the three daily buses that connect the two towns. **HUELGOAT** itself was the ancestral home of the Kerouac family, as in Jack Kerouac of *On The Road* fame; it still makes a pleasant overnight stop, next to its own small **lake**.

While there may be doubt as to whether the "Argoat", the great forest supposed to have stretched the length of prehistoric inland Brittany, ever existed, the antiquity of Huelgoat cannot be questioned. Until 1987, this was a staggering landscape of trees, giant boulders and waterfalls tangled together in primeval chaos. Just how fragile it really was, just how miraculous had been its long survival, was demonstrated by the **hurricane** of that October, which smashed it to smithereens in the space of fifteen minutes.

After two decades of restoration, the forest has now returned to a fairly close approximation of its former glories. Once again, it's possible to walk for several kilometres along the various paths that lead into the depths of the woods, and in spring and autumn in particular Huelgoat merits a substantial detour.

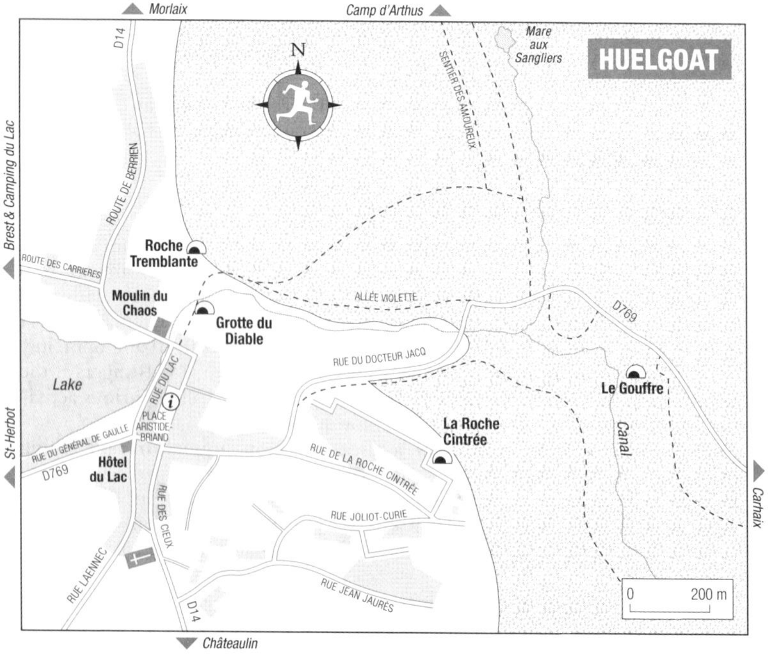

The strange granite formations of Huelgoat have survived better than the trees, and a half-hour stroll close to the village enables you to scramble over, among, and even under a number of inconceivably large specimens. At the **Grotte du Diable** ("Devil's Cave"), a short way along the main path from the former watermill known as the Moulin du Chaos, just below the road bridge, you can make a somewhat perilous descent, between the rocks, to a subterranean stream.

A hundred or so metres further on, at an open-air auditorium used for occasional performances, the path crosses the stream. Near the top of a small hill on the far side, the **Roche Tremblante** ("trembling rock") is supposed to wobble at the slightest prod; in reality, it seems to remain disappointingly stable despite the strenuous efforts of every passing walker. Just beyond that, in a lovely sunny garden at the foot of the hill, the *Crêperie de la Roche Tremblante* (ⓣ02.98.99.98.08) serves snacks and drinks to visitors in summer only.

Further into the forest, not far from the waterfall known as the **Mare aux Sangliers**, the **Camp d'Arthus** has been identified as a Gallo-Roman *oppidum*, or hillfort, large enough to be a settlement for a whole community rather than just a military encampment. Until the hurricane, it was also the spitting image of Astérix the Gaul's fictional village. Nowadays it's not nearly so recognizable, although the obliteration of the tree cover enabled archeologists to get a clearer view of its history.

Practicalities

Huelgoat's **tourist office** is at 18 place Aristide-Briand in town (July & Aug Mon–Sat 10am–12.30pm & 2–5pm; Sept–June Mon–Sat 10–11.45am & 2.30–4.30pm; ⓣ02.98.99.72.32, ⓦtourismehuelgoat.fr), supplies walking maps of the forest. The **hotel** *du Lac*, beside the lake at 9 rue du Général-de-Gaulle (ⓣ02.98.99.71.14; ❸; closed Mon Sept–June, plus mid-Jan to mid-Feb), offers well-refurbished rooms and an inexpensive grill **restaurant**, serving chicken or

▲ Forêt de Huelgoat

pizza from €8, steaks from €12 and a menu at €28. Also alongside the lake, on the road towards Brest, the two-star *Camping du Lac* (Ⓣ02.98.99.72.50; closed Sept–June) is complete with swimming pool.

Five kilometres south of Huelgoat in the small village of **PLOUYÉ**, the *Ti Elise* (Ⓣ02.98.99.96.44) is a **bar** well known in these parts for its concerts of traditional Breton music.

Lac de Guerlédan and around

Although between Carhaix and Pontivy the **Nantes–Brest canal** is limited to canoeists, it's worth some effort to follow on land, particularly for the scenery around the artificial **Lac de Guerlédan**, between **Gouarec** and **Mur-de-Bretagne**. Along this 15km stretch the **N164** skirts the edge of the **Forêt de Quénécan**, within which lies the lake, created when the Barrage of Guerlédan was completed in 1928. It's a beautiful section of the river, if a little over-popular with British camper-caravanners, but peaceful enough nonetheless. Approaching by road, the canal path is easiest joined at Gouarec. En route, you pass the rather subdued (and unmemorable) town of **ROSTRENEN**, whose old facades are given a little life at the Tuesday **market**.

Gouarec

At **GOUAREC**, the River Blavet and the canal meet in a confusing swirl of water that shoots off, edged by footpaths, in the most unlikely directions. The old houses of the town are barely disturbed by traffic or development, nor are there great numbers of tourists.

Sadly, Gouarec has lost its one hotel, but there's a well-positioned, British-run two-star **campsite**, the *Tost Aven* (Ⓣ02.96.24.85.42, Ⓦbrittanycamping.com; closed late Sept to early May), next to the canal and away from the main road, which also rents bikes.

St-Gelven

Just off the N164 near the village of **ST-GELVEN**, 5km east of Gouarec, the beautiful **Abbaye de Bon-Repos** nestles beside the water at the end of an avenue of ancient trees. Most of what now survives of this twelfth-century Cistercian abbey, largely destroyed during the French Revolution, are its former outbuildings. These are home to an absolutely irresistible, inexpensive **hotel-restaurant**, the ravishing *Jardins de l'Abbaye* (Ⓣ02.96.24.95.77, Ⓦabbaye.jardin.free.fr; ❸; closed Tues eve & Wed in low season). Porthole-like windows pierce the thick slate walls of its six cosy guest rooms, to look out across extensive riverfront grounds to the dramatic wooded slopes beyond. Menus in its **restaurant** start at €14.50 for lunch and €18.50 for dinner.

The ruins of the abbey are open to visitors (March to mid-June & mid-Sept to Oct daily 2–6pm; mid-June to mid-Sept daily 11am–7pm; €3.50; Ⓣ02.96.24.82.20, Ⓦbon-repos.com), and also play host to son et lumière spectacles on the first two weekends in August (Ⓣ02.96.24.85.28, Ⓦwww.pays-conomor.com; €18), while its grounds are taken over by an **organic farmers' market** on Fridays from Easter to November.

A little further down the lane, a tiny stone bridge crosses the canal, and the towpath squeezes alongside meadows that are popular with picnickers. Next to the far side of the bridge, the *Café de l'Abbaye* (Ⓣ02.96.24.86.56; closed Mon, plus mid-Sept to mid-Oct) is a rural brasserie with nice outdoor seating.

Beau Rivage

From just west of **CAUREL** and 7km east of St-Gelven, the brief loop of the D111 leads to tiny sandy beaches – a bit too tiny in season. At the spot known justifiably as **Beau Rivage** stands the *Hôtel Beau Rivage* (Ⓣ02.96.28.52.15; ❸; closed Mon & Tues). It may not be at all prepossessing as a building, and the bedrooms though new and well equipped are carpeted all the way up the wall in the worst French tradition, but it commands magnificent views of the lake and serves great food, with dinner menus from €19 and even crêpes for breakfast. *L'Embarcadère* **restaurant** here (Ⓣ02.96.28.52.64) serves good meals on its own terrace, and also serves as the base for two glass-topped sightseeing boats, the *Duc de Guerlédan I* and *II*, which offer pleasure cruises (€12) as well as three-hour dinner trips (€37–59) on the Lac de Guerlédan to no very fixed schedule between March and mid-October (Vedettes de Guerlédan Ⓣ02.96.28.52.64, Ⓦguerledan.com).

Beau Rivage is also a very popular spot for **waterskiing** (Ⓣ02.99.21.11.16, Ⓦskiguerledan.fr), and holds several **campsites** too, including the four-star *Nautic International* (Ⓣ02.96.28.57.94, Ⓦcampingnautic.fr; closed Oct to mid-May), with heated swimming pool and offering plenty of water sports, and the simpler, two-star *Les Pins* (Ⓣ02.96.28.52.22; closed Oct–March).

Mur-de-Bretagne

MUR-DE-BRETAGNE, set back from the eastern end of the lake, is a lively place with a wide and colourful pedestrianized zone around its church. As the nearest town to the barrage – just 2km distant – it holds the regional **tourist office,** at 1 place de l'Église (July–Aug Mon–Sat 10am–12.30pm & 2–6.30pm, Sept–June Mon–Fri 10am–noon & 2–5pm; Ⓣ02.96.28.51.41, Ⓦwwwguerledan.fr), which can help organize bike rides, horseriding, canoeing and jet-skiing.

The *Auberge Grand'Maison* on the left as you climb to the centre at 1 rue Léon-le-Cerf (Ⓣ02.96.28.51.10, Ⓦwww.auberge-grand-maison.com; ❸), has clean and homely **rooms**, and a good restaurant downstairs. The local **campsite**, the *Rond-Point du Lac* (Ⓣ02.96.26.08.99; closed mid-Sept to mid-June), has facilities for windsurfing and horseriding.

If you'd rather eat by the lake, get one of the thick wooden tables at *Merlin les Pieds dans l'Eau* (Ⓣ02.97.27.52.36), at **ST-AIGNAN** 3km southwest, where there is also camping and pedalo rental.

The central canal

Beyond the barrage of Guerlédan, the historic town of **Pontivy** is the central junction of the Nantes–Brest canal, where the course of the canal breaks off once more from the Blavet and you can again take **barges** – all the way to the Loire. Until you get as far as **Josselin**, with its imposing waterfront ducal castle, none of the towns en route is all that enthralling, but there are some quirky rural attractions nearby, such as the enigmatic statue known as the *Venus de Quinipily* near **Baud**.

Pontivy

PONTIVY owes much of its appearance, and its size, to the canal. When the waterway opened, the small medieval centre was expanded, redesigned and given broad avenues to fit its new role. It was even renamed **Napoléonville** for a time, in honour of the instigator of its new prosperity, and still uses the name fairly interchangeably.

These days it is a bright market town, its twisting old streets contrasting with the stately riverside promenades. At the north end of the town, occupying a low eminence above the main through road, is the **Château de Rohan**, built by the lord of Josselin in the late fifteenth century (April–June & Sept Wed–Sun 10am–noon & 2–6pm; July & Aug daily 10.30am–6.30pm; Oct–Nov & Feb–March Wed–Sun 2–6pm; €6). Used in summer for low-key cultural events and temporary exhibitions, the castle still belongs to the Josselin family. Behind its impressive facade, complete with deep moat and two forbidding towers looking out over the river, the structure rather peters out.

Practicalities

Pontivy's *gare SNCF* is close to the River Blavet and roughly ten minutes' walk south of the helpful local **tourist office**, which is housed in a cottage that was once a leprosy hospital at 61 rue du Général-de-Gaulle, immediately below the castle (Mon–Sat 10am–noon & 2–6pm; Ⓣ02.97.25.04.10, Ⓦpontivy.fr). Central **hotels** include the spruce but inexpensive *Porhoët*, very near the tourist office at 41 rue du Général-de-Gaulle (Ⓣ02.97.25.34.88, Ⓦhoteldepontivy.com; ❷), which has a bar but no restaurant, and the opulent *Europe*, 12 rue François-Mitterand (Ⓣ02.97.25.11.14, Ⓦhotellerieurope.com; ❹). In addition, there's a smart **hostel**, 2km from the *gare SNCF* on the Île des Récollets (Ⓣ02.97.25.58.27, Ⓦfuaj.org/Pontivy; €12.60; by reservation only at weekends in low season), which also serves cheap meals. The best **restaurant** in town is *La Pommeraie*, 17 quai du Couvent (Ⓣ02.97.25.60.09; closed Sun & Mon), where lunch menus start at €19, and there's a great €32 dinner menu.

West from Pontivy: along the Blavet

If you choose to follow the **River Blavet** southwest from Pontivy towards Lorient – rather than the canal – take the time to go by the smaller roads along the valley itself. The Blavet connects the canal with the sea, and once linked Lorient to the other two great ports of Brittany, Brest and Nantes.

Quistinic

The D159 to **QUISTINIC** passes through lush green countryside, its hedgerows full of flowers, where by June there's already been one harvest and grass is growing up around the fresh haystacks. The ivy-clad church of **St-Mathurin** in Quistinic is the scene of a *pardon* (in the second week of May) that dates from Roman times. The devotion to the saint is strongly evident on the village's war memorial, too – his name is that of almost half the victims.

You can **camp** on the edge of Quistinic, near the river at the two-star *Île de Minazen* (ⓣ02.97.39.70.99; closed mid-Sept to mid-June).

Baud: the Venus de Quinipily

The main reason to go on to **BAUD**, a major road junction just east of the river, is to see the **Venus de Quinipily**. Signposted off the Hennebont road, 2km out of town, the Venus is a crude statue that at first glance looks Egyptian. Once known as the "Iron Lady", it is of unknown but ancient origin. It stands on, or rather nestles its ample buttocks against, a high plinth above a kind of sarcophagus, commanding the valley in the gardens of what was once a château. Behind its stiff pose and dress, the statue has an odd informality, a half-smile on the otherwise impassive face. It used to be the object of "impure rites" and was at least twice thrown into the Blavet by Christian authorities, only to be fished out by locals eager to reindulge. It may itself have been in some way "improper" before it was recarved, perhaps literally "dressed", some time in the eighteenth century.

The **gardens** around the statue are luxuriantly fertile, while the various farmhouses and outbuildings are adorned with splendid flowers. To visit, you pay a small fee at the gatehouse (daily: May–Oct 10am–7pm, Nov–April 11am–5pm; €3).

Rooms to suit all price ranges can be found at the *Relais de la Forêt* (ⓣ02.97.51.01.77, ⓦhotel-restaurant-aurelaisdelaforet.fr; ❷; restaurant closed Sun eve), opposite the town hall at 19 rue de la Mairie in Baud, and the similarly inexpensive *Auberge du Cheval Blanc*, a Logis de France nearby at 16 rue de Pontivy (ⓣ02.97.51.00.85; ❷; closed Jan; restaurant closed Mon lunch and all Jan, plus Sat lunch & Sun eve Sept–June). Both hotels have **restaurants**, where menus start at around €15.

Camors

CAMORS, just south of Baud, has a smart square-towered **church**, with a weathercock on top and a little megalith set in the wall. You can spend the night here at the *Hôtel-Restaurant Ar Brug*, at 14 rue Principale opposite the church (ⓣ02.97.39.20.10; ❷), which has rather run-of-the-mill rooms, but also an excellent restaurant that doesn't scrimp on the portions. There's a two-star **campsite**, *du Petit Bois* (ⓣ02.97.39.18.36; closed Sept–June), at one end of the series of forests that grow bleaker and harsher eastwards to become the Lanvaux Moors.

Just 100m from the campsite, the Camors Adventure Forest is an exhilarating arboreal **adventure park**, in which participants clamber, swing and leap from tree to tree, around a demanding circuit (April to mid-Nov: daily during school holidays 9.30am–6pm, otherwise Wed–Sun same hours; adults €20, under-16s €16; by reservation only, on ⓣ02.97.39.28.69; ⓦcamors-adventure-forest.com).

Josselin

The three Rapunzel towers of the **Château de Rohan** at **JOSSELIN**, embedded in a vast sheet of stone above the water, are the most impressive sight along the Nantes–Brest canal. However, they turn out on close inspection to be no more than a facade. The building behind was built in the last century, the bulk of the original castle having been demolished by Richelieu in 1629 in punishment for Henri de Rohan's leadership of the Huguenots. The Rohan family, still in possession, used to own a third of Brittany, though the present incumbent contents himself with the position of local mayor.

Tours of the oppressively formal apartments of the ducal residence are not very compelling, even if it does contain the table on which the Edict of Nantes was signed in 1598. But the duchess's collection of ancient **dolls**, around six hundred in total, housed in the **Musée des Poupées**, behind the castle, is something special (early April to mid-July daily 2–6pm; mid-July to Aug daily 11am–6pm; Sept daily 2–5.30pm; Oct Sat, Sun & hols 2–5.30pm; tours and museum entry €7 each, combined ticket €12; ⓦchateaujosselin.com).

The **town** itself is full of medieval splendours, from the castle ramparts to the gargoyles of the basilica of **Notre Dame du Roncier**, as well as the half-timbered houses in between. The basilica was built on the spot where in the ninth century a peasant supposedly found a statue of the Virgin under a bramble bush. The statue was burned during the Revolution, but an important *pardon* is held each year on September 8. As ever, the religious procession and open-air services are solemn in the extreme, but there's a lot of other stuff going on to keep you entertained.

One of the most famous episodes of late chivalry, the **Battle of the Thirty**, took place nearby in 1351. Rivalry between the French garrison at Josselin and the English at Ploërmel led to a challenge being issued to settle differences in a combat of thirty unmounted knights from each side. The French won, killing the English leader Bemborough. The actual battle site, marked by a small monument, is now isolated between the two carriageways of the N24 from Josselin to Ploërmel.

Practicalities

Josselin's **tourist office** is in a superb old house on the place de la Congrégation, up in town next to the castle entrance (April–June & Sept Mon–Sat 10am–noon & 2–6pm, Sun 2–6pm; July & Aug daily 10am–6.30pm; Oct–March Mon–Fri 10am–noon & 2–6pm; ⓣ02.97.22.36.43, ⓦjosselin.com).

The lovely ★ *Hôtel du Chateau*, a Logis de France facing the castle from across the river at 1 rue du Général-de-Gaulle (ⓣ02.97.22.20.11, ⓦwww.hotel-chateau.com; ❸; closed Feb), makes a perfect place to **stay**. Rooms with views of the château are slightly more expensive, but worth it – the whole place looks fabulous lit up at night – and the food, with dinner menus from €16, is first-rate. The nearest good **campsite** is the three-star *Bas de la Lande* (ⓣ02.97.22.22.20, ⓦwww.guegon.fr; closed Nov–March), half an hour's walk from the castle, south of the river and west of town in Guégon, where some simple chalets are also available for rental, by the week in summer. There's also the **Gîte d'étape de l'Écluse**, right below the castle walls, where a dorm bed for the night costs around €11.20, and you can also rent canoes or kayaks (ⓣ02.97.22.24.17; closed Oct–April).

Guéhenno

GUÉHENNO, 10km south of Josselin on the D123, holds one of Brittany's largest and finest **calvaries**. Built in 1550, the figures include the cock that crowed to expose Peter's denials, Mary Magdalene with the shroud and a recumbent Christ in the crypt. Its appeal is enhanced by the naivety of its amateur restoration. After damage caused by Revolutionary soldiers in 1794 – who amused themselves by playing boules with the heads of the statues – all the sculptors approached for the work demanded exorbitant fees, so the parish priest and his assistant decided to undertake the task themselves.

Kerguéhennec Sculpture Park

Another unusual sculptural endeavour, this time contemporary, takes place at the **Domaine de Kerguéhennec**, signposted a short way off the D11 near St-Jean-Brévelay, 7km west of Guéhenno. This innovatory **sculpture park** (daily except Mon: mid-Jan to June & Sept to mid-Dec 11am–6pm; July & Aug 10am–7pm; free; Ⓣ02.97.60.44.44, Ⓦart-kerguehennec.com) is progressively building up a fascinating permanent collection.

Among the first pieces to be installed, back in 1986, was a massive railway sleeper painstakingly stripped down by Giuseppe Penone to reveal the young sapling within. Since then the park has acquired works by leading international sculptors, many of whom have served as artists-in-residence, and become an increasingly compelling stop. Its setting is the lawns, woods and lake of an early eighteenth-century château; studios and indoor workshops in the outbuildings are used by visiting artists.

Lizio

Nine kilometres east from Guéhenno, off the D151, the little village of **LIZIO** has also set itself up as a centre for arts and crafts, with ceramic and weaving workshops as its speciality. For most of the year, you might pass along its single curving street of stone cottages without seeing a sign of life; on the second Sunday in August, however, it's the scene of a **Festival Artisanal**, featuring street theatre (and pancakes).

If you do take the trouble to stop in Lizio, you may spot that one venerable old cottage, from the outside looking much like the rest, houses an **Insectarium** (April–Sept daily 10am–12.30pm & 1.30–6.30pm; Oct–March Wed, Sat & Sun 1.30–6pm; €6; Ⓦinsectariumdelizio.fr). Creepy-crawlies within include all sorts of hairy spiders, giant millipedes, huge iridescent butterflies, praying mantises that look like dead leaves and stick insects in amazing colours. It's a little expensive for twenty minutes on the verge of nausea, but kids will probably love it.

Various farmers in the nearby countryside, who welcome visitors, are working to re-create traditional skills such as beekeeping and cider-making, and one is even rearing wild boars for food. For details of them all, and an overview of long-lost agricultural techniques and implements, call in at the **Eco-Musée des Vieux Métiers**, 4km out of Lizio on the D174 towards Ploërmel (2nd fortnight of Feb, April–June, mid-Sept to Oct & 2nd fortnight of Dec daily 2–6pm; July to mid-Sept daily 10am–noon & 2–7pm; closed Jan to mid-Feb, all March & Nov to mid-Dec; €6; Ⓦecomuseelizio.com).

Lizio has no hotels, but it does have a couple of restaurants. There's also a tiny two-star municipal **campsite**, *Le Val Jouin* (closed mid-Oct to mid-June), as well as several **gîtes** in the immediate area (all information on Ⓣ02.97.74.92.67 or Ⓦlizio.fr).

Ploërmel

PLOËRMEL, whose English garrison was defeated by Josselin in the fourteenth-century Battle of the Thirty (see p.321), is still not quite a match for its rival. It's not on the canal, and neither is it any longer served by trains. Attractions are the artificial **Étang au Duc**, well stocked with fish, 2km to the north, and an interesting array of houses: James II is said to have spent a few days of his exile in one on rue Francs-Bourgeois, while the **Maison des Marmosets** on rue Beaumanoir has some elaborate carvings.

Ploërmel's **tourist office**, 5 rue du Val (July & Aug Mon–Sat 9.30am–7pm, Sun 10am–12.30pm; Sept–June Mon–Sat 10am–12.30pm & 2–6.30pm ⓣ02.97.74.02.70, ⓦwww.ploermel.com), holds a nice model of the town as it looked in 1500. A couple of good-value **hotels** – *St-Marc*, near the long-defunct railway station at 1 place de St-Marc (ⓣ02.97.74.00.01, ⓦhotel-restaurant-saintmarc.com; ❶; restaurant closed Sun eve), and the very fancy *Cobh*, behind a yellow facade at 10 rue des Forges (ⓣ02.97.74.00.49, ⓦhotel-lecobh.com; ❹), where dinner menus start at €25 – make suitable bases for venturing further away from the canal, up into Paimpont forest.

The Forêt de Paimpont

A definite magic still lingers about the **FORÊT DE PAIMPONT**. Though now just forty square kilometres in extent, it seems to retain the secrets of a forest once much larger, and everywhere recalls legends of the vanished Argoat, the great primeval forest of Brittany. The one French claimant to an Arthurian past that carries any real conviction, it is just as frequently known by its Arthurian name of **Brocéliande**. Its central village, **Paimpont**, is much the nicest of the little settlements scattered in and around the woodlands.

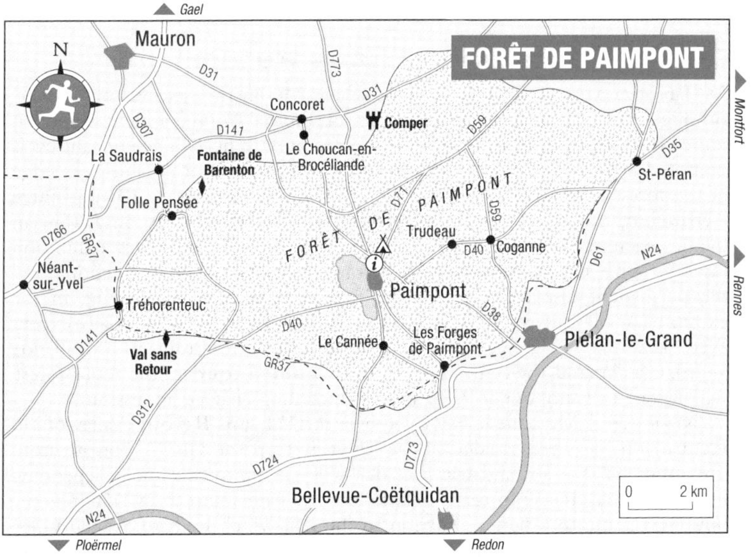

The Fontaine de Barenton

Medieval Breton minstrels, like their Welsh counterparts, set the tales of King Arthur and the Holy Grail both in *Grande Bretagne* and here in *Petite Bretagne*. The particular significance of Brocéliande was as the forest where **Merlin** made his home; some say that he is still here, in "Merlin's stone", where he was imprisoned by the enchantress Viviane.

The stone is next to the **Fontaine de Barenton**, a lonely spot high in the woods that is far from easy to find. Turn off the main road into the forest from **Concoret** (a village notable for having once supposedly had the Devil as its rector) at La Saudrais, and you will come to the village of **Folle Pensée**. Go past the few farmhouses, rather than up the hill, and you arrive at a small car park. Follow the wide, gravelled path from its far end, then turn right onto another wide footpath at the first trail intersection. Take the next branch left, and then turn right again at the next junction. The *fontaine* is a couple of hundred metres on, set in a muddy clearing amid the oak trees, and filled with the most delicious water imaginable.

Legend has it that, if after drinking from the *fontaine*, you splash water on to the stone slab, you instantly summon a mighty storm, together with roaring lions and a horseman in black armour. This story dates back at least to the fifth century and is recounted, somewhat sceptically, in Robert Wace's *Romance of the Rose*, written around 1160:

> Hunters repair (to the fountain) in sultry weather; and drawing water with their horns, they sprinkle the stone for the purposes of having rain, which is then wont to fall, they say, throughout the forest around; but why I know not. There too fairies are to be seen (if the Bretons tell truth), and many other wonders happen. I went thither on purpose to see these marvels. I saw the forest and the land, and I sought for the marvels, but I found none. I went like a fool, and so I came back. I sought after folly, and found myself a fool for my pains.

The parish priest of Concoret and his congregation are reported nonetheless to have successfully ended a drought by this means in 1835, and a procession endorsed by the church went to the spring as recently as 1925.

Comper and the Val sans Retour

At Barenton, you are at the very spot where Merlin first set eyes on Viviane, although you are not at the Fountain of Eternal Youth, which is hidden somewhere nearby and accessible only to the pure in heart. The enchantress is supposed to have been born at the château at **COMPER**, at the northern edge of the forest near Concoret. Today it serves as the **Centre de l'Imaginaire Arthurien**, hosting different exhibitions and entertainments on Arthurian themes each summer. Only pay to go in if the year's temporary exhibition interests you – the château itself dates largely from the nineteenth century, and the permanent displays of pointlessly posed mannequins are boring in the extreme (April–June & Oct Thurs–Mon 10am–5.30pm; July–Sept daily except Wed 10am–7pm; €5.50; Ⓣ02.97.22.79.96, Ⓦcentre-arthurien-broceliande.com). On demand, the centre also organizes **guided tours** of the actual forest, which start in Paimpont at 9.30am (€13, including château admission).

Viviane's rival, Morgane le Fay, ruled over the **Val sans Retour** (Valley of No Return) on the western edge of the forest, just off the GR37 footpath from Tréhorenteuc. For a round-trip hike that will take up to two hours, depending how soon you choose to turn back, follow the path south from Tréhorenteuc until you come to a signed junction to the left, which leads to a steep valley from which exits are barred by thickets of gorse and giant furze on the rocks above. At one point it skirts an overgrown table of rock, the **Rocher des Faux Amants** ("Rock of the False Lovers") – from which the seductress Morgane was wont to entice unwary and faithless youths.

Paimpont and other forest villages

PAIMPONT village is the most obvious and enjoyable base for exploring the forest. Consisting of little more than a single little street of stone cottages, it's right at the centre of the woods, backing onto a marshy lake whose shores are thick with wild mushrooms (*cèpes*). There's superb walking to be enjoyed in almost any direction; the best megalithic site in the vicinity is undoubtedly the **Site des Pierres Droites**, a stone circle not far to the south. Paimpont's **tourist office** is alongside the lakeside abbey (Feb–June & Sept–Dec daily except Mon 10am–noon & 2–5pm; July & Aug daily 10am–12.30pm & 2–6pm; Ⓣ02.99.07.84.23, Ⓦpaimpont.fr).

Standards have slipped recently at Paimpont's one hotel, the *Relais de Brocéliande*, and it is no longer recommendable; for the moment, the best alternative is the *Bruyères*, at 10 rue de Brocéliande in the tiny but much less attractive village of **PLÉLAN-LE-GRAND**, 6km southeast (Ⓣ02.99.06.81.38, Ⓦhoteldesbruyeres.canalblog.com; ❶; restaurant closed Tues eve & Wed), where the cheapest rooms are not en suite, and the restaurant offers satisfactory menus from €15. There's also a reasonable hotel in **MAURON**, a rambling, charming country town at the northern edge of the forest – the *Brambily*, in the centre at 14 place Henri-Thebault (Ⓣ02.97.22.61.67, Ⓦhotel-lebrambily.com; ❸; restaurant closed Sun eve).

The forest holds several appealing **B&Bs**, including the *Corne de Cerf* in Le Cannée 3km south of Paimpont (Ⓣ02.99.07.84.19, Ⓦcorneducerf.bcld.net; ❸), and the the *Gîte de Coganne*, just off the D40 4km northwest (Ⓣ02.99.61.88.15, Ⓦgitecoganne.com; ❸), where with advance warning they'll cook you a dinner of gourmet crêpes. A lovely rural **hostel** is located at Le Choucan-en-Brocéliande, 5km northwest towards Concoret (Ⓣ02.97.22.76.75, Ⓦfuaj.org/choucan-en-broceliande; dorm beds €10.70; closed mid-Sept to May). **Campsites** include the attractive, well-wooded two-star municipal site on the edge of Paimpont village (Ⓣ02.97.07.89.16, Ⓦwww.camping-paimpont-broceliande.com; closed Oct–March).

The best restaurant in the vicinity is the *Auberge des Forges de Paimpont*, housed in the former canteen of the ironworks beside the lake at Plélan-le-Grand (Ⓣ02.99.06.81.07; closed Mon, 2nd fortnight of Sept, Sun eve & Tues eve in low season), where lunch menus start at €11 and dinners are superb.

Montfort-sur-Meu

At **MONTFORT-SUR-MEU**, northeast of the forest and 25km west of Rennes, an illuminating **Eco-Musée** at 2 rue de Château provides background information on the region (Mon–Fri 9am–noon & 2–6pm, April–Sept also Sat & Sun 2–6pm; €4; Ⓦecomusee-montfort.com). Set in the one surviving tower of what in the fourteenth century was a complete walled town, it holds – as well as the usual small-town museum assortment of costumed dolls – fascinating displays on varying aspects of local ecology, economy and history. It also runs workshops, where children are taught traditional crafts with materials such as cow dung, and where sculptors explain their work to casual visitors.

Montfort is on the railway, with a reasonable **hotel**, the *Relais de la Cane*, 2 rue de la Gare (Ⓣ02.99.09.00.07, Ⓦhotel-le-relais-de-la-cane.fr; ❷), close by the **gare SNCF**.

Malestroit, Rochefort and La Gacilly

If you follow the canal southeast from Josselin, as opposed to venturing into the Forêt de Paimpont, the next significant town you reach is the small but appealing **Malestroit**. Beyond that, if you are not actually travelling on the canal – which at this stage is the **River Oust** – the D764 on the south bank, or the D146/149 on the north, will keep you parallel for much of its course towards Redon. Along the way there are two worthwhile detours: south of the canal to **Rochefort-en-Terre**, or north to **La Gacilly**.

Malestroit and around

Although not a lot happens in **MALESTROIT**, founded in 987 AD – apart from the **Pont du Rock** music festival (Ⓦaupontdurock.com), on the last weekend of July – the town is full of unexpected and enjoyable corners. As you come into the main square, the **place du Bouffay** in front of the church, the houses are covered with unlikely carvings – an anxious bagpipe-playing hare looks over its shoulder at a dragon's head on one beam, while an oblivious sow in a blue buckled belt threads her distaff on another. The church itself is decorated with drunkards and acrobats outside, torturing demons and erupting towers within; a placard outside explains the various allegories. The only ancient walls without adornment are the ruins of the **Chapelle de la Madeleine**, where one of the many temporary truces of the Hundred Years War was signed.

Beside the grey canal, the matching grey-slate tiles on the turreted rooftops bulge and dip, while on its central island overgrown houses stand next to the stern walls of an old mill.

Practicalities

If you arrive in Malestroit by barge – this being a good stretch to travel on the water – you'll moor very near the town centre. The **tourist office** stands alongside the main square at 17 place du Bouffay (mid-June to mid-Sept Mon–Sat 9am–7pm, Sun 10am–4pm; mid-Sept to mid-June Mon–Sat 9.30am–12.30pm & 2.30–6.30pm; Ⓣ02.97.75.14.57, Ⓦmalestroit.com); they can provide details of **boat rental**. The nearby **gare routière** is served by buses from Vannes.

Malestroit's only **hotel** is the exceptionally cheap, somewhat plain, but good-value *Cap Horn*, 1 Faubourg St-Michel (Ⓣ02.97.75.13.01, Ⓦhotel-malestroit.com; ❶; closed Wed). Across the river, down below the bridge in the Impasse d'Abattoir next to the swimming pool, there's a two-star **campsite**, *La Daufresne* (Ⓣ02.97.75.13.33; closed mid-Sept to April). The *Vieille Auberge* opposite the church at 9 place de Bouffay (Ⓣ02.97.75.20.35) serves simple, hearty **meals**.

The Musée de la Résistance Bretonne

Two kilometres west of Malestroit, the village of **ST-MARCEL** hosts the **Musée de la Résistance Bretonne** (April to mid-June daily 10am–noon & 2–6pm; mid-June to mid-Sept daily 10am–7pm; mid-Sept to March daily except Tues 10am–noon & 2–6pm; €7 Ⓦresistance-bretonne.com). This museum stands on the site of a June 1944 battle in which the Breton *maquis* (resistance), joined by Free French forces parachuted in from England, successfully diverted the local German troops from the main Normandy invasion movements.

The museum's greatest strength is its presentation of the pressures that made so many French collaborate: the reconstructed street corner overwhelmed by the brooding presence of the occupiers; the big colourful propaganda posters offering work in Germany, announcing executions of *maquisards*, equating resistance with aiding US and British big business; and, against these, the low-budget, shoddily printed Resistance pamphlets. All the labelling is in French, which non-speakers may find frustrating.

Rochefort-en-Terre

ROCHEFORT-EN-TERRE overlooks the River Arz from a high eminence 17km south of Malestroit. While arguably a prettified and polished version of its neighbour, and something of a tourist trap with its little antique shops and expensive restaurants, it ranks among the most delightful villages in Brittany. Every available stone surface, from the window ledges to the picturesque wishing well, is permanently bedecked in flowers, to the extent that Rochefort has been banned since 1967 from taking part in regional and national contests for the town with the best floral decorations (*villes fleuries*).

The flowery tradition originated with the painter Alfred Klots, who was born in France to a wealthy American family in 1875, and who bought Rochefort's ruined **château** in 1907. Perched on the town's highest point, the castle is open to visitors (April & May Sat & Sun 2–6.30pm; June & Sept daily 2–6.30pm; July & Aug daily 10am–6.30pm; €4), though not until you go through its dramatic gateway do you find out that in fact that gateway is all that survives of the original fifteenth-century structure. Instead, the castle as it stands today was cobbled together by Klots using pieces from various other local ruins. It contains his own unremarkable paintings, along with those of his son, plus family memorabilia such as the "Cardinal Room", where a US cardinal once stayed and appears to have forgotten to take his clothes and suitcase when he left. The highlights are Klots' former studio, a detached building with magnificent views over the surrounding hills and gorges, and garden terraces on all sides.

At the bottom end of town, the church of **Notre Dame de Tronchaye** holds a Black Virgin that was found hidden from Norman invaders in a hollow tree in the twelfth century, and is the object of a pilgrimage on the first Sunday after August 15. More interesting, though, is the **Lac Bleu**, just to the south, where the deep galleries of some ancient **slate quarries** are the home of blind butterflies and long-eared bats.

Practicalities

Rochefort's **tourist office** is in the central place du Puits (Jan to mid-June & mid-Sept to Nov Tues–Sat 10am–1pm & 2–5pm; 2nd fortnight of June & 1st fortnight of Sept Mon & Tues 10am–1pm & 2–6pm, Wed–Fri 9.30am–6.30pm, Sat 2–6pm, Sun 10am–1pm; July & Aug Mon–Fri 9.30am–6.30pm, Sat 2–6pm, Sun 10am–1pm; Dec Tues–Sat 2–7pm; ⓣ02.97.43.33.57, ⓦrochefort-en-terre .com). The one **hotel** in town, *Le Pélican* in the place des Halles: (ⓣ02.97.43.38.48, ⓦhotel-pelican-rochefort.com; ❻ including dinner; closed mid-Jan to mid-Feb), offers reasonable rooms and insists guests dine in its restaurant. There's also a very grand country-house hotel, set in magnificent gardens 4km northwest of town, the *Château de Talhouët* (ⓣ02.97.43.34.72, ⓦchateaudetalhoet.com; ❼–❾; closed first three weeks of Jan & 2nd fortnight of Nov), which holds half a dozen plush bedrooms furnished according to various themes; dinner costs €47. The three-star municipal **campsite**, *Le Moulin Neuf*, is in the chemin de Bogeais (ⓣ02.97.43.37.52; closed mid-Sept to mid-May). The *Creperie La*

Terrasse, 4 rue St-Michel (Ⓣ02.97.43.35.56; closed Jan–March) is a good option for a cheap meal.

At the village of **ST-VINCENT-SUR-OUST**, on the D764 halfway between Rochefort and Redon, a **hostel**, *Ty Kendalc'h* (Ⓣ02.99.91.28.55; closed Jan), serves as a centre for **Breton music and dance**, although accommodation is only available for groups.

The Parc de Préhistoire de Bretagne

Two kilometres southeast of Rochefort, outside the small community of **MALANSAC**, the very heavily publicized **Parc de Préhistoire de Bretagne** is a theme park aimed overwhelmingly at children (April–Sept daily 10.30am–7pm, last admission 5pm; Oct to early Nov Sun 1–6.30pm; Ⓦprehistoire-bretagne.com; €10). Separate landscaped areas contain dioramas of gigantic (if stationary) dinosaurs, and human beings at various stages in their evolution; the story ends shortly after a bunch of deformed but enthusiastic Neanderthals hit on the idea of erecting a few megaliths.

La Gacilly and around

Fourteen kilometres north of the canal, **LA GACILLY** makes a good base for walking trips in search of megaliths, sleepy villages and countryside. The town itself has prospered recently thanks to the creation of a beauty-products industry based on the abundantly proliferating flowers in the Aff valley. It's also a centre for many active craftsworkers; a walk down the old stone steps of the cobbled street that runs parallel to the main road between town centre and river is both a pleasure in itself and an opportunity to look in on their workshops. The only real disappointment is that the riverfront is not accessible to walkers, though you can enjoy views of it from a couple of restaurants, and rent boats to take out on it, costing from €25 for 1 hour up to €115 for a full day (Ⓣ02.99.72.41.11, Ⓦbateaux-fluviaux-bretagne.com).

Practicalities

Up in the town centre, the *Europ'Hôtel*, 15 place du Square (Ⓣ02.99.08.11.15, Ⓦhotel-lagacilly.com; ❷; closed Sun eve Oct–April), is an extremely hospitable Logis, with quiet and comfortable **rooms** in what used to be the separate *Hôtel du Square*, reached through the long gardens at the back. Alternatively, the *chambre d'hôte* (Ⓣ02.99.70.07.40, Ⓦmanoir-pommery.com; ❸) in the sixteenth-century Manoir de Pommery, 7km east in **Sixt-sur-Aff**, provides ideal countryside **B&B** accommodation, with dinner at €20.

The Megaliths of St-Just

Around 10km east of La Gacilly, in the vicinity of the village of **ST-JUST**, the small windswept **Cojoux** moor is rich in ancient megalithic remains. Only recently have they received much attention, as archeologists have gradually uncovered all sorts of ancient tombs and sacred sites. In summer, a small **visitor centre** (May & June Wed–Sun 2–6pm; €5; Ⓣ02.99.72.69.25, Ⓦlandes-de-cojoux.com), aimed largely at local schoolchildren, explains the latest discoveries, and also organizes **walking tours**. In any case, it's a rewarding area to ramble around yourself; the larger menhirs and so on are signposted along dirt tracks and footpaths, and you'll probably stumble upon a few lesser ones by chance.

Redon

Thirty-four kilometres east of Malestroit, at the junction of the rivers Oust and Vilaine, on the Nantes–Brest canal, linked by rail to Rennes, Vannes and Nantes, and at the intersection of six major roads, **REDON** is not a place it's easy to avoid. And you shouldn't try to, either. A wonderful mess of water and locks – the canal manages to cross the Vilaine at right angles in one of the more complex links – the town has history, charm and life. It's among the best stops along the whole canal.

Arrival and information

Redon's friendly and helpful **tourist office** is in the place de la République, north across the railway tracks from the town centre (July & Aug Mon–Sat 9am–7pm, Sun 10am–1pm & 4–6pm; Sept–June Mon & Wed–Fri 9.30am–noon & 2–6pm, Tues 2–6pm, Sat 10am–12.30pm & 3–5pm; ⓣ02.99.71.06.04, ⓦtourisme-pays-redon.com); in summer they have an annexe in the port. The **gare SNCF** is five minutes' walk west. **Internet access** is available at E'scape Zone, across from the tourist office at 5 place de Bretagne (ⓣ02.99.72.43.10; daily noon–midnight; €4 per hr).

Bicycles can be rented from BoutiCycle Chedaleux, 19 rue Briangaud (Mon–Sat 9am–noon & 2–7pm; ⓣ02.99.72.19.95), and **barges** from Locaboat Plaisance, 12 quai Jean-Bart (ⓣ02.99.72.15.80, ⓦbretagne-plaisance.fr). In addition, Vedettes Jaunes (ⓣ02.97.45.02.81, ⓦvedettesjaunes.com) run **river cruises** along the Vilaine from the Arzal dam – which is as close as they can get to the sea – upstream past La Roche-Bernard to Redon (very irregular schedule; 2hr 30min). Tickets can be reserved at the tourist office.

Accommodation

Redon's **hotels** are mostly concentrated in the town and near the *gare SNCF* rather than in the port area, but it's small enough that it makes little difference where you stay. The off-white *France* looks down on the canal from 30 rue Duguesclin, at the corner with the quai de Brest (ⓣ02.99.71.06.11, ⓦlefrance.chez-alice.fr; ❷); its renovated rooms, nearly all of which have en-suite bathrooms, offer considerable comfort for the price. Across (or rather under) the railway tracks from the tourist office, the *Asther*, 14 rue des Douves (ⓣ02.99.71.10.91, ⓦasther-hotel.com; ❷), is set above a brasserie, *Le Théâtre*. A little nearer the station, the *Chandouineau*, 1 rue Thiers (ⓣ02.99.71.02.04, ⓦhotel-restaurant-chandouineau.com; ❹; closed Sat & Sun eve), is an upmarket establishment with just seven bedrooms, and a gourmet restaurant.

The Town

Founded in 832 AD by St Conwoïon at the instigation of Nominoë, the first king of Brittany, Redon was a place of pilgrimage until the seventeenth century. Its Benedictine abbey is now the focus of the church of **St-Sauveur** – the rounded angles of the dumpy twelfth-century Romanesque lantern tower are unique in Brittany. All but obscured by later roofs and the high choir, the four-storey belfry is best seen from the adjacent cloisters. The later Gothic tower was entirely separated from the main building by a fire in 1780. Every Friday and Saturday from the end of June to the end of July, Redon puts on a large-scale son et lumière re-enactment of ten of the earliest years of its history, from 835 until 845 AD.

Under the chapel of Joan of Arc, the church crypt holds the tomb of Pierre l'Hospital, the judge who condemned **Gilles de Rais** to be hanged in 1440 for satanism and the most infamous orgies. Gilles had fought alongside Joan, burned for heresy, witchcraft and sorcery in 1431, and in both cases the court procedures were irregular to say the least. Legends of Gilles' atrocities were the source for tales of the monstrous wife-murderer **Bluebeard**.

Until World War I Redon was the seaport for Rennes. Its industrial docks – or what remains of them – are therefore on the Vilaine, while the canal, even in the very centre of town, is almost totally rural, its towpaths shaded avenues. Ship-owners' homes from the seventeenth and eighteenth centuries can be seen in the port area – walk via quai Jean-Bart next to the *bassin* (pleasure port) along the **Croix des Marins promenade**, returning along quai Duguay-Trouin beside the river, where you'll also find the *Attis*, a US boat that was used in the Normandy landings, and being no longer seaworthy is now moored here permanently. A rusted wrought-iron workbridge, equipped with a crane rolling on tracks, still crosses the river, but the main users of the port now are **cruise ships**, which come from 40km downstream at the Arzal dam.

Flowers abound throughout Redon, which achieves regular success in *villes fleuries* – in 1983, it won the national first prize. As late as October, swathes of chrysanthemums in autumn tints hang from balconies and the numerous iron bridges.

Eating, drinking and entertainment

La Bogue, in a flowery mansion in place du Parlement at 3 rue des États (☎02.99.71.12.95; closed Sun eve & Mon), is a friendly and good-value **fish restaurant**. Its cheapest, €23 menu features a *cassolette* of snails with *petits pois* as one of its four courses; the most expensive, at €60, is a sumptuous feast. Elsewhere, *L'Akène*, 10 rue de Jeu-de-Paume (☎02.99.71.25.15; closed Tues eve, plus Wed eve in winter), is a crêperie in an equally lovely old house in an alleyway close to the port; you must try the rhubarb jam crêpe. Further delicious crêpes are available at Monday's large **market**, which sprawls through most of town on both sides of the railway tracks.

Redon also holds plenty of **bars and pubs**. At the *Cubana Café* on avenue Jean Burel in St-Nicolas-de-Redon, across the Vilaine from the port (☎02.99.71.30.64), where themed rooms include the *Mille et une nuits*, incorporating real sand, you can drink cocktails, eat tapas and take Latin dance classes on Saturdays. The season at the modern *Canal* **theatre** (☎02.99.71.09.50), near the main square, runs from September to May.

Châteaubriant

Sixty kilometres east of Redon, and the same distance north of Nantes, the fortified town of **CHÂTEAUBRIANT** guards the border of Brittany and Anjou. While it's not a place to go out of your way to see, and the flat surrounding countryside holds precious little of interest, a couple of hours spent wandering in and around its venerable **Château** makes a welcome interruption to a day spent travelling.

The castle walls still encircle the crest of a knoll just east of the town proper, although only the entrance keep (*donjon d'entrée*) remains of the original tenth-century structure. Simply stroll through that mighty gateway to find a disparate assembly of buildings of different eras, in similarly assorted states of repair, interspersed with peaceful lawns and formal gardens. The most complete edifice is a self-contained Renaissance château, built from 1521 onwards, and equipped with a sort of secular cloisters. To see the apartments inside, join a **guided tour** (mid-May to mid-Sept daily except Tues, 11am, 2.30pm & 4pm; mid-Sept to mid-May Sat & Sun 3.30pm; €3.50).

Practicalities

Châteaubriant's **tourist office** is in the centre of the old town, just north of the church, at 22 rue du Couéré (Mon 2–6pm, Tues–Fri 9.30am–12.30pm & 2–6pm, Sat 9.30am–12.30pm; ⓣ02.40.28.20.90, ⓦtourisme-chateaubriant.fr). Close to the tourist office, the *Hôtel du Pont St-Jean*, 5 rue Denieul et Gastineau (ⓣ02.40.28.04.54; ➊) has inexpensive **rooms**, while the *Le Poêlon d'Or*, nearby at 30 rue du 11-Novembre (ⓣ02.40.81.43.33; closed Sun eve & Mon, plus last week in Feb and first fortnight in Aug), is an excellent little homely restaurant where menus start at €17.

Nantes

Over the last decade the rejuvenated, go-ahead city of **NANTES** has transformed itself into a likeable metropolis that deserves to figure on any tourist itinerary. At the heart of this ambitious regeneration project stands a must-see attraction, the **Machines de l'Île** – home of the Grand Éléphant – but the city as a whole is also scrubbed, gleaming, and suffused with a remarkable energy.

As the capital of an independent Brittany, Nantes was a considerable medieval centre. Great wealth came later, however, when it prospered from colonial expeditions, and was by the end of the eighteenth century the principal port of France. Huge fortunes were made via the city's involvement in the slave trade; an estimated 500,000 African slaves were carried to the Americas in vessels based here, and even after abolition in 1817 the trade continued illegally. Subsequently the port declined, and heavy industry and wine production became more important. At the start of the twentieth the city had become known as "Nantes the Grey".

Although Nantes today is no longer even in Brittany – it was transferred to the Pays de la Loire in 1962 – its inhabitants still consider it to be an integral part of the province. Once you've seen the machines, the **Château des Ducs** and the **Beaux Arts** museum are well worth visiting, but this is also a place to enjoy a little urban excitement in this predominantly slow-paced region.

Arrival and information

Nantes' **gare SNCF**, a little way east of the château, is served by fast trains between Paris and Brittany – a dozen TGVs daily reach Paris in as little as two hours – and is the terminus for the local line westwards to St-Nazaire, La Baule and Croisic. The station has two exits; for most facilities (tramway, buses, hotels) use *Accès Nord*.

There are two main **bus** stations. The one just south of the centre on allée Baco, near place Ricordeau, is used by buses heading south and southwest, while the one where the cours des 50 Otages meets rue de l'Hôtel de Ville serves routes that stay north of the river. **Trams** run along the old riverfront, past the *gare SNCF* and the two bus stations. Flat-fare tickets, at €1.50, are valid for one hour, rather than just a single journey, though one-day tickets are also available for €3.50. Tickets must be bought at tram stations, not on board.

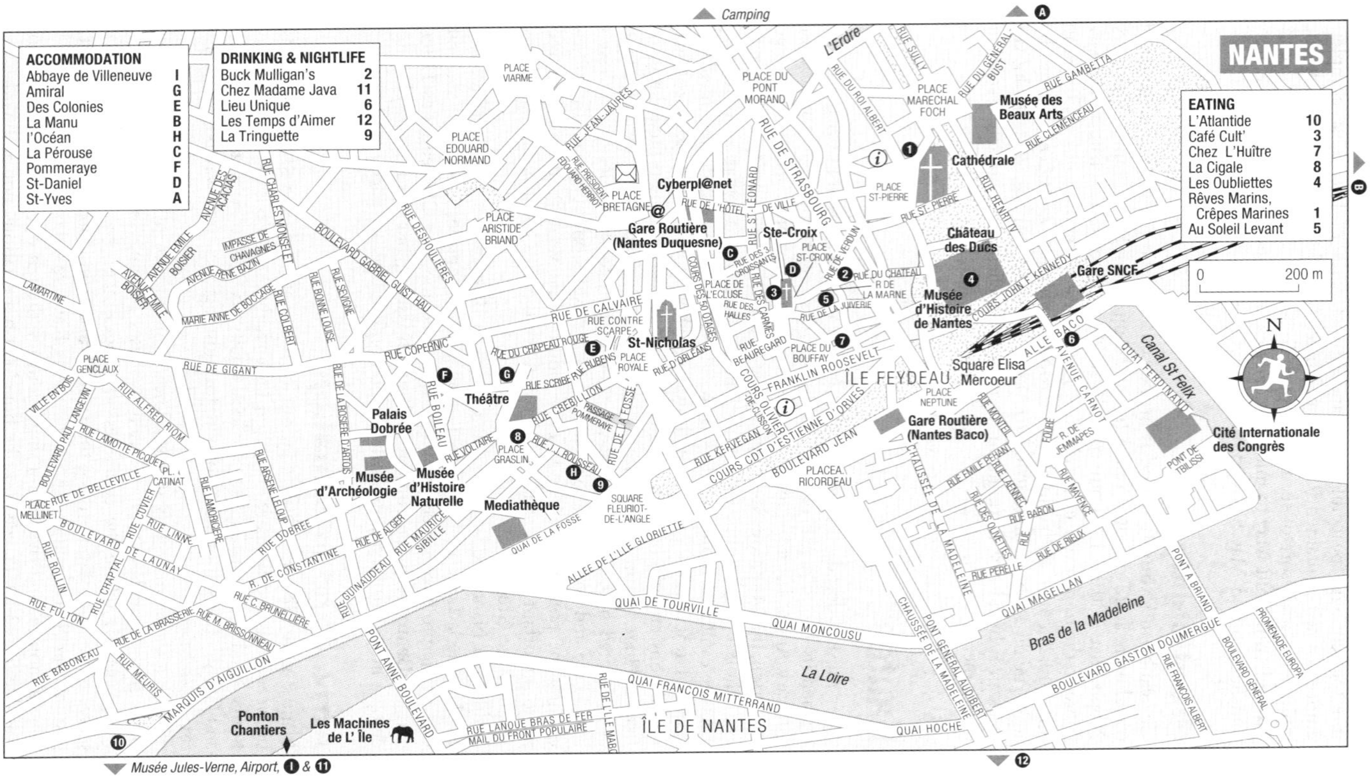
NANTES
ACCOMMODATION
Abbaye de Villeneuve I
Amiral G
Des Colonies E
La Manu B
l'Océan H
La Pérouse C
Pommeraye F
St-Daniel D
St-Yves A
DRINKING & NIGHTLIFE
Buck Mulligan's 2
Chez Madame Java 11
Lieu Unique 6
Les Temps d'Aimer 12
La Tringuette 9
EATING
L'Atlantide 10
Café Cult' 3
Chez L'Huître 7
La Cigale 8
Les Oubliettes 4
Rêves Marins, Crêpes Marines 1
Au Soleil Levant 5
0 200 m
N
Camping
Musée Jules-Verne, Airport, 1 & 11
L'Erdre
La Loire
Bras de la Madeleine
Canal St Felix
ÎLE FEYDEAU
ÎLE DE NANTES
Cathédrale
Musée des Beaux Arts
Château des Ducs
Musée d'Histoire de Nantes
Gare SNCF
Square Elisa Mercoeur
Gare Routière (Nantes Baco)
Cité Internationale des Congrès
Ste-Croix
St-Nicholas
Cyberpl@net
Gare Routière (Nantes Duquesne)
Théâtre
Palais Dobrée
Musée d'Archéologie
Musée d'Histoire Naturelle
Mediathèque
Ponton Chantiers
Les Machines de L' Île
PLACE DU PONT MORAND
PLACE MARECHAL FOCH
PLACE ST-PIERRE
PLACE BRETAGNE
PLACE EDOUARD NORMAND
PLACE VIARME
PLACE ARISTIDE BRIAND
PLACE ROYALE
PLACE GRASLIN
PLACE DU BOUFFAY
PLACE NEPTUNE
PLACEA RICORDEAU
PLACE GENCLAUX
PLACE MELLINET
SQUARE FLEURIOT-DE-L'ANGLE
RUE DE STRASBOURG
COURS JOHN F KENNEDY
COURS FRANKLIN ROOSEVELT
COURS OLIVIER DE-CLISSON
COURS CDT D'ESTIENNE D'ORVES
COURS DES 50 OTAGES
BOULEVARD JEAN
CHAUSSÉE DE LA MADELEINE
QUAI DE TOURVILLE
QUAI MONCOUSU
QUAI MAGELLAN
QUAI FRANCOIS MITTERRAND
QUAI HOCHE
QUAI DE LA FOSSE
QUAI FERDINAND
PONT ANNE BOULEVARD
PONT GENERAL AUDIBERT
PONT A BRIAND
BOULEVARD GASTON DOUMERGUE
BOULEVARD GENERAL
PROMENADE EUROPA
MARQUIS D'AIGUILLON
BOULEVARD GABRIEL GUIST HAU
BOULEVARD DE LAUNAY
AVENUE CARNOT
ALLE BACO
RUE DE CALVAIRE
RUE DE GIGANT
RUE BOILEAU
RUE CREBILLON
RUE DE LA FOSSE
RUE JEAN-JAURES
RUE HENRI IV
RUE GAMBETTA
RUE CLEMENCEAU
RUE SULLY
RUE DU ROI ALBERT
ALLEE DE L'ILE GLORIETTE

Services to Nantes' **airport** (Ⓦnantes.aeroport.fr), 12km southwest and connected by regular buses, include daily Air France flights from London City Airport.

Nantes has **tourist offices** at 3 cours Olivier-de-Clisson (Mon–Wed, Fri & Sat 10am–6pm, Thurs 10.30am–6pm; Ⓣ08.92.46.40.44, Ⓦnantes-tourisme.com), and next to the cathedral at 2 place St-Pierre (Tues, Wed & Fri–Sun 10am–1pm & 2–6pm, Thurs 10.30am–1pm & 2–6pm). Both sell the **Pass Nantes**, available in 24-hour (€18), 48-hour (€28) and 72-hour (€36) versions, which grants unrestricted use of local transport and some car parks, and free admission to several museums and attractions. There's internet access at **Cyberpl@net**, 18 rue de l'Arche Sèche (Mon–Sat 10am–2am, Sun 2–10pm; Ⓣ02.51.82.47.97, Ⓦcyberplanet.fr; €3 per hr).

Under the Bicloo scheme (Ⓦwww.bicloo.nantesmetropole.fr), **bikes** are available to rent from docking stations all over the city; the first half hour is free.

Accommodation

Although it has plenty of **hotels** to suit all budgets, Nantes is one of those cities where you won't necessarily stumble upon a suitable place just by walking or driving around at whim. Instead, there are two main concentrations; one, as ever, in the immediate vicinity of the *gare SNCF*, and one in the narrow streets around the place Graslin. Surprisingly few are in the older part of town. The tourist office runs a booking service (Ⓣ08.92.46.40.44, Ⓦwww.resanantes.com).

Hotels

Abbaye de Villeneuve rte de la Roche sur Yonne, Les Sorinières Ⓣ02.40.04.40.25, Ⓦabbayedevilleneuve.com. Nantes' only four-star hotel, housed in a restored eighteenth-century *abbaye* 7km south of town, off the A83. Gorgeously lavish rooms, a circular swimming pool and spa, and a superb restaurant. ⑤–⑨

Amiral 26bis rue Scribe Ⓣ02.40.69.20.21, Ⓦhotel-nantes.fr. Well-maintained little hotel on a lively pedestrianized street just north of pl Graslin, and perfect for young night owls. All rooms have TV, bath and double-glazing, though some noise still creeps in. Mon–Fri ⑤, Sat & Sun ③

Des Colonies 5 rue du Chapeau Rouge Ⓣ02.40.48.79.76, Ⓦhoteldescolonies.fr. Spruce, good-value hotel a couple of blocks up from pl Graslin, within walking distance of everything. The lobby doubles as an art gallery. Discounts at weekends. No restaurant. ④

l'Océan 11 rue Maréchal-de-Lattre-de-Tassigny Ⓣ02.40.69.73.51, Ⓦwww.hotel-nantes.com. A pleasant hotel, with helpful management, just below pl Graslin near the Médiathèque. All rooms have TV and shower, while a private toilet costs only €2 extra. Parking space is available around the back. No restaurant, breakfast served in room only. Closed last two weeks of Dec. ②

La Pérouse 3 allée Duquesne Ⓣ02.40.89.75.00, Ⓦhotel-laperouse.fr. Superb contemporary building ingeniously integrated with the older architecture that surrounds it – right down to its leaning north-facing side. The interior is decorated with 1930s furniture, stucco walls and high-tech touches like flat-screen TVs and wi-fi. An original, comfortable and friendly place to stay, with excellent breakfasts to boot. ⑤

Pommeraye 2 rue Boileau Ⓣ02.40.48.78.79, Ⓦhotel-pommeraye.com. Extremely good-value modern boutique hotel with large, designer-decor rooms, beautiful bathrooms and free parking; good buffet breakfast for €9.40. ④

St-Daniel 4 rue du Bouffay Ⓣ02.40.47.41.25, Ⓦwww.hotel-saintdaniel.com. These simple but pleasant and well-lit rooms, all en-suite, are located on a cobbled street just off the pl du Bouffay in the very heart of the old city, and are much in demand in summer. Street-side rooms are sound-proofed. Breakfast is just €4. ③

St-Yves 154 rue du Général-Buat Ⓣ02.40.74.48.42, Ⓦhotel-saintyves.fr. Very attractive, great value little ten-room hotel, 10min walk north of the railway station, with friendly staff, a nice garden and big breakfasts for €6.50. ②

Hostel and campsite

La Manu 2 pl de la Manufacture Ⓣ02.40.29.29.20, Ⓦfuaj.org/nantes. Nantes' hostel, which has internet access and a cafeteria,

River cruises from Nantes

Bateaux Nantais offer **river cruises** from Nantes, both on the **Loire**, departing from the Ponton Chantiers on the Île de Nantes, and on the **Erdre**, departing from the *gare fluviale*, on the quai de la Motte-Rouge a little way north of the centre. Typical options range from a circumnavigation of the Île de Nantes (€9), a 1hr 45min cruise on the Erdre (€10), or a three-hour trip on a floating restaurant for lunch (noon) or dinner (8pm), for €89. For details and reservations, contact ⓣ02.40.14.51.14 or ⓦwww.bateaux-nantais.fr.

is housed in a postmodern former tobacco factory a few hundred metres east of the *gare SNCF* and a 5min ride from the centre on tramway #1. Beds in 4- or 6-bed dorms for €17.40 including breakfast. Reception daily 8am–noon & 4–10.30pm, closed mid-Dec to early Jan.

Du Petit Port 21 bd du Petit-Port (ⓣ02.40.74.47.94, ⓦnge-nantes.fr. This well-managed, four-star campsite with swimming pool, occupies a pleasant tree-shaded setting north of the city centre on tram route #2 (stop "Morrhonnière"). Open all year.

The City

Huge redevelopment schemes are currently attempting to shift the focus of Nantes back towards the **Loire**, the original source of its riches. As recently as the 1930s, the river crossed the city in seven separate channels, but German labour as part of reparations for World War I filled in five of them. For the moment, however, the main distinction still lies between the older **medieval city**, concentrated around the cathedral and with the château prominent in its southeast corner, and the elegant **nineteenth-century town** to the west, across the cours de 50 Otages. In a sense, that division has an additional political significance, for Nantes is not solely Breton. As trade along the Loire made the French influence on the city ever more significant, from the end of the eighteenth century onwards this newer area earned the nickname of "little Paris".

Place Royale, at the heart of the nineteenth-century town, was first laid out in the 1790s; damaged by bombing in 1943, it has now been restored. **Place Graslin**, 200m west, dates from the same period; the Corinthian portico of its **theatre** contrasts with the 1895 Art Nouveau of the delightful *La Cigale*, opposite, embellished with mosaics and mirrors and still a popular brasserie (see p.338).

A spectacular nineteenth-century multi-level indoor shopping centre, the **Passage Pommeraye**, drops down three flights of stairs towards the river on nearby rue Crebillon. The scale of its architectural embellishments is extraordinary; each of the gas lamps that light the central area is held by an individually crafted marble cherub. Although the building itself remains impressive, business is not exactly booming, and the presence of the odd shop selling candles or ethnic jewellery only adds to its run-down feel.

Many of the streets in the two principal regions of the city have been semi-pedestrianized, and they abound in pavement cafés, brasseries and shops. Just south of them both, the elongated **Île Feydeau** is no longer an island, being now surrounded not by water, but by busy roads. Even so, its eighteenth-century houses, seen at their best in rue Kervegan, retain a certain Baroque charm.

The Château des Ducs

Though no longer on the waterfront, the **Château des Ducs** still preserves the form in which it was built by two of the last rulers of independent Brittany,

François II and his daughter Duchess Anne, born here in 1477. The list of famous people who have been guests or prisoners, defenders or belligerents, of the castle is impressive. It includes Gilles de Rais (Bluebeard), publicly executed in 1440; Machiavelli in 1498; the firebrand Scottish preacher John Knox as a galley slave in 1547–49; and Bonnie Prince Charlie in 1745. The most significant act in the castle, was the signing of the **Edict of Nantes** in 1598 by Henri IV. The edict ended the Wars of Religion by granting a certain degree of toleration to the Protestants, but had far more crucial consequences when it was revoked by Louis XIV in 1685. To their credit, the people of Nantes took no part in the subsequent general massacres of the Huguenots.

The stout **ramparts** of the château remain pretty much intact, and most of the encircling moat is filled with water, surrounded by well-tended lawns that make a popular spot for lunchtime picnics. Following extensive restoration, visitors can pass through the walls, and also stroll atop them for fine views over the city, for no charge (July & Aug daily 9am–8pm; Sept–June daily 10am–7pm).

The rather incongruous potpourri of buildings within includes a major exhibition space used for year-long displays on differing subjects; the nice *Oubliettes* café/restaurant (see p.338); and the new, high-tech **Musée d'Histoire de Nantes** (July & Aug daily 9.30am–7pm; Sept–June daily except Tues 10am–6pm; €5, €8 combined with temporary exhibitions; Ⓦchateau-nantes.fr). Spreading through 32 rooms and seven "themes", the latter covers local history in exhaustive detail. Highlights include a fascinating scale model of the city in the thirteenth century, and a determined attempt to come to terms with Nantes' slave-trading past, displaying pitiful trinkets that were used to buy slaves in Africa.

The cathedral

The fifteenth-century **Cathédrale de St-Pierre-et-St-Paul** stands 200m north of the château (Easter to mid-July Sat 10am–12.30pm & 3–6pm, Sun 3–6pm; mid-July to Aug Tues–Fri 3–6pm, Sat 10am–12.30pm & 3–6pm, Sun 3–6pm; Sept–Easter Sat & Sun 3–6pm). Made to seem especially light and soaring by its clean white stone, it contains the tomb of François II, the last duke of Brittany, and his wife, Margaret, the parents of Duchess Anne – with somewhat grating symbols of Power, Strength and Justice for him and Fidelity, Prudence and Temperance for her. This imposing monument is illuminated by a superb modern stained-glass window devoted to Breton and Nantais saints.

Les Machines de l'Île

Inaugurated in 2007, and centering on the fabulous **Grand Éléphant**, the **Machines de l'Île** is a truly world-class attraction. The "machines" of the name are the astonishing contraptions created by designer/engineer François Delarozière and artist Pierre Orefice; the "island" is the Île de Nantes, a 3km-long, whale-shaped island in the Loire that has remained neglected ever since the city's shipbuilding industry closed down in 1987. Part *hommage* to the sci-fi creations of Jules Verne and the blueprints of Leonardo da Vinci, part street-theatre extravaganza, this is the lynchpin of Nantes' urban regeneration; far from an enclosed theme park, it's open to any passer-by (see p.337 for visitor information). While the actual machines are kept and constructed in vast hangars, the elephant emerges for regular walks. Visitors can pay to enter the indoor workshops, or to ride on the elephant, but you can also simply see the elephant for free, and follow it on its pachydermic perambulations along the huge esplanade outside.

Twelve metres high and eight metres wide, the elephant itself is made largely from American tulipwood. Although it's phenomenally realistic, down to the

▲ The magnificent Grand Éléphant at the Machines de l'Île

articulation of its joints as it "walks", and its trunk as it flexes and sprays water, its mechanical underbelly is not hidden away; that you can see how it all works is part of the fun. It's basically a replica of the Sultan's Elephant, which stopped London in its tracks when it spent a week exploring the city in 2006, though this version is re-jigged to carry passengers. You don't have to sit down as you ride; instead you can wander through its hollow belly and climb the spiral stairs within to reach the balconies and vantage points around its canopied howdah.

The exuberant creativity of the whole thing is breathtaking. Originally commissioned to celebrate the centenary of Nantes native Jules Verne's death, the elephant has a madcap Victorian flavour, combining Verne's charm and adventure with a modern steam-punk aesthetic. The crackpot relish about the details – the intricate sculpting and painting of every wooden surface, the wear and tear on the massive leather ears – makes it clear this whole undertaking is prompted by love not money.

Inside the main hangar, the **Workshop** can be viewed from an overhead walkway, while the **Gallery** displays a changing assortment of completed machines. At the time of writing, these were the various components of the multi-tiered Marine Worlds carousel, due to be fully assembled and operational in 2011. Those visitors who volunteer quickly enough – mostly but not necessarily children – get to ride such oddball devices as the Giant Crab, the Bus of the Abyss, and the Reverse-Propelling Squid. It also displays blueprints and models of **L'Arbre aux Herons** ("the Heron Tree"), a steel tree fifty metres in diameter by 22 metres high, topped by two herons, which will ultimately be erected beside the Loire. Visitors will be able to walk up the branches of the tree, pausing at a café amid the hanging foliage, and ride in baskets suspended from the herons' wings.

A full-scale sample branch of the Heron Tree spreads at the front of the whole complex. Alongside stands an earlier fairground carousel known as **Le Manège**

d'Andréa, created by the same team in 1999 and peopled by similarly bizarre apparitions (ages 2–12 only; Mon & Tues 3–7pm, Wed–Sun 11am–12.30pm & 2.30–7pm; one ticket €2, ten tickets €15).

The Museums

The **Musée des Beaux Arts**, east of the cathedral at 10 rue Clemenceau, displays its paintings in excellent modern galleries, and hosts a high standard of temporary exhibitions (Mon, Wed & Fri–Sun 10am–6pm, Thurs 10am–8pm; €3.50, €2 after 4.30pm). Not all its Renaissance and contemporary works are on show at any one time, but you should be able to take in canvases ranging from a gorgeous *David Triumphant* by Delaunay and Léon Comerre's disturbing *Le Déluge*, a writhing orgy of drowning flesh, to Chagall's *Le Cheval Rouge* and one of Monet's *Nymphéas*.

Rue Voltaire runs west of the place Graslin, leading to the **Musée d'Histoire Naturelle** at no. 12 (daily except Tues 10am–6pm; €3.50; Ⓦwww.museum.nantes.fr). Recently overhauled, this centres on an old-fashioned collection of oddities, including stuffed specimens of virtually every bird and animal imaginable. An eccentric "Old Irish"-style mansion at 18 rue Voltaire nearby is known as the **Palais Dobrée** (Tues–Fri 1.30–5.30pm, Sat & Sun 2.30–5.30pm; €3, free on Sun). This was home to Thomas Dobrée (1810–95), who accumulated oddments including a little reliquary of beaten gold that contains Duchess Anne's heart. An ugly new building in the grounds serves as the **Musée d'Archéologie**

Machines de l'Île: practical information

The Machines de l'Île are ten minutes' walk southwest from the tourist office, across the northern arm of the Loire, and clearly signposted. The abundant parking space is not easy to find – once you're in the immediate vicinity, follow signs to "Les Chantiers".

Opening hours

Opening hours vary enormously throughout the year; check Ⓦwww.lesmachines-nantes.fr or Ⓣ08.10.12.12.25 for up-to-date information.

Early Jan to mid-Feb: closed

Second half of Feb: daily except Mon 2–7pm

March to mid-April: Wed–Fri 2–6pm, Sat & Sun 2–7pm

Mid-April to early May & late May to June: Tues–Fri 10am–6pm, Sat & Sun 10am–7pm

Middle fortnight of May: Mon–Fri 10am–6pm, Sat & Sun 10am–7pm

July & Aug: daily 10am–8pm

Sept to early Nov: Tues–Fri 10am–6 pm, Sat & Sun 10am–7pm

Early Nov to late Dec: Wed–Fri 2–6pm, Sat & Sun 2–7pm

Late Dec to early Jan: Daily except Mon 2–7pm

Tickets and reservations

The ticket office shuts one hour before the site closes. Elephant rides cannot be reserved in advance; tickets are sold for same-day rides only, with a limit of 49 passengers per ride. Provided those times fall within that day's opening hours, rides are scheduled for 10.30am, 11.15am, noon, 12.45pm, 3.30pm, 4.15pm, 5pm & 5.45pm.

Tickets for the Gallery *or* an elephant ride cost €6.50 for adults and €5 for under-18s. Either ticket gives access to the Workshop and the branch of the Heron Tree. Only the Gallery is free with the Pass Nantes (see p.333). Note that you can see the elephant close-up – which is actually more exciting than riding it, though kids won't believe it – and ride the Manège d'Andréa carousel, without paying for admission.

(same hours & ticket), holding a quite nicely displayed but rather meagre collection of Greek, Egyptian and Etruscan artefacts.

Disappointingly dry despite its proximity to the river, the **Musée Jules-Vernes**, at 3 rue de l'Hermitage a kilometre southwest of the centre, commemorates the birthplace of the first serious writer of science fiction (daily except Tues: July & Aug 10am–6pm, Sept–June 10am–noon & 2–6pm, Sun 2–6pm; €3).

Eating

Unlike hotels, **restaurants** fill the winding lanes of the old city. It shouldn't take you long to find somewhere once you start wandering the central pedestrian streets. Nantes is large enough to have all sorts of ethnic alternatives as well, with North African, Italian, Chinese, Vietnamese and Indian places concentrated especially along the rue de la Juiverie.

L'Atlantide Centre des Salorges, 16 quai Ernest-Renaud T 02.40.73.23.23, W restaurant-atlantide.net. Designer restaurant, with big river views from the fourth floor of a modern block, serving the contemporary French cuisine of chef Jean-Yves Gueho. Fish is the speciality, but expect quirky twists like the bananas braised in beer. Menus at €27, €55 and €75. Closed Sat lunch & all Sun, plus late July to late Aug.

Café Cult' 2 rue des Carmes T 02.40.47.18.49. Friendly, good-value café housed in a beautiful old half-timbered house. They serve two-course lunches for just €11 and cheap drinks later on, when it becomes a lively bar. Until 2am, closed Sun.

Chez L'Huître 5 rue des Petites-Écuries T 02.51.82.02.02. Much as the name suggests, this lovely little restaurant, with outdoor seating on a pedestrian street, specializes in oysters of all sizes and provenance, priced at €9–11 per half-dozen. The *apérihuître* consists of six oysters and a glass of Muscadet for €5.50; there's also a €15.90 set menu. Open until late nightly, closed Sun lunch.

La Cigale 4 pl Graslin T 02.51.84.94.94, W www.lacigale.com. Fabulous late-nineteenth-century brasserie, offering fine meals in opulent Belle Époque surroundings, with seating either at tiled terrace tables or in a more formal indoor dining room. Fish is a speciality, with lunch options like the €16.90 *tartare de thon* or "River Runs Through It" salmon platter. Assorted set menus are served until midnight in keeping with the tradition of providing post-performance refreshments for patrons of the theatre opposite. Daily 7.30am–12.30am.

Les Oubliettes 4 pl Marc Elder T 02.51.82.67.04, W lesoubliettes.fr. Despite the address, this little daytime-only restaurant is splendidly and very spaciously set in the château courtyard, a world away from the city traffic, with seating both indoors and in the open air. Breakfast, tea and good-value lunches, with large *plats* and specials for around €10.

Rêves Marins, Crêpes Marines 2 rue de Roi Albert T 02.40.47.00.96. Boat-themed crêperie, with a frequently changing menu of seriously original *galettes*, including braised duck and lobster in saffron. Closed Sun & Mon.

Au Soleil Levant 12 rue de la Juiverie T 02.40.35.68.65. One of several Asian options along a little pedestrian street, with seating both indoors and out, this Japanese restaurant serves good-quality sushi, sashimi, maki rolls and noodles in all sorts of combinations, with full dinners €11.50–21, and lunch menus as cheap as €9.50, for either soup plus brochettes or raw fish. Closed Mon lunch.

Drinking and nightlife

By regional standards, Nantes by night is very lively indeed. Most of the action takes place in the alleyways of the medieval city, where students pack the **bars** until the small hours, though fancier but less atmospheric cafés surround place Graslin to the west.

Buck Mulligan's 12 rue du Château T 02.40.20.02.72. Irish-themed bar with genuine Irish owners and a dingy, dungeon-like setting, tucked away close to the château. Organizes plenty of events, from quiz nights to live music.

Chez Madame Java 118 rue Basse-Île T 02.40.04.20.88. Colourful and laid-back wine bar, with different food on offer most days and a garden out back for the summer. Live samba and reggae every second Sun in the winter.

Lieu Unique quai Ferdinand Favre ⓣ02.51.82.15.00 ⓦwww.lelieuunique.com. As unique as its name proclaims, this former LU biscuit factory now plays host to concerts, theatre, dance, art exhibitions, a bookshop, a fair brasserie and a great bar, open until late.
Les Temps d'Aimer 14 rue Alexandre-Fourny ⓣ02.40.89.48.60, ⓦletandem.com. Nantes' premier gay club, just south of the centre on the Île de Nantes, puts on a wide programme of events and shows. Nightly midnight–7am.
La Tringuette 3 quai de la Fosse ⓣ02.51.72.39.05. This hip central bar, with indoor and outdoor seating and friendly English-speaking owners, serves *tartines* and *croques monsieur* to go with its fine *aperitifs*, and gets especially lively on market day, Sat, when DJs play. Mon–Fri 8.30am–10pm, Sat 7.30am–8pm.

Around Nantes

The Loire **wine** region, responsible for two classic dry whites, Gros-Plant and Muscadet, lies immediately upstream (east) from Nantes. Any **vineyard** should be happy to give you a *dégustation*. Most operate on a very small scale; the largest, however, the **Chasseloir vineyard** at **ST-FIACRE-SUR-MAINE** (Mon–Sat 9am–6pm; ⓣ02.40.54.81.15, ⓦchereau-carre.fr), is perhaps the most interesting. This occupies the grounds of a former château, with fifty acres of vines – some a century old. The vineyard sells mostly within the catering trade, but anyone is welcome to visit their cellars, which are decorated with painted Rabelaisian carvings and candelabras made from vine roots.

Clisson

The town of **CLISSON**, the crossroads of the three ancient duchies of Brittany, Anjou and Poitou, perches 20km southeast of Nantes above the point where the Sèvre meets the Maine. This was remodelled by two French architects in the nineteenth century into a close approximation of an Italian hill town. The fact that they already had the raw material of a ruined fortress (May–Sept daily 11am–6.30pm; Oct–April Wed–Sun 2–5.30pm; €2.20), a covered market hall and a magnificent situation makes it a sight not to be missed. The best **place to stay** is the *Hôtel de la Gare*, on place de la Gare (ⓣ02.40.36.16.55; ③).

Travel details

Trains

No east–west railway line crosses central Brittany; however, certain towns can be reached by train.
Carhaix to: Guingamp (6 daily; 1hr).
Châteaubriant to: Rennes (4 daily; 1hr 10min).
Châteaulin to: Brest (7 daily; 1hr); Quimper (7 daily; 20min).
Loudéac to: St-Brieuc (5 daily; 1hr); Vannes (2 daily; 1hr 20min).
Nantes to: Paris (15 TGVs daily; 2hr 5min); Quimper (2 daily; 2hr 40min); Rennes (6 daily; 1hr 40min).
Pontivy to: St-Brieuc (3 daily; 1hr 15min); Vannes (2 daily; 55min).
Redon to: Nantes (10 daily; 45min); Quimper (10 daily; 1hr 45min); Rennes (18 daily; 40min); Vannes (10 daily; 30min).

Buses

Carhaix to: Morlaix (3 daily; 1hr 30min), via Huelgoat (30min); Quimper (1 daily; 1hr 20min) via Châteauneuf-du-Faou (30min) and Châteaulin (50min).
Châteaulin to: Châteauneuf-du-Faou (2 daily; 30min); Pleyben (2 daily; 15min).
Nantes to: Pornic (7 daily; 1hr 10min); Rennes (5 daily; 1hr); St-Nazaire (2 daily; 40min); Vannes (1 daily; 2hr 40min).
Pontivy to: Rennes (4 daily; 2hr) via Josselin (30min) and Ploërmel (45min).
Vannes to: Elven (3 daily; 25min); Malestroit (3 daily; 45min); Ploërmel (3 daily; 1hr); Pontivy (8 daily; 1hr 20min).

7

The South Coast

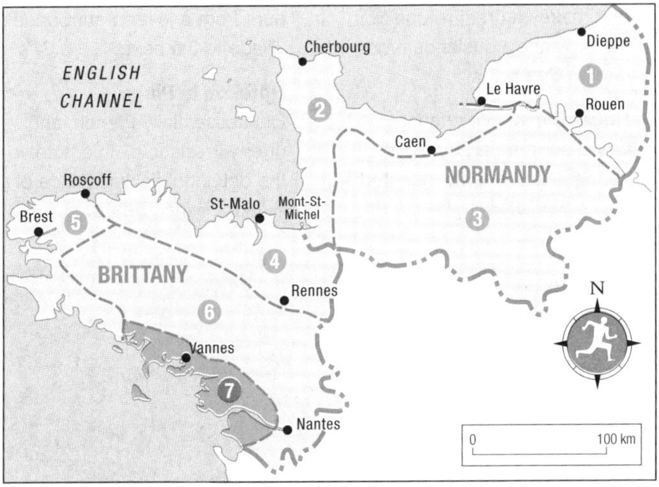

CHAPTER 7

Highlights

* **The Inter-Celtic Festival** The world's largest pan-Celtic jamboree, held every August, turns sleepy Lorient into Brittany's liveliest town. See p.346

* **De la Criée** Fabulous quayside fish restaurant in Quiberon, serving whatever's freshest from each day's catch. See p.353

* **Sauzon** Tiny seaside village on the lovely island of Belle-Île that makes a great refuge from the province's busier summer resorts. See p.356

* **Houat** Diminutive offshore island surrounded by sandy beaches and deeply indented coves. See p.357

* **The megaliths of Carnac** Said to be the oldest inhabited spot on earth, Carnac is still surrounded by relics of its ancient past. See p.361

* **Gavrinis** Brittany's most impressive pyramids crown this speck of an island in the land-locked Golfe du Morbihan. See p.368

* **The Grande-Brière** Eerie, mist-swathed marshes, just in from the sea, where you can punt from one reed-surrounded village to the next. See p.377

* **Hôtel de la Plage** Quintessentially French, and utterly irresistible, little hotel in the delightful fishing village of Piriac-sur-mer. See p.380

▲ Boat in the Golfe du Morbihan

7

The South Coast

Brittany's **southern coast** takes in several of the province's most famous sites, and also offers its warmest swimming. The whole coast is a succession of natural and human wonders. If you have any interest in prehistory, then the concentration of **megaliths** around the **Morbihan** should prove irresistible. **Carnac**, the most important site, may well be Europe's oldest settlement; the sun has risen more than two million times over its extraordinary alignments of menhirs. **Locmariaquer**, too, has a gigantic ancient stone, said by some to be the key to a prehistoric astronomical observatory, while the most beautifully positioned of all is the great tumulus on **Gavrinis**, one of the fifty or so islets scattered around the **Gulf of Morbihan**'s inland sea.

As for more hedonistic pastimes, in theory the best of the south's **beaches** are around the Gulf of Morbihan, and at **La Baule.** Not surprisingly, therefore, these areas are very popular with tourists, and you can be hard-pushed to find a room in summer – or to escape the crowds. La Baule is also the one resort in Brittany to be conspicuously affected and overpriced, and almost entirely lacks the character of the rest of the region. Excellent, lower-key alternatives can be found close by at **Le Croisic** and **Piriac-sur-mer**, and all along the south coast: at Carnac and Locmariaquer; at **Quiberon**; and out on the **islands** of **Groix** and **Belle-Île**. The largest Breton island, Belle-Île is a perfect microcosm of the province – a beautiful place with grand countryside and a couple of lively towns.

The south coast is also host to Brittany's most compelling **festival**, the ten-day **Inter-Celtic** gathering at **Lorient** in August. The end of July sees a **jazz festival** at the main Morbihan town, **Vannes**.

Lorient and its estuary

Brittany's fourth largest city, **LORIENT**, lies on an immense natural harbour protected from the ocean by the Île de Groix and strategically located at the junction of the rivers Scorff, Ter and Blavet. A functional, rather depressing port today, it was once a key base for French colonialism, and was founded in the mid-seventeenth century (in what its charter called a "vague, vain and useless place") for trading operations by the Compagnie des Indes, an equivalent of the Dutch and English East India Companies. The port's name was originally *L'Orient* ("The East"), and came from a mighty trading vessel, the *Soleil d'Orient*, which was the first ship to be built in its nascent dockyards.

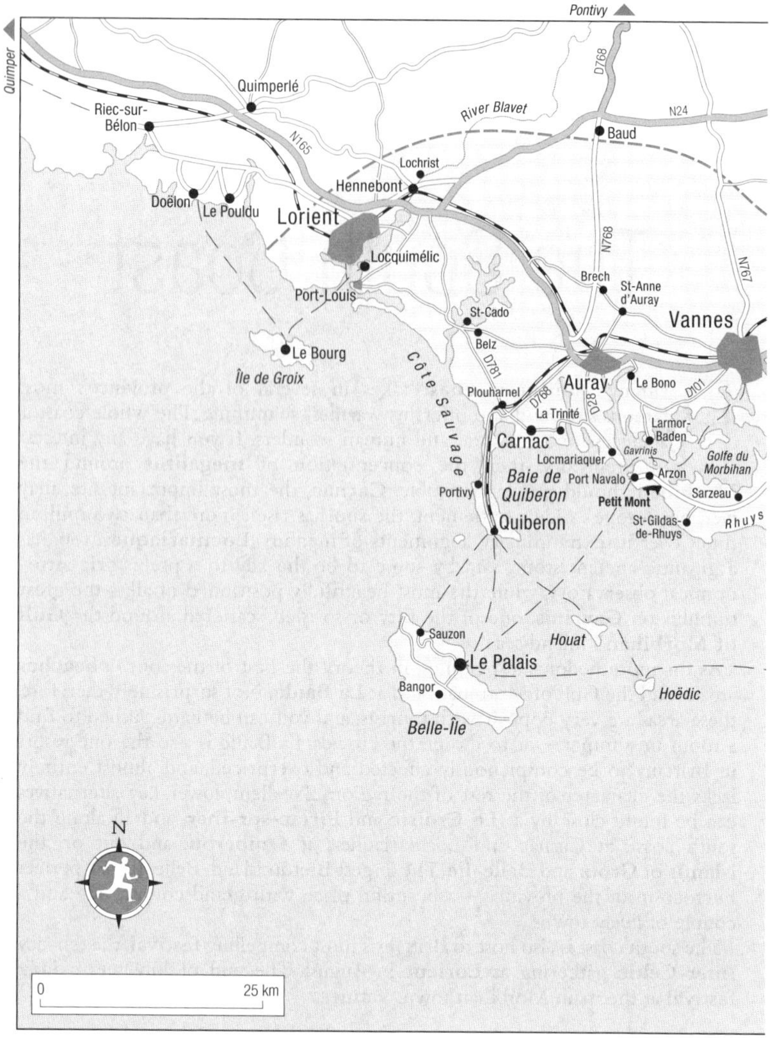

Arrival and information

Lorient's **tourist office**, beside the pleasure port on the quai de Rohan (early April to early July & late Aug to late Sept, Mon–Fri 10am–noon & 2–6pm, Sat 10am–noon & 2–5pm; early July to late Aug Mon–Sat 9.30am–1pm & 2–7pm, Sun 10am–1pm, except during the festival, when it's daily 9am–8pm; late Sept to early April Mon–Fri 10am–noon & 2–5pm, Sat 10am–1pm; ⓣ 02.97.84.78.00, ⓦ www.lorient-tourisme.fr), can provide full details on local boat trips, and organizes some excursions itself. **Ferries** to the Île de Groix see p.348. The **gare SNCF** is roughly 1km north of the centre.

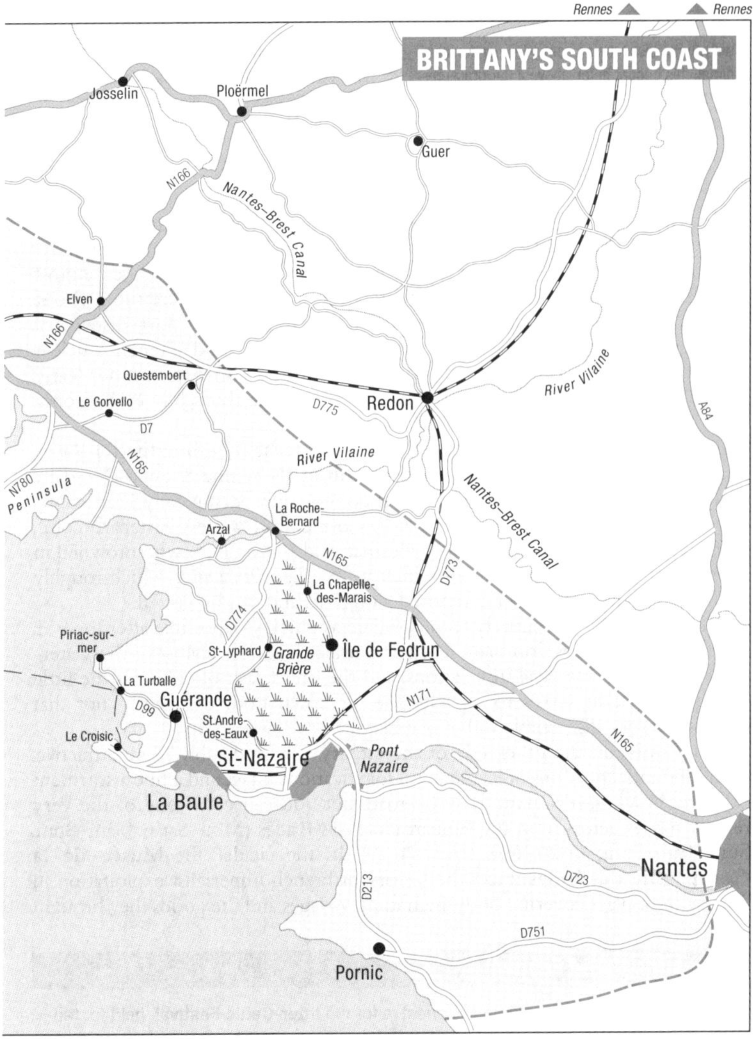

Accommodation

Lorient holds a surprisingly large number of **hotels**, though demand is of course high during the Inter-Celtic Festival. Reasonable central options include several along rue Lazare-Carnot as it curves away south of the tourist office.

Hostel 41 rue Victor-Schoelcher Ⓣ02.97.37.11.65, Ⓦfuaj.org/lorient. Inexpensive hostel beside the River Ter, 3km out on bus line C1 from the *gare SNCF*, which as well as €13.60 dorm beds, table tennis and a small bar, offers camping space in summer.

Maison des Gens de Mer 14 bd Louis-Nail Ⓣ02.97.37.11.28, Ⓦlesgensdemer.fr. Used primarily by fishing crews, this spruce modern hotel, south of the centre by the fishing port, may not have sea views, but it does hold an excellent fish restaurant. ③

Pecheurs 7 rue Jean Lagarde ⓣ02.97.21.19.24, ⓦwww.hotel-lespecheurs.com. While undeniably minimal, this budget hotel, above a bar/brasserie around the corner from rue Lazare-Carnot, is still perfectly presentable. ❶

Victor Hugo 36 rue Lazare-Carnot ⓣ02.97.21.16.24, ⓦwww.hotelvictorhugo-lorient.com. Good-value hotel, which as well as clean, sound-proofed, en-suite rooms has a pleasant restaurant. ❸

The Town

Little remains in the town itself to suggest the plundered wealth that used to arrive here. During the last war, Lorient was a major target for the Allies; the Germans held out until May 1945, by which time the city was almost completely destroyed. The only substantial traces to survive were the **U-boat pens**, a couple of kilometres south of the centre in the port district of **Kéroman**, which were subsequently expanded to hold French nuclear submarines. They're now open for fascinating **guided tours** in summer (early July to late Sept daily 1.30–6.30pm; English-language tours July & Aug only, Wed–Fri 1.30pm; €7.50; ⓣ02.97.84.78.06).

The adjoining **Cité de la Voile Éric Tabarly**, at the mouth of the Ter River, is a large, modern, interactive museum of **sailing** (Feb–June & Sept–Dec daily except Mon 10am–6pm, open Mon in school hols; July & Aug daily 10am–8pm; closed Jan; last admission 1hr 30min before closing; €11; ⓦcitevoile-tabarly.com). M Tabarly himself was a champion yachtsman and Breton hero who drowned in 1998. Several of his yachts – all of which were called *Pen Duick*, which roughly means "little black head" – are moored alongside, and can be visited.

As Lorient had to be entirely reconstructed as quickly as possible after the war, drab concrete facades dominate its central urban landscape. Most of the waterfront is taken up by naval installations, and the one splash of colour is the little pleasure port that serves to separate the old town from the new – not that there's any very discernible difference between the two.

Port-Louis, on the other side of the estuary, is considerably more attractive, with substantial portions of its medieval fortifications intact and a fine assortment of sandy beaches. It's 20km away by road, but you can catch one of the very regular ferries across from the Embarcadère des Rades (Mon–Sat 6.45am–8pm, Sun 10am–7pm; €1.20; ⓣ02.97.21.28.29). In the citadel, the **Musée de la Compagnie des Indes** traces the history of French imperialist exploitation in Asia, with displays covering both the trading voyages and the goods they brought

The Inter-Celtic Festival

The main reason visitors come to Lorient is for the **Inter-Celtic Festival**, held for ten days from the first Friday to the second Sunday in August. This is the biggest Celtic event in Brittany, or anywhere else for that matter, with representation from all the Celtic nations of Europe – Brittany, Ireland, Scotland, Wales, Cornwall, the Isle of Man, Asturias and Galicia. In a genuine celebration of cultural solidarity, well over half a million people come to more than a hundred different shows, five languages mingle, and Scotch and Guinness flow with French and Spanish wines and ciders. There is a certain competitive element, with championships in various categories, but the feeling of mutual enthusiasm and conviviality is paramount. The various activities – embracing music, dance and literature – take place all over the city, with mass celebrations around both the central place Jules-Ferry and the fishing harbour, and the biggest concerts at the local football stadium, the Parc du Moustoir.

For full schedules, which are not usually finalized until June, see ⓦfestival-interceltique.com. Tickets for the largest events should be reserved well in advance.

home (Feb–April & Sept to mid-Dec, daily except Tues 1.30–6pm; May–Aug daily 10am–6.30pm; closed mid-Dec to Jan; €5.50; Ⓦmusee.lorient.fr).

Eating and drinking

Le Pic, just south of the *gare SNCF* at 2 bd Maréchal-Franchet-d'Esperey (Ⓣ02.97.21.18.29; closed Sat lunch & Sun), is an imaginative little **restaurant**, with varied menus from €19. More central alternatives include the *Café Leffe* (Ⓣ02.97.21.21.30; closed Jan), in the same building as the tourist office, facing the port, which is particularly strong on seafood.

Celts are famed for their **pubs**, and there's a fine selection in Lorient: you can get good, hearty meat and fish dishes at *Tavarn ar Roue Morvan* on place Polig-Monjarret (Ⓣ02.97.21.61.57; closed Sun except during festival) as well as home-made cider and live traditional music; *Galway Inn* on 18 rue Belgique (Ⓣ02.97.64.50.77) is the Irish-Celtic alternative, with Guinness and rock instead.

The Île de Groix

The steep-sided, eight-kilometre-long rock of the **Île de Groix**, which shields Lorient 10km out to sea from the mouth of the Blavet estuary, is a sort of little sister to the better-known island of Belle-Île (see p.353). With its own crop of lovely beaches, and its own throngs of summer visitors – not to mention a similar abundance of exclusive holiday homes – it's in no way inferior to its larger neighbour, however, and taking a day-trip out from the Lorient area is well worth the effort.

Groix flourished during the seventeenth and eighteenth centuries in tandem with Lorient, and was even the target of invasions by both the English (in 1663) and the Dutch (in 1774). Subsequently, after the island's first proper port was constructed in 1792, it became a major centre for catching and canning tuna. That industry has long since gone into decline, however, and Groix now makes its living from summer tourism, with beach-lovers joined both by birdwatchers in search of migratory species, and by geologists, who come to study its peculiar rock formations.

Ferries dock at **PORT-TUDY**, where a former tuna cannery houses the **Eco-Musée**, chronicling the island's history since the Bronze Age (April–June & Sept–Nov daily except Mon 10am–12.30pm & 2–5pm; July & Aug daily except Mon 9.30am–12.30pm & 3–7pm; Dec–March Wed, Sat & Sun 10am–12.30pm & 2–5pm; €5; Ⓦecomusee.groix.free.fr). While the more general displays are interesting enough, the museum's real strong point is in its depiction of the patterns and traditions of individual lives. Countless personal and family sagas are covered in exhaustive detail upstairs, from birth and the acquisition of language (which meant Breton until World War I), through school, apprenticeship and marriage, all the way to death.

About 500m uphill from the port is the largest of the island's 27 villages, **LE BOURG** (also known as Loctudy, or even, simply, Groix). Although it's attractive enough, with a tuna-fish weathervane topping its little church, a more obvious way to spend a day on Groix is to tour its dramatic coastline. The easiest way to do this is to rent a **bicycle** from one of several outlets at the port, costing around €12 per day. Crossing the island north to south takes barely ten minutes by bike; east to west requires more like an hour, especially as it can be hard to spot which coastal paths will prove negotiable, and which merely peter out into the sand.

At their tallest, at the **Pointe du Grognon** in the northwest, the **cliffs** of Groix rise 50m out of the sea; that may not sound all that high, but only Belle-Île in Brittany surpasses it. Much of the western tip serves as a bird sanctuary; the southeastern corner, by contrast, close to the **Pointe des Chats** and its little lighthouse, is renowned for its unusual green-tinged mineral deposits.

The best **beaches** are also at the eastern end of the island. Locals claim that the **Plage des Grandes Sables**, jutting out into the sea, is the only convex beach in Europe. Palpable nonsense that may be, but it is a beautiful little unsheltered strip of sand that offers calm swimming (supervised by lifeguards in summer), with pleasure boats bobbing at anchor just off shore. The next group of beaches to the south are even better, a succession of little sandy coves tucked between the rocks known collectively as **Les Sables Rouges**.

Getting to Groix

It takes 45 minutes to reach the Île de Groix by **boat** from the south quay of Lorient's pleasure port, near the tourist office (Compagnie-Océane; 4–9 sailings daily all year; adults €29.65 return, under-25s €18.45, over-60s €22.70, small cars €137 return; ⓣ08.20.05.61.56, ⓦwww.compagnie-oceane.fr). In recent years the first daily departure from Lorient has ranged from 7.30am in July and August up to 9am in winter.

Additional services are offered in summer only by the Société Morbihannaise de Navigation (ⓣ08.20.05.60.00, ⓦwww.smn-navigation.fr). They operate from **Locmiquélic**, directly across the estuary from Lorient, north of Port St-Louis (mid-June to early Sept only; Thurs, Sat & Sun; departs Locmiquélic 8.30am, departs Groix 7.50pm), and tiny **Doëlan**, 20km west of Lorient and 5km west of le Pouldu (mid-June to mid-July & late Aug to mid-Sept daily except Mon departs Doëlan 10.30am, departs Groix 5.45pm; mid-July to late Aug, departs Doëlan Tues, Wed & Fri 8.30am, 10.30am & 5.45pm, Thurs, Sat & Sun 10.30am & 6.50pm; departs Groix Tues & Wed 4.45pm or 6.50pm, Thurs, Sat & Sun 5.45pm). Adults pay €26 return, under-15s pay €18.

Information and accommodation

Groix's **tourist office** is the first building you come to on the quayside at **Port-Tudy** (April–June & Sept Mon–Fri 9.30am–12.30pm & 2–5.30pm, Sat 9.30am–12.30pm, Sun 9.30–11.30am; July & Aug Mon–Sat 9am–1pm & 2.30–6.30pm, Sun 9.30–11.30am; Oct to early Nov Tues–Fri 9am–noon; ⓣ02.97.86.53.08, ⓦwww.lorient-tourisme.fr). Three **hotels** stand nearby: the pink pastel *de l'Escale* (ⓣ02.82.8097.29, ⓦhoteldelescale.com; ❸; closed mid-Dec to mid-Jan), which has rather characterless but perfectly adequate guest rooms inside and café seating outside; the fancier *Ty Mad* (ⓣ02.97.86.80.19, ⓦtymad.com; ❸; closed Dec–Feb), set back behind an attractive lawn, which serves good seafood meals in the open air, and has a pool; and the *de la Jetée* (ⓣ02.97.86.80.82, ⓦhoteldelajetee.fr; ❸; closed Jan to mid-March), at the far right end of the port, which holds somewhat faded rooms with great sea views. The **restaurant** here, *Le Pub de la Jetée* (ⓣ02.97.86.59.42; closed Nov to mid-March), is the best for seafood-lovers, with its simple menu dominated by oysters of various sizes; half a dozen can be had for around €8.

Up the hill in **Le Bourg**, the **hotel-restaurant** *de la Marine*, 7 rue Générale-de-Gaulle (ⓣ02.97.86.80.05, ⓦhoteldelamarine.com; ❷; closed Jan to mid-Feb, plus Sun eve & Mon in low season), is a large, well-furnished house that offers comfortable rooms, most but not all en-suite, and serves delicious fish dinners in its front garden, including burbot brochettes and fish couscous on menus starting at €17.

A few hundred metres east of town, close to the sea en route towards the small beach at the Pointe de la Croix, the **Fort du Méné** holds a simple but beautifully sited summer-only **hostel** (ⓣ02.97.86.81.38, ⓦfuaj.org/Ile-de-Groix;

€10.70; closed Oct–March), with a **campsite** alongside (☎02.97.86.81.13; closed Oct–April). The nicest campsite on the island, however, is further on – the lovely three-star *Les Sables Rouges* (☎02.97.86.81.32, Ⓦcampingdessablesrouges.com; closed mid-Sept to April), above the beaches at the southeast corner.

Hennebont

The old walled town of **HENNEBONT** stands a few kilometres upstream from Lorient, at the point where the River Blavet first starts to widen into the estuary. The fortifications, and especially the main gate, the Porte Broerec'h, are imposing, and from the top of the ramparts there are wide views of the river below. What you see of the old city within, however, is entirely residential – an assortment of washing-lines, budgies and garden sheds. All the public buildings were destroyed by wartime bombing, and now not even a bar (or rented room) is to be found in the former centre.

The one time Hennebont comes alive is at the **Thursday market**, held below the ramparts and through the squares by the church. It's one of the largest in the region, with a heady mix of good fresh food, crêpes and delicacies from around the world, alongside livestock, flowers, carpets and clothes. On other days, the only places where you'll find any activity are along the **place Maréchal-Foch** (in front of the basilica) and the **quai du Pont-Neuf** beside the river.

Immediately north of the centre, on rue Victor-Hugo on the east bank of the Blavet, the **Haras National** or National Stud, is home to fifty superb stallions, as well as a museum on the history of the horse (April Mon–Fri 9.30am–12.30pm & 2–6pm, Sat & Sun 2–6pm; May–June & Sept Mon, Sat & Sun 2–6pm, Tues–Fri 9.30am–12.30pm & 2–6pm; July & Aug daily 10am–7pm; €7.10; Ⓦharas-hennebont.fr).

Practicalities

Hennebont's **tourist office** is in the town centre, at 9 place Maréchal-Foch (mid-June to mid-Sept Mon–Sat 9am–7pm, Sun 10am–12.30pm; mid-Sept to mid-June Mon–Sat 9am–12.30pm & 1.30–6pm; ☎02.97.36.24.52, Ⓦwww.hennebont.fr). The **gare SNCF** is 1km west, on the other side of the Blavet. If you decide to **stay** – and few people do – the best bet is the very good-value, renovated *Hôtel-Restaurant du Centre*, 44 rue du Maréchal-Joffre (☎02.97.36.21.44; ❶; closed Sun eve & Mon), which is as central as its name implies. The seafood-dominated menus in its restaurant are uniformly superb, starting at €15 and with a €26 *Menu du Terroir* featuring hot oysters. The local two-star **campsite**, *Camping Municipal de St-Caradec* (☎02.97.36.21.73; closed mid-Sept to mid-June), has a prime site on the riverbank opposite the fortifications.

Lochrist

At **LOCHRIST**, just north of Hennebont, the great chimneys of the town's **ironworks** stand, smokeless and silent, looking down on the Blavet. Strikes and demonstrations failed to prevent the foundry's closure in 1966, and the only work since then has been to convert it into the **Eco-Musée Industriel des Forges** (March–May & Sept–Dec Mon–Fri 10am–noon & 2–6pm, Sun 2–6pm; June Mon–Fri 10am–noon & 2–6pm, Sat & Sun 2–6pm; July & Aug Mon–Fri 10am–6.30pm, Sat & Sun 2–6.30pm; €5), which documents its hundred-year history from the workers' point of view. Some of the men made redundant contributed their memories and tools; for others turning their workplace into a museum was adding insult to injury. It is in fact excellent, both in content and presentation – though in view of the joyful pictures of successful strikes in the 1930s, its very existence seems a sad defeat.

St-Cado

Fifteen kilometres southeast of Hennebont, or 12km east of Port-Louis, a large bridge spans the broad estuary of the **Etel** River. A short detour north of the village of **BELZ** on the eastern shore brings you to the delightful islet of **ST-CADO**, a round speck on the water dotted with perhaps twenty white-painted houses.

From the mainland, you walk across a spindly little bridge to reach the island itself. Its main feature is a **twelfth-century chapel** on the site of a Romanesque predecessor built by St Cado around the sixth century. Cado, a prince of "Glamorgant", returned in due course to his native Wales and was martyred, but Welsh pilgrims still make their way to this pretty little spot. As Cado is a patron saint of the deaf, it's said that hearing problems can be cured by lying on his stone "bed" inside the chapel. A little fountain behind the chapel only emerges from the sea at low tide.

There's nowhere to stay on St-Cado, nor are there any restaurants; just a couple of **bars** facing it from the quayside on the mainland, such as *Les Asturies*, 10 rue de la Jetée, which serve *moules frites* and similar snacks. Between May and September it's possible to rent **boats** by the hour, day or week from St-Cado Plaisance (Ⓣ02.97.55.46.57, Ⓦsaintcado-plaisance.com).

The Quiberon peninsula

The **Presqu'île de Quiberon** is as close to being an island as any peninsula could conceivably be; the long causeway of sand that links it to the mainland narrows to as little as 50m in places. In the past this was always a strategic military location. The English held the peninsula for eight bloody days in 1746; Chouans (see p.394) and royalists landed here in 1795 in the hope of destroying the Revolution, only to be sealed in and slaughtered; and the defoliation that

▲ St-Cado

threatens the dunes today is in part the result of German fortifications constructed during the last war. The peninsula is now packed with tourists during the summer. They come not so much to visit the towns, which, other than **Quiberon** itself, are generally featureless, but to use them as a base for trips out to **Belle-Île** or around the contrasting coastline.

The coast here has two quite distinct characters. The **Côte Sauvage**, facing the Atlantic to the west, is a bleak rocky heathland, lashed by heavy seas. Though it's renowned as a destination for expert **surfers**, it's also notorious as the scene of innumerable drownings. The sheltered eastern side, however – the **Baie de Quiberon** – contains safe sandy beaches, as well as one of the many Thalasso-therapy Institutes that line the Breton coast.

Portivy

Just after the D768 curves around the bay outside **PLOUHARNEL**, and starts to descend the peninsula, it crosses the tracks of the Tire-Bouchon train line down to Quiberon. Beyond that, the isthmus of Penthièvre stretches for roughly 3km, with windsurfers launching into the Baie de Quiberon from the embankment on its eastern side, and kite-fliers perched on the west where the sea's too rough to enter.

In the village of **PORTIVY**, tucked into the only real shelter along the Côte Sauvage just beyond the slender neck of the *presqu'île*, you can arrange **surfing** lessons with the École de Surf de Bretagne, 6 av de l'Océan (Ⓣ02.97.52.41.18, Ⓦboard-kulture.com), or **sea-kayaking lessons** with Sillages École de Kayak, 18 rue de Rouzenn (Ⓣ06.81.26.75,08, Ⓦwww.kayak-sillages.com).

A charming **hotel**, *La Taverne*, faces the port at 11 place St-Ivy (Ⓣ02.97.30.91.61; ❸; closed Nov–Jan), with good sea views from most rooms, while there's also a **campsite** just outside Portivy, the two-star *Port Blanc* on the route du Port Blanc (Ⓣ02.97.30.91.30; closed mid-Sept to mid-June). Other two-star sites nearby include the *Camping Municipal de Penthièvre* (Ⓣ02.97.52.33.86; closed Oct to mid-April), and the *Camping Municipal de Kerhostin* (Ⓣ02.97.30.95.25; closed Sept–April).

Quiberon

Much of the peninsula has become built up over the years, but it still holds only one true town, **QUIBERON**, at its southern tip. Its most active area, **Port-Maria**, is home to the **gare maritime** for the islands of Belle-Île, Houat and Hoëdic, as well as a fishing harbour, with a lovely sheltered **beach** nearby.

Arrival and information

If you're **driving** in, expect traffic delays all along the single narrow road down the peninsula; there's very little parking for ferry passengers down by the port, so you may well have to park at the huge Sémaphore car park at the north end of town, and catch a free shuttle bus for the remaining 1.5km to the waterfront. In July and August, the special Tire Bouchon train links Quiberon's **gare SNCF**, which is a short way above the town proper, with Auray. (The name, which means "corkscrew", refers to the bottleneck at the mouth of the peninsula rather than any circuitousness in the route.) Bus #1 (TIM; Ⓣ02.97.24.26.20) runs right to the *gare maritime* from Vannes, via Auray and Carnac.

The **tourist office**, at 14 rue de Verdun (July & Aug daily 9am–1pm & 2–7pm; Sept–June Mon–Sat 9am–12.30pm & 2–5.30pm; Ⓣ02.25.13.56.00, Ⓦquiberon.com), has a 24-hour computer terminal outside showing which hotels are full, hour by hour. **Bicycles** can be rented from Cycl'omar, 47 place Hoche (ⓣ02.97.50.26.00, ⓦcyclomar.com).

Accommodation

For most of the year, it's hard to get a **room** in Quiberon. In July and August, the whole peninsula is packed, while in winter it's so quiet that virtually all its facilities close down. The nicest area to stay is along the seafront in **Port-Maria**, where several good hotel-restaurants face the Belle-Île ferry terminal.

Hotels

Bellevue rue de Tiviec ⓣ02.97.50.16.28, ⓦbellevuequiberon.com. Relatively quiet Logis de France, set slightly back from the sea near the casino 500m east of the port, with its own pool and a restaurant where you can either opt for *demi-pension* or pay à la carte. Closed Oct–March. ④

Au Bon Accueil 6 quai de Houat ⓣ02.97.50.07.92. Seafront hotel that's Port-Maria's best option for budget travellers. The rooms are basic but inexpensive, and there's a particularly good restaurant downstairs (see opposite). Closed mid-Nov to mid-Feb. ②

De la Mer 8 quai de Houat ⓣ02.97.50.09.05, ⓦhotel-de-la-mer.fr. Blue-trimmed hotel with a lift at the western end of Port-Maria's seafront strip, offering an adequate standard of comfort and sea views from some rooms, but rather poor en-suite bathrooms. The heated swimming pool is open only during summer, and the *Turbotin* restaurant is recommended. Closed mid-Nov to mid-Feb & Thurs. ④

Neptune 4 quai de Houat ⓣ02.97.50.09.62. The best value around. All rooms have either sea or garden views – some with private balconies – and there's a very good restaurant (see opposite) with terrace overlooking the water. Closed Jan to mid-Feb, plus Mon in low season. ④

L'Océan 7 quai de l'Océan ⓣ02.97.50.07.58, ⓦhotel-de-locean.com. Attractive little hotel in the port, with multicoloured pastel shutters, reasonable rooms – not quite all are en suite, and some are a little drab – and views over the port. The friendly owners rent out bikes and offer private parking. Closed Oct–March. ③

Hostel and campsites

Camping du Conguel bd de la Teignouse ⓣ02.97.50.19.11, ⓦcampingduconguel.com. Beachfront four-star site east of Quiberon, where the large pool has elaborate water slides. Closed Nov–March.

Camping Do-Mi-Si-La-Mi 31 rue de la Vierge, St-Julien Plage ⓣ02.97.50.22.52, ⓦdomisilami.com. Verdant three-star site, 100m from the beach along the sheltered east coast near Quiberon town. Closed Nov–March.

Camping Municipal Kerné ⓣ02.97.50.05.07. The only campsite on the Côte Sauvage, just outside a small village 2km northwest of central Quiberon. Closed Sept–June.

Filets Bleus 45 rue du Roc'h-Priol ⓣ02.97.50.15.54, ⓦfuaj.org/quiberon. Well-situated but fairly basic hostel, in which some rooms don't have a window. Better to camp under the pine trees in the back. €10.70, camping €5.70 or €7.50 if you use the tents they provide. Closed Oct–March.

The Town

Quiberon town centres on a busy little park with a miniature golf course, but few of the streets further back hold anything of great interest. The exception is the little hill that leads down to the port from the **gare SNCF**, where you can browse in some surprisingly good clothes and antique shops.

From the ferry terminal and the fishing harbour – once famous for its sardines – a long curve of fine sandy **beach** stretches away east, lined for several hundred metres with bars, cafés and restaurants. The slopes that climb back from the sea are largely residential, with modern holiday apartments scattered amid fine villas.

Port-Haliguen, the other port, is on the eastern coast. Today, it's an active marina, with a little commercial fishing. Boats from the islands occasionally shelter here, and use it for embarkation in rough weather. Captain Alfred Dreyfus disembarked here on his return from Devil's Island in 1899.

Eating and drinking

The most appealing area in which to browse the menus in search of a good **meal** is along the waterfront in **Port-Maria**, where a row of seafood restaurants compete to attract ferry passengers. Hotel owners are very insistent on persuading guests to pay for half-board, but there are plenty of alternatives to choose from if you manage to escape their clutches.

To stock up on provisions, try the morning **markets** at Kerhostin at the neck of the peninsula 5km north of Quiberon on Wednesday, at St-Pierre-Quiberon just south of Kerhostin on Thursday, and in Quiberon itself on Saturday.

Au Bon Accueil 6 quai de Houat ⓣ02.97.50.07.92. Friendly dining room with something of the atmosphere and decor of a village bar, serving good fish soup and seafood specialities such as *cassolette de la mer* on menus that start at €19. Closed Wed in low season.

Chaumine 36 pl de Manémeur ⓣ02.97.50.17.67. Manémeur is technically a separate village to Quiberon, though it's not too far to walk around the headland west of the port. Set close to the menhir in the main square, this lovely little fish restaurant serves menus from €18, with a €27 option featuring salmon braised in champagne. Closed Mon, plus Sun eve in low season; closed altogether early Nov to March.

De la Criée 11 quai de l'Océan ⓣ02.97.30.53.09. Truly superb local fish restaurant, serving changing fish specialities every day, fresh from the morning's catch; make your choice from the baskets arrayed along the front. For €21, you can get either the one set menu, which may include ling and sea bass, for example, and fish smoked on the premises, or a great seafood couscous. Closed both Sun eve & Mon in low season, plus Jan.

Neptune 4 quai de Houat ⓣ02.97.50.09.62. Hotel dining room that serves exceptionally good seafood menus at €18 and €21. The portions are small, but the food is exquisite. Closed Jan & Mon in low season.

Belle-Île

The island of **Belle-Île**, 15km offshore, due south of Quiberon, is a gorgeous place. Considerably larger than the other Breton islands, it has less of an island feel, with its bus tours and traffic, but its towns – **Le Palais**, **Sauzon** and **Bangor** – are consistently lovely, and it offers wonderful opportunities for walking and cycling.

The physical geography of Belle-Île mirrors that of Brittany as a whole. On the landward side it is rich and fertile, interrupted by deep estuaries with tiny ports; facing the ocean, along its own Côte Sauvage, sparse heather-covered cliffs trail rocky crags out into the sea.

With the island measuring 17km east to west and up to 10km north to south, some kind of transport is essential, even if you just come for a day-trip: rental bikes and cars are readily available at the island port of **Le Palais**, while for a hefty price you can also take a small car over on the ferries.

Belle-Île once belonged to the monks of Redon, and later to the ambitious Nicholas Fouquet, Louis XIV's minister, whose hubris in buying it in 1658 contributed to his downfall at the hands of the Three Musketeers three years later. It was subsequently captured by the English in 1752, who swapped it for Menorca in 1761 in an unrepeatable bargain deal. Along the way Belle-Île has seen a fair number of distinguished exiles. The citadel prison at Le Palais closed only in 1961, having numbered among its inmates an astonishing succession of state enemies and revolutionary heroes – including the son of Toussaint L'Ouverture of Haiti, Ben Bella of Algeria, and even, for a brief period after 1848, Karl Marx. Less involuntarily, such celebrated figures as the painters Monet and Matisse, the writers Flaubert and Proust, and the actress Sarah Bernhardt all spent time on the island.

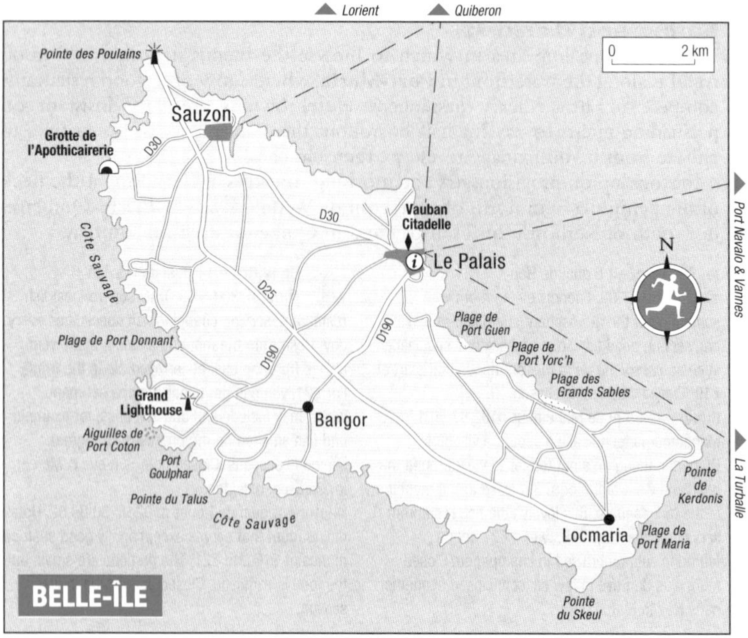

Le Palais

As you dock at the pleasant little harbour town of **LE PALAIS**, the abrupt star-shaped fortifications of the **Citadelle** are the first thing you see, towering above the port. Once you've explored the few little streets of the town proper, it's well worth crossing the small lock and climbing up to have a closer look. Now the very picture of tranquility, the fortress is surrounded by lawns, flowers and ornate topiary. Constructed along stylish and ordered lines by the great builder Vauban early in the eighteenth century, it is startling in size – filled with doorways leading to mysterious cellars and underground passages, endless sequences of rooms and dungeons and deserted cells. Though largely empty, the structure is quite sound, and fitted with sturdy new floors.

An informative **museum** (daily: April–June, Sept & Oct 9.30am–6pm; July & Aug 9am–7pm; Nov–March 9.30am–noon & 2–5pm; €6.10; ⓦcitadellevauban.com) documents the island's history, including its involvement in Dumas' tales of *The Three Musketeers* (which feature an account of the death of Porthos on the island). Displays cover Vauban himself, and also the 78 Acadian families who settled here in 1765 after the defeat of French Canada – part of the mass migration that was also responsible for populating Louisiana, in what's now the southern US, with "Cajuns". There's disappointingly little explanation of perhaps the prison's most enigmatic inmates, however: the Le Voisin family of poisoners, incarcerated here in perpetual silence in 1682.

Arrival and information

The **tourist office** for the whole island is right beside the ferry dock in Le Palais (July & Aug Mon–Sat 8.45am–7pm, Sun 8.45am–1pm; Sept–June Mon–Sat 9am–12.30pm & 2–6pm; ⓣ02.97.31.81.93, ⓦwww.belle-ile.com). Several waterfront outlets rent **bicycles** at around €12 per day, including Didier Banet (ⓣ02.97.31.84.74, ⓦwww.location2roues.com) and A Loca Scoot (ⓣ02.97.31.49.94, ⓦvelo-scooter-belle-ile.fr), which rents scooters and **mopeds** as well. **Cars**, costing from around €62 per day, can be rented at the port from Locatourisle (ⓣ02.97.31.83.56, ⓦlocatourisle.com) or Belle-Île Tourisme (ⓣ02.97.31.28.69, ⓦbelle-isle-tourisme.com). Belle-Île also has its own **bus** system, operated by Taol Mor (ⓣ02.97.31.32.32, ⓦtaol-mor.com), centred in Le Palais and offering around eight daily connections in summer to each of Sauzon, Bangor and Locmaria.

Accommodation and Eating

Hotels in Le Palais include a row of appealing options side by side along the quai de l'Acadie, while there are also several campsites and a hostel nearby

Hotels and B&Bs

Atlantique quai de l'Acadie ⓣ02.97.31.80.11, ⓦhotel-atlantique.com. Well priced waterfront hotel, charging extra for those rooms that have sea views, and home to the top-notch *Atlantique* restaurant, with a great-value €17 menu that offers duck terrine or salmon in a beetroot coulis followed by steamed or grilled fish or grilled meat. ❸

Château Bordénéo Bordénéo ⓣ02.97.31.53.00 ⓦchateau-bordeneo.fr. Delightful luxury B&B, just northwest of town, with a lovely garden and indoor pool. ❽

Getting to Belle-Île

All the schedules and fares given below are liable to change; check with operators before you set off.

Throughout the year, **Compagnie-Océane** (ⓣ02.20.05.61.56, or, from outside France, 02.97.35.02.00, ⓦwww.compagnie-oceane.fr) sends at least seven **ferries** daily – and up to fifteen in high summer – from **Port-Maria**, at the southernmost tip of the Quiberon peninsula, to **Le Palais** on Belle-Île. The first departure each day is almost always at 7.45am, and the crossing normally takes 45 minutes, though the high-speed vessel *Locmaria 56* makes up to five crossings daily between mid-April and August in just twenty minutes. The adult return fare is €28.15; under-25s pay €17, and over-60s €22.55. Small cars can be taken on the slower crossings only, for €134.30 return, while bikes cost €16.70 return. Despite the high number of sailings, it's advisable to reserve in advance on the website if you plan to travel during a peak period such as Easter or high summer.

Between early July and the end of August, the same company also sends the *Locmaria 56* on one daily trip to **Sauzon** from **Port-Maria**, for the same fare, though in recent years it has departed at around 8pm and thus only been useful for visitors spending at least one night on the island.

From early April until September, **Compagnie des Îles** (ⓣ02.25.13.41.40, ⓦcompagniedesiles.com) also connects Port-Maria with both **Le Palais** and **Sauzon**, operating two services daily except Monday for most of the season, and three daily between mid-July and late August (adults €26 return, under-15s €18). The same company also sails direct to **Le Palais** from **La Turballe** (ⓣ02.25.13.41.80), between Piriac and Guérande on the coast not far north of La Baule. The crossing takes 1 hour 45 minutes (sporadic sailings May to mid-July & late Aug to end Sept; early July to late Aug daily; departs 8.15am; adults €37 return, under-15s €24.50). Between early July and late Aug, they also run day-trips from **Le Croisic** (ⓣ02.25.13.41.70; same fares), departing at 8am.

Navix (ⓣ02.25.13.21.00, ⓦnavix.fr) also operate day-trips to the island. These run twice weekly in April, stepping up to daily from May until late September, from **Vannes** (8am) and **Port-Navalo** (9.10am), and twice daily between mid-July and late August from La Trinité (8am & 10.30am). Adults pay €32 return, under-15s €22.

Frégate quai de l'Acadie ⓣ02.97.31.54.16. Simple quayside hotel, facing the ferry above a nice little outdoor bar/restaurant. Closed mid-Nov to March. ❸

Grand Hôtel de Bretagne quai de l'Acadie ⓣ02.97.31.80.14, ⓦhotel-de-bretagne.fr. Fancy option by the ferry dock, where sea-view rooms cost extra, and there's an excellent sea-view restaurant. ❹

Vauban 1 rue des Remparts ⓣ02.97.31.45.42, ⓦhotelvauban.com. Friendly Logis de France hotel, a little way back from the port, but still enjoying sea views. Closed early Nov to early March. ❹

Hostel and campsite

Camping de l'Océan ⓣ02.97.31.83.86, ⓦcamping-ocean-belle-ile.com. Despite the name, this pleasant, three-star, year-round campsite is 500m directly inland from the port; it offers rental chalets as well as tent camping.

Hostel Haute-Boulogne ⓣ02.97.31.81.33, ⓦfuaj.org/belle-ile-en-mer. Despite holding almost a hundred dorm beds – at €12.50 per night – Belle-Île's hostel is always wildly oversubscribed. It's located a short way out of town along the clifftops from the citadelle. Closed Oct.

Sauzon

SAUZON, Belle-Île's second town, is also on the island's sheltered north coast. A beautiful little village, it's arrayed along one side of the mouth of a slender estuary, 6km west of Le Palais (and a 20min ride on bus #1). There's next to nothing to see here, but if you're staying any length of time, and you've got your own transport, it's a lovely spot in which to base yourself.

In a magnificent setting, next to its eponymous little lighthouse on the headland at the very tip of the estuary, the *Phare* is a good, inexpensive fourteen-room **hotel** (ⓣ02.97.31.60.36, ⓦhotelduphare.blogspot.com; ❸; closed Nov–March), which serves delicious fish dinners with menus at €17.20 and €29.10. There's also a very fancy, comfortable **B&B** slightly uphill nearby, a large pink house known as *La Touline* (ⓣ02.97.31.69.69, ⓦhostellerielatouline.com; ❻; closed Oct to late March). In addition, Sauzon can offer two two-star **campsites**, *Pen Prad* (ⓣ02.97.31.64.82, ⓦwww.sauzon.fr; closed Oct–March) and *La Source* (ⓣ02.97.31.60.95, ⓦwww.belleile-lasource.com; closed early Oct to mid-March).

As for **eating**, *Le Petit Baigneur*, rampe des Glycines (ⓣ02.97.31.67.74; closed Mon in low season), is a pretty little restaurant set slightly back from the port near the far end, serving à la carte mussels for €15 and meat or fish dishes for a little more, or you can simply buy tasty take-away sandwiches or ice cream at the friendly quayside *Professional de Glacier*, to enjoy on the harbour-front benches.

Around the island

Although exploring Belle-Île is an absolute joy, it's too large to see the whole island in a single day. A magnificent **coastal footpath** winds around the entire shoreline, but day-trippers are unlikely to get any further from Le Palais on foot than either Sauzon to the northwest, or the succession of sandy **beaches** like the plage de Port Guen to the southeast.

With a car or bicycle, the best plan is to head to the island's southern side, then hike along at least part of the Côte Sauvage. Note that you can't cycle on the coastal footpath, while many of the officially recommended cycle routes are on dirt roads that can be heavy going. Also, don't put too much faith in island maps that show lots of little villages; most simply don't exist, and only Sauzon, Bangor, and Locmaria at the eastern end hold facilities of any kind.

For an overview of the island, the obvious first stop is the **Grand Lighthouse**, set amid the fields, 2km west of Bangor. Dating from 1835, and hollow like a chimney, it commands a sweeping panorama of the craggy western coastline just beyond – assuming you have the energy to climb its 247 steps, the last fifty or so of which are up ladders (daily except Sat 11am–1pm & 3–5pm; €2).

The only place where a road runs along the Côte Sauvage, and even here just for a few hundred metres, is immediately west of the lighthouse. It ends at the car park for the **Aiguilles de Port-Coton** formation just offshore, where a savage sea foams amid the pinnacles of rock. It's a lovely spot, where you can escape the crowds, and watch the turmoil from different angles, by walking out along any of several spindle-thin cliff-top promontories. An easy twenty-minute stroll leads to the pretty beach of **Port-Donnant** 1km north, which despite appearances is unsafe for swimming.

A couple of **hotels** stand just short of the Aiguilles. The luxurious *Castel Clara*, a spa resort above Port Goulphar, was a favourite retreat for former President Mitterrand, who came for a farewell visit shortly before his death in 1996 (Ⓣ02.97.31.84.21, Ⓦcastel-clara.com; ➒; closed mid-Jan to mid-Feb). Perched nearer the ocean, the more affordable orange-pink *Grand Large* (Ⓣ02.97.31.80.92, Ⓦhotelgrandlarge.com; ➎; closed Nov to late March), charges premium rates for its finest sea views.

The next point where there's access to the coast by road is 5km north of the Aiguilles. A precarious oceanfront cave here is known as the **Grotte de l'Apothicairerie** because it used to be filled with the nests of cormorants, arranged like the jars on a pharmacist's shelves. Once again it's a ravishing spectacle. Vestiges of ancient stairways to the cave are clearly visible, but none leads all the way down, and signs warn of "mortal danger" should you attempt the descent. In summer, guided **birdwatching tours** start from the car park (mid-July to mid-Aug daily 10am & 4pm; €5; Ⓣ06.78.72.28.99). Here again there's a hotel, the faceless, modern and eerily quiet *L'Apothicairerie* (Ⓣ02.97.31.62.62, Ⓦhotelapothicairerie.com; ➎; closed Oct–March, except New Year), where sea-view rooms once again cost considerably more.

The **D30 inland** from the cave leads along a miniature tree-lined valley sheltered from the Atlantic winds. If you take the **D25** back towards Le Palais you pass the two **menhirs**, Jean and Jeanne, said to be lovers petrified as punishment for wanting to meet before their marriage. Another (larger) menhir used to lie near these two – it was broken up to help construct the road that separates them.

The **Pointe des Poulains**, at the northwestern tip of the island where the Côte Sauvage comes to an end, is an exposed little headland that holds a picturesque little lighthouse-cum-cottage and is all but separated from the rest of the island at high tide. The road comes to an end just short of the slender sandy spit that leads to the point, alongside the country estate where actress and celebrity **Sarah Bernhardt** used to spend her summers.

Houat and Hoëdic

Houat and **Hoëdic**, two smaller and much quieter islands to the east of Belle-Île, can also be reached by ferries from Quiberon and elsewhere. Though most visitors come to the islands on day-trips, to seek out their magnificent – and usually all but empty – golden **beaches**, both offer facilities for extended stays.

The Île de Houat

The island of **Houat**, which means "duck" in Breton, measures 5km from east to west, and much less than half that north to south. It's an idyllic spot, populated largely by rabbits and lizards, with hardly a tree to its name. Most of what marginally higher ground it has to offer consists of open heathland, with its thin covering of turf petering out at the head of pink granite cliffs which look down on long sandy beaches and lovely little coves.

Boats draw in at **Port St-Gildas**, a not especially picturesque little harbour just below the island's one "town", the flowery village of **HOUAT**. A private house to the right of the road up into the village rents out poor-quality **bicycles** at around €14 per day (ⓣ02.97.30.66.64), but the island is small enough for walking to be a pleasure, and it's not in any case legal to cycle along the coastal footpaths. The finest **beaches** lie to the east and south, in the shape of the sheltered **Tréac'h er Gourèd** that runs the full length of the eastern shoreline, and the **Tréac'h Salus** nearby.

During the 1980s, the islanders tried to boost their economy by raising lobsters in tanks in a large shed-like building known as the *écloserie*, 1km southwest of Houat. That experiment never proved profitable, so the structure now serves instead as the **Eclosarium** (July & Aug daily 10am–6pm, Easter–June & Sept daily 10am–noon & 2–5pm; €4), a museum dedicated almost exclusively to the microscopic marine world of **phytoplankton**, the organisms responsible for producing eighty percent of earth's oxygen. It's more interesting than it might sound, with a healthy dose of local history thrown in. Fetid-looking vials demonstrate how algae is cultivated locally, for use in products such as shower gel, sun cream, moisturizer and even pasta – if you're tempted, the gift shop sells them at discounted prices.

Practicalities

Two small **hotels** offer Houat's most comfortable accommodation. At the edge of town, overlooking the harbour, the *Hôtel-Restaurant des Îles* (ⓣ02.97.30.68.02, ⓦhouat.chez.com; ❸; closed Nov–Jan) offers tasteful sea-view rooms and serves good food both indoors and out on its terrace; it's a great spot for lunch, with the main set menu costing €17.50. Alternatively, *L'Ezenn*, on the main

Getting to Houat and Hoëdic

From **Quiberon-Port-Maria**, Compagnie-Océane (ⓣ08.20.05.61.56, or, from outside France, 02.97.35.02.00; ⓦwww.compagnie-oceane.fr) run between one and six ferries to **Houat** and **Hoëdic** daily all year, to widely varying schedules (40min to Houat, another 25min to Hoëdic; adults €29.65 return, under-25s €18.45, over-60s €22.70). There's usually a 9am sailing from Quiberon in summer, but in low season the day's only service can be in the afternoon, making a day-trip impossible.

Compagnie des Îles (ⓦcompagniedesiles.com) run day-trips to both islands (adults €26 return, under-15s €18 return) from **Vannes** (ⓣ08.25.13.41.00), **Locmariaquer** (ⓣ08.25.13.41.30) and **Port Navalo** (ⓣ08.25.13.41.20). Between mid-July and the end of August, boats leave Vannes at 8.15am & 9.30am; Locmariaquer at 10.45am; and Port Navalo at 9.15am & 11am. Otherwise, sailings increase from a level of one per week in April until they become daily in mid-July, and then decrease once more in September; the departure times are always 10am from Vannes, 10.45am from Locmariaquer and 11am from Port Navalo.

The same company also sails from **La Turballe** (ⓣ08.25.13.41.80), to both Hoëdic (1hr 15min; adults €29 return, under-15s €19 return) and Houat (1hr 45min; adults €33 return, under-15s €22 return). The annual schedule follows much the same pattern (sporadic sailings May to mid-July & late Aug to end Sept; early July to late Aug daily; departs 8.15am). Between early July and late August, they also run day-trips from **Le Croisic** (ⓣ08.25.13.41.70; same fares), departing at 8am.

Finally, Navix (ⓣ08.25.13.21.00, ⓦnavix.fr) run day-trips to Houat only on Wednesdays between mid-July and mid-August, leaving **La Trinité** at 8.45am (adults €28 return, under-15s €18).

road above the Tréac'h er Gouréd beach (Ⓣ02.97.30.69.73; ❸; closed Feb), has excellent modernized rooms but no restaurant. **Camping** among the dunes is illegal, to protect the fragile environment, but there's a municipal campsite, again just back from the Tréac'h er Gouréd beach (Ⓣ02.97.30.68.04; closed Oct–May).

The Île de Hoëdic

At a mere 2.5km end to end, Hoëdic – in Breton, the "duckling" to Houat's "duck" – is that much tinier still. It's such a sleepy place, the story goes, that during the eighteenth century the rector of Hoëdic lost not only his sense of time but also his calendar, and ended up reducing Lent from forty days down to a more manageable three.

The island's sole settlement – **HOËDIC**, naturally – stands right in the centre, a short walk up from the ferry landing at **Port-Argol**. Other than the appealing nineteenth-century church of St-Goustan, the only activity is to walk off in search of **beaches**. The best are to the south and east; take care how far you stroll out at low tide, as some patches become isolated offshore sandbanks when the sea comes in.

Hoëdic boasts just one **hotel**, *Les Cardinaux* (Ⓣ02.97.52.37.27, Ⓔdominic .trarieux2005@orange.fr; ❻; closed Sun eve & Mon in winter, plus all Feb and first half of Oct), which offers extensive sea views and insists on half-board. There's also a large, well-equipped municipal **campsite** (Ⓣ02.97.52.48.88; closed Sept–June), between the harbour and the village, plus a dozen or so **gîtes**, rented year-round by the week through the Mairie (Ⓣ02.97.52.48.88).

Carnac

CARNAC is the most important prehistoric site in Europe – in fact this spot is thought to have been continuously inhabited longer than anywhere else in the world. Its **alignments** of two thousand or so menhirs stretch over 4km, with great burial tumuli dotted amid them. In use since at least 5700 BC, the site long predates Knossos, the Pyramids, Stonehenge and the great Egyptian temples of the same name at Karnak.

The **town** of Carnac is split into two distinct halves – the popular seaside resort of Carnac-Plage and, further inland, Carnac-Ville near the alignments. It's an amalgam that can verge on the ridiculous, with rows of shops named Supermarché des Druides and the like. For all that, Carnac is a relaxed and attractive place, and any commercialization doesn't intrude on the megaliths themselves. Fortunately, the ancient builders had the foresight to construct their monuments well back from the sea.

Arrival and information

In July and August, when the Tire Bouchon **rail** link runs between Auray and Quiberon, trains call at **Plouharnel**, 4km northwest of Carnac and connected by buses. The main bus stop is near the main **tourist office**, which is slightly back from the main beach at 74 av des Druides in Carnac-Plage (July & Aug Mon–Sat 9am–7pm, Sun 3–7pm; Sept–June Mon–Sat 9.30am–12.30pm & 2–6pm; Ⓣ02.97.52.13.52, Ⓦot-carnac.fr). An annexe in the place de l'Église in town is open between April and September (Mon–Sat 9.30am–12.30pm & 2–6pm). **Bicycles** can be rented from *Le Randonneur*, 20 av des Druides,

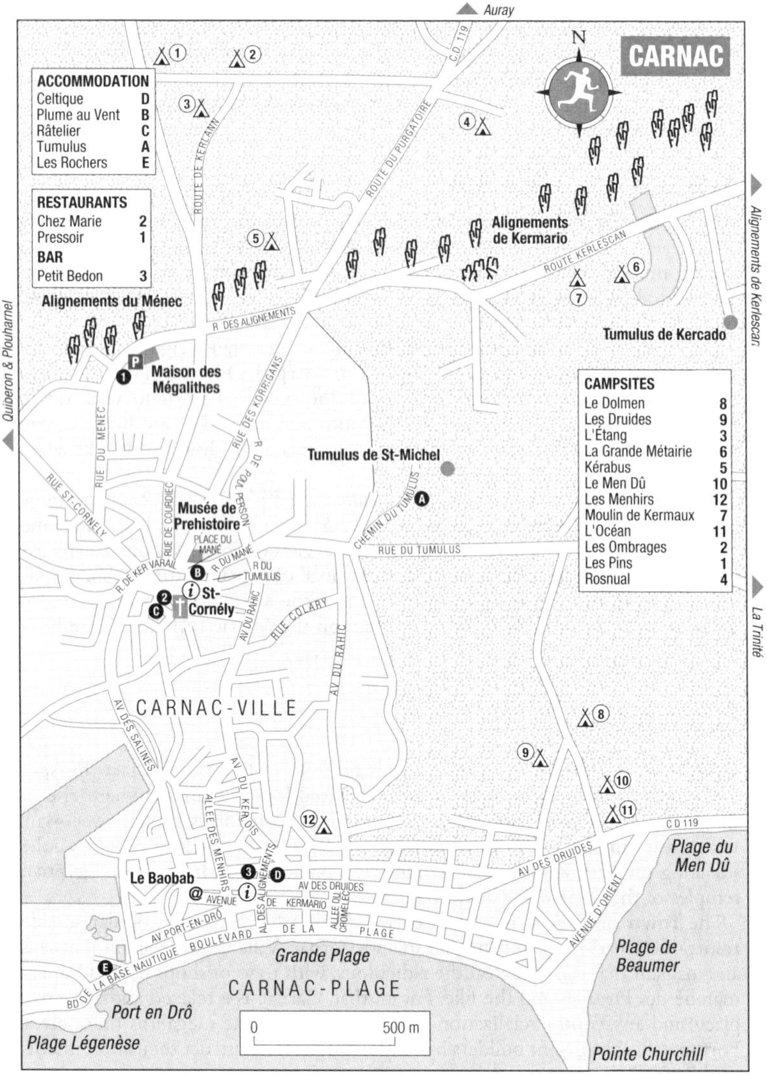

Carnac-Plage (☎02.97.52.02.55), or local campsites like the *Grande Métairie* (see opposite), which also arranges horseback tours.

Accommodation

Hotel prices in Carnac are among the most expensive in all Brittany, and rooms are at a premium in July and August, when you can expect higher rates and intense pressure to take half-board (*demi-pension*). Carnac-Ville tends to be marginally cheaper than Carnac-Plage, although the distinction is blurred where the two merge. As befits such a family-oriented place, Carnac also features as many as twenty **campsites** (see map above).

Hotels and B&Bs

Celtique 82 av des Druides, Carnac-Plage T 02.97.52.14.15, W hotel-celtique.com. One of the best luxury options, by the beach at Carnac-Plage and affiliated to Best Western. Facilities include an indoor pool, spa and billiard room. 6

Plume au Vent 4 venelle Notre-Dame, Carnac-Ville T 06.16.98.34.79, W plume-au-vent.com. Brilliantly decorated B&B, drawing tastefully on the nautical theme (for once), with pastel colours and a great collection of found artefacts. It also has a very warm welcome and a prized location in the heart of Carnac-Ville. 5

Râtelier 4 chemin de Douët, Carnac-Ville T 02.97.52.05.04, W le-ratelier.com. Old, ivy-clad stone hotel with comfortable rooms characterized by rustic colours and open wooden beams; some have showers but not toilets. Top-quality food on menus that start from €20. Restaurant closed Tues & Wed Oct–Easter, hotel closed mid-Nov to mid-Dec & all Jan. 3

Rochers 6 bd de la Base Nautique, Carnac-Plage T 02.97.52.10.09, W www.les-rochers.com. Well-kept, family-friendly hotel offering the best value by the beach, especially if you are looking for sea-view balconies. Closed Nov–Easter. 5

Tumulus Chemin du Tumulus T 02.97.52.08.21, W hotel-tumulus.com. Fancy hotel, east of town alongside the Tumulus St-Michel, which has been entirely renovated and has a heated pool and another fine restaurant. Closed early Nov to mid-Feb. 8

Campsites

Dolmen T 02.97.52.12.35, W campingledolmen.com. Central three-star site, immediately north of Carnac-Plage but still an easy walk from the sea. Closed Oct–March.

Grande Métairie T 02.97.52.24.01, W lagrandemetairie.com. Expensive four-star site near the Kercado tumulus, which offers tennis, horseriding and a swimming pool. Closed early Sept to late March.

Men Dû T 02.97.52.04.23, W camping-mendu.com. Two-star site near the sea, just inland from the plage du Men Dû. Closed Oct–March.

The alignments

All sorts of conjectures have been advanced about the **Carnac megaliths**. One ancient story said they were petrified Roman soldiers; more recently, US soldiers in the last war allegedly believed them to be German anti-tank obstructions. The general consensus today is that they had a religious significance connected with their use as some sort of astronomical observatory. One expert, the late Professor Thom, saw the alignments as part of a unified system for recording such phenomena as the extreme points of the lunar and solar cycles. According to this hypothesis, the Carnac stones provided a grid system – a kind

Seeing the stones

Thanks to increasing numbers of visitors (and despite vehement local opposition), the principal alignments are fenced off. The area is being allowed to revegetate at a natural pace, but there's no predicting how long that will take, and even when it's complete access will probably still be restricted. Currently you are allowed to walk freely around the best-preserved sites from October to March (daily 10am–5pm); between April and September access is on guided tours only (€4.50), some of which are in English (in recent years, Wed–Fri at 10.30am). To pick up the tour schedule, see some interesting displays, examine a model of the entire site, and buy books and maps, call in at the official visitor centre, the **Maison des Mégalithes**, across the road from the Alignements de Menec (daily: May & June 9am–7pm, July & Aug 9am–8pm, Sept–April 10am–5pm; T 02.97.52.29.81).

You get a much better sense of the alignments when you're able to walk among them, and touch the stones. However, it is possible to see them pretty well from outside the fences, especially if you take time to walk the parallel footpaths, like the one from the Maison that follows the wilder, northern side of the Ménec and Kermario alignments. That said, from this (or, indeed almost any) distance, the individual stones tend to look like no more than stumps in the heather.

of Neolithic graph paper – for plotting heavenly movements, and hence to determine the siting of other stones (see Contexts, p.386).

However, it's hard to see real consistency in the size or shape of the stones, or enough regularity in the lines to pinpoint their direction. Local tradition has it that new stones were added to the lines, illuminated by fire, each June. An annual ceremony in which willing participants set up one stone does sound more plausible than a vast programme of slave labour to erect them all at once. In any case, the physical aspect and orientation of the stones may have been subsidiary to their metaphysical significance; perhaps no practical purpose or precise pattern was involved, and their importance was entirely symbolic.

The way you see them today cannot be said to be authentic. Having been used for generations as a source of ready-quarried stone, they were later also surreptitiously removed by farmers attempting to prevent academics and tourists damaging precious crops. Not only is it impossible to say how many stones have disappeared, but those that remain are not necessarily in their original positions – small holes filled with pink concrete at the base of the stones denote those that have been restored or re-erected.

The **menhirs** range in size from mere stumps to five-metre-high blocks; some stand alone, others in circles known as **cromlechs**, or in approximate lines. In addition there are **dolmens**, groups of standing stones roofed with further stones across the top, which are generally assumed to be burial chambers. And there are tumuli – most notably the **Tumulus de St-Michel**, near the town centre, a vast artificial mound containing rudimentary graves. It used to be possible for visitors to enter subterranean passages that tunnelled beneath the St-Michel tumulus, but it's now considered too unstable to do so; the history museum in Vannes has some exquisite jadeite axes found buried within.

Taken all together, the stones make up three distinct major alignments, all running roughly northeast–southwest, but each with a slightly separate orientation. These are the **Alignements de Ménec**, "the place of stones" or "place of remembrance", with 1169 stones in eleven rows; the **Alignements de Kermario**, "the place of the dead", with 1029 menhirs in ten rows; and the **Alignements de Kerlescan**, "the place of burning", with 555 menhirs in thirteen lines. All three run parallel to the sea beside the Route des Alignements and Route de Kerlescan, 1km or so north of Carnac-Ville.

The Museum of Prehistory

Carnac's **Musée de Préhistoire** (May, June & Sept daily except Tues 10am–12.30pm & 2–6pm; July & Aug daily 10am–6pm; Oct–April daily except Tues 10am–12.30pm & 2–5pm; €5; Ⓦwww.museedecarnac.com) is at 10 place de la Chapelle, Carnac-Ville. It's a disappointingly dry museum of archeology that's likely to leave anyone whose command of French is less than perfect almost completely in the dark as to what all the fuss is about. Tracing the history of the area from earliest times, it starts with 450,000-year-old chipping tools and leads by way of the Neanderthals to the megalith-builders and beyond. As well as authentic physical relics, such as the original "twisted dolmen" of Luffang, with a carving of an octopus-like divinity guaranteed to chill the blood of any devotee of H.P. Lovecraft, there are reproductions and casts of the carvings at Locmariaquer, a scale model of the Alignements de Ménec, and diagrams of how the stones may have been moved into place.

The town and the beaches

Carnac itself, divided between the original **Carnac-Ville** and the seaside resort of **Carnac-Plage**, is extremely popular and crowded, swarming with holiday-makers in July and August. For most of these, the alignments are only a sideshow. But, as a holiday centre, Carnac has its special charm, especially in late spring and early autumn, when it is less crowded – and cheaper. The town and seafront remain well wooded, and the tree-lined avenues and gardens are a delight. The climate is mild enough for the Mediterranean mimosa and evergreen oak to grow alongside the native stone pine and cypress.

Near the Museum of Prehistory, in the centre of Carnac-Ville, the **church of St-Cornély** is dedicated to the patron saint of horned animals. Archeologists believe the custom of bringing diseased cattle to Carnac to be cured, still honoured at the saint's *pardon* on the second Sunday in September, dates back as far as the Romans. The Romans also had heated seawater baths here; today the **Thalassotherapy Centre** is an ultramodern building where, among other things, they treat *maladies de civilisation*.

Carnac's five **beaches** extend for nearly 3km. The largest – logically enough, the Grande Plage – runs the full length of the built-up area known as Carnac-Plage. For much of the way it's hidden from view by the slightly raised line of dunes that separates it from the boulevard de la Plage, which is in turn very low-key; the parallel avenue des Druides, a couple of blocks inland, is much busier, with shops and restaurants.

Further west, nearer the yacht club, the small **plage Légenèse** is reputed to be the beach on which the ill-fated *Chouan* royalists landed in 1795. The two most attractive beaches, usually counted together as one of the five, are **plages Men Dû** and **Beaumer**, which lie to the east towards La Trinité beyond Pointe Churchill. They're especially popular with **kite-surfers**.

Eating and drinking

Most of the **restaurants** worth recommending in Carnac are in the hotels, as described on p.361, but *Chez Marie*, facing St-Cornély church at 3 place de l'Église (Ⓣ02.97.52.07.93; closed Nov–Easter), and the *Pressoir* by the Ménec *alignements* (Ⓣ02.97.52.01.86; closed Sept–Easter) are worthwhile crêperies.

There's a **market** in Carnac-Ville on Wednesday and Sunday mornings; in the surrounding area, Locmariaquer holds them on Tuesday and Saturday, La Trinité on Tuesday and Friday, and Auray on Monday. Avenue des Druides has a few **bars**, such as the *Petit Bedon* at no.108 (Ⓣ02.97.52.11.62, Ⓦlepetitbedon.org), which starts off the evening playing predominantly rock, but has covered most musical styles by the time it closes at 4am.

La Trinité

An alternative base to Carnac is **LA TRINITÉ**, three or four kilometres east along the coast, around the sweep of Beaumer bay. The town itself is uninteresting – a modern and very upmarket yacht harbour without a proper beach – but has achieved fame as the former home of yachtsman Eric Tabarley (see p.346), and as the birthplace of Jean-Marie Le Pen, founder of France's ultra-right National Front.

La Trinité does at least hold some high-quality **hotel-restaurants**, among them the *Ostrea*, facing the port at 34 cours des Quais (Ⓣ02.97.55.73.23, Ⓦhotel-ostrea.com; ❹; closed Dec to mid-Feb, plus Sun eve & Mon in low season), where you dine on a sea-view terrace, and a crop of four-star **campsites** nearby, including the attractive *Camping La Baie* on the plage de Kervillen (Ⓣ02.97.55.73.42, Ⓦwww.camping-la-baie.com; closed mid-Sept to late April).

Locmariaquer

LOCMARIAQUER stands right at the mouth of the Gulf of Morbihan, its cape separated by only a few hundred metres from the tip of the Rhuys peninsula across the water. On the ocean side, it has a long sandy beach, popular not only with swimmers but also with beachcombers and shellfish-scavengers; on the Gulf side, it has a small tidal port. Like Carnac, however, the main reason to go out of your way to visit Locmariaquer is for its fine crop of megaliths.

Menhirs and dolmens

Locmariaquer's principal megalithic site, 500m out of town (daily: May & June 10am–6pm, July & Aug 10am–7pm; Sept–April 10am–12.30pm & 2–5.15pm; €5, under-18s free; Ⓦlocmariaquer.monuments-nationaux.fr), was thought until 1991 to hold two monuments – the broken fragments of the largest known menhir, and a massive dolmen. Then archeologists realized that the car park for visitors had inadvertently been created atop a third, even larger relic. Now known as **Er Grah**, it consists of a series of partially reconstructed stone terraces, the purpose of which remains unknown.

There's no mistaking the **Grand Menhir Brise**, a huge column of stone that some believe was the crucial central point of the megalithic observatory of the Morbihan (see Contexts, p.387). Having originally stood twenty metres tall, and weighed 347 tonnes, it's thought to have been toppled deliberately around the time the two neighbouring structures were built, and currently lies on the ground in four pieces (a possible fifth is missing). An estimated workforce of between two and four thousand people was required to move it.

Alongside the Grand Menhir, the **Table des Marchand** is a dolmen or table-like structure that when erected stood exposed to the air, but later became covered by a tumulus. It's once more open to the elements, but visitors can go inside, along a narrow passage comprised of massive curving menhirs chinked with smaller pebbles, and stand beneath its huge roof. Carvings overhead seem to depict ploughing, which may well have been a recent innovation at the time they were made. During the 1980s, it was discovered that this roof is part of the same stone as that on the tumulus at Gavrinis and on another local dolmen – the carvings match like a jigsaw. That constitutes a fresh puzzle for the archeologists, as it suggests that the builders did not revere the stones in themselves. In addition, the stone at the end of the central chamber was originally erected as a stand-alone menhir, so the "table" must have been built around an earlier monument.

Locmariaquer's other megaliths remain open at all times – and open to the weather as well, so watch out for muddy and waterlogged underground passages, and take a torch if you want to explore them thoroughly. The most interesting are the **Dolmen des Pierres Plates**, at the end of the town beach, with what

Boats from Locmariaquer

Boat trips set out from Locmariaquer in all directions, for which rival companies sell tickets both in the town centre and at the port further down towards the narrow straits, with precise departure points depending on the level of the tides. Both Vedettes Angélus (Ⓣ02.97.57.30.29, Ⓦvedettes-angelus.com), and Compagnie des Îles (Ⓣ08.25.13.41.30, Ⓦcompagniedesiles.com) run gulf tours, as detailed on p.369; the latter also offers day-trips to the Île de Houat (see p.357).

In July and August, regular ferries (Ⓣ02.97.57.72.63; €8.50) cross to Port Navalo on the Rhuys peninsula (see p.376), carrying bikes but not cars.

looks like an octopus divinity deep in its long chamber, and the **Dolmen de Mané-Rethual**, a long covered tunnel leading to a burial chamber capped with a huge rock, reached along a narrow footpath that starts behind the phone boxes next to the Mairie/tourist office. At a third dolmen, the **Mané-Lud**, a horse's skull was found on top of each stone during excavations.

Practicalities

The local **tourist office** is at 1 rue de la Victoire (April–June & Sept Mon–Sat 9am–noon & 2–5.30pm; July & Aug Mon–Sat 9am–1pm & 2–6pm, Sun 10am–1pm; Oct–March Mon–Fri 9am–noon & 2–5.30pm, Sat 9.30am–12.30pm; ⓣ02.97.57.33.05, ⓦot-locmariaquer.com). There are a couple of reasonable small **hotels** in Locmariaquer, both with good restaurants. *L'Escale* (ⓣ02.97.57.32.51, ⓦescale-hotel.com; ❸; closed Oct–March) is right on the waterfront at 2 place Dariorigum, so you get a great view from its terrace as you feast on oysters and mussels, while the *Lautram* is set slightly back from the sea, facing the church on place de l'Église (ⓣ02.97.57.31.32, ⓦhotel-golfe-morbihan.com; ❷; closed Oct–March). The food at the *Lautram* is superb, and there's a family room, but the cheaper rooms are pretty minimal.

Campsites include the excellent two-star *Ferme Fleurie* (ⓣ02.97.57.34.06, ⓦcampinglafermefleurie.com; closed Nov to mid-March), 1km northwest towards Kerinis, and the two-star, summer-only *Lann Brick* (ⓣ02.97.57.32.79, ⓦcamping-lannbrick.com; closed Nov to mid-March), 1.5km further on, nearer the beach.

Auray and around

The old town of **AURAY** may not quite have the cachet (or the walls) of its neighbour Vannes, but it's a lot less crowded, and in many way its medieval streets are just as attractive. Into the bargain, it's also much cheaper than Quiberon and Carnac, but usefully placed for combining visits both south to the Quiberon peninsula and east to the Gulf of Morbihan.

The natural centre of town these days is the **place de la République**, with its eighteenth-century Hôtel de Ville and adjoining **covered market**. In a nearby square, along rue du Lait, the seventeenth-century **church of St-Gildas** has a fine Renaissance porch, while on Mondays an open-air market fills the surrounding streets with colour – and stops all traffic for a considerable radius.

However, Auray's showpiece is undoubtedly the ancient quarter of **St-Goustan**, just a couple of minutes' pleasant stroll away down by the river, with its delightful, albeit restored, fifteenth- and sixteenth-century houses. This bend in the River Loch, an early defended site, made a natural setting for a town – and, with its easy access to the gulf, it soon became one of the busiest ports of Brittany. Today, as you look at it from the Promenade du Loch on the opposite bank, with the diminutive seventeenth-century stone bridge still spanning the river, it is not difficult to imagine it in its heyday. In 1776, Benjamin Franklin landed here on his way to seek the help of Louis XVI in the American War of Independence; Auray is also said to have been the last place Julius Caesar reached in his conquest of Gaul.

On the northern edge of town, the imposing and evocative **Abbaye de Chartreuse** (daily except Tues 2–5.10pm; free) houses a David d'Angers mausoleum of black-and-white marble, commemorating the failed Chouan landing at Quiberon in 1795 (see p.350). For Bretons, the event was something more than an attempt at a royalist restoration, with strong undertones of a struggle for independence.

Two kilometres further north, a group of reconstructed farm buildings forms the **Eco-Musée St-Degan** (March–June, Sept & Oct daily 2–5.30pm; July & Aug daily 10am–7pm; Nov–Feb school holidays only, daily 2–5.30pm; €5; ⓦecomusee-st-degan.fr), which sets out to represent local peasant life a century ago, It's a bit determinedly rustic and charming, but at least it attempts to escape the glass cases and wax models of most folk museums.

Practicalities

Auray's **tourist office** is at 20 rue du Lait, very near the Hôtel de Ville on place de la République (July & Aug Mon–Sat 9am–7pm, Sun 9am–noon; Sept–June Mon–Fri 9am–noon & 2–6pm, Sat 9am–noon, plus Sun 2–6pm April–June; ⓣ02.97.24.09.75, ⓦwww.auray-tourisme.com). The **gare SNCF** is twenty minutes' walk northeast of the centre; east–west routes run year-round, but the Tire-Bouchon line heads south to Quiberon via Plouharnel during July and August only. Buses run from the station through the centre of Auray and on to La Trinité, Carnac and the *gare SNCF* at Quiberon.

Although the waterfront of the St-Goustan port is lined with brasseries and crêperies, mostly named after Benjamin Franklin, sadly there's no **hotel** right there. However, a short walk along the quayside brings you to the nice little *Marin* at 1 place du Rolland (ⓣ02.97.24.14.58, ⓦhotel-lemarin.com; ④; closed Jan), which offers smart, well-equipped rooms above a brasserie. Alternative options up in Auray proper include the nicely refurbished *Celtic*, 38 rue Georges-Clemenceau (ⓣ02.97.24.05.37, ⓦceltic-hotel.fr; ④), and the cheaper, more basic *Cadoudal*, 9 place Notre-Dame (ⓣ02.97.24.14.65, ⓦhotellecadoudal-auray.com; ②).

Le Bono

Three kilometres south of St-Goustan, and still officially within Auray, the main road down the Auray estuary, the D101, crosses the River Bono on a high bridge. Visible way below it to the left is a beautiful iron bridge. A side turning before the river leads across that bridge into **LE BONO**, a harbour village that looks almost ludicrously idyllic seen from one of the *vedettes* out in the gulf. At the south end of the higher bridge, the refurbished **hotel** *Alicia*, 1 rue du Générale-de-Gaulle (ⓣ02.97.57.88.65, ⓦhotel-alicia.com; ③; closed Jan, plus Sun eve & Mon Oct–March), is perched high above the river. Its very comfortable rooms are equipped with balconies, several of which enjoy river views, and there's an excellent **restaurant**, serving exquisite food on menus from €22.

Ste-Anne d'Auray

The town of **STE-ANNE D'AURAY**, 7km northeast of Auray, has been a centre for pilgrimage since 1623, when a local peasant, one Nicolazic, discovered a statue of St Anne (the mother of Mary). He claimed that the saint directed him to the spot where it was buried, and instructed him to build a church. Twenty years later, on his deathbed, the ecclesiastical authorities were still interrogating Nicolazic, but the church had already been built and pilgrims were arriving. Nicolazic was an illiterate peasant who spoke no French; it is a testimony to his obduracy that his claims were eventually accepted against the opposition of sceptical clergy and nobility. To this day, Nicolazic has not been canonized, but the pilgrimage earned papal approval when Pope John Paul II visited in 1996.

On St Anne's feast day, July 26, the town hosts one of the largest of the Breton *pardons*. Well over 25,000 pilgrims gather to hear Mass in the church, mount the *scala sancta* on their knees and buy trinkets and snacks from the street stalls.

Ste-Anne is also home to a vast **Monument aux Morts**, erected by public subscription in honour of the 250,000 Breton dead of World War I. One in fourteen of the population died, the highest proportion of any region involved. A crypt topped by a dome with a granite altar, the monument is surrounded by a huge and sombre wall that must be 200m long, covered with inscriptions to the dead. Even that does not have space to list them all by name, often just cataloguing the horrific death tallies of tiny and obscure villages.

Practicalities

Ste-Anne is a sad and solemn place. Away from the spacious promenades for the pilgrims, the town, is small, low and drab; not a place for a long stay, although there is no shortage of **hotels**. Among the best value in the centre are the *Moderne*, 8 rue de Vannes (Ⓣ02.97.57.66.55, Ⓦhotel-le-moderne.com; ❸; closed late Dec to late Jan, plus Sat in winter), and the *Croix Blanche*, nearby at 25 rue de Vannes (Ⓣ02.97.57.64.44, Ⓦhotel-lacroixblanche.com; ❸; closed Jan, plus Sun eve & Mon in low season), both of which have good restaurants.

The Golfe du Morbihan

Beautiful, popular, and yet remarkably unspoiled by tourism, the sheltered **Golfe du Morbihan** – the word means "little sea" in Breton – is one of the loveliest stretches of Brittany's coast. Its only large town, medieval **Vannes**, is well worth visiting, but its endlessly indented shoreline is the major attraction, with superb vistas at every turn, and countless secluded **beaches**.

By popular tradition, the gulf holds 365 scattered **islands** – one for every day of the year. For centuries, though, the waters have been rising, and the figure now is more like one for each week. Of these, some thirty are owned by film stars and the like, while two – the **Île aux Moines** and **Île d'Arz** – have regular ferry services and permanent populations, and end up extremely crowded in summer. Others are better, and a **boat tour** around them, or at least a trip out to **Gavrinis**, near the mouth of the gulf, ranks among the most enjoyable activities southern Brittany has to offer.

As the boats thread their way through the baffling muddle of channels, you swiftly lose track of which is island and which is mainland; and everywhere there are **megalithic ruins**, stone circles disappearing beneath the water and solitary menhirs on small hillocks. At the time when they were built, the sea level was around 5m lower than today, and the islands may have been mounds amid the marshlands. Flaubert evocatively described Celtic mercenaries far off in Carthage pining for the Morbihan – *Les Celtes regrettaient trois pierres brutes, sous un ciel plouvieux, dans un golfe remplie d'îlots* – not that the Celts actually set up the stones in the first place.

Larmor-Baden

LARMOR-BADEN, near the eastern tip of the Auray estuary and the departure point for trips to Gavrinis, is a subdued little town, set at the bottom of a long slope of fields of dazzling sunflowers. The port looks out on the tangle of islands in the Gulf of Morbihan, which at this point is so narrow that Arzon on the Rhuys peninsula (see p.376) appears to be on just another nearby island. It's not

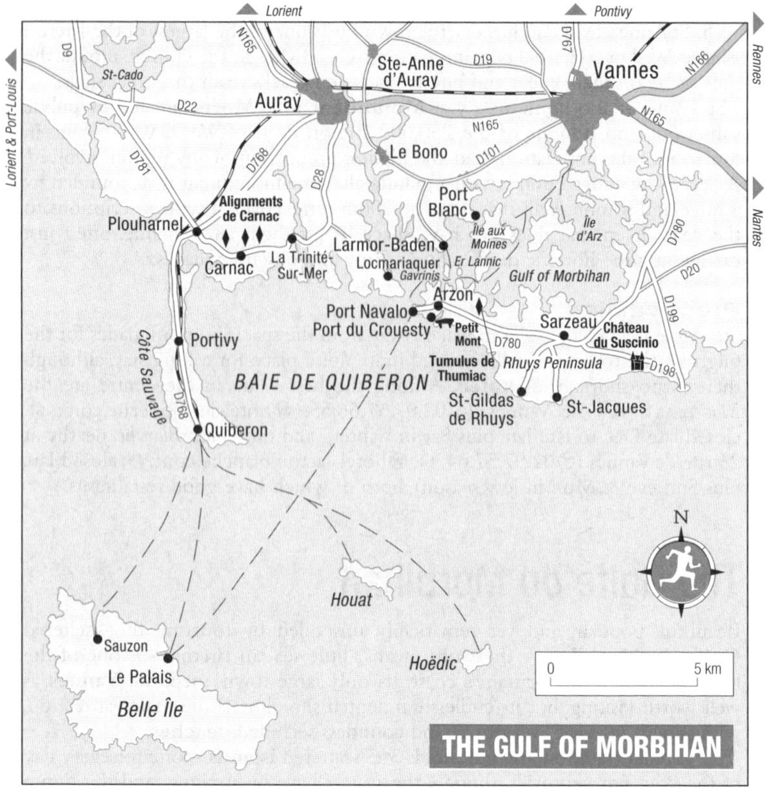

an inspiring place to stay – neither a resort nor a town – but there's a three-star beachfront **campsite**, *Les Algues* (ⓣ02.97.65.55.47, ⓦwww.larmor-plage.com; closed mid-Sept to mid-June), and a fair number of **hotels** including the *Auberge du Parc Fétan*, 17 rue de Berder (ⓣ02.97.57.04.38, ⓦhotel-parcfetan.com; ❸).

Gavrinis

The reason to visit the island of **Gavrinis**, which can only be reached on guided boat tours from Larmor-Baden, is its **megalithic site**. The most impressive and remarkable in Brittany, it would be memorable just for its location. But it really is extraordinary as a structure, standing comparison with Newgrange in Ireland and – in shape as well as size and age – with the earliest pyramids of Egypt.

It is essentially a **tumulus**, an earth mound covering a stone cairn and "passage grave". However, in 1981 half of the mound was peeled back and, using the original stones around the entrance as a basis, the side of the cairn that faces the water was reconstructed to make a facade resembling a step-pyramid. At the time it was built, Gavrinis probably wasn't an island, but a high eminence commanding the mouths of two adjacent rivers. Groups of visitors are now shepherded through the doorway and along a straight passageway that at fourteen metres is said to be the longest known, to reach a slightly enlarged chamber at the far end. The corridor is oriented so the rising sun at the winter solstice shines directly on the far wall.

Inside, every stone of both passage and chamber is covered in carvings, with a restricted "alphabet" of fingerprint whorls, axe-heads and other conventional signs, including the spirals familiar in Ireland but seen only here in Brittany. The roof is made from the self-same piece of carved stone as covers the Table des Marchand in Locmariaquer (see p.364). No one knows the purpose of the three holes leading to a recessed niche in one of the walls of the chamber. Some medieval monks were buried in the mound, but the cairn itself seems never to have been a grave.

From Gavrinis, you can look across to the half-submerged stone circle on the tiny island of **Er Lanic**, which rests on its skirt of mud like an abandoned hovercraft. It has been identified as a major centre for the manufacture of ceremonial axes, using stone brought from Port Navalo.

Practicalities

Gavrinis can be visited between March and November only. The **ferry** ride from Larmor-Baden is a fifteen-minute battle against fierce swirling currents.

Gulf tours

In season, dozens of boats leave for **gulf tours** each day from Vannes, Port Navalo, La Trinité, Locmariaquer, Auray, Le Bono and Larmor-Baden. Options include:

Compagnie des Îles ⓣ08.25.13.41.00, ⓦcompagniedesiles.com. Gulf tours (€15–29) from **Vannes** (daily: early April to Sept 9.30am, 10.30am, 2pm & 5pm; July & Aug also 11.30am & 4pm; Feb & Oct usually but not always 10.30am & 4pm). They also operate a more limited programme of cruises from **Port Navalo** (ⓣ08.25.13.41.20), **Locmariaquer** (ⓣ08.25.13.41.30), and Port Haliguen in **Quiberon** (ⓣ08.25.13.41.40). The price of each cruise generally depends on the number of stops you make, with possibilities of getting off at Île aux Moines and Île d'Arz.

Izenah Croisières ⓣ02.97.57.23.24 or 02.97.26.31.45, ⓦwww.izenah-croisieres.com. Gulf tours from **Port Blanc** at **Baden** in summer (April–Sept daily 10am, plus various other departures at increasing frequency in summer; €10–23), and a year-round ferry service to the Île aux Moines (daily every 30min: July & Aug 7am–10pm, Sept–June 7am–7.30pm; €4 return).

Navix ⓣ08.25.13.21.00, ⓦnavix.fr. Based in **Vannes**, they run up to six deluxe half-day (€22.50) and full-day (€29) tours around the gulf every day between mid-April and September (first departure: mid-April to late June 8.45am; late June to late Aug 9am; late Aug to end of Sept 10am). They also offer **lunch cruises** aboard the *Mor Bihan* from Vannes (daily: mid-April until early July & late Aug until the end of Sept 12.30pm; early July to late Aug 1pm); and **dinner cruises** (early July until late Aug daily 8.30pm; 8pm on certain dates otherwise). These cost €24 and €26 respectively, plus the cost of your meal, which varies from €25 to €31 according to your choice of menu. Much the same programme of tours, at the same prices, also departs from **Port Navalo** (first departure daily: early July to late Aug 9.45am; early April to early July & late Aug until mid-Sept 10.15am; ⓣ08.25.13.21.20). There's a slightly smaller selection from **Locmariaquer** (first departure mid-April to mid-Sept daily 10am; ⓣ08.25.13.21.30), with prices ranging €14–29. Between early July and late August, Navix also operates daily from either **Auray** (departures at 9am & 2.15pm; ⓣ08.25.13.21.40;) or **Le Bono** (departures at 9.15am & 2.30pm), as well as **La Trinité** (daily 9am & 1.45pm; ⓣ08.25.13.21.50), with cruises costing €22.50–29. They also go to **Belle-Île** (see p.353; April–Sept; €32 return) from Vannes and **Port Navalo**, and **Houat** (see p.357; mid-July to mid-Aug; €28) from **La Trinité**.

Vedettes Angelus ⓣ02.97.57.30.29, ⓦvedettes-angelus.com. Up to five gulf tours of varying lengths daily from Locmariaquer (mid-April to Sept; first departure 10am; €13–25).

Tides permitting, the service operates at half-hourly intervals, and the cost includes both ferry ride and a guided tour of the cairn (April, June & Sept daily 9.30am–12.30pm & 1.30–6.30pm; May Mon–Fri 1.30–6.30pm, Sat & Sun 9.30am–12.30pm & 1.30–6.30pm; July & Aug daily 9.30am–12.30pm & 1.30–7pm; March, Oct & Nov daily except Wed 1.30–5pm; €12: Ⓣ02.97.57.19.38, Ⓦgavrinis.info). The last boat of the morning usually leaves Larmor-Baden at noon in July and August, and at 11am otherwise; the last afternoon boat leaves at 3pm or 3.30pm daily, depending on how busy things are. In addition, most gulf cruises sail close enough to the island to give a view of the cairn, but do not land.

Vannes

Thanks to its position at the head of the Golfe du Morbihan, **VANNES**, 20km east of Auray, is southern Brittany's major tourist town. Modern Vannes is such a large and thriving community that the small size of the old walled town at its core, **Vieux Vannes**, may well come as a surprise. Its focal point, the old gateway of the **Porte St-Vincent** on its southern side, commands a busy little square at the head of the long canalized port that provides access to the gulf itself. Inside the ramparts, the old centre of chaotic streets – crammed around the cathedral, and enclosed by gardens and a tiny stream – is largely pedestrianized, in refreshing contrast to the somewhat insane road system beyond.

It was from Vannes that the great Breton warrior hero Nominoë (see p.389) set out to unify Brittany at the start of the ninth century; defeating the Franks, he pushed the borders beyond Nantes and Rennes, where they remained until

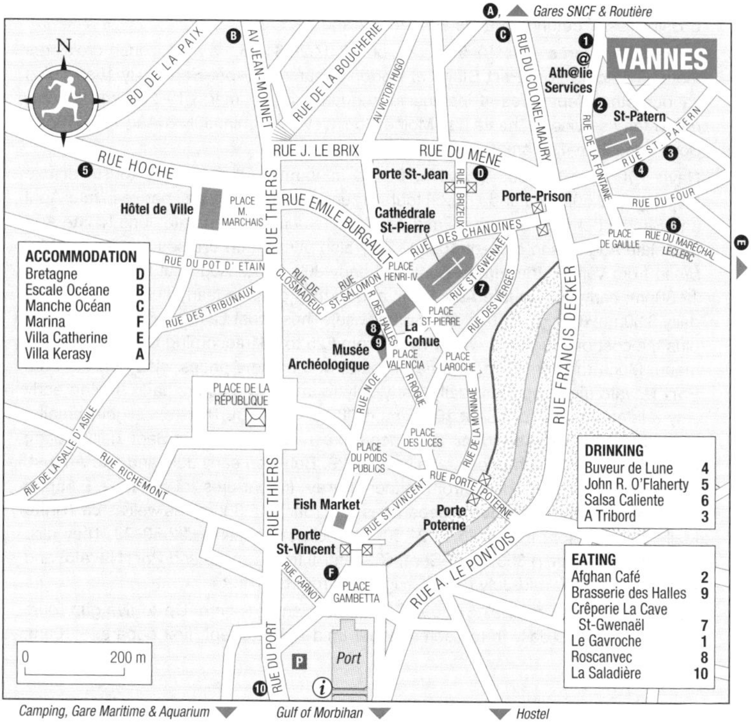

the French Revolution nearly a millennium later. Here too, the Breton *États* assembled in 1532 to ratify the Act of Union with France, in the building known as La Cohue; and here, also, 22 of the royalists captured at Quiberon (see p.351) were executed in the Jardins de la Garrène in 1795. Parisian soldiers fired the shots because local regiments refused.

Arrival and information

Vannes' **gare SNCF** and **gare routière** (CTM; ⓣ02.97.01.22.01, ⓦlactm.com) face each other across avenue Favrel et Lincy, 25 minutes' walk north of the centre. **Parking** in town can be a problem; there's a large underground car park on the west side of the port, near the southern edge of the old town, with plenty more quayside parking south of that. Quai Tabarly here is also home to the new, modern **tourist office** (July & Aug Mon–Sat 9am–7pm, Sun 10am–6pm; Sept–June Mon–Sat 9.30am–12.30pm & 2–6pm; ⓣ08.25.13.56.10, ⓦwww.tourisme-vannes.com).

Boats around the gulf operate from the **gare maritime**, a little way south of the centre on the parc du Golfe, by Navix (ⓣ08.25.13.21.00, ⓦnavix.fr) and Compagnie des Îles (ⓣ08.25.13.41.00, ⓦcompagniedesiles.com), among others (see box, p.369).

Accommodation

Although Vannes offers a more extensive choice of **hotels** than anywhere else around the Golfe du Morbihan, most, unfortunately, are well away from the centre. The liveliest area to stay is **place Gambetta** overlooking the port, the one part of Vannes that stays busy well into the evening all year.

Hotels and B&Bs

Le Bretagne 36 rue du Méné ⓣ02.97.47.20.21, ⓦhotel-lebretagne-vannes.com. Reasonable and friendly hotel just outside the walls, around the corner from the Porte-Prison, with nicely refitted en-suite rooms. ❸

Escale Océania av Jean-Monnet ⓣ02.97.47.59.60, ⓦoceaniahotels.com. Dependable upscale hotel a short walk northwest of the walled town, offering 65 large, soundproofed, en-suite and a/c rooms, plus an adequate restaurant that's closed at weekends. ❺

Manche Océan 31 rue du Colonel-Maury ⓣ02.97.47.26.46, ⓦmanche-ocean.com. Ordinary but perfectly acceptable modern rooms between the station and the walled town, used mainly by tour groups. Small-scale buffet breakfasts for €8.50. ❻

Marina 4 pl Gambetta ⓣ02.97.47.00.10, ⓔlemarinahotel@aol.com. Fifteen pleasantly refurbished rooms – double glazed to keep the noise out – above a busy bar right by the port with sea views and morning sun. En-suite facilities cost €5 extra. ❷

Villa Catherine 89 av du president Édouard-Herriot ⓣ02.97.42.48.59, ⓦvilla-catherine.fr. Charming four-room B&B, in a late nineteenth-century townhouse, which has been entirely restored using ecologically sustainable materials, and serves an entirely organic breakfast. ❺

Villa Kerasy 20 av Favrel et Lancy ⓣ02.97.68.36.83, ⓦwww.villakerasy.com. A top-of-the-range luxury hotel and Indian spa, with its finest rooms leading onto a Japanese garden. Service and surroundings are very good, though there's no restaurant. ❽

Hostel and campsite

Camping Conleau av du Maréchal-Juin ⓣ02.97.63.13.88, ⓔcamping@mairie-vannes.fr. This very pleasant three-star municipal campsite, the closest to central Vannes, is set right beside the gulf at the far end of ave du Maréchal-Juin, 2km southwest of the centre. Closed Oct–March.

Centre International de Séjour rte de Moustérian, Séné ⓣ02.97.66.94.25, ⓦlesasterides.com. Budget hostel, with dorm beds at €12.50, 4km southeast of the town centre on bus route #4 from pl de la République. Closed July & Aug.

The Town

Modern Vannes centres on **place de la République**; the administrative headquarters were shifted outside the medieval city during the nineteenth-century craze for urbanization. The grandest of the public buildings here, guarded by a pair of sleek and dignified bronze lions, is the **Hôtel de Ville** at the top of rue Thiers.

By day, however, the cobbled streets of the old city, especially in the area around the cathedral, are the chief source of pleasure, as well as being where most of Vannes' busy commercial life takes place. With their skew-windowed and half-timbered houses – most overhanging and witch-hatted, some tumbling down, some newly propped-up and painted – they amply repay time spent wandering. **Place Henri-IV** in particular, with its charming fifteenth- and sixteenth-century gabled houses, is stunning, as are the views from it down the narrow side streets. Here and there, it's possible to climb up onto the **ramparts** to admire the views, though much of the way you have to trace the circuit around the outside instead, from the far side of what used to be the city moat, which now consists of neat and colourful flowerbeds. Near the **Porte Poterne**, the "back gate", an old slate-roofed wash-house survives.

La Cohue, which fills a block between rue des Halles and place St-Pierre, and takes its name from a word meaning "bustling crowd", currently houses the **Musée des Beaux Arts** (daily: mid-June to Sept 10am–6pm; Oct to mid-June 1.30–6pm; €4.20, or €6 with history museum), having served at various times over the past 750 years as High Court and assembly room, prison, Revolutionary tribunal, theatre and marketplace. Upstairs there's a dull collection of paintings and engravings, heavy on worthy Breton artists such as J.-F. Boucher and Jean Frélaut, while the main gallery downstairs stages different temporary exhibitions.

The **Cathédrale St-Pierre** is a rather forbidding place, with its stern main altar almost imprisoned by four solemn grey pillars. Light, purple through the new stained glass, spears in to illuminate the finger of the Blessed Pierre Rogue, who was guillotined in the main square on March 3, 1796. Opposite this desiccated digit is the black-lidded sarcophagus that marks the tomb of the fifteenth-century Spanish Dominican preacher St Vincent Ferrier. For a small fee, you can in summer examine the assorted **treasure** in the chapterhouse, which includes a twelfth-century wedding chest, brightly decorated with enigmatic scenes of romantic chivalry.

▲ Vannes

A sombre fifteenth-century private mansion at 2 rue Noé, the Château Gaillard, holds Vannes' **Musée d'Histoire et Archéologie** (mid-May to mid-June daily 1.30–6pm, mid-June to Sept daily 10am–6pm; otherwise by appointment only, ⓣ02.97.01.63.00; €4.20, or €6 with Beaux Arts museum). Until recently, it was solely an archeological museum, focused on what's said to be one of the world's finest collections of prehistoric artefacts. However, although it certainly holds some elegant stone axes, for example, they're simply arrayed in formal patterns in glass cases. The museum's upper floors, designed to illustrate daily life in the Middle Ages, are more entertaining, and feature an interesting wood-panelled room, featuring 57 separate scenes of the lives of the "Desert Fathers", painted in 1606.

The Parc du Golfe

Vannes' major modern tourist attraction, the **parc du Golfe**, is located around 1km, or ten to fifteen minutes' walk, south of place Gambetta along the west (right) bank of the port. **Free shuttle buses** do the trip every fifteen minutes or so between 10am and 7pm from Monday to Saturday in July and August.

The main feature here is a modern **aquarium** that claims to have the best collection of tropical fish in Europe (daily: April–June & Sept 10am–noon & 2–6pm; July & Aug 9am–7.30pm; Oct–March 2–6pm, except school hols 10am–noon & 2–6pm; adults €10.30, under-12s €7.20; ⓦaquarium-du-golfe.com). Some of its specimens are certainly pretty extraordinary: four-eyed fish from Venezuela that can see simultaneously above and below the surface of the water, and are also divided into four sexes for good measure; cave fish from Mexico that by contrast have no eyes at all; and *arowana* from Guyana, which jump two metres out of the water to catch birds. A Nile crocodile found in the Paris sewers in 1984 shares its tank with a group of piranhas, while elsewhere there's a huge tank of black- and white-tipped sharks. Most species are identified with their French and Latin names, not necessarily their English ones.

Alongside the aquarium, the separate **Jardin aux Papillons**, or Butterfly Garden, consists of a huge glass dome containing hundreds of free-flying butterflies (same hours; adults €8.60, under-12s €6, or €15.10 and €10.60 respectively for combined ticket with aquarium; ⓦjardinauxpapillons.com).

Eating

Dining out in old Vannes can be expensive, whether you eat in the intimate little restaurants along the rue des Halles, or down by the port. Other, cheaper restaurants abound in the St-Patern quarter, outside the walls in the northeast, where rue de la Fontaine holds some simple Chinese and North African places.

The city's excellent **fish market** is held in the covered hall on place de la Poissonnerie every morning between Tuesday and Saturday. A general market spreads slightly higher up on the streets towards the cathedral on Wednesday and Saturday.

Afghan Café 12 rue de la Fontaine ⓣ02.97.42.77.77. This excellent restaurant provides a rare opportunity to try good Afghan cuisine, which centres around rice with fish, meat or vegetarian dishes and cardamon tea. Count on €25 a head, and demand is high, so book ahead. Dinner only, closed Mon.

Brasserie des Halles 9 rue des Halles ⓣ02.97.54.08.34. Inexpensive brasserie, open until midnight, which manages to squeeze a few tables out onto the pavement. For €11 you can get a bowl of mussels, for €19.50 a seafood *choucroute*, and there's a wide range of mainly fishy dishes at similar prices. Closed Sat lunch & Sun eve.

Crêperie La Cave St-Gwenaël 23 rue St-Gwenaël ⓣ02.97.47.47.94. Atmospheric, good-value crêperie in the cellar of a lovely old house, alongside the cathedral. Closed Sun, plus Mon Sept–June & all Jan.

Le Gavroche 17 rue de la Fontaine Pasteur ⓣ02.97.54.03.54. A true godsend for meat-lovers in a region dominated by fish restaurants. Here you can feast on truly excellent meat-packed menus starting at a mere €15, where the steaks are cooked to perfection and original starters such as pig's trotters – along with the complementary glass of potent home-made rum – will put hairs on your chest. Closed Sun & Mon.

Roscanvec 17 rue des Halles ⓣ02.97.47.15.96, ⓦroscanvec.com. Absolutely superb formal gourmet restaurant, in a lovely half-timbered house in the old town, with dining on two levels and also outdoors. Lunch at €20 is a bargain, while even the cheapest dinner menu, at €30, features unusual dishes such as *carbonara d'huîtres,* beautifully prepared and presented. For the standard, even the €60 "Hédoniste" menu is a bargain. Closed Sun in summer, Sun eve & all Mon Sept–June.

La Saladière 36 rue du Port ⓣ02.97.42.52.10. Large, tasty, fresh-made salads for €11–15, in an inexpensive restaurant just west of the port and tourist office, which also serves full lunch menus from €10 and dinner from €17. Closed Sun in low season.

Drinking and entertainment

The St-Patern quarter offers the highest single concentration of **bars** in the town centre, though most of them are low-key affairs. Otherwise, place Gambetta is usually lively. At the end of July, the open-air concerts of the **Vannes Jazz Festival** take place in the Théâtre de Verdure.

Buveur de Lune 8 rue St-Patern ⓣ02.97.54.32.32. A relaxed and good-natured spot for a drink with the night sky across the ceiling and fairly priced drinks. Closed Mon & Tues.

John R O'Flaherty 22 rue Hoche ⓣ02.97.42.40.11. A real Irish pub with the right ales on tap, various bits of junk on the walls and traditional Irish folk live on Friday nights. Closed Sun.

Salsa Caliente 27 rue du Maréchal Leclerc ⓣ02.97.47.04.53. Latino bar decorated with all things Cuban, where you can listen to the occasional live band and drink *mojitos* and other cocktails made, of course, with Cuban rum.

A Tribord 28 rue St-Patern ⓣ02.97.42.76.94. Lively, old-fashioned French bar, with a bit of a nautical theme, and serving snacks as well as drinks.

Listings

Bicycle rental Cycles Le Mellec, pl de la Madeleine, 51 rue Jean Gougaud ⓣ02.97.63.00.24.

Car rental Some of the main companies have offices at the *gare SNCF*, including: Avis ⓣ02.97.47.54.54; Budget ⓣ02.97.54.25.22; and Europcar ⓣ02.97.69.05.05.

Cinemas Cinéville Parc-Lann, rue Boucicaut and La Garenne, 12bis rue A. Le Pontois: both ⓣ08.92.70.21.31.

Pharmacie 19 rue Thiers ⓣ02.97.47.20.57 (Mon–Sat 8.45am–12.15pm & 2–7pm).

Post office 25 pl de la République ⓣ02.97.68.30.20 (Mon–Wed & Fri 8.30am–6.30pm, Thurs 8.30am–1.15pm & 2.30–6.30pm; Sat 8.30am–12.15pm).

Swimming pools Piscine Municipale, rue Winston Churchill ⓣ02.97.62.69.00; Piscine Municipale VanOcéa, 20 rue Émile Jourdan ⓣ02.97.62.68.00.

The southern shore: the Rhuys peninsula

Though the tip of the **Presqu'île de Rhuys** is just a few hundred metres across the mouth of the Gulf of Morbihan from Locmariaquer, it somehow seems to mark a distinctly southwards shift in climate. The Côte Sauvage is lost and in its wake appear pomegranates, fig trees, camellias, even vineyards (Rhuys produces the only truly Breton wine), along with cultivated oysters down below in the mud.

Unfortunately, due to fierce currents in the gulf, swimming from the north side of the peninsula is very unsafe. The **ocean beaches**, however, make much more promising destinations if you're hoping to sunbathe or play in the water. Fabulously long and sandy, they break out intermittently to either side of **St-Gildas-de-Rhuys**, amid the glittering gold- and silver-coloured rocks.

For details on the entire peninsula, call in at the **information centre**, just off the main D780 as you come into **Sarzeau** (July & Aug Mon–Sat 9am–12.30pm & 2–7pm, Sun 10am–1pm; Sept–June Mon–Sat 9.30am–12.30pm & 2–6pm, Sun 10am–12.30pm; Ⓣ02.97.26.45.26, Ⓦwww.rhuys.com).

Sarzeau and the Château de Suscinio

The D780 runs through the heart of the Rhuys peninsula, with no sea views to speak of. As it starts an extravagant curve south of **SARZEAU**, a short detour south along the D198 leads to the impressive fourteenth-century **Château de Suscinio** (daily: April–Sept 10am–7pm; Feb, March & Oct 10am–noon & 2–6pm; Nov–Jan 10am–noon & 2–5pm; €7; Ⓦsuscinio.info), set in marshland at the edge of a tiny village. Despite its redoubtable size, this completely moated castle never had any defensive purpose or military significance. Originally a hunting lodge of the dukes of Brittany, it has been very heavily restored, and now showcases the extensive remains of a remarkable medieval patterned **tiled floor**, which dates from 1330 and may well be the oldest in all France. You can also stroll around its high ramparts, and visit for musical or theatrical performances on summer evenings.

Sarzeau's nicest **hotel** is the *Connétable*, 3 place Richemont (Ⓣ02.97.41.85.48, Ⓦpagesperso-orange.fr/hotelfermine; ❸), though the cheapest rooms are not en suite. Its decent restaurant has lots of outdoor seating on the pretty square, and serves lunch from €12, dinner from €20. The best local **campsite**. *de la Plage*, is beside a long sandy beach just southeast of the castle (Ⓣ02.97.41.73.56, Ⓦcamping-de-la-plage.com; closed Nov–March).

St-Gildas-de-Rhuys

At **ST-GILDAS-DE-RHUYS**, 6km southwest of Sarzeau, Pierre Abelard, the theologian/lover of Héloïse, was abbot for a period from 1126, having been exiled from Paris. "I live in a wild country where every day brings new perils", he wrote to Héloïse, eventually fleeing after his brother monks – hedonists unimpressed by his stern scholasticism – attempted to poison him.

Beachfront **campsites** near the village include the luxurious four-star *Menhir* (Ⓣ02.97.45.22.88, Ⓦcamping-bretagnesud.com; closed early Sept to April), but there's no hotel.

The Tumulus de Thumiac and the Petit Mont

Just north of the main road as the peninsula narrows towards its western tip, the **Tumulus de Thumiac** is also known as the Butte de César, or "Caesar's Mount". Climb its summit to gaze out over the gulf, and you're standing where Julius Caesar supposedly watched the sea battle in which the Romans defeated the Veneti (see p.388) – the only naval victory they ever won away from the Mediterranean and out on the ocean. In fact, excavations in the nineteenth century revealed a 5000-year-old burial, complete with 32 stone axes and a pearl necklace.

Another ancient tumulus, the **Petit Mont**, stands in glorious isolation a little further along, on a slender promontory to the south that has been left entirely undeveloped. There's free access to the footpaths that circle the headland both halfway up – at which level they're lined by high hedges that almost entirely obscure any potential views – and along the coast at its base, which is a longer walk but serves up tremendous views out to sea, across the gulf, and also along the magnificent beaches on the southern shore of the peninsula.

The Petit Mont is topped by an exposed **prehistoric cairn** (April–June & Sept daily except Wed 2.30–6.30pm, tours 2.45pm & 4.30pm; July & Aug daily 11am–6.30pm, frequent tours; €6), much like those at Gavrinis and Barnenez, except that a German bunker was deliberately and destructively built into it in 1943, in order to be inconspicuous from the air. Visitors enter the cairn's deepest chamber, where 6000-year-old carvings can just about be discerned, by way of the bunker, which now holds displays on the site's history.

Arzon and Port Navalo

The pleasant little village of **ARZON** stands at the far western end of the peninsula. Immediately before the centre, however, the **Port du Crouesty** is a desperately unattractive modern marina, dominated by the hideous crab-like *Hôtel Miramar* (Ⓣ02.97.53.49.00, Ⓦmiramarcrouesty.com; ❾; closed mid-Nov to Dec). On first glance, **PORT NAVALO** at the very tip has little more character, but there's a cute beach tucked into the headland.

The best-value local **hotel** is the *Glann Ar Mor*, 27 rue des Fontaines in Port Navalo (Ⓣ02.97.53.88.30, Ⓦglannarmor.fr; ❹; closed mid-Nov to early Feb). For details of the **gulf cruises** from here, see p.369.

East of Vannes

Though Gavrinis and the Morbihan islands are the most exciting excursions from Vannes, various sights inland, **east of the city**, can fill a day's round-trip. Vannes' **traffic system** will do its damnedest to prevent you leaving the city in any direction, however, so you can't be too choosy about where you end up. Public transport is, as ever, not a viable alternative.

The Château de Largoët

The ruins of the **Château de Largoët**, also known as the Elven Towers, perch on an eminence in a small forest around 12km northeast of Vannes (May Sat & Sun 2.20–6.30pm; June & Sept daily except Tues 10.30am–12.10pm & 2.20–6.30pm; July & Aug daily 10.30am–12.10pm & 2.20–6.30pm; €4; Ⓦforteresselargoet.free.fr). Still guarded by its old gatehouse, carved all over with granite bunnies, the castle consists mainly of two stark towers, inside which the wooden flooring has long since rotted away to leave the shafts open to the sky. The *donjon* proper is topped by a finger-like watchtower, one of the highest in the country at over 45m, where from 1474 until 1476 the Breton Duke François imprisoned the future English king, Henry VII.

Le Gorvello and Questembert

A dozen kilometres due east of Vannes, the D7 passes straight through the beautiful village of **LE GORVELLO**. Bedecked with potted geraniums and huge azaleas, it has at its centre a perfect roadside cross.

Another 15km on, larger **QUESTEMBERT** centres on a low-roofed wooden market hall dating from 1675. Its ivy-coated **hotel** *Le Bretagne*, 13 rue St-Michel (Ⓣ02.97.26.11.12, Ⓦresidence-le-bretagne.com; ❻; closed second half of Nov & second half of Jan), is a renowned rendezvous for gourmets, with lavish rooms and a sumptuous, Michelin-starred **restaurant** (closed Mon, plus Sun eve & Tues lunch Oct–April), doing wonderful things with foie gras, sole and truffles on menus at €90, €120 and €165.

La Roche-Bernard

The southern shoreline of the Rhuys peninsula segues imperceptibly into the northern bank of the estuary of the Vilaine, which flows into the sea roughly 30km southeast of Vannes. When Viking longboats used the river to access the heart of Brittany, approaches to the Vilaine were guarded by the fortified settlement of **LA ROCHE-BERNARD** on the south bank, where the harbour continued to serve as what the French call the *avant-port* for Redon and Rennes into the twentieth century. Thanks to a massive dam near **ARZAL**, 5km downstream, sea-going vessels can no longer enter the Vilaine, but La Roche-Bernard remains a pretty little village that's well worth the detour down from the mighty suspension bridge that carries the N165 autoroute towards Nantes.

Most of the village stands atop the rocky headland that gave it its name, and fine medieval buildings cluster around the lovely little central place du Bouffay. Down at water level, a delightful promenade leads beside the river, where assorted quirky sculptures and memorials include a one-third-scale model of the mizzen mast of *La Couronne*, an enormous French naval galleon constructed here at the start of the eighteenth century.

Up in town, the flower-bedecked **hotel-restaurant** *Auberge des Deux Magots*, 1–2 place du Bouffay (ⓣ02.99.90.60.75, ⓦauberge-les2magots.com; ❸; closed Mon, plus last two weeks in June & Oct, and Sun eve Sept–June), serves a good-value €15 menu, and others up to €50. Down by the harbour, the *Petit Marin* (ⓣ02.99.90.79.41) is a large, inexpensive brasserie/crêperie with a waterfront terrace, while *Les Copains d'à Bord* (ⓣ02.99.90.81.03; closed Tues eve & Wed), a restaurant aboard a permanently moored boat, offers menus at €17–27. A charming **campsite**, *Le Pâtis* (ⓣ02.99.90.60.13, ⓦcamping-larochebernard.com; closed mid-Oct to mid-March), stretches along the riverbank, and rents out canoes, kayaks and motorboats.

In season, **river trips** set off to explore the broad estuary waters as far downstream as the dam, offering close-up views of the densely wooded slopes along the north bank (July & Aug 1–3 times each afternoon, April–June & Sept by reservation only; €10; ⓣ02.97.45.02.81, ⓦvedettesjaunes.com).

The Grande-Brière

South of the **River Vilaine**, you leave the Morbihan, and technically you leave Brittany as well, entering the *département* of Loire Atlantique. The roads veer firmly east and south, to Nantes and La Baule respectively. Inland between them, as you approach the wide Loire estuary, lie the otherworldly marshes of the **Grande-Brière**.

These eighty square kilometres of peat bog have for centuries been deemed to be the common property of all who live in them. The scattered population, the *Brièroise*, make their living by fishing for eels, gathering reeds and – on the nine days permitted each year – cutting the peat. The few villages are known as *îles*, being hard granite outcrops in the boggy wastes. Most consist of a circular road around the inside of a ring of thatched cottages, slightly raised above the waters on to which they back. For easy access to the watery flatlands, filled with lilies and irises and browsed by Shetland ponies, each village is encircled by its own canal, or *curée*. The houses themselves typically consist of two rooms and a stable, with a door on the north side and windows on the south. A few crops are grown in the adjacent fields, which always remain above high water.

Though this can be a captivating region for unhurried exploration, if you're simply passing through, the waterways are not very visible from the road unless you pause on one of the occasional humpback bridges. Instead, the widely touted attractions are taking a tour in either a horse-drawn **calèche** or a **punt**, known as a *chaland* or a *blain*. Both typically cost €8 for around 45 minutes, and you can also rent a punt for around €20 per hour, and pole your way through the bullrushes. Operators include Briére-Evasion, in **ST-LYPHARD** (Ⓣ02.40.91.41.96, Ⓦbriere-evasion.com), and La Chaussée Neuve, based 6km northeast of La Baule at **ST-ANDRÉ-DES-EAUX** (Ⓣ02.40.91.59.36, Ⓦbrieremahe.free.fr).

Much of the Grande-Brière is a **bird sanctuary**, home to vast numbers of waterfowl. The principal **tourist office** is on the northern fringes of the marshes, at 38 rue de la Brière in the village of **LA-CHAPELLE-DES-MARAIS** (June–Sept daily 10am–1pm & 2–6pm; Oct–May Mon–Fri 10am–1pm & 2–6pm, Sat 10am–1pm & 2–5pm; Ⓣ02.40.66.85.01, Ⓦwww.parc-naturel-briere.fr).

The most authentic surviving village, known as both **ST-JOACHIM** and **ÎLE DE FEDRUN**, is filled with traditional dwellings, and also holds a small, pricey **hotel**, *La Mare Aux Oiseaux*, 162 Île de Fedrun (Ⓣ02.40.88.53.01, Ⓦmareauxoiseaux.fr; ❼; closed Jan & March), where dinner menus start at €39.

The coast at the mouth of the Loire

There is something very surreal about emerging from the Brière to the coast at **La Baule**. For this is Brittany's most upmarket pocket – an imposing, moneyed landscape where the dunes are bonded together no longer with scrub and pines but with massive apartment blocks and luxury hotels. Nearby, **Guérande** is a superb medieval walled town, while **Piriac-sur-mer**, and to a lesser extent **Le Croisic**, are less frenetic alternatives. **St-Nazaire**, however, guarding the mouth of the Loire itself, is a run-down industrial port.

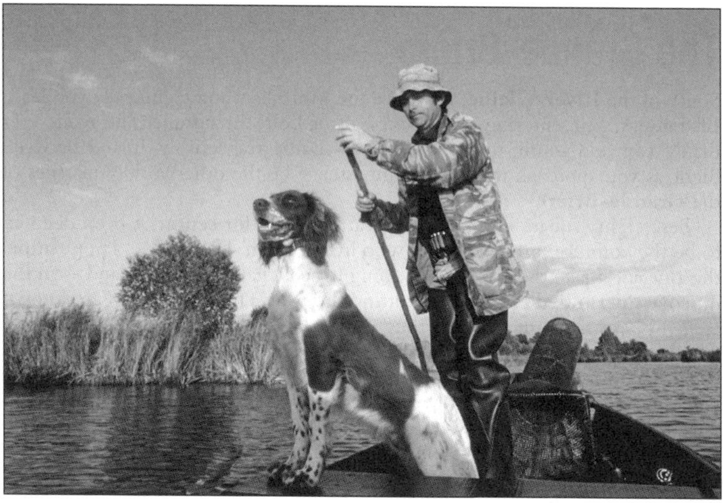

▲ Fisherman on the Grande-Brière

Guérande

No visitor to the region should miss the gorgeous walled town of **GUÉRANDE**, inland on the southwestern edge of the marshes of the Grande-Brière. Guérande derived its fortune from controlling the saltpans that form a chequerboard across the surrounding inlets. This "white country" is composed of bizarre-looking *oeillets*, each seventy to eighty square metres, in which sea-water has been collected and evaporated since Roman times, leaving piles of white salt.

Guérande, a tiny little place, is still entirely enclosed by its stout fifteenth-century **ramparts**. A spacious promenade leads right the way around the outside, passing four fortified gateways; for half its length, the broad old moat remains filled with water.

Within the walls, pedestrians throng the narrow cobbled streets during high season; the main souvenir on sale is locally produced salt, but abundant shops sell trinkets from all over the world, and there are lots of restaurants and crêperies. So long as the crowds aren't too oppressive, it makes a great day out, with the old houses bright with windowboxes. On Wednesdays and Saturdays, a market is in full swing in the centre, next to the **church of St-Aubin**.

You can only gain access to the top of the walls, and even then only to a short stretch that has no views into the town, via the disappointing **museum** of local history inside Guérande's original main entrance, the **Porte St-Michel** on its east side (April–Sept Mon 2.30–7pm, Tues–Sun 10am–12.30pm & 2.30–7pm; Oct Mon 2–6pm, Tues–Sun 10am–noon & 2–6pm; €4).

Practicalities

Guérande's **tourist office** is just outside the Porte St-Michel at 1 place du Marché au Bois (June & Sept Mon–Sat 9.30am–12.30pm & 1.30–6pm, Sun 10am–1pm & 3–5pm; July & Aug Mon–Sat 9.30am–7pm, Sun 10am–1pm & 3–5pm; Oct–May Mon–Sat 9.30am–12.30pm & 1.30–6pm; Ⓣ08.20.15.00.44, Ⓦot-guerande.fr). There's metered **parking** right here, or the free Guesny car park is a short walk away.

Near St-Aubin church, but tucked out of sight behind the market, the pretty *Roc-Maria*, 1 rue du Vieux Marché aux Grains (Ⓣ02.40.24.90.51, Ⓦhotel-creperie-rocmaria.com; ❹; closed Mon in low season), is a lovely little village **hotel** that offers cosy rooms above a crêperie in a fifteenth-century town house. Opposite the porte Vannetoise and the most impressive stretch of ramparts, to the north, *Les Voyageurs*, 1 place du 8 Mai (Ⓣ02.40.24.90.13; ❸; closed late Dec to late Jan, plus Sun eve & Mon), is a *logis* serving reasonable menus from €14. A short way further around the walls, near the tourist office, the *Remparts*, 14–15 bd du Nord (Ⓣ02.40.24.90.69; ❷; closed early Nov to mid-March; restaurant closed Sun eve & Mon Sept–July), offers less appealing rooms but better food.

Of the many central **restaurants**, the *Vieux Logis*, set within the walled garden of a grand old house facing the main church doors at 1 place de la Psalette (Ⓣ02.40.62.09.73), has something to suit every palette, with traditional menus from €25 at dinner, plus a separate crêperie/pizzeria.

Piriac-sur-mer

Still readily recognizable as an old fishing village, but lively all through summer with holidaying families, **PIRIAC-SUR-MER**, 13km west from Guérande is a ravishing old-fashioned seaside resort that knocks the socks off its giant neighbour La Baule. Although the adjacent headland offers fine sandy **beaches** within a couple of minutes' walk from the centre, the village itself turns its back on the Atlantic, preferring to face the protective jetty that curls back into the little bay to shield its small fishing fleet and summer array of yachts.

Practicalities

Recently spruced up by energetic young management, the red-striped *de la Plage*, at no. 2 on the quiet seafront place du Lehn (Ⓣ02.40.23.50.05, Ⓦhoteldelaplage-piriac.com; ❷; closed Oct–March), is just the most perfect French seaside **hotel** imaginable. The cheapest rooms lack en-suite facilities, but all are cheery and comfortable, and almost all have views of the sea. A friendly little café takes up most the ground floor, including the terrace. Alternatively, the *de la Poste*, a few streets in from the sea in a large house at 26 rue de la Plage (Ⓣ02.40.23.50.90, Ⓦpiriac-hoteldelaposte.com; ❸; closed Jan, restaurant closed Mon in low season), is a renovated *logis* with good rooms, serving menus from €27. The shady four-star *Parc du Guibel* (Ⓣ02.40.23.52.67, Ⓦparcduguibel.com; closed Oct–March), further on towards Mesquer, is one of several good local **campsites**, and has its own waterpark.

Piriac's twisting narrow lanes are crammed with **cafés**, **crêperies** and **brasseries**, as well as bucket-and-spade shops and ice-cream and candyfloss stalls. *La Vigie* (Ⓣ02.40.60.39.62, Ⓦlavigie.eu) is a good **restaurant** right beside by the port, where you can dine on oysters and mussels at the water's edge for around €20, while the flower-bedecked *St-Michel* (Ⓣ02.40.15.50.15), is a charming crêperie whose courtyard tables take up most of place de la Chope, between the old granite church and the beach.

La Baule

LA BAULE is certainly a place apart from its rival Breton resorts, almost any of which can seem appealingly rustic and shambolic by comparison. Sited on the long stretch of dunes that link the former island of Le Croisic to the mainland, it owes its existence to a violent storm in 1779 that engulfed the old town of Escoublac in silt from the Loire, and thereby created a wonderful crescent of sandy beach that's sometimes claimed to be the largest in Europe. That has survived, albeit now lined for several kilometres with a Riviera-style spread of palm-tree-fronted hotels and residences.

Neither La Baule's permanence nor its affluence seems in any doubt these days. This is a resort that very firmly imagines itself in the south of France: around the crab-shaped bay, bronzed nymphettes and medallion men stride across the sands against a backdrop of cruising lifeguards, horse-dung removers and fantastically priced cocktails. It can be fun if you feel like a break from the more subdued Breton attractions – and the beach is undeniably impressive. It's not a place to imagine you're going to enjoy strolling around in search of hidden charms, however; the backstreets have an oddly rural feel, but hold nothing of any interest.

Practicalities

La Baule's **tourist office** is away from the seafront at 8 place de la Victoire, close to the *gare routière* (July & Aug daily 9.30am–7.30pm; Sept–June Mon & Wed–Sat 9.15am–12.30pm & 2–6pm, Tues 10.15am–12.30pm & 2–6pm, Sun 10am–1pm; Ⓣ02.40.24.34.44, Ⓦlabaule.fr). Its main **gare SNCF**, served by TGVs from Paris, is La-Baule-Escoublac on place Rhin-et-Danube.

Few of the **hotels** are cheap, particularly in high season, and in low season more than half are closed. Relatively lower-priced options near the main *gare SNCF* include the comfortable *Marini*, 22 av Clemenceau (Ⓣ02.40.60.23.29, Ⓦhotel-marini.com; ❹), which has a lift and a swimming pool, while the *Mascotte*, 26 av Marie-Louise (Ⓣ02.40.60.26.55, Ⓦla-mascotte.fr; ❹; closed

Dec–Feb), is a quieter and classier option less than 100m back from the beach. The finest of the many local **campsites**, 2km from the sea, is the four-star *La Roseraie*, 20 av Sohier (Ⓣ02.40.60.46.66, Ⓦwww.laroseraie.com; closed Oct–March), which has a waterpark.

Right in the centre, set back less than 50m from the sea and not far from the tourist office, the *Lutetia* at 13 av Olivier Guichard (Ⓣ02.40.60.25.81, Ⓦwww.lutetia-rossini.com; ❻), has fancy rooms, but more importantly is home to the *Rossini* **restaurant** (closed Sun eve, Mon & Tues lunch), which offers magnificent fish cookery on full menus that start at €26.

Le Croisic

The small port of **LE CROISIC**, sheltering from the ocean around the corner of the headland, but stretching right across the peninsula, is an attractive alternative to La Baule. These days it's basically a pleasure port, but fishing boats do still sail from its harbour, near the very slender mouth of the bay, and there's a modern **fish market** near the long Tréhic jetty, where you can watch the day's catch being auctioned. The hills to either side of the harbour, Mont Lenigo and Mont Esprit, are not natural; they were formed from the ballast left by salt-trading ships.

Le Croisic holds a couple of excellent **hotels**: *Castel Moor*, 500m beyond the town centre towards the end of the headland, on the sheltered side (Ⓣ02.40.23.24.18, Ⓦcastel-moor.com; ❹; closed Jan), where there's a good restaurant, and *Les Nids*, set slightly back from the ocean side of the peninsula at 15 rue Pasteur (Ⓣ02.40.23.00.63, Ⓦhotellesnids.com; ❺; closed mid-Nov to March), which has its own small indoor swimming pool.

Close by, all around the rocky sea coast known as the **Grande Côte**, are a whole range of **campsites**, including the *Océan* (Ⓣ02.40.23.07.69, Ⓦcamping-ocean.com; closed Oct–March; around €18).

For equally good beaches, you could alternatively go east from La Baule to **PORNICHET** (though its overpriced, aseptic marina is worth avoiding) or to tiny **ST-MARC**, where in 1953 Jacques Tati filmed *Monsieur Hulot's Holiday*.

St-Nazaire

The best sandy coves in the region, bizarrely enough, are on the outskirts of **ST-NAZAIRE**: 1km west of town, they're linked by wooded paths and almost deserted. But the city itself is gloomy, distinguishable from afar by the black silhouettes of its mighty cranes and the soaring arch of the Loire bridge. Bombed to extinction in World War II, its shipyards, in more or less continuous operation since they built Julius Caesar's fleet, are closing all around it.

The one reason you might choose to stay in St-Nazaire is the relative ease of finding an inexpensive **hotel**. Modern, well-equipped options include the *Touraine*, 4 av de la République (Ⓣ02.40.22.47.56, Ⓦhotel-de-touraine.com; ❶), and the smarter, soundproofed *Korali*, opposite the station on place de la Gare (Ⓣ02.40.01.89.89, Ⓦwww.hotelkorali.fr; ❸), which has a nice **restaurant**.

South of the Loire

From St-Nazaire you can cross the mouth of the Loire via an inspired piece of engineering, the **Pont St-Nazaire**. This is a great elongated S-curve of a suspension bridge, its lines only visible at an acute angle at either end.

From this high viewpoint (up to 131m), you can see that the **Loire** is a definite climatic dividing line (a point regularly confirmed by French television weather bulletins). To the north of the river, the houses have steep grey-slate roofs against the storms; to the south, in the Pays de Retz, the roofs are flat and red-tiled. Nonetheless, vast deposits of Loire silt have affected both banks of the huge estuary – they buried the ancient town of Montoise on the southern side just as they did Escoublac to the north.

As you continue **south** along the coast, Brittany begins to slip away. Dolmens stand above the ocean, and the rocky coast is interspersed with bathing beaches, but the climate, the architecture, the countryside and, most obvious of all, the vineyards make it clear that this is the start of the south.

Pornic

The **Pays de Retz** coast is developed for most of its length – an almost unbroken line of holiday flats, Pepsi, *frites* and crêpes stands. **PORNIC**, the nicest of the resorts, has a functional fishing port and one of "Bluebeard" Gilles de Rais' many castles. It is a small place: you can walk beyond the harbour and along the cliffs to a tiny beach where the rock walls glitter from phosphorescent sea water.

Good-value **hotels** hereabouts include the seafront *Sablons*, at 13 rue des Sablons in Ste-Marie-sur-mer (ⓣ02.40.82.09.14, ⓦhotelesablons.com; ❹; restaurant closed Sun eve, all Mon & Tues lunch mid-Sept to mid-June), which serves good menus from €20.

Travel details

Trains

Auray to: Tire-Bouchon line (July & Aug 10 daily) to Plouharnel (20min) and Quiberon (40min).
Le Croisic to: La Baule (10 daily; 15min); Nantes (10 daily; 1hr 10min); Paris (4 daily TGVs; 3hr 15min); St-Nazaire (10 daily; 30min).
Pornic to: Nantes (2 daily; 1hr), with connections to Paris.
Vannes to: Auray (13 daily; 15min); Lorient (13 daily; 40min), with connections to Quimper (13 daily; 1hr 40min).

Buses

Auray to: Carnac (9 daily; 30min); Quiberon (10 daily; 1hr); Vannes (8 daily; 30min).
Lorient to: Pontivy (2 daily; 1hr 40min).
Vannes to: Arzon (4 daily; 50min); Auray (8 daily; 30min); Carnac (7 daily; 1hr 20min); La Roche-Bernard (3 daily; 1hr); Ploërmel (3 daily; 1hr 10min) via Elven (20min); Pontivy (9 daily; 1hr 10min); Quiberon (7 daily; 2hr).

Ferries

Belle-Île Ferry services detailed on p.355.
Groix Ferry services detailed on p.348.
Gulf of Morbihan For details of gulf tours and trips to the islands see p.369.
Houat and Hoëdic Ferry services detailed on p.358.
Lorient Shuttle service to Port-Louis (6.30am–8pm, every 30min; ⓣ02.97.21.28.29).

Contexts

Contexts

History

Although Brittany and Normandy have belonged to the French state for almost five hundred years, they have been distinct entities throughout recorded history, and their traditions and interests remain separate.

Brittany, for most of the five millennia during which its past can be traced, drew its cultural links and influences not inland, from the rest of France, but from the Atlantic seaboard. Isolated both by the difficulty of its marsh and moorland terrain, and its sheer distance from the heartland of Europe, it was nonetheless at the centre of a sophisticated prehistoric culture intimately connected with those of Britain and Ireland. It is populated today by descendants of the Celtic immigrants who arrived from Britain and Ireland around the time that the Romans were leaving Gaul. The "golden age" of Brittany came in the fifteenth century, when it was ruled as an independent duchy, but it was subsequently absorbed into France.

The economic decline of the province in recent centuries is attributed by Breton nationalists wholly to the union with France. Other factors, inevitably, were also at play, but it's certainly true that the rulers of France often ignored or oppressed their westernmost region, and even the current revival of Brittany's fortunes owes much to the conscious attempt to revive the old pan-Celtic trading routes.

Normandy has no equivalent prehistoric relics, and only very briefly was it an independent nation. Its founders were the Vikings who raided along the Seine in the ninth century. These Northmen gave the region its name, and brought it military glory in the great Norman age of the eleventh century, when William conquered England and his nobles controlled swaths of land as far afield as Sicily and the Near East. They were also responsible for the cathedrals, castles and monasteries that still stand as the most enduring monuments of Normandy's past.

The Normans blended into the general mass of the population, both in France and in England, and Normandy itself was surrendered to Louis IX by Henry III of England in 1259. After the Hundred Years War, the province was firmly integrated into France, and all but disappears from history until the Allied invasion of 1944.

The megaliths of Brittany

Megalithic sites can be found all around the Mediterranean, and along the Atlantic shoreline from Spain to Scandinavia. Among the most significant are Newgrange in Ireland, Stonehenge in England and the Ring of Brodgar in the Orkneys. However, there was not one, single megalith-building "civilization", and neither did the practice necessarily originate in the Mediterranean and spread out to the "barbarian" outposts of Europe. In fact, the tumuli, alignments and single standing stones of Brittany are of pre-eminent importance.

Late Stone Age settlements had been established along the Breton coast by around 6000 BC. Soon afterwards, the culture responsible either started building megaliths, or was displaced by megalith-building newcomers. Dated at 5700 BC, the tumulus of Kercado at **Carnac**, in southern Brittany, appears to be the earliest stone construction in Europe, predating even the Egyptian pyramids.

Little is known of the **people** who erected the megaliths. Those few skeletons that have been found in the graves seem to indicate a short, dark, hairy race with a life expectancy of no more than the mid-30s. All that's certain is that their civilization was long-lasting; the earliest and the latest constructions at Carnac are over five thousand years apart.

As for the **purpose** of the stones, there are far more theories than definite conclusions. Flaubert commented: "those who like mythology see them as the Pillars of Hercules; those who like natural history see here a symbol of the Python...lovers of astronomy see a zodiac". In the eighteenth century, for example, enthusiasts managed to see snakes in everything, and declared the megalithic sites to be remnants of some Druidic serpent cult; in fact the stones were already ancient before the Druids appeared.

These days, the most fashionable **theories** – with the general public at least – see the megaliths as part of a vast system of **astronomical measurement**, record-keeping and prediction. Precise measurements of sites all over Europe suggest that they share a standard measure of length, the "megalithic yard" – equivalent to 83 modern centimetres. In Brittany, the argument goes, the now fallen Grand Menhir of Locmariaquer was erected, using this prehistoric calibration, as a "universal lunar foresight". Its alignments with eight other sites are said to correspond to the eight extreme points of the rising and setting of the moon during its 18.61-year cycle. The Golfe de Morbihan made an ideal location for such a marking stone – set on a lagoon surrounded by low peninsulas, the menhir was visible from all directions. Once the need for the Grand Menhir was decided upon, it would then have taken hundreds of years of careful observation of the moon to fix precise positions for all the relevant sites. It is thought that this was done by lighting fires on the top of high poles at trial points on the crucial nights every nine years. The alignments of Carnac are thus explained as the graph paper, as it were, on which the lunar movements were plotted.

While certainly appealing, this "megalithic observatory" is by no means universally accepted. Controversy rages as to whether the Grand Menhir ever stood or, if it did, whether it fell or was broken up before the eight supposedly associated sites came into being. In addition, advocates are accused of ignoring the fact that the sea level in southern Brittany 6600 years ago was 10m lower than it is today.

In any case, the stones at Carnac have been so greatly eroded that perhaps it is little more than wishful thinking to imagine that their original size, shape and orientation can be accurately determined. They have been knocked down and pulled out by farmers seeking to cultivate the land; they have been quarried for use in making roads; they have been removed by landowners angry at the trespass of tourists and scientists; nineteenth-century pseudo-scientists have tampered with them, re-erecting some and shifting others; and what may have gone on in much earlier periods is anyone's guess.

An alternative approach, more popular with conventional archeologists, places much greater emphasis on sociological factors. This argues that the stones date from the great period of transition when humankind was changing from a predatory role to a productive one, and that they can only have been put in place by the coordinated efforts of a large and stable **community**. Some suggest that the megaliths were erected by Neolithic settlers, who generation by generation advanced across Europe from the east bringing advances in agriculture. Whether these technologically advanced newcomers displaced Brittany's previous inhabitants, or simply taught them new skills, remains unknown. The pattern all over the world, however, seems to be that people do not simply learn to plant seeds and grow crops, but they acquire a whole cultural package in the process, taking in prayers, beliefs and rituals along with new forms of social organization.

It takes a substantial community, with a settled economy and the capacity to create a large agricultural surplus, to erect large monuments. Their construction could also have demonstrated that the group responsible was "favoured" by the gods, and thus of "pure" or "noble" lineage.

An experiment in 1979 demonstrated that it takes 260 people, using rollers, to set up a 32,000-kilogramme stone, together with a large number of auxiliaries to provide food and shelter. It's surely inconceivable that entire alignments like those at Carnac could have been erected in one go. Instead, each stone or small group was presumably shaped, transported and put in place during a quiet period in the farming calendar. Perhaps the process involved an annual festival, to celebrate a successful harvest; or perhaps it was a more sombre, fearful ritual. Either way, the social significance of constructing these lines, mounds and circles may well have been of greater importance than any physical characteristics of the arrangements themselves.

Despite the pervasive legends, the megaliths cannot be attributed to the Celts. Even so, theological parallels have been drawn between ancient and modern **Breton beliefs**. It is argued that there is a specifically Breton attitude to death, dating back thousands of years, in which the living are in everyday communication with the dead. The phenomenon of the "parish close" (described on p.264) is said to mirror the design of the ancient passage graves, with the Christian ossuary serving the same function as the buried passageways of the old tombs – a link between the place of the dead and the place of the living.

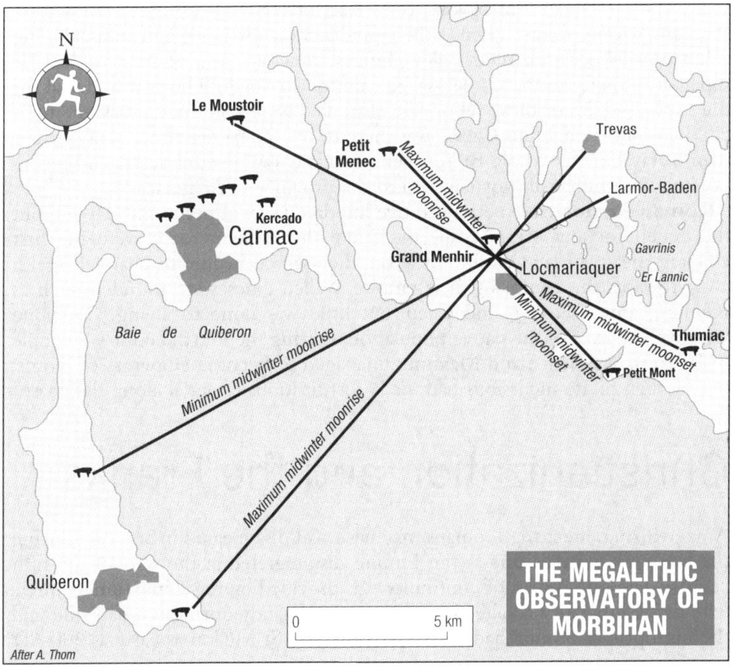

Celts and Romans

While Brittany in particular prospered during the **Bronze Age**, and was a major manufacturer of bronze axes that were distributed throughout Atlantic Europe, its peoples were left behind by the technological advances of the **Iron Age**, and became increasingly peripheral from 700 BC onwards. The economy turned instead towards supplying raw materials to the more developed cultures of Germany and southern France, and it is as traders in **tin and copper** that both the Bretons and the Normans make their first appearance in recorded history. Small trading ports emerged all along the Atlantic coast, and the routes went up the rivers Loire and Seine. The tin itself was mined in both Brittany and Cornwall, and the Seine became important as the "Tin Road", the most direct means for the metals to be transported towards the heart of Europe. Iron Age forts, such as the one of which traces survive in the forest of Huelgoat, show evidence of large-scale, stable communities even far inland.

That was why the **Romans**' top priority, when they came to Gaul centuries later, was to secure control of the Seine valley and tie the province firmly into the network of empire. Brittany, less accessible to the invading armies, was able to put up a more spirited resistance, although sadly there was no such last-ditch rebel stronghold as Astérix's fictional village. The **Breton Gauls**, descendants of a first influx of Celts, were divided into five major tribes, each of which controlled an area roughly corresponding to a modern *département*.

The most powerful of these tribes were the **Veneti**, based in the Morbihan with what is now Vannes as their capital. The decisive sea battle in which they were defeated in 56 BC took place around the Golfe du Morbihan, and was the only major naval battle the Romans ever won outside the Mediterranean. Ocean-going expeditions beyond the Pillars of Hercules were not among the Romans' strong points – hence their predilection for roads and foot-slogging – but on this occasion their galleys, built somewhere near St-Nazaire, had far superior mobility to the leather-sailed ships of the Veneti. The cost of defeat for the tribes was severe; those who were not killed were sold into slavery, and their children mutilated. Julius Caesar was there to see the battle; he went no further than Auray, but the whole Breton peninsula was swiftly conquered, and incorporated with much of Normandy into the province of Armorica.

Roman Armorica experienced five hundred years of peace, though without the benefit of any great prosperity. While the Roman roads were the first efficient means of land communication, they served mainly to channel wealth away towards the centre of their empire. Walled cities were founded, such as Rennes, Vannes, Rouen and Caen, but little was done to change, let alone improve, the lives of the native population. During the fourth century, a couple of Bretons, Magnence and Maximus, managed to become emperors of Rome, but by then pirate incursions had made fortifications essential along the coast.

Christianization and the Franks

Any civilizing effect the Romans may have had disappeared in any case during the **barbarian invasions** as the Empire disintegrated at the start of the fifth century. The one thread of continuity was provided by the **Christian** Church. The first Christians had already arrived in Normandy during Roman rule, and the bishopric at Rouen had been established by St Mellon as early as 300 AD.

They were followed in the fifth and sixth centuries by waves of **Celtic immigrants** crossing from Britain to Brittany. Traditional history considered these to be "Dark Ages" of terror and chaos throughout Europe, with the immigrants as no more than panic-stricken refugees. However, evidence of stable diplomatic and trading contact across the Channel suggests a much more ordered process of movement and interchange.

The vigorous Welsh and Irish missionaries named their new lands **Little Britain**, and their Christianity supplanted the old Celtic and Roman gods. That process is remembered in myth in terms of the confrontation of elemental forces – the Devil grappling with the Archangel Michael from Dol to Mont-St-Michel, St Pol driving out the "laidly worm" from the Île de Batz – which surely symbolize the forcible expulsion of paganism. Often the changes were little more than superficial: crosses were erected on top of menhirs, mystical springs and wells became the sites of churches, Christian processions such as *pardons* traced circuits of megalithic sites, and ancient tales of magic and witchcraft were retold as stories of Jesus and the saints. The names of innumerable Celtic religious leaders – Malo, Brieuc, Pol – have survived in place names, even if the Church has never officially recognized them as saints.

Cultural links with Britain and Ireland meant that Brittany played an important role in **Arthurian legends**. Breton minstrels, like their Welsh counterparts, did much to popularize the tales in the Middle Ages. None of the local sites that claim to be Arthur's Camelot carries much conviction, although Tristan who loved Iseult came from Brittany (the lovers may have hidden at Trémazan castle in Finistère), as did King Ban and his son Lancelot. Sir Galahad found the Holy Grail somewhere in Brocéliande Forest, said also to be the home of such diverse residents as Merlin, Morgane le Fay and the Fisher King.

Such legends reflect the fact that, for all this time, central Brittany was an almost impenetrable wilderness. The region as a whole was split into two separate petty monarchies, **Dumnonia** in the north and **Cornubia** (the basis of Cornouaille) in the south. Charlemagne amalgamated the two by force under **Frankish control** in 799, after they had consistently failed to pay tribute. When the Frankish Empire began to fall apart, their appointee as governor, **Nominoë**, seized the opportunity to become the first ruler of an independent Brittany, by defeating the Frankish leader Charles the Bald in the Battle of Redon (near modern La Bataille) in 845.

Without Celtic immigration on anything like the same scale, it took longer for **Normandy** to become fully Christianized. It was only when it too came under the control of Charlemagne's **Carolingian** dynasty that the newly founded monasteries of Jumièges and St-Wandrille became pre-eminent.

Over the succeeding centuries, as the authority of the Franks weakened, the **Vikings** repeatedly raided along the Seine, while similar raids on the Breton coast drove many monks into exile across the Channel. Major Viking incursions took place in the second half of the ninth century, interspersed with attempts to conquer England. The Vikings came more often and for longer, until in 911 King Charles the Simple acknowledged the inevitable and granted their leader **Rollo** formal title to the **Duchy of Normandy**. In their adopted French homeland, the pagan Scandinavians acquired the culture, language and religion of their new subjects so rapidly that spoken Norse died out in Rouen by the time of Rollo's grandson, Duke Richard I. Even so, they were still seen as a race apart.

A few years later, in 932, the Breton prince known as Alain Barbetorte returned from England to re-establish control over Brittany, and many of its monasteries were subsequently rebuilt in the new Romanesque style.

The Normans

During the eleventh century, **the Normans** became one of the most significant forces in Europe. Not only did the dukes of Normandy invade and conquer England, but Norman mercenaries and adventurers fought to gain lands for themselves wherever they could. They insinuated themselves into the wars of Italy, individually acquiring control of Aversa, Apulia and Calabria, as well as most of Sicily, their greatest prize. They took part in the Church's wars, too, fighting in Greece against Byzantium, and in the First Crusade – which in 1098 saw the Norman leader Bohemond take Antioch.

Duke William's **invasion of England** is portrayed by the Bayeux Tapestry as a just struggle: the result solely of William's conviction that he was the rightful heir to Edward the Confessor, a succession acknowledged under oath by Harold. Be that as it may, the sheer speed of what proved to be such a permanent conquest indicates the extent of Norman power at the time. Having crossed the Channel to defeat the usurper Harold in September 1066 in the **Battle of Hastings**, the Conqueror was crowned king in Westminster Abbey on Christmas Day, and by the next Easter was secure enough to be able to return to Normandy. Almost paradoxically, the Norsemen from France finally freed England from the threat of invasion from Scandinavia, which had persisted for centuries. English attention was thus reorientated towards the mainland of Europe – a shift that was to have a major impact on history.

The Norman capacity for **organization** was primarily responsible not just for these military triumphs, but also for the consolidation of power and wealth that followed. The Domesday Book, which catalogued the riches of England, was paralleled by a similar undertaking in Sicily, the *Catalogus Baronum*. William's son Henry introduced trial by jury in the king's courts – justice that had to be paid for. Henry II established the Exchequer to collect royal revenue.

Intellectually, too, the Normans were dominant; the Abbey of Bec-Hellouin, for example, was a renowned centre of learning, inspired first by Lanfranc and then by the theologian Anselm, each of whom moved on to become archbishop of Canterbury. And **architecturally**, the wealth and technical expertise of the Normans made possible the construction of such lasting monuments as the cathedrals of Bayeux, Coutances and Durham, and the monasteries of Mont-St-Michel, Jumièges and Caen.

The twelfth-century "**Anglo-Normans**" who invaded Ireland were recognizably descended from the army of the Conqueror, and Norman French remained the legal and administrative language of England until 1400. Elsewhere the mark of the conquerors was less distinct. The Norman kings of Sicily ruled a cosmopolitan society dependent largely on the skills of Muslim craftsmen. Their architecture barely resembles what is thought of today as "Norman", and the Norman bloodline soon vanished into the general population of Sicily.

However, for the duchy and the kingdom on either side of the Channel, the shared rulers made close connections inevitable. The Norman lords in England required luxury items to be imported. Flemish weavers were encouraged to settle in London and East Anglia, and gradually the centre of affluence and importance shifted away from Normandy. By the time Henry II, great-grandson of William the Conqueror, inherited the throne, England was a major power and the seeds of the Hundred Years War had been sown. Fifteen years later Château Gaillard on the Seine was taken by **Philippe Auguste**, and Normandy for the first time became part of France.

The Hundred Years War

While Normandy was at the height of its power, **Bretons** lived in constant fear of invasion by their belligerent neighbours. Although their own leaders had managed to prevent a parallel Viking takeover of Brittany, it was at the price of numerous **warlords** setting up their own private strongholds. Their emergence seriously weakened the authority of Nominoë's successors, and the resultant anarchy devastated the Breton economy. Frequent power bids by the Norman English and the kings of France – now referred to as the **Hundred Years War** – hardly helped the situation.

Bertrand du Guesclin, born in 1321 in the unprepossessing town of Broons, south of Dinan, ranks among the outstanding medieval military geniuses. After an ignominious start, when his father disowned him because of his ugliness, he developed his novel approach to war as an outlaw chief in the heart of Brittany. With little truck for chivalric conventions, he simplified the chaotic feudal map, and in a bewildering succession of French and Spanish campaigns earned the command of the French army. Eschewing prearranged battles in favour of ambush and general guerrilla tactics, he taught the French to fight dirty. Nobles were forced to dismount and fight on foot, while the fact that his soldiers were paid ensured that they did not alienate the peasantry by plundering. This formidable man also developed the use of gunpowder, in tandem with new assault techniques capable of devastating the strongest fortresses.

Thanks to du Guesclin's strategies, by 1377 the English had been driven almost completely out of France. Virtually every town and castle in Brittany and Normandy seems to have some du Guesclin connection; not only did he live, besiege or fight almost everywhere, but after his death in 1380 parts of his body were buried in no fewer than four different cities. Yet, despite his myriad intrigues and battles, Brittany benefited very little from his activities.

The Hundred Years War resurfaced after du Guesclin's death, with much of the fighting in Normandy. Henry V of England recaptured the province step by step, until by 1420 he was in a position to demand recognition of his claim to the French throne. Eight years later, the French were defending their last significant stronghold, Orléans on the Loire, when the extraordinary figure of **Joan of Arc** (see p.81) appeared on the scene and relieved the siege of the city. Through moral inspiration as much as military leadership, she ensured that the mass of ordinary, miserable peasants, not to mention the demoralized soldiers of the French army, made the enemy occupation untenable. Within two astonishing years, the Dauphin had been crowned, to become King Charles VII of France. Joan herself was captured by the Burgundian allies of the occupiers, tried by a French bishop and an English commander, and burned at the stake as a witch in Rouen. Nonetheless, in 1449, Charles VII was able to make a triumphal entry into the regional capital. Within twelve months this latest 32-year English occupation of Normandy was at an end.

The Duchy of Brittany

As the second phase of the Hundred Years War began, Breton involvement was minimal. Between 1399 and 1442, **Duc Jean V** remained neutral, allowing the economy of the province to prosper. Fishing, shipbuilding and sail manufacture developed, accompanied by a flowering of the arts that saw the construction of the Kreisker chapel and the church of Folgoët.

Although involvement in the Anglo-French conflict was inevitable, Jean's heirs for a time continued to rule over a successful and **independent duchy**. Arthur III, duke in the mid-fifteenth century, had fought alongside Joan of Arc, but he used his connections with the French army to protect Breton autonomy. His successor, however, Duc François II, was less astute. Brittany, the last large region of present-day France to resist agglomeration, was a very desirable prize for King Louis XI. In looking for allies beyond France, François antagonized and alarmed the French. A pretext was eventually found for the royal army to invade Brittany, where the Breton army was defeated at St-Aubin-du-Cormier in 1488. Duc François was forced to concede to the French king the right to determine his own daughter's marriage, and died of shame (so the story goes) within a few weeks.

François's heiress, **Duchess Anne**, was the last ruler of an independent Brittany. At first she defied the treaty of 1488, and attempted to forge an alliance against the French, first by becoming engaged to the Prince of Wales, and then by marrying Maximilian of Austria by proxy in 1490. However, Charles VIII of France (himself in theory married to Maximilian's daughter) demanded adherence to the treaty, captured Nantes, advanced north and west and proposed to Anne.

By and large the population preferred a royal wedding to death by starvation or massacre, and it duly took place on September 16, 1491. Anne bemoaned "Must I thus be so unfortunate and friendless as to have to enter into marriage with a man who has so ill-treated me?" – and then, to the amazement of all, the couple actually fell in love with each other. Despite the marriage, the duchy remained independent, but Anne was contractually obliged to marry Charles's successor should he die before they produced an heir. When Charles duly bumped his head and died in 1498, his successor, Louis XII, divorced his wife and married Anne. This time Anne's position was considerably stronger, and in the contract she laid down conditions that remained a source of Breton pride and frustration for many centuries. The three main clauses stipulated that no taxes could be imposed without the consent of the Breton *États*; conscripts were only to fight for the defence of Brittany; and Bretons could only be tried in their own courts. When Anne died, Bretons mourned a genuinely loved leader.

In 1514, the still independent duchy passed to Anne's daughter Claude, whom the future François I of France married with every intention of incorporating Brittany into his kingdom. This he did, and the permanent **union of Brittany and France** was endorsed by the Breton *États* at Vannes in 1532. In theory, the act confirmed Anne's stipulations that all the rights and privileges of Brittany would be observed and safeguarded as inviolable. However, it was rarely honoured, and its subsequent violation by successive French kings and governments has been the source of conflict ever since.

The ancien régime

As the French Crown consolidated its power and began to centralize its economy, the ports of the two western provinces developed, serving the **colonial interests** of the state. As early as 1364, sailors from **Dieppe** had established Petit Dieppe in what is now Sierra Leone. **Le Havre** was founded in 1517 to be France's premier Atlantic port and, between intermittent attacks and takeovers by the English, became a centre for the coffee and cotton markets. Sailors from Granville, Dieppe and Cherbourg set up colonies in Brazil, Canada, Florida and Louisiana.

In Brittany, **St-Malo** and **Lorient** were the two top trading ports; the latter benefitted whenever the English harassed Channel ports and shipping. **Jacques Cartier** of St-Malo sailed up the St Lawrence River and added Canada to the possessions of France. Nantes too was an important base for trade with the Americas, India and the Middle East, with **slaves** an especially profitable "commodity". Though the business of exploitation and battles with rival foreign ships was motivated by private profit, the net result was very much to the advantage of the state.

Thanks to its early contacts with England, and the cosmopolitan nature of its Channel ports, Normandy became one of the main **Protestant** centres of France, with Caen and its university having very active Huguenot populations. The region was therefore in the front line when the **Wars of Religion** flared up in 1561–63, and again in 1574–76. When the Edict of Nantes, with its privileges and immunities for Protestants, was revoked, large-scale Huguenot emigration took place, seriously damaging the local textile industry.

Brittany on the other hand had a minimal Protestant presence, and the Wars of Religion were only significant as a cover for a brief attempt to win back independence. Breton linen manufacture had taken advantage of the lack of French tolls and customs dues, and only declined much later, when England, post-Industrial Revolution, flooded the market with mass-produced textiles.

Although the power of the French kings increased over the centuries, outlying regions were not always entirely under royal control. The rural nobles were persistently lawless, and intermittent **peasant revolts** took place. In 1675 Louis XIV's finance minister put a tax on tobacco, pewter and all legal documents to raise money for the war with Holland. The ensuing "Stamped Paper" revolt, which started with riots in Nantes, Rennes and Guingamp, soon spread to the country, with the peasants making very similar demands to those of the revolutionaries over a hundred years later. The aristocracy took great delight in brutally crushing the uprising, pillaging several towns and stringing up insurgents and bystanders from every tree.

The reign of **Louis XIV** saw numerous infringements of Breton liberties, including the uprooting of vines throughout the province on the grounds that the people were all drunkards. If the Bretons could not get revenge they could at least be entertained by court scandals. In 1650 Louis's Superintendent of Finance, **Nicolas Fouquet**, bought the entire island of Belle-Île and fortified it as his own private kingdom. The alarmed king had to send D'Artagnan and the three musketeers to arrest him before his ambitions went any further.

While taxes on Brittany increased in the early eighteenth century, Normandy found new prosperity by feeding Paris. Lacemaking too became a major regional industry, and several abbeys that had been closed during the Wars of Religion were now revitalized. However, by 1763 France had lost Canada and given up all pretensions to India. The ports declined and trade fell off as England became the workshop of the world.

Revolution

At first, the people of both Brittany and Normandy welcomed the **French Revolution**. Breton representatives at the États Généraux in Paris seized the opportunity to air all Brittany's grievances, and the "Club Breton" they formed was the basis of the **Jacobins**. Caen, meanwhile, became the centre of the bourgeois **Girondist** faction. In August 1789 it was a Breton *député* who proposed the abolition of privileges. However, under the Convention it became clear that the price to be paid for the elimination of the *ancien régime* was further reductions in local autonomy and the suppression of the Breton language.

Neither province was sympathetic to the execution of the king – 30,000 people took to the streets in Rouen to express their opposition. The Girondins came out worst in the factional infighting at the Convention. Some Girondist deputies managed to flee the edict of June 2, 1793 which ordered their arrest, but the army they organized to march on Paris was defeated at Pacy-sur-Eure. The final major Norman contribution to Revolutionary history was provided that same day by **Charlotte Corday** of Caen, when she stabbed Jean-Paul Marat in his bath.

The concerted attack on religion and the clergy was not happily received, particularly in Brittany where the Church was closely bound up with the region's independent identity. An attempt to conscript an army of 300,000 Bretons was deeply resented. The popular image of the Revolution in Brittany was now further damaged by the brief **Reign of Terror** in 1793 of Carrier, the Convention's representative in Nantes. Under the slogan "all the rich, all the merchants are counter-revolutionaries", he killed perhaps 13,000 people in three months, by such methods as throwing prisoners into the Loire tied together in pairs. This was done without Tribunal sanction or approval, and Carrier was himself guillotined before the end of the year.

All this made Brittany an inevitable focal point for the Royalist **counter-revolution** known as the *Chouannerie*. A vast invasion force of exiled and foreign nobility, backed by the English, was supposed to sweep through France, rallying all dissenters to the royalist flag. In the event only 8000 landed at Quiberon in 1795, and they could not even escape from the self-imposed trap of the peninsula. Instead, they devastated what little they could before being brutally massacred. Much local support was motivated by the age-old desire to win back independence, but Breton *Chouans* ("screech owls") fighting elsewhere ended up being abandoned to years of quixotic and doomed guerrilla warfare.

A rebel army continued to fight sporadically in the Cotentin and the Bocage until 1800, while in Brittany another **royalist revolt** in 1799 was easily crushed. In 1804, Cadoudal, "the last *Chouan*", was captured and executed in Paris, where he had gone to kidnap Napoléon – having refused the emperor's offer of a generalship if he surrendered.

The nineteenth century

Normandy at the beginning of the nineteenth century remained wealthy, despite the crippling of its ports by the blockade imposed by the European coalition against Napoléon. Proportionally, five times as many of its people were eligible, as property owners, to vote as in the impoverished mountain areas of the south, while its agriculture accounted for eleven percent of France's produce on six percent of its land. Only industry remained relatively unadvanced.

When protectionist tariffs were removed from grain in 1828, and Normandy was forced to compete with other producers, widespread **rural arson and tax riots** ensued. But, when the revolution of 1848 offered the prospect of socialism, the deeply conservative Catholic peasantry showed little enthusiasm for change. Even the re-emergence of a rural textile industry in the 1840s, relying on outworkers brutally exploited by the capitalists of Rouen, added no radical impetus.

The advent of the **railways** and the patronage of the imperial court encouraged the development of Normandy's resorts, while along the Seine watermills provided the power for major spinning centres at Louviers, Évreux and Elbeuf. Serious decline did not come until the 1880s, when **rural depopulation** was brought on by emigration combined with a low birth rate – and a high death rate in which excessive drinking played a part.

Nineteenth-century Brittany was no longer an official entity, save as five *départements* of France. The railways were of negative benefit, submitting the province to competition from more heavily industrialized regions, while the Nantes–Brest canal did not achieve the expected success, and **emigration** increased from here too. Culturally, the century witnessed a revival of Breton language, customs and folklore, but the initiative came from intellectuals rather than from the mainly illiterate masses.

Around the turn of the **twentieth century** both provinces experienced a surge of artistic creativity, with painters such as Gauguin in Pont-Aven and Monet in Giverny, and such writers as Marcel Proust in Normandy and Pierre Loti in Brittany.

As everywhere in Europe, this idyll was shattered by the **Great War**. Although far from the actual front, both Brittany and Normandy were dramatically affected. Brittany, for its size, suffered the heaviest death toll of anywhere in the world. The vast memorial at Ste-Anne-d'Auray is testimony to the extent of the loss, while a parallel spiritual grief can be seen in the dramatic growth in Normandy of the cult of the recently dead Thérèse of Lisieux.

World War II and the Battle of Normandy

That the **beaches of Normandy** were chosen as the site of the Allied invasion of Europe in June 1944 was by no means inevitable. Far from the major disputed areas and communication routes of Europe, Normandy had seen almost no military activity since the Hundred Years War. But in that blazing summer six armies and millions of men fought bloody battles across the placid Norman countryside. Much of the province was in ruins by the time Hitler's defensive line was broken and the road to Paris cleared.

France had surrendered to the Germans in 1940. A year later, the fascist armies turned east to invade the Soviet Union. America and Britain declared full support for the Soviets but resisting Stalin's demand for a second front. In 1942 the two western powers promised a landing in northern France, but all that ensued was an abortive commando raid on Dieppe (see p.56). By the time the second front materialized, the tide of the war had already been turned at Stalingrad.

The Germans had meanwhile fortified the whole northwest seaboard of Europe. Their **Atlantic Wall** was constructed from spring 1942 onwards by the Todt organization, previously responsible for building the German *Autobahn* network. Although it used thirteen million cubic metres of concrete, and 1.2 million tons of steel, it was never an unbroken continuous line, and the senior German officer in France later described it as a "giant bluff".

From the Allied point of view, any invasion site had to lie within range of air support from Britain, which meant anywhere from Rotterdam to St-Malo. Nonetheless, the Nazis expected the attack to come at the Channel's narrowest point, across the Straits of Dover. The **D-Day invasion** of June 6, 1944, was presaged by months of intensive aerial bombardment across Europe, without concentrating too obviously on the chosen landing sites. In the event, the Nazis vastly overestimated Allied resources – two weeks after D-Day Rommel still thought the Normandy landings might be no more than a preliminary diversion to a larger-scale assault around Calais. After all, as a British photographic survey of the whole Norman coast – even prewar holiday snaps had been requisitioned – had conclusively established, none of the Norman channel ports was susceptible to easy capture.

As a result, the landings used amphibious craft to storm the **beaches** of Normandy, rather than its ports. On Utah Beach, the Atlantic Wall lasted for little more than five minutes; on Gold, Juno and Sword beaches, it was overrun in about an hour; and even on Omaha, where the sea turned red with blood, it took less than a day for the Allies to storm through.

Albert Speer summed up the failure of the wall by saying: "A fortnight after the first landings by the enemy, this costly effort was brought to nothing by an idea of simple genius…the invasion forces brought their own harbours with them". These "**Mulberry**" **harbours**, as described on p.127, proved the key to the Allied victory.

The basic plan was for the British and Commonwealth forces under Montgomery to strike for Caen, the pivot around which the Americans (whose General Eisenhower was in overall command) were to swing following their own landings further west. Not everything went smoothly. There are appalling stories of armoured cars full of men plunging straight to the bottom of the sea as they rolled off landing craft unable to get close enough to the shore. Many early objectives took much longer to capture than was originally envisaged – the British took weeks rather than hours to reach Caen, while American hopes of a rapid seizure of the deep-water port at Cherbourg were thwarted. Most notorious of all, the opportunity to capture the bulk of the German army, which was all but surrounded in the "Falaise pocket", was lost.

Almost five thousand of the 156,000 soldiers who landed on D-Day itself were killed. In all, between June 6 and August 22 1944, a total of 124,400 US soldiers and 82,300 from the UK and Canada lost their lives.

Military historians say that man for man the German army was the more effective fighting force; but with their sheer weight of resources the Allies achieved a fairly rapid victory. Crucially, the concentration of German air power on the eastern front meant that there was never a significant German air presence over Normandy. Parachutists, reconnaissance flights and air support for ground troops were all able to operate virtually unimpeded, as too were the bombing raids on Norman towns and on every bridge across the Seine west of Paris. Furthermore, the muddled enemy command, in which generals at the front were obliged to follow broad directives from Berlin, caused an American general to comment, "one's imagination boggled at what the German army might have done to us without Hitler working so effectively for our side".

Within a few days of D-Day, the leader of the Free French, **General de Gaulle** was able to return to France, making an emotional first speech at Bayeux, while a seasick Winston Churchill sailed up to Deauville in a destroyer and "took a plug at the Hun". At the end of July, General Patton's Third Army broke out across Brittany from Avranches with the aid of 30,000 **French Resistance** fighters, and on August 25 Allied divisions entered Paris, where the German garrison had already been routed by the Resistance. In the east the Red Army were sweeping back the Axis powers.

Though the war in Europe still had several bloody months to run – Hitler made a desperate last attempt to smash the western front during the Ardennes offensive of December 1944 – the road to Berlin was finally opening up.

Postwar: the Breton resurgence

The war left most of **Normandy** in ruins: while the province remained relatively prosperous in terms of its produce, decades of reconstruction were required. The development of private transport also meant that Normandy became ever more filled with the second homes of the rich. This has often been resented – the movie actor Jean Gabin, for example, was literally besieged in his new country house by hundreds of peasants insisting that he had "too much land", and was obliged to sell some of it off.

Meanwhile, very little was happening in **postwar Brittany** save ever-increasing migration from the countryside to the main towns, and from there, often, out of the province altogether. By the 1950s some 300,000 Bretons lived in Paris, industry was almost exclusively limited to the Loire estuary, and agriculture was dogged by archaic marketing and distribution.

However, since the late 1960s Brittany has experienced considerable economic regeneration, due in part to the initiatives of **Alexis Gourvennec**. He first came to prominence at the age of 24, in 1961, when he led a group of fellow farmers into Morlaix to occupy the government's regional offices in an effective (if violent) protest at exploitation by middlemen. The act set the pace for his lifetime's concern – to obtain the best possible price for Breton agricultural produce. To this end he lobbied Paris for a deep-water port at Roscoff, and once that was built his farmers' cooperative set up Brittany Ferries to carry Breton artichokes and cabbages to English markets (see box, p.258).

Brittany Ferries has prospered, thanks to the British and Irish entry to the EC upon which Gourvennec had gambled. Yet, despite Gourvennec's enthusiasm for his Celtic cousins, there have been several instances of ugly **protectionism** – attacking British lorries importing meat, violently breaking up strikes in Brittany and forcibly preventing Townsend Thorensen from starting a rival ferry service to St-Malo.

In 1973 a semi-decentralized **regional administration** was set up to provide an intermediate level between the *départements* and the State. Normandy, being rich, became two regions – *Basse*, with its capital in Caen, and *Haute*, centred on Rouen – while Brittany was a single entity, but lost the Loire-Atlantique *département*, which included what was traditionally its principal city, **Nantes**. The new boundaries had no impact on people's perception of the provinces, though they did start to have some practical consequence when the Socialist government increased regional powers in 1981.

Fishing and **agriculture** remain the mainstays of the Breton economy, though the former has never benefited from an equivalent to Gourvennec. Both arenas have been subject to increasingly bitter intra-European disputes. The economic survival of Breton fishermen in particular has been seriously threatened by a flood of cheap imports from the factory-fishing trawlers of the former Soviet Union. In 1994, five thousand fishermen rioted in the streets of Rennes, and a stray flare set light to the roof of the ancient Breton Parliament.

Thirty percent of fish caught by British vessels are exported to Europe through French ports, and Channel ports have been repeatedly blockaded, with hypermarkets being ransacked and Scottish fish landed at Roscoff destroyed by angry mobs. In response to a threat by trawlermen wishing to fish for scallops and spider crabs, to blockade the Channel Islands, the French government reduced the tax burden on self-employed fishermen, and set minimum prices for cod, haddock, coley and monkfish.

Despite the loss of its traditional industrial centres on the Loire estuary, including the shipbuilding town of St-Nazaire, Brittany has nonetheless managed to expand its industrial base, with the advent of a Citroën plant at Rennes being one high-profile example. The development of the ultra-fast Paris–Brest TGV rail link in particular, inaugurated in 1989, has made a considerable difference. Growth in Normandy has been less spectacular, but the region entered the twenty-first century with something of a resurgence, spearheaded by the high-tech facilities of Caen.

Politically, Bretons always used to supply an above-average proportion of the national conservative vote, with the most traditional, rural, areas being the most conservative of all. In recent national elections, however, the region has come to favour the left.

The **separatist movement**, as a positive celebration of the Breton nation rather than a reactionary throwback, has never been all that powerful. In 1932 a bomb in Rennes destroyed the monument to Franco-Breton unity, and since 1966 the Front de Libération de Bretagne has intermittently attacked such targets as the nuclear power station in the Monts d'Arrée, and the Hall of Mirrors at the palace of Versailles in 1978. They were joined in 2000 by the shadowy **Breton Liberation Army** (ARB), which carried out a succession of bombings that culminated with an explosion that killed an employee at a *McDonald's* restaurant outside Dinan.

The emphasis for most Breton activists these days is on cultural pride rather than militancy. The idea is to establish a clear and vital sense of national identity – to create, as one leader put it, "the spiritual basis for a new political thrust". Although overall use of the Breton language may be declining, it is taught in schools, and great stress has been placed on its historical and artistic significance.

Perhaps the biggest ongoing story in recent years has been the catastrophic succession of **oil spills** along the coastline. Ever since the foundering of the *Torrey Canyon* off Ouessant in 1967, and the devastation when the *Amoco Cadiz* sank off northern Finistère in 1978, Bretons have come to dread the coming of the *marées noires* or "black tides". Another major disaster came at the end of 1999, when the Maltese super-tanker *Erika* sank off southern Brittany, releasing around 23,000 tonnes of pollutants into the Atlantic ocean.

Ongoing controversy has also centred on Cogema's UP3 nuclear reprocessing plant at **Cap de la Hague**, near Cherbourg in Normandy. The state-owned facility "reprocesses" spent nuclear fuel from power stations all over the world, and in doing so discharges 230 million litres of nuclear waste each year into the Atlantic. Analysis of the ocean floor in the vicinity has shown it to be so contaminated that legally the stones on the sea bed should themselves be classified as controlled nuclear waste. **Greenpeace** researchers have labelled the La Hague plant as "the single largest source of radioactive contamination in the European Union", and also "the single largest source of aerial radioactivity in the world". The French authorities continue to stonewall on the issue, proud of the fact that 75 percent of the country's electricity is produced by nuclear power stations.

Tourism to both regions remains strong, despite such factors as the recession, the decline in cross-Channel ferry routes since the advent of the Channel Tunnel and the "toxic seaweed" crisis of 2009 (see p.235). More visitors than ever seem to be touring Normandy's invasion beaches, even though 2009's commemorations of the 65th anniversary of D-Day, attended by presidents Obama and Sarkozy, were inevitably attended by fewer veterans than before. 2009 also saw the prospect raised that **Brittany** will finally return to its historic borders; a widely accepted report into the administrative reorganization of France recommended that Nantes and the entire Loire-Atlantique department should be re-integrated into the province.

Books

Both Brittany and Normandy have been written about extensively, in literature and history. Books that played a helpful or enjoyable role in preparing this guide are listed below; those marked ⋆ are especially recommended.

Prehistory and megaliths

Aubrey Burl *Megalithic Brittany.* Detailed guide to the prehistoric sites of Brittany, area by area. Very precise on how to find each site, and what you see when you get there, but little historical or theoretical overview.

⋆ **John Michell** *Megalithomania.* General popularizing work about megaliths everywhere, with a lot of entertaining descriptions of how visitors have reacted to them.

Mark Patton *Statements in Stone.* Sober, scientific account of Brittany's megalithic heritage, reappraised in the light of archeological discoveries.

A. Thom and A.S. Thom *Megalithic Remains in Britain and Brittany.* A scientific rather than anecdotal account of the Thoms' extensive analysis. The mathematics and astronomy can be a bit overpowering without necessarily convincing you of anything.

⋆ **Uderzo and Goscinny** *Astérix the Gaul.* Breton history mixed together in a magic cauldron.

History and politics

John Ardagh *France in the New Century: Portrait of a Changing Society.* Detailed journalistic survey of modern France, with an interesting and relevant section on "Brittany's revival".

Alfred Cobban *A History of Modern France.* Very thorough, three-volume political history from Louis XIV to de Gaulle.

Patrick Galliou and Michael Jones *The Bretons.* Accessible and illuminating account of Breton history from the megaliths, through the Romans, as far as the union with France.

⋆ **Frank McLynn** *1066: The Year of The Three Battles.* Myth-busting exploration of what really happened in 1066, which reveals how close the Norman invasion came to failure.

François Neveux *A Brief History of the Normans: The Conquests That Changed the Face of Europe.* Accessible overview of who the Normans were, how they rose to prominence and what became of them.

Graham Robb *The Discovery Of France.* Captivating study of the evolution and "civilization" of France since the Revolution, which makes a superb antidote to conventional narratives of kings and state affairs.

Barbara Tuchman *Distant Mirror.* A history of the fourteenth century as experienced by a French nobleman. Makes sense of the human complexities of the Hundred Years War.

⋆ **Mark Twain** *Joan of Arc.* Little-known fictionalized biography of Joan by America's greatest nineteenth-century writer; quite extraordinarily hagiographic considering his normal scorn for religion.

Ian W. Walker *Harold: The Last Anglo-Saxon King.* This first full-length biography puts flesh on the bones of the man whom William defeated at the Battle of Hastings.

Theodore Zeldin *France 1845–1945*. Five thematic volumes on French history.

The Normandy landings

Stephen Ambrose *D-Day*. Six hundred-page extravaganza by the doyen of American historians, chronicling the minutiae of the Normandy landings.

Anthony Beevor *D-Day: The Battle For Normandy*. This consistently absorbing re-appraisal has instantly become the definitive account of the Allied invasion of Normandy.

Paul Fussell *The Boys' Crusade: American GIs in Europe – Chaos and Fear in World War Two*. This short reflection on the lives of the young American soldiers who took part in the D-Day campaign is heavily coloured by Fussell's own wartime experiences, which makes for a fascinating polemic.

Max Hastings *Overlord*. Balanced and objective history of D-Day and its aftermath; Hastings distances himself thoroughly from propaganda and myth-making.

John Keegan *Six Armies in Normandy*. A fascinating military history, which combines the personal and the public to original effect. Each of the participating armies in the Battle of Normandy is followed during the most crucial phase of its involvement; some of the lesser details of the conflict are missed, but the overall sweep is compelling.

Studs Terkel *The Good War*. Excellent collection of interviews with participants of every rank and nation, including civilians, in World War II.

Art and architecture

Henry Adams *Mont-St-Michel and Chartres*. Extraordinary, idiosyncratic account of the two medieval masterpieces, attempting through prayer, song and sheer imagination to understand the society and the people that created them. A tribute to Norman wisdom.

John Ardagh *Writers' France*. Entertaining anecdotes about most of the writers mentioned in this book, with colour photos.

Christina Björk *Linnea in Monet's Garden*. A Swedish book for children, which tells the story of a young girl achieving her unlikely lifetime's dream of visiting Monet's home in Giverny. A well-illustrated introduction to the Impressionists.

Claire Joyes *Monet at Giverny*. Large-format account of Monet's years at Giverny, combining biography with good reproductions of the famous waterlilies.

Brittany in fiction

Honoré de Balzac *The Chouans*. A hectic and crazily romantic story of the royalist *Chouan* rebellion shortly after the Revolution, set mainly in Fougères.

Alexandre Dumas *The Three Musketeers*. Brilliant swashbuckling romance with peripheral Breton scenes on Belle-Île and elsewhere.

Victor Hugo *Ninety-Three*. Rather more restrained, but still compelling, *Chouan* novel.

Jack Kerouac *Satori in Paris*...and in Brittany. Inconsequential anecdotes.

Pierre Loti *An Iceland Fisherman*. Much-acclaimed nineteenth-century realist novel (filmed in 1924), focusing on the whaling fleets that sailed from Paimpol, and now finally available in translation.

Normandy in fiction

Julian Barnes *Flaubert's Parrot*. A lightweight novel which rambles around the life of Flaubert, with much of the action taking place in Rouen and along the Seine.

Peter Benson *Odo's Hanging*. Delicate but dramatic fictionalized account of the human stories behind the creation of the Bayeux Tapestry.

Gustave Flaubert *Bouvard and Pécuchet*. Two petits-bourgeois retire to a village between Caen and Falaise and attempt to practise every science of the time. Very funny or dead boring, according to taste.

Gustave Flaubert *Madame Bovary*. "The first modern novel", by the Rouennais writer. Drawn from a real-life story from Ry (see p.91) it contains little that is specifically Norman, however.

Marcel Proust *In Remembrance of Things Past*. Dense, dreamily disturbing autobiographical trilogy, evocative of almost everything except the places in Normandy and Brittany to which his memories take him back.

Julian Rathbone *The Last English King*. Lyrical and extremely readable fictionalized version of the Norman Conquest, as told by King Harold's one surviving bodyguard. The Normans themselves are depicted as heartless villains.

Jean-Paul Sartre *Nausea*. Sartre's relentlessly gloomy description of just how unpleasant it was to drag out one's existence in Le Havre (or "Bouville") in the 1930s.

Henry Treece *Hounds of the King and Man with a Sword*. Classic children's fiction that provides a vivid picture of the Normans and their world.

Breton myth and folk tales

Pierre-Jakez Hélias *The Horse of Pride*. This deeply reactionary and sentimental account of a Breton childhood in the Bigouden district of the early twentieth century has sold over two million copies in France.

Professor Anatole Le Braz *Celtic Legends of the Beyond: A Celtic Book of the Dead*. The definitive text on Breton myths centred on Ankou and the prescience of death.

F.M. Luzel *Celtic Folk-Tales from Armorica*. A collection of timeless Breton fairy stories, in English, and complete with commentaries.

W.Y. Evans Wentz *The Fairy Faith in Celtic Countries*. Bizarre survey of similarities and differences in folk beliefs and religion between Celtic nations, with extensive details about Brittany.

Breton music

Drawing richly in its themes, style and instrumentation on the common Celtic heritage of the Atlantic seaboard, Breton **music** has remained for centuries a unifying and inspiring part of the culture of the province. It has survived the union with France and the general attempt by the French state to suppress indigenous art and language.

However, attempting to pin even an approximate date on the origins of traditional Breton music is a haphazard business. No literature survives in the native tongue prior to the fifteenth century, although wandering Breton minstrels, known as *conteurs*, had enjoyed great popularity abroad long before that. Many of the songs they wrote were translated into French, being otherwise unintelligible to audiences outside Brittany, but unfortunately both versions have vanished with time. Only a number of Norse and English translations, probably dating from the twelfth century, escaped destruction. These works tell of romances won and lost, acrimonious relationships between fathers and their sons, and the testing of potential lovers.

The historical record of Breton music begins with the publication of **Barzaz-Breiz**, a collection of traditional songs and poems, in 1839. Compiled by a nobleman, Hersart de la Villemarqué, from his discussions with fishermen, farmers and oyster-and-pancake women, it has come to be acknowledged as a treasure of Breton folk culture. Serious doubts have been raised as to its authenticity – many sceptics believe Villemarqué doctored those parts of the material he found distasteful, and even composed portions of it himself – but it is unquestionably a work of linguistic brilliance and great beauty, and its appearance triggered the serious study of popular Breton culture. Following in La Villemarqué's footsteps, the far more scrupulous folklorist **Francois-Marie Luzel** (1821–95) published four large volumes of ballads and songs, and three volumes of folk tales, between 1868 and 1890.

During the last hundred years, and especially since World War II, Brittany's traditional music and folk culture has been a major vehicle for the expression of Breton national identity. Countless Breton music and dance clubs were formed all over Brittany and beyond (notably Paris). In order to bequeath this rich and unique culture to future generations, huge effort was put into collecting and recording Breton music and songs, and **Dastum**, a central library of Breton music, song and folklore, was established. Like its Irish and Scottish counterparts, Breton music remains popular with all ages.

Styles and instrumentation

According to the harpist Alan Stivell, "Breton music is a Celtic music… While other Europeans favour a diatonic scale, Celtic musics have a tendency to go back to a pentatonic scale". Produced for example by playing just the black keys on a keyboard, the pentatonic scale has five tones to the octave. Its widespread use is what gives not only traditional Breton music, but also Gregorian chant and traditional Scottish, Irish and Chinese music, their distinctively melancholy, minor-key sound.

Perhaps the most quintessentially Breton of all instruments is the **bombarde**, a double-reed descendant of the medieval shawm. While it looks like a shortened version of the oboe, its tone is more vigorous and bracing; depending on your mood, it can sound like either a hypnotic trance-inducing paean to the gods, or a sackful of weasels being yanked through a mincer. Traditionally, the *bombarde* is played either solo or as part of a duet or *couple*, alongside a **biniou** or bagpipe. Brittany boasts two principal kinds of bagpipe: the **biniou braz** or "big bagpipe" is the Scottish bagpipe with three drones, while the **biniou koz** or "old bagpipe" is much smaller, has a single drone, and its piercing sound is an octave higher. In a *couple*, the *bombarde* can be played in unison with the *biniou* or in a call-and-response alternation known as *kan ha diskan*, in which the opening and closing phrases overlap. Other than the drone(s) of the *biniou*, there are no harmonies.

Pipe-bands or **bagadou** are very popular, and pipe-band competitions attract large crowds. The first-ever Breton pipe band was only put together in the 1940s, but there are more than a hundred on the circuit today. Their precise size and make-up varies, but as a rule they consist of around twenty-five musicians: eight *binious* (*braz*), ten *bombardes*, and seven drums, of which four are snare drums, two tenor drums and one a bass drum. Most *bagadou* include both traditional and composed material in their repertoire, and the most accomplished are renowned for their innovation and range. Thus **Bagad Men ha Tan** have collaborated with Senegalese percussionists, while **Bagad Kemper** have expanded to include a brass section, and have recorded with traditional vocalists, jazz musicians and rock groups.

While the *biniou* and *bombarde* were traditionally played outdoors, the **telenn** or **Breton harp** began life in the Middle Ages as an indoor, courtly instrument. Its use had dwindled almost to extinction before the Breton cultural resurgence of the nineteenth and twentieth centuries. Although Jord Cochevelou achieved local fame as both a maker of, and a composer for, the Breton harp, it was his son **Alan Stivell** who brought it to worldwide fame, with his milestone 1972 recording *Renaissance of the Celtic Harp*. Several other Breton harpists are worth looking out for, such as the group **An Triskell**, which features the virtuoso brothers Pol and Herve Queffeleant, **Dominig Bouchaud**, **Kristen Nogues** and **Myrzhin**, who has played with Afro-Celt Sound System among others.

Instruments more familiar to outsiders include the **violin**, which is descended from the medieval rebec (*rebed* in Breton). Very common in Brittany until a century ago, this only returned to prominence with the folk revival of the 1960s, and the increasing influence of Irish bands. The best-known Breton practitioners are **Jacky Molard**, **Christian Lemaitre** and **Fanch Landreau**. The **guitar** too has become ubiquitous, whether played solo or as part of larger groups; **Dan Ar Braz**, **Soig Siberil** and **Jacques Pellen** are equally renowned in both roles. In addition, the **accordion** has enjoyed a certain popularity ever since it was brought to Brittany by soldiers returning from the trenches of World War I; **Yann-Fanch Perroches** is the best-known modern practitioner.

Until the 1960s, Breton **songs** were normally sung unaccompanied, often by solo performers. Performances and recordings of either unaccompanied, or minimally accompanied, singing remain common. Traditional songs fall into several distinct categories, including **gwerziou**, sombre or serious ballads; **soniou**, lighter songs about love, for instance, or drinking; and sacred songs, known as **kanticou**. Deeply rooted and beautiful, this latter style has been enhanced by the twentieth-century development of combining **church organ** with *bombarde* to produce haunting renditions of religious music. At the same time, Breton **singer-songwriters** are producing original material of high quality. Pre-eminent among them is **Gilles Servat**, who sings in both Breton and French, and mixes his own protest songs and modern chansons with long-established Breton pieces.

Traditional dance music

Each of the many different rhythms in **Breton dance tunes** tends to be associated with different dance steps, and to originate from a distinct region of Brittany. The most common form of dance music has long been that performed by **sonneurs de couple**, a pair of musicians playing *bombarde* and *biniou*. While following the same melody line, with a drone from the *biniou*, they pursue a steadily accelerating tempo, each taking turns in call and response. The second player chimes in with the last three or so notes of the first player, and then vice versa, each musician overlapping and covering as the other pauses for breath.

The purely vocal counterpart to this is known as **kan ha diskan**. Once again intended as dance music, it's performed by a pair of "call-and-response" singers. In its basic form, the two unaccompanied singers – the *kaner* and the *diskaner* – alternate phrases, joining each other at the end of each phrase. As there were no amplifiers in the past, singers used a high-pitched nasal tone to ensure that their voices would carry. They might also give dancers the odd break by performing a *gwerz*, or ballad, again unaccompanied.

Such traditional accompaniments have been increasingly supplanted by four- or five-piece **folk groups**, who add fiddle and accordion, and sometimes electric bass and drums, to the *bombarde*, and less often the *biniou*. As the tunes are reinterpreted, the *gwerz* singers are giving way to folk-style singer-songwriters, with guitar backing. Purists might regret the changes, but they have probably ensured the survival of *festou-noz*, with the enthusiastic participation of musicians and dancers of all ages.

Festou-noz

The liveliest setting in which to hear traditional Breton music is a *Fest-Noz* or "Night Feast", a night of serious dancing (and drinking). A *Fest-Noz* (plural *Festou-noz*) was originally an outdoor music-and-dance event, and thus especially suited to the summer months. Nowadays, however, *Festou-noz* take place year round, usually in large halls but also in barns in rural areas. Once the

Live music and festivals

Visitors to Brittany get the chance to enjoy Breton music at several annual festivals. The most famous of these is the Lorient festival inter-Celtique. Others include Quimper's Festival de Cornouaille (mid–late July), Rennes's Tombées de la Nuit (early July), and the intimate Printemps de Châteauneuf-du-Faou (Easter Sunday).

In addition, most Breton towns and villages have cafés and pubs that offer live music. Try:

Brest *Les Dubliners, Café le Triskel* and *the Bar Écossais.*

Douarnenez *Le Pourquois Pas.*

Gouarec (near Gourin) *Bar de Daoulas.*

Lorient *Galway Inn* and *Tavarn ar Roue Morvan.*

Plouyé *Ti Elise.*

Plouhinec (near Lorient) *Café de la Barre.*

Quimper *Ceili Bar.*

Rennes *Barantic.*

evening gets underway, people dance in great circles, often in their hundreds, hour after hour, sometimes lively and leaping, sometimes slow and graceful with their little fingers intertwined. Joining in is an exhilarating experience – it's easy to learn, just copy what everyone else does.

Festou-noz have nurtured successive generations of Breton musicians, and served as a springboard for bands such as **Strobinell**, with their line-up of *bombarde*, *biniou*, violin, flute and guitar, who eventually move on to join the festival and concert circuit. Over the years, an electrified *Fest-noz* sound has also developed, complete with drum kit, as epitomized by bands like **Bleizi Ruz** (Red Wolves) and **Sonerien Du** (Black Musicians). The most musically innovative band of all, **Gwerz**, started out by making several CDs of traditional songs and instrumentals, using *bombarde*, *biniou*, clarinet, violin and guitars; members these days concentrate on solo projects.

Contemporary Breton Music

Breton music has come a long way since **Alan Stivell** led one of Europe's first folk-rock bands in the late 1960s. Stivell played harp and bagpipes alongside Dan Ar Braz on electric and acoustic guitar, performing a repertoire that drew on wider Celtic traditions. Both artists still perform and record separately in the folk-rock idiom.

Thirty years on, groups such as Gwerz and latterly **Skolvan** have added subtle jazz and Eastern European touches to their interpretations of Breton music, while Gwerz's singer **Erik Marchand** has been even bolder, performing *gwerziou* with a Romanian gypsy band and playing with Sardinian and Gallego musicians. Marchand is emblematic of a steady modern flow of innovative cross-cultural music from Breton musicians, due in no small part to the fact that more Bretons live in Paris – one of the great hubs of world music – than in any city in Brittany. Notable collaborations include those of **Kerhun** with Moroccan Gnawa musicians, and the Breton/Algerian confluences to be found in the music of Cheb Mami, Thalweg, Mugar, Idir and Tayfa.

An exhilarating creativity pervades current Breton "roots" music. **Manau** and **Denez Prigent** have mixed techno and club sounds with traditional airs and ballads, while Prigent has also presented very contemporary messages within the ancient tradition of *gwerziou*. His work with Lisa Gerrard (for the movie soundtrack *Black Hawk Down*) and Nabil Khalidi has produced thrilling new blends and textures. Similarly, **Bagad Kemper** have performed and recorded with the South African Zulu rock group Johnny Clegg & Savuka, as well as splicing together jazz horns including saxophone, guitarists and a singer with a full pipe band. Meanwhile **Didier Squiban's** *Breton Piano Trilogy* displays classically polished solo piano jazz variations on traditional Breton themes.

Breton singing too is exploring new territory, from the dramatic Brechtian cabaret delivery of **Marthe Vassallo's** *gwerziou*, with their stark and lurid accordion accompaniment, to the bluesy, surreal, satirical, darkly poetic songs of **Bernez Tangi** and **Denez Abernot**.

Websites

To listen to Breton music online, access radio station **Arvorig FM** (Ⓦarvorigfm.com). To buy it, go to the website of the **Ar Bed Keltiek** music and book shop

(Ⓦarbedkeltiek.com); to record companies such as Gallomusic (Ⓦgallomusic.fr); or to general retailers like Amazon (Ⓦamazon.fr) and FNAC (Ⓦfnac.com). *Festou-noz* are well publicized locally with posters and leaflets, but you can also find up-to-the minute listings on Ⓦtamm-kreiz.com and Ⓦfest-noz.net.

By Paul Matheson, drawing on an original piece by Raymond Travers.

Recommended discography

Compilations

Breton Music For Dummies (Keltia Musique)

Fest Vraz (Keltia Musique)

Bombarde and biniou

Youenn Le Bihan (*bombarde*) and **Patrick Molard** (*biniou koz*) *Er Bolom Koh*

Patrick Molard (*biniou braz*) *Deliou*

Bagadou (Pipe-bands)

Bagad Bleimor *Sonerezh Geltiek*

Bagad Kemper *Hep Diskrog; Azeliz Iza*

Bagad Men Ha Tan & Doudou N'Diaye Rose *Dakar*

Telenn

Dominig Bouchaud *L'Ancre d'Argent*

Alan Stivell *Renaissance of the Celtic Harp; Trema'n Inis; 1 Douar*

Triskell *Rowan Tree*

Violin

Christian Lemaitre, Jacky Molard, Fanch Landreau et al. *Archétype*

Jacky Molard, Patrick Molard & Jacques Pellen *Triptyque*

Guitar

Dan Ar Braz *Xavier Grall chanté par Dan Ar Braz*

Jacques Pelenn *Les Tombées de la Nuit*

Soig Siberil *Gwenojenn*

Church music

Anne Auffret, Jean Baron & Michel Ghesquiere *Sacred Music from Brittany*

Anne Auffret, Daniel Le Feon & Loik Le Griguer *Pardoniou*

Yann-Fanch Kemener & Anne Auffret *Roue Gralon/Ni ho Salud!*

Vocal

Annie Ebrel *Tre ho ti ha ma hini*

Yann-Fanch Kemener & Didier Squiban *Enez Eusa*

Erik Marchand & Thierry Robin *Songs of Central Brittany*

Denez Prigent *Live Holl a-gevret!*

Marthe Vassallo & Philippe Ollivier (aka "Bugel Koar") *Ar Solier*

Dance music

Various *Kan ha Diskan*

Various *Voix de Bretagne*

Festou-noz

Bleizi Ruz *En Concert*

Frères Guichen *Dreams Of Brittany*

Gwerz *Live*

Pennou Skoulm *Fest-noz*

Sonerien Du *Steir*

Singer-songwriters

Louis Capart *Patience; Rives Gauches de Bretagne et d'Ailleurs*

Gilles Servat *Les Albums de la Jeunesse; Je Vous Emporte Dans Ma Coeur*

Triskell/Gilles Servat *L'Albatros Fou*

Contemporary Breton Sounds

Denez Abernot *Tri Miz Noz*

Bernez Tangi *Eured an Diaoul*

Cheb Mami *Meli Meli*

Kerhun et les Gnawa *Lila-Noz*

Erik Marchand *Kan*

Erik Marchand et le Taraf de Caransebes *Dor; Sag an Tan Ell*

Ozan Trio *Prizioù*

Les Ramoneurs de Menhir *Dañs an Diaoul*

Red Cardell *Le Banquet du Cristal*

Storlok *Stok ha Stok*

Tayfa *Assif*

Language

Language

Language

Although **Breton** (see box, p.422) is still a living language, every encounter you have with local people in both Brittany and Normandy will almost certainly be conducted in **French**. Thanks to the number of words and structures it shares with English, French can seem deceptively familiar, but it's not a particularly easy language to pick up. The bare essentials, however, are not difficult to master, and can make all the difference. Even just saying "Bonjour Madame" or "Bonjour Monsieur" when you go into a shop, and then pointing, will usually get you a smile and helpful service. People working in hotels, restaurants and tourist offices almost always speak some English, and tend to use it even if you're trying in French – be grateful, not insulted.

Pronunciation

One easy rule to remember is that **consonants** at the ends of words are usually silent. *Pas plus tard* (not later) is thus pronounced "pa-plu-tarr". But when the following word begins with a vowel, you run the two together: *pas après* (not after) becomes "pazaprey".

Vowels are the hardest sounds to get right. Roughly:

a as in h**a**t
e as in g**e**t
é between g**e**t and g**a**te
è between g**e**t and g**u**t
eu like the **u** in h**u**rt
i as in mach**i**ne
o as in h**o**t
o, au as in **o**ver
ou as in f**oo**d
u as in a pursed-lip version of **u**se

More awkward are the **combinations in/im, en/em, an/am, on/om, un/um** at the ends of words, or followed by consonants other than **n** or **m**. Again, roughly:

in/im like the an in **an**xious
an/am, en/em like the on in D**on**caster when said with a nasal accent
on/om like the on in Doncaster said by someone with a heavy cold
un/um like the u in **u**nderstand

Consonants are much as in English, except that: *ch* is always "sh", *c* is "s", *h* is silent, *th* is the same as "t", *ll* is mostly like the "y" in yes, *w* is "v" and *r* is growled (or rolled).

Basic words and phrases

French nouns are divided into masculine and feminine. This causes difficulties with adjectives, whose endings have to change to suit the nouns they qualify – you can talk about *un château blanc* (a white castle), for example, but *une tour blanche* (a white tower). If you're not sure, stick to the simpler masculine form – as used in this glossary.

Phrasebooks and courses

Rough Guide French Phrasebook (Rough Guides). Mini-dictionary-style phrasebook with both English–French and French–English sections, along with cultural tips for tricky situations and a menu reader.

Harrap's Mini French Dictionary (Harrap). Surprisingly comprehensive French–English and English–French dicitionary, with a brief guide to grammar and pronunciation.

Breakthrough French (Palgrave Macmillan). Excellent teach-yourself course, in three levels.

Get Into French Course Pack (BBC Worldwide). BBC beginners' course, with book, CD and CD-Rom. See also ⓦwww.bbc.co.uk/languages/french for a free, 24-part online audio course, "French Steps".

Essentials

hello (morning or afternoon)	bonjour
hello (evening)	bonsoir
good night	bonne nuit
goodbye	au revoir
thank you	merci
please	s'il vous plaît
sorry	pardon/Je m'excuse
excuse me	pardon
yes	oui
no	non
OK/agreed	d'accord
help!	au secours!
here	ici
there	là
this one	ceci
that one	celà
open	ouvert
closed	fermé
big	grand
small	petit
more	plus
less	moins
a little	un peu
a lot	beaucoup
cheap	bon marché
expensive	cher
good	bon
bad	mauvais
hot	chaud
cold	froid
with	avec
without	sans
entrance	entrée
exit	sortie
man	un homme
woman	une femme (pronounced "fam")

Numbers

1	un
2	deux
3	trois
4	quatre
5	cinq
6	six
7	sept
8	huit
9	neuf
10	dix
11	onze
12	douze
13	treize
14	quatorze
15	quinze
16	seize
17	dix-sept
18	dix-huit
19	dix-neuf
20	vingt

21	vingt-et-un	95	quatre-vingt-quinze
22	vingt-deux	100	cent
30	trente	101	cent-et-un
40	quarante	200	deux cents
50	cinquante	300	trois cents
60	soixante	500	cinq cents
70	soixante-dix	1000	mille
75	soixante-quinze	2000	deux milles
80	quatre-vingts	5000	cinq milles
90	quatre-vingt-dix	1,000,000	un million

Time

today	aujourd'hui	now	maintenant
yesterday	hier	later	plus tard
tomorrow	demain	at one o'clock	à une heure
in the morning	le matin	at three o'clock	à trois heures
in the afternoon	l'après-midi	at ten-thirty	à dix heures et demie
in the evening	le soir	at midday	à midi

Days and dates

January	janvier	Sunday	dimanche
February	février	Monday	lundi
March	mars	Tuesday	mardi
April	avril	Wednesday	mercredi
May	mai	Thursday	jeudi
June	juin	Friday	vendredi
July	juillet	Saturday	samedi
August	août	August 1	le premier août
September	septembre	March 2	le deux mars
October	octobre	July 14	le quatorze juillet
November	novembre	November 23	le vingt-trois novembre
December	décembre	2009	deux mille neuf

Talking to people

When addressing people a simple *bonjour* is not enough; you should always use *Monsieur* for a man, *Madame* for a woman, *Mademoiselle* for a young woman or girl. This isn't as formal as it seems, and it has its uses when you've forgotten someone's name or want to attract someone's attention.

Do you speak English?	Parlez-vous anglais?	I'm...	Je suis...
		...English	...anglais[e]
How do you say it in French?	Comment ça se dit en français?	...Irish	...irlandais[e]
		...Scottish	...écossais[e]
What's your name?	Comment vous appelez-vous?	...Welsh	...gallois[e]
		...American	...américain[e]
My name is...	Je m'appelle ...	...Australian	...australien[ne]

...Canadian	...canadien[ne]
...a New Zealander	...néo-zélandais[e]
...South African	...sud-africain[e]
I understand	Je comprends
I don't understand	Je ne comprends pas
Can you speak slower?	S'il vous plaît, parlez moins vite
How are you?	Comment allez-vous?/ Ça va?
Fine, thanks	Très bien, merci
I don't know	Je ne sais pas
Let's go	Allons-y
See you tomorrow	À demain
See you soon	À bientôt
Leave me alone (aggressive)	Fichez-moi la paix!
Please help me	Aidez-moi, s'il vous plaît

Finding the way

bus	autobus/bus/car
bus station	gare routière
bus stop	arrêt
car	voiture
train/taxi/ferry	train/taxi/bac
boat	bâteau
plane	avion
shuttle	navette
train station	gare (SNCF)
platform	quai
What time does it leave?	Il part à quelle heure?
What time does it arrive?	Il arrive à quelle heure?
a ticket to...	un billet pour...
single ticket	aller simple
return ticket	aller retour
validate your ticket	compostez votre billet
valid for	valable pour
ticket office	vente de billets
how many kilometres?	combien de kilomètres?
how many hours?	combien d'heures?
hitchhiking	autostop
on foot	à pied
Where are you going?	Vous allez où?
I'm going to...	Je vais à...
I want to get off at...	Je voudrais descendre à...
the road to...	la route pour...
near	près/pas loin
far	loin
left	à gauche
right	à droite
straight on	tout droit
on the other side of	à l'autre côté de
on the corner of	à l'angle de
next to	à côté de
behind	derrière
in front of	devant
before	avant
after	après
under	sous
to cross	traverser
bridge	pont
town centre	centre ville
all through roads (road sign)	toutes directions
other destinations (road sign)	autres directions
upper town	ville haute/haute ville
lower town	ville basse/basse ville
old town	vieille ville

Questions and requests

The simplest way of asking a question is to start with *s'il vous plaît* (please), then name the thing you want in an interrogative tone of voice. For example:

Where is there a bakery?	S'il vous plaît, la boulangerie?
Which way is it to the Eiffel Tower?	S'il vous plaît, la route pour la tour Eiffel?
Can we have a room for two	S'il vous plaît, une chambre pour deux?
Can I have a kilo of oranges?	S'il vous plaît, un kilo d'oranges?

Question words

where?	où?
how?	comment?
how many/how much?	combien?
when?	quand?
why?	pourquoi?
at what time?	à quelle heure?
what is/which is?	quel est?

Accommodation

a room for one/two persons	une chambre pour une/deux personne(s)
a double bed	un grand lit/un lit matriomonial
a room with two single beds/twin	une chambre à deux lits
a room with a shower	une chambre avec douche
a room with a bath	une chambre avec salle de bain
for one/two/three nights	pour une/deux/trois nuits
Can I see it?	Je peux la voir?
a room on the courtyard	une chambre sur la cour
a room over the street	une chambre sur la rue
first floor	premier étage
second floor	deuxième étage
with a view	avec vue
key	clef
to iron	repasser
do laundry	faire la lessive
sheets	draps
blankets	couvertures
quiet	calme
noisy	bruyant
hot water	eau chaude
cold water	eau froide
Is breakfast included?	Est-ce que le petit déjeuner est compris?
I would like breakfast	Je voudrais prendre le petit déjeuner
I don't want breakfast	Je ne veux pas de petit déjeuner
bed and breakfast	chambre d'hôte
Can we camp here?	On peut camper ici?
campsite	camping/terrain de camping
tent	tente
tent space	emplacement
hostel	foyer
youth hostel	auberge de jeunesse

Driving

service station	garage
service	service
to park the car	garer la voiture
car park	un parking
no parking	défense de stationner/stationnement interdit
petrol/gas station	poste d'essence
fuel	essence
unleaded	sans plomb
leaded	super
diesel	gazole
(to) fill it up	faire le plein
oil	huile
air line	ligne à air
put air in the tyres	gonfler les pneus
battery	batterie
the battery is dead	la batterie est morte
plugs	bougies
to break down	tomber en panne
gas can	bidon
insurance	assurance
green card	carte verte
traffic lights	feux
red light	feu rouge
green light	feu vert

Cycling

to adjust	raxler
ball bearing	le roulement à billes
battery	la pile
bent	tordu
bicycle	le vélo
bottom bracket	le logement du pédalier
brake cable	le cable
brakes	les freins
broken	cassé
bulb	l'ampoule
chain	la chaîne
cotter pin	la clavette
to deflate	dégonfler
dérailleur	le dérailleur
frame	le cadre
gears	les vitesses
grease	la graisse
handlebars	le guidon
to inflate	gonfler
inner tube	la chambre à air
loose	déserré
to lower	baisser
mudguard	le garde-boue
pannier	le pannier
pedal	le pédale
pump	la pompe
puncture	la crevaison
rack	le porte-bagages
to raise	remonter
to repair	réparer
saddle	la selle
to screw	visser/serrer
spanner	la clef (mécanique)
spoke	le rayon
to straighten	rédresser
stuck	coincé
tight	serré
toe clips	les cale-pieds
tyre	le pneu
wheel	la roue

Health matters

doctor	médecin
I don't feel well	Je ne me sens pas bien
medicines	médicaments
prescription	ordonnance
I feel sick	Je suis malade
I have a headache	J'ai mal à la tête
stomach ache	mal à l'estomac
period	règles
pain	douleur
it hurts	ça fait mal
chemist/pharmacist	pharmacie
hospital	hôpital
condom	préservatif
morning-after pill /emergency contraceptive	pilule du lendemain
I'm allergic to...	Je suis allergique à...

Other needs

bakery	boulangerie
food shop	alimentation
delicatessen	charcuterie, traiteur
cake shop	pâtisserie
cheese shop	fromagerie
supermarket	supermarché
to eat	manger
to drink	boire
tasting, eg wine tasting	dégustation
camping gas	camping gaz
tobacconist	tabac
stamps	timbres
bank	banque
money	argent
toilets	toilettes
police	police
telephone	téléphone
cinema	cinéma
theatre	théâtre
to reserve/book	réserver

Restaurant phrases

I'd like to reserve a table	Je voudrais réserver une table
for two people, at eight thirty	pour deux personnes, à vingt heures et demie
I'm having the €30 set menu	Je prendrai le menu à trente euros
Waiter!	monsieur/madame!/ s'il vous plaît!
the bill/check please	l'addition, s'il vous plaît

A food glossary

Basic terms

l'addition	bill/check
beurre	butter
bio or biologique	organic
bouteille	bottle
carafe d'eau	jug of water
la carte	the menu
chauffé	heated
couteau	knife
cru	raw
cuillère	spoon
cuit	cooked
emballé	wrapped
à emporter	takeaway
entrée	starter
formule	lunchtime set menu
fourchette	fork
fumé	smoked
huile	oil
lait	milk
moutarde	mustard
œuf	egg
offert	free
pain	bread
pimenté	spicy
plat	main course
poivre	pepper
salé	salted/savoury
sel	salt
sucre	sugar
sucré	sweet
table	table
verre	glass
vinaigre	vinegar

Snacks

un sandwich/ une baguette	a sandwich
au jambon	with ham
au fromage	with cheese
au saucisson	with sausage
à l'ail	with garlic
au poivre	with pepper
au pâté (de campagne)	with pâté (country style)
croque-monsieur	grilled cheese and ham sandwich
croque-madame	grilled cheese and bacon, sausage, chicken or egg sandwich
pain bagnat	bread roll with egg, olives, salad, tuna, anchovies and olive oil
panini	toasted Italian sandwich
tartine	buttered bread or open sandwich

œufs	eggs	**omelette**	omelette
au plat	fried	**nature**	plain
à la coque	boiled	**aux fines herbes**	with herbs
durs	hard-boiled	**au fromage**	with cheese
brouillés	scrambled		

Pasta (*pâtes*), pancakes (*crêpes*) and flans (*tartes*)

nouilles	noodles	**pissaladière**	tart of fried onions with anchovies and black olives
pâtes fraîches	fresh pasta	**tarte flambée**	thin pizza-like pastry topped with onion, cream and bacon or other combinations
crêpe au sucre/ aux œufs	pancake with sugar/eggs		
galette	buckwheat pancake		
socca	thin chickpea flour pancake		
panisse	thick chickpea flour pancake		

Soups (*soupes*)

baudroie	fish soup with vegetables, garlic and herbs	**potage**	thick vegetable soup
bisque	shellfish soup	**potée auvergnate**	cabbage and meat soup
bouillabaisse	soup with five fish	**rouille**	red pepper, garlic and saffron mayonnaise served with fish soup
bouillon	broth or stock	**soupe à l'oignon**	onion soup with rich cheese topping
bourride	thick fish soup	**velouté**	thick soup, usually fish or poultry
consommé	clear soup		
garbure	potato, cabbage and meat soup		
pistou	parmesan, basil and garlic paste added to soup		

Starters (*hors d'œuvres*)

assiette anglaise	plate of cold meats	**escargots**	snails
assiette composée	mixed salad plate, usually cold meat and vegetables	**hors d'œuvres**	combination of the above plus smoked or marinated fish
crudités	raw vegetables with dressings		

Fish (*poisson*), seafood (*fruits de mer*) and shellfish (*crustaces* or *coquillages*)

amandes	clams	**anchois**	anchovies
aiglefin	small haddock or fresh cod	**anguilles**	eels
		barbue	brill

bar	bass
baudroie	monkfish or anglerfish
bigorneau	periwinkle
brème	bream
bulot	whelk
cabillaud	cod
calmar	squid
carrelet	plaice
claire	type of oyster
colin	hake
congre	conger eel
coques	cockles
coquilles St-Jacques	scallops
crabe	crab
crevettes grises	shrimp
crevettes roses	prawns
daurade	sea bream
écrevisses	crayfish
éperlan	smelt or whitebait
favou(ille)	tiny crab
flétan	halibut
friture	assorted fried fish
gambas	king prawns
hareng	herring
homard	lobster
huîtres	oysters
julienne	ling
langouste	spiny lobster
langoustines	saltwater crayfish (scampi)
lieu	pollock
limande	lemon sole
lotte	burbot
lotte de mer	monkfish
louvine, loubine	similar to sea bass
loup de mer	sea bass
maquereau	mackerel
merlan	whiting
moules (marinières)	mussels (with shallots in white wine sauce)
oursin	sea urchin
palourdes	clams
poissons de roche	fish from shoreline rocks
praires	small clams
raie	skate
rouget	red mullet
saumon	salmon
sole	sole
St Pierre	John Dory
thon	tuna
tourteau	crab
truite	trout
turbot	turbot
violet	sea squirt

Fish dishes and terms

aïoli	garlic mayonnaise served with salt cod and other fish
anchoïade	anchovy paste or sauce
arête	fish bone
assiette de fruits de mer	seafood platter
assiette de pêcheur	assorted fish
beignet	fritter
darne	fillet or steak
la douzaine	a dozen
frit	fried
friture	deep-fried small fish
fumé	smoked
fumet	fish stock
gigot de mer	large fish baked whole
grillé	grilled
hollandaise	butter and vinegar sauce
à la meunière	in a butter, lemon and parsley sauce
mousse/mousseline	mousse
pané	breaded
poutargue	mullet roe paste
raïto	red wine, olive, caper, garlic and shallot sauce
quenelles	light dumplings
thermidor	lobster grilled in its shell with cream sauce

Meat (*viande*) and poultry (*volaille*)

agneau (de pré-salé)	lamb (grazed on salt marshes)
andouille /andouillette	tripe sausage
bavette	French cut of beef equivalent to flank
bifteck	steak
bœuf	beef
boudin blanc	sausage of white meats
boudin noir	black pudding
caille	quail
canard	duck
caneton	duckling
contrefilet	sirloin roast
coquelet	cockerel
dinde/dindon	turkey
entrecôte	rib steak
faux filet	sirloin steak
foie	liver
foie gras	(duck/goose) liver
gibier	game
gigot (d'agneau)	leg (of lamb)
grenouilles (cuisses de)	frogs (legs)
grillade	grilled meat
hâchis	chopped meat, mince or hamburger
langue	tongue
lapin/lapereau	rabbit/young rabbit
lard/lardons	bacon/diced bacon
lièvre	hare
merguez	spicy, red sausage
mouton	mutton
museau de veau	calf's muzzle
oie	goose
onglet	French cut of beef steak that makes a prime steak
os	bone
poitrine	breast
porc	pork
poulet	chicken
poussin	baby chicken
ris	sweetbreads
rognons	kidneys
rognons blancs	testicles
sanglier	wild boar
steak	steak
tête de veau	calf's head (in jelly)
tournedos	thick slices of fillet
tripes	tripe
tripoux	mutton tripe
veau	veal
venaison	venison
volaille	poultry

Meat and poultry dishes and terms

aïado	roast shoulder of lamb stuffed with garlic and other ingredients
aile	wing
au feu de bois	cooked over wood fire
au four	baked
baeckoffe	Alsatian hotpot of pork, mutton and beef baked with potato layers
blanquette, daube, navarin, ragoût, estouffade, hochepôt	types of stew
blanquette de veau	veal in cream and mushroom sauce
bœuf bourguignon	beef stew with Burgundy, onions and mushrooms
canard à l'orange	roast duck with an orange and wine sauce
canard pâté de périgourdin foie gras	roast duck with prunes and truffles
carré	best end of neck, chop or cutlet
cassoulet	casserole of beans, sausages and duck /goose

choucroute	pickled cabbage with peppercorns, sausages, bacon and salami
civet	game stew
confit	meat preserve
côte	chop, cutlet or rib
cou	neck
coq au vin	chicken slow-cooked with wine, onions and mushrooms
cuisse	thigh or leg
épaule	shoulder
en croûte	in pastry
farci	stuffed
grillade	grilled meat
garni	with vegetables
gésier	gizzard
grillé	grilled
hâchis	chopped meat or mince hamburger
magret de canard	duck breast
marmite	casserole
médaillon	round piece
mijoté	stewed
pavé	thick slice
pieds et paques	mutton or pork tripe and trotters
poêlé	pan-fried
poulet de Bresse	chicken from Bresse – the best
râble	saddle
rôti	roast
sauté	lightly fried in butter
steak au poivre (vert/rouge)	steak in a black (green/red) peppercorn sauce
steak tartare	raw chopped beef, topped with a raw egg yolk
tagine	North African casserole
tournedos	beef fillet with foie gras rossini and truffles
viennoise	fried in egg and breadcrumbs

Terms for steaks

bleu	almost raw
saignant	rare
à point	medium rare
bien cuit	well done
très bien cuit	very well done
brochette	kebab

Garnishes and sauces

américaine	white wine, cognac and tomato
arlésienne au porto	with tomatoes, onions, aubergines, potatoes and rice in port
auvergnat	with cabbage, sausage and bacon
béarnaise	sauce of egg yolks, white wine, shallots and vinegar
beurre blanc	sauce of white wine and shallots, with butter
bonne femme	with mushroom, bacon, potato and onions
bordelaise	in a red wine, shallot and bone-marrow sauce
boulangère	baked with potatoes and onions
bourgeoise	with carrots, onions, bacon, celery and braised lettuce
chasseur	white wine, mushrooms and shallots
châtelaine	with artichoke hearts and chestnut purée
diable	strong mustard seasoning
forestière	with bacon and mushroom

fricassée	rich, creamy sauce
mornay	cheese sauce
pays d'auge	cream and cider
périgourdine	with foie gras and possibly truffles
piquante	gherkins or capers, vinegar and shallots
provençale	tomatoes, garlic, olive oil and herbs
savoyarde	with gruyère cheese
véronique	grapes, wine and cream

Vegetables (*légumes*), herbs (*herbes*) and spices (*épices*)

ail	garlic
algue	seaweed
anis	aniseed
artichaut	artichoke
asperge	asparagus
avocat	avocado
basilic	basil
betterave	beetroot
blette/bette	Swiss chard
cannelle	cinnamon
capre	caper
cardon	cardoon, a beet related to artichoke
carotte	carrot
céleri	celery
champignons, cèpes, ceps, girolles, chanterelles, pleurotes	mushrooms
chou (rouge)	(red) cabbage
choufleur	cauliflower
concombre	cucumber
cornichon	gherkin
echalotes	shallots
endive	chicory
épinard	spinach
estragon	tarragon
fenouil	fennel
férigoule	thyme (in Provençal)
fèves	broad beans
flageolets	flageolet beans
gingembre	ginger
haricots	haricot beans
verts	string beans
rouges	kidney beans
beurres	butter beans
laurier	bay leaf
lentilles	lentils
maïs	maize (corn)
menthe	mint
moutarde	mustard
oignon	onion
panais	parsnip
pélandron	type of string bean
pâte	pasta or pastry
persil	parsley
petits pois	peas
piment rouge/vert	red/green chilli pepper
pois chiche	chick peas
pois mange-tout	snow peas
pignons	pine nuts
poireau	leek
poivron (vert, rouge)	sweet pepper (green, red)
pommes de terre	potatoes
primeurs	spring vegetables
radis	radish
riz	rice
safran	saffron
salade verte	green salad
sarrasin	buckwheat
tomate	tomato
truffes	truffles

Vegetable dishes and terms

alicot	puréed potato with cheese
allumettes	very thin chips
à l'anglaise	boiled
beignet	fritter
duxelles	fried mushrooms and shallots with cream
farci	stuffed
feuille	leaf
fines herbes	mixture of tarragon, parsley and chives
gratiné	browned with cheese or butter
à la grecque	cooked in oil and lemon
jardinière	with mixed diced vegetables
mousseline	mashed potato with cream and eggs
à la parisienne	sautéed potatoes, with white wine and shallot sauce
parmentier	with potatoes
petits farcis	stuffed tomatoes, aubergines, courgettes and peppers
râpée	grated or shredded
sauté	lightly fried in butter
à la vapeur	steamed
en verdure	garnished with green vegetables

Fruit (*fruit*) and nuts (*noix*)

abricot	apricot
acajou	cashew nut
amande	almond
ananas	pineapple
banane	banana
brugnon, nectarine	nectarine
cacahouète	peanut
cassis	blackcurrant
cérise	cherry
citron	lemon
citron vert	lime
datte	date
figue	fig
fraise (de bois)	strawberry (wild)
framboise	raspberry
fruit de la passion	passion fruit
grenade	pomegranate
groseille	redcurrant
mangue	mango
marron	chestnut
melon	melon
mirabelle	small yellow plum
myrtille	bilberry
noisette	hazelnut
noix	walnuts; nuts
orange	orange
pamplemousse	grapefruit
pastèque	watermelon
pêche	peach
pistache	pistachio
poire	pear
pomme	apple
prune	plum
pruneau	prune
raisin	grape
reine-claude	greengage

Fruit dishes and terms

agrumes	citrus fruits
beignet	fritter
compôte	stewed fruit
coulis	sauce of puréed fruit
crème de marrons	chestnut purée
flambé	set aflame in alcohol
fougasse	bread flavoured with orange-flower water or almonds (can be savoury)
frappé	iced

Desserts (*desserts* or *entremets*) and pastries (*pâtisserie*)

bombe	moulded ice-cream dessert
brioche	sweet, high yeast breakfast roll loaf
calisson	almond sweet
charlotte	custard and fruit in lining of almond fingers

Breton

Breton is one of the Celtic family of languages, linked with Welsh and Gaelic even if it's not mutually comprehensible, and especially closely tied with Cornish. Its strong oral tradition ranges from medieval minstrels to modern singers and musicians.

Current estimates put the number of people who understand spoken Breton at between 400,000 and 800,000. However, only perhaps a third of those actually speak the language with any fluency or frequency. You're very unlikely to find it spoken as a first, day-to-day language; the only conceivable possibilities are among the very old, or in exceptionally remote parts of Finistère. For centuries it was efficiently suppressed by the state; its use was forbidden for official and legal purposes, and even Breton-speaking parents would seek to enhance their children's prospects by bringing them up to speak French. Although Breton is now taught in some schools once again, and there is even a Breton regional bank, learning the language is not really a viable prospect for visitors who do not already have a good grounding in another Celtic language.

However, as you travel through the province it's interesting to note the roots of Breton **place names**, many of which have a simple meaning in the language. The list of Breton words below includes some of the most common, as well as a few everyday words and greetings.

Breton vocabulary

aber	estuary
avel	wind
bihan	little
bran	hill
braz	big
Breizh	Brittany
creach	height
cromlech	stone circle
dol/taol	table
dour	water
du	black
enez	island
gavre	goat
goat/coat/koat	forest
goaz	stream
gwenn	white
hen	old
heol	sun
hir	long
kastell	castle
kenavo	goodbye
ker	town, village
koz	old
lan	church, holy place
lann	heath
lech	flat stone
loc	isolated, holy place
mad	good
men	stone
menez	mountain
mario	dead
menhir	long stone
meur	big
mor	sea
nevez	new
parc	field
penn	end, head
plou	parish
pors	port, farmyard
roch	stone
ster	river
stivel	fountain, spring
ti	house
traez	sand, beach
trugarez	thank you
trou	valley
wrach	witch
ya	yes

chichi	doughnut shaped in a stick
clafoutis	heavy custard and fruit tart
crème Chantilly	vanilla-flavoured and sweetened whipped cream
crème fraîche	sour cream
crème pâtissière	thick, eggy pastry filling
crêpe suzette	thin pancake with orange juice and liqueur
fromage blanc	cream cheese
gaufre	waffle
glace	ice cream
Île flottante/ œufs à la neige	whipped egg-white floating on custard
macaron	macaroon
madeleine	small sponge cake
marrons Mont Blanc	chestnut purée and cream on a rum-soaked sponge cake
mousse au chocolat	chocolate mousse
omelette norvégienne	baked alaska
palmier	caramelized puff pastry
parfait	frozen mousse, sometimes ice cream
petit-suisse	a smooth mixture of cream and curds
petits fours	bite-sized cakes/pastries
poires belle hélène	pears and ice cream in chocolate sauce
tarte tatin	upside-down apple tart
tarte tropezienne	sponge cake filled with custard cream topped with nuts
tiramisu	mascarpone cheese, chocolate and cream
yaourt/yogourt	yoghurt

Glossary

abbaye	abbey
aber	estuary
accueil	reception
arrêt d'autobus	bus stop
Assemblée Nationale	the French parliament
auberge de jeunesse	(AJ) youth hostel
autobus	city bus
autoroute	motorway/freeway
banque	bank
bassin	harbour basin
Beaux-arts	fine arts school (and often museum)
bibliothèque	library
bistro	small restaurant or bar
bois	wood
boulangerie	baker
brasserie	café/restaurant
bureau de change	money exchange
calvaire	("calvary") a cluster of religious statues standing on a single base, usually topped by a Crucifixion, as found in many Breton churchyards.
car	coach, bus
cave	(wine) cellar
centre ville	town centre
chambre d'hôte	B&B
charcuterie	delicatessen
chasse, chasse gardée	hunting grounds beware/keep out
château	castle or mansion
cimetière	cemetery
citadelle	fortified city
cloître	cloister
confiserie	sweet shop
consigne	left luggage
couvent	monastery
crêperie	pancake restaurant
dégustation	tasting

département	administrative division equivalent to an English county
dolmen	megalithic stone "table"
donjon	castle keep
église	church
enclos	group of church buildings
enclos paroissial	("parish close") a walled churchyard that incorporates a church, acemetery, a calvary and an ossuary.
entrée	entrance
fermeture	closing time/period
forêt	forest
formule	lunchtime set menu
fouilles	archeological excavations
foyer	residential hostel for young workers or students
gare routière	bus station
gare	SNCF train station
gîte d'étape	countryside hostel
grotte	cave
halles	covered market
hôpital	hospital
hôtel	hotel – but also used for an aristocratic town house or mansion
Hôtel de Ville	town hall
île	island
jours fériés	public holidays
mairie	town hall
maison	literally a house – can also be an office or base of an organization
marché	market
menhir	single megalithic stone
office du tourisme (OT)	tourist office
ouverture	opening time/period
pardon	procession
pâtisserie	pastry shop
pharmacie	chemist
place	square
plage	beach
plat du jour	daily special on menu
porte	gate
poste	post office
presqu'île	peninsula
privé	private
PTT	post office
quartier	quarter or district of a town
Relais Routier	truck-stop restaurant
rez-de-chaussée	ground floor (UK), first floor (US)
RN route nationale	(main road)
salon de thé	tearoom
SI	tourist office (see syndicat d'initiative below)
SNCF	French railways
syndicat d'initiative (SI)	tourist office
tabac	bar or shop selling stamps, cigarettes, etc
tour	tower
traiteur	delicatessen
Vauban	famous seventeenth-century military architect
zone bleue	parking zone
zone piétonnière	pedestrian zone

Travel store

ROUGH GUIDES World Coverage

Travel

Andorra The Pyrenees, Pyrenees & Andorra Map, Spain
Antigua The Caribbean
Argentina Argentina, Argentina Map, Buenos Aires, South America on a Budget
Aruba The Caribbean
Australia Australia, Australia Map, East Coast Australia, Melbourne, Sydney, Tasmania
Austria Austria, Europe on a Budget, Vienna
Bahamas The Bahamas, The Caribbean
Barbados Barbados DIR, The Caribbean
Belgium Belgium & Luxembourg, Bruges DIR, Brussels, Brussels Map, Europe on a Budget
Belize Belize, Central America on a Budget, Guatemala & Belize Map
Benin West Africa
Bolivia Bolivia, South America on a Budget
Brazil Brazil, Rio, South America on a Budget
British Virgin Islands The Caribbean
Brunei Malaysia, Singapore & Brunei [1 title], Southeast Asia on a Budget
Bulgaria Bulgaria, Europe on a Budget
Burkina Faso West Africa
Cambodia Cambodia, Southeast Asia on a Budget, Vietnam, Laos & Cambodia Map [1 Map]
Cameroon West Africa
Canada Canada, Pacific Northwest, Toronto, Toronto Map, Vancouver
Cape Verde West Africa
Cayman Islands The Caribbean
Chile Chile, Chile Map, South America on a Budget
China Beijing, China, Hong Kong & Macau, Hong Kong & Macau DIR, Shanghai
Colombia South America on a Budget
Costa Rica Central America on a Budget, Costa Rica, Costa Rica & Panama Map
Croatia Croatia, Croatia Map, Europe on a Budget
Cuba Cuba, Cuba Map, The Caribbean, Havana
Cyprus Cyprus, Cyprus Map
Czech Republic The Czech Republic, Czech & Slovak Republics, Europe on a Budget, Prague, Prague DIR, Prague Map
Denmark Copenhagen, Denmark, Europe on a Budget, Scandinavia
Dominica The Caribbean
Dominican Republic Dominican Republic, The Caribbean
Ecuador Ecuador, South America on a Budget
Egypt Egypt, Egypt Map
El Salvador Central America on a Budget
England Britain, Camping in Britain, Devon & Cornwall, Dorset, Hampshire and The Isle of Wight [1 title], England, Europe on a Budget, The Lake District, London, London DIR, London Map, London Mini Guide, Walks In London & Southeast England
Estonia The Baltic States, Europe on a Budget
Fiji Fiji
Finland Europe on a Budget, Finland, Scandinavia
France Brittany & Normandy, Corsica, Corsica Map, The Dordogne & the Lot, Europe on a Budget, France, France Map, Languedoc & Roussillon, The Loire, Paris, Paris DIR, Paris Map, Paris Mini Guide, Provence & the Côte d'Azur, The Pyrenees, Pyrenees & Andorra Map
French Guiana South America on a Budget
Gambia The Gambia, West Africa
Germany Berlin, Berlin Map, Europe on a Budget, Germany, Germany Map
Ghana West Africa
Gibraltar Spain
Greece Athens Map, Crete, Crete Map, Europe on a Budget, Greece, Greece Map, Greek Islands, Ionian Islands
Guadeloupe The Caribbean
Guatemala Central America on a Budget, Guatemala, Guatemala & Belize Map
Guinea West Africa
Guinea-Bissau West Africa
Guyana South America on a Budget
Holland see The Netherlands
Honduras Central America on a Budget
Hungary Budapest, Europe on a Budget, Hungary
Iceland Iceland, Iceland Map
India Goa, India, India Map, Kerala, Rajasthan, Delhi & Agra [1 title], South India, South India Map
Indonesia Bali & Lombok, Southeast Asia on a Budget
Ireland Dublin DIR, Dublin Map, Europe on a Budget, Ireland, Ireland Map
Israel Jerusalem
Italy Europe on a Budget, Florence DIR, Florence & Siena Map, Florence & the best of Tuscany, Italy, The Italian Lakes, Naples & the Amalfi Coast, Rome, Rome DIR, Rome Map, Sardinia, Sicily, Sicily Map, Tuscany & Umbria, Tuscany Map, Venice, Venice DIR, Venice Map
Jamaica Jamaica, The Caribbean
Japan Japan, Tokyo
Jordan Jordan
Kenya Kenya, Kenya Map
Korea Korea
Laos Laos, Southeast Asia on a Budget, Vietnam, Laos & Cambodia Map [1 Map]
Latvia The Baltic States, Europe on a Budget
Lithuania The Baltic States, Europe on a Budget
Luxembourg Belgium & Luxembourg, Europe on a Budget
Malaysia Malaysia Map, Malaysia, Singapore & Brunei [1 title], Southeast Asia on a Budget
Mali West Africa
Malta Malta & Gozo DIR
Martinique The Caribbean
Mauritania West Africa
Mexico Baja California, Baja California, Cancún & Cozumel DIR, Mexico, Mexico Map, Yucatán, Yucatán Peninsula Map
Monaco France, Provence & the Côte d'Azur
Montenegro Montenegro
Morocco Europe on a Budget, Marrakesh DIR, Marrakesh Map, Morocco, Morocco Map,
Nepal Nepal
Netherlands Amsterdam, Amsterdam DIR, Amsterdam Map, Europe on a Budget, The Netherlands
Netherlands Antilles The Caribbean
New Zealand New Zealand, New Zealand Map

DIR: Rough Guide **DIRECTIONS** for short breaks

Nicaragua Central America on a Budget
Niger West Africa
Nigeria West Africa
Norway Europe on a Budget, Norway, Scandinavia
Panama Central America on a Budget, Costa Rica & Panama Map, Panama
Paraguay South America on a Budget
Peru Peru, Peru Map, South America on a Budget
Philippines The Philippines, Southeast Asia on a Budget,
Poland Europe on a Budget, Poland
Portugal Algarve DIR, The Algarve Map, Europe on a Budget, Lisbon DIR, Lisbon Map, Madeira DIR, Portugal, Portugal Map, Spain & Portugal Map
Puerto Rico The Caribbean, Puerto Rico
Romania Europe on a Budget, Romania
Russia Europe on a Budget, Moscow, St Petersburg
St Kitts & Nevis The Caribbean
St Lucia The Caribbean
St Vincent & the Grenadines The Caribbean
Scotland Britain, Camping in Britain, Edinburgh DIR, Europe on a Budget, Scotland, Scottish Highlands & Islands
Senegal West Africa
Serbia Montenegro Europe on a Budget
Sierra Leone West Africa
Singapore Malaysia, Singapore & Brunei [1 title], Singapore, Singapore DIR, Southeast Asia on a Budget
Slovakia Czech & Slovak Republics, Europe on a Budget
Slovenia Europe on a Budget, Slovenia
South Africa Cape Town & the Garden Route, South Africa, South Africa Map
Spain Andalucía, Andalucía Map, Barcelona, Barcelona DIR, Barcelona Map, Europe on a Budget, Ibiza & Formentera DIR, Gran Canaria DIR, Madrid DIR, Lanzarote & Fuerteventura DIR Madrid Map, Mallorca & Menorca, Mallorca DIR, Mallorca Map, The Pyrenees, Pyrenees & Andorra Map, Spain, Spain & Portugal Map, Tenerife & La Gomera DIR
Sri Lanka Sri Lanka, Sri Lanka Map
Suriname South America on a Budget
Sweden Europe on a Budget, Scandinavia, Sweden
Switzerland Europe on a Budget, Switzerland
Taiwan Taiwan
Tanzania Tanzania, Zanzibar
Thailand Bangkok, Southeast Asia on a Budget, Thailand, Thailand Map, Thailand Beaches & Islands
Togo West Africa
Trinidad & Tobago The Caribbean, Trinidad & Tobago
Tunisia Tunisia, Tunisia Map
Turkey Europe on a Budget, Istanbul, Turkey, Turkey Map
Turks and Caicos Islands The Bahamas, The Caribbean
United Arab Emirates Dubai DIR, Dubai & UAE Map [1 title]
United Kingdom Britain, Devon & Cornwall, Edinburgh DIR England, Europe on a Budget, The Lake District, London, London DIR, London Map, London Mini Guide, Scotland, Scottish Highlands & Islands, Wales, Walks In London & Southeast England
United States Alaska, Boston, California, California Map, Chicago, Colorado, Florida, Florida Map, The Grand Canyon, Hawaii, Los Angeles, Los Angeles Map, Los Angeles and Southern California, Maui DIR, Miami & South Florida, New England, New England Map, New Orleans & Cajun Country, New Orleans DIR, New York City, NYC DIR, NYC Map, New York City Mini Guide, Oregon & Washington, Orlando & Walt Disney World® DIR, San Francisco, San Francisco DIR, San Francisco Map, Seattle, Southwest USA, USA, Washington DC, Yellowstone & the Grand Tetons National Park, Yosemite National Park
Uruguay South America on a Budget
US Virgin Islands The Bahamas, The Caribbean
Venezuela South America on a Budget
Vietnam Southeast Asia on a Budget, Vietnam, Vietnam, Laos & Cambodia Map [1 Map],
Wales Britain, Camping in Britain, Europe on a Budget, Wales
First-Time Series FT Africa, FT Around the World, FT Asia, FT Europe, FT Latin America
Inspirational guides Earthbound, Clean Breaks, Make the Most of Your Time on Earth, Ultimate Adventures, World Party
Travel Specials Camping in Britain, Travel with Babies & Young Children, Walks in London & SE England

ROUGH GUIDES Don't Just Travel

Computers Cloud Computing, FWD this link, The Internet, iPhone, iPods & iTunes, Macs & OS X, Website Directory
Film & TV American Independent Film, British Cult Comedy, Comedy Movies, Cult Movies, Film, Film Musicals, Film Noir, Gangster Movies, Horror Movies, Sci-Fi Movies, Westerns
Lifestyle Babies & Toddlers, Brain Training, Food, Girl Stuff, Green Living, Happiness, Men's Health, Pregnancy & Birth, Running, Saving & Selling Online, Sex, Weddings
Music The Beatles, The Best Music You've Never Heard, Blues, Bob Dylan, Book of Playlists, Classical Music, Heavy Metal, Jimi Hendrix, Led Zeppelin, Nirvana, Opera, Pink Floyd, The Rolling Stones, Soul and R&B, Velvet Underground, World Music
Popular Culture Anime, Classic Novels, Conspiracy Theories, Crime Fiction, The Da Vinci Code, Graphic Novels, Hidden Treasures, His Dark Materials, Hitchhiker's Guide to the Galaxy, The Lost Symbol, Manga, Next Big Thing, Shakespeare, True Crime, Tutankhamun, Unexplained Phenomena, Videogames
Science The Brain, Climate Change, The Earth, Energy Crisis, Evolution, Future, Genes & Cloning, The Universe, Weather

Small print and

Index

A Rough Guide to Rough Guides

Published in 1982, the first Rough Guide – to Greece – was a student scheme that became a publishing phenomenon. Mark Ellingham, a recent graduate in English from Bristol University, had been travelling in Greece the previous summer and couldn't find the right guidebook. With a small group of friends he wrote his own guide, combining a highly contemporary, journalistic style with a thoroughly practical approach to travellers' needs.

The immediate success of the book spawned a series that rapidly covered dozens of destinations. And, in addition to impecunious backpackers, Rough Guides soon acquired a much broader and older readership that relished the guides' wit and inquisitiveness as much as their enthusiastic, critical approach and value-for-money ethos.

These days, Rough Guides include recommendations from shoestring to luxury and cover more than 200 destinations around the globe, including almost every country in the Americas and Europe, more than half of Africa and most of Asia and Australasia. Our ever-growing team of authors and photographers is spread all over the world, particularly in Europe, the US and Australia.

In the early 1990s, Rough Guides branched out of travel, with the publication of Rough Guides to World Music, Classical Music and the Internet. All three have become benchmark titles in their fields, spearheading the publication of a wide range of books under the Rough Guide name.

Including the travel series, Rough Guides now number more than 350 titles, covering: phrasebooks, waterproof maps, music guides from Opera to Heavy Metal, reference works as diverse as Conspiracy Theories and Shakespeare, and popular culture books from iPods to Poker. Rough Guides also produce a series of more than 120 World Music CDs in partnership with World Music Network.

Visit www.roughguides.com to see our latest publications.

Rough Guide travel images are available for commercial licensing at www.roughguidespictures.com

Rough Guide credits

Text editors: Alice Park and Alison Roberts
Layout: Jessica Subramanian
Cartography: Alakananda Roy
Picture editor: Mark Thomas
Production: Rebecca Short
Proofreader: Anita Sach
Cover design: Dan May and Chloë Roberts
Editorial: Ruth Blackmore, Andy Turner, Keith Drew, Edward Aves, Lucy White, Jo Kirby, James Smart, Natasha Foges, Róisín Cameron, Lara Kavanagh, James Rice, Emma Traynor, Emma Gibbs, Kathryn Lane, Monica Woods, Mani Ramaswamy, Harry Wilson, Lucy Cowie, Joe Staines, Peter Buckley, Matthew Milton, Tracy Hopkins, Ruth Tidball; **Delhi** Madhavi Singh, Karen D'Souza, Lubna Shaheen
Design & Pictures: **London** Scott Stickland, Dan May, Diana Jarvis, Nicole Newman, Sarah Cummins, Emily Taylor; **Delhi** Umesh Aggarwal, Ajay Verma, Ankur Guha, Pradeep Thapliyal, Sachin Tanwar, Anita Singh, Nikhil Agarwal, Sachin Gupta.
Production: Liz Cherry
Cartography: **London** Ed Wright, Katie Lloyd-Jones; **Delhi** Rajesh Chhibber, Ashutosh Bharti, Rajesh Mishra, Animesh Pathak, Jasbir Sandhu, Karobi Gogoi, Swati Handoo, Deshpal Dabas
Online: **London** Faye Hellon, Jeanette Angell, Fergus Day, Justine Bright, Clare Bryson, Aine Fearon, Adrian Low, Ezgi Celebi; **Delhi** Amit Verma, Rahul Kumar, Narender Kumar, Ravi Yadav, Debojit Borah, Rakesh Kumar, Ganesh Sharma, Shisir Basumatari
Marketing & Publicity: **London** Liz Statham, Louise Maher, Jess Carter, Vanessa Godden, Vivienne Watton, Anna Paynton, Rachel Sprackett, Laura Vipond; **New York** Katy Ball, Judi Powers; **Delhi** Ragini Govind
Reference Director: Andrew Lockett
Operations Assistant: Becky Doyle
Operations Manager: Helen Atkinson
Publishing Director (Travel): Clare Currie
Commercial Manager: Gino Magnotta
Managing Director: John Duhigg

Publishing information

This eleventh edition published May 2010 by
Rough Guides Ltd,
80 Strand, London WC2R 0RL
14 Local Shopping Centre, Panchsheel Park, New Delhi 110017, India
Distributed by the Penguin Group
Penguin Books Ltd,
80 Strand, London WC2R 0RL
Penguin Group (USA)
375 Hudson Street, NY 10014, USA
Penguin Group (Australia)
250 Camberwell Road, Camberwell, Victoria 3124, Australia
Penguin Group (Canada)
195 Harry Walker Parkway N, Newmarket, ON, L3Y 7B3 Canada
Penguin Group (NZ)
67 Apollo Drive, Mairangi Bay, Auckland 1310, New Zealand
Cover concept by Peter Dyer.

Typeset in Bembo and Helvetica to an original design by Henry Iles.

Printed in Singapore

440pp includes index

A catalogue record for this book is available from the British Library

ISBN: 978-1-84836-480-6

3 5 7 9 8 6 4 2

Help us update

We've gone to a lot of effort to ensure that the eleventh edition of **The Rough Guide to Brittany and Normandy** is accurate and up-to-date. However, things change – places get "discovered", opening hours are notoriously fickle, restaurants and rooms raise prices or lower standards. If you feel we've got it wrong or left something out, we'd like to know, and if you can remember the address, the price, the hours, the phone number, so much the better.

Please send your comments with the subject line "**Rough Guide Brittany and Normandy Update**" to Ⓔ mail@roughguides.com. We'll credit all contributions and send a copy of the next edition (or any other Rough Guide if you prefer) for the very best emails.

Have your questions answered and tell others about your trip at Ⓦ www.roughguides.com

Acknowledgements

Greg Ward would like to thank: first and foremost, thanks and love to my wife Sam, for life in general, for a great road trip, and for all her ideas and support.

Thanks also to everyone at Rough Guides, and above all to the text editors who did so much to make the book the best it could be, Alice Park and Alison Roberts.

Readers' letters

Many thanks to all those readers who sent in updates via e-mail or letters:

Mrs N. Amos, Zoe Barlow, Samuel Best-Shaw, Inda Bevis, Stephen Bidwell, John Bradley, Christopher Clayton, Dick Conroy, Franzeca Drouin, Mrs Arlene Hansell, Laura Henderson, George Hudson, Peter Kellow, Gerry Maffre, Nigel Malcolm-Smith, David Maloney, Mark McMaster, Pamela and Christopher Nye, Chris O'Driscoll, Robert Page, Simon Phillips, Graham W. Ryder, Ron and Enid Samuel, Lindsay Simpson and Lelia Thornton.

Photo credits

All photography by Greg Ward © Rough Guides except the following:

Title page

Finistère © Herve Hughes/Hemis/Axiom

Full page

Honfleur © Paul Williams/Alamy

Introduction

Bakery sign © Nicole Duplaix/Getty
Le Petit Andelys on the Seine © Philippe Body/Getty
Audierne Bay © Herve Lenain/Getty Images
Bessin port © John Frumm/Hemis/Axiom

Things not to miss

01 The Grand Éléphant © Greg Ward
02 Cycling © Ian Cumming/Axiom
03 Giverny gardens © Anneke Schram/istock
07 Inter-Celtic Festival © Marion Kaplan/Alamy
08 Bayeux Tapestry © Hemis/Alamy
09 Nantes-Brest Canal © Greg Ward
10 Honfleur © Ellen Rooney/Axiom
13 Rouen © Hemis/Alamy
14 St Malo © Sylvain Grandadam/Getty
18 D-Day beaches © ICP/Alamy
19 Île de Sein © Greg Ward

Feasting in northern France

Plate of seafood © Bon Appetit/Alamy
Galette with scallops © directphoto.bz/Alamy
Men farming oyster beds © Hemis/Alamy
Cider for sale in Honfleur © CW Images/Alamy
Cheeses on a market stall © Paul Williams/Alamy

Megaliths and monuments

Mont St-Michel © Bertrand Rieger/Getty Images
Dolmen interior © Steve Mansfield/Alamy
Josselin Château © Suzanne & Nick Geary/Getty

Black and whites

p.165 Abbaye de Bec-Hellouin © Paul Collis/Alamy
p.183 Cows in the Suisse Normane © Hemis/Alamy
p.227 The Château at Vitre © FAN Travelstock/Alamy
p.336 Grand Éléphant © Greg Ward
p.372 Vannes © Greg Ward
p.378 Fisherman on the Grand-Briere © Hemis/Alamy

Index

Map entries are in colour.

D

E

F

M

N

O

P

Q

R

S

INDEX